THE EARLY MARRIAGES OF STRAFFORD COUNTY NEW HAMPSHIRE 1630-1870

SUPPLEMENT #2

Robert Sayward Canney

HERITAGE BOOKS
2008

HERITAGE BOOKS
AN IMPRINT OF HERITAGE BOOKS, INC.

Books, CDs, and more—Worldwide

For our listing of thousands of titles see our website at
www.HeritageBooks.com

Published 2008 by
HERITAGE BOOKS, INC.
Publishing Division
100 Railroad Ave. #104
Westminster, Maryland 21157

Copyright © 2000 Robert Sayward Canney

Other books by the author:
The Early Marriages of Strafford County, New Hampshire, 1630-1850
The Early Marriages of Strafford County, New Hampshire, 1630-1860
The Early Marriages of Strafford County, New Hampshire, Supplement, 1630-1870
The Early Marriages of Strafford County, New Hampshire, Second Supplement, 1630-1870

All rights reserved. No part of this book may be reproduced or transmitted in any form or by any means, electronic or mechanical, including photocopying, recording or by any information storage and retrieval system without written permission from the author, except for the inclusion of brief quotations in a review.

International Standard Book Numbers
Paperbound: 978-0-7884-1651-4
Clothbound: 978-0-7884-7189-6

INTRODUCTION

This supplemental volume presents a combination of previously unrecorded marriages and updated entries from the previous edition. The updated information within the old entries is designated by underlining.

The material has been gathered from town records, Piscataqua Pioneer files, census records, private manuscripts, and published town histories. The marriages are arranged, first, by the groom's surname and then chronologically by marriage date. Parentage, birth and death dates, and the official performing the ceremony are included when available.

While most recorded marriages occurred in Strafford County, a small number took place in southern York County, Maine, and northern Rockingham County, New Hampshire, but are included due to their connection with Strafford County families.

ABBOTT, Samuel, of Wolfeboro, b. June 22, 1767, d. 1823, m. Dec. 14, 1789, in Wolfeboro, Annie Varney, b. May 13, 1769, dau. of Moses.

ABBOTT, Elisha, b. Jan. 30, 1805, d. Apr. 23, 1898, m. int. June 1826, in Tuftonboro, Harriet Tate, of Tuftonboro, d. Sept. 6, 1876, aged 69.

ABBOTT, Thomas H., m. (1) int. Aug. 19, 1827, in Dover, Paulina Thomas, m. (2) Lydia P. ----, d. June 23, 1849, aged 36.

ABBOTT, Richard, of Effingham, d. Nov. 26, 1871, aged 65, m. June 21, 1833, in Wolfeboro, Jane Young, of Wolfeboro, d. Dec. 29, 1871, aged 67.

ABBOTT, Philbrook R., m. Jan. 16, 1842, by Rev. Aaron Ayer, Mrs. Elizabeth G. Smith, b. Nov. 25, 1804, d. Jan. 10, 1889, both of Dover.

ABBOTT, Asa, d. Sep. 3, 1894, aged 79, m. (pub. Sep. 19, 1843, is Ossipee), Sarah H. Moody, d. Sep. 30, 1905, aged 42.

ABBOTT, Ichabod, b. Nov. 13, 1823, d. Mar. 11, 1897, m. (1) (pub. Mar. 17, 1846, in Great Falls), Ann Barnes, b. July 6, 1820, d. Feb. 7, 1851, m. (2) (pub. Feb. 10, 1852, in Great Falls), Rosetta Wentworth, b. Aug. 17, 1833, d. Dec. 10, 1899.

ABBOTT, Andrew, of North Berwick, Me., m. Apr. 9, 1848, in Lebanon, Me., Betsey Jones, d. Mar. 9, 1868.

ABBOTT, Elias H. P., of Moultonboro, son of Paul, b. Oct. 21, 1831, d. Mar. 12, 1895, m. June 20, 1852, in Sandwich, Mary Jane Glines, of Sandwich.

ABBOTT, John W., of Dover, son of Elisha, b. Sept. 29, 1831, d. Aug. 2, 1931, aged 99, m. Nov. 22, 1853, by Elder Elias Hutchins, Emily B. Cheswell, of Newmarket, d. Mar. 29, 1888, aged 59, dau. of Thomas.

ABBOTT, Benjamin F. Jr., m. (pub. Jan. 27, 1859, in Great Falls), Mrs. Amelia J. Mears, d. Feb. 15, 1895, aged 71, both of Ossipee.

ABBOTT, John H., m. (1) Oct. 29, 1861, by Rev. James Rand, Mrs. Eliza A. (Dexter) Lane, wid. of George W., dau. of George G., m. (2) Oct. 23, 1865, in Great Falls, Mrs. Mary E. Perkins, both of Dover.

ABBOTT, Alpheus P., of Dover, m. Dec. 2, 1863, in Portsmouth, Mary Eliza Folsom, of Newmarket.

ABBOTT, Ivory, m. Apr. 19, 1864, in Ossipee, Amelia A. Lewis.

ABBOTT, Isaac F., of Dover, b. Nov. 1, 1842, d. Jan. 14, 1895, m. Oct. 10, 1867, in Dover, Lizzie J. Cushman, of Brunswick, Me., b. July 14, 1843, d. Mar. 18, 1892.

ABBOTT, Thomas, of Durham, m. May 14, 1868, by Rev. Robert S. Stubbs, Mrs. Lorana Murray, of Dover.

ABBOTT, Nathaniel R., of Berwick, Me., m. (pub. Jan. 27, 1870, in Great Falls), Phebe J. Clark, of Brookfield.

ADAMS, Dr. Nathaniel, m. (1) Feb. 23, 1800, by Rev. Isaac Hasey, Hannah Owen Hasey, dau. of Rev. Isaac, m. int. Sep. 4, 1822, in Berwick, Me., Anna Dunkins, of Berwick, Me.

ADAMS, George, of Durham, b. 1829, d. 1900, m. (1) June 16, 1853, in Newburyport, Mass., Sarah C. Plummer, of Newburyport, Mass., b. 1832, d. 1858, dau. of Ebenezer, m. (2) Mary Elizabeth Libby, b. 1840, d. 1931, dau. of James.

ADAMS, John Q., son of Mark, d. Sep. 6, 1918, aged 83, m. Jul. 9, 1859, in Gilmanton, Mary C. Freeman, d. Jan. 3, 1917, aged 80, dau. of Oliver.

ADAMS, Francis P., of Newfield, Me., m. (pub. Dec. 4, 1862, in Ossipee), Susan P. Brown, of Wolfeboro.

ADAMS, John T., m. Apr. 30, 1863, in Middleton, Mary S. Bradbury, both of Middleton.

ADAMS, Charles W., U.S.N., m. (pub. Jan. 26, 1865, in Portsmouth), Caroline C. Hartshorn, dau. of James F.

ADAMS, Asahel L., m. May 2, 1866, in Sandwich, Lucy Straw.

ADEL, Elbridge T., m. May 2, 1865, in Dover, Abbie M. Mudgett, both of Somersworth.

AKERMAN, Phinehas, m. Dec. 20, 1800, in Barrington, Sally Allard, both of Farmington.

ALEXANDER, Ira, of New York, m. Dec. 28, 1863, in Great Falls, Mary Jane Dennett, of Portsmouth.

ALEXANDER, William, son of Thomas, m. May 15, 1864, by Rev. Alvan Tobey, Elizabeth Casey, dau. of Peter.

ALLARD, John W., of Dover, son of William, m. Oct. 22, 1864, in Durham, Frances L. Demeritt, of Durham, dau. of Rev. William.

ALLARD, John P., of Eaton, m. Feb. 27, 1865, in Effingham, Lucretia Durgin, of Freedom.

ALLEN, Jacob, son of Edward, will 1752, m. (1) Feb. 5, 1701/02, by Rev. John Pike, Martha Dame, b. Mar. 29. 1683, d. Jun 22, 1716, dau. of William, m. (2) early as 1718, Mary (Spencer) Jones, wid. of Joseph, dau. of Moses.

ALLEN, Robert, son of Francis, b. July 24, 1710, m. (pub. Dec. 19, 1730), Catherine Furbish, b. 1708, dau. of Daniel.

ALLEN, Ezekiel, son of Francis, m. Oct. 14, 1751, Mary Needham, d. Jan. 6, 1796.

ALLEN, Jedediah, m. in 1754, in Hampton, Sarah Peasley, d. Oct. 2, 1817, dau. of John.

ALLEN, Solomon, son of Robert, b. Sept. 28, 1731, d. Dec. 17, 1826, m. Nov. 10, 1757, Catharine Neal, b. July 28, 1730, d. Mar. 13, 1814, dau. of Andrew.

ALLEN, Elijah, son of Francis, b. Mar. 12, 1720, d. Nov. 3, 1795, m. (1) Elizabeth Reed, m. (2) Dec. 10, 1760, Elizabeth (Dennett) Jenkins, wid. of Jabez, b. June 23, 1721, d. Nov. 3, 1795, dau. of Ebenezer.

ALLEN, Col. Joshua, son of Nathan, b. 1754, d. May 13, 1817, m. Feb. 13, 1777, by Rev. Joseph Haven, Martha Varney, d. June 1, 1822.

ALLEN, Daniel, son of Elijah, d. Nov. 28, 1810, m. Feb. 1780, Abigail Allen, b. Mar. 10, 1761, d. Sept. 28, 1834, dau. of Solomon.

ALLEN, Jacob, son of Elijah, b. June 1, 1758, d. Feb. 28, 1844, m. Mar. 17, 1784, Dorcas Allen, b. Mar. 15, 1759, d. Apr. 19, 1843, dau. of Solomon.

ALLEN, Samuel, son of William, b. Mar. 24, 1761, d. Nov. 22, 1846, m. Nov 8., 1785, by Rev. Joseph Haven, Sarah Ham, b. Dec. 9, 1761, d. Jan. 2, 1828, both of Rochester.

ALLEN, James, son of Solomon, b. Apr. 10, 1771, d. June 28, 1858, m. Jan. 18, 1796, Hannah Heard, d. July 20, 1850, dau. of James.

ALLEN, Elijah, son of Solomon, b. July 13, 1775, d. Sept. 15, 1855, m. near 1799, Lois Hill, b. in 1778, d. Apr. 13, 1848, dau. of Mark.

ALLEN, Ephraim, son of Solomon, b. Oct. 20, 1777, d. Nov. 14, 1869, m. int. Nov. 10, 1805, Lydia Furbish, b. Jan. 5, 1788, d. Oct. 28, 1878.

ALLEN, Rev. Eben, b. Dec. 30, 1794, d. May 14, 1881, m. Oct. 16, 1817, in Tamworth, Thankful Ellis, both of Ossipee.

ALLEN, Asa, son of Ephraim, b. Dec. 29, 1780, d. Apr. 28, 1866, m. July 5, 1821, in Berwick, Lydia Buffum, b. May 17, 1792, d. Aug. 1, 1853, dau. of Joshua and Patience, of Berwick, Me.

ALLEN, Isaac Jr., son of Daniel, b. 1799, d. Aug. 8, 1854, m. Sept. 2, 1821, Sarah Clark.

ALLEN, Charles, of Lee, m. (1) int. Oct. 29, 1829, in Lee, Hannah Gilman, of Gilford, m. (2) Mary ----, d. Sep. 4, 1869, aged 38.

ALLEN, Isaiah, son of Elijah, b. Jan. 10, 1802, d. Mar. 27, 1875, m. Nov. 18, 1829, Cyclene Hurd, of Sanford, Me., b. Feb. 26, 1803, d. Nov. 29, 1882, dau. of Jacob.

ALLEN, Andrew, son of Ephraim, b. Sept. 9, 1806, d. Jan. 27, 1900, m. int. Nov. 6, 1830, Judith Cole, b. Nov. 20, 1808, d. 1879.

ALLEN, Francis, son of Daniel, b. Mar. 19, 1802, d. Apr. 3, 1872, m. int. Sept. 17, 1831, Hannah Parsons, of Sanford, Me., b. Feb. 25, 1801, d. Nov. 6, 1885, dau. of John.

ALLEN, Solomon, son of Jedediah, m. int. Oct. 22, 1831, Lucinda Allen, b. Feb. 6, 1811, dau. of Elijah.

ALLEN, George Washington, son of Jacob, b. June 17, 1807, d. Sept. 8, 1868, aged 61, m. (1) Jan. 31, 1832, by Rev. John Osborne, Mrs. Susan C. Brewster, b. 1807, d. 1835, both of Lee, m. (2) (pub. June 27, 1837, in Great Falls) Mary Jane Brewster, d. Mar. 28, 1875, aged 63.

ALLEN, Solomon, son of Elijah, b. July 17, 1807, d. Aug. 26, 1887, m. int. Apr. 20, 1833, Mercy Tripp, b. 1815, d. Feb 17, 1883, dau. of Robert.

ALLEN, Charles, m. Jan. 12, 1834, in Brookfield, Adeline Trickey, of Brookfield, d. Oct. 22, 1853, aged 46, dau. of William.

ALLEN, Thomas Jefferson, son of Jacob, b. Nov. 28, 1802, d. Dec. 12, 1857, m. Mar. 9, 1834, in N. Berwick, Me., Apphia Allen, b. Nov. 26, 1811, d. May 14, 1872, dau. of Daniel.

ALLEN, Samuel Furbish, son of Daniel, b. Oct. 1807, d. 1872, m. Mar. 25, 1835, Louisa Hatch, b. 1816, d. Jan. 1, 1886.

ALLEN, William, son of Ephraim, b. July 1808, d. May 2, 1895, m. Nov. 1, 1835, Sarah Ann Furbish.

ALLEN, Ephraim, son of Ephraim, b. Feb. 18, 1812, d. May 3, 1872, m. int. Oct. 20, 1837, Catherine Allen, b. Mar. 14, 1814, d. Sept. 30, 1866, dau. of Elijah.

ALLEN, Asa, of Lee, son of Samuel, d. Dec. 5, 1861, aged 53, m. (pub. Jan. 29, 1839, in Wakefield), Patience C. Piper, of Tuftonboro, b. Oct. 5, 1814, d. Sep. 3, 1853, aged 38, dau. of John.

ALLEN, Lyman, m. Nov. 25, 1839, by Rev. Silas Green, Vienna Emily Piper, b. Jan. 16, 1821, dau. of John, both of Dover.

ALLEN, Lewis, son of Jedediah, of Limington, Me., b. Feb. 6, 1806, d. Oct. 17, 1850, m. Oct. 1, 1840, in N. Berwick, Me., Phebe Jenkins, b. Nov. 25, 1811, d. Sept. 29, 1874, dau. of Joshua, of Berwick, Me.

ALLEN, Solomon, son of Ephraim, b. June 21, 1818, d. Mar. 10, 1875, m. Dec. 2, 1841, Dorothy Hatch, of Wells, Me., b. Feb. 9, 1825, d. Nov. 24, 1894.

ALLEN, David, son of Elijah, b. June 6, 1819, d. Jan. 11, 1885, m. (1) Aug. 25, 1844, Keziah G. Allen, b. Dec. 1, 1825, d. Mar. 4, 1854, dau. of Ephraim, m. (2) Dec. 11, 1857, Sarah Jane Page, b. July 14, 1823, d. Sept. 1, 1904, dau. of David.

ALLEN, Elijah, son of Elijah, b. Mar. 27, 1822, d. June 4, 1880, m. (1) Oct. 31, 1844, Louisa L. Allen, b. Feb. 22, 1827, d. Oct. 28, 1855, dau. of Ephraim, m. (2) July 6, 1858, Ruth W. Tobie, of Sanford, Me.

ALLEN, James L., son of Samuel, d. Oct. 18, 1898, aged 72, m. Sept. 5, 1847, by Rev. Theodore Wells, Mary Ann Hoitt, both of Barrington.

ALLEN, Nahum Perkins, son of Ephraim, b. June 21, 1829, d. Oct. 29, 1916, m. Oct. 7, 1858, in Dover, Laura J. Tripp, b. May 25, 1841, d. Oct. 20, 1916, dau. of Capt. Theodore, both of Sanford, Me.

ALLEN, Thomas, d. Sept. 23, 1881, aged 50, m. (pub. Aug. 18, 1859, in Somersworth), Mary Ann McCrillis, b. 1838, d. 1918, both of N. Berwick, Me.

ALLEY, Samuel, son of Garlen L., d. Dec. 12, 1918, aged 76, m. Dec. 19, 1867, by Rev. Robert S. Stubbs, Sarah C. (Leighton) Quimby, wid. of Joseph C., b. 1817, d. Mar. 12, 1907.

AMAZEEN, Christopher C., of Newcastle, m. (pub. Dec. 17, 1863, in Portsmouth), Mary E. Brown, of N. Berwick, Me.

AMAZEEN, George E., m. Nov. 19, 1866, in Alton, Clara A. Merrow, both of Farmington.

AMBROSE, Oliver L., son of Jesse, m. Dec. 27, 1864, Abby C. Weed, both of Sandwich.

ANDREWS, James, son of Daniel, d. Jan. 31, 1900, aged 70, m. (pub. Jul. 11, 1861, in Berwick, Me.), Caroline Hill, d. May 5, 1909, aged 70.

ANDREWS, Albert, of Berwick, Me., b. 1835, d. 1915, m. June 21, 1866, in Great Falls, Almena Webber, of Great Falls.

ANDREWS, Hiram E., of Great Falls, m. Nov. 26, 1866, in Great Falls, Eliza E. Manahan, of Sanford, Me.

ANDREWS, Howard, of Lynn, Mass., m. Nov. 22, 1867, by Rev. Alden Sherwin, Mary J. Hatch, of Wolfeboro.

ANDREWS, Frank B., of Amesbury, Mass., m. Dec. 25, 1868, by Rev. Robert Stubbs, Anna V. Cook, of Dover.

APPLEBEE, Thomas, son of Hawley, b. July 19, 1764, d. Mar. 2, 1841, aged 84, m. (1) June 9, 1785, by Rev. Matthew Merriam, Molly Goodwin, m. (2) Judith Rines, b. 1769, d. Nov. 23, 1859, dau., of Henry.

APPLEBEE, Hiram, son of James, b. 1836, d. 1861, m. July 4, 1855, in Acton, Me., Betsey Jane Evans, b. 1830, d. Feb. 12, 1860, dau. of Joseph G.

APPLEBEE, Theodore S., b. Sep. 26, 1841, d. Jan. 16, 1928, m. Aug. 6, 1864, in Dover, Augusta Leighton, b. Mar. 2, 1848, both of Dover.

APPLEBEE, Oliver H., m. Sep. 22, 1866, by Rev. James Rand, Ellen C. Rains, d. Mar. 10, 1892, aged 48, dau. of Samuel.

ARLEN, John, m. Jan. 13, 1807, in Barrington, Polly Cater, both of Barrington.

ARLEN, Isaac, m. June 4, 1814, in Barrington, Patience Gray, both of Barrington.

ARLIN, Edward, m. Mar. 9, 1837, by Rev. William S. Locke, Matilda Perkins, both of Barrington.

ARLIN, William, m. (1) Caroline ----, d. July 1, 1847, aged 30, m. (2) Oct. 24, 1847, in Barrington, Phebe Jane Cate.

ARLIN, David W., m. (1) Nov. 25, 1847, in Barnstead, Betsey Hayes, d. June 10, 1848, aged 20, both of Barrington, m. (2) (pub. Dec. 30, 1851, in Haverhill, Mass.) Pamelia B. Griffin, of Vershire, Vt.

ARLIN, Edward, m. Nov. 15, 1848, by Rev. Theodore Wells, Eliza Willey, both of Barrington.

ARLIN, John W., son of John, d. Aug. 26, 1908, aged 83, m. May 24, 1849, by Elder Samuel Sherburne, Sarah Hoitt, d. May 7, 1908, aged 75, dau. of Benjamin, both of Barrington.

ASHTON, James F., of Dover, d. Aug. 16, 1893, aged 89, m. July 3, 1858, in Dover, Mary Demeritt, of Durham, d. Apr. 21, 1884, aged 80.

ASHTON, Benjamin F., son of James, d. Nov. 4, 1876, aged 28, m. Dec. 21, 1864, in Dover, Lizzie L. Parcher, of Waterboro, Me., b. Apr. 30, 1844, d. June 8, 1906.

ASPINWALL, William K., m. Sept. 26, 1862, in Rollinsford, Mrs. Mary B. Weed, both of Rollinsford.

ASPINWALL, John G., aged 21, m. Jan. 23, 1865, in W. Milton, Frances P. Perkins, aged 16, both of Middleton.

ATWATER, Constant L. T., m. Feb. 20, 1864, in Dover, Ellen M. Langley, both of Newburyport, Mass.

ATWOOD, Charles H., of Sandwich, son of Harrison, aged 21, m. Aug. 7, 1864, in Strafford, Eliza B. Stevenson, aged 20, of Tamworth.

AUSTIN, Jacob K., m. July 21, 1866, in Dover, Mary C. Witham, both of Dover.

AUSTIN, Joseph, of Rollinsford, m. July 31, 1869, in Salmon Falls, Mrs. Anna Perkins, of York, Me.
AVERILL, Benjamin, m. Apr. 6, 1868, in Great Falls, Lizzie Hutchinson.
AVERILL, Trask W., m. (pub. Dec. 8, 1870, in Farmington), Almena A. Runnals, both of Farmington.
AVERY, David, b. Mar. 18, 1815, d. Feb. 24, 1904, m. June 1, 1836, by Rev. Nathaniel Berry, Sally L. Holmes, d. Oct. 29, 1861, aged 40, both of Strafford.
AVERY, Henry C., son of John, d. Feb. 15, 1892, aged 57, m. Nov. 21, 1860, in Alton, Emma R. Sawyer, d. Dec. 17, 1958, aged 79, dau. of Rev. Seth, both of Alton.
AVERY, George W., son of Daniel E., d. June 8, 1911, aged 72, m. Nov. 18, 1862, in Dover, Eliza G. Trickey, d. Feb. 17, 1916, aged 78, dau. of Lemuel G., both of Dover.
AVERY, Lewis C., m. Mar. 18, 1866, in Barnstead, Ruth H. Canney, b. Dec. 18, 1837, d. Dec. 30, 1905, dau. of Joseph, both of Barnstead.
AVERY, Joseph Howard, b. 1844, d. 1937, m. (1) May 26, 1866, in Milton, Thesta D. Hanscomb, b. 1846, d. 1875, m. (2) Emma C. --- -, b. 1841, d. 1933.
AVERY, Solomon, m. Aug. 28, 1866, in Dover, Ellen L. McDuffee, d. Apr. 4, 1901, aged 59, dau. of Thomas.
AYERS, Joseph, of Barrington, m. Apr. 4, 1837, in Wolfeboro, Susan W. Piper, of Wolfeboro, b. Oct. 26, 1806, dau. of John.
AYERS, Levi, d. Mar. 20, 1885, aged 73, m. (pub. Sept. 5, 1837, in Ossipee), Salley Welch, b. Jan. 20, 1818, d. Jan. 1, 1901, both of Tuftonboro.
AYERS, Charles W., m. Aug. 7, 1867, in Great Falls, Addie E. Carpenter, of Exeter.
AYERS, John H., m. Sept. 13, 1866, by Rev. James Rand, Emma A. Fogg, both of Rollinsford.
BABB, Benjamin, m. June 28, 1779, by Rev. Joseph Haven, Hannah Furber, d. Dec. 20, 1830, aged 85.
BABB, Moses, b. in 1753, d. in 1837, m. Aug. 22, 1780, by Rev. Joseph Haven, Maribah Lock, d. Feb. 22, 1849, aged 97, both of Barrington.
BABB, John, m. Nov. 25, 1790, by Rev. Benjamin Balch, Mary Hodgdon, both of Barrington.
BABB, William, d. Dec. 15, 1825, aged 60, m. Dec. 10, 1791, by Rev. Benjamin Balch, Esther Hodgdon, both of Barrington.

BABB, Charles, m. Jan. 1793, Hannah Church, dau. of Ebenezer, both of Barrington.

BABB, Thomas, m. Oct. 3, 1799, by Rev. Benjamin Balch, Lydia Ham, both of Barrington.

BABB, David, m. Nov. 10, 1803, in Barrington, Anna Felker, both of Barrington.

BABB, Richard, m. Nov. 22, 1804, by Rev. Benjamin Balch, Hannah Felker, d. Feb. 28, 1848, aged 66, both of Barrington.

BABB, William 3rd, m. Sept. 4, 1806, by Rev. Benjamin Balch, Lydia Cate, both of Barrington.

BABB, Sampson, m. Oct. 19, 1809, in Barrington, Betsey Raymond, both of Barrington.

BABB, Isaac, of Barrington, d. Aug. 4, 1848, aged 50, m. Feb. 5, 1826, by Elder Enoch Place, Lucinda Leighton, of Strafford, d. 1840, aged 40.

BABB, Joseph T., b. Dec. 28, 1803, d. May 4, 1892, m. (1) Feb. 1, 1827, by Rev. Enoch Place, Abigail F. Cater, dau. of John, both of Barrington, m. (2) Nov. 14, 1838, Mary B. Tebbets, m. (3) Jan. 30, 1844, by Rev. Enoch Place, Abigail Kimball, of Strafford, b. Jan. 16, 1817, d. Jan. 3, 1882.

BABB, Benjamin Franklin, of Barrington, b. 1807, d. Oct. 24, 1851, m. May 1, 1828, by Rev. Enoch Place, Mary Huckins, of Madbury, b. 1804, d. May 27, 1858.

BABB, Joel, of Strafford, m. June 18, 1829, by Rev. John Winkley, Charlotte Babb, of Barrington, d. Dec. 19, 1843, aged 39.

BABB, John, of Barrington, m. Nov. 28, 1833, in Barrington, by Rev. Samuel H. Merrill, Mary Mason, of Somersworth.

BABB, Asahel, d. Aug. 5, 1886, aged 74, m. Jan. 29, 1835, by Elder Enoch Place, Lydia Berry, dau. of Benjamin, d. Jan. 24, 1887, aged 78, both of Strafford.

BABB, Joseph T., m. Nov. 14, 1838, in Barrington, Mary B. Tibbets, both of Barrington.

BABB, Isaac, m. int. Nov. 10, 1841, in Dover, Martha Cater, b. Jan. 10, 1824, dau. of Daniel.

BABB, Thomas, of New Durham, aged 74, m. (1) ----, m. (2) Nov. 14, 1844, by Elder Enoch Place, Mrs. Abigail (Clark) Sampson, of Strafford, aged 45, wid. of Jonathan.

BABB, George W., m. Apr. 8, 1860, by Rev. John Winkley, Sarah E. Foss, both of Strafford.

BABB, John L., of Strafford, b. Apr. 17, 1842, d. July 7, 1923, m. June 8, 1862, in New Durham, Sarah A. Nutter, of Barnstead.

BABB, Richard F., b Feb. 25, 1843, d. Apr. 11, 1912, m. Sep. 19, 1863, by Rev. John Winkley. Mary F. Hartford, of Somersworth, b. Feb. 7, 1843, d. Oct. 9, 1922.

BABB, John A., of Dover, m. Jan. 4, 1866, by Rev. Francis E. Abbott, Mary E. Bickford, of Rochester.

BADGER, Elder Joseph, son of Peaslee, b. Aug. 16, 1792, d. May 12, 1852, m. (1) July 21, 1816, by Elder Enoch Place, Mary Peavey, of Farmington, b. Feb. 26, 1798, d. Apr. 4, 1820, dau. of Col. Anthony, m. (2) Mar. 21, 1821, Eliza Maria Sterling, of Lima, NY.

BADGER, John P., m. Oct. 26, 1870, in Dover, Adelaid Hussey, both of Dover.

BAILEY, James H., m. Aug. 10, 1867, by Rev. Robert S. Stubbs, Fanny W. Beacher, both of Rochester.

BAKER, James Willard, son of John., d. Nov. 28, 1880, m. (1) Jan. 15, 1846, by Elder Enoch Place, Mary Elizabeth Place, d. Aug. 13, 1890, aged 67, dau of Elder Enoch, both of Strafford, m. (2) ? Nov. 13, 1891, in Dover, Lydia E. O'Conner.

BAKER, Eben F., of Dover, m. Jan. 1, 1865, in Dover, Darinda A. Hill, of Great Falls.

BAKER, Asa S., of Dover, m. May 1, 1865, in Dover, Sarah A. Meader, of Rochester.

BAKER, Frank H., of Dover, m. July 11, 1870, in Augusta, Me., Sarah Butler, of Augusta, Me.

BALCH, Thomas, son of Rev. Benjamin, of Seabrook, Mass., b. Oct. 2, 1765, m. (1) Nov. 10, 1793, by Rev. Benjamin Balch, Elizabeth Kingman, b. Aug. 16, 1774, d. Apr. 21, 1802, dau. of John, m. (2) Dec. 6, 1803, by Rev. Benjamin Balch, Judith Swain, of Gilmanton, b. Aug. 10, 1793.

BALL, Dr. Charles G., m. Mar. 6, 1864, in Dover, Lizzie P. Hammett, of Dover.

BANFIELD, J. Stewart, of Dover, m. Oct. 1, 1867, in Brooklyn, N.Y., Hattie R. Smith, of Brooklyn, N.Y.

BANFILL, A. L., of Conway, m. July 28, 1867, in Tuftonboro, Eliza A. Roberts, b. 1845, d. 1916, dau. of William.

BANKS, Israel, of Parsonsfield, Me., m. June 24, 1849, by Rev. Levi B. Tasker, in Sandwich, Elvira B. Moulton, of Sandwich.

BANKS, Edwin, of N. Haven, Me., son of William, m. Aug. 14, 1864, by Rev. Alvan Tobey, Julia M. Willey, of Newmarket, dau. of Benjamin.

BARKER, Dudley, of Alton, d. 31 Dec. 1881, aged 79, m. (pub. Mar. 14, 1837, in Alton), Betsey Willey, of New Durham, d. Mar. 1, 1884, aged 71.

BARKER, Dr. Charles G., m. Oct. 10, 1862, in Wakefield, Ellen M. Grover.

BARKER, S. Augustine, of Boston, m. (pub. Dec. 3, 1863, in Wolfeboro), Melissa Jane Furber, dau. of John.

BARKER, Joy W., son of Ira, d. Nov. 28, 1905, aged 68, m. Mar. 22, 1866, in Rochester, Maria M. Horne, both of Derry.

BARNES, Benjamin Jr., m. Apr. 4, 1864, by Rev. James Rand, Mary E. Meader, d. Mar. 25, 1928, aged 84, dau. of Isaac, both of Dover.

BARNES, David H., of Dover, m. May 17, 1868, in Winchenden, Mass., Martha A. Sweetser, of Winchenden, Mass.

BARROWS, William H., of Manchester, m. Jan. 21, 1865, in Lowell, Mass., Lizzie J. Hanson, of Barrington.

BARROWS, Alvah G., m. Nov. 26, 1866, in Farmington, Lizzie B. Ricker, both of Milton.

BARROWS, Orin R., of Lovell, Me., m. Mar. 23, 1868, in Great Falls, Sophronia Johnson, of Great Falls.

BARTER, Paul, m. Sept. 4, 1805, in Barrington, Mrs. Elizabeth Berry, both of Barrington.

BARTLETT, Joseph, b. Feb. 27, 1738, d. 1808, m. Oct. 12, 1762, Sarah Morse.

BARTLETT, Jonathan, son of Col. Thomas, d. Oct. 25, 1852, aged 72, m. Feb. 2, 1809, by Rev. John Osborne, Love Laskey, of Lee, b. Dec. 12, 1789, d. Aug. 7, 1884, dau. of William.

BARTLETT, Alfred, of Lee, son of Josiah, b. Aug. 30, 1820, d. Aug. 16, 1887, aged 66, m. (1) Nov. 14, 1844, by Rev. Mr. Thompson, Mary M. Furber, of Lee, dau. of John, d. Nov. 24, 1857, aged 34, m. (2) (pub. Nov. 1, 1860, in Dover), Louisa W. Cushing, d. June 7, 1861, aged 26, dau. of Samuel H.

BARTLETT, Jonathan L., m. June 11, 1866, in Nottingham, Sarah A. Simpson.

BATCHELDER, Davis Jr., m. Nov. 28, 1787, Sarah Hull, dau. of Richard.

BATCHELDER, Abraham, of Northwood, m. Jan. 1, 1804, by Rev. Benjamin Balch, Hannah Caldwell, of Barrington.

BATCHELDER, Nathaniel, of Gilmanton, m. Dec. 25, 1816, by Elder Enoch Place, Jane Dame, of Barrington, dau. of Jonathan.

BATEMAN, John H., m. Dec. 16, 1868, in Dover, Sarah E. Foss, both of Strafford.

BATES, John W., of Great Falls, d. May 23, 1901, aged 69, m. (pub. Jun. 21, 1853, in Eliot, Me.), Sophia E. Thompson, of Solon, Me., d. Mar. 1, 1873, aged 38.

BATES, George S., m. July 27, 1864, in Great Falls, Laura A. Legro, d. Sep. 6, 1903, aged 63, both of Great Falls.

BAXTER, Charles N., of Rollinsford, m. Oct. 9, 1869, in Salmon Falls, Ella N. Stanley, of Lynn, Mass.

BAXTER, Nahum W., m. Sept. 11, 1870, in Dalmon Falls, Jennie Cochran, both of Salmon Falls.

BAXTER, John M., m. (pub) Dec. 29, 1870, in Great Falls), Abby M. Jones.

BAYLES, Abial, d. Mar. 14, 1909, aged 69, m. (pub. Jan. 12, 1860, in Great Falls), Mary Odel.

BEACHAM, George A., son of Asa, b. Oct. 10, 1826, d. Mar. 11, 1866, m. Jan. 27, 1856, in Rochester, Mary Frances Canney, b. Sept. 23, 1830, d. Mar. 10, 1913, dau. of Moses.

BEACHAM, John E., son of Simon F., b. 1843, d. 1918, m. (pub. Mar. 19, 1863, in Ossipee), Annie E. Chick, b. 1847, d. 1901.

BEALS, William W., m. May 7, 1865, in E. Boston, Ellen A. Wiggin, of Dover.

BEAN, Benjamin m. near 1774, Rachel Gilman, d. 1815.

BEAN, Andrew, m. Feb. 5, 1792, by Rev. Jeremiah Shaw, Betty Sinclair, of Sandwich, d. May 1, 1859, aged 88.

BEAN, Benning M., of Moultonboro, d. Feb. 9, 1866, aged 84, m. Feb. 28, 1818, by Rev. Jeremiah Shaw, Lydia Adams, of Centre Harbor, d. 1866, aged 73.

BEAN, Josiah, son of Benjamin, d. Dec. 13, 1847, aged 50, m. int. Nov. 1822, in Tuftonboro, Anna Kinnison, d. Sept. 29, 1862, aged 73, both of Tufttonboro.

BEAN, Elder Silas F., of Tuftonboro, b. Oct. 3, 1807, d. Mar. 6, 1890, m. (1) 1836, Ursula A. Seavey, d. Jan. 1, 1846, aged 27, dau. of Joseph M. Seavey, m. (2) (pub. Apr. 4, 1848, in Ossipee), Mary Ann Abbott, of Ossipee, b. June 26, 1829, d. Sept. 14, 1902.

BEAN, James G., m. Oct. 18, 1857, in Sandwich, Mrs. Elizabeth J. Rogers.

BEAN, Henry F., of Old Town, Me., m. (pub. Dec. 31, 1857, in Great Falls), Ellen F. Roberts, of Rochester, d. Jul. 25, 1928, aged 86, dau. of Dudley.

BEAN, Jonathan M., of Dover, m. Dec. 4, 1858, in Dover, Calantha D. Walker, of Newmarket, b. 1838, d. 1861.

BEAN, Joseph D., of Alfred, Me., m. Feb. 24, 1863, in Waterboro, Me., Jennie Gray, of Dover.

BEAN, Edmund C., m. (pub. June 2, 1864, in Portsmouth), Olive W. Dame, both of Newington.

BEAN, Enos, m. Sept. 15, 1866, by Rev. James Rand, Mrs. Mary Lunt, both of Dover.

BEAN, George W., of Farmington, m. (pub. Dec. 29, 1870), in Great Falls), Mary E. Goodwin, of Lebanon, Me.

BECK, Samuel, of New Durham, m. Jan. 7, 1808, by Rev. Benjamin Randall, Betsey Davis, of Alton, dau. of Zebulon.

BEECHER, John A., m. Dec. 16, 1869, in Rochester, Ella H. Sanborn.

BEEDE, Thomas, son of Jacob, b. Dec. 26, 1788, d. Mar. 24, 1866, m. (1) Susannah Rogers, m. (2) Sept. 1, 1853, by Rev. Levi B. Tasker, in Sandwich, Mrs. Ruth R. (Smith) Prescott, b. Nov. 17, 1813, d. Feb. 24, 1888, dau. of Isaac, both of Sandwich

BEEDE, J.C., m. Oct. 13, 1866, in Center Sandwich, Clara E. Copp.

BEEDLE (BETLE?), John, m. Dec. 31, 1818, in Lebanon, Me., Polly Mills.

BEEDLE, Henry, of Somersworth, son of Ivory, b. Aug. 6, 1824, d. June 11, 1897, m. (1) (pub. Jan. 18, 1848, in Parsonsfield, Me.), Mary Jane Burbank, of Parsonsfield, Me., d. Nov. 16, 1854, aged 31, dau. of David, m. (2) int. Dec. 25, 1855, in Rollinsford, Mary D. Emery, in S. Berwick, Me., b. Dec. 21, 1822, d. Dec. 29, 1902.

BELL, Charles H., m. (pub. June 13, 1867, in Exeter), Mrs. Mary E. Gilman.

BENN, George W., of Dover, m. June 23, 1868, in Kalamazoo, Mich., Letitia J. Shaw, of Kalamazoo, Mich.

BENNETT, John Jr., d. June 1, 1876, aged 81, m. Oct. 24, 1819, by Rev. Joseph Boodey, Ruth Elkins, d. Dec. 2, 1862, aged 74, both of New Durham.

BENNETT, David D., of Northwood, d. Oct. 11, 1866, aged 77, m. Mar. 13, 1820, by Elder Enoch Place, Sarah T. Collins, of Barrington, b. 1797, d. 1873.

BENNETT, Ebenezer L. of Northwood, d. Jun. 10, 1883, aged 87, m. Aug. 30, 1820, by Rev. John Osborne, Catherine T. (Gile) Stevens, of Lee, d. Apr. 6, 1860, aged 68, wid. of Joseph.

BENNETT, James, of New Durham, son of Abraham, b. Feb. 23, 1816, d. Nov. 21, 1894, m. 1844, Betsey N. Davis, b. July 16, 1822, d. Dec. 11, 1910.

BENNETT, John E., son of John, d. Apr. 6, 1900, aged 76, m. (pub. Dec. 15, 1846, in Tuftonboro), Hannah Welch, d. Sept. 8, 1899, aged 77, dau. of Adriel, both of Tuftonboro.

BENNETT, George P., b. 1827, d. 1864, m. Oct. 1, 1848, by Rev. Charles N. Smith, Abigail P. Straw, b. 1827, d. Apr. 8, 1889, dau. of Moses, both of Dover.

BENNETT, James M., of Moultonboro, aged 25, m. Nov. 11, 1850, by Rev. Levi B. Tasker, in Sandwich, Susan Cook, of Dover, aged 21.

BENNETT, Augustus, m. Nov. 28, 1864, in Dover, Viola Nason, both of S. Berwick, Me.

BENNETT, Josiah C., of Sandwich, m. Feb. 5, 1865, in Dover, Nancy L. Richardson, of Rochester, dau. of Capt. Ephraim.

BENNETT, Frank H., m. May 1, 1865, in Dover, Emily A. Hill, both of Northwood.

BENNETT, Tuttle, m. July 3, 1865, in Northwood, Mary A. Holmes, both of Nottingham.

BENNETT, John S., of Bucksport, Me., m. Feb. 22, 1866, in Newmarket, Albertine Hatch, of Portsmouth.

BENNETT, George W., m. June 27, 1870, in Dover, Coridle Young, both of Dover.

BENSON, Ephraim C., b. Mar. 18, 1840, d. Dec. 5, 1918, m. Aug. 17, 1865, in Dover, Florence E. Caverly, b. Sept. 7, 1846, both of W. Peru, Me.

BENTLY, Thomas, of Rollinsford, b. June 19, 1835, d. Feb. 26, 1911, m. July 3, 1865, in Great Falls, Ruth A. Dore, of S. Berwick, Me., b. Oct. 31, 1838, d. Oct. 25, 1910.

BENTLY, Joseph, m. July 4, 1870, in Berwick, Me., Lizzie Banks, both of Nottingham.

BERRY, Thomas, m. Nov. 27, 1777, in Barrington, Tamsin Stanton, both of Barrington.

BERRY, Stephen, m. Dec. 4, 1777, in Barrington, Judith Foss, both of Barrington.

BERRY, George Jr., d. Sep. 10, 1835, aged 70, m. Nov. 29, 1787, by Rev. Benjamin Balch, Hannah Evans, d. Jun. 19, 1844, aged 81, both of Barrington.

BERRY, Richard, d. Sep. 13, 1825, m. Feb. 11, 1790, by Rev. Benjamin Balch, Olly Seavey, both of Barrington.

BERRY, John Jr., d. Sep. 4, 1815, aged 30, m. Apr. 5, 1804, by Rev. Benjamin Balch, Betsey Elliot, both of Barrington.

BERRY, William, d. May 16, 1878, aged 91, m. Oct. 30, 1806, by Rev. Benjamin Randall, Sarah Hall, d. Sept. 3, 1845, aged 62, <u>dau. of Joseph</u>, both of Barrington.

BERRY, Joseph, m. Dec. 1, 1814, by Rev. Paul Jewett, Abigail Fall.

BERRY, Jeremiah, d. May 20, 1817, aged 62, m. (1) Tamson ----, d. Nov. 26, 1807, aged 48, m. (2) Feb. 2, 1808, in Barrington, Hannah Cate, both of Barrington.

BERRY, Jeremiah, m. Mar. 26, 1808, in Barrington, Joanna Felker, both of Barrington.

BERRY, Stephen Jr., m. Jan. 19, 1809, in Barrington, Betsey Foss, both of Barrington.

BERRY, Levi, son of Benjamin, b. 1787, m. Oct. 26, 1809, in Barrington, <u>Mrs</u>. Margaret <u>(Freese)</u> Moulton, <u>wid. of Moses, both of Barrington</u>.

BERRY, Paul, of Strafford, b. 1806, d. Feb 27, 1884, m. <u>(1)</u> Apr. 8 1830, by Rev. Enoch Place, Hannah Brock, of Barnstead, d. Oct. 21, 1845, aged 42, <u>m. (2) Abigail ----, d. Feb. 2, 1891, aged 71</u>.

BERRY, George 3rd, m. Feb. 23, 1811, by Rev. Micajah Otis, Esther Johnson, both of Barrington.

BERRY, Jonathan, m. Aug. 2, 1812, in Barrington, Betty Fowler, both of Barrington.

BERRY, Ezra, of Barrington, m. <u>(1)</u> Feb. 9, 1819, by Elder Enoch Place, Elizabeth Pearl, of Rochester, <u>d. Mar. 19</u>, 1832, aged 33, dau. of Ebenezer, m. (2) Nov. 11, 1832, by Rev. Samuel Sherburne, Mary Pearl, both of Barrington.

BERRY, Woodbury, <u>son of Richard</u>, m. Feb. 20, 1823, by Elder Enoch Place, Lovey Brown, d. Nov. 6, 1842, aged 40, both of Barrington.

BERRY, Jonathan <u>Neal, d. Oct. 1, 1881, aged 78</u>, m. Mar. 9, 1828, Eliza Berry, <u>d. Aug. 6, 1881, aged 81</u>, both of Moulton.

BERRY, Alexander S., of Strafford, m. <u>(1)</u> Apr. 30, 1835, by Elder Enoch Place, Belinda Jenness, of Rochester, dau. of John, <u>m. (2) int. Mar. 23, 1867, in Brookfield, Mrs. Mary A. Nute, wid. of Isaac</u>.

BERRY, Meshack, of Strafford, d. May 6, 1864, aged 61, m. <u>(1)</u> Sept. 11, 1823, by Rev. Joseph Boodey, Eliza Kimball, of Alton, d. Oct. 16, 1853, aged 48, <u>m. (2) Jane ----, b. May 4, 1836, d. May 5, 1916</u>.

BERRY, Rev. Nathaniel, son of Benjamin, d. Oct. 19, 1865, aged 77, m. (1) Nabby ----, d. Sept. 18, 1823, aged 32, m. (2) Aug. 15,

1824, by Rev. Joseph Boodey, Mary C. Young, d. May 1, 1857, aged 55, both of Farmington.

BERRY, Richard, of Strafford, son of Richard, d. Sept. 1875, aged 83, m. (1) Lois ----, d. June 14, 1824, m. (2) Aug. 26, 1824, by Elder Enoch Place, Sally Stockbridge, of Barrington.

BERRY, John, of Dover, d. Apr. 7, 1851, aged 57, m. Nov. 12, 1824, by Elder Enoch Place, Rachel Hayes, of Strafford.

BERRY, Stephen F., d. Mar. 16, 1852, aged 41, m. int. Sept. 25, 1831, in Dover, Hannah Bunker, dau. of John.

BERRY, Enoch, m. (1) Nov. 15, 1831, by Rev. John G. Dow, Eliza Hurd, d. June 6, 1867, aged 61, both of Dover, m. (2) (pub. Dec. 17, 1868, in New Durham), Mrs. Sarah Ann C. Ela, both of New Durham, wid. of George, d. Feb. 5, 1854, aged 38.

BERRY, Nicholas, son of Thomas, d. Oct. 17, 1855, aged 71, m. (1) Hannah ----, d. Aug. 11, 1829, aged 41, m. (2) Oct. 7, 1832, by Rev. Nathaniel Berry, Abigail Cornell, d. Apr. 2, 1873, aged 81, both of Strafford.

BERRY, Lieut. William, d. Feb. 22, 1894, aged 88, m. Dec. 1832, by Rev. John Winkley, Polly Hayes, d. Aug. 5, 1883, aged 75, both of Strafford.

BERRY, Edward, b. Apr. 8, 1803, d. Jul. 22, 1887, m. Nov. 27, 1834, by Rev. John Winkley, Jane Foss, b. Jan. 16, 1805, d. Feb. 1, 1885, dau. of Joshua, both of Strafford.

BERRY, Alexander S., of Strafford, m. Apr. 30, 1835, by Elder Enoch Place, Belinda Jenness, of Rochester, dau. of John.

BERRY, James M., d. Apr. 6, 1895, aged 80, m. Mar. 31, 1839, by Rev. John Winkley, Sarah C. Hayes, d. Dec. 28, 1863, aged 59, both of Strafford.

BERRY, Jesse C., son of george, d. Jan. 11, 1891, aged 77, m. (pub. Nov. 12, 1839, in Strafford), Jane H. Sanders, d. Jul. 22, 1867, aged 48, dau. of Daniel, both of Strafford.

BERRY, Ezekiel H., son of Stephen, d. Mar. 25, 1849, aged 31, m. Dec. 11, 1841, by Rev. John Winkley, Mary Hayes, b. Oct. 7, 1818, d. Apr. 17, 1891, both of Strafford.

BERRY, George, 2nd, of Strafford, son of John, m. Dec. 22, 1842, by Elder Enoch Place, Mary Danforth, of Somersworth, d. Mar. 28, 1888, aged 63, dau. of Coleman.

BEERY, Ezra, of Barrington, m. Mar. 10, 1843, in Lebanon, Me., Sarah Johnson, of Somerset.

BERRY, Jotham S., of Portsmouth, m. before May 10, 1845, in Portsmouth, Judith Wallingford.

BERRY, Lemuel, m. Nov. 27, 1846, by Elder Samuel Sherburne, Olive Hoitt, both of Barrington.

BERRY, Stephen B., b. 1825, d. 1906, m. (1) Sarah A. Holmes, d. Apr. 16, 1852, aged 23, dau. of Noah, m. (2) Apr. 26, 1853, by Rev. John Winkley, Eliza Brewster, b. 1820, d. 1904, both of Barnstead.

BERRY, Paul, d. Feb. 27, 1884, aged 78, m. Nov. 19, 1857, in Dover, Abby Berry, d. Feb. 2, 1891, aged 72, dau. of Richard.

BERRY, John B., of New Durham, b. 1836, d. 1881, m. Nov. 1, 1859, in Dover, Vianna F. Horn, of Farmington, b. 1844, d. Mar. 29, 1912.

BERRY, Eliphalet C., m. Sept. 16, 1862, in Barrington, Nancy B. Chesley, both of Barrington.

BERRY, Levi R., of Dover, m. Apr. 11, 1863, in Great Falls, Mary J. Durgin, of W. Newfield, Me.

BERRY, Edwin E., of New Durham, m. Feb. 2, 1864, in Dover, Emma J. Hurd, of Dover, dau. of John S.

BERRY, Samuel, of Tamworth, m. Nov. 14, 1864, in Strafford, Vienna Pitman.

BERRY, Eben C., of Strafford, m. Jan. 17, 1865, in Rochester, Abbie Felker, of Barrington.

BERRY, John E., of Wolfeboro, b. Nov. 13, 1830, d. June 17, 1913, m. Jan. 27, 1866, in Wolfeboro, Olive M. Chesley, of Alton, b. Aug. 11, 1848, d. Dec. 5, 1883.

BERRY, Joel F., m. Mar. 7, 1866, in Rochester, Frances M. Foss, both of Strafford.

BERRY, Alonzo F., m. Aug. 20, 1866, in Barrington, Olive A. Brown, both of Barrington.

BERRY, Nathaniel H., of Farmington, m. Oct. 6, 1866, in Rochester, Fannie D. Durgin, of Parsonsfield, Me.

BERRY, Alonzo J., m. Nov. 25, 1866, in Dover, Anabel Gerrish, both of Dover.

BERRY, Lovell F., of Strafford, m. July 18, 1867, Melissa A. Hartford, of Somersworth, b. Oct. 28, 1844, d. Jan. 10, 1912, aged 67, dau. of Samuel.

BERRY, Frank J., of Watertown, Mass., m. May 20, 1868, by Rev. Robert S. Stubbs, Sarah H. Ross, of Dover.

BERRY, Joseph F., of Dover, son of Oliver, b. 1845, d. 1934, m. Aug. 25, 1868, in Dover, Josephine M. Reynolds, of Madbury, d. July 14, 1925, aged 82.

BERRY, Charles F., of New Durham, m. (pub. July 14, 1870, in Rochester), Martha A. Trickey.

BERRY, Eben C., of Farmington, m. Oct. 6, 1870, in Dover, Celissa A. Buzzell, of Quincy, Mass.

BICKFORD, Andrew, of Durham, son of Benjamin, d. Apr. 2, 1831, aged 80, m. Aug. 28, 1777, by Dr. Belknap, Rebecca Canney, of Dover, dau. of Thomas.

5) BICKFORD, John, son of Joshua, d. Dec. 20, 1832, aged 69, m. 1785, Mehitable Leathers.

BICKFORD, John, 3rd, b. 1766, m. Nov. 19, 1788, by Rev. Joseph Haven, Sarah Nutter, d. July 28, 1840, aged 77, both of Rochester.

BICKFORD, Samuel, of New Durham, m. Jun. 25, 1794, in Brookfield, Comfort York, of Middleton.

BICKFORD, Nathaniel, son of Jonathan, b. 1774, d. Dec. 1, 1853, m. int. Feb. 1801, in Tuftonboro, Mary Bean, of Tuftonboro, b. 1780, d. Feb. 23, 1860, dau. of Benjamin.

6) BICKFORD, Gershom, of Wolfeboro, son of Jonathan, d. Oct. 1854, aged 73, m. (1) int. May 1808, in Tuftonboro, Elizabeth Bean, of Tuftonboro, d. Apr. 13, 1852, aged 68, m. (2) May 2, 1853, in Wolfeboro, Mary Jackson, of Tamworth.

BICKFORD, Aaron, of Rochester, son of John, b. 1790, d. Oct. 15, 1852, m. (1) May 12, 1814, by Elder Enoch Place, Temperance Thompson, of Wakefield, d. June 21, 1823, aged 28, m. (2) Patience Jenness, b. 1803, d. Apr. 1, 1890, dau. of William.

BICKFORD, Isaac, son of John, b. 1807, d. Jun. 14, 1878, m. Sep. 19, 1834, in Lebanon, ME, Sarah Jenness, b. 1804, d. 1869.

6) BICKFORD, Robert, of Durham, son of Robert, b. Mar. 3, 1805, d. Apr. 11, 1876, m. (1) Dec. 15, 1831, Elizabeth ----, m. (2) Nov. 4, 1867, by Rev. Alvan Tobey, Sarah (Clay) Clark, of Newmarket, aged 46, of Newmarket, dau. of John.

BICKFORD, Dr. Alphonzo, son of Thomas, b. Dec. 12, 1817, d. Dec. 31, 1869, m. May 29, 1838, by Rev. Alvin Tobey, Mary J. Smith, of Durham, dau. of Maj. Winthrop.

BICKFORD, Orin W., m. (1) Mar. 9, 1836, in Lebanon, Me., Catherine Gerrish, m. (2) (pub. Feb. 26, 1857, in Somerset), Lydia S. Hamilton, m. (3) Jul. 11, 1867, in Lebanon, Me., Mrs. Judith (Gerrish) Wiles, dau. of James.

BICKFORD, David, m. Feb. 24, 1840, in Barrington, by Rev. Samuel Nichols, Susanna Marden, both of Barrington.

BICKFORD, Charles D., m. (pub. Jan. 19, 1847, in Rochester), Mrs. Susan (Ham) Meserve, d. July 4, 1847, aged 23, wid. of John C., both of Rochester.

BICKFORD, John T., of Rochester, m. Mar. 17, 1853, in Lebanon, Me., Phebe H. Hayes, of Strafford.

BICKFORD, Thomas, m. Jul. 28, 1857, Eliza Cushing, d. Jul. 3, 1887, dau. of Jonathan.

BICKFORD, Marquis J., son of James, d. Feb. 25, 1864, aged 24, m. Jan. 7, 1862, in Ossipee, Sarah C. Hodgdon, of Tuftonboro.

BICKFORD, Charles D., of Roxbury, Mass., m. June 16, 1862, Judith A. Davis, of Madbury, b. Mar. 15, 1842, d. Nov. 18, 1906, dau. of Samuel.

BICKFORD, Clark, of Boston, Mass., m. July 3, 1862, Mary A. Downing, of New Durham.

BICKFORD, J. M., m. (pub. Jan. 8, 1863, in Great Falls), Emma F. Twombly, both of New Durham.

BICKFORD, E. A., m. Feb. 13, 1864, in Great Falls, Eliza J. Ward, both of Great Falls.

BICKFORD, David, m. July 4, 1864, in Rochester, Wealthy A. C. Smith, of Loudon, d. Aug. 11, 1904, aged 62, dau. of Rawson J.

BICKFORD, Merrill D., of Parsonsfield, Me., m. Mar. 7, 1866, in Dover, Clara A. Davis, dau. of E. S. Davis.

BICKFORD, Paul P., of Madison, m. Apr. 28, 1867, in Conway, Eliza A. Rand, of Dover, dau. of Leonard S.

BICKFORD, Edward, of Laconia, m. Nov. 28, 1867, in Salmon Falls, Jennie E. Horn, of Rollinsford.

BICKFORD, Charles W., son of John, d. Aug. 8, 1908, aged 65, m. May 28, 1868, in Rochester, m. Louise Henderson, dau. of Charles, both of Rochester.

BICKFORD, George A., of Rochester, m. Dec. 13, 1868, in Rochester, Lavina H. Scruton, of Farmington.

BILLINGS, Oliver, of Lebanon, Me., m. Sep. 3, 1851, in Lebanon, Me., Sarah Thompson, of No. Berwick, Me.

BIXBY, Avery D., of Manchester, m. June 6, 1867, in Rochester, Sarah A. Perkins, of Wakefield.

BLACKMAR, Charles E., d. Sep. 30, 1907, aged 74, m. Feb. 4, 1859, in North Berwick, Me., Eliza A. Tuttle, both of Rochester.

BLACKMAR, Dr. John, m. Oct. 22, 1863, in Effingham, Ellen S. Dearborn, of Effingham, dau. of J. Shephard Dearborn.

BLAISDELL, John M., m. Nov. 22, 1863, in Great Falls, Sophia H. Dame, both of Rochester.

BLAISDELL, Joseph B., of S. Berwick, Me., m. Dec. 7, 1865, in Great Falls, Adelaide A. Delano, of Great Falls.

BLAISDELL, George W., m. (pub. Jan. 27, 1870, in Great Falls), Julia E. Bell, both of Lebanon, Me.

BLAISDELL, Jonathan W., of Lebanon, Me., m. July 4, 1870, in Dover, Georgia Parker, of E. Rochester.

BLAISDELL, Charles, m. (pub. Aug. 11, 1870, in Great Falls), Sophia Mills.

BLAKE, John, m. Oct. 1, 1772, in Barrington, Rachel Marden, b. Oct. 16, 1751, dau. of James.

BLAKE, Joseph, of Barnstead, b. Apr. 13, 1820, d. Mar. 8, 1893, m. (pub. Jan. 23, 1849, in Strafford), Alice G. Perkins, of Strafford, b. Apr. 21, 1822, d. Feb. 12, 1910.

BLAKE, William H., of Berwick, Me., m. May 14, 1854, in Lebanon, Me., Mary McCrillis.

BLAKE, F. Warren, of Pittsfield, m. June 21, 1866, in Kingston, R. I., Mary L. Judkins, of Kingston, R. I.

BLANCHARD, Jacob S. m. Mar. 1866, in Lee, Placentia C. Meserve, both of Lee.

BLOOD, Ira A., m. May 31, 1870, in Great Falls, Emma M. Martin.

BLUNT, Capt. A. E., of Cleveland, Tenn., m. Aug. 10, 1865, in Wolfeboro, Susan P. Hall, dau. of Dr. J. F. Hall.

BODGE, Samuel, of Lee, m. Sept. 28, 1777, by Dr. Belknap, Rebecca Gear, of Barrington, d. Oct. 2, 1830.

BODGE, Stephen W., of Madbury, son of Samuel, d. July 16, 1868, aged 72, m. Oct. 27, 1821, by Rev. John Osborne, Sarah Williams, of Lee.

BODGE, Jeremiah, of Madbury, son of Andrew, d. Jul. 15, 1844, aged 28, m. int. Oct. 22, 1842, in Lee, Mary Ann Gear, of Lee.

BODGE, Andrew J., of Dover, m. July 29, 1862, in Strafford, Mary M. Parshley, of Strafford, dau. of Ebenezer.

BODGE, George W., of Madbury, m. Dec. 31, 1864, in Barnstead, Eliza E. Blaisdell, of Barnstead.

BODGE, J. F., m. Aug. 26, 1866, in Tamworth, M. M. Robinson (was this a second marriage?).

BODGE, Alfred, d. Mar. 16, 1891, aged 57, m. Jan. 26, 1867, in Melvin Village, Mary E. Estes, d. Aug. 14, 1877, aged 80, both of Wolfeboro.

BODWELL, James, m. Dec. 26, 1846, in Lebanon, Me., Dorcas Jordan, both of Berwick, Me.

BODWELL, Elisha Allen, of Saco, Me., m. Nov. 14, 1849, by Rev. Levi B. Tasker, in Sandwich, Grace B. Robinson, of Sandwich.

BODWELL, Frank, m. (pub. Dec. 15, 1870, in Great Falls), Ella G. Libby, both of Great Falls.

BOLO, Peter Jr., of Dover, m. Apr. 30, 1812, by Micajah Otis, Sarah Felker, of Barrington.

3) **BOODEY**, Rev. Joseph, son of Azariah, b. May 16, 1752, d. Jan. 7, 1824, m. Olive Drew, b. June 3, 1752, d. Jan. 23, 1826.

BOODEY, George S., of Strafford, son of Ira, b. 1839, d. May 30, 1869, aged 30, m. Apr. 1, 1860, by Rev. John Winkley, Eliza J. Carter, of Barrington, b. 1842, d. 1906.

BOODEY, John O., b 1842, d. 1914, m. Nov. 27, 1863, in Dover, Orissa O. Hanson, b. Mar. 24, 1845, d. Jan. 31, 1909, both of Strafford.

BOOTHBY, Johnson, of Waterville, Me., m. Dec. 24, 1861, in Dover, L. Abbie Haines. of N. Wolfeboro.

BOOTHBY, Henry J., m. Sept. 12, 1864, in Ossipee, Maria A. Morton, both of Conway.

BOOTHBY, C. S., of Saco, Me., m. Mar. 29, 1866, in Dover, Lillie G. Remick, of Biddeford, Me.

BOOTHBY, G. F., of Saco, Me., m. Mar. 29, 1866, in Dover, Ellen D. Cobb, of Biddeford, Me.

BOSTON, Oliver, b. 1838, d. 1914, m. Nov. 21, 1866, by Rev. James Rand, Mary E. Cooper, b. 1839, d. 1897, both of S. Berwick, Me.

BOSTON, William, of Biddeford, Me., m. May 14, 1869, in Dover, Bell Hanks, of Augusta, Me.

BOSTON, James W., m. (pub. June 16, 1870, in Rochester), Lizzie S. McIlroy, both of Rochester.

BOURNE, Rev. George W., of Sanford, Me., m. Dec. 29, 1840, by Rev. Daniel Lancaster, Wealthy C. B. Ham, d. Apr. 20, 1842, aged 29, dau. of John.

BOWMAN, Eli E., m. (pub. Mar. 17, 1864, in Milton), Lydia Mayhew.

BOYCE, James, son of Richard, b. Feb. 13, 1758, m. Jan. 28, 1773, by Rev. Isaac Hasey, Hannah Garland.

BRACKETT, Lorenzo D., of Biddeford, Me., m. Feb. 4, 1864, in Salmon Falls, Julia A. Sawyer, of Saco, Me.

BRACKETT, Joseph, m. Dec. 31, 1864, in New Durham, Mary E. Wilkinson, both of New Durham.

BRACKETT, Hiram, of New Durham, m. July 12, 1865, in Farmington, Mary J. French, of Farmington, dau. of Jeremiah.

BRACKETT, Henry H., of Somersworth, d. Dec. 28, 1906, aged 63, m. May 2, 1867, in Rochester, Emma Leeman, of Saco, Me.
BRACKETT, Arthur B., m. Oct. 28, 1867, in Newmarket, Martha Anderson.
BRACKETT, Charles A., of Great Falls, m. (pub. July 30, 1868, in Great Falls), Susan K. Drew, of Biddeford, Me.
BRADLEY, William, of Bedford, Mass., m. Apr. 15, 1849, by Rev. Levi B. Tasker, in Sandwich, Sarah Ann Morse, of Sandwich, dau. of Benjamin.
BRADWICK, Albert, of Vallejo, Calif., m. Oct. 25, 1864, in Dover, Amanda Henderson, of Dover.
BRAGDON, Charles, of Rochester, son of Amos, d. June 14, 1893, aged 77, m. (1) July 14, 1844, by Rev. Nathaniel Barker, Susan Adams, of Milton, d. Mar. 11, 1845, aged 23, dau. of Ebenezer, m. (2) Dec. 17, 1846, by Elder Elias Hutchins, Rosamond P. Adams, d. Oct. 28, 1847, aged 23, dau. of Ebenezer.
BRAGDON, John F., m. Aug. 12, 1867, in Salmon Falls, Emily A. Hatch, both of Wells, Me.
BRAZEER, John, m. Apr. 26, 1797, by Rev. Benjamin Balch, Mary Meader, both of Barrington.
BRESLAUER, Victor, m. (pub. Mar. 25, 1869, in Dover), Ann E. Pearl.
BREWSTER, Daniel, m. Jan. 31, 1793, by Rev. Benjamin Balch, Sally Furber, both of Barrington.
BREWSTER, Timothy, m. Jan. 21, 1795, by Rev. Benjamin Balch, Lydia Hayes, both of Barrington.
BREWSTER, Daniel, m. Mar. 24, 1798, by Rev. William Hooper, Jenny Lane, d. Nov. 18, 1831, both of Lee.
BREWSTER, Paul L., of Dover, d. Apr. 10, 1828, aged 29, m. (1) in 1825, in Barrington, Temperance Spinney, of Dover, d. May 7, 1826, aged 28, m. (2) Dec. 22, 1827, by Rev. John Osborne, Susannah C. Wiggin, of Lee.
BREWSTER, Joseph H., of Barrington, m. Jan. 4, 1829, by Rev. Cephas H. Kent, Lydia Garland, of Rochester.
BREWSTER, Joseph, of Ossipee, m. (pub. Sep. 8, 1829, in Wakefield), Mrs. Nancy C. Moulton, of Wakefield, wid. of Jonathan, b. 1799, d. Dec. 8, 1867, aged 68.
BREWSTER, George W., son of Paul, d. July 4, 1897, aged 85, m. Apr. 16, 1840, by Elder Enoch Place, Phebe Leighton Ham, d. Dec. 23, 1853, aged 41, dau. of George, both of Strafford.

BREWSTER, Eli V., son of George F., b. <u>Mar. 24</u>, 1824, d. Mar. 18, 1903, m. (1) June 3, 1847, by Rev. Hiram Stevens, Mary D. Tasker, b. Mar. 10, 1807, d. Sept. 22, 1866, dau. of Ebenezer, m. (2) Oct. 3, 1867, Freelove J. Hayes, b. 1825, d. Jan. 27, 1908, dau. of Joseph.

BREWSTER, Daniel J., m. Jan. 9, 1864, in Dover, <u>Mrs</u>. Georgie A. (Lord) Hall, wid. of George W., <u>both of Barrington</u>.

BREWSTER, Timothy M., m. Mar. 29, 1864, by Rev. James Rand, Mary Ann Libbey, d. Oct. 25, 1887, aged 69, dau. of Jeremiah, <u>both of Dover</u>.

BREWSTER, Gilman T., of Strafford, m. Oct. 27, 1866, in Great Falls, Hattie E. Hayes, of Rochester, dau. of John S.

BRIARD, Samuel, <u>d. Oct. 25, 1847, aged 50</u>, m. int. Mar. 1822, in Tuftonboro, Lydia Moulton, <u>d. Nov. 14, 1869, aged 78</u>, both of Tuftonboro.

BRIDGE, William H., of Nottingham, m. May 15, 1868, in Nottingham, Fannie E. Kelley, of Northwood.

BRIER, David B., m. (pub. Jan. 22, 1863, in Sandwich), Mary P. Gilman.

3) **BROCK**, Isaac, of Barrington, son of Nicholas, d. Sept. 2, 1860, aged 80, m. July 6, 1802, in Barrington, Polly Young, of Dover, d. Mar. 2, 1859, aged 77.

BROCK, John, d. Feb. 16, 1849, aged 69, m. near 1805, in Barrington, Lydia Tuttle, both of Barrington.

BROCK, Capt. Ephraim, d. Jun. 2, 1862, aged 76, m. (1) July 11, 1806, in Barrington, Hannah Brassbridge, d. June 8, 1852, aged 77, both of Barrington, m. (2) (pub. Nov. 23, 1852, in Strafford), Polly Scruton.

3) BROCK, Ralph, son of Nicholas, d. Mar. 5, 1858, aged 68, m. (1) Aug. 30, 1810, <u>in Barrington</u>, Dorothy Young, b. Dec. 1, 1791, d. Oct. 23, 1847, dau. of William, <u>both of Barrington</u>, m. (2) Nov. 5, 1848, by Rev. Charles N. Smith, Mrs. Elizabeth Demeritt, of Madbury.

3) BROCK, Nicholas Jr., m. Mar. 7, 1811, in Barrington, Nancy Arlin, both of Barrington.

BROCK, William, <u>son of William, b. Mar. 19, 1782</u>, m. Jul. 13, 1812, by Rev. Jonathan Tompson.

<u>4)</u> BROCK, Rev. Hezekiah H., of Utica, N.Y., son of Isaac, d. Dec. 30, 1851, aged 31, m. June 17, 1850, by Rev. Homer Barrows, Susan M. Tuttle, of Dover, d. July 17, 1854, aged 28.

BROCK, Oliver, m. Mar. 31, 1862, by Rev. Enoch Place, Hannah Saunders, both of Strafford.

BROCK, John F., m. Jan. 5, 1863, in Dover, Susan M. Evans, d. Aug. 15, 1918, aged 84, dau. of William, both of Rochester.

BROCK, Harrison, of Rochester, d. Feb. 2, 1883, aged 42, m. Dec. 13, 1864, by Rev. Enoch Place, Martha J. Carley, of Farmington.

BROCK, Edward H., m. Apr. 23, 1868, in Lynn, Mass., Edna E. Caswell, both of Lynn, Mass.

BROOKS, Capt. Ephraim, b. Aug. 15, 1798, d. Dec. 23, 1875, m. int. Jan. 27, 1821, in Lebanon, Me., Perlina Lord, of South Berwick, Me., b. Apr. 30, 1795, d. Jul. 19, 1890.

BROWN, Edward, m. May 6, 1799, by Rev. Benjamin Balch, Patty Willey, both of Barrington.

BROWN, Joseph, m. (1) June 1, 1799, in Wakefield, Polly Demeritt, of Ossipee, m. (2) Nov. 15, 1804, in Barrington, Molly Cater, both of Barrington.

BROWN, Israel, m. June 13, 1799, by Rev. Benjamin Balch, Temperence Peavey, both of Barrington.

BROWN, Mark, m. June 7, 1812, in Barrington, Olive Twombly.

BROWN, Richardson, m. (1) Mehitable ----, d. Mar. 23, 1817, aged 32, m. (2) Dec. 12, 1817, by Rev. Jeremiah Shaw, Tamson Abbott, both of Tuftonboro.

BROWN, John, d. May 26, 1865, aged 79, m. Nov. 28, 1813, by Rev. Joseph Boody, Sarah (Hanson) Brown, d. June 16, 1868, aged 77, both of Barrington.

BROWN, John P., of Strafford, m. Apr. 27, 1835, by Rev. John Winkley, Nancy Twombly, of Barrington, d. Apr. 10, 1848, aged 36.

BROWN, Joseph, m. Aug. 27, 1835, in Barrington, Jane Howard, dau. of John.

BROWN, Samuel, m. Sept. 15, 1839, by Rev. Samuel Nichols, Joanna Arlen, both of Barrington.

BROWN, John N., d. Oct. 1, 1877, aged 63, m. Jun. 25, 1846, by Elder Elias Hutchins, Lydia Leighton, d. Aug. 12, 1881, aged 66.

BROWN, Joseph, of Northwood, son of Samuel, d. May 27, 1871, aged 49, m. June 1, 1849, by Rev. John Winkley, Melissa Ann Berry, of Strafford.

BROWN, Edmond K., of Ossipee, son of Adam T., d. July 10, 1865, aged 39, m. (1) July 4, 1849, in Great Falls, Sarah Jane Dore, d. May 14, 1861, aged 32, both of Ossipee, m. (2) July 14, 1862, by

Rev. James Rand, Abbie K. Ayers, of Salem, Mass., d. Oct. 13, 1872, aged 46.

BROWN, John L., d. May 23, 1876, m. Apr. 21, 1855, in Farmington, Mary E. Twombly.

BROWN, Nahum, m. Nov. 27, 1861, in Great Falls, Mary L. Brown, both of Somersworth.

BROWN, S. S., of Boston, Mass., m. Dec. 7, 1861, in Wakefield, Hannah Woodman, of Wakefield.

BROWN, Sgt. Jared P., m. Oct. 8, 1863, in Strafford, Sarah J. Brown, of Strafford.

BROWN, Frank S., of Boston, Mass., m. Nov. 16, 1863, in Rochester, Annie M. McDuffee, of Rochester, dau. of John.

BROWN, Charles A., m. Apr. 5, 1864, in Berwick, Me., Eliza J. Sweanor (?), of Somersworth.

BROWN, Charles W., m. June 23, 1864, in Conway, Mary Ann Brown, d. Oct. 29, 1897, aged 57, dau. of Thomas, both of Rochester.

BROWN, Frank W., of Lovell, Me., m. Apr. 25, 1867, in Great Falls, Phebe H. Kingman.

BROWN, Oscar E., m. July 4, 1867, in New Durham, Mary A. Jenness.

BROWN, Phylander, of Stowe, Me., m. Dec. 21, 1867, in Dover, Mrs. Mary J. Taylor, of Sheffield, Vt.

BROWN Israel B., of Strafford, m. Feb. 16, 1869, in Strafford, Rhoda Otis, of Northwood.

BROWN, Orange S., of Great Falls, m. (pub. June 10, 1869, in Great Falls), Mattie E. Seiders, of Waldoboro, Me.

BROWN, Charles E., m. (pub. July 8, 1869, in Great Falls), Lizzie H. Hussey.

BRYANT, A. W., of Stoneham, Mass., aged 24, m. May 8, 1851, by Rev. Levi B. Tasker, in Sandwich, Lucy A. Marston, of Sandwich, aged 28, d. Nov. 3, 1899, dau. of Caleb or Caleb M.

BRYANT, Silas J. m. Apr. 7, 1859, in Sandwich, Mary Ann Brown, both of Sandwich.

BRYANT, Perley B., m. Dec. 21, 1861, in Dover, Isabella Drew, both of Dover.

BRYANT, James Jr., m. May 14, 1862, in Tamworth, Ceceline G. Smith, dau. of Col Aaron G., both of Tamworth.

BRYANT, Edwin A., of Woburn, Mass., m. Mar. 21, 1866, in Dover, Isabella (Drew) Bryant, wid. of Lt. Perley B., b. May 1, 1842, d. July 5, 1878, dau. of Samuel.

BRYANT, James M., m. (pub. July 22, 1869, in Rochester), Sarah E. Ricker, both of Somersworth.

BRYER, James R. aged 24, son of James, m. Apr. 7, 1859, in Sandwich, Rhoda E. Bennett, aged 19, both of Sandwich.

BUCK, Dr. Jeremiah Crosby, of Acton, Me., d. Mar. 15, 1885, aged 63, m. Jan. 16, 1850, in Milton, Eunice C. Swasey, of Milton, d. Aug. 5, 1893, aged 66, dau. of Deac. Charles.

BUCK, John C., son of Dr. Reuben, b. 1826, d. June 30, 1896, m. Dec. 14, 1867, in Lebanon, Me., Hannah B. Brackett, b. 1836, d. July 30, 1921, dau. of Benjamin.

BUEL, Charles C., of Dover, m. May 8, 1828, by Elder Enoch Place, Tammy Willey, of Strafford, d. Feb. 6, 1851, aged 49, dau. of Isaac.

BUFFUM, Henry, m. Dec. 22, 1867, in N. Berwick, Me., Susan Hatch, both of N. Berwick, Me.

BUMFORD, John, m. Nov. 27, 1806, by Rev. Benjamin Balch, Patty Tebbets, both of Barrington.

BUNCE, Charles H., of Dover, son of George, d. Jan. 30, 1887, aged 62, m. Feb. 28, 1866, in Dover, Mary E. Bickford, of Ossipee, d. June 3, 1883, aged 62.

BUNCE, Peter, of Dover, m. May 12, 1868, in Wolfeboro, Georgia A. Bickford, of Tuftonboro.

BUNCE, George F., m. Apr. 18, 1870, in Dover, Sarah E. Wentworth, both of Dover.

BUNKER, Samuel, of Pittsfield, m. Feb. 12, 1791, in Barrington, Betsey Hill, of Barrington.

BUNKER, Joseph, son of Benjamin, m. (1) (pub. Jan. 27, 1807), Betsey Hawkins, of Barrington, d. May 23, 1832, aged 45.

BUNKER, John, m. Nov. 23, 1809, in Barrington, Mary Babb, both of Barrington.

BUNKER, Joseph, m. (2) Mar. 16, 1834, by Elder Enoch Place, Mrs. Betsey Wentworth, d. Oct. 21, 1861, aged 68, both of Strafford.

6) BUNKER, Ephraim, Jr., of Durham, son of John, d. July 9, 1883, aged 67, m. Oct. 19, 1837, by Elder Enoch Place, Olive Berry, of Strafford, d. Sept. 30, 1884, aged 74, dau. of Benjamin.

6) BUNKER, Valentine, of Durham, son of William, d. Oct. 18, 1852, aged 25, m. Jan. 17, 1850, by Rev. Arthur Caverno, Lavina Freeman, of Dover, d. Mar. 16, 1854, aged 22.

BUNKER, Daniel C., of Durham, son of Richard, m. Feb. 26, 1865, by Rev. Alvan Tobey, Helen D. Twilight, of Exeter, dau. of William.

BUNKER, George W., of Durham, son of Ephraim, m. Jan. 1, 1866, in Durham, Louisa E. Foster, of Holliston, Mass., dau. of Ira.

BUNKER, George F., m. Feb. 12, 1866, in Dover, Nancy S. Thompson, both of Durham.

BUNKER, Charles H., of Durham, son of Ephraim, m. 1867, in W. Newbury, Mass., Annie R. Mathes, of Rollinsford, dau. of George A.

BUNKER, Charles, of Durham, son of William, m. Mar. 25, 1868, by Rev. Alvan Tobey, Mary P. Twilight, of Vershire, Vt., dau. of Asa O.

BUNKER, James E., of Durham, son of Richard, m. Sept. 25, 1868, by Rev. Alvan Tobey, Belinder A. George, of Weare, Me., dau. of Stenford W.

BUNKER, Charles E., m. Aug. 24, 1870, in Dover, Orissa J. Davis, both of Dover.

BURBANK, Col. Robert Ingalls, of Boston, Mass., m. July 8, 1862, in Dover, Lizzie Wheeler Christie, of Dover, dau. of Daniel M.

BURBANK, George, of Boston, Mass., m. (pub. Nov. 13, 1862, in Wolfeboro), Hannah J. Rust, dau. of H. B. Rust.

BURKE, James, m. Nov. 12, 1795, in Brookfield, Elizabeth Willey, both of Brookfield.

BURKE, James Jr., son of James, b. 1816, d. 1872, m. (1) May 10, 1837, in Wolfeboro, Esther Willey, b. 1819, d. 1857, both of Wolfeboro, m. (2) Elizabeth ----, b. 1826, d. 1867.

BURKE, Samuel R., m. Mar. 23, 1862, in Tamworth, Carrie M. Atkinson, both of Madison.

BURKE, Thomas F., of Boston, Mass., m. Sept. 1, 1863, in S. Berwick, Me., Clara A. Billings, of N. Berwick, Me.

BURKE, James M., of S. Berwick, Me., m. (pub. Dec. 1, 1870, in Great Falls), Sarah E. Grant, of W. Newfield, Me.

BURLEIGH, Jonathan H., of Tuftonboro, son of Jacob, d. June 7, 1901, aged 87, m. Jan. 14, 1839, in Wolfeboro, Caroline Tebbets, of Wolfeboro, d. Oct. 21, 1905, aged 86.

BURLEIGH, Micajah C., of South Berwick, Me., d. Mar. 7, 1881, aged 63, m. (pub. Dec. 21, 1847), in Great Falls), Mary F. Russell, d. Nov. 29, 1889, aged 68, dau. of Richard.

BURLEIGH, Joseph T., m. Dec. 6, 1865, in Ossipee, Mary Young, d. Oct. 16, 1866, aged 23, dau. of John.

BURLEY, Daniel W., nephew of Daniel (born Caswell), m. int. Dec. 26, 1852, in Lee, Margaret Ann Lock, both of Lee.

BURLEY, Charles Henry, of Dover, son of John, d. Oct. 29, 1915, aged 85, m. (1) (pub. Sept. 12, 1854, in Newmarket), Olive Russell, m. (2) Feb. 21, 1867, in Dover, Dora J. Thompson, of Franklin, m. (3) Sept. 9, 1894, in Dover, Sarah Jane Morrill, of Moultonboro, b. 1827.

BURLEY, Thomas C., of Brookfield, aged 35, m. Jan. 16, 1858, in Brookfield, Susan Moulton, of Wakefield.

BURLEY, Joseph F., of Dover, m. Nov. 28, 1867, in Dover, Mary E. Wade, of Freeport, Me.

BURLEY, Samuel D., m. Dec. 24, 1867, by Rev. Robert S. Stubbs, Clara Styles, both of Dover.

BURNHAM, George, m. Apr. 23, 1772, in Brookfield, Sarah Rogers.

4) BURNHAM, Rev. Jeremiah, son of John, d. Aug. 21, 1784, m. (1) Apr. 21, 1749, by Rev. J. Adams, in Newington, Elizabeth Adams, d. June 2, 1753, aged 22, dau. of Matthew, both of Oyster River, m. (2) Mar. 14, 1756, Abigail Emerson, d. Sept. 2, 1800, aged 66, dau. of Timothy.

BURNHAM, William H.Y., m. (1) June 10, 1824, by Elder Enoch Place, Hannah Foye, d. Dec. 19, 1825, aged 28, both of Strafford, m. (2) Susan ----, b. 1788, d. 1869.

BURNHAM, George Washington, d. Jun. 5, 1860, aged 57, m. Jan. 18, 1827, by Rev. Joseph Boodey, Sally David, d. Jun. 3, 1860, aged 51, both of New Durham.

BURNHAM, Nathaniel W., of Milton, son of Dudley, m. Feb. 10, 1833, by Rev. Nathaniel Berry, Ruth Davis, of New Durham.

BURNHAM, Winthrop, d. Aug. 13, 1890, aged 83, m. (1) Mary ----, d. Mar. 25, 1842, aged 39, m. (2) int. Aug. 13, 1843, in Dover, Martha Decater.

BURNHAM, Jeremiah P., son of Joseph, b. Sept. 8, 1822, d. Sept. 25, 1849, m. (1) int. Dec. 22, 1844, in Dover, Mary Ann Cate, b. June 8, 1821, d. Jan. 2, 1847, aged 25, dau. of John, m. (2) Aug. 5, 1848, by Rev. Charles N. Smith, Mary A. Canney, b. Apr. 23, 1827, d. Aug. 15, 1879, dau. of Joshua.

BURNHAM, Charles, aged 24, m. Aug. 10, 1856, in Sandwich, Mary E. Leavitt, aged 22, both of Sandwich.

BURNHAM, Charles S., of Middleton, m. Aug. 20, 1864, in Farmington, Ellen H. Pinkham, of Farmington, dau. of Thomas.

BURNHAM, Joseph W., of Bath, Me., m. Mar. 12, 1865, in Dover, Frances E. Willey, of Wakefield.

BURNHAM, Royal R., m. Apr. 3, 1865, in Dover, Emily A. Foss, both of Portland, Me.

BURNHAM, Calvin S., of Epping, m. (pub. Oct. 28, 1869, in Epping), Mrs. Hannah S. (Twombly) Kimball, wid. of William, dau. of Reuben.

BURNHAM, John M., m. Oct. 29, 1870, by Rev. Elmer Hewitt, Abby J. Moulton, both of Dover.

BURNS, Matthew, m. June 20, 1866, in Rochester, Mrs. Bedelia Martin, both of Milton.

BURROWS, Joseph, m. Nov. 25, 1773, Rev. Isaac Hasey, Alice Farnham.

BURROWS, James, son of David, b. May 7, 1823, d. Oct. 30, 1899, m. (pub. Feb. 24, 1852, in Rochester), Lorania Blaisdell, b. July 11, 1826, d. Oct. 1, 1910, both of Dover.

BURROWS, Warren, of Middleton, aged 22, m. Mar. 7, 1857, in Brookfield, Abigail M. Willey, aged 16, of Brookfield.

BURROWS, (BURROUGHS), Charles L., m. Apr. 6, 1870, in Dover, Lucretia Pinkham, both of Dover.

BURT, Andrew J., of Providence, R. I., m. Sept. 26, 1868, in Charlestown, Mass., Sarah F. Nute, of Charlestown, Mass.

BUTLER, James, m. Aug. 1820, by Rev. Micajah Otis, Patience Newton.

BUTLER, Frederick, of Haverhill, Mass., m. Apr. 25, 1865, in Dover, Sarah J. Card, of Dover.

BUTLER, Horace, of Iowa, m. Sept. 13, 1866, in Wolfeboro, Rosa J. Furber, dau. of Jethro.

BUTLER, Benjamin H., of Berwick, Me., m. (pub. May 13, 1869, in Salmon Falls), Ellen G. Brooks, of Salmon Falls.

BUTLER, George E., m. (pub. Sept. 15, 1870, in Rochester), Julia A. Small, d Oct. 23, 1919, aged 70, dau. of James B.

BUTTERFIELD, Ira A., m. Dec. 23, 1868, in Dover, Eliza J. Granville, both of Dover.

4) **BUZZELL**, John, Jr., son of John, m. Jan. 4, 1724/5, by Rev. Hugh Adams, Sarah Wibird.

BUZZELL, James, m. Nov. 18, 1778, in Barrington, Margery Buzzell, both of Barrington.

BUZZELL, Henry, m. Feb. 14, 1780, in Barrington, Louise Buzzell, both of Barrington.

BUZZELL, Rev. Aaron, b. Nov. 1764, d. Oct. 21, 1854, m. (1) in 1786, Eunice Buzzell, d. Aug. 17, 1798, m. (2) Jan. 14, 1799, by Rev. Benjamin Randall, Miriam Flanders, d. Mar. 24, 1850, both of Alton.

BUZZELL, Levi, m. Nov. 17, 1788, by Rev. Benjamin Balch, Isett Buzzell, both of Barrington.

BUZZELL, Moses, m. Nov. 17, 1788, by Rev. Benjamin Balch, Sarah Caverno, both of Barrington.

BUZZELL, Jacob, b. Apr. 10, 1773, d. Nov. 16, 1831, m. near 1794, Elizabeth ----, b. Apr. 30, 1772.

BUZZELL, Elder Hezekiah D., d. Sept. 6, 1858, aged 80, m. (1) 1796, Polly Flanders, d. 1850, m. (2) Jan. 9, 1849, in Tuftonboro, Mrs. Charlotte (Clark) Tibbetts, wid. of Levi, d. July 1, 1850, aged 66.

BUZZELL, Benjamin, m. Mar. 1801, in Barrington, Prudence Richards, both of Alton.

BUZZELL, Miles, of Barrington, d. May 7, 1856, aged 68, m. 1811, by Rev. John Osborne, Deliverance Snell, of Lee, d. Sept. 27, 1841, aged 55, dau. of John.

BUZZELL, Ebenezer, son of Jacob, b. Jan. 19, 1795, d. Jan. 28, 1877, aged 82, m. (1) Mar. 17, 1822, by Rev. William Demeritt, Hannah Caldwell, b. Mar. 12, 1803, d. Feb. 20, 1846, aged 43, dau. of Nathaniel, m. (2) Nov. 5, 1846, by Rev. Homer Barrows, Deborah Palmer, of Dover, d. Feb. 2, 1877, aged 75.

BUZZELL, Jeremiah, son of John, b. 1791, d. Jul. 2, 1858, m. Jul. 9, 1822, by Rev. Federall Burt, Ann Winkley, b. Jan. 27, 1796, d. Dec. 11, 1871, aged 75, dau. of William.

BUZZELL, Dr. James M., son of Elder John, d. May 12, 1868, aged 66, m. Sept. 10, 1825, Susan Thompson, b. June 20, 1800, d. Feb. 3, 1873, dau. of Job, both of Lee.

BUZZELL, Dr. Aaron, of Deerfield, son of Elder John, m. Sept. 22, 1825, by Elder Enoch Place, Hannah E. Leighton of Strafford, d. Nov. 21, 1844, dau. of Andrew.

BUZZELL, Aaron, b. 1803, d.1889, m. May 27, 1844, by Rev. Nathaniel Berry, Rhoda B. Blaisdell, b. 1819, d. 1888, both of Gilford.

BUZZELL, Smith E., d. Feb. 10, 1873, aged 62, m. Dec. 24, 1845, by Elder Samuel Sherburne, Mary E. Jenkins, both of Lee.

BUZZELL, William Caldwell, of Boston, Mass., son of Ebenezer, b. Apr. 8, 1823, m. Sept. 18, 1847, by Rev. Theodore Wells, Ann Maria Fernald, of Barrington, dau. of John S.

BUZZELL, Dr. Andrew J. H., son of Dr. Aaron, m. Apr. 16, 1854, in Dover, Sarah Ann Wendell, d. Aug. 22, 1869, aged 37, dau. of Oliver F.

BUZZELL, John M., m. (pub. Mar. 20, 1862, in Ossipee), Mrs. Julia A. Abbott.

BUZZELL, Samuel H., of Farmington, m. Dec. 15, 1862, in Dover, Josie M. Fernald, of Wolfeboro.

BUZZELL, D. O., of Barrington, m. Oct. 20, 1863, in Barrington, M. A. Neal, of Newburyport, Mass.

BUZZELL, John H., of Ossipee, m. (pub. May 12, 1864, in Center Ossipee), Sarah G. Bailey, of E. Kingston.

BUZZELL, John H., of Barrington, m. Nov. 14, 1866, in Dover, Annie E. Emerson, of Lee.

BUZZELL, Dr. John, of Methuem, Mass., m. Dec. 21, 1870, in Union, Mrs. Adeline D. P. Arling, of Middleton.

CALDER, Alexander R., of Chinguaconsey, Canada, m. (pub. June 1, 1865, in Troy, N.Y.), Sarah M. Copp, of Wakefield.

CALDWELL, William, m. Mar. 29, 1804, by Rev. Benjamin Balch, Anna Buzzell, both of Barrington.

CALDWELL, William, of Barrington, son of Nathaniel, b. Apr. 16, 1801, d. Sept. 28, 1854, aged 53, m. Sept. 26, 1823, by Rev. John Osborne, Abigail Tebbets, of Madbury, d. Apr. 18, 1877, aged 75 yrs., 3 mos., dau. of Israel.

CALDWELL, John, of Barrington, son of Nathaniel, b. Nov. 25, 1805, m. int. Dec. 18, 1830, in Lee, Sally Langley, of Lee.

CALDWELL, Alexander, of Newburyport, m. Sept. 22, 1847, by Rev. Mr. J. E. Farwell, Elizabeth H. True, of Barrington.

CAME, George B., of Portsmouth, m. Jan. 22, 1870, in N. Berwick, Me., Augusta Hill, of N. Berwick, Me.

6) **CANNEY**, Ichabod, son of Isaac, b. 1770, d. Jan. 13, 1855, m. (1) Jan. 12, 1792, Sarah Hanson, b. Apr. 25, 1765, dau. of Stephen, m. (2) Oct. 4, 1820, Nancy (Church) Marden, wid. of John, b. Nov. 10, 1790, d. Apr. 23, 1854, dau. of Nathaniel.

6) CANNEY, Jacob, son of Isaac, of Madbury, b. Feb. 20, 1776, d. Dec. 8, 1857, m. (1) Apr. 10, 1805, Sarah J. Jenness, of Rochester, b. 1781, d. 1844, m. (2) Sarah H. ----, b. 1783, d. 1851.

6) CANNEY, Samuel, son of Isaac, b. Oct. 1781, d. May 1846, m. June 2, 1806, by Rev. Benjamin Balch, Olive Ayers, b. Oct. 1782, d. July 30, 1866, both of Barrington.

6) CANNEY, Francis S., of Barrington, son of Isaac, m. Mar. 28, 1811, Deborah Nutter, of Rochester.

8) CANNEY, Albert Jenness, son of Joseph, d. May 1925, aged 85, m. (1) Mar. 6, 1863, in Alton, Ellen A. Woodman, b. 1844, d. 1867, dau. of Jeremiah, m. (2) Jan. 1, 1877, in Northbridge, Mass.,

Emma Frances Chapin, b. Oct. 10, 1853, d. May 27, 1881, dau. of John C., m. (3) ---- ----.

8) CANNEY, Andrew Jackson, son of Isaac, b. Oct. 21, 1843, d. July 28, 1918, m. June 1, 1867, in New Durham, Caroline Ham, b. June 29, 1847, d. Dec. 22, 1945, dau. of Samuel D., both of Farmington.

CANNON, Dr. Hiram, m. int. Nov. 28, 1807, Calista Haines.

CAPON, Timothy, m. Nov. 28, 1833, in Barrington, Sally Hanscomb, both of Barrington.

CARD, James W., m. Sept. 1, 1866, in Farmington, Ella Tebbetts, of Farmington, dau. of Alvin C.

CARLETON, Carey F., of Bradford, Mass., m. May 31, 1863, in Farmington, Mary E. Downing, of Farmington.

CARLETON, James, m. Apr. 8, 1869, in Dover, Annie M. Parcher, both of Dover.

CARPENTER, Nicholas, m. Sep. 8, 1761, Miriam Davis.

CARPENTER, Benjamin, m. June 17, 1787, by Rev. Benjamin Balch, Hannah Leathers, both of Barrington.

CARPENTER, George M., of Boston, Mass., m. May 9, 1865, in Rochester, Lucy A. Meserve, of Rochester.

CARPENTER, Alonzo, of Waterboro, Me., m. Nov. 10, 1866, in Dover, Isabella Mandaville, of Dover.

CARR, Moses, Jr., of Somersworth, son of Moses, b. May 28, 1746, m. Nov. 13, 1782, by Rev. Matthew Merriam, Hannah Hamilton, of Berwick, Me., d. 1843, aged 82, dau. of Jonathan.

CARR, George W., of Somerville, Mass., m. Apr. 14, 1870, in Rochester, Sarah F. W. Mathes, of Rochester.

CARROLL, Robert, of Sanford, Me., m. June 29, 1868, in Newmarket, Mrs. Olivea Brown, of Newmarket.

CARTER, John, m. Feb. 21, 1794, by Rev. Benjamin Balch, Lydia Coffin, both of Dover.

CARTER, Sanborn B., of Ossipee, d. July 8, 1881, aged 62, m. Aug. 29, 1865, by Rev. Asa Piper, Mrs. Mary Sweat, of Wakefield, d. Jan. 5, 1903, aged 74.

CARTER, James F., of Northwood, m. May 10, 1867, in Gonic, Mrs. Lanora F. Perkins, of Barrington.

2) **CARTLAND**, Joseph, son of John, d. Jan. 21, 1807, m. (1) Nov. 7, 1745, Lydia Allen, b. July 12, 1717, d. June 1758, dau. of Francis, m. (2) Oct. 27, 1763, Anne Hanson, d. Dec. 10, 1816, dau. of Tobias.

CASWELL, Richard, son of Robert, b. Dec. 28, 1721, d. 1810, m. (1) early as 1750, Abigail ----, d. Mar. 3, 1790, m. (2) July 12, 1795, Meribah (Patch) Marshall, wid. of John.
CASWELL, Joseph, d. Feb. 9, 1846, aged 91, m. Mar. 13, 1779, by Rev. Isaac Smith, Lydia Evans, d. July 19, 1850, aged 93.
CASWELL, Isaac, of Strafford, son of Joseph, d. June 17, 1861, aged 63, m. Nov. 23, 1824, Lucy Witham, of Middleton, d. Apr. 1, 1862, aged 58.
CASWELL, Thomas, d. Sept. 21, 1875, aged 74, m. Dec. 23, 1824, by Elder Enoch Place, Sally Evans, d. Jan. 11, 1864, aged 62, dau. of Lemuel, both of Strafford.
CASWELL, Enoch B., of Northwood, son of Timothy, m. May 27, 1827, by Elder Enoch Place, Joanna Boodey, of Barrington.
CASWELL, Andrew, d. Mar. 19, 1853, aged 48, m. Oct. 21, 1827, by Elder Enoch Place, Mary Jane Waldron, b. 1806, d. 1906, both of Strafford.
CASWELL, James, M., of Strafford, son of Andrew, b. Jan. 27, 1828, d. Jan. 12, 1902, m. (1) Sarah Ann ----, d. Jan. 18, 1853, aged 28, m. (2) Mar. 17, 1856, by Elder Enoch Place, Abby J. Drew, of Barrington, b. Jan. 11, 1835, d. Apr. 30, 1925, dau. of Timothy.
CASWELL, John G., of Strafford, b. 1814, d. 1891, m. Dec. 28, 1862, in Strafford, Mrs. Louisa A. Manson, of Barrington, b. 1836, d. 1906..
CASWELL, Charles A., m. Apr. 7, 1867, in Dover, Sarah E. Caverno.
CASWELL, Newell F., m. Sept. 24, 1868, in Dover, Mary G. Tanner, both of Dover.
CATE, John, son of Capt. William, m. Oct. 17, 1762, in Barrington, Mary Garland, b. May 26, 1744, dau. of John.
CATE, Richard, of Barrington, m. Nov. 16, 1790, in Barrington, Mary Rand, of Rye.
CATE, Paul, b. 1773, m. July 17, 1796, in Barrington, by Rev. Benjamin Balch, Susannah Davis, b. 1777, dau. of Thomas, both of Barrington.
CATE, Benjamin, of Barrington, m. Sept. 22, 1796, by Rev. Benjamin Balch, Deborah Giles, of Rochester.
CATE, Ebenezer, m. Nov. 17, 1796, by Rev. Benjamin Balch, Abigail Cate, both of Barrington.
CATE, Joseph, m. Apr. 14, 1801, by Rev. Benjamin Balch, Elizabeth Parshley, both of Barrington.
CATE, Samuel, b. Nov. 6, 1770, m. Sept. 27, 1801, in Barrington, Ruth Young (?), b. Aug. 31, 1777.

CATE, Isaac, m. Nov. 26, 1801, by Rev. Benjamin Balch, Phebe Haines, both of Barrington.

CATE, Joseph, m. Mar. 29, 1802, in Barrington, Sally Randel, both of Barrington.

CATE, Samuel, of Alton, m. (1) Sept. 16, 1821, by Rev. Federal Burt, Catherine Jenkins, of Madbury, b. 1800, d. 1825, m. (2) Mar. 19, 1826, by Elder Thomas Flanders, Sophia Sawyer, dau. of Enoch, both of Alton.

CATE, Daniel, m. Feb. 9, 1825, by Elder Enoch Place, Betsey Peavey, d. Apr. 28, 1863, aged 80, dau. of Joseph, both of Strafford.

CATE, William T., of Brookfield, b. Jan. 8, 1802, d. Aug. 4, 1890, m. (1) Sept. 1, 1827, in Wolfeboro, Betsey Cate, of Wolfeboro, b. May 2, 1807, d. Nov. 12, 1854, aged 47, m. (2) (pub. Apr. 23, 1863, in Ossipee), Mrs. Mary G. (Colby) Stillings, of Ossipee, wid. of Isaac G., d. May 31, 1882, aged 84.

CATE, Joseph Jr., of Barrington, son of Capt. Joseph, m. Nov. 24, 1830, by Elder Enoch Place, Susan B. Garland, of Strafford, d. Mar. 13, 1831, aged 18.

CATE, Eleazer, d. Mar. 13, 1865, aged 53, m. (1) Apr. 11, 1844, by Rev. Elijah Mason, Mary Susan Young, d. Sept. 25, 1853, aged 33, dau. of Jonathan, m. (2) May 15, 1855, by Rev. Thomas G. Salter, Lydia B. Miles, of Madbury, dau. of Abraham.

CATE, Oliver B., son of John, d. Mar. 8, 1887, aged 54, m. (1) Aug. 7, 1852, in Ossipee, Joanna Wentworth, both of Somersworth, m. (2) (pub. Feb. 22, 1855), in Somersworth), Hannah Colbath, d. Jan. 24, 1909, aged 78.

CATE, Joshua Neal, b. 1828, m. Oct. 4, 1854, in Brookfield, Betsey A. Cotton, b. 1831, of Wolfeboro.

CATE, David O., of Rollinsford, m. Oct. 19, 1862, in Gilmanton Iron Works, Emily A. Gilman, of Gilmanton.

CATE, Joseph W., of Strafford, m. Dec. 31, 1862, in Barrington, Hannah J. Lane, of Lee, d. Jan. 27, 1890, aged 57.

CATE, Charles G., of Alton, m. Feb. 11, 1864, in Alton, Carrie C. Ricker, of S. Berwick, Me.

CATE, Levi A., m. July 25, 1864, in Dover, Ellen A. Reed, both of Durham.

CATER, John, of Barrington, son of John, d. Oct. 2, 1863, aged 88, m. (1) Aug. 18, 1796, by Rev. Joseph Haven, Susanna Holmes, d. Jan. 17, 1800, aged 42, m. (2) Mrs. Mary Grover, d. Feb. 25, 1837, aged 58, m. (3) int. Feb. 24, 1839, in Dover, Mary Leighton, d. Feb. 20, 1864, aged 74.

CATER, Joseph, m. Oct. 14, 1798, by Rev. Benjamin Balch, Genna Otis, both of Barrington.

CATER, Capt. Joel, d. Jan. 16, 1877, aged 78, m. (1) July 16, 1818, by Elder Enoch Place, Miriam Babb, d. Jan. 1, 1828, aged 31, both of Barrington, m. (2) Feb. 9, 1829, by Elder Enoch Place, Ann Babb, d. Mar. 11, 1880, aged 71, both of Dover.

CATER, Ephraim, of Barrington, b. Jan. 9, 1800, d. Nov. 20, 1887, aged 87, m. Oct. 25, 1821, by Elder Enoch Place, Charlotte Otis, of Strafford, b. Sept. 19, 1800, d. July 29, 1878, aged 77.

CATER, John Jr., b. Aug. 15, 1802, d. Dec. 17, 1862, aged 61, m. Sept. 5, 1822, by Elder Enoch Place, Abigail Babb, b. Nov. 26, 1799, d. Dec. 13, 1879, aged 80, both of Barrington.

CATER, Cyrus, b. Nov. 22, 1805, m. Mar. 13, 1828, by Elder Enoch Place, Olive W. Woodhouse, b. Apr. 7, 1807, both of Dover.

CATER, Horace G., son of John Jr., b. Sept. 1, 1824, d. Apr. 13, 1903, aged 78, m. Apr. 30, 1848, in Barrington, Elizabeth Lucy Hayes, d. May 20, 1905, aged 78, dau. of Jacob, both of Barrington.

CATER, John B., son of John, b. July 25, 1829, m. Jan. 1, 1851, by Rev. Thomas J. Greenwood, Abby H. Woodus, d. Jan. 23, 1891, aged 60, dau. of John F.

CATER, George F., of Barrington, m. Jan. 1, 1862, in Barrington, Almira O. Meader, of Rochester.

CATER, John A., m. Oct. 20, 1863, in Barrington, Mary E. Leighton.

CATER, James H., m. Sept. 24, 1867, in Rochester, Mary H. Goodall.

CAVERLY, Moses Jr., of Portsmouth, b. 1719, m. Mar. 12, 1740, in Portsmouth, Hannah Johnson, d. 1802.

CAVERLY, Charles, m. Mar. 16, 1786, by Rev. Benjamin Balch, Molly Danielson, both of Barrington.

CAVERLY, William, m. Apr. 24, 1794, by Rev. Benjamin Balch, Polly Holmes, both of Barrington.

CAVERLY, John, d. Feb. 6, 1849, aged 76, m. June 19, 1794, by Rev. Joseph Haven, Sarah Varney, d. Jan. 3, 1835, aged 56, both of Rochester.

CAVERLY, John, m. Oct. 11, 1795, by Rev. Benjamin Balch, Betsey Holmes, both of Barrington.

CAVERLY, John, m. Mar. 25, 1803, by Rev. Benjamin Balch, Molly Tennys, both of Barrington.

CAVERLY, Samuel, son of Lt. John, d. June 4, 1852, aged 79, m. Sept. 13, 1811, in Barrington, Hannah Hanson, d. Sept. 2, 1872, aged 79.

CAVERLY, Rev. John 4th, of Barrington, son of Lt. John, b. Aug. 23, 1789, d. Mar. 23, 1863, aged 73, m. (1) Dec. 27, 1818, by Rev. Joseph Boodey, Nancy French, of New Durham, b. Sept. 9, 1795, d. Jan. 22, 1855, aged 59, m. (2) ---- ----.

CAVERLY, m. Dec. 22, 1819, in Barrington, Anna Brown, both of Barrington.

CAVERLY, Joel, of Strafford, son of Ephraim, d. Jan. 12, 1892, aged 80, m. Oct. 30, 1836, by Elder Samuel Sherburne, Mary S. Caverly, of Barrington, d. Oct. 15, 1904, aged 86.

CAVERLY, Capt. Azariah, son of Lt. John, d. Dec. 14, 1843, aged 51, m. (1) Sally Adams, d. May 28, 1830, aged 38, m. (2) Sept. 23, 1832, by Elder Enoch Place, Eliza Tasker, b. 1813, d. 1870, both of Strafford.

CAVERLY, Asa, d. mar. 13, 1887, aged 74, m. Oct. 27, 1833, by Rev. John Winkley, Susan Bunker, d. Apr. 3, 1892, aged 81, both of Strafford.

CAVERLY, Asa, of Strafford, son of Elder John, m. (1) July 29, 1835, by Elder Enoch Place, Abigail Young, of Barrington, d. Nov. 11, 1854, aged 46, dau. of Isaac.

CAVERLY, Robert Boodey, son of Lt. John, b. July 19, 1809, d. Aug. 12, 1846, m. (1) June 1837, by Rev. David Root, Clara W. Carr, b. June 18, 1815, d. May 11, 1841, dau. of Andrew, m. (2) ---- ----.

CAVERLY, Richard, m. Dec. 27, 1838, by Rev. John Winkley, Hannah Vanduzza, both of Barrington.

CAVERLY, Ephraim H., d. Apr. 19, 1891, aged 85, m. Apr. 12, 1840, by Elder Enoch Place, Mary Jane Critchet, d. Sept. 20, 1892, aged 76, dau. of Richard.

CAVERLY, Thomas C., son of Elder John, b. July 1, 1807, d. Nov. 27, 1863, m. May 7, 1843, by Elder Enoch Place, Susan Demeritt Place, dau. of Elder Enoch, both of Strafford.

CAVERLY, Nathaniel Jr., of Barrington, d. Aug. 26, 1845, m. int. Sept. 29, 1844, in Lebanon, Me., Nancy Jane Ricker, d. May 6, 1873, dau. of Ezekiel.

CAVERLY, Charles H., d. Jun. 19, 1873, aged 49, m. Feb. 19, 1845, by Rev. John Winkley, Phoebe Durgin, d. Mar. 29, 1862, aged 41, both of Strafford.

CAVERLY, Mason, son of Rufus, b. Apr. 2, 1829, m. May 4, 1851, by Rev. Homer Barrows, Caroline A. Fisher.

CAVERLY, Seth William, son of Col. Joseph, b. Oct. 22, 1834, d. Nov. 26, 1904, m. June 30, 1855, in Barrington, Asenath Abigail Boodey, b. Feb. 17, 1838, d. Nov. 13, 1917, both of Strafford.

CAVERLY, John B., of Rollinsford, b. Dec. 24, 1835, d. May 14, 1928, m. Aug. 23, 1857, in Nottingham, Hannah H. Hill, of Barrington.

CAVERLY, Asa, d. Dec. 2, 1886, aged 85, m. (1) Abigail Young, of Barrington, d. Nov. 11, 1854, aged 46, dau. of Isaac, m. (2) Apr. 11, 1859, by Elder Enoch Place, Betsey Y. Sanders, d. Jan. 4, 1890, aged 66.

CAVERLY, Daniel E., son of Richard, b. Aug. 9, 1839, d. Oct. 2, 1921, m. Aug. 21, 1865, in Tuftonboro, Sarah E. Fernald, b. Apr. 30, 1843, d. Mar. 19, 1886, both of Tuftonboro.

CAVERLY, Robert B., of Strafford, m. Oct. 26, 1865, in Epping, Mary H. E. Wilson, of Epping.

CAVERLY, George W., m. Oct. 17, 1870, in Dover, Lizzie A. Seward, both of Strafford.

CAVERNO, Jeremiah, son of John, d. Aug. 25, 1825, aged 59, m. June 22, 1790, by Rev. Benjamin Balch, Peggy Brewster, d. Feb. 21, 1854, aged 86, both of Barrington.

CAVERNO, Rev. Arthur, son of Jeremiah, d. July 15, 1876, aged 75, m. (1) Dec. 11, 1823, by Elder Enoch Place, Olive H. Foss, d. Jan. 30, 1854, aged 50, both of Strafford, m. (2) (pub. Feb. 22, 1855, in Bath), Mrs. Isabel J. Soule, of Bath, d. Mar. 22, 1883, aged 62.

CAVERNO, Jeremiah, of Strafford, m. (pub. Apr. 17, 1829, in Barrington), Dolla K. Balch, of Barrington, b. Sept. 10, 1799, dau. of Thomas.

CAVERNO, George W., son of Jeremiah, d. Mar. 22, 1875, aged 72, m. June 29, 1831, by Rev. William Demeritt, Hannah Ricker, d. Aug. 3, 1833, aged 23.

CAVERNO, George S., of Strafford, d. Oct. 21, 1916, aged 74, m. Jan. 30, 1867, in Dover, Ida S. Hanson, of Dover, d. Oct. 21, 1918, aged 78.

CHADWICK, John, m. (pub. Feb. 13, 1827, in Middleton), Elizabeth B. Pike, both of Middleton.

4) **CHAMBERLAIN**, Col. Jacob, son of William, b. 1738, d. 1816, m. early as 1763, Alice ----, b. 1743, d. 1804.

CHAMBERLAIN, John, m. Mar. 30, 1774, in Brookfield, Mary Jackson.

CHAMBERLAIN, Jason, son of William, b. Feb. 9, 1756, d. Jan. 29, 1823, m. in 1780, Mary Brewster, d. Mar. 9, 1830, aged 69, dau. of Daniel.

CHAMBERLAIN, Ephraim, Jr., son of Col. Jacob, b. Mar. 21, 1773, d. 1840, m. Dec. 5, 1793, by Rev. Joseph Haven, Mary Davis, of New Durham, b. July 2, 1778, d. 1855, dau. of Eleazer.

CHAMBERLAIN, John, m. Aug. 6, 1794, in Brookfield, Joanna Banfield, both of Middleton.

CHAMBERLAIN, William, d. Oct. 7, 1861, aged 79, m. Sept. 12, 1811, in Wolfeboro, Betsey Adams Horne, b. Feb. 4, 1793, d. Oct. 17, 1835, dau. of John, both of Wolfeboro.

CHAMBERLAIN, Col. Josiah, son of Thomas, d. Jul. 19, 1823, m. Jun. 30, 1820, in Wolfeboro, Betsey Guppy, of Wolfeboro, b. Dec. 29, 1797, dau. of William.

CHAMBERLAIN, Lt. George, b. 1814, d. 1904, m. Dec. 18, 1836, by Rev. Joseph Boodey, Keziah Jenkins, of New Durham, d. Nov. 9, 1888, aged 74.

CHAMBERLAIN, Joshua P., of Alton, son of Jacob, d. Sept. 8, 1891, aged 76, m. Sept. 29, 1839, by Elder Enoch Place, Sally Sloper, b. May 18, 1813, d. Mar. 6, 1894, dau. of William, of Strafford.

CHAMBERLAIN, Thomas, of Brookfield, m. (pub. Sept. 1, 1846, in Wolfeboro), Nancy Horne, of Wolfeboro, b. Aug. 13, 1787, d. Feb. 19, 1879 (was this a second marriage?)

CHAMBERLAIN, Charles Burnham, of Lebanon, Me., son of James, b. Mar. 19, 1830, m. (pub. Oct. 19, 1852, in Somersworth), Sarah Smith Cooper, of Wakefield, b. Oct. 12, 1825.

CHAMBERLAIN, Horatio G., of New Durham, m. Oct. 8, 1862, in Strafford, Augusta Jane Ricker, of Farmington.

CHAMBERLAIN, Dr. Jonas, m. Oct. 16, 1862, in New Durham, Mary S. Burley.

CHAMBERLAIN, John S., of New Durham, m. Feb. 21, 1863, in Alton, Susan E. Spead, of Newmarket.

CHAMBERLAIN, John F., of Dover, m. Nov. 30, 1863, by Rev. James Rand, Josephine A. Horn, of Wolfeboro.

CHAMBERLAIN, Charles Edward, m. Aug. 15, 1865, in Manchester, Henrietta L. Osgood, both of Dover.

CHAMBERLAIN, Ivory Jenkins, of Alton, m. June 5, 1866, in Lee, Georgianna O. Hoitt, of Lee, b. Nov. 4, 1837, d. Aug. 9, 1914, dau. of Gorham D.

CHAMBERLAIN, Josiah W., m. (pub. Nov. 29, 1866, in Wolfeboro), Fannie E. Weeks.

CHAMBERLAIN, Asa, m. Feb. 16, 1867, in Alton, Betsey Stevens, both of Alton.

CHAMBERLAIN, Edward B., of Dover, m. May 19, 1867, by Rev. George T. Day, Mrs. Hannah P. Smith, of Candia.

CHAMPION, Alvah, of Dover, m. Dec. 1827, by Elder David Blaisdell, Adah Jones, of Lebanon, Me.

CHAMPION, Levi, of Lowell, Mass., d. Oct. 5, 1897, aged 88, m. July 10, 1831, by Rev. John Osborne, Nancy N. Doe, of Lee, d. Aug. 18, 1885, aged 75.

CHAMPION, Lorenzo L., d. Mar. 17, 1899, aged 72, m. (1) Hannah ----, d. July 24, 1857, aged 22, m. (2) (pub. Oct. 22, 1857, in Effingham), Sabrina S. Day, d. Dec. 6, 1900, aged 67, both of Effingham.

CHAMPION, Charles W., of Dover, m. Mar. 20, 1865, in Dover, Carrie Berry, of Portland, Me.

CHAMPION, Alvah, m. Oct. 14, 1869, in Dover, Sophronia Wiggin, both of Dover.

CHANDLER, William E., m. (pub. Jan. 21, 1869, in Portsmouth), Nellie Holmes, dau. of Joseph.

CHAPMAN, Edward A., of York, Me., m. (pub. Jan. 7, 1864, in Portsmouth), Maria Somerby, dau. of Sherburne.

CHAPMAN, Capt. C. L., m. Dec. 27, 1865, in Great Falls, Fannie Brown.

CHAPMAN, Edward T., m. Feb. 20, 1867, by Rev. Charles Tenny, Abby E. Vickery, both of Dover.

CHASE, Samuel, m. Apr. 1, 1787, by Rev. Isaac Hasey, Amy Kilgore.

2) CHASE, James, b. 1768, d. Sep. 14, 1801, m. near 1795, Elizabeth Gage, d. Sep. 30, 1813, aged 39, dau. of Moses.

CHASE, Nathaniel, b. 1781, d. 1861, m. Feb. 8, 1807, in Wolfeboro, Susannah Rust, b. 1787, d. 1856, both of Wolfeboro.

CHASE, Josiah W., of Wolfeboro, son of Nathaniel, b. 1803, d. 1891, m. Apr. 3, 1828, in Wolfeboro, Abigail Chase, of Alton, b. 1807, d. 1874.

CHASE, Daniel, son of Isaac, b. July 5, 1805, m. Mar. 30, 1829, in Conway, Abigail H. Garland, b. Jan. 29, 1811.

CHASE, James Monroe, son of Edmund, d. Jul. 21, 1888, aged 67, m. (pub. Dec. 1, 1840, in Great Falls), Betsey S. Heath, d. Sep. 8, 1891, dau. of John.

CHASE, Sewell J., m. int. Nov. 22, 1855, in Lebanon, Me., Eliza Hussey, of Acton, Me.

CHASE, Joseph T., of Fall River, Mass., m. Oct. 22, 1866, in Dover, Ellen J. Corson, of Barrington.
CHASE, Arthur W., of Haverhill, Mass., son of Frederick, m. May 1, 1867, by Rev. Isaac C. White, Julia F. Parker, of N. Andover, Mass., dau. of Nathan.
CHASE, James W., of No. Berwick, Me., m. May 15, 1869, in Lebanon, Me., Louise S. Worster.
CHASE, Charles F., of Dover, m. Aug. 21, 1869, in Dover, Susan Marden, of Dunkirk, N.Y.
CHELLIS, Charles B., m. (pub. Aug. 11, 1870, in Great Falls), Louisa Buck, both of Salmon Falls.
CHENEY, Elder Oren Burbank, m. int. Jul. 10, 1847, in Lebanon, Me., Nancy S. Perkins, of New Hampton, N. H., d. Feb. 21, 1886, aged 72.
CHENEY, Perley C. J., of Boston, Mass., m. July 25, 1866, in S. Berwick, Me., Anna A. Cater, of Rollinsford.
CHENEY, Andrew J., m. Aug. 10, 1867, in Great Falls, Lydia S. Rogers, both of Salmon Falls.
5) **CHESLEY**, James, son of Thomas, b. Jan. 25, 1750, d. Jan. 13, 1851, m. near 1772, Elizabeth Downing Furber, d. Feb. 6, 1838, aged 79, dau. of Richard.
6) CHESLEY, Lemuel, of Lee, son of Lemuel, d. Mar. 27, 1855, aged 90, m. Oct. 9, 1793, by Rev. William Hooper, Love Hull, of Northwood, d. 1872, aged 102, dau. of Richard.
CHESLEY, Samuel, b. Mar. 1, 1772, d. Feb. 10, 1863, m. Mar. 2, 1797, Nancy Perkins, b. Apr. 26, 1775, d. Nov. 17, 1856.
CHESLEY, Ebenezer, m. Dec. 21, 1797, by Rev. Benjamin Balch, Hannah Pearl, both of Rochester.
6) CHESLEY, Paul, of Durham, son of Philip, d. July 9, 1840, aged 57, m. (1) July 17, 1803, by Rev. William Hooper, Sally Hooper, dau. of Rev. William, m. (2) Apr. 3, 1816, Polly Demeritt, dau. of Andrew.
CHESLEY, Samuel 2nd, of Madbury, son of Paul, d. June 27, 1887, aged 83, m. Sept. 25, 1825, by Rev. John Brodhead, Mehitable Demeritt, of Durham, d. Sept. 15, 1868, aged 68, dau. of Joseph.
7) CHESLEY, Dr. James C., of Barrington, son of Joseph, d. Nov. 19, 1893, aged 70, m. Mar. 9, 1845, in Barrington, Mariah L. Roberson, d. Jan. 19, 1895, aged 71, both of Barrington.
CHESLEY, Joseph W., m. (1) Aug. 3, 1845, Mary Jane Swain, m. (2) June 30, 1846, by Elder Samuel Sherburne, Margaret A. Swain, both of Barrington.

CHESLEY, Joshua R., son of Joseph R., d. May 16, 1902, aged 73, m. Dec. 23, 1849, by Elder Samuel Sherburne, Mary E. Swain, d. July 29, 1898, aged 66, dau. of Daniel, both of Barrington.
CHESLEY, Benjamin, of Farmington, d. Nov. 17, 1890, aged 72, m. (1) June 26, 1858, in Dover, Mary A. Chamberlain, of New Durham, d. Dec. 13, 1863, aged 34, m. (2) April 30, 1866, in Rochester, Mrs. Betsey H. Goodwin, d. Mar. 14, 1879, aged 57.
CHESLEY, David G., m. Feb. 24, 1862, in Barrington, Nancy Twombly, both of Barnstead.
CHESLEY, John B., m. Jan. 7, 1863, in Gilmanton, Mary H. Moore, both of Barnstead.
CHESLEY, George S., of Lee, d. Jun. 12, 1878, aged 40, m. Jan. 4, 1864, in Hampton, Sarah Fannie Palmer, of Hampton.
CHESLEY, Asa G., of Barrington, son of Asa, b. Jan. 26, 1839, d. July 4, 1920, m. Nov. 15, 1864, in Barrington, Deborah M. Canney, b. May 29, 1849, d. July 19, 1930, dau. of James.
CHESLEY, Freeman, of Barrington, m. Sept. 21, 1865, in Barrington, Cornelia R. Welsh, of Deerfield.
CHESLEY, Harry J., of Wolfeboro, m. Nov. 4, 1865, in Farmington, Alice M. Hartford, of Lebanon, Me.
CHESLEY, J. Edwin, m. Sept. 3, 1866, in Rochester, Lizzie W. Horne.
CHESLEY, Samuel, m. Sept. 16, 1869, in Dover, Mrs. Mary B. Jenness, both of Dover.
CHESLEY, George E., of Lee, son of Thomas, b. 1833, d. 1925, m. Sep. 15, 1877, in Lee, Abbie H. Pettingill, of Haverhill, Mass., b. 1844, d. 1923.
CHESWELL, Paul W., m. Aug. 2, 1857, by Elder Elias Hutchins, Ann Augusta Edgerly, b. 1840, dau. of Jacob, both of Durham.
CHESWELL, Thomas E., d. Mar. 23, 1923, aged 79, m. Dec. 22, 1862, in Dover, Mary F. Wentworth, both of Dover.
CHICK, Aaron, son of Aaron, Jr., d. Mar 16, 1851, m. (1) Jul. 25, 1793, Susannah Fogg, b. Apr. 29, 1771, d. Dec. 28, 1797, aged 28, dau. of James, m. (2) Dec. 5, 1804 in Lebanon, Me., Abigail Libbey, b. Jul. 23, 1775, d. Mar. 29, 1817, aged 42, dau. of Jeremiah.
CHICK, Samuel, of Eliot, Me., m. Mar. 6, 1806, Ursula Nute, of Dover, b. Jan. 8, 1785, d. Dec. 27, 1868.
CHICK, Thomas, d. May 3, 1826, aged 34, m. May 27, 1813, by Rev. Joseph Boody, in Barrington, Mary Holmes, d. May 12, 1860, aged 67, dau. of John.

CHICK, Capt. Simon F., m. (1) Nov. 7, 1824, Mary Jane Pray, b. Feb. 25, 1808, d. May 2, 1836, dau. of Samuel, m (2) Apr. 27, 1837, Ann B. Pray, of Shapleigh, Me., b. Nov. 10, 1810, d. May 14, 1877.

CHICK, Freeman, son of Simon F., b. Feb. 8, 1838, d. Feb. 8, 1887, m. Jan. 31, 1861, in Lebanon, Me.,m Amanda J. Clark, d. Jan. 1887.

CHICK Winthrop F., d. Aug. 25, 1898, aged 76, m. (1) Mar. 23, 1847, in Effingham, Huldah Jane Drake, d. May 9, 1853, aged 25, m. (2) Rose L. ----, d. May 13, 1887, aged 61.

CHICK, Alvin, of Lebanon, Me., son of Simon F., b. Mar. 12, 1833, d. Aug. 22, 1865, aged 32, m. Sep. 8, 1857, by Rev. Thomas J. Greenwood, Maria F. Woodman, of Nottingham, d. May 1, 1877, aged 44.

CHICK, Freeman, of Lebanon, Me., d. Feb. 8, 1887, aged 49, m. Jan. 31, 1861, by Rev. Benjamin F. Parsons, Frances A. Clark, d. Jan. 26, 1887, aged 49, dau. of David M., both of Somersworth.

CHICK, John, of Somersworth, m. Feb. 23, 1861, in Lebanon, Me., Elizabeth Lord, d. Sep. 3, 1914, aged 76.

CHICK, James W., m. Nov. 1, 1866, in Effingham, Hannah A. Bean, both of Effingham.

CHICK, Almon Howard, aged 24, son of Simon F., b. Oct. 3, 1843, m. int. Oct. 3, 1867, in Lebanon, Me., Joan Lord, aged 22, dau. of Elbin.

3) **CHURCH**, Jonathan, son of John, b. July 25, 1708, d. 1774, m. Dec. 11, 1740, Abigail Hanson, of Dover, dau. of Nathaniel.

CHURCH, William, of Pittstown, m. June 23, 1799, by Rev. Benjamin Balch, Sarah Daniels, of Barrington.

5) CHURCH, Nathaniel, son of Nathaniel, b. Sept. 8, 1799, d. Feb. 22, 1850, m. Jan. 23, 1827, by Rev. William Demeritt, Patience Hanson, d. Apr. 18, 1886, aged 80, dau. of Isaac.

CHURCHILL, Thomas Lindsay, of Brookfield, b. 1822, m. (1) (pub. Mar. 16, 1847, in Wakefield), Sarah A. Stackpole, of Somersworth, m. (2) int. Sep. 3, 1867, in Brookfield, Nancy M. Seward, of Boston, Mass., aged 35.

CHURCHILL, Albert, m. June 28, 1863, in Dover, Belinda E. Colbath, both of Dover.

CILLEY, David T., m. Aug. 30, 1863, in Deerfield, Sylvira L. Tuttle, dau. of Rev. A. Tuttle, both of Nottingham.

CILLEY, William P., m. (pub. Nov. 18, 1869, in Great Falls), Sarah F. Yeaton, both of Rochester.

CLARK, Deac. Enoch P., d. Dec. 17, 1825, aged 62, m. Sept. 12, 1789, by Rev. James Miltmore, Polly Robinson, d. 1833, aged 65.

CLARK, Levi, b. Mar. 11, 1769, d. Feb. 9, 1862, aged 89, m. June 6, 1790, Love Wiggin, b. Jan. 14, 1768.

CLARK, Jonathan, m. Jan. 31, 1792, by Rev. Benjamin Balch, Sarah Hall, both of Barrington.

CLARK, Enoch, d. 1825, m. Aug. 17, 1792, by Rev. Benjamin Balch, Susannah Canney, of Madbury, d. 1811, dau. of Isaac.

CLARK, Rev. Jeremiah, d. June 17, 1857, aged 82, m. Sarah Hill, b. Sept. 15, 1777, d. May 26, 1857, dau. of Andrew.

CLARK, James of Barrington, m. Nov. 28, 1799, by Rev. Joseph Haven, Elizabeth McNeal, of Rochester, d. Nov. 1, 1822, aged 40.

CLARK, Daniel, Jr., of Exeter, d. Apr. 14, 1829, aged 50, m. Jan. 28, 1802, by Rev. Joseph Haven, Rachel Wiggin, of Rochester.

CLARK, Jacob, m. Sept. 15, 1804, by Rev. Benjamin Balch, Genny Gray, both of Barrington.

CLARK, Rev. Peter, of Gilmanton, son of Samuel, b. Oct. 8, 1781, d. Nov. 25, 1865, m. (1) Nov. 28, 1805, Mary Morrison, d. Sept. 25, 1841, m. (2) in 1849, Mrs. Abigail E. Ware.

CLARK, Rev. Mayhew, of Wakefield, m. June 4, 1807, in Wakefield, Betty Horne, of Wolfeboro.

CLARK, Ebenezer, m. Oct. 29, 1807, by Rev. Isaac Hasey, Sally Smith, dau. of Ichabod.

CLARK, John, m. Nov. 17, 1808, in Barrington, Eleanor Berry, both of Barrington.

CLARK, John Jr., d. Sept. 27, 1819, m. July 18, 1816, by Elder Enoch Place, Betsey Caverly, both of Barrington

CLARK, William S., of Barnstead. d. Feb. 15, 1875, aged 75, m. Dec. 26, 1822, by Elder Enoch Place, Judith Hanson, of Strafford, d. Feb. 1, 1865, aged 61.

CLARK, Jonathan Jr., of Strafford, d. May 4, 1826, m. Mar. 20, 1823, by Elder Enoch Place, Polly Varney, of Milton.

CLARK, Oliver, son of James, b. Dec. 12, 1805, d. Apr. 12, 1839, m. May 5, 1833, by Rev. Abner Flanders, Ruth Delano.

CLARK, Rufus, m. int. Nov. 10, 1833, in Lebanon, Me., Hannah Chick, b. Dec. 23, 1811, dau. of Aaron.

CLARK, James V., of Strafford, son of Ebenezer, b. June 5, 1809, d. July 14, 1880, aged 71, m. Apr. 15, 1835, by Rev. Jared Perkins, Elizabeth Nute, of Dover, b. Jan. 23, 1809, d. Feb. 16, 1892.

CLARK, Hiram, b. 1810, d. 1898, m. July 9, 1837, Mrs. Adah (Downs) Jones, wid. of Thomas, b. 1809, d. 1880.

CLARK, Timothy L., b. 1815, d. Jan. 4, 1892, m. Jun. 27, 1844, by
Rev. John Winkley, Patience M. Leighton, b. 1820, d. May 18,
1905, both of Strafford.

CLARK, Albert G., m. May 27, 1846, in Wakefield, Mary A. Cook,
b. Nov. 21, 1821, d. Dec. 7, 1864, dau. of John.

CLARK, Richard H., son of James, b. Apr. 4, 1823, d. Oct. 10, 1852,
m. Jan. 23, 1848, by Rev. Joseph Loring, Lois Brackett, of
Somersworth.

CLARK, Levi, of Berwick, Me., son of James, b. 1819, d. 1881, m.
(1) Apr. 23, 1848, by Rev. Samuel Kelley, Hannah P. Downs, of
Dover, b. 1820, d. Dec. 27, 1867, m. (2) Aug. 2, 1870, in Malden,
Mass., Sarah W. Clark, b. 1833, d. 1904, dau. of James.

CLARK, James, m. Feb. 26, 1849, in Barrington, Anna M. Downing,
of Barrington.

CLARK, Alonzo F., of Alton, m. int. Jun. 4, 1853, in Lebanon, Me.,
Eunice T. Goodwin.

CLARK, William, m. (pub. June 24, 1858, in Somersworth), Olive
W. Hammond, b. 1836, d. 1915, both of N. Berwick, Me.

CLARK, Charles T., son of Sylvester, d. May 4, 1917, aged 74, m.
(pub. Aug. 15, 1861, in Great Falls), Ellen F. Hoyt, d. Jan. 26,
1903, aged 60, dau. of Lewis, both of Rochester.

CLARK, John D., m. June 29, 1862, in Strafford, Almira E. Tuttle, d.
Dec. 2, 1867, aged 71, dau. of Enoch..

CLARK, George H., m. Mar. 3, 1864, in Great Falls, Margaret
Honners, both of Somersworth.

CLARK, John, m. June 14, 1865, in Dover, Nellie E. Stanton, both of
N. Berwick, Me.

CLARK, Rev. John W., of Dover, m. Jan. 17, 1866, in Boston, Mass.,
Margaret T. Hubbard, of Exeter.

CLARK, James F., of Rochester, m. July 11, 1866, in Milton, Jennie
L. Tuttle, of Middleton.

CLARK, George G., m. Dec. 9, 1866, in Great Falls, Susie M.
Staples, both of Tuftonboro.

CLARK, Charles A. W., son of William, d. May 2, 1916, aged 76, m.
Nov. 16, 1874, in Barnstead, Ruth H. (Canney) Avery, b. Dec.
1837, d. Dec. 30, 1905, wid. of Lewis, dau. of Joseph.

CLARK, William D., of Great Falls, b. Nov. 8, 1843, d. Feb. 17,
1919, m. Mar. 5, 1868, in Great Falls, L. Augusta Piper, of
Tuftonboro, b. Mar. 18, 1839, d. Mar. 31, 1907.

CLARK, Sanborn B., of Ossipee, m. (pub. Oct. 8, 1868, in
Wakefield), Mrs. Mary A. Sweat, of Wakefield.

CLARK, Robert I., aged 78, m. (pub. Oct. 8, 1868, in Wakefield), Ann Pinkham, aged 65, (this is his 5th, her 1st).

CLARK, Charles E., of Brookfield, aged 25, m. int. Feb. 24, 1869, in Brookfield, Ella M. Willand, of Tuftonboro, aged 19.

CLARK, George E., of Dover, m. Mar. 3, 1869, in Dover, Elizabeth Gilman, of Effingham.

CLARK, Orrin R., of Dover, m. July 7, 1869, in Dover, Lovie D. Hayes, of Madison.

CLARK, George W., d. May 24, 1912, aged 77, m. Aug. 3, 1869, in Dover, Nellie Brooks, both of Dover.

CLARK, Charles H., of Dover, son of John S., d. Sept. 30, 1918, aged 67, m. Feb. 21, 1870, in Dover, Georgia A. Dolliver, of Bangor, Me.

CLARK, George G. m. June 20, 1870, in Dover, Mary F. E. Lock, both of Dover.

CLARK, Benjamin L., m. (pub. Dec. 8, 1870, in Great Falls), Luella J. Ricker, both of Berwick, Me.

CLARK, James F., of Brookfield, aged 20, m. int. Jan. 13, 1871, in Brookfield, Saddie A. Abbott, of No. Berwick, Me., aged 21.

CLARK, Charles A. W., m. Nov. 16, 1874, in Barnstead, Ruth H. (Canney) Avery, b. Dec. 1837, d. Dec. 30, 1905, wid. of Lewis, dau. of Joseph.

CLARKE, Linus Everett, m. Jan. 6, 1867, in Dover, Mary Ellen Hill, both of Melrose, Mass.

CLARKE, Frederick M., m. (pub. June 3, 1869, in Great Falls), Susan H. Nute, both of Berwick, Me.

CLAY, Samuel, of Lee, m. Mar. 22, 1788, in Barrington, Esther Hall, of Barrington.

CLAY, John, m. Oct. 21, 1790, by Rev. Benjamin Balch, Abigail Glover, both of Barrington.

CLAY, Jonathan, m. Aug. 1, 1833, in Barrington, Susan Brown, of Barrington.

CLAY, Arthur G., d. Nov. 22, 1867, aged 30, m. (pub. Jan. 16, 1862, in Ossipee), Olive E. Tebbets, d. Dec. 12, 1886, aged 49.

CLAY, Francis S., of Barrington, m. (pub. Sept. 21, 1865, in Lowell, Mass.), Margaret Mahoney, of Lowell, Mass.

CLAY, John, of Barrington, son of John, m. Dec. 25, 1868, by Rev. Alvan Tobey, Mary A. Glover, of Lee, dau. of Plumer.

CLAY, Charles H., of Farmington, m. May 2, 1869, in Bristol, Eva Call, of Bristol.

CLEMENTS, William Jr., m. Oct. 18, 1841, by Rev. Aaron Ayer, Elizabeth B. Canney, b. May 1824, d. Oct. 21, 1847, dau. of Isaac.

CLEMENTS, Joseph H., d. Nov. 4, 1874, aged 55, m. Aug. 17, 1844, in Lebanon, Me., Betsey Ann Clements, d. June 5, 1885, aged 71, both of Somersworth.

CLIFFORD, James, of Loudon, m. Oct. 31, 1813, in Barrington, Peggy Hanscom, of Barrington.

CLIFFORD, Simon J., of S. Hampton, m. Jan. 13, 1865, in Dover, Paulina Goodwin, of S. Berwick, Me.

CLOUGH, Josiah, of Northwood, d. Apr. 29, 1856, aged 92, m. Apr. 19, 1785, by Rev. Isaac Smith, Mary Young, of Gilmanton.

CLOUGH, William, of Northwood, m. Dec. 6, 1792, by Rev. Benjamin Balch, Sarah Swain, of Barrington.

CLOUGH, Jonathan, b. Nov. 28, 1797, d. Dec. 2, 1865, m. May 22, 1823, by Rev. Jeremiah Shaw, Hannah Ambrose, b. June 26, 1803, d. Nov. 7, 1859.

CLOUGH, Micajah S., d. Feb. 13, 1815, aged 67, m. Jan. 2, 1827, by Elder Enoch Place, Mrs. Deborah Ricker, d. Nov. 27, 1875, aged 88, both of Barrington.

CLOUGH, Jonathan C., d. Nov. 8, 1856, aged 44, m. int. Oct. 8, 1837, in Dover, Sarah A. Hanson, b. Oct. 12, 1814, d. Sept. 14, 1897, dau. of Ebenezer.

CLOUGH, Jesse W., of Wolfeboro, m. May 29, 1848, in Wolfeboro, Sabrina Wentworth, of Berwick, Me., d. Apr. 12, 1894, dau. of Benjamin.

CLOUGH, Jonathan A., of Dover, d. Apr. 28, 1893, aged 63, m. (pub. Sept. 6, 1853, in Portsmouth), Sarah L. Nutter, of Eliot, Me., d. Sept. 14, 1897, aged 73.

CLOUGH, Josiah E., m. Nov. 13, 1853, in Lebanon, Me., Mary E. Carley, both of Rochester.

CLOUGH, Nathaniel, m. Dec. 25, 1867, in Rochester, Mary D. Pinkham.

CLOUGH, David E., m. Jan. 8, 1868, in Alton, Rosetta B. Miller, both of Alton.

CLOUGH, Frank B., m. Dec. 23, 1868, in Dover, Julia A. Nute, both of Dover.

CLOUGH, William, of Barnstead, m. (pub. July 21, 1870, in Strafford), Mrs. Nancy L. Clark, of Strafford.

CLOUTMAN, Eliphalet, son of John, b. Mar. 17, 1753, d. Oct. 1, 1838, m. (1) Feb. 1, 1776, by Rev. David Tenny, Hannah Hayes, b. Sept. 8, 1755, d. Jan. 12, 1832, aged 76, dau. of Robert, m. (2) Feb.

25, 1833, in Lebanon, Me., Sarah Berry, b. Apr. 22, 1793, d. Apr. 17, 1845, dau. of Jeremiah.

CLOUTMAN, Asa, of Wakefield, d. Feb. 1885, aged 74, m. (1) Mar. 11, 1833, in Middleton, Syrene Hanson, of Middleton, d. Sept. 9, 1867, aged 54, m. (2) (pub. Nov. 26, 1868, in Northwood), Mrs. Polly Davis, wid. of Daniel W., d. Feb. 1, 1890, aged 75.

CLOUTMAN, Samuel S., of Middleton, son of William M., b. Jul. 1826, m. (pub. Apr. 20, 1852, in Middleton), Caroline W. Pearl, of Farmington, d. Feb. 7, 1867, dau. of Levi.

COBB, Bensley P., of Somersworth, m. Apr. 3, 1840, by Elder Enoch Place, Martha Ann Foss, of Strafford, dau. of Ephraim.

COBB, Frank M., of Mechanics Falls, Me., m. Dec. 28, 1864, in Gonic, Hannah H. Currier, of Gonic, dau. of William.

COBBETT, Charles A. A., m. Jan. 5, 1867, in Rochester, Mary A. Ransom, both of Rochester.

COBURN, Frank F., of Haverhill, Mass., m. Aug. 26, 1867, by Rev. Robert S. Stubbs, Carrie Nancy Cleaves, of Dover, b. June 2, 1838, d. Apr. 12, 1925, dau. of Thaddeus P.

COCKING, Charles R., d. Mar. 11, 1902, m. Sept. 16, 1864, in Roxbury, Mass., Marianna Davis, b. Apr. 28, 1847, dau. of Samuel, both of Madbury.

COCKING, Edward H., of Dover, m. Dec. 31, 1868, in Dover, Sarah M. Foss, of Madbury.

COE, Joseph W., of Durham, m. (pub. Dec. 11, 1862, in Lawrence, Mass.), Hattie S. Churchill, of Lawrence, Mass.

COFFIN, Eliphalet, son of Tristram, b. Jan. 13, 1689, m. Feb. 11, 1710, Judith Noyes.

COFFIN, Benjamin, son of Maj. Jonathan, b. 1777, d. 1844, m. Jan. 2, 1800, by Rev. Isaac Smith, Eunice Kelley, b. 1781, d. 1853.

COFFIN, Jonathan, of Tuftonboro, son of Maj. Jonathan, b. Jan. 28, 1781, d. Apr. 25, 1862, m. (1) int. Feb. 1803, in Tuftonboro, Sally Gilman, of Alton, dau. of Moses, m. (2) Lydia Nay, d. Apr. 10, 1879, aged 85, dau. of Joseph.

COFFIN, Moses, son of Maj. Jonathan, m. int. June 1808, in Tuftonboro, Fanny Foss, both of Tuftonboro.

COFFIN, Rev. Stephen, of Alton, son of Jonathan, b. Mar. 8, 1792, d. Mar. 4, 1867, m. (1) Jan. 15, 1815, by Rev. Joseph Boodey, Phebe Ayers, of Barnstead, b. 1783, d. 1817, m. (2) Deborah Philbrick, dau. of Deac. David, d. Oct. 4, 1838, aged 38, m. (2) Apr. 3, 1839, by Elder Enoch Place, Caroline E. Foss, of Poughkeepsie, N.Y., d. Jan. 24, 1880, aged 76.

COFFIN, Isaac P., of Alton, b. 1814, d. 1878, m. (pub. Mar. 26, 1839, in Barnstead), Phebe R. Clough, of Gilmanton, b. 1815, d. 1894.

COFFIN, Francis T., of Pittsburgh, Pa., m. June 14, 1865, in Alton, Mary F. Mooney, of Alton.

COFFIN, Benjamin, of Boston, Mass, m. Oct. 19, 1867, by Rev. Alden Sherwin, Henrietta Hodgkins, of Dover.

COGSWELL, John, of Landaff, m. Dec. 1, 1814, by Rev. Isaac Smith, Mrs. Ruth Butler, wid. of Gen. Henry.

COGSWELL, Rev. Fredrick, son of Judge Thomas, b. Mar. 23, 1792, d. July 1857, m. May 18, 1817, Hannah Rogers Peavey, d. July 9, 1853, dau. of Col. Anthony.

COGSWELL, Franklin, m. Aug. 24, 1864, in Rochester, Mary A. Moody, both of Newmarket.

COLBATH, Dudley, b. Nov. 1, 1792, d. Feb. 23, 1832, m. Jul. 23, 1823, in Lebanon, Me., Hannah Dunnel, b. Jul. 12, 1793, d. Jun. 20, 1831.

COLBATH, James A., of Somersworth, m. Aug. 12, 1827, by Rev. Joseph Hilliard, Eunice Witherell, of Berwick, Me., d. June 1, 1853, aged 44.

COLBATH, Washington, of Middleton, son of Samuel, m. Oct. 30, 1831, in Farmington, Electra Jane Varney, of Farmington.

COLBATH, King, of Porter, Me., d. Nov. 25, 1904, aged 85, m. Sep. 30, 1845, by Rev. John Parkman, Emily Guppey, d. Oct. 12, 1899, aged 69, dau. of Benjamin F.

COLBATH, William, aged 31, of Dover, m. int. Nov. 16, 1855, in Brookfield, Mary Jane Churchill, of Brookfield, aged 23.

COLBATH, John, m. int. Jul. 9, 1860, in Lebanon, Me., Almira Emery, of Sanford.

COLBATH, Joseph W., of Exeter, m. Feb. 12, 1862, in Dover, Martha F. Hussey, of Rochester.

COLBATH, Jonathan F., of Alton, m. Mar. 14, 1862, in Alton, Annette J. Pease, of Gilmanton.

COLBATH, Levi F., of Dover, m. Dec. 31, 1866, in Dover, Annie M. Turner, of Lawrence, Mass., d. Aug. 10, 1868, aged 23, dau. of Levi G.

COLBATH, Benjamin R., of Middleton, m. (pub. Nov. 12, 1868, in Middleton), Betsey Foss, of Farmington.

COLBATH, John L., of Farmington, m. May 27, 1870, in Dover, Sarah L. Batson, of New Castle.

COLBY, Elder John J. G., of Ossipee, b. Apr. 7, 1796, d. June 5, 1877, aged 81, m. Nov. 24, 1830, by Rev. Isaac Willey, Camela Abby Horne, of Rochester, b. July 2, 1809, d. Aug. 4, 1886.

COLBY, Samuel S. of Wakefield, b. 1816, d. Dec. 9, 1884, m. (pub. Jan. 3, 1843, in Wakefield), Betsey Jenness, b. 1799, d. Apr. 10, 1878.

COLBY, Ira M., of Warner, m. Sept. 26, 1866, by Rev. Francis E. Abbott, Amanda J. Conner, of Dover.

COLE, William, of Somersworth, m. int. Nov. 1823, Susanna Corson, of Dover.

COLE, Benjamin James, son of Isaac, m. Jun. 17, 1838, Mehitable A. Batchelder, dau. of Nathan.

COLE, John W., d. Jan. 15, 1871, aged 65, m. July 29, 1849, by Elder Elias Hutchins, Rachel A. Woodman, d. Apr. 26, 1894, aged 62.

COLE, John W., m. July 16, 1862, in Dover, Frances K. West, both of Dover.

COLE, Al S., of Eliot, Me., m. (pub. Jan. 7, 1864, in Portsmouth), Caroline A. Varney.

COLE, William H., m. Nov. 28, 1866, in Great Falls, Margaret A. Kidder, both of Great Falls.

COLE, Nathan H., of Swamscott, Mass., m. July 4, 1869, in Dover, Emma Gilman, of Effingham.

COLE, Henry C., m. (pub. Oct. 20, 1870, in Farmington), Alice M. Remick, of Kittery.

COLEMAN, John Jones, m. Jan. 14, 1810, by Elder Isaac Townsend, Eliza Neal.

4) COLEMAN, James son of Woodman, b. Nov. 13, 1787, d. Oct. 18, 1834, m. 1817, Mary G. Meserve, b. Mar. 2, 1798, d. Nov. 23, 1830, aged 32, dau. of Ebenezer.

COLEMAN, Charles, m. Mar. 4, 1817, in Wakefield, Eliza (Neal) Coleman, of Brookfield, wid. of John Jones, d. Oct. 5, 1862, aged 67.

COLEMAN, Edwin, m. Jan. 1, 1863, in Dover, Carrie M. Pinkham.

COLEMAN, Oliver W., son of Oliver, b. 1838, d. Jan. 15, 1912, m. July 4, 1863, in Dover, Emma Davis, b. 1845, d. Feb. 21, 1912, dau. of Henry D.

COLEMAN, James W., m. Jan. 14, 1866, in Newington, Mary E. Nutter, dau. of Charles W., both of Newington.

COLEMAN, Henry J., m. (pub. May 31, 1866, in Wolfeboro), Eliza Warren.

COLEMAN, John L. O., of Portsmouth, m. Aug. 5, 1866, in W. Alton, Annie S. Morrill, of Gilford.

COLEMAN, James H., m. Dec. 9, 1866, in Dover, Martha A. Clements.

COLLINS, Richard, m. June 15, 1794, by Rev. Benjamin Balch, Patience Tuttle, both of Barrington.

COLLINS, Rev. John, of Auburn, Me., m. (pub. Jan. 8, 1863, in Great Falls), Louisa S. Horne, of Great Falls.

COLLY, Richard, of Stratham, m. Sep. 1814, by Rev. William Hooper, Sarah Leathers, of Madbury, d. Jan. 2, 1859, aged 84.

COLOMY, Daniel Jr., d. Jan. 29, 1875, aged 44, m. (pub. Feb. 11, 1851), in Haverhill, Mass.), Dorothy S. Locke, b. June 19, 1832, d. Aug. 11, 1906, aged 74, dau. of Benjamin B., both of New Durham.

COLOMY, William H., m. (pub. Mar. 1, 1866, in Rochester), Lizzie Littlefield, both of Farmington.

CONNOR, Badger P., of Ossipee, m. (1) (pub. Jan. 5, 1860, in Great Falls), Mary S. Wood, d. 1861, aged 18, dau. of John B., m. (2) Aug. 17, 1862, in Somersworth, Mrs. Jane R. Bickford.

CONNOR, John, m. Dec. 29, 1862, in Great Falls, Lydia Goodwin, both of Rollinsford.

CONNOR, Isaiah C., m. Jan. 6, 1864, in Great Falls, Lizzie Goodwin, both of Dover.

CONVERSE, Joshua, b. June 15, 1813, d. Apr. 5, 1891, m. Aug. 30, 1869, in Wakefield, Hannah Jane Dearborn, b. Apr. 21, 1837, d. Nov. 4, 1891, dau. of Joseph Jr.

CONVERSE, Abraham, m. June 2, 1874, in Wakefield, Elizabeth S. Converse, b. Apr. 20, 1836, d. Apr. 27, 1891, dau. of Joseph Jr.

COOK, Joseph, son of Joseph, b. Aug. 15, 1754, m. Nov. 24, 1777, by Rev. Joseph Haven, Anna Young, d. Jun. 23, 1805, aged 74.

COOK, Peter, d. Mar. 2, 1832, m. Dec. 31, 1789, by Rev. Benjamin Balch, Patience Smith, both of Barrington.

COOK, Amos, m. int. Aug. 14, 1819, in Lebanon, Me., Deborah Lord.

COOK, Peter, m. July 7, 1828, by Elder Enoch Place, Margery Durgin, d. Jan. 23, 1853, aged 84, both of Strafford.

COOK, Hiram, of Milton, m. Apr. 9, 1829, in Middleton, Hannah Wiggin Rines, of Middleton, b. Apr. 27, 1807.

COOK, Capt. Peter J. Jr., of Wakefield, b. 1807, d. 1880, m. (1) (pub. May 12, 1829, in Effingham), Mahala Sanders, of Effingham, d. Apr. 17, 1843, aged 37, dau. of Nathaniel, m (2) Jan. 28, 1845, in Brookfield, Patience Downing, b. 1800, d. 1883, dau. of Samuel.

COOK, John, m. (1) Dorothy S. ----, d. Jun. 16, 1836, aged 30, m. (2) int. Feb. 4, 1838, in Dover, Esther F. Bickford, d. Jul. 3, 1885, aged 76.

COOK, John A., of Wakefield, son of John, b. 1819, d. Mar. 18, ----, m. May 28, 1846, in Wolfeboro, Sarah H. Young, of Wolfeboro, b. 1816, d. Feb. 5, 1893.

COOK, John I., of Wolfeboro, d. Aug. 18, 1925, aged 84, m. (pub. Aug. 30, 1860, in New Durham), Maria A. H. Davis, of Milton.

COOK, William H., of Somersworth, m. May 18, 1862, in Dover, Nancy C. Ramsbottom, of Rochester.

COOK, John H., of Milton, m. Feb. 13, 1864, in Middleton, Martha Young, of Alton.

COOK, Jeremiah B., m. July 10, 1864, in Milton, Emily R. Whitehouse, of Milton.

COOK, Mark F., m. July 21, 1866, in W. Milton, P. Abbie Colomey, both of Farmington.

COOK, Daniel D., of Middleton, son of John, aged 50, m. (1) ---- ----, m. (2) June 28, 1868, by Rev. Alvan Tobey, Annie Chamberlain, of Rhode Island.

COOK, David D., of Epping, m. (pub. Aug. 6, 1868, in Durham), Mrs. Annie Chamberlain, of Newmarket.

COOKE, Thomas F., m. Dec. 2, 1868, in Farmington, C. Augusta Edgerly, dau. of Judge Josiah B.

COOLEY, Almon P., m. (pub. June 30, 1864, in Tamworth), Sarah E. Wilkinson.

COOMBS, Isaac, m. Aug. 21, 1867, in Dover, Lydia Richardson, both of Boston, Mass.

COOPER, Richard, d. Aug. 10, 1857, aged 54, m. May 17, 1820, by Rev. Joseph Boodey, Polly Libbey, d. Nov. 28, 1878, aged 77, both of Alton.

COOPER, Ivory, b. May 1, 1834, d. Apr. 25, 1884, m. int. Nov. 12, 1861, in Rollinsford, Anna Maria Neal, b. 1841, d. 1923, both of S. Berwick, Me.

COOPER, Warren S., of Farmington, m. Feb. 9, 1867, in Wolfeboro, Laura E. Drew, of Wolfeboro.

COPP, Capt. Tristram, of Tuftonboro, d. Apr. 10, 1847, aged 79, m. July 8, 1794, by Rev. Joseph Haven, Priscilla Bickford.

COPP, William H., of Tuftonboro, son of Tristram, d. Mar. 14, 1841, aged 76, m. Dec. 1795, in Wolfeboro, Elizabeth Blake, of Wolfeboro, d. Aug. 27, 1844, aged 69.

COPP, Moses, son of Tristram, d. Apr. 4, 1862, aged 90, m. int. Sept. 1800, in Tuftonboro, Betsey Wiggin, d. Sept. 1862, aged 86, both of Tuftonboro.

COPP, Elder Roger, son of Samuel, b. May 21, 1781, d. Feb. 16, 1860, m. Apr. 5, 1810, by Elder John Blaisdell, Nabby Blaisdell, b. Mar. 3, 1786.

COPP, Jonathan, of Tuftonboro, son of Tristram, b. Apr. 19, 1799, d. Apr. 30, 1871, m. Feb. 28, 1825, by Hatevil Knight, Hannah Hayes, d. Dec. 23, 1874, aged 72, dau. of Deac. Hayes.

COPP, Isaac N., of Tuftonboro, son of William H., d. May 13, 1887, aged 87, m. int. Sept. 1827, in Tuftonboro, Hannah H. Rogers, of Wolfeboro, d. Nov. 12, 1884, aged 78.

COPP, William, son of William H., d. Sept. 24, 1857, aged 50, m. (pub. Dec. 31, 1831, in Tuftonboro), Hannah W. Morrill.

COPP, Dearborn, son of William, b. Mar. 10, 1811, d. Mar. 4, 1896, m. (1) (pub. Mar. 10, 1835, in Tuftonboro), Elizabeth G. Burley, d. Mar. 11, 1864, aged 51, m. (2) Sarah M. ----, d. May 10, 1882, aged 53.

COPP, Stephen L., of Gilford, m. Sept. 4, 1851, by Rev. Levi B. Tasker, in Sandwich, Mary B. True, of Moultonboro.

COPP, Reuben H., of Farmington, son of Isaac, d. Apr. 20, 1899, aged 74, m. (1) Oct. 31, 1853, by Elder Elias Hutchins, Hannah J. Burke, of Wolfeboro, d. Dec. 16, 1865, aged 33, dau. of Stephen, m. (2) Dec. 26, 1866, in Farmington, Betsey J. Burke.

COPP, Frederick A., m. June 1862, in Wakefield, by Rev. Nathaniel Barker, Emily Paul.

COPP, Enoch Byron, m. (pub. Sept. 4, 1862, in Ossipee), Mrs. Lydia Sceggel.

COPP, N. Hayes, son of Jonathan, d. Oct. 21, 1883, aged 46, m. Jan. 31, 1866, in Rochester, Rebecca B. Colcord, of Rochester, d. Apr. 14, 1882, aged 35.

CORSON, Joseph, m. Nov. 13, 1803, by Rev. Joseph Haven, Lydia Ricker, b. Sep. 6, 1776, dau. of David, both of Rochester.

CORSON, Ephraim, of Lebanon, Me., b. 1792, d. 1845, m. Nov. 20, 1823, by Rev. Joseph Haven, Mary Johnson, of Rochester, b. 1800, d. 1882.

CORSON, Robert S., son of Robert, d. 1885, aged 68, m. (pub. Dec. 28, 1841, in Ossipee), Sarah Nay, b. 1817, d. Feb. 15, 1908, dau. of Joseph.

CORSON, Eli, of New Durham, m. May 31, 1852, in Middleton, Angelina Perkins, of Middleton.

CORSON, Aaron Flagg, son of John Jr., d. Jul. 28, 1901, aged 68, m. Nov. 21, 1855, in Milton, Abby Horne, d. Jan. 25, 1905, aged 65.

CORSON, David S., son of Samuel, d. Feb. 11, 1916, aged 79, m. (pub. Feb. 28, 1856, in Great Falls), Jane Meader.

CORSON, George E., of Lebanon, Me., son of Nathaniel, d. Feb. 20, 1897, aged 60, m. (pub. Aug. 30, 1860, in New Durham), Lucretia Perkins, of Jackson.

CORSON, Charles, m. (pub. May 31, 1866, in Wolfeboro), Sarah Colby.

CORSON, William A., m. July 31, 1866, in Rochester, Carrie Williams, both of Rochester.

CORSON, Elbridge H., of Rochester, m. Dec. 25, 1866, by Rev. James Rand, Eliza A. Wiggin, of S. Berwick, Me.

CORSON, John S., son of John Jr., b. May 21, 1845, d. Nov. 18, 1923, m. Mar. 30, 1867, in Milton, Lorana Duntley, b. Mar. 7, 1846, d. Jan. 11, 1911, dau. of Hazen.

CORSON, George M., b. 1842, m. (1) Oct. 7, 1868, in Milton, Julia H. Cummins, d. 1869, m. (2) Nov. 29, 1871, Draxcy A. Pierce.

CORSON, John R., m. Oct. 9, 1868, in Great Falls, A. Amanda Chase, both of E. Rochester.

CORSON, William W., of Boston, Mass., m. (pub. Sept. 9, 1869, in Great Falls), Sarah L. Horn, of Great Falls.

CORSON, William F., b. July 11, 1835, d. May 16, 1876, m. Jan. 29, 1870, in Gonic, Eliza Ann Cumming, both of Lebanon, Me.

COTTLE, Joshua Jr., of Brookfield, m. Apr. 29, 1846, by Rev. William K. Lucus, Martha Weeks, of Wakefield.

COTTON, N. Franklin, of Moultonboro, son of John, b. Aug. 12, 1835, d. Feb. 18, 1862, m. Mar. 22, 1857, in Sandwich, Lydia A. Ethridge, of Sandwich.

COTTON, Ira M., m. Nov. 4, 1862, in Newington, Martha Adeline Hoyt.

COTTON, Joel F., b. Apr. 2, 1839, d. Sept. 21, 1887, m. Mar. 9, 1864, in Strafford, Lavinia Gilman, both of Moultonboro.

COTTON, William W., m. (pub. Feb. 1, 1866, in Portsmouth), Annie M. Moses, dau. of J. Woodman Moses, both of Portsmouth.

COURSER, William M., of Warner, m. July 27, 1869, in Dover, Mary E. Wentworth, of Wolfeboro.

COUSENS, Israel, of Dover, m. Jan. 29, 1868, by Rev. Robert S. Stubbs, Mrs. Tryphina Kimball, of Lyman, Me.

COWAN, Dr. James Wellington, b. Jun. 23, 1814, d. Jul. 22, 1848, m. Oct. 5, 1837, by Rev. David Root, Elizabeth Hodgdon, b. Oct. 15, 1819, d. Jan. 18, 1888, dau. of William.

COWELL, John, son of Ichabod, d. Jan. 26, 1793, aged 31, m. Dec. 1, 1783, by Rev. Isaac Hasey, Martha Kilgore.

COWELL, Edmond, son of Ichabod, b. Oct. 31, 1766, d. Nov. 24, 1850, m. Jan. 1, 1787, by Rev. Isaac Hasey, Comfort Corson, b. May 1766, d. Jan. 25, 1856.

COWELL, Ichabod, d. Nov. 30, 1873, aged 86, m. Dec. 22, 1811, by Rev. Isaac Hasey, Rebecca Clark, d. Sept. 3, 1873, aged 81.

COWELL, John, m. d. Nov. 20, 1843, m. Sept. 6, 1814, by Rev. Paul Jewett, Mercy Clark, d. Sept. 29, 1872.

COWELL, Edmond Clark, son of Edmond, b. Mar. 20, 1799, d. Aug. 7, 1839, m. Dec. 2, 1821, Mary Wentworth, b. Mar. 15, 1802, d. Feb. 13, 1889.

COWELL, Elder David B., of Lebanon, Me., son of Edmond, b. Dec. 20, 1806, d. Apr. 15, 1884, m. Jan. 6, 1841, Christina B. Coffin, of Wolfeboro, b. Sept. 24, 1821, d. Oct. 8, 1862, dau. of Stephen.

COWELL, Edmund Eustis, son of Isaac, b. Oct. 25, 1825, d. Aug. 3, 1898, m. Feb. 1858, Elizabeth Jane (Chamberlain) Hussey, wid. of Alexander, b. Nov. 24, 1829, d. May 18, 1923, dau. of Samuel.

COWELL, Mark H., d. Sept. 17, 1862, m. (pub. May 20, 1858, in Great Falls), Mary J. Adams, of Dexter, Me.

COWELL, Edwin J., of Great Falls, m. (pub. Aug. 26, 1869, in Great Falls), E. Tewksbury, of Stewartston.

CRAGIN, Samuel, of Boston, Mass., m. Jan. 1, 1870, in Great Falls, Mary A. Ricker, of Somersworth, b. Dec. 9, 1842, d. May 13, 1907, dau. of Stephen.

CRAM, John P., of Dover, m. Aug. 21, 1872, in Lebanon, Me., Albertina Waldron.

CRAWFORD, Aaron Stuart, of Lowell, Mass, m. Oct. 7, 1840, in Barrington, by Rev. Samuel Nichols, Elizabeth Locke, of Barrington, b. Dec. 12, 1817, dau. of Elisha.

CRITCHERSON, Charles M., son of William, b. 1843, m. int. Mar. 26, 1864, in Lee, Sarah F. Glover, b. 1843, dau. of William P., both of Lee.

CRITCHET, Samuel, m. Dec. 5, 1816, by Elder Enoch Place, Lydia Clark, d. May 26, 1860, aged 70, both of Barrington.

CRITCHET, Reuben, son of Richard P., d. Jul. 11, 1882, aged 86, m. Jul. 1, 1821, by Elder Enoch Place, Betsey Dame, d. Feb. 2, 1875.

CRICHETT, John, m. Feb. 9, 1843, in Barrington, Lucy Maria Young, both of Barrington.
CROCKETT, Edmond, m. Mar. 5, 1799, by Rev. Joseph Haven, Abigail Davis, dau. of Zebulon, both of Alton.
CROCKETT, Jacob, b. 1781, d. 1845, m. Jan. 7, 1813, by Rev. Joseph Boodey, Betsey Brackett, d. Mar. 11, 1844, aged 49, both of Alton.
CROCKETT, William C., of Freedom, b. 1810, d. Oct. 8, 1843, aged 33, m. (pub. June 11, 1833, in Alton), Martha T. Roberts, of Alton, b. Feb. 28, 1796, d. Nov. 5, 1865, dau. of Joseph.
CROCKETT, Nathaniel, of Dover, m. Sept. 27, 1864, in S. Berwick, Me., Dorcas Welch, of Rollinsford.
CROSBY, John M., d. Apr. 21, 1919, aged 77, m. Oct. 28, 1869, in Dover, Sarah Ida B. Mathes, dau. of Samuel H.
CROSS, Richard, b. 1770, d. Feb. 1, 1825, m. Nov. 3, 1805, by Rev. Joseph Haven, Abigail (Place) Brewster, wid. of John Jr., dau. of John, both of Rochester.
CROSS, Joseph H., of Somersworth, b. 1820, d. July 1, 1850, m. Jan. 29, 1842, by James Hanson, J.P., Elmira M. Place, b. 1823, d. Jan. 11, 1854, of Rochester, dau. of George.
CROSS, Nathaniel, son of Joseph, d. May 15, 1907, aged 78, m. May 7, 1856, in Rochester, Jane C. Stillings.
CROSS, Timothy E., of Dover, m. Sept. 17, 1865, in Portsmouth, Mrs. Bridget O'Brian, of Newmarket.
CROSSLAND, Joseph, m. July 18, 1870, in Dover, Minerva A. Tibbetts, both of Dover.
CUMMINGS, Samuel F., m. Jan. 19, 1845, in Wakefield, Nancy B. Neal, both of Brookfield.
CUMMINGS, Joseph F., of Salem, Mass., son of Albert G., m. Apr. 6, 1864, by Rev. Alvan Tobey, Sarah E. Davis, of Lee, dau. of Timothy G.
CUNNINGHAM, John J., of Charlestown, Mass., m. Feb. 26, 1868, in Newmarket, Abbie L. Davis, of Lee.
CURLEY, Michael J., of Boston, Mass., m. July 4, 1865, in Great Falls, Martha J. Roberts, of Berwick, Me.
CURRIER, William, b. 1793, d. Aug. 1, 1865, m. (1) Aug. 11, 1816, by Rev. Micajah Otis, Nancy Henderson, b. 1798, d. 1825, dau. of Richmond, of Rochester, m. (2) Sept. 13, 1826, by Rev. Isaac Willey, Mehitable Hayes, b. 1798, d. 1899, dau. of Nathaniel, both of Rochester.

CURRIER, Artemus, of Gilmanton, m. Jan. 28, 1864, in S. Berwick, Me., Mrs. Olive M. (Lougee) Potter, of Alton, wid. of John M.

CURRIER, John W., m. June 29, 1865, in Alton, Mary S. Savage, dau. of Col. George D., both of Alton.

CURRIER, Charles E., of E. Rochester, m. (pub. Nov. 10, 1870, in Great Falls), Alice H. Yeaton, of Rochester.

CURTIS, Edmund, m. Oct. 23, 1803, in Dover, Lydia Gage, dau. of Moses.

CURTIS, Elijah, m. Nov. 26, 1815, in Lebanon, Me., Elizabeth Wentworth.

CURTIS, Joseph, m. Dec. 5, 1815, in Lebanon, Me., Rachel Wentworth.

CURTIS, Tristram B., of Brookfield, m. (1) int. May 30, 1838, in Lebanon, Me., Abigail Hersom, d. 1842, m. (2) (pub. Sep. 19, 1843, in Tamworth), Irene Johnson, of Tamworth.

CURTIS, Maxwell T., of Portsmouth, m. Jan. 4, 1865, in Rochester, Mary J. Hayes, dau. of Watson.

CURTIS, Erastus H., of Rochester, m. Jan. 29, 1866, in Lebanon, Me., Theodoisa M. Libbey.

4) **CUSHING**, Samuel W., son of Daniel, b. Apr. 9, 1802, d. Oct. 21, 1864, m. June 21, 1834, Mrs. Asenath (Hayes) Hyde, of Tamworth, wid. of Jacob, d. Sept. 15, 1861, aged 49, dau. of Enoch.

CUSHING, Thomas A., m. Aug. 31, 1865, in Great Falls, Harriet E. Morrill, dau. of Jacob, both of Great Falls.

CUTLER, Charles, of Somersworth, m. Sep. 16, 1832, in Lebanon, Me., Flavilla Ann Foss.

CUTTER, George T., of Medford, Mass., son of Gershom, m. Nov. 25, 1847, in Lebanon, Me., Abba E. Blaisdell, dau. of Samuel.

CUTTING, Simon R., m. Oct. 21, 1869, in Dover, Alice N. Brawn, both of Dover.

CUTTS, Thomas J. son of Thomas J., b. July 6, 1839, d. Mar. 15, 1933, m. Sept. 23, 1862, in Milton, Lydia Merrill Jewett, b. Sept. 22, 1842, d. May 19, 1922, dau. of Asa.

DAME, John, m. Feb. 11, 1795, by Rev. Benjamin Balch, Phebe Ayers, both of Barrington.

DAME, Paul, d. Feb. 24, 1822, aged 50, m. int. Oct. 1800, in Tuftonboro, Betsey (White) Canney, wid. of William, b. Apr. 1, 1773, d. Oct. 25, 1854.

DAME, Isaac, d. Jan. 14, 1870, aged 62, m. (pub. Sept. 4, 1827, in Tuftonboro), Polly Coffin, d. Apr 2, 1877, aged 68.

DAME, William, m. Mar. 30, 1834, by Rev. Enoch Place, Nancy Cater, d. July 4, 1841, aged 30, both of Strafford.

DAME, Asa C., of Barrington, d. Aug. 12, 1862, aged 45, m. (1) July 4, 1848, by Rev. Theodore Wells, Caroline A. Buzzell, d. Apr. 1858, aged 31, m. (2) Dec. 11, 1858, in Dover, Mrs. Mary Berry, of Strafford.

8) DAME, Greenleaf, son of Hunking G., b. July 19, 1820, d. July 19, 1850, m. Sept. 4, 1848, by Rev. Elias Hutchins, Charlotte Cheswell, of Durham, b. 1825, dau. of Paul.

DAME, James C. of Dover, m. (pub. Jan. 2, 1862, in Concord), Lucinda B. Freeman, of Concord.

DAME, William, son of Joseph, b. Sept. 7, 1827, d. July 27, 1887, m. May 24, 1862, in Dover, Drusilla Glidden, b. Feb. 1824, d. Sept. 23, 1895, both of Dover.

DAME, John W., of Rochester, m. Dec. 2, 1862, in Dover, Mary J. C. Hanson, of Dover.

DAME, William H. of Rochester, son of Joseph, d. Oct. 21, 1893, aged 51, m. Nov. 12, 1863, in Rochester, Nancy E. Witham, of Milton.

DAME, John W., m. Sept. 17, 1864, in Dover, Mary A. Glidden, d. Jan. 31, 1919, aged 79, dau. of Jacob, both of Dover.

DAME, Melvin A., of Strafford, m. Mar. 7, 1865, in Strafford, Hester A. Brown, of New Hampton.

DAME, Albert W., m. Sept. 21, 1867, in Dover, Addie A. Roberts, both of Farmington.

DAME, Charles H., of Farmington, son of Daniel, d. Nov. 20, 1901, aged 67, m. Jan. 1, 1868, in W. Milton, Annie P. Nute, of W. Milton.

DAME, John T. Jr., of Dover, m. (pub. Sept. 22, 1870, in Exeter), Susie A. Doe, of Newmarket.

DANFORTH, George O., of Cambridge, Mass., m. Dec. 5, 1844, by Rev. Joseph Loring, Olive M. Goodwin, dau. of Benjamin.

DANFORTH, Henry W., son of Noah, d. Mar. 14, 1881, aged 60, m. (1) Betsey Caverly, d. Aug. 26, 1850, aged 30, dau. of Capt. Ezeriah, m. (2) Nov. 15, 1851, by Rev. Justin Spaulding, Eliza J. Clark, b. Mar. 23, 1818, d. Feb. 18, 1897, dau. of Joseph.

DANFORTH, John H., of Dover, m. Sept. 28, 1867, by Rev. Robert S. Stubbs, Anna M. Lovering, of Freedom.

3) **DANIEL**, Samuel, son of John, m. Dec. 30, 1756, Elizabeth Noble, d. Dec. 3, 1825, aged 96.

DANIELS, Joseph, b. Mar. 12, 1752, m. Apr. 9, 1778, in Barrington, Sarah Leathers, b. Oct. 16, 1743.

DANIELS, John, m. Apr. 28, 1797, by Rev. Benjamin Balch, Lovey Waldron, both of Barrington.

DANIELS, Arthur, of Madbury, m. Dec. 25, 1806, by Rev. Benjamin Balch, Hannah Caverly, of Barrington.

DANIELS, Clement Jr., m. Oct. 21, 1812, by Rev. Abner Clark, Nabby Foss, of Barrington.

DANIELS, Hayes, m. July 9, 1826, in Lee, by Rev. John Osborne, Mehitable Daniels, d. Nov. 13, 1862, aged 88, both of Dover.

DANIELS, Samuel, m. (1) Sarah ----, d. Jan. 3, 1826, aged 21, m. (2) Apr. 6, 1829, by Elder Enoch Place, Olive Libbey, both of Strafford.

DANIELS, John D., m. Sept. 15, 1864, in Dover, Esther G. Tuttle, both of Nottingham.

DANIELSON, Arthur (sometimes called McDanielson), m. Jan. 31, 1735, in Barrington, Lydia Drew, dau. of William.

DANIELSON, Charles, son of Arthur, b. June 29, 1746, m. near 1770, Hannah ----, b. Oct. 12, 1749.

3) **DAVIS**, Samuel, son of Col. James, b. Sept. 26, 1693, d. 1788, m. early as 1719, Martha Chesley, b. 1692, d. Apr. 1, 1796, aged 104, dau. of Thomas.

DAVIS, Thomas, m. Feb. 6, 1794, by Rev. Benjamin Balch, Abigail Jones, both of Barrington,

DAVIS, John, m. Nov. 26, 1802, in Barrington, Betsey Howard, both of Barrington.

DAVIS, John, of New Durham, son of John, b. 1785, d. Oct. 31, 1865, m. Nov. 9, 1806, by Rev. Benjamin Randall, Lydia Canney, of Farmington, d. Oct. 17, 1850, aged 62.

DAVIS, Nathaniel, of Middleton, son of Eleazer, b. 1778, d. 1857, m. int. Feb. 4, 1810, in Milton, Elizabeth Tuttle, of Milton, b. 1783, d. 1815, m. (2) Clarissa ----, b. 1788, d. 1868.

DAVIS, Noah, of Epping, d. May 8, 1872, aged 79, m. Jul. 14, 1814, by Rev. John Osborne, Sally Noble, of Lee, d. May 28, 1865, aged 72.

DAVIS, Clement M., son of John, b. Sept. 1, 1795, d. Jan. 15, 1877, m. July 12, 1817, by Rev. John Osborne, Sarah J. (Davis) Stevens, b. Mar. 5, 1798, d. Jan. 14, 1871, both of Durham.

DAVIS, Solomon 2nd, of Nottingham, son of John, b. Apr. 20, 1794, m. Apr. 30, 1819, Abigail Hall, of Barrington, b. Aug. 31, 1797, dau. of Daniel.

DAVIS, Capt. Zebulon, of Lee, d. Nov. 21, 1868, aged 67, m. (1) int. Dec. 28, 1822, in Lee, Rebecca Page, of Rochester, d. Sep. 19, 1831, aged 28, m. (2) Jun. 25, 1832, in Lee, Sally Huckins, d. Mar. 28, 1884, aged 73, both of Lee.

DAVIS, Daniel, son of John, of Lee, b. Nov. 16, 1802, m. Mar. 30, 1826, Caroline Teague, b. Mar. 1, 1795, d. Feb. 22, 1882.

DAVIS, John, of Alfred, Me., m. Dec. 3, 1826, in Lebanon, Me., Lucy Ricker.

DAVIS, Eleazer 3rd, b. Jan. 30, 1806, d. June 27, 1888, m. (1) Sept. 23, 1830, in Middleton, Martha Davis, b. Aug. 28, 1806, d. Sept. 2, 1847, both of New Durham, m. (2) Eliza ----, b. June 18, 1813, d. May 4, 1885.

DAVIS, Samuel L., b. 1813, d. 1884, m. (1) Apr. 7, 1831, in Middleton, Mahalah Cate, b. 1806, d. 1856, both of Alton.

DAVIS, Daniel W., d. Apr. 2, 1859, aged 59, m. (pub. Oct. 4, 1831, in Middleton), Mary Perkins, d. Feb. 1, 1890, aged 75, both of Middleton.

DAVIS, Ira, of Center Harbor, m. Mar. 4, 1832, in Lebanon, Me., Mary Lord.

DAVIS, Weare, of Lee, son of Capt. Zebulon, d. Jul. 22, 1893, aged 77, m. Jan. 29, 1839, Sarah Dockham, of Durham, d. Apr. 10, 1890, aged 79.

DAVIS, William H., m. int. 1845, Mahala Kimball, d. Feb. 2, 1874.

DAVIS, Alonzo, of Newfield, Me., son of Daniel, d. Nov. 17, 1889, aged 60, m. (pub. Oct. 5, 1847, in Great Falls), Marion Wilson, d. Dec. 22, 1910, aged 81.

DAVIS, John W., of Somersworth, m. Mar. 19, 1848, in Lebanon, Me., Mary L. Corson.

DAVIS, Luther W., son of Moses, d. May 12, 1864, aged 28, m. July 4, 1857, Mrs. Lizzie P. Hayes.

DAVIS, William H., son of George, d. May 22, 1891, aged 59, m. Dec. 15, 1857, in Wakefield, Elizabeth A. Caverly, b. 1828, d. July 12, 1881, aged 53, both of Tuftonboro.

DAVIS, Albert W., of Lee, son of Noah, b. 1832, d. May 26, 1909, m. int. Dec. 21, 1858, in Lee, Isabel A. Tilton, of Deerfield, b. 1835, d. Feb. 19, 1860.

DAVIS, Eleazer, m. Apr. 12, 1861, Sarah Ann Waldron, dau. of Wells.

DAVIS, Nathaniel N., of Famington, m. Nov. 13, 1862, in Alton, Amanda F. Richardson, of Barrington.

DAVIS, George N., of Farmington, m. Jan. 10, 1863, in Farmington, Angela A. Small, of Madbury.

DAVIS, B. Parker, of Newburyport, Mass., m. May 27, 1863, by Rev. John W. Tilton, Jessie M. S. Swett, of Tuftonboro.

DAVIS, Albion L., m. Apr. 26, 1866, in Effingham, Emma S. Drake.

DAVIS, William F., of Lowell, Mass., m. July 23, 1867, in Exeter, Caroline E. Kelley, dau. of John.

DAVIS, Frank E., of Wakefield, m. Aug. 30, 1867, in Wakefield, Mary O. Bearse, of Sanford, Me.

DAVIS, Charles T., m. Oct. 14, 1867, in Great Falls, Abbie J. Moore, of Springvale, Me.

DAVIS, Samuel Caverno, of Madbury, son of Samuel, b. Mar. 15, 1842, m. Sept. 30, 1868, Frances Tuttle, of Dover, d. Nov. 20, 1887, dau. of Thomas.

DAVIS, George E., of Lawrence, Mass., m. Oct. 20, 1869, in Farmington, Ari Pearl Hayes, of Farmington.

DAVIS, Lewis B., of Rochester, son of Charles F., d. Oct. 11, 1893, aged 50, m. (pub. Dec. 22, 1870, in Rochester), Mrs. Sarah B. Smith, of Strafford.

DAVIS, John B., m. Sept. 10, 1873, in Farmington, Mrs. Patience (Colomy) Rollins, wid. of John T.

DAY, John, of Great Falls, m. Feb. 17, 1866, in Dover, Octavie Wallace, of Dover.

DEARBORN, Charles H. of New Durham, m (1) (pub. Sep. 28, 1847, in Lebanon, Me.), Almira Chamberlain, of Lebanon, Me., d. Oct. 29, 1870, aged 51, m. (2) int. Jan. 8, 1874, in Lebanon, Me., Mary A. Wentworth.

DEARBORN, Abraham, of Exeter, m. (pub. Oct. 6, 1864, in Haverhill, Mass.), Hannah O. Walker, of Durham, dau. of Nathan.

DEARBORN, John F., m. (pub. May 11, 1865, in Portsmouth), Mrs. Eliza A. Reynolds, of Newmarket.

DEARBORN, William B., of Boston, Mass., m. Sept. 11, 1865, in Dover, Laura A. Roberts, of Rochester.

DEARBORN, Stephen H., m. (pub. Nov. 16, 1865, in Gilmanton), Emma O. Prescott, both of Alfred.

DEARBORN, Warren S., m. (pub. Sept. 13, 1866, in Northwood), Mary E. Foss, both of Strafford.

DEARBORN, John E., of Hampton, m. Feb. 7, 1867, by Rev. James Rand, Elvira A. Johnson, of Parsonsfield, Me., d. Apr. 21, 1927, aged 77, dau. of Dennis.

DEARBORN, Samuel, m. (pub. Apr. 25, 1867, by Rev. Cummins Paris, in Effingham), Emma Nichols, both of Effingham.

DEARBORN, Henry F., m. (pub. June 13, 1867, in Exeter), Helen M. Whitten, of Rochester.

DEARBORN, Emulus M., m. Sept. 24, 1868, in Great Falls, Anna L. Prescott, both of Vienna, Me.

DEBERTRAM, George, of Buffalo, N.Y., m. Oct. 3, 1864, by Rev. James Rand, Susan T. Neal, of Rochester.

DECATER, George, d. Feb. 6, 1856, aged 41, m. (1) Belinda ----, d. Jan. 18, 1848, aged 25, m. (2) Jan. 27, 1849, in Dover, Betsey Burnham.

DEERING, Thomas C., m. (1) Apr. 1, 1858, in Rollinsford, Mary Deering, m. (2) int. Apr. 10, 1872, in Lebanon, Me., Mrs. Lizzie P. Davis.

DEERING, Capt. George A., of Saco, Me., m. June 18, 1868, in Dover, Annie E. Swain, of Dover.

DELAND, Samuel, d. June 20, 1870, aged 58, m. Dec. 26, 1839, by Rev. George O. Cotton, Lydia P. Doe, d. Sept. 23, 1876, aged 62.

DELAND, Ambrose, of Wolfeboro, m. (1) Aug. 13, 1849, in Wolfeboro, Hannah Evans, of Alton, b. 1810, d. 1852, m. (2) in 1858, in Wolfeboro, Rosannah Wiggin.

DELAND, Samuel J., son of John, d. Mar. 5, 1895, aged 80, m. Apr. 24, 1851, by Elder Joseph Spinney, Maria Cowell, both of Brookfield.

DELANO, James C., m. int. Jan. 13, 1838, in Lebanon, Me., Abigail A. Goodwin.

DELANY, Joseph, m. Mar. 9, 1854, in Dover, Olive Ham, d. Nov. 26, 1857, aged 39, dau. of Joshua.

DELANY, John W., m. Sept. 6, 1862, in Dover, Nancy E. Jacobs, both of Dover.

DELANY, Charles R., of Dover, m. Sept. 22, 1862, in Manchester, Jennie A. Clough, of Rye.

DELOID, Charles H., of Boston, Mass., m. Dec. 25, 1866, in Dover, Elizabeth C. Mack, of Dover.

2) DEMERITT, Job, b. Mar. 29, 1705, d. Aug. 7, 1772, m. early as 1734, Mary Buzzell, d. Nov. 30, 1799, aged 91, dau. of John.

3) DEMERITT, Solomon, son of Job, d. Apr. 5, 1828, aged 94, m. Ann Demeritt, d. Jan. 18, 1797, aged 61, dau. of William.

4) DEMERITT, Ebenezer, of Madbury, son of Ebenezer, b. Feb. 15, 1759, d. June 15, 1808, m. May 25, 1780, by Dr. Belknap, Elizabeth Young, b. Oct. 22, 1760, d. 1822, dau. of Nathaniel.

4) DEMERITT, Robert, son of Job, d. Feb. 14, 1839, aged 78, m. Oct. 26, 1786, by Rev. Benjamin Balch, Deborah Twombly, both of Barrington.
DEMERITT, John, m. Sept. 19, 1799, by Rev. William Hooper, Abigail Leathers, d. July 27, 1847, aged 67, dau. of Robert.
4) DEMERITT, Eli, of Madbury, son of Solomon, m. June 9, 1800, by Rev. William Hooper, Deborah Bunker, of Durham, d. Feb. 2, 1828, dau. of Zechariah.
4) DEMERITT, Solomon, son of Solomon, m. May 24, 1801, by Rev. Benjamin Balch, Kezia Hall, d. Dec. 31, 1857, aged 77, dau. of Isaac, both of Barrington.
DEMERITT, Samuel, m. Sept. 5, 1805, by Rev. Benjamin Balch, Rachel Berry, both of Barrington.
DEMERITT, Daniel, m. July 18, 1811, by Rev. Joseph Boodey, Betsey Demeritt, d. June 4, 1853, aged 64.
DEMERITT, Samuel, of Nottingham, d. Nov. 28, 1834, aged 40, m. Nov. 12, 1820, by Elder Enoch Place, Rhoda Seward, of Barrington, dau. of George.
5) DEMERITT, Ebenezer Thompson, son of Jonathan, b. Apr. 7, 1792, d. Sept. 26, 1863, m. (1) Oct. 28, 1821, by Rev. J. W. Clary, Hannah Y. Demeritt, d. Mar. 14, 1830, aged 43 yrs., 1 mo., 9 das., dau. of Ebenezer, m. (2) Dec. 24, 1831, Sophia Young, d. Jan. 8, 1870, aged 75 yrs., 11 mos., 4 das., dau. of Timothy.
DEMERITT, Jacob I., d. June 1, 1831, aged 26, m. Aug. 13, 1828, by Rev. Isaac Willey, Elizabeth Evans, both of Rochester.
DEMERITT, Ebenezer, b. May 9, 1808, d. Oct. 5, 1839, m. Sept. 5, 1828, Sally Stokes, b. Apr. 12, 1808, d. Apr. 9, 1879.
DEMERITT, Alfred, m. June 23, 1833, Mary E. Torr, d. July 28, 1875, aged 62, dau. of Benjamin, both of Madbury.
5) DEMERITT, James Young, son of Ebenezer, b. Dec. 25, 1788, d. July 18, 1847, aged 58, m. Aug. 27, 1843, by Elder Enoch Place, Matilda Rowe, b. May 12, 1807, d. June 17, 1880, both of Madbury.
DEMERITT, Shepard F., d. Apr. 23, 1908, aged 80, m. (pub. Jan. 6, 1852, in Effingham), Martha E. Thurston, b. Dec. 9, 1835, d. Oct. 16, 1860, both of Effingham.
DEMERITT, Samuel E., of Dover, d. Jan. 22, 1911, aged 81, m. (pub. Sep. 27, 1860, in Great Falls,), Lucy A. Dockham, of Wolfeboro, d. Mar. 22, 1903, aged 73, dau. of Mark R.

DEMERITT, J. J., of Dover, m. Aug. 13, 1862, in Newmarket, Frances R. Osgood, of Madbury.

DEMERITT, Seorim, of Dover, son of Jacob J., d. Apr. 10, 1908, aged 70, m. Apr. 4, 1867, in Dover, Fanny A. Joy, of N. Berwick, Me.

DEMERITT, Albert W., of N. Hampton, m. Apr. 4, 1867, in Dover, Maria Varney, of Barrington.

DEMERITT, Edwin, of Durham, son of Stephen P., m. Dec. 18, 1868, in Boston, Mass., Frances A. Norton, of Portsmouth.

DEMERITT, Andrew W., m. July 6, 1869, in Dover, Carrie A. Dorman, both of Northwood.

DEMERITT, A. M., of Strafford, m. Nov. 26, 1869, in Dover, Martha L. Maxwell, of Norridgewock, Me.

DEMERITT, James Young, of Dover, son of James, d. June 28, 1913, aged 67, m. Sept. 14, 1870, in Dover, Martha C. Ward, of Rumney, d. June 17, 1927, aged 80.

DENNETT, Joseph C., m. Apr. 5, 1855, in Newmarket, Harriet Greene.

DENNIS, William B., m. May 7, 1867, in Dover, Leah Helen Goodwin, d. June 1, 1917, aged 68, both of Dover.

DEWEY, Lt. Com. George, m. Oct. 24, 1867, in Portsmouth, Susie Boardman Goodwin, dau. of Hon. Ichabod.

DIAMOND, Daniel H., of Laconia, m. Sept. 26, 1867, by Rev. Robert S. Stubbs, Margaret White, of Portland, Me.

DICEY, George W., of Effingham, m. July 19, 1866, in Union, Susan A. Durrell, of Union.

DICKSON, Everett E., son of Benjamin, d. Dec. 25, 1895, aged 45, m. (pub. Dec. 22, 1870, in Wolfeboro), Ada F. Stackpole, b. Feb. 10, 1852, d. Jan. 21, 1929.

DILLINGHAM, Seth, of No. Berwick, Me., m. int., Clara Butler.

DILLINGHAM, Paul, m. Dec. 12, 1824, by Elder Zebedee Delano, in Lebanon, Me., Sabina Libbey, both of Berwick, Me.

DILLINGHAM, John L., m. (1) Sep. 5, 1850, in Lebanon, Me., Miriam F. Perkins, m. (2) int. Aug. 28, 1880, Emily A. (Chase) Peirce, of No. Berwick, Me.

DIMICK, Edwin Merrill, of Concord, m. (pub. June 24, 1869, in Great Falls), Mrs. Ellen M. Cater, of Dover.

DIXON, Charles A., of Lebanon, Me., m. Oct. 22, 1867, in Rochester, Elizabeth M. Baker, of Milton.

DODGE, Charles E., of Raymond, m. Mar. 6, 1866, in Dover, Hannah A. Durgin, of S. Berwick, Me.

DODGE, Charles A., of Readville, Mass., m. Aug. 13, 1870, in Lebanon, Me., Frances D. Wentworth, of Great Falls.

4) **DOE**, Ebenezer, son of Benjamin, b. Dec. 14, 1758, d. Oct. 23, 1839, m. (1) Apr. 27, 1788, Hannah Chesley, b. Dec. 28, 1766, d. Dec. 20, 1808, dau. of Joseph, m. (2) Jan. 18, 1810, Susanna Joy, b. Sept. 5, 1774, d. June 26, 1845, dau. of Deac. Samuel.

DOLBY, Henry J., m. Nov. 9, 1865, in Farmington, Ellen A. Pinkham, both of Alton.

4) **DORE**, Henry, son of Henry, b. 1749, bpt. Aug. 20, 1749, d. Mar. 14, 1839, m. May 27, 1773, by Rev. Isaac Hasey, Frances Stevens, b. 1753, d. Apr. 2, 1828.

4) DORE, Jonathan, son of John, m. (1) Nov. 15, 1773, by Dr. Belknap, Eunice Downs, m. (2) Aug. 24, 1786, Rebecca Garland, dau. of Dodavah.

5) DORE, Abijah, son of Henry, bpt. Sept. 28, 1788, d. Apr. 8, 1860, aged 72, m. July 11, 1811, by Rev. Isaac Hasey, Eunice Legro, b. June 25, 1789, d. Mar. 3, 1855, dau. of Thomas.

DORE, William, of Lebanon, Me., d. Jan. 20, 1858, aged 65, m. May 20, 1816, by Rev. Joseph Hilliard, Agnes Guptill.

DORE, William, m. Apr. 8, 1827, in Lebanon, Me., Rosannah Ellis.

DORE, Brackett, m. (1) Oct. 24, 1844, in Lebanon, Me., Lydia Mills, of Rochester, m. (2) 1855, in Somersworth, Judith G. Hill, of Somersworth.

DORE, John C., d. Nov. 4, 1880, aged 44, m. int. Sep. 13, 1856, in Lebanon, Me., Julia A. Corlis, d. Jul. 12, 1925, aged 86, both of Milton.

DORE (DORR), George, of Milton, m. Dec. 15, 1862, in Milton, Mrs. Lydia C. Legro, of Kingston.

DORE, Charles H., of Alton, m. Mar. 12, 1866, by Rev. James Rand, Onissa E. Adams, of New Durham.

DORE, Charles A., son of Oliver, d. Mar. 26, 1910, aged 70, m. Mar. 26, 1866, in Dover, J. Abbie Leavitt, both of Dover.

DORE, James Freeman, son of Eliphalet P., b. Oct. 3, 1843, d. Nov. 24, 1912, m. Jun. 26, 1870, in Milton, Sarah Elizabeth Maddox, d. Sep. 13, 1920, aged 74, dau. of Stephen.

DOTY, Simeon W., b. Nov. 10, 1824, d. Nov. 10, 1900, m. Nov. 25, 1869, in Dover, Eliza Flood, b. Feb. 8, 1831, d. Dec. 17, 1906, both of Dover.

DOW, Taylor, of Gilmanton, m. July 4, 1825, by Elder Enoch Place, Abigail Foss, of Strafford, dau. of Timothy.

DOW, Dr. Enoch C., son of Josiah, b. 1813, d. Jan. 4, 1876, aged 63, m. (1) (pub. Dec. 28, 1841, in Tuftonboro), Martha M. Palmer, d. Oct. 18, 1861, aged 49, m. (2) Jan. 27, 1863, in Rochester, Lucy Ann Tebbets, b. 1830, d. Sept. 4, 1913, dau. of Leonard.

DOW, Isaac, m. (pub. June 26, 1862, in Portsmouth), Abby W. Beane, both of Newington.

DOW, George E., m. (pub. June 4, 1863, in Moultonboro), Julia Nelson, both of Moultonboro.

DOW, John P., m. July 5, 1865, in Strafford, Mary E. Morrison, both of Northwood.

DOW, Cyrus P., of Sanbornville, m. Aug. 17, 1865, in Conway, Delia E. Hayford, of Tamworth.

DOW, John H., of Newington, m. (pub. Aug. 9, 1866, in Newington), Mrs. Mary A. Leavitt, of Portsmouth.

DOW, George Prince, m. Dec. 13, 1866, in Wakefield, by Rev. Daniel Tappan, Adah B. Tappan, of Salem, Mass., dau. of Rev. Daniel D.

DOWNING, David R., m. Dec. 6, 1849, in Milton, Nancy Peavey, d. Apr. 19, 1875, aged 71, dau. of Oliver.

DOWNING, John E. 2nd, of Great Falls, m. (pub. July 30, 1868, in Salmon Falls), Lizzie A. Durgin, of Waterboro, Me.

DOWNING, William J., m. Nov. 6, 1868, in Dover, Mrs. Jane C. French, both of Durham.

DOWNING, John B., m. (pub. Apr. 29, 1869, in Farmington), Mrs. Betsey B. (Lord) Legro, wid. of Benjamin F., both of Farmington.

DOWNING, William H., m. (pub. Dec. 1, 1870, in Rochester), Laura Palmer, both of Rochester.

DOWNS, Stephen, son of Daniel, d. Apr. 1, 1811, aged 36, m. Nov. 10, 1796, by Rev. Isaac Willey, Elizabeth Jones, b. Jul. 28, 1776, d. Jul. 22, 1858, dau. of Reuben.

DOWNS, Peter, m. int. May 18, 1811, in Lebanon, Me., Eunice Reynolds.

DOWNS, James, son of Moses, b. May 16, 1793, d. Oct. 3, 1882, aged 89, m. Nov. 11, 1813, by Rev. Joseph Boodey, Judith Wentworth, b. Jun. 30, 1792, d. Apr. 13, 1867, both of Milton.

DOWNS, Moses, d. Feb. 14, 1870, aged 64, m. Feb. 22, 1838, Rebecca (Wentworth) Blaisdell, wid. of Elijah, b. May 18, 1805, d. Feb. 14, 1870, dau. of John. (was this a second marriage?)

DOWNS, George B., m. (pub. Apr. 3, 1862, in Farmington), Sarah A. Horn.

DOWNS, Horace P., of Tamworth, m. Mar. 21, 1863, in Great Falls, Sylvina Guptill, of Great Falls.

DOWNS, Jefferson P., of Berwick, Me., m. June 25, 1866, in Rochester, Dorcas A. Austin, of Somersworth.

DOWNS, Moses J., of Milton, m. (pub. Dec. 15, 1870, in Great Falls), Sarah R. Horne, of Rochester.

DRAKE, John, d. Dec. 10, 1836, aged 68, m. July 21, 1804, by Rev. Jeremiah Shaw, Mary Bean, d. July 10, 1843, aged 66.

DRAKE, Maj. Joseph, of Effingham, d. Aug. 20, 1844, aged 47, m. Nov. 26, 1822, in Tamworth, Mary Clark, of Tamworth, d. Jan. 27, 1872, aged 72.

DRAKE, Bradley, d. Apr. 10, 1865, aged 49, m. (1) Emeline ----, d. 1849, aged 26, m. (2) Sally ----, d. Sept. 14, 1860, aged 44, m. (3) Jan. 23, 1861, in Effingham, Marintha A. Towle, both of Effingham.

DRAKE, Cyrus K., b. Oct. 15, 1819, d. Aug. 1, 1892, m. (1) (pub. Nov. 9, 1841, in Effingham), Caroline L. Morse, b. Dec. 9, 1821, d. May 7, 1870, both of Effingham, m. (2) Mary Eastman, b. Apr. 19, 1841, d. Apr. 5, 1897.

DRAKE, Frank K., of Cambridgeport, Mass., m. Mar. 21, 1867, in Lawrence, Mass., Attie A. Horne, of Lawrence, Mass.

DRAKE, Enoch, of Boston, Mass., m. (pub. Dec. 17, 1868, in Rochester), Clara L. Rand, of Rochester.

DREW, John, son of John, b. 1766, d. Sep. 7, 1827, m. Dec. 29, 1789, Lydia Butler, b. Feb. 3, 1768, d. Mar. 7, 1830, dau. of Samuel.

DREW, Jonathan, of Durham, b. Jul. 28, 1782, m. Oct. 8, 1806, in Barrington, Elizabeth Winkley, b. Feb. 16, 1783, dau. of Samuel.

DREW, Andrew, m. Sep. 18, 1785, in Brookfield, Joanna Hodgdon.

DREW, Elijah, of Coxhall, Me., m. Dec. 1, 1785, by Rev. Benjamin Balch, Elizabeth Holmes, of Barrington.

DREW, Silas, m. Oct. 11, 1792, by Rev. Benjamin Balch, Lydia Cate, both of Barrington.

DREW, Jacob, m. Mar. 26, 1793, by Rev. Benjamin Balch, Anna Davison, both of Barrington.

DREW, Robert, of Madbury, m. June 8, 1801, by Rev. Benjamin Balch, Sally Pinkham, of Barrington.

6) DREW, Shadrach, of Dover, son of Joseph, b. Dec. 7, 1773, d. Aug. 30, 1860, m. Jan. 20, 1803, by Rev. Benjamin Balch, Martha

Winkley, of Barrington, b. May 16, 1771, d. Jun 18, 1859, dau. of Francis.

6) DREW, Joseph, of Alton, son of John, b. Nov. 2, 1776, d. Mar. 14, 1846, m. Jan. 24, 1805, by Rev. Joseph Haven, Leah Jones, of Farmington, b. 1784, d. 1853.

DREW, Jonathan, of Durham, b. July 28, 1782, m. Oct. 8, 1808, in Barrington, Elizabeth Winkley, b. Feb. 16, 1783, dau. of Samuel.

DREW, Lemuel, m. Feb. 25, 1821, by Elder Enoch Place, Lois Hall, dau. of Benjamin, both of Barrington.

DREW, Nathan, d. Nov. 25, 1859, aged 83, m. Apr. 1822, Sally S. ----, of Portsmouth, b. Aug. 18, 1780, d. Oct. 5, 1848.

DREW, Jeremiah O., son of Moses, b. Jan. 29, 1806, d. Jan. 1, 1885, m. int. Aug. 28, 1825, in Dover, Tamson Whitehouse, b. May 24, 1808, d. Jan. 20, 1895, aged 86, dau. of Reuben.

DREW, Deac. John B., d. Apr. 24, 1871, aged 64, m. June 23, 1830, by Elder Enoch Place, Anna Hurd Drew, d. Aug. 13, 1869, aged 61, dau. of Mesheck.

DREW, Joseph S., son of Jonathan, b. Aug. 12, 1811, d. Apr. 22, 1874, m. int. Mar. 24, 1833, in Dover, Mary Jane Raynes, d. Jan. 29, 1842, aged 31, dau. of Eliot.

DREW, John T., b. Apr. 11, 1811, m. May 13, 1833, by Rev. John Winkley, Alice Waterhouse, b. Jan. 11, 1817, both of Barrington.

DREW, Swain, m. Nov. 28, 1833, by Elder Samuel Sherburne, Matilda Hall, b. Mar. 4, 1812, dau. of Daniel.

DREW, Horatio, son of Jonathan, b. Dec. 3, 1814, m. int. Oct. 18, 1835, in Dover, Mary Piper.

DREW, Silas, b. Nov. 10, 1810, in Strafford, Vt., m. Oct. 22, 1836, by Elder Enoch Place, Eliza Jane Caverly, b. Jan. 13, 1816, d. Apr. 8, 1873, aged 57, dau. of Moses, both of Barrington.

DREW, Jonas F., of Dover, m. int. June 28, 1845, in Dover, Sarah Jane Hoitt, of Windham, Mass.

DREW, Jonathan R., son of Jonathan, b. Apr. 14, 1821, m. Nov. 20, 1846, by Rev. Theodore Wells, Elizabeth H. Hayes, d. July 6, 1872, aged 44, both of Barrington.

DREW, Henry A., of Durham, d. Jun. 10, 1916, aged 90, m. (1) Feb. 1, 1853, by Rev. Alvin Tobey, Sarah Tuttle, of Strafford, b. Jul. 15, 1825, d. Jun. 9, 1865, aged 40, dau. of William, m. (2) int. Sep. 18, 1868, in Brookfield, Emeline Dyer, b. Feb. 10, 1829, d. Dec. 16, 1887.

DREW, Daniel W., of Barrington, son of John T., b. Mar. 20, 1837, m. Sept. 15, 1862, in Dover, Lavinia H. Twombly, of Madbury.

DREW, Maj. William P., d. Oct. 12, 1868, aged 49, m. Dec. 24, 1862, in Tuftonboro, Augusta M. Canney, b. Apr. 4, 1846, d. Apr. 16, 1869, dau. of Ira, both of Tuftonboro.

DREW, Charles A., of Durham, son of Lemuel, m. Jan. 6, 1864, in Durham, Mary E. Foss, dau. of Leonard.

DREW, Henry L., of Dover, son of Benjamin, d. Feb. 1, 1912, aged 75, m. Nov. 26, 1864, in Dover, Mary L. Joice, of Fitchburg, Mass.

DREW, Thomas F., m. Dec. 20, 1865, in Exeter, Amanda S. Spurling, both of Dover.

DREW, Henry A., of Strafford, m. July 28, 1866, in Kensington, M. Abby Shaw, of Kensington.

DREW, Meshach T., m. Feb. 16, 1867, in Gonic, Lydia A. Ham, d. Jul. 19, 1911, aged 68, dau. of Samuel, both of Rochester.

DREW, Charles H., of Somersworth, m. Mar. 20, 1867, in Somersworth, Lucy E. Virgin, of Rumford, Me.

DREW, Isaac M., of Dover, m. Sept. 22, 1867, in Great Falls, Marcia A. Leonard, of S. Berwick, Me.

DREW, William B., of Durham, son of William, m. Dec. 13, 1867, by Rev. Alvan Tobey, Sarah S. Ayers, of Dover, dau. of Joseph.

DREW, William, of Dover, m. Dec. 19, 1867, in Durham, Susan L. Ayers, of Barrington.

DREW, Joseph, m. Jan. 15, 1868, in Strafford, Almira A. Wentworth, both of Strafford.

DREW, John S., m. Nov. 13, 1869, in Dover, Abby D. Chamberlain, both of Dover.

DREW, Manning A., of Boston, Mass., m. Sept. 1, 1870, in Dover, Isabel A. Flanders, of Dover.

DROWN, Moses, of Rochester, m. Mar. 15, 1788, in Barrington, Hannah Hatch, of Lebanon, Me.

DROWN, Solomon, m. July 1806, in Barrington, Charity Evans, both of Rochester.

DUBE, L. A., m. (pub. Apr. 26, 1866, in Great Falls), Julia Barber.

DUDLEY, Stephen Jr., m. Jan. 10, 1782, by Rev. Isaac Smith, Molly Gilman, dau. of John.

DUDLEY, Joseph, b. Jan. 2, 1822, d. Apr. 29, 1887, m. Jan. 30, 1847, by Rev. S. J. Spaulding, Jane G. Hamilton, b. June 30, 1829, d. Oct. 17, 1827, dau. of Rufus, both of Somersworth.

DUDLEY, Otis B., of Alton, aged 66, m. (1) ---- ----, m. (2) Mar. 6, 1867, by Rev. Isaac C. White, Sarah C. Young, of Durham, aged 48.

DUESBURY, Frederic W., of Lowell, Mass., m. Jan. 28, 1869, in Dover, Susan A. Hope, of Dover.
DUNHAM, William H., m. Jan. 14, 1862, in Dover, Huldah F. Gray.
DUNN, Frank, son of Samuel, m. (1) July 6, 1857, in Newmarket, Abigail Canney, d. May 14, 1860, aged 20, dau. of Jacob.
DUNNELS, John, d. Sep. 13, 1836, aged 80, m. Dec. 28, 1794, by Rev. Isaac Hasey, Polly Farnham.
DUNNELLS, Joseph, m. Nov. 29, 1866, in Great Falls, Clara M. Davis, both of Newfield, Me.
DUNTLEY, Amos G. of Milton, d. Nov. 23, 1922, aged 78, m. Nov. 31, 1867, by Rev. Asa Piper, Mary P. Sawyer, of Wakefield.
DUNTLEY, J. Leighton, of Rochester, m. Feb. 15, 1868, in Strafford, M. Augusta Miles, of Strafford.
DURANT, Valentine, son of William, b. Sept. 16, 1782, m. July 1, 1806, by Rev. William Hooper, Hannah Tuttle, d. Feb. 3, 1865, aged 78, both of Dover.
DURANT, Charles J., m. Nov. 3, 1864, in Farmington, Carrie S. Gray, both of Farmington.
1) **DURGIN**, William, b. 1643, living in 1694, dead in 1703, m. (1) Martha Cross, dau. of Robert, m. (2) June 25, 1672, Catherine (Matthews) Footman, wid. of Thomas, d. Sept. 1705, aged 67, dau. of Francis.
DURGIN, Thomas, m. Mar. 19, 1778, in Barrington, Mary Howe, both of Barrington.
DURGIN, Samuel Jr., m. 1840, Sarah Elizabeth Buzzell, d. July 29, 1844, aged 23, dau. of Miles.
DURGIN, Simeon, son of Silas, d. Jan. 20, 1902, aged 73, m. (1) (pub. Nov. 7, 1854, in Newburyport, Mass.), Mary Jane Mooney, b. 1830, d. 1858, both of Alton, m. (2) Elizabeth W. ----, b. 1830, d. 1932.
DURGIN, Henry S., of Epping, m. Mar. 23, 1862, in Durham, Janette Young, of Madbury.
DURGIN, Horace J., m. Apr. 16, 1862, in Dover, Sarah F. Bradeen, both of Dover.
DURGIN, George W., d. Feb. 19, 1907, aged 72, m. Feb. 23, 1864, in Dover, Sarah E. D. Gray, both of Dover.
DURGIN, James W., of New Durham, m. Jan. 27, 1866, in Dover, Hannah M. Varney, of Dover.
DURGIN, James B., m. June 3, 1866, in Gilmanton, Augusta E. Pease, both of Gilmanton.

DURGIN, Albert F., of Greenland, m. Aug. 20, 1868, by Rev. Robert S. Stubbs, Mrs. Almira P. Wentworth, of Dover, d. July 4, 1887, aged 48, dau. of Jonathan.

DURGIN, David C., of Strafford, m. (pub. Dec. 8, 1870, in Portsmouth), Annie E. Holt, of Portsmouth.

DURRELL, Nathaniel, b. 1804, d. Jul. 11, 1876, m. Oct. 19, 1828, in Wakefield, Mahala Whitehouse, d. Aug. 3, 1876, aged 72, both of Wakefield.

DUSTIN, Adrian C., m. Sept. 22, 1868, in Dover, Mary F. Berry, both of Strafford.

DUSTIN, Albert B., of New York City, m. Dec. 24, 1868, by Rev. Robert S. Stubbs, Abbie L. Card, of Dover.

DYER, Albert P., m. Dec. 25, 1869, in Dover, Mary Ann Davis, both of Dover.

EARL, Anthony, of Lynn, Mass., m. Dec. 17, 1867, in N. Berwick, Me., Julia A. Snow.

EARLE, Timothy K., of Worcester, Mass., m. Oct. 10, 1867, in Dover, Caroline C. Osborne, of Dover, dau. of Daniel.

EASTMAN, William, of Tamworth, m. Jul. 28, 1827, in Tamworth, Louise Burleigh, of Ossipee, d. Aug. 11, 1842, dau. of James.

EASTMAN, George Albion, son of William, b. Feb. 14, 1829, d. Mar. 6, 1910, m. (pub. Jan. 22, 1850, in Somersworth), Joanna Estes, b. Apr. 16, 1832, d. Dec. 22, 1885.

EASTMAN, John m. (pub. Dec. 17, 1863, in Portsmouth), Alice A. C. Trefethen, of Newcastle.

EASTMAN, George H., m. (1) Lydia A. ----, d. Dec. 30, 1862, aged 18, m. (2) May 16, 1866, in Strafford, Roxanna Andrews, of Stowe, Me.

EASTMAN, John C., of Lowell, Mass., m. (pub. June 17, 1869, in Farmington), Sarah F. Adams, of Gilmanton.

EASTMAN, Edwin, of Newmarket, m. (pub. Oct. 13, 1870, in Great Falls), Mrs. Phebe Brackett, of Great Falls.

EATON, Jonathan, of Gilford, m. Sept. 3, 1824, in Middleton, Nancy N. Libbey, of Alton, dau. of Benjamin.

EATON, Alvin, of No. Reading, Mass., m. Apr. 28, 1841, in Lebanon, Me., Harriet Goodwin.

EATON, Thomas, of No. Reading, Mass., m. Apr. 28, 1842, in Lebanon, Me., Mary E. Goodwin.

EATON, Rev. Benjamin F., m. Apr. 5, 1867, in St. Peters, Minn., Ellen N. Kennard, both of Dover.

EDGECOMB, John F., of Wakefield, m. Jan. 3, 1870, in Union, Clara E. Brackett, of Facton, Me.

3) **EDGERLY**, James, son of Samuel, b. 1704, m. (1) in 1730, Eleanor Sawyer, widow, d. in 1734, m. (2) in 1736, Rachel Stanwood.

5) EDGERLY, Thomas C., son of Sgt. Thomas, b. Dec. 4, 1773, d. Nov. 24, 1845, m. 1797, Hannah Libbey, d. Mar. 9, 1853, aged 72, dau. of Abraham.

EDGERLY, Silas, m. Dec. 28, 1797, by Rev. Benjamin Balch, Molly Winkley, b. Aug. 3, 1777, dau. of Samuel, both of Barrington.

5) EDGERLY, John, son of Sgt. Thomas, b. June 8, 1784, d. 1841, m. in 1809, Anna Watson, dau. of David.

5) EDGERLY, William P., son of Sgt. Thomas, b. Oct. 12, 1787, d. 1871, m. July 22, 1810, Anna Chase, dau. of Jonathan.

6) EDGERLY, Thomas T., son of Josiah, b. Jan. 21, 1794, d. Feb. 1, 1848, m. Oct. 31, 1813, by Rev. Joseph Boodey, Sarah Roberts, d. Dec. 19, 1850, aged 58, dau. of John, both of Farmington.

6) EDGERLY, Moses, of Wolfeboro, m. Feb. 25, 1822, in Wolfeboro, Sally Stillings, of Ossipee.

6) EDGERLY, Nathaniel G., son of Joseph, b. Apr. 10, 1809, m. (1) Aug. 5, 1830, in Wolfeboro, Mary Furber, both of Wolfeboro, m. (2) ---- ----.

6) EDGERLY, Josiah B., son of Josiah, b. Aug. 14, 1800, m. (1) Jan. 31, 1833, by Nathaniel Berry, Cordelia Waldron, d. Aug. 23, 1854, aged 43, dau. of Jeremiah, both of Farmington, m. (2) Feb. 5, 1856, Eliza J. Hayes.

6) EDGERLY, Rev. David S., of New Durham, son of Jeremiah, b. Apr. 18, 1818, m. (1) Nov. 17, 1836, by Rev. Nathaniel Berry, Olive W. Place, of Alton, d. Apr. 22, 1848, aged 31, dau. of Moses, m. (2) July 22, 1851, by Elder Elias Hutchins, Almira Boody Chamberlain, d. Feb. 18, 1869, aged 37, dau. of Samuel F., m. (3) Sept. 27, 1870, Attilo Jane Winslow, d. Mar. 23, 1888.

EDGERLY, Charles G., of Wolfeboro, b. 1813, d. 1901, m. (pub. Jan. 1, 1839, in Tuftonboro), Mary S. Wiggin, of Tuftonboro, b. 1816, d. 1852.

6) EDGERLY, John, son of John, b. Oct. 29, 1815, m. (pub. Oct. 18, 1842, in Tuftonboro), Eliza Ann Caverly.

6) EDGERLY, James, son of Daniel, b. Mar. 13, 1804, m. Oct. 20, 1843, Anna H. Wedgewood, b. Dec. 24, 1812, d. Sept. 29, 1866, dau. of Lot.

6) EDGERLY, Nathaniel G., son of Joseph, b. Apr. 10, 1809, m. (1) Mary Furber, m. (2) July 26, 1848, by Rev. Oliver Ayer, Cynthia Lord.

6) EDGERLY, Albert L., son of John and Anna, b. June 10, 1825, d. Jan. 29, 1903, aged 77, m. Oct. 12, 1848, in Tuftonboro, Nancy M. Hersey, of Tuftonboro, d. May 26, 1891, aged 69, dau. of James.

6) EDGERLY, John C., of Wolfeboro, son of Daniel, b. Nov. 21, 1820, m. Oct. 7, 1849, by Elder Josiah Glines, Mary J. Deland, of New Durham.

EDGERLY, James B., m. (pub. Feb. 5, 1850, in Durham), Sophronia D. Durgin, d. Nov. 1886, aged 68, dau. of John, both of Durham.

EDGERLY, George J., of Farmington, b. 1825, m. Mar. 10, 1855, in Brookfield, Lois M. Piper, b. 1832, of Brookfield.

EDGERLY, John H., m. Sep. 16, 1856, in Farmington, Elizabeth A. Dame, d. Jul. 2, 1913, aged 78, dau. of John V.

EDGERLY, John, of Tamworth, m. (pub. Jan. 9, 1861, in Effingham), Abby A. Dore, of Ossipee, dau. of Ezekiel.

EDGERLY, Charles R. son of John, d. Feb. 16, 1907, aged 81, m. Apr. 8, 1863, by Rev. James Rand, Mary Jane Kelley, both of Dover.

EDGERLY, James B. of Farmington, m. Apr. 30, 1863, in S. Berwick, Me., Mary J. Fernald, of S. Berwick, Me.

EDGERLY, Daniel W., of Farmington, m. Mar. 26, 1864, in Strafford, Ellen A. Hanson, of Strafford.

EDGERLY, Thomas H., of Rochester, m. Mar. 11, 1868, in Alton, Helen A. Nute, of Alton.

EDGERLY, Charles E. of Meredith, son of William, aged 29, m. May 31, 1870, in Newmarket, Sarah A. Thompson, of Durham, aged 18, dau. of Jacob B.

EDGERLY, Henry I, m. Dec. 25, 1870, in Dover, Sarah A. Whitten, both of Farmington.

7) EDGERLY, James A., son of James, b. May 15, 1846, d. Feb. 8, 1908, aged 61, m. Nov. 19, 1874, in Rochester, Annie A. Wood.

EDWARDS, George, of Boston, Mass., m. (pub. Sept. 29, 1864, in Wolfeboro), Sarah E. Hunt.

EDWARDS, Sidney S., of N. Andover, Mass., m. Oct. 16, 1867, in Great Falls, Sarah E. Whitehouse, of Rollinsford.

ELA, John Whittier, son of John, b. Feb. 5, 1776, d. 1801, m. 1793, Mehitable Dame, of Durham.

1) ELA, Nathaniel Whittier, son of John, b. Feb. 5, 1776, d. Feb. 21, 1843, m. Nov. 7, 1790, Esther Emerson, b. Apr. 22, 1766, d. Feb. 28, 1826.

ELA, Joseph, m. (pub. Feb. 4, 1834, in Meredith), Sally Miller Moulton, d. 1878, aged 65, dau. of Jonathan, both of Meredith.

ELKINS, Amasa V., m. (pub. May 12, 1864, in Newcastle), Lydia A. Downs, both of Farmington.

ELKINS, Cyrus, m. Mar. 5, 1867, in Farmington, Martha A. Foote, of Newburyport, Mass., dau. of Lewis.

ELLIS, Jacob, m. Jun. 15, 1786, by Rev. Isaac Hasey, Sarah Whitehouse.

ELLIS, Edward, m. Jan. 13, 1791, by Rev. Benjamin Balch, Olly Foye, both of Barrington.

ELLIS, Jonathan Jr., of Rochester, m. Mar. 16, 1810, in Lebanon, Me., Jane Hartford.

ELLIS, John, of Rochester, b. 1793, d. 1862, m. May 12, 1816, by Rev. Joseph Boodey, Olive Bickford, of New Durham, d. Feb. 2, 1879, aged 78.

ELLIS, Moses, of Rochester, m. Nov. 21, 1822, in Lebanon, Me., Mary Shorey.

ELLIS, Moses, b. 1800, d. 1884, m. July 5, 1827, by Rev. Joseph Boodey, Hannah W. Bickford, b. 1801, d. 1860, both of Alton.

ELLIS, Moses A., son of Moses, d. July 19, 1910, aged 73, m. (pub. July 8, 1858, in Barnstead), Mrs. Sarah M. Lougee, both of Alton.

ELLIS, William C., of Boston, Mass., m. Oct. 22, 1866, in Portsmouth, Mary Harriet Ham, dau. of Henry.

ELLIS, Walter B., of Rochester, d. Oct. 12, 1916, aged 86, m. May 9, 1869, in Strafford, Joanna Keating, of Strafford.

ELLISON, James, m. Apr. 13, 1848, by Elder Samuel Sherburne, Abigail Randall, both of Nottingham.

ELLISON, William H., m. Apr. 20, 1867, in Nottingham, Hannah M. Critcherson, both of Lee.

ELWELL, George S., b. 1835, m. July 1860, Orrville E. Harriman.

ELWELL, Josiah, m. Mar. 22, 1863, in Dover, Abbie Hobbs, both of S. Berwick, Me.

ELWELL, John F., m. July 22, 1866, in Dover, Hattie H. T. Holbrook, both of Somersworth.

3) EMERSON, Solomon, d. Oct. 10, 1800, "aged 91" (see *N.H. Gazette-Portsmouth*), m. (1) early as 1735, Elizabeth Smith, b. Apr. 29, 1712, dau. of Samuel, m. (2) Mary Meader, wid. of Samuel.

4) EMERSON, Samuel, d. Sept. 29, 1854, aged 90, son of Solomon, m. (1) Ann Dow, m. (2) Lois McCoy.
5) EMERSON, Smith, son of Capt. Smith, b. May 12, 1776, m. Bridget Buzzell, d. Mar. 13, 1827, aged 46.
EMERSON, Joseph, m. Nov. 24, 1791, by Rev. Benjamin Balch, ---- Hayes, both of Barrington.
5) EMERSON, Moses, son of Solomon, b. Dec. 1781, d. Mar. 12, 1834, m. Nov. 17, 1803, by Rev. John Osborne, Rosemon Nutter, of Lee, d. Feb. 22, 1870, aged 80, dau. of Lemuel.
EMERSON, Seth R., of Alton, d. Feb. 10, 1891, aged 64, m. (1) Emily Ann Rollins, b. Jun. 25, 1830, d. Aug. 3, 1855, aged 25, dau. of Ichabod, m. (2) Nov. 25, 1858, in Guilford, Emily O. Grant, of Guilford, d. Jan. 6, 1910, aged 70.
7) EMERSON, John Place, son of Timothy, b. July 28, 1832, d. July 24, 1889, m. Aug. 26, 1860, Mary M. Bunker, d. Dec. 24, 1924, aged 85, dau. of Ephraim.
EMERSON, Dr. James, of New Ipswich, m. Jan. 22, 1862, in Barnstead, Laura Dennett, of Barnstead.
6) EMERSON, John O., of Dover, son of Moses, b. Nov. 9, 1835, m. (1) Sarah Langley, m. (2) Oct. 26, 1869, in Dover, Clara L. Wentworth, of Rollingford.
EMERSON Albert S., m. Aug. 4, 1864, in Gilmanton, Ann E. Norris, both of Alton.
EMERSON, Charles W., of Durham, m. May 27, 1865, by Rev. Ezra Haskell, Mary A. Randlett, of Stratham.
EMERSON, Charles, of Farmington, m. May 20, 1866, in Farmington, Vienna E. Dolby, of Alton, dau. of Isaac.
EMERSON, Laverne, of Madbury, son of Solomon, m. Apr. 7, 1868, by Rev. Alvan Tobey, Electa A. Lane, of Lee, dau. of Alexander Seavey.
EMERSON, John, of Durham, son of Joshua, aged 35, m. June 15, 1868, by Rev. Alvan Tobey, Abby A. Brewster, of Barrington, aged 35, dau. of Samuel.
EMERSON, Robert F., of Addison, Me., son of Joseph D., d. Mar. 6, 1914, aged 70, m. (pub. Apr. 22, 1869, in E. Rochester), Evelyn R. Corson, of E. Rochester.
EMERSON, Edgar L., of Dover, m. (pub. July 21, 1870, in Portsmouth), Sophronia Preston, of Portsmouth.
EMERSON, Daniel, of Madbury, m. Dec. 8, 1873, in Barrington, Mrs. Sarah A. (Demeritt) Pierce, of Barrington, wid. of Andrew D., b. Apr. 17, 1832, d. Jan. 21, 1903.

EMERY, Joseph, son of Job, b. Feb. 24, 1702, d. Jul. 1, 1793, m. Oct. 10, 1726, Mehitable Stacy, b. Feb. 4, 1705, d. Oct. 27, 1788.

5) EMERY, Samuel, son of Simon, b. 1732, m. (1) Apr. 15, 1756, by Rev. John Morse, Abigail Shackleve(?), m. (2) Jan. 29, 1785, Abigail Ferguson.

EMERY, Thomas, m. Sep. 8, 1796, by Rev. Isaac Hasey, Sarah Nock.

EMERY, Caleb, d. Sep. 12, 1785, m. int. May 15, 1813, in Lebanon, Me., Betsey Hurd, of Cornish, Me., b. Jun. 10, 1786.

EMERY, Noah, of Waterboro, Me., m. Oct. 29, 1815, in Lebanon, Me., Sally Dixon.

EMERY, Joseph, son of William, b. Feb. 4, 1795, d. Oct. 21, 1878, m. Jul. 4, 1816, by Rev. Jonathan Tompson, Matilda Nason.

EMERY, Shem, d. June 24, 1882, aged 68, m. Oct. 21, 1841, Dorcas Witham, d. Oct. 30, 1887, aged 71, dau. of Josiah, both of Somersworth.

EMERY, John, of Somersworth, m. Apr. 29, 1849, by Rev. Thomas Greenwood, Mary Jane Hill, of Dover, d. Dec. 6, 1907, aged 83, dau. of William.

EMERY, William, m. May 26, 1852, in Lebanon, Me., Harriet W. Fall.

EMERY, Jacob P., of Waterboro, Me., m. Nov. 24, 1859, in Lebanon, Me., Susan E. Fall, b. Jan. 26, 1838, dau. of Adoniram.

EMERY, Samuel H., m. (pub. Jan. 7, 1864, in Portsmouth), Mary E. Sias.

EMERY, John W., of Madbury, m. Mar. 28, 1864, in Dover, Evelyn F. Pinkham, of Dover.

EMERY, John H., of Lebanon, Me., m. Aug. 10, 1867, in Great Falls or Somersworth, Lizzie J. West, of Wakefield.

EMERY, Edwin A., m. (pub. Nov. 14, 1867, in West Milton), Sarah F. Jenkins, both of Milton.

ENGLAND, Thomas, m. Jan. 3, 1870, in Dover, Ellen F. Hartfield, both of Dover.

ESTERBROOK, Marcus M., of Sherburne, Vt., son of Richard, m. Aug. 3, 1864, in Durham, Emeline Paul, of Durham, dau. of Ellison.

ESTERBROOK, Dr. L. D., m. Dec. 9, 1869, in Durham, Emma J. Davis, both of Galveston, Tex.

ESTES, George, b. Oct. 29, 1785, m. Sep. 24, 1807, by Rev. Isaac Hasey, Sally Ricker, b. Aug. 30, 1781, dau. of Simon.

ESTES, Levi, son of George, b. Jan. 10, 1814, m. Mar. 4, 1840, Mrs. Betsey Woodsom, d. Feb. 13, 1857, aged 60.

ESTES, Leonard, of Dover, m. May 11, 1867, in Great Falls, Esther F. Brown.
EVANS, Benjamin, b. 1750, d. 1844, m. Dec. 16, 1771, by Ephraim Ricker, Elizabeth Ricker, d. Nov. 1, 1829, aged 78, dau. of Elizabeth Marden.
EVANS, Benjamin, son of Benjamin, b. Mar. 1, 1777, d. 1838, m. Oct. 1, 1799, Hannah Lucas, b. 1779, d. 1851, both of Wolfeboro.
EVANS, Nicholas, m. Mar. 6, 1821, by Rev. Micajah Otis, Deborah Twombly, both of Barrington.
EVANS, Daniel J. of Farmington, m. Nov. 15, 1849, by Elder Enoch Place, Lovina Foss, of Rochester, d. Sep. 30, 1855, aged 25.
EVANS, Albert, of Strafford, son of Lemuel, d. Dec. 2, 1905, aged 81, m. Jan. 9, 1850, by Elder Samuel Sherburne, Elizabeth Ann Swain, of Barrington, d. Nov. 11, 1910, aged 90, dau. of Israel.
EVANS, Dudley P., son of William, b. May 20, 1830, d. Nov. 8, 1892, m. (pub. Oct. 7, 1858, in Alton), Martha C. Kimball, d. Aug. 2, 1876, aged 38, dau. of Nehemiah, both of Alton.
EVANS, Henry, m. (pub. Jun. 27, 1861, in Great Falls), Isabel Blodgett, d. Dec. 3, 1903, aged 62, dau. of Wilber D.
EVANS, William, of Rochester, m. Mar. 28, 1865, in Dover, Rebecca Hayes, of Lowell, Mass.
EVANS, Edward E., son of William, d. Feb. 28, 1918, aged 78, m. Apr. 5, 1866, in Rochester, Mary A. Vickery, both of Rochester.
EVANS, Charles W., of Rochester, m. Nov. 22, 1866, in Rochester, Clara A. Young, of Farmington.
EVANS, John W., m. July 3, 1867, in Rochester, Melvina Farnham, both of Wakefield.
EVANS, Ingalls, m. (pub. July 11, 1867, in Milton), Lizzie H. Parker, both of Stoneham, Me.
EVANS, Charles E., of Strafford, d. Apr. 17, 1924, aged 83, m. Apr. 24, 1869, by Rev. John Winkley, Lavina Thompson, of Barrington.
EVANS, Albert Levi, of Wakefield, b. 1844, d. 1914, m. (1) Apr. 14, 1870, in Peabody, Mass., Hattie M. Goodale, of Peabody, Mass., b. 1851, d. 1884, m. (2) Mary M. Wadleigh, b. 1857, d. 1897.
EVANS, Charles M., son of Jeremiah, d. Nov. 21, 1910, aged 62, m. (pub. July 14, 1870, in Rochester), Amanda Clough.
FALL, Tristram Jr., b. May 8, 1740, d. Feb. 7, 1792, m. Nov. 15, 1759, by Rev. John Morse, Martha Pray, dau. of John.
FALL, Tristram, son of Ebenezer, d. Mar. 23, 1854, aged 78, m. Aug. 8, 1796, by Rev. Matthew Merriam, Anna Lord, dau. of Hemphrey.

FALL, Daniel, son of Ebenezer, d. Dec. 26, 1853, aged 62, m. Jul. 15, 1815, by Rev. Paul Jewett, Lucy Moody, d. Dec. 3, 1850, aged 57.

FALL, Ebenezer, son of Daniel, b. May 9, 1816, d. Apr. 25, 1883, m. (1) May 13, 1841, by Rev. Joseph Loring, Abra W. Fall, b. Jan. 17, 1820, d. Sep. 20, 1845, dau. of George Jr., m. (2) Nov. 20, 1847, by Rev. Joseph Loring, Dorcas D. Horne, b. 1825, d. 1912, dau. of Richard.

FALL, Ivory Jr., son of Ivory, b. Aug. 16, 1820, m. int. Sep. 13, 1845, in Lebanon, Me., Abby Fernald, b. Mar. 6, 1819, dau. of James.

FALL, Ebenezer, b. May 9, 1816, m. (1) Abra W. ----, m. (2) Nov. 20, 1847, by Rev. Joseph Loring, Dorcas Downs Horne.

FALL, Isaac W., son of George Jr., b. Jan. 9, 1830, d. Feb. 17, 1855, m. int. Mar. 6, 1852, in Lebanon, Me., Mary E. Clark, b. May 26, 1834, d. May 30, 1882, aged 59, dau. of George, Jr.

FALL, William A., son of Adoniram C., b. Apr. 5, 1834, m. (pub. May 15, 1856, in Somersworth), Martha A. Linscott.

FALL, Edward E, d. Aug. 11, 1906, aged 73, m. (1) (pub. May 24, 1860, in Wolfeboro), Martha C. Welch, d. Nov. 29, 1886, aged 53, both of Tuftonboro, m. (2) Ann E. ----, d. Dec. 17, 1903, aged 64.

FALL, Nathaniel F., son of Adoniram C., b. Dec. 6, 1831, m. Jan. 1, 1863, in Lebanon, Me., Betsey Coffin, of Waterboro, Me.

FALL, Frank, m. Mar. 26, 1866, in Ossipee, Emma F. Chick.

FALL, Joseph O., m. Jan. 27, 1867, in Ossipee, Lydia A. Chick, of Ossipee.

FALL, John A., of Berwick, Me., b. 1845, d. May 26, 1921, aged 76, m. (pub. July 22, 1869, in Rochester), Susie A. Lord, of Somersworth, b. 1851.

FARNHAM, Mathew, m. Jan. 15, 1795, by Rev. Isaac Hasey, Catharine Austin.

FARNHAM, Gaius, m. Feb. 6, 1800, by Rev. Isaac Hasey, Polly Gerrish.

FARNHAM, Enoch, son of David, bpt. Oct. 22, 1780, m. int. Jul. 20, 1800, in Lebanon, Me., Sally Worster.

FARNHAM, Jeremiah, son of David, bpt. Jul. 28, 1786, m. int. Jun. 18, 1808, in Lebanon, Me., Fanny Stacey.

FARNHAM, David, of Acton, Me., b. 1808, d. 1882, m. Apr. 16, 1835, Rowena Dearborn, d. Sept. 6, 1900, aged 86, dau. of Nathaniel.

FARNHAM, John Gates, d. Sept. 30, 1864, aged 54, m. June 5, 1842, by Elder A. K. Moulton, Louisa Whitten, d. Dec. 11, 1842, aged 62, both of Dover.

FARNHAM, Ezra, son of John, b. Oct. 10, 1831, d. July 26, 1884, m. June 3, 1855, in Acton, Me., Harriet A. Hubbard, b. Jan. 18, 1837, d. Mar. 10, <u>1929</u>, both of Acton, Me.

FARNHAM, Edwin P., of Wakefield, m. Aug. 10, 1867, in Rochestert, Mary C. Ricker, of Rollinsford.

FARNHAM, Henry C., <u>d. Apr. 6, 1935, aged 87</u>, m. Feb. 20, 1869, in Dover, Lizzie S. Merrill, <u>both of Dover</u>.

FARNHAM, Orin L., m. (pub. Nov. 18, 1869, in Great Falls), Nettie Moore, both of Great Falls.

FARNSWORTH, Thomas, of Dover, m. Sept. 1, 1867, in Orange, Wisc., Marietta Weed, of Orange, Wisc.

FARRINGTON, <u>Joseph H.</u> of Rochester, <u>d. Dec. 10, 1895, aged 59</u>, m. (pub. May 22, 1862, in Portsmouth), Susan A. Clough, of Lowell, Mass.

FELCH, Daniel, son of Simeon, aged 19, m. Apr. 27, 1851, by Rev. Levi B. Tasker, in Sandwich, Judith B. George, aged 18, dau. of Levi, both of Sandwich.

FELKER, Isaiah, son of Michael, b. 1750, d. Jan. 1828, m. Mercy Church, b. 1754, dau. of <u>Ebenezer</u>.

FELKER, Joseph <u>Jr.</u>, son of Charles, m. Dec. 13, 1810, <u>in Barrington</u>, Rebecca Leathers, <u>both of Barrington.</u>

FELKER, <u>Capt.</u> John, son of William, b. May 26, 1801, d. Mar. 23, 1872, m. Nov. 24, 1824, Mehitable Winkley, b. June 24, 1802, d. Jan. 28, 1894, dau. of Benjamin.

FELKER, Capt. William, of Barrington, son of William, d. <u>Apr. 27,</u> 1842, aged 75, m. Oct. 26, 1826, Mrs. Susan Holmes, of Rochester, d. May 17, 1841, aged 42.

FELKER, Elias R., d. Apr. 24, 1844, aged 26, m. Feb. 9, 1843, in Dover, Rebecca O. Barrows, <u>d. May 14, 1871, aged 49.</u>

FELKER, Samuel, m. Mar. 7, 1844, by Elder Enoch Place, Hannah H. Varney, d. Mar. 28, 1882, aged 62, <u>dau. of Elias</u>, both of Barrington.

FELKER, B. Frank, son of John, d. Jan. 20, 1917, aged 78, m. Aug. 31, 1862, in Barrington, Hattie S. Berry, both of Barrington.

FELKER, S. Francis, <u>of Rochester</u>, m. June 29, 1867, by Rev. Robert S. Stubbs, Jennie L. Tibbetts, <u>of Langford, Me.</u>

FELLOWS, <u>Capt.</u> Stephen <u>Jr.</u>, m. May 2, 1808, in Tamworth, Peggy McGaffy, d. June 9, 1823, aged 38, both of Sandwich.

FELLOWS, Edward H., m. Jan. 6, 1866, in Dover, Mary Shearden, <u>both of Dover.</u>

FELLOWS, William, of Hamstead, m. Dec. 3, 1868, in Dover, Fannie M. C. Perkins, of Dover.

FELLOWS, Charles S., of Wakefield, b. 1844, son of John, m. May 4, 1869, by Rev. Alvan Tobey, Annie (Sherburne) Demeritt, widow, b. 1834, dau. of Isaac.

FERGUSON, Charles P., of Springvale, Me., m. Feb. 8, 1864, in Dover, Mary A. Chase, of Dover.

FERNALD, Tobias, son of Nathaniel, b. Aug. 25, 1703, m. Jan. 30, 1729, by Rev. Jos. Adams, Abigail Smith, both of Kittery, Me.

FERNALD, William, m. Aug. 6, 1797, in Brookfield, Betsey Johnson.

FERNALD, Joel, d. Oct. 1856, m. int. Nov. 24, 1821, in Dover, Katharine Clark.

FERNALD, William, son of James, b. Dec. 4, 1821, m. Jun. 16, 1842, Nancy C. Mason, d. Oct. 3, 1869.

FERNALD, Dr. John S., of Barrington, b. May 1, 1800, d. Jan. 4, 1864, m. (1) Dec. 17, 1826, Sarah Ann Paul, b. Aug. 30, 1802, d. Apr. 16, 1838, dau. of James, m. (2) July 19, 1840, by Rev. Samuel Nichols, Mary Ann Meserve, b. Nov. 19, 1811, d. May 18, 1899, both of Barrington.

FERNALD, Joseph, d. Dec. 3, 1884, aged 81, m. Feb. 11, 1827, by Elder Enoch Place, Lydia Perry, d. Apr. 12, 1871, aged 66, dau. of Humphrey, both of Barrington.

FERNALD, Isaac, of Barrington, b. 1809, m (1) (pub. Dec. 11, 1827, in Milton), Polly Drew, of Milton, m. (2) int. Jun. 25, 1864, in Lee, Mrs. Nancy Drew, b. 1841, both of Lee.

FERNALD, Samuel Pray, of Ossipee, b. May 25, 1809, d. June 9, 1888, m. (pub. May 1, 1838, in Tuftonboro), Hannah E. Palmer, of Tuftonboro, b. Sept. 12, 1810, d. July 1, 1888.

FERNALD, Ira, of Eaton, m. int. Jan. 8, 1843, in Lebanon, Me., Clarissa Jane Hodgdon, d. Dec. 3, 1843, dau. of Isaac.

FERNALD, William P., of Exeter, m. Dec. 10, 1844, Mary Ann Sanborn, of Somersworth, d. Apr. 14, 1905, aged 72, dau. of Perkins.

FERNALD, Daniel Jr., d. Oct. 5, 1905, aged 82, m. (1) Dec. 9, 1847, by Elder Josiah Glines, Sarah H. Caverly, d. Oct. 13, 1868, aged 47, both of Tuftonboro, m. (2) Lizzie ----, d. Mar. 5, 1889, aged 39.

FERNALD, Oliver, m. 1853, in Somersworth, Catherine A. Pendergast, of Great Falls.

FERNALD, John Quincy, son of Deac. Thomas, b. Jun. 19, 1832, d. Mar. 30, 1891, m. Nov. 12, 1853, in Lebanon, Me., Sarah Lord, of Lebanon, Me., b. Jan. 20, 1835.

FERNALD, Thomas J., son of Thomas, b. Jan. 11, 1830, m. int. Mar. 28, 1856, in Lebanon, Me., Vanna Goodwin, b. Oct. 16, 1831, dau. of Jacob.

FERNALD, Charles A., b. 1857, m. int. Dec. 1, 1861, in Lee, Mary E. Randall, b. 1845, both of Lee.

FERNALD, Giles, m. (pub. Aug. 7, 1862, in Salem, Mass.), Lydia Ann Brown, of Moultonboro.

FERNALD, John F., son of John Y., b. Apr. 4, 1848, d. Dec. 20, 1916, m. Jan. 1, 1869, by Rev. Robert S. Stubbs, Viola U. Jackson, b. July 9, 1847, d. Nov. 8, 1909, both of Ossipee.

FERNALD, Edwin L, m. Mar. 24, 1869, in Dover, Ella Adelia Jones, d. Aug. 21, 1913, aged 62, dau. of Ephraim M., both of Dover.

FERNALD, Matthew C., of Eliot, Me., m. (pub. Sept. 9, 1869, in Wakefield), Augusta H. Leavitt, of Wakefield.

FERRIN, Moses, b. 1756, d. Jan. 15, 1843, m. (1) Mary Dellan, m. (2) Sept. 8, 1784, by Rev. Nathaniel Ewer, Asenath Robinson, m. (3) Jane Blazo.

FIELD, John, m. Nov. 14, 1813, by Rev. Joseph Boody, Patty Sewards.

FIFIELD, Charles, of Somersworth, m. Nov. 30, 1833, in Lebanon, Me., Emily Plumer.

FIFIELD, Charles N., son of Charles, d. Mar. 10, 1892, aged 79, m. int. Sep. 23, 1838, in Dover, Betsey N. Nutter, d. Feb. 8, 1911, aged 43, dau. of John H.

FISH, Ira, son of John, b. Jan. 4, 1790, d. May 24, 1872, m. (1) Nov. 11, 1813, by Rev. Joseph Boodey, Louisa Twombley, b. Dec. 6, 1792, d. Dec. 1816, both of Milton, m. (2) Mar. 6, 1820, by Rev. Joseph Boodey, Mrs. Abra Dearborn, of Milton, wid. of Dr. Ebenezer.

FISHER, Samuel C., of Francistown, son of Matthew, b. Nov. 29, 1822, d. July 10, 1909, m. (1) Nov. 11, 1847, by Rev. William P. Tilden, Mary Elizabeth Barnes, b. Sept. 16, 1826, d. Nov. 29, 1852, dau. of Benjamin, m. (2) July 20, 1864, in Dover, Sarah J. Christie, b. Mar. 27, 1830, d. Feb. 2, 1898, dau. of Daniel M., m. (3) Apr. 15, 1899, in Dover, Emily Bacon.

FISHER, Erastus E., m. Dec. 13, 1865, in Dover, Sarah E. Place, both of Dover.

FITZGERALD, Daniel, d. 1799, m. Mar. 2, 1770, by Dr. Jeremy Belknap, Elizabeth Allen, b. Feb. 24, 1753, dau. of Ezekiel, both of Kittery.

FLAGG, William, son of George W., d. Apr. 12, 1908, aged 69, m. Jan. 16, 1862, in Dover, Eveline Bickford, d. May 25, 1914, aged 77, dau. of Aaron, both of Rochester.

FLAGG, Joshua G., son of William, d. Apr. 3, 1907, aged 72, m. Dec. 18, 1862, in Dover, Emily C. Hussey, d. Aug. 21, 1909, aged 72, dau. of Moses, both of Dover.

FLAGG, Charles W., of Rochester, m. May 30, 1867, in Providence R.I., Emma F. Ramsbottom, of Providence, R.I.

FLANDERS, Enoch, of Alton, son of Ezekiel, b. 1801, d. 1873, m. June 11, 1823, Dorothy L. Witham, of Alton, b. 1801, d. 1874.

FLETCHER, Wesley H., m. Sept. 10, 1870, in Dover, Nellie M. Peck, both of Portland, Me.

FLINT, Charles, m. Feb. 20, 1822, in Lebanon, Me., Anna Horne, d. Mar. 16, 1838, dau. of Elnah.

FLINT, Luther, of Candia, m. Oct. 30, 1855, in Newmarket, Mary J. Leavitt, of Newmarket.

FLOOD, Lawrence, m. Feb. 24, 1869, in Rochester, Emily Richards, both of Rochester.

FOLSOM, Jacob, m. June 4, 1787, by Rev. Nathaniel Ewer, Elizabeth Smart, d. Aug. 22, 1867, aged 97.

FOLSOM, Capt. Isaac, of New Durham, m. June 4, 1815, by Rev. Joseph Boodey, Mercy Winkley, of Alton, dau. of Mark H.

FOLSOM, George L., d. June 9, 1915, aged 72, m. Mar. 13, 1867, by Rev. Francis E. Abbott, Nellie E. Otis, of Boston, Mass., dau. of A. H. Otis.

FOOT, George E., son of Henry, b. 1840, d. 1893, m. June 3, 1866, in Dover, Sarah A. Rollins, b. 1848, d. 1900, both of Dover.

FOOTE, Capt. William L., of Somersworth, d. July 6, 1866, aged 75, m. (1) Judith ----, b. Sept. 30, 1800, d. Mar. 29, 1824, m. (2) Feb. 13, 1825, by Rev. Zebedee Delano, Mary P. Wood, b. Jan. 11, 1798, d. Mar. 27, 1888.

FORD, Edwin H., of Pembroke, Mass, m. (pub. Feb. 23, 1865, in Wolfeboro), Susan C. Young, of Wolfeboro.

FORD, Steven S., of Manchester, m. Aug. 22, 1868, in Dover, Abbie Perkins, of Rollinsford.

FORD, Daniel, m. Sept. 13, 1869, in Dover, Mrs. Jane Drew.

FOSS, Capt. Joshua, b. June 12, 1738, m. Sept. 18, 1764, in Barrington, Abigail ----, b. Mar. 4, 1743.

FOSS, Moses, m. Feb. 19, 1778, in Barrington, Molly Daniels, both of Barrington.

FOSS, Richard T., d. Jun. 11, 1862, aged 53, m. May 7, 1833, by Rev. John Winkley, Mary Ann Clark, d. Apr. 15, 1884, aged 72, both of Strafford.

FOSS, George, of Barrington, d. Jan. 29, 1844, aged 86, m. Feb. 18, 1780, by Dr. Belknap, Lois Drew, d. Oct. 11, 1822.

FOSS, Moses, d. Dec. 1826, aged 80, m. Mar. 1781, Molly Drew, d. Oct. 30, 1827, dau. of David, both of Barrington.

FOSS, Richard, son of George, b. May 15, 1760, d. Mar. 25, 1802, m. Nov. 28, 1782, by Rev. Joseph Haven, Marcy Berry, b. Apr. 10, 1755, d. Oct. 30, 1827.

FOSS, Maj. Samuel, d. Sept. 24, 1825, aged 65, m. Feb. 27, 1783, by Rev. Joseph Haven, Marcy Berry.

FOSS, William, son of George, b. May 15, 1760, d. Feb. 3, 1830, m. (1) Apr. 21, 1785, by Rev. Benjamin Balch, Elizabeth Hayes, b. Aug. 12, 1767, d. Aug. 20, 1806, both of Barrington, m. (2) Margaret Babb, d. Oct. 6, 1836, aged 62.

FOSS, John, m. Sept. 20, 1785, by Rev. Benjamin Balch, Abigail Foss, both of Barrington.

FOSS, Joshua 3rd, of Barrington, d. Feb. 18, 1844, aged 79, m. Nov. 7, 1785, by Rev. Benjamin Balch, Elizabeth Hunt, of Rye.

FOSS, John Sr., m. Feb. 11, 1787, by Rev. Benjamin Balch, Susannah Hayes, both of Barrington.

FOSS, William, m. July 1, 1787, by Rev. Benjamin Balch, Polly Kingman, both of Barrington.

FOSS, Timothy, d. May 15, 1854, aged 92, m. (1) Aug. 6, 1787, Abigail Blake, b. Mar. 12, 1768, d. Jan. 28, 1840, dau. of William, both of Barrington, m. (2) July 9, 1840, by Elder Enoch Place, Mrs. Judith A. Sheppard, of Strafford.

FOSS, James Jr., m. Nov. 27, 1787, by Rev. Benjamin Balch, Abigail Marden, both of Barrington.

FOSS, John 3rd, m. Jan. 15, 1789, by Rev. Benjamin Balch, Meribah Babb, both of Barrington.

FOSS, Samuel, d. Jan. 19, 1826, aged 59, m. Nov. 25, 1789, in Barrington, Betsey Babb, b. July 17, 1771, d. Feb. 12, 1871, aged 99, dau. of William.

FOSS, Nathan, d. June 30, 1843, aged 75, m. Mar. 7, 1790, in Barrington, by Rev. Benjamin Balch, Alice Babb, d. May 20, 1859, aged 90, both of Barrington.

FOSS, Joseph, of Barrington, m. June 5, 1791, in Barrington, Bettey Turas (?), of Northwood.

FOSS, John 5th, m. Aug. 21, 1791, in Barrington, Dolley Babb, both of Barrington.

FOSS, Joshua, m. Nov. 17, 1791, by Rev. Benjamin Balch, Lydia Daniels, both of Barrington.

FOSS, Dr. John, son of Thomas, b. Apr. 11, 1767, d. Sept. 19, 1848, m. Oct. 23, 1794, by Rev. Benjamin Randall, Sarah Twombly, b. Feb. 26, 1775, d. Dec. 17, 1822, dau. of Andrew, both of Barrington.

FOSS, Lt. George, d. Dec. 30, 1831, aged 49, m. (1) Nov. 21, 1799, Betsey Canney, b. Mar. 12, 1778, m. (2) July 27, 1807, by Rev. Caleb Sherman, Alice Holland, d. Dec. 23, 1831, aged 46.

FOSS, Ichabod, m. Nov. 21, 1802, by Rev. Benjamin Balch, Sarah Rowe, both of Barrington.

FOSS, Samuel, m. Feb. 15, 1803, in Barrington, Abigail Reed, both of Rochester.

FOSS, David, m. Apr. 14, 1803, by Rev. Benjamin Balch, Margaret Ham, both of Barrington.

FOSS, Elisha, m. Dec. 1806, in Barrington, Polly Bryant, both of Barrington.

FOSS, Elisha, m. Dec. 29, 1808, in Barrington, Nabby Johnson, both of Barrington.

FOSS, Nathaniel, m. May 4, 1809, in Barrington, Rebecca Hawkins, both of Barrington.

FOSS, Ralph, m. Oct. 26, 1809, in Barrington, Sally Foss, both of Barrington.

FOSS, Benjamin, son of Dr. John, d. Dec. 30, 1849, aged 58, m. (1) Nov. 3, 1811, by Rev. Moses Cheney, Patience Horn, d. Nov. 2, 1836, aged 43, both of Farmington, m. (2) Mar. 22, 1837, by Elder Enoch Place, Mrs. Joanna Otis, of Strafford, wid. of Capt. Stephen, d. July 15, 1852, aged 58.

FOSS, William, d. Mar. 27, 1846, aged 63, m. (1) Mary Downs, d. Sept. 1828, aged 44, dau. of Moses, m. (2) int. July 18, 1830, in Lebanon, Me., Polly Corson.

FOSS, Stephen, m. Nov. 21, 1811, in Barrington, Dorothy Foss, both of Barrington.

FOSS, George Jr., d. Nov. 11, 1841, aged 58, m. Jan. 21, 1812, by Rev. Joseph Boody, Jane Hill, both of Barrington.

FOSS, Enoch, d. Aug. 3, 1858, aged 73, m. Nov. 17, 1812, by Rev. Micajah Otis, Hannah Hill, both of Barrington.

FOSS, Job, m. Nov. 11, 1813, by Rev. Joseph Boody, Abigail Foss, both of Barrington.

FOSS, John, of Milton, b. 1789, d. 1869, m. Dec. 7, 1815, by Rev. Joseph Haven, Lydia Wingate, of Farmington, b. 1786, d. 1862.

FOSS, David B., d. Jan. 18, 1864, aged 70, m. Mar. 21, 1816, by Elder Enoch Place, Susanna Sampson, of Rochester, d. Mar. 23, 1863, aged 69, dau. of Dr. Nehemiah.

FOSS, James Seavey, of Rochester, b. June 21, 1787, d. Sept. 19, 1860, m. Sept. 1, 1816, by Elder Enoch Place, Sally Hodsdon, of Barrington, b. in 1798, d. Dec. 31, 1848.

FOSS, Col. Oliver S., son of George, b. June 6, 1800, d. Oct. 4, 1841, aged 41, m. (pub. Sept. 26, 1820, in Dover), Sarah Ann Sawyer, b. Oct. 17, 1802, d. Nov. 4, 1830, dau. of Jacob.

FOSS, Israel Jr., of Strafford, d. Mar. 31, 1879, aged 79, m. (1) Feb. 17, 1824, by Elder Enoch Place, Hannah Thompson, of Barrington, d. Jan. 9, 1827, aged 25, dau. of Noah, m. (2) July 3, 1828, by Elder Enoch Place, Sarah Leighton, d. May 11, 1876, aged 72, both of Strafford.

FOSS, Eliphalet, son of James, d. Dec. 5, 1853, aged 57, m. Dec. 15, 1825, by Elder Enoch Place, Mary A. Foss, d. Sept. 19, 1838, aged 33, dau. of James, both of Barrington.

FOSS, Eliphalet, d. Sept. 1884, aged 82, m. Jan. 10, 1828, by Elder Enoch Place, Nancy Leighton, d. Aug. 3, 1862, aged 57, dau. of Jonathan, both of Strafford.

FOSS, David, b. Dec. 11, 1860, aged 62, m. (1) Apr. 2, 1828, by Rev. Mr. Hawes, Mary Brock, d. Oct. 26, 1845, aged 40, both of Dover, m. (2) Aug. 31, 1846, by Rev. Homer Barrows, Mrs. Ann Hall.

FOSS, Israel Jr., d. Mar. 3, 1879, aged 79, m. (2) Jul. 3, 1828, by Elder Enoch Place, Sarah Leighton, d. Apr. 15, 1880, aged 79, both of Strafford.

FOSS, John S., d. Feb. 25, 1859, aged 62, m. int. Oct. 1828, in Tuftonboro, Sally Morrill, d. Nov. 21, 1854, aged 43, both of Tuftonboro.

FOSS, Lemuel, d. Jan. 23, 1867, aged 72, m. Dec. 4, 1828, by Elder Enoch Place, Sarah Foss, d. June 1, 1862, aged 55, dau. of Mark, both of Strafford.

FOSS, Elder Andrew T., of Dover, b. 1803, m. (pub. Feb. 24, 1829, in Parsonsfield), Mary Morrill.

FOSS, Daniel, of Barrington, son of David, b. July 4, 1803, d. Oct. 29, 1861, aged 58 yrs., 4 mos., m. Oct. 31, 1829, by Rev. Isaac

Willey, Mary Ann Tebbetts, of Strafford, d. Sept. 7, 1885, aged 74 yrs., 2 mos.

FOSS, Enos H., m. (1) Sally Berry, d. Mar. 10, 1830, aged 22, m. (2) Mar. 17, 1831, by Elder Enoch Place, Sarah Pearl, both of Strafford.

FOSS, Richard, m. May 7, 1833, by Rev. John Winkley, Mary Ann Clark, d. Sept. 7, 1855, aged 70, both of Strafford.

FOSS, Green O., of Rutland, Mass., d. Mar. 10, 1853, aged 42, m. Aug. 15, 1833, in Barrington, Maria Foss, of Barrington, d. Sept. 1848, aged 38.

FOSS, Jacob D., son of David B., m. Sept. 18, 1837, by Rev. John Winkley, Hannah Foss, both of Boston, Mass.

FOSS, Dennis, d. Aug. 29, 1893, aged 81, m. Dec. 3, 1837, by Elder Rnoch Place, Patience Scruton, b. Oct. 1, 1813, d. Jun. 21, 1891, dau. of Michael, both of Strafford.

FOSS, Jeremiah J., m. Dec. 20, 1838, by Elder Enoch Place, Martha Hayes, b. June 18, 1801, d. Nov. 21, 1858, aged 57, both of Strafford.

FOSS, Sylvanus C., d. July 19, 1904, aged 83, m. June 6, 1839, by Elder Enoch Place, Lydia D. Foss, d. Nov. 11, 1887, aged 67, both of Strafford.

FOSS, Joel S., m. Jan. 10, 1841, by Elder Enoch Place, Deborah Jane Sloper, d. July 5, 1898, aged 79, dau. of William, both of Strafford.

FOSS, Warren, son of William, b. Feb. 10, 1815, d. Jan. 6, 1893, aged 77, m. (pub. Feb. 9, 1841, in Strafford), Deborah Jane Sloper, d. July 5, 1898, aged 79, dau. of William, both of Strafford.

FOSS, Tadoc W., son of George, b. July 2, 1808, d. Jan. 2, 1875, aged 66, m. int. Apr. 7, 1841, in Dover, Sarah Horn.

FOSS, Nehemiah, b. Jul. 18, 1818, d. Dec. 19, 1903, aged 85, m. Oct. 3, 1841, by Elder, Enoch Place, Sarah Jane Leighton, b. Jul. 24, 1824, d. May 26, 1880, both of Strafford.

FOSS, Horace, d. 1901, m. Jul. 3, 1843, by Rev. John Winkley, Betsey F. Berry, d. Mar. 13, 1914, aged 93, both of Strafford.

FOSS, Thomas C., d. July 23, 1854, aged 38, m. int. Aug. 4, 1844, in Dover, Margaret Ann Sayward, d. June 23, 1900, aged 76, both of Dover.

FOSS, Oliver, son of William, b. June 26, 1810, m. Jan. 2, 1845, by Elder Mahew Clark, Betsey Perkins.

FOSS Dennis, of Strafford, m. Dec. 16, 1845, by Elder Samuel Sherburne, Hannah Peavey, of Barrington.

FOSS, Daniel, m. (1) int. Mar. 2, 1846, in Dover, Sophronia A. Randall, d. Feb. 5, 1856, aged 34, m. (2) Oct. 17, 1856, in Dover, Mary Jane Otis, both of Milton.

FOSS, Andrew W., son of Silas, d. Dec. 29, 1904, aged 83, m. (pub. July 14, 1846, in Barrington), Abigail Place, dau. of James, both of Rochester.

FOSS, Erastus Dearborn, d. Mar. 15, 1853, aged 28, m. July 11, 1847, by Elder Enoch Place, Frances Marion Merrill, d. Jan. 13, 1850, aged 22, both of Strafford.

FOSS, Enos George, b. 1816, d. Nov. 14, 1908, aged 92, m. (1) Apr. 9, 1848, by Rev. Homer Barrows, Sarah Berry, d. Oct. 13, 1869, aged 51, both of Strafford, m. (2) June 16, 1870, Sarah J. (Boswell) Wood, b. 1828, d. Feb. 17, 1912, dau. of Joseph.

FOSS, Rev. Tobias, aged 35, son of William, b. Feb. 2, 1813, m. Apr. 13, 1848, by Elder Enoch Place, Margaret Sloper, aged 35, both of Strafford.

FOSS, Jonas S., m. June 11, 1848, in Barrington, by Rev. Theodore Wells, Martha J. Foss, d. Feb. 26, 1875, aged 45, both of Barrington.

FOSS, John W., m. Nov. 25, 1849, by Rev. Theodore Wells, Priscilla M. Foss, both of Barrington.

FOSS, Joseph Otis, son of Isaac, b. Aug. 16, 1821, d. Jan. 16, 1887, aged 65, m. near 1850, Ariana E. Boodey, d. Aug. 9, 1885, aged 56.

FOSS, Richard Waldron, son of James B., d. Oct. 6, 1901, aged 74, m. Nov. 27, 1851, by Elder Enoch Place, Emily Y. Place, d. Sept. 21, 1883, aged 51, dau. of James.

FOSS, Darius, b. 1829, d. Apr. 29, 1898, m. (1) Dec. 14, 1851, by Rev. Homer Barrows, Almira N. Goodall, b. 1830, d. Feb. 20, 1893, m. (2) Apr. 5, 1894, in Dover, Myra Perry, b. 1843, d. Oct. 31, 1924, dau. of Frank W.

FOSS, Aaron W., m. near 1852, Elizabeth D. Caverly, b. 1833, dau. of Elder John.

FOSS, Cyrus Kingsbury, b. Jan. 10, 1828, d. Aug. 20, 1902, m. (pub. Jan. 13, 1852, in New Durham), Mary E. Hill, d. Jun. 21, 1905, aged 74, dau. of Joseph, both of Strafford.

FOSS, John C., m. May 24, 1852, by Elder Enoch Place, Mary E. Montgomery, d. Apr. 13, 1862, aged 43, dau. of Capt. Paul, both of Strafford.

FOSS, William B., of Strafford, son of William, d. Dec. 1, 1896, aged 78, m. May 25, 1852, by Elder Elias Hutchins, Sarah J. Haines, of Wolfeboro, d. Feb. 7, 1890, aged 60, dau. of James.

FOSS, Isaac B., of Strafford, b. 1829, d. 1871, m. Sep. 15, 1852, by Rev. John Winkley, Mary Jane Mace, of Dover, b. 1827, d. 1913.

FOSS, Joel, m. Dec. 18, 1853, by Rev. John Winkley, Mary I. Thompson, both of Strafford.

FOSS, Clement B., son of Israel, d. Mar. 30, 1856, aged 31, m. Oct. 2, 1854, by Rev. John Winkley, Sarah A. Locke, both of Strafford.

FOSS, John T., m. Sept. 15, 1855, in Newmarket, Almira Plummer, both of Newmarket.

FOSS, Joshua H., m. Feb. 10, 1856, in Barrington, Mrs. Eliza Ann (Foss) Varney, wid. of Elias Jr., both of Barrington.

FOSS, Ham, son of Daniel, d. Apr. 18, 1916, aged 86, m. July 17, 1856, in Rochester, Mrs. Lucy Hanson, both of Rochester.

FOSS, Jacob K., of Barrington, m. Feb. 23, 1862, in Strafford, Ann Maria Pearl, of Rochester.

FOSS, Eliphalet, of Strafford, m. Aug. 12, 1863, by Rev. James Rand, Cynthia D. Rand, of Farmington.

FOSS, Dr. David, m. (pub. Sept. 3, 1863, in Rochester), Leah M. Osborne.

FOSS, Jonathan, aged 73, m. Nov. 11, 1863, in Barnstead, Olive Ann Canney, aged 16.

FOSS, William H., of Strafford, m. Dec. 13, 1863, in Strafford, Fanny D. Boston, of Barrington.

FOSS, William H., of Dover, m. June 5, 1864, in Rochester, Adelaide Foss, of Gonic.

FOSS, Albert H., m. July 4, 1865, in Strafford, Lizzie M. Hall.

FOSS, Daniel B., of Madbury, m. Mar. 6, 1866, in Great Falls, Elizabeth A. Simpson, of Berwick, Me.

FOSS, George W., m. Mar. 10, 1866, by Rev. John Winkley, Mary Jane Foss, both of Strafford.

FOSS, George W., m. Mar. 10, 1866, by Rev. John Winkley, Hannah Foss, both of Strafford.

FOSS, Joel N., of Strafford, m. July 21, 1866, in Barrington, Livonia J. Gray, of Barrington.

FOSS, Hiram B., of Strafford, m. (pub. July 26, 1866, in Effingham), Mrs. Serena A. Jenness, of Eaton.

FOSS, Cotton, m. Jan. 20, 1867, in Straffortd, Vienna S. Berry.

FOSS, Samuel A., m. Feb. 21, 1867, in Barrington, Abbie D. Roberts.

FOSS, Isaac A., of Rochester, b. 1846, d. 1906, m. (pub. Apr. 18, 1867, in Great Falls), Flora J. Berrey, of Strafford, b. 1850, d. 1931.

FOSS, Edwin J., of Nottingham, m. (pub. Jan. 30, 1868, in Strafford), Viola Berry, of Strafford.

FOSS, Jacob W., son of Dennis, b. Jul. 27, 1846, d. Jan. 25, 1912, aged 65, m. Apr. 28, 1868, in Dover, Louisa A. Scruton, b. Oct. 27, 1846, d. Jan. 11, 1933, both of Strafford.

FOSS, Marshall B., of Madbury, b. 1847, d. 1923, m. June 2, 1868, in Dover, by Rev. Alden Sherwin, Mrs. Julia M. Banks, b. 1848, d. 1923, of Rockland, Me.

FOSS, Warren, of Dover, m. Aug. 5, 1868, in Great Falls, Mercy E. Demeritt, of Strafford.

FOSS, Nathaniel, of Milton, aged 21, m. Sept. 18, 1868, in Wakefield, by Rev. Asa Piper, Mary Ellen Drew, of Brookfield, aged 19.

FOSS, Mark, of Strafford, m. (pub. Jan. 20, 1870, in Newmarket), Emily Locke, of Epping.

FOSS, Rufus S., of Barnstead, m. (pub. Dec. 8, 1870, in Great Falls), Mary E. Tasker, of Strafford.

FOSS, James H., of Barrington, m. Apr. 17, 1874, in Dover, Mrs. Lucretia W. (Brooks) Dill, of Rochester, d. Mar. 12, 1912, aged 64, dau. of Samuel.

FOSTER, Rev. J. C., of Beverly, Mass., m. May 1, 1866, in Dover, Julia A. Gould, of Dover.

FOSTER, Rev. Caleb C., of Tunbridge, Vt., son of Moses B., d. July 4, 1914, aged 77, m. July 14, 1869, in Dover, Mary Anna Flanders, of Dover.

FOWLER, Jonathan, b. Sept. 5, 1769, m. Apr. 13, 1789, in Barrington, Elizabeth Cate, both of Barrington.

FOWLER, James H., of Cambridge, Mass., m. July 21, 1853, by Rev. Levi B. Tasker, in Sandwich, Sarah L. Smith, of Sandwich, dau. of Simeon.

FOWLER, John F., of Newmarket, m. Nov. 19, 1863, in Dover, Dorcas A. Winn, of Great Falls.

FOWLER, Alonzo, m. May 31, 1865, in Freedom, Vina Smart, both of Freedom.

FOX, Ira, of Wolfeboro, d. Nov. 21, 1853, aged 53, m. int. Oct. 1827, in Tuftonboro, Cyntihia Tebbetts, of Tuftonboro, d. June 10, 1873, aged 68.

FOX, Ira, m. Jan. 1, 1864, in Lebanon, Me., Emeline Dore.

FOX, Augustus, m. (pub. Apr. 21, 1864, in Portsmouth), Lauretta M. Hanson, of Portsmouth.

FOYE, Aaron, son of Eli, d. Aug. 1876, aged 78, m. Susannah Jones, b. Dec. 25, 1797, dau. of William.

FOYE, Eli, d. Oct. 1826, aged 60, m. Jan. 14, 1794, by Rev. Benjamin Balch, Sally Drew, d. May 1842, aged 70, both of Barrington.

FOYE, Joshua R., d. May 16, 1865, aged 69, m. (1) Mary F. ----, d. May 6, 1849, aged 45, m. (2) (pub. June 4, 1850, in Great Falls), Mrs. Sarah Batchelder.

FOYE, Merritt S., of great Falls, m. int. Nov. 22, 1856, in Lebanon, Me., Mary E. Goodwin.

FRANCIS, Robert W., m. (1) (pub. Oct. 2, 1856, in Durham), Mary A. Venner, of Durham, m. (2) Aug. 10, 1856, in Durham, Mary A. Varney, dau. of Thomas.

FREEMAN, David, of Barrington, m. int. Mar. 23, 1845, in Dover, Hannah H. Gray, of Dover.

FREEMAN, Miles, m. May 11, 1845, in Barrington, Lucinda Willey, both of Barrington.

FREEMAN, Henry D., of Dover, m. int. May 5, 1855, in Lebanon, Me., Phebe Nason.

FREEMAN, Samuel, of Chelsea, Mass., m. Mar. 24, 1864, in Great Falls, Annie A. Nelson, of Newfield.

FREEMAN, Edmund J., m. Aug. 17, 1864, by Rev. Ezra Haskell, Fanny H. Horne, dau. of Moses, both of Dover.

FREEMAN, Charles F., m. Jan. 29, 1869, by Rev. Robert S. Stubbs, Carrie A. Frost, both of Dover.

FREEMAN, Charles S., m. June 30, 1869, in St. Louis, Mo., Harriet A. Jenkins, of Milton.

FRENCH, William, d. Jan. 29, 1863, aged 69, m. Sept. 30, 1815, by Rev. John Osborne, Rebecca Ricker, d. Jan. 19, 1886, aged 89, both of Durham.

FRENCH, Joseph Y., of Newmarket, m. May 21, 1846, by Rev. John Parkman, Elizabeth R. (Hayes) Parshley, of Dover, wid. of John G., d. Feb. 11, 1849, aged 34.

FRENCH, Charles W., son of Joseph, b. 1816, d. 1850, m. Nov. 29, 1846, by Rev. Hezekiah D. Buzzell, Mary Willey, b. 1814, d. Feb. 9, 1890, both of New Durham.

FRENCH, Dr. George F., of Alexandria, Va., m. Oct. 14, 1862, in Washington, D.C., Clara A. Hill, dau. of Dr. Levi G.

FRENCH, George W. Jr., m. July 9, 1865, in Dover, Lizzie J. French, both of Newmarket.
FRENCH, Samuel D., of Newmarket, m. Nov. 23, 1869, in Dover, Carrie G. Stilson, of Dover, dau. of James.
FRENCH, Napoleon B., m. (pub. Feb. 3, 1870, in Great Falls), Mary H. Stanton.
FROST, John, son of Charles, d. Feb. 25, 1732, m. Sept. 4, 1702, by Joseph Hammon, Esq., Mary Pepperell, b. Sept. 5, 1685, d. 1766.
FROST, Reuben, m. Feb. 23, 1815, in Lebanon, Me., Lydia Austin.
FROST, Joseph Sheaf, of Milton, m. int. Feb. 12, 1820, in Lebanon, Me., Betsey Lord.
FROST, Alexander Raitt, of Rollinsford, d. Nov. 30, 1898, aged 65, m. (pub. Nov. 8, 1853, in South Berwick, Me.), Melissa Harvey, of South Berwick, Me., d. Aug. 4, 1878, aged 44, dau. of Stephen.
FROST, Joseph A., of Lawrence, Mass., m. Feb. 26, 1862, in Dover, Della P. Alvord, of Hope, Me.
FROST, Howard, of Sanford, Me., m. (pub. Nov. 6, 1862, in Ossipee), Lydia F. Roles.
FROST, Marcellus, of Newcastle, m. Nov. 25, 1863, in Dover, Susan M. Tuttle, of Dover.
FROST, Samuel B., m. May 24, 1864, in Dover, Annie L. Chase, both of Dover.
FROST, Leonard F., of Haverhill, Mass., m. Jan. 20, 1868, in Dover, Esther Grant, of Wells, Me.
FROST, David, m. May 9, 1868, by Rev. Robert S. Stubbs, Laura C. Chapman, both of Dover.
FROST, John, of Salem, Mass., m. Nov. 12, 1868, in Dover, Mrs. Nancy Odiorne, of Durham.
FROST, Leonard, of Eliot, Me., m. (pub. June 16, 1870, in Great Falls), Nellie F. Shapleigh, of Great Falls.
FRYE, Benjamin, b. Dec. 13, 1794, d. May 27, 1864, m. May 4, 1823, in Lebanon, Me., Jane Furbish, bpt. Jun. 16, 1802, d. Jan. 26, 1879, aged 76, dau. of Daniel.
FRYE, James, of Shapleigh, Me., b. Aug. 28, 1808, d. Jun. 13, 1852, m. Nov. 14, 1830, in Lebanon, Me., Elizabeth J. Burrows, b. 1810, d. Sep. 14, 1894.
FRYE, John, son of Benjamin, b. Mar. 24, 1824, m. Oct. 1849, in Lebanon, Me., Catherine T. Gerrish.
FRYE, Nathaniel, d. Dec. 20, 1898, m. (1) Jan. 12, 1853, by Rev. Levi B. Tasker, in Sandwich, Eliza A. Tappan, both of Sandwich, m. (2) Nov. 30, 1882, Mrs. Mariah J. Hoag. wid. of Uriah J.

FRYE, Russell E., m. Oct. 10, 1867, by Rev. Robert S. Stubbs, Mary S. Gilmore, both of Dover.

FRYE, Frank O., of Dover, m. (pub. May 27, 1869, in Rochester), Jennie C. Kenniston, of Saco, Me.

FRYE, Joseph W., m. Dec. 2, 1869, in Dover, Carrie J. Locke, both of Dover.

FURBER, Richard, of Rochester, m. Oct. 12, 1786, by Rev. Benjamin Balch, Polly Powers, of Madbury.

FURBER, Pierce Powers, of Farmington, b. Aug. 20, 1788, m. Oct. 12, 1811, in Barrington, Mehitable Winkley, b. Aug. 5, 1789, dau. of Samuel.

FURBER, Richard Jr., of Barrington, m. Jan. 19, 1812, by Rev. Enos George, Mary Winkley, of Barrington, dau. of Samuel.

FURBER, Col. Edmund, d. July 4, 1881, aged 91, m. (1) Mar. 13, 1817, by Rev. Joseph Haven, Deborah Walker, d. 1845, aged 50, both of Farmington, m. (2) Mar. 21, 1847, by Rev. Homer Barrows, Elizabeth L. Babb, b. 1805, d. 1887.

FURBER, Isaac, of Lee, m. int. Jan. 23, 1824, in Lee, Mary Smith, of Brentwood.

FURBER, William L., of Wolfeboro, m. Oct. 14, 1845, in Wolfeboro, Louisa A. Cate, of Brookfield, d. Jan. 6, 1907, aged 84, dau. of Samuel.

FURBER, Benjamin F., of Alton, son of Edward, d. Sept. 8, 1904, aged 82, m. June 4, 1853, in Dover, Sarah J. Babb, of Dover, b. 1831, d. 1874, dau. of Benjamin F.

FURBER, Frank B., m. Feb. 18, 1874, in Lee, Isabella F. Demeritt, both of Lee.

FURBISH, Richard Jr., son of Richard, m. May 26, 1793, by Rev. Isaac Hasey, Hannah Blaisdell.

FURBISH, Nathaniel, m. Nov. 24, 1822, in Lebanon, Me., Jane McCrillis.

FURBISH, David, m. int. Nov. 15, 1832, in Lebanon, Me., Sophia Jones.

FURBISH, Giles William, m. May 21, 1837, in Lebanon, Me., Sabra Furbish.

FURBISH, Stephen, m. Nov. 28, 1839, in Lebanon, Me., Sally B. Wentworth.

FURBUSH, John, m. Jun. 1, 1828, in Lebanon, Me., Ann Furbush.

FURBUSH, Joseph 2nd, m. int. May 25, 1833, in Lebanon, Me., Lucinda Chase, of No. Berwick, Me.

FURBUSH, Joseph, m. Jun. 14, 1832, in Lebanon, Me., Polly Nichols.

FURBUSH, Richard, m. int. Oct. 4, 1832, in Lebanon, Me., Phebe Chase, of No. Berwick, Me.

FURBUSH, Webber, of Rome, m. int. Feb. 21, 1822, in Lebanon, Me., Betsey Furbush.

FURBUSH, Joseph, m. Nov. 23, 1847, by Rev. Charles Corson, Elizabeth Austin.

FURBUSH, George F., m. int. Mar. 11, 1861, in Lebanon, Me., Louisa N. Fernald.

FURBUSH, David, aged 68, of New Durham, m. Nov. 13, 1875, in Middleton, Mrs. Martha A. Perkins, aged 54, of Middleton. [Was this a second marriage?]

FURNESS, Robert, son of Patrick, b. May 11, 1788, d. Mar. 27, 1840, m. Apr. 14, 1814, Mary French, of Durham, b. Oct. 16, 1791, d. May 22, 1885.

FURNESS, Edward, son of Patrick, d. Jan. 5, 1822, m. May 27, 1816, Charlotte Dutch, of Newmarket, b. July 25, 1794, d. Apr. 5, 1874.

FURNESS, Charles E., m. Mar. 12, 1869, in Rochester, Mary E. Foss, both of Manchester.

GAGE, Moses, son of Moses, d. 1846, aged 83, m. Apr. 2, 1794, in Wakefield, Dolly Dearborn, d. Dec. 6, 1858, aged 84, both of Wakefield.

GAGE, James, son of John, b. 1779, d. Feb. 23, 1836, m. early as 1803, Elizabeth Hussey, d. Sep. 8, 1855, aged 70.

GAGE, Jonathan, son of Moses, d. Jul. 22, 1840, aged 70, m. May 22, 1818, by Rev. J. W. Clary, Elizabeth Ham, b. Jun. 3, 1783, d. Jul. 11, 1862.

GAGE, William H., of Lowell, Mass., d. Jan. 25, 1856, aged 49, m. Aug. 21, 1836, Harriet C. Libbey, d. May 3, 1885, aged 75.

GAGE, Moses, b. 1818, d. 1919, m. Jun. 20, 1841, by Rev. Elihu Scott, Elizabeth Hussey, d. Feb. 10, 1855, aged 34.

GALE, Stephen, of Gilmanton, m. Nov. 26, 1805, in Louden, Sarah Drew, of Barrington.

GALE, James, m. Aug. 4, 1864, in Effingham, Jennie M. Clark, both of Malden, Mass.

GALE, William, m. Apr. 29, 1865, in Dover, Emma T. Salmon, of Rochester.

GALE, Nathaniel S., m. May 8, 1866, in Laconia, Emily A. Peaslee, both of Gilmanton.

GALLIGAN, James or John, of Cincinnati, Ohio, m. Mar. 1, 1869, by Rev. Robert S. Stubbs, Isadore V. Nute, of Dover.

GANNETT, Matthew, son of Matthew, m. Dec. 17, 1824, in Tamworth, Betsey Goodwin, d. Jun. 10, 1849, aged 48, both of Tamworth.

GANNETT, William G., of Tamworth, son of Matthew or Matthew Jr., aged 31, d. Aug. 12, 1896, m. Jun. 3, 1857, in Sandwich, Sarah Quimby, of Sandwich, aged 21, d. Nov. 24, 1895, dau. of J. Smith Quimby.

GARDNER, Benjamin J., 78 yrs., of Tamworth, m. Jan. 31, 1863, in Tamworth, Mrs. Deborah Howard, 72 yrs., of Porter.

GARDNER, Charles B., m. Jan. 16, 1868, in Dover, Mary N. Tucker, both of Dover.

GARDNER, James A., m. Jan. 13, 1869, by Rev. Francis E. Abbott, Alta Augusta Moulton.

GARLAND, Thomas, of Lee, d. 1832, m. Aug. 6, 1777, Hannah Ham, b. 1758, d. May 16, 1844, dau. of Joseph.

GARLAND, Samuel, m. Jan. 26, 1786, by Rev. Benjamin Balch, Abigail Drew, both of Barrington.

GARLAND, Dodavah, son of Ebenezer, m. Jul. 20, 1789, by Rev. Isaac Hasey, Esther Bartlett.

GARLAND, Benjamin, m. Jan. 18, 1790, by Rev. Benjamin Balch, Polly Balch, both of Barrington.

GARLAND, Nathaniel, of Somersworth, son of Nathaniel, b. Jun. 7, 1765, m. Feb. 25, 1790, by Rev. Joseph Haven, Hannah Witherell, of Rochester.

GARLAND, Isaac, m. Nov. 24, 1795, by Rev. Benjamin Balch, Lydia Babb, both of Barrington.

GARLAND, James, m. Dec. 11, 1800, by Rev. Joseph Haven, Abigail Jenness, d. Mar. 28, 1828, aged 49, both of Rochester.

GARLAND, John, of Rochester, m. Feb. 8, 1829, by Rev. Cephas H. Kent, Polly Ham, of Barrington.

GARLAND, Charles D., of Newmarket, m. Nov. 6, 1844, in Brookfield, Lucy Dearborn, of Durham.

GARLAND, Eli, m. (1) Dec. 10, 1850, by Elder Josiah Glines, Abigail Corson, b. 1832, d. 1854, dau. of James, both of New Durham, m. (2) int. Nov. 12, 1855, in New Durham, Sarah Jane Cotton, of New Durham, d. July 1877, aged 44.

GARLAND, Nathaniel B., of Moultonboro, aged 21, m. May 26, 1852, by Rev. Levi B. Tasker, in Sandwich, Lydia Bennett, of Moultonboro, aged 18.

GARLAND, John W., of Newton, Mass., m. Apr. 4, 1867, by Rev. James Rand, Olive J. Leighton, of Great Falls.

GARVIN, William R., m. Apr. 2, 1862, in Rollinsford, Frances H. Yeaton, dau. of Leavitt H., both of Rollinsford..

GEAR, Samuel, m. May 4, 1790, by Rev. Benjamin Balch, Abigail Sherbourn, d. Feb. 2, 1844, aged 78, both of Barrington.

GEAR, James, of Lee, m. int. Mar. 31, 1843, in Lee, Abigail Watson, of Barrington, d. Oct. 27, 1867, aged 41.

GEAR, Daniel, m. Apr. 24, 1863, in Barrington, Rosina Brock, both of Barrington.

GEAR, David, m. Jan. 2, 1866, in Strafford, Frances J. Chesley, both of Barrington.

GEAR, James W., of Methuen, Mass., son of William, m. Jan. 19, 1869, by Rev. Alvan Tobey, Annie P. Hodgdon, of Greenland, dau. of Charles.

GEORGE, Jesse, of E. Rochester, m. Mar. 10, 1866, in E. Rochester, Elizabeth Booth, of Whitney, England.

4) **GERRISH**, Andrew, son of Timothy, b. Aug. 4, 1724, m. before 1748, Hannah Norton, b. 1720, d. 1790, dau. of Capt. Constant Norton.

GERRISH, John, m. int. Mar. 27, 1785, by Rev. Isaac Hasey, Elizabeth Warren.

GERRISH, Benjamin Jr., of Berwick, Me., b. 1758, d. 1792, m. Dec. 23, 1788, Miriam (Raitt) Ferguson, wid. of William, b. Jun. 29, 1762, d. 1832, dau. of Alexander.

GERRISH, William, m. Apr. 1, 1793, by Rev. Isaac Hasey, Molly Knox.

GERRISH, George, m. Feb. 11, 1799, by Rev. Isaac Hasey, Elizabeth Thompson Furbish.

GERRISH, Levi, m. int. Oct. 5, 1805, in Lebanon, Me., Betsey Yeaton.

GERRISH, James, m. int. Oct. 24, 1817, in Lebanon, Me., Sophia Goodwin.

GERRISH, Nathaniel, son of John, m. Feb. 7, 1819, in Salem, Mass., Fanny Millet.

GERRISH, Ivory, m. May 14, 1820, in Lebanon, Me., Dorothy Farnham.

GERRISH, John, m. int. Feb. 3, 1821, in Lebanon, Me., Elizabeth Gerrish.

GERRISH, Timothy, m. Jul. 1824, by Rev. James Weston, Betsey Nichols.

GERRISH, John Jr., m. Dec. 25, 1828, in Lebanon, Me., Hannah Blaisdell, dau. of Jonathan.

GERRISH, Hiram, m. May 3, 1842, in Lebanon, Me., Sophia Lord.

GERRISH, Daniel, m. Oct. 27, 1842, in Lebanon, Me., Sally Hodgon.

GERRISH, Jacob Goodwin, m. Apr. 30, 1848, in Lebanon, Me., Mary Elizabeth Goodwin.

GERRISH, Ebenezer T., m. int. May 13, 1854, in Lebanon, Hannah E. Wingate, of Rochester.

GERRISH, Elisha Proctor, m. Oct. 14, 1856, in Lebanon, Me., Elizabeth M. Hersom.

GERRISH, James M., m. int. Mar. 15, 1858, in Lebanon, Me., Phebe H. Hobbs, of Sanford, Me.

GERRISH, Benjamin F., m. June 11, 1863, in Wakefield, Ruth B. Stevens, both of Middleton.

GERRISH, C. H., of Madbury, m. Oct. 17, 1867, in Strafford, Sarah E. Shepard, of Strafford.

GERRISH, Aurin J., of Deerfield, m. Nov. 8, 1867, by Rev. Alden Sherwin, Josephine S. Jenness, of Dover.

GERRISH, Alphonzo D., of Berwick, Me., son of William H., d. Jan. 5, 1915, aged 68, m. (pub. June 17, 1869, in S. Berwick, Me.), Mary E. Smith, of Rochester.

GERRISH, J. E., of Northwood, m. (pub. July 7, 1870, in Strafford), Fanny Campbell, of Reading, Mass.

GERRISH, Oliver F., m. July 10, 1870, in Portsmouth, Florence Louisa Norton.

GIBBS, John W., of Lebanon, Me., m. Apr. 25, 1867, in Great Falls, Sarah C. Jones, of Middleton.

GILMAN, Col. David, of Newmarket, b. Jun. 9, 1735, d. May 9, 1827, m. (1) Betsey ----, m. (2) Jul. 21, 1778, by Rev. Nathaniel Ewer, Sarah (Smith) Hilton, d. Dec. 1788, m. (3) Betsey Ayer, widow.

GILMAN, Porter, m. Apr. 3, 1786, in Brookfield, Hannah Hall.

GILMAN, David, b. Aug. 19, 1779, d. 1847, m. early as 1799, Rhoda Hunt, b. Sept. 27, 1779, d. 1860.

GILMAN, Stephen, of Alton, m. Sep. 30, 1811, by Rev. Isaac Smith, Mary S. Gale, of Gilmanton, d. May 24, 1829, aged 37.

GILMAN, Daniel (David), of Eaton, m. Mar. 14, 1821, in Lebanon, Me., Hannah Jackson.

GILMAN, Manoah G. W., of Alton, son of Levi, b. 1821, d. 1864, m. (pub. Jan. 31, 1843, in Gilford), Mercy Grant, of Gilford, b. 1815, d. 1861.

GILMAN, Adarial, of Quincy, Ill., son of Avery, d. Nov. 18, 1889, aged 67, m. (1) Aug. 30, 1855, in Dover, Elizabeth T. Gilman, of Dover, b. Oct. 23, 1825, d. May 29, 1856, aged 31, dau. of Theophilius, m. (2) Sarah H. Gilman, d. Feb. 9, 1879, aged 54, dau. of Theophilius.

GILMAN, Benjamin, of Wakefield, aged 40, m. Oct. 30, 1858, in Brookfield, Mary A. Pike, of Wolfeboro, aged 30.

GILMAN, William B., of Somersworth, m. Nov. 6, 1859, in Tuftonboro, Maria E. Abbott, of Ossipee, d. Feb. 5, 1915, aged 78.

GILMAN, Daniel F., m. (pub. Dec. 4, 1862, in Alton), Jennie M. Edgerly, of New Durham.

GILMAN, Phineas G., of Ossipee, d. Aug. 4, 1867, aged 24, m. May 6, 1866, in Ossipee, Jennie L. Clark, of Tuftonboro.

GILMAN, Charles H., m. Oct. 12, 1867, in Sandwich, Emma E. Magoon.

GILMAN, Lawrence A., m. June 18, 1868, in Great Falls, Hattie A. Foss, both of Great Falls.

GILMAN, George, of New Durham, m. July 15, 1868, in Alton, Clara Mooney, of Alton, dau. of Charles.

GILMAN, Daniel W., of Denmark, Me., m. Feb. 27, 1869, in Great Falls, Isabel B. Drew, of Great Falls.

GILMAN, Joseph W., m. Nov. 8, 1869, in Dover, Martha A. Gale, both of Kingston.

GILPATRICK, John, b. 1805, d. Mar. 13, 1890, m. Sept. 9, 1835, in Dover, by Rev. Daniel P. Cill, Abigail Young, d. May 8, 1847, aged 33, dau. of John.

GILPATRICK, William H., m. (pub. Apr. 26, 1866, in Northwood), Mrs. Nancy J. Leighton. (was this a second marriage?)

GLIDDEN, Caleb, m. Nov. 16, 1798, by Rev. Isaac Smith, Dolly Gilman, dau. of Jonathan, both of Gilmanton.

GLIDDEN, George, m. (1) (pub. June 7, 1836, in Alton), Lucy Ann Flanders, d. 1851, m. (2) (pub. Aug. 16, 1853, in Gilmanton), Mrs. Adaline L. (Flanders) Sawyer, of Gilmanton, wid. of Noah L., d. Jun. 26, 1892, aged 72, dau. of Jedediah.

GLIDDEN, Levi, son of Benjamin, d. Apr. 3, 1902, aged 79, m. pub. Jul. 14, 1846, in Wolfeboro, Livona Dow, both of Alton.

GLIDDEN, Edmund C., of Dover, m. July 7, 1861, in Rochester, Mary Abby Morse, of Tuftonboro, d. Feb. 12, 1864, aged 25.

GLIDDEN, Rev. Noah, of Gilmanton, m. Jan. 19, 1863, in Alton, Martha A. Marden, of Epsom.

GLIDDEN, Joseph, aged 60, m. Apr. 5, 1863, in Tamworth, Mrs. Elizabeth Thompson, aged 21.

GLIDDEN, Howard M., of Lee, son of <u>Deac</u>. Guy, b. 1842, d. 1918, m. int. Dec. 1865, in Lee, m. Jan. 3, 1867, in Burnham, Mabelle F. Wiggin, of Durham, b. 1845, <u>d. 1912</u>, dau. of Nathaniel P.

GLIDDEN, John, of Brookfield, aged 55, m. int. Jan. 29, 1866, in Brookfield, Mrs. Mary J. Emery, widow, of Wolfeboro, aged 37.

GLIDDEN, Henry S., m. Apr. 4, 1866, in Dover, <u>Sarah</u> Ella Walker, <u>b. 1848, d. Jan. 13, 1930, dau. of Stephen, both of Dover</u>.

GLIDDEN, Howard M., of Lee, <u>son of Guy</u>, b. 1842, m. int. Dec. 1865, in Lee, <u>m. Jan. 3, 1867, in Durham</u>, Mabelle F. Wiggin, of Durham, b. 1845, <u>dau. of Nathaniel P</u>.

GLIDDEN, Charles R., <u>of Ossipee</u>, m. Feb. 26, 1870, in Dover, Mary A. Knights, <u>of Lee</u>.

GLINES, Asahel, of Moultonboro, m. Feb. 23, 1859, in Sandwich, Lydia Ann Foss, of Sandwich, <u>dau. of David</u>.

GLOVER, George, d. Apr. 14, 1879, aged 57, m. June <u>16</u>, 1843, by Elder Samuel Sherburne, Hannah Clay, <u>both of Barrington</u>.

GOING, Samuel, m. int. Jan. 1801, in Lebanon, Me., Mary Brackett.

GOING, George 2nd, m. Jan. 19, 1828, in Lebanon, Me., Anna Abbott, both of Sanford, Me.

GOLDSMITH, William H., <u>b. Feb. 12, 1841, d. July 28, 1918</u>, m. (pub. Mar. 18, 1858, in Ossipee), Martha Hodgdon.

GOLDSMITH, James A., <u>b. June 5, 1832, d. Dec. 8, 1902</u>, m. (pub. Oct. 11, 1860, in Ossipee), Amerette F. Thompson, <u>b. Oct. 6, 1839, d. Sept. 17, 1917</u>.

GOLDSMITH, Abner, m. Sept. 12, 1867, in Ossipee, Mrs. Lavinia Goldsmith, wid. of Jonathan, d. Jan. 2, 1877, aged 77.

GOOCH, Deac. Joseph, of Alton, <u>b. 1793, d. 1875, m. (1) Nancy N. ---, b. 1794, d. 1848</u>, m. <u>(2)</u> Nov. 29, 1849, by Elder William K. Lucas, Susan Stevens, of New Durham, d. Jan. 1882, aged 82.

GOODHUE, Thomas, of Brookfield, aged 22, m. int. Nov. 27, 1867, in Brookfield, Sarah E. Witham, of Brookfield, aged 19.

GOODRICH, James A., of Berwick, Me., d. Oct. 14, 1847, aged 72, m. Aug. 2, 1803, by Rev. Joseph Haven, Sarah Twombly, of Milton, <u>b. Mar. 15, 1785</u>, d. Sep. 11, 1846, aged 61, <u>dau. of Samuel</u>.

GOODRICH, Samuel, m. Jul. 7, 1816, in Lebanon, Me., Molly Lord.

GOODRICH, Elisha, m. Aug. 2, 1821, in Lebanon, Me., Lois Brown.

GOODRICH, Isaac, of Berwick, Me., b. 1818, d. 1872, m. int. Feb. 26, 1843, in Lebanon, Me., Betsey Wallingford, b. 1811, d. 1884.

GOODRICH, James L., d. Jul. 26, 1861, aged 36, m. (1) Sarah ----, d. Nov. 18, 1846, aged 24, m. (2) (pub. Apr. 5, 1853, in Somersworth), Mary E. Sanborn, d. Dec. 28, 1908, aged 77, both of Berwick, Me.

GOODWIN, Moses, m. Aug. 19, 1773, by Rev. Isaac Hasey, Abigail Blaisdell.

GOODWIN, Elder William Jr., d. Sep. 12, 1817, aged 41, m. Feb. 18, 1796, by Rev. Matthew Merriam, Molly Yeaton, b. Apr. 25, 1772, dau. of Richard.

GOODWIN, Ephraim, m. Jun. 23, 1802, by Elder Zebedee Delano, Polly Lord.

GOODWIN, Ebenezer, d. Jan. 12, 1864, aged 84, m. (1) Feb. 17, 1807, Mary Fernald, b. Sep. 11, 1779, d. Feb. 9, 1832, dau. of Capt. Mark, m. (2) Keziah ----, d. Mar. 8, 1877, aged 87.

GOODWIN, John, m. Sep. 22, 1811, in Lebanon, Me., Anna Lord.

GOODWIN, Jacob Jr., m. Oct. 24, 1819, in Lebanon, Me., Ruth Blaisdell.

GOODWIN, Ivory, m. int. Nov. 13, 1819, in Lebanon, Me., Relief Jones.

GOODWIN, Elisha Jr., m. (1) Jun. 10, 1821, in Lebanon, Me., Sally Worster, m. (2) Jul. 30, 1842, in Lebanon, Me., Julian Ann Hanscom.

GOODWIN, Benjamin, m. (1) int. Sep. 8, 1821, in Lebanon, Me., Olive Moody, m. (2) int. Dec. 21, 1828, in Lebanon, Me., Mrs. Amy Shapleigh.

GOODWIN, Daniel, m. Dec. 12, 1821, in Lebanon, Me., Charlotte Wentworth.

GOODWIN, Urban, son of Simeon, b. Jan. 1, 1793, m. Jan. 10, 1822, Peazy Horn.

GOODWIN, Otis, m. Jan. 3, 1828, in Lebanon, Me., Charlotte Nisbett.

GOODWIN, Tristram F., m. Jan. 8, 1829, by Elder Zebedee Delano, Miriam B. Wood.

GOODWIN, Mark, m. Sep. 1, 1831, by Rev. Daniel Reynolds, Lydia Wentworth.

GOODWIN, Waldron, son of Jacob, b. May 31, 1806, m. int. Apr. 20, 1833, in Lebanon, Me., Sarah Jane Goodwin.

GOODWIN, Amos, m. int. Jun. 8, 1833, in Lebanon, Me., Julian Smith.

GOODWIN, John, m. May 10, 1835, in Lebanon, Me., Amy Smith.

GOODWIN, Capt. Luther, m. int. Apr. 30, 1836, in Lebanon, Me., Ruth Ricker.

GOODWIN, Wentworth, m. (1) Mar. 26, 1820, Sally Gowell, m. (2) Jan. 11, 1837, in Lebanon, Me., Betsey Gowell.

GOODWIN, William, m. int. Oct. 14, 1837, in Lebanon, Me., Lydia Jones.

GOODWIN, Charles E., m. Dec. 24, 1837, by Elder Zebedee Delano, Dorcas Goodwin, of No. Berwick, Me.

GOODWIN, William, of Shapleigh, Me., m. Sep. 19, 1838, in Lebanon, Me., Hannah Goodwin.

GOODWIN, Moses, of Acton, Mass., m. Feb. 3, 1839, in Lebanon, Me., Katherine M. Clark.

GOODWIN, Thomas L., of Somersworth, m. Apr. 18, 1841, by Elder David H. Lord, Betsey Wentworth.

GOODWIN, Thomas, of Rochester, m. May 9, 1841, in Lebanon, Me., Mary Tebbets.

GOODWIN, Ephraim L., m. Aug. 28, 1841, by Rev. Theodore Stevens, Elizabeth L. Goodwin.

GOODWIN, Nahum G., m. Oct. 14, 1848, in Lebanon, Me., Melissa Jane Glidden.

GOODWIN, Blaisdell J., m. May 28, 1849, by Elden Oren B. Chaney, Julia Ann Worster.

GOODWIN, Amaziah, m. int. Feb. 16, 1850, in Lebanon, Me., Hannah Drew.

GOODWIN, Charles E., d. May 8, 1877, aged 46, m. Nov. 25, 1857, in Sandwich, Lucinda B. Mudgett, both of Sandwich.

GOODWIN, Nathan, of Tamworth, m. (pub. July 18, 1861, in Ossipee), Mrs. Mary E. Brimmer, b. Sept. 29, 1823, d. Dec. 28, 1884.

GOODWIN, Richard H., m. Jan. 7, 1862, by Elder John H. Garmon, Susan J. Nowell, of Sanford, Me.

GOODWIN, Jeremiah, m. Mar. 26, 1862, by Rev. James Rand, Esther A. Cooper, both of S. Berwick, Me.

GOODWIN, John A., of Milton, m. (pub. May 15, 1862, in Concord), Mrs. Pamelia Ann (Davis) Pinkham, wid. of James H.

GOODWIN, Edward L., of W. Milton, m. July 4, 1862, in Lee, Emily M. Hersey, of Tuftonboro.

GOODWIN, Naham F., m. int. Oct. 13, 1862, in Lebanon, Me., Amanda F. Hall, of No. Berwick, Me.

GOODWIN, John H., of Berwick, Me., m. Dec. 31, 1863, in S. Berwick, Me., Eugene F. Pike, of S. Berwick, Me.

GOODWIN, Lorenzo D., m. May 13, 1865, in Lebanon, Me., Mary E. Butler.
GOODWIN, Edwin R., b. 1838, d. 1894, m. July 4, 1865, in Andover, Mass., Helen L. Watt, b. 1842, d. 1926, both of S. Berwick, Me.
GOODWIN, George Millett, of Lebanon, Me., m. Dec. 5, 1865, in Dover, Hannah Connacher, of Great Falls, b. Oct. 26, 1838, m. (2) Oct. 19, 1875, by Rev. Samuel Lord, Emma C. Horne.
GOODWIN, Samuel H., d. Jan. 13, 1918, aged 73, m. Apr. 3, 1866, in Dover, Helen E. Gowen, both of Dover.
GOODWIN, Charles W., of Acton, Me., m. (pub. Nov. 15, 1866, in E. Rochester), Luella Barton, of Cambridge, Mass.
GOODWIN, Frederick A., m. Nov. 20, 1866, by Rev. Ezra Haskell, Nellie Booker, both of Gardner, Me.
GOODWIN, Albion N., son of Asa, d. June 16, 1910, aged 65, m. Jan. 30, 1867, in Dover, Elma P. Glidden, both of Rochester.
GOODWIN, Joseph W., b. 1838, d. 1915, m. June 19, 1867, in Wolfeboro, Nellie A. Furber, b. 1846, d. 1921, dau. of Jethro.
GOODWIN, Henry H., of Dover, m. June 25, 1867, in Great Falls, Belle Davis, dau. of Owen W.
GOODWIN, James M. m. Dec. 19, 1867, in Lebanon, Me., Ellen M. Carroll, of Sanford, Me.
GOODWIN, Horace J., of S. Berwick, Me., m. Mar. 17, 1869, in Dover, Electra J. Bragdon, of York, Me.
GOODWIN, Fred J., of W. Lebanon, Me., m. Mar. 28, 1869, in Great Falls, Ellen Burke, of Rochester.
GOODWIN, Charles E., m. (pub. Aug. 5, 1869, in Great Falls), Lizzie M. Smith, dau. of Edward A., both of Great Falls.
GOODWIN, Elisha, of Wolfeboro, m. Sept. 2, 1869, in Boston, Mass., M. A. Smith, of Boston, Mass.
GOODWIN, Benjamin F., m. (1) int. Oct. 13, 1869, in Lebanon, Me., Elizabeth Morrison, m. (2) Apr. 13, 1875, in Milton, Emma A. Wentworth, of Acton, Me.
GOODWIN, Lucius S., m. (pub. Jan. 27, 1870, in Great Falls), Sarah C. Wheeler.
GOODWIN, Charles E., m. May 2, 1870, in Dover, Sarah F. Fall, both of S. Berwick, Me.
GOODWIN, John A., of Farmington, m. Aug. 13, 1870, in Dover, Abbie M. Tibbetts, of Dover.
GOOKIN, John, m. Feb. 11, 1866, in Great Falls, Lucy Andrews.
GORDING, Daniel C., of Perkinsville, Vt., m. int. Aug. 15, 1834, in Lebanon, Me., Rebecca Tebbets.

GORDON, William, m. Dec. 18, 1862, in Dover, Agnes A. Nalty, both of Saco, Me.

GORDON, Ebenezer H. Jr., of Lawrence, Mass., son of Ebenezer, m. Jan. 24, 1864, in Dover, Lucy A. Chapman, of Newmarket.

GORDON, Ezra B., m. Mar. 23, 1864, in Rochester, Eliza Riddy, of Great Falls.

GORDON, Henry, m. (pub. Apr. 27, 1865, in Portsmouth), Sarah F. Allard, of Newington.

GORDON, Charles C., of Saco, Me., m. Oct. 9, 1869, in Dover, Nellie G. Percy, of Biddeford, Me.

GOULD, Robert, d. May 16, 1882, aged 58, m. (pub. Dec. 15, 1846, in Great Falls), Mary Wiggin, d. Sept. 8, 1890, aged 64.

GOVE, Jonathan, m. (pub. Nov. 29, 1866, in Amesbury, Mass.), Mrs. Mercy R. Holeman, both of Nottingham.

GOWELL, Benjamin, d. 1825, m. Sep. 1, 1774, by Rev. Matthew Merriam, Susanna Pike, dau. of Thomas, d. Aug. 22, 1844, both of Berwick, Me.

GOWELL, Benjamin Jr., b. 1784, d. Nov. 23, 1838, m. int. Dec. 17, 1808, in Lebanon, Me., Olive Ricker, d. Nov. 21, 1851.

GOWELL, John, m. Feb. 17, 1818, in Lebanon, Me., Lucy Frost, d. 1878.

GOWELL, Benjamin, m. int. Jun. 1, 1868, in Lebanon, Me., Lydia A. Willand, d. Jan. 22, 1889.

GOWEN, Ezckicl Jr., m. May 4, 1812, in Lebanon, Me., Love Frost, both of Sanford, Me.

GOWEN, James, d. Apr. 17, 1865, m. int. Jan. 3, 1818, in Lebanon, Me., Nabby Hanscom, d. Jun. 11, 1876, aged 81.

GOWEN, Daniel, m. int. Sep. 5, 1818, in Lebanon, Me., Abigail Libbey, d. Jun. 11, 1876, aged 81.

GOWEN, Walter, of Sanford, Me., d. Jul. 19, 1887, m. Dec. 5, 1822, by Elder Zebedee Delano, Catharine Hanscom, d. Apr. 20, 1832, dau. of Isaac.

GOWEN, Horace, m. (1) July 23, 1865, in Dover, Jennie A. Perkins, both of Dover, m. (2) July 6, 1869, in Dover, Sarah F. Roberts, of Rollinsford.

GRAHAM, James, m. May 1, 1864, in Rochester, Mrs. Catherine H. (Wallace) Clark, d. Apr. 1, 1896, aged 71, dau. of Thomas, both of Rochester.

GRANT, William Jr., of Lebanon, Me., son of William, b. 1745, d. 1820, m. Nov. 23, 1769, Mary Wentworth.

GRANT, Paul, m. Jan. 12, 1809, in Barrington, Alice Sloper, both of Barrington.

GRANT, John, m. Mar. 15, 1821, by Elder John Blaisdell, Eunice Jones, d. Jun. 17, 1877.

GRANT, William, of York, Me., m. int. Jun. 7, 1823, in Lebanon, Me., Theodotia Langton.

GRANT, Joseph, m. int. Jun. 10, 1827, in Lebanon, Me., Sarah C. Merrill, of Brownfield, Me.

GRANT, Daniel Jr., m. Dec. 31, 1827, in Lebanon, Me., Susan Foss.

GRANT, Joseph, m. int. Feb. 10, 1830, in Lebanon, Me., Mary A. Merrill, of Brownfield, Me.

GRANT, Eli, d. July 16, 1886, aged 77, m. (1) July 31, 1831, by Rev. John G. Dow, Mary Ann Snell, d. Dec. 25, 1843, aged 32, both of Dover, m. (2) Dec. 25, 1845, by Rev. Oliver Ayer, Harriet E. Snell, d. Sept. 14, 1851, aged 39, m. (3) Pamelia Varney, d. Jan. 26, 1895, aged 64.

GRANT, Samuel, son of Capt. Daniel, b. Jan. 28, 1813, m. Mar. 31, 1833, in Lebanon, Me., Esther Hanson, d. Oct. 2, 1860.

GRANT, Daniel, m. int. Nov. 11, 1834, in Lebanon, Me., Sarah Ricker, dau. of Moses.

GRANT, Moses Ricker, son of Capt. Daniel, b. Aug. 24, 1810, d. Feb. 23, 1859, m. Jun. 4, 1843, in Lebanon, Me., Esther Ann Blaisdell, d. Oct. 2, 1860.

GRANT, Edward, m. int. May 14, 1847, in Lebanon, Me., Sophia Downs, of Somersworth.

GRANT, Joseph Leavitt, m. Mar. 29, 1851, by Elder Elias Hutchins, Julia (Hanscom) Sargent, wid. of Amos, b. June 14, 1823, dau. of Alpheus.

GRANT, Henry, d. July 11, 1881, aged 42, m. Oct. 6, 1855, by Elder Elias Hutchins, Ruth E. Chase, d. Sept. 6, 1862, aged 23, both of Dover.

GRANT, Charles, m. int. May 22, 1858, in Lebanon, Me., Huldah E. Thompson, of Kennebunk, Me.

GRANT, John, m. Jan. 6, 1864, in Great Falls, Statira A. Quimby, d. Feb. 4, 1912, aged 67, dau. of James M., both of Great Falls.

GRANT, James Weston, son of Joseph, b. Nov. 16, 1833, m. int. May 22, 1865, in Lebanon, Me., Lucinda T. Freeman, of Augusta, Me.

GRANT, Lucian H., son of Micah, d. Sept. 21, 1899, aged 59, m. (1) May 19, 1866, by Rev. James Rand, Emeline S. Witham, dau. of Joseph, both of Dover, m. (2) Jan. 27, 1893, in Dover, Elizabeth Mullen, of Ireland.

GRANT, Henry, m. May 23, 1866, in Rochester, Flora M. Smith, of Gilsum.

GRANT, Henry, m. Nov. 21, 1867, by Rev. Robert S. Stubbs, Louisa H. Chase, both of Dover.

GRANT, Isaiah, of Acton, Me., d. Mar. 24, 1886, m. int. Sep. 15, 1868, in Lebanon, Me., Mary A. Worster.

GRANT, Edward F., m. Feb. 6, 1869, by Rev. Robert S. Stubbs, Sarah Hurd, both of Dover.

GRANT, Daniel, of Great Falls, m. (pub. Aug. 19, 1869, in Great Falls), Fannie A. Sterritt, of Hodgdon, Me.

GRANT, Tristram, m. (pub. May 5, 1870, in Great Falls), Mrs. Sophia B. (Curtis) Jenkins, wid. of Martin B.

GRAVES, Lyford T., of Brentwood, m. Sept. 28, 1865, in Dover, Abbie F. Downs, of Dover.

GRAY, William Jr., m. Jan. 23, 1777, in Barrington, Abigail Leighton, both of Barrington.

GRAY, Samuel, d. Mar. 8, 1824, m. Jan. 1785, Abigail Brown, both of Barrington.

GRAY, John, m. Dec. 3, 1786, by Rev. Benjamin Balch, Lydia Foss, d. July 11, 1845, aged 81, dau. of Thomas, both of Barrington.

GRAY, Rev. Robert, b. Oct. 9, 1761, d. Aug. 25, 1822, m. (1) Mar. 27, 1787, in Charlestown, Mass., Lydia Tufts, d. Aug. 31, 1801, aged 39, dau. of John, m. (2) Aug. 24, 1802, Susanna Hoar, divorced in 1816, m. (3) Polly (Chesley) Jones, wid. of John Jr., d. Mar. 23, 1858, aged 85.

GRAY, Stephen, m. int. Dec. 10, 1799, in Farmington, Charity Allard, both of Farmington.

GRAY, Ebenezer, m. Aug. 30, 1804, by Rev. Benjamin Balch, Deborah Hodgdon, both of Barrington.

GRAY, William, m. Mar. 17, 1805, in Barrington, Sally Clark, both of Barrington.

GRAY, Henry, of Barrington, m. Dec. 31, 1812, in Barrington, Dorothy Otis, of Rochester.

GRAY, William, of Farmington, d. Mar. 20, 1866, aged 74, m. (pub. Sept. 25, 1813, in Barrington), Polly Gray, of Barrington, d. Sept. 12, 1867, aged 78.

GRAY, Samuel Jr., m. Dec. 21, 1815, by Rev. Micajah Otis, Keziah Roberts, both of Barrington.

GRAY, Reuben, d. Sept. 28, 1848, aged 63, m. Feb. 8, 1816, by Rev. Micajah Otis, Mrs. Tamson (Hodgdon) Foss, wid. of Daniel, both of Barrington.

GRAY, William, of Strafford, son of Eben, d. Sep. 23, 1887, aged 83, m. (1) Polly Gray, d. Jan. 26, 1822, aged 28, m. (2) Oct. 15, 1826, by Elder Enoch Place, Sarah F. Gray, of Barrington.

GRAY, Edward Tyler, b. Dec. 28, 1796, d. Mar. 17, 1874, m. Mar. 11, 1823, Deborah W. Sprague.

GRAY, Thomas, of Barnstead, m. July 4, 1833, by Rev. Reuben H. Deming, in Dover, Olive Frost Davis, of Dover.

GRAY, John, son of Samuel, d. Jan. 4, 1878, aged 79, m. near 1838, Dorothy Otis, d. Mar. 18, 1866, aged 67.

GRAY, Jeremiah, son of George, d. Feb. 13, 1845, aged 28, m. (1) int. Oct. 6, 1839, in Dover, Elizabeth Cook, m. (2) Hannah H. ----, d. Oct. 23, 1886, aged 84.

GRAY, George W., m. Nov. 14, 1840, in Barrington, by Rev. Samuel Nichols, Susan G. Cate, both of Barrington.

GRAY, Edward Augustus, son of Edward T., b. Apr. 16, 1824, d. Jun. 28, 1878, m. Nov. 2, 1846, in Lebanon, Me., Mary Ann Corson.

GRAY, Enoch W., b. 1816, d. 1874, m. (1) July 9, 1848, by Elder Samuel Sherburne, Deborah H. Foss, b. 1813, d. Feb. 10, 1854, both of Barrington, m. (2) Meribah Hayes, b. 1821, d. 1907.

GRAY, Dennis, d. Apr. 12, 1908, aged 78, m. int. Dec. 9, 1849, in Dover, Lydia Perkins, d. Nov. 10, 1861, aged 36.

GRAY, Moses Franklin, of Farmington, son of James, d. Apr. 15, 1864, aged 37, m. Mar. 23, 1856, in Rochester, Julia A. Hatch, of Dorchester, Mass.

GRAY, Paul, of Rochester, m. Dec. 15, 1861, by Rev. John Winkley, Fanny B. Berry, of Farmington.

GRAY, Smith W., of Farmington, son of John, d. July 8, 1910, aged 72, m. Mar. 15, 1862, by Rev. James Rand, Delia A. Tuttle, of Dover.

GRAY, Levi L., of Strafford, m. Aug. 7, 1862, in Rochester, Lucy Horne, of Rochester.

GRAY, Warren G., of Jackson, m. Jan. 31, 1865, in Tamworth, Amanda Hatch, of Bartlett.

GRAY, Solomon S., m. Mar. 8, 1865, in Dover, Hannah J. Davis, both of Dover.

GRAY, Charles F., m. May 25, 1867, in Great Falls, Eliza L. Clay, both of Dover.

GRAY, John, m. July 9, 1867, in Rochester, Hannah Otis, of Farmington.

GRAY, George W., son of James F., d. Aug. 5, 1916, aged 76, m. Mar. 13, 1869, in Dover, Emily J. Lord, both of Dover.

GRAY, Henry S., son of Simon L., d. Aug. 13, 1892, aged 46, m. Oct. 9, 1869, in Dover, Fanny C. Libbey, both of Dover.

GREEN, Oliver, of Chichester, m. Feb. 18, 1829, by Elder Enoch Place, Eleanor R. Dame, of Strafford, dau. of Jonathan.

GREEN, John Roberts, d. Oct. 13, 1872, m. Oct. 9, 1868, in Lebanon, Me., Abbie A. Chase.

GREENE, Moses H., of Haverhill, Mass., m. Jan. 31, 1870, in Farmington, Ella G. Roberts, of Farmington, dau. of George E.

GREENLEAF, Albert F., son of Joshua, m. (1) Nov. 21, 1866, in Dover, Louisa F. Hartford, both of Rochester, m. (2) June 1, 1890, in Dover, Mrs. Ella J. Blaisdell.

GREENVILLE, Capt. John W., m. Sept. 9, 1866, in Effingham, Olive J. Huckins, both of Effingham.

GRIFFIN, Simon, m. Nov. 9, 1806, by Rev. Benjamin Balch, Lydia Hoitt, both of Northwood.

GRIFFIN, James J., of Lee, son of John, b. Oct. 1, 1813, m. (1) int. Sept. 3, 1838, in Lee, Lucinda Nutter, of Barnstead, m. (2) int. June 14, 1847, in Lee, Irena McDaniel, of Barrington, d. Dec. 29, 1878, aged 59, dau. of John.

GRIMES, William, m. Nov. 21, 1865, in Dover, Mary C. Chase, both of Dover.

GROVER, Henry W. B., son of George, b. Dec. 28, 1805, d. June 22, 1882, m. (1) Sept. 28, 1828, Rebecca Linscott, of Eaton, b. Sept. 7, 1805, d. Feb. 10, 1860, m. (2) Aug. 3, 1862, Emeline (Woodhouse) Pendergast, widow, dau. of John.

GROVER, Henry, of Milbury, Mass., m. July 24, 1862, in Durham, Sarah E. Grover, of Durham.

4) **GUPPEY**, James, d. Apr. 17, 1821, aged 40, m. in 1801, Abigail Burrows, d. Jan. 17, 1872, aged 87, dau. of Thomas

GUPPEY, Benjamin F. son of William, b. 1795, d. Dec. 19, 1855, m. Feb. 1821, Martha A. Warren, d. June 24, 1866, aged 67.

GUPPEY, Benjamin, m. Apr. 25, 1822, in Brookfield, Martha Warren, both of Brookfield.

GUPPEY, George F., son of James, m. int. Nov. 28, 1835, in Dover, Abigail F. York, d. June 26, 1868, aged 57, both of Dover.

GUPPEY, Oliver C., d. Feb. 13, 1867, aged 50, son of James, m. int. Feb. 10, 1839, in Dover, Elizabeth W. Drew, b. Jan. 2, 1815, d. Sept. 12, 1870.

GUPPEY, Thomas B., d. July 11, 1856, aged 44, son of James, m. int. Sept. 7, 1842, in Dover, Emeline Pinkham.

GUPPEY, George N., m. Aug. 23, 1866, in Dover, Louisa A. Preston, dau. of William, both of Berwick, Me.
GUPPEY, James E., m. Oct. 21, 1866, in Dover, Ellen A. Quimby, both of Dover.
GUPPEY, John, m. Nov. 26, 1868, by Rev. Robert S. Stubbs, Annie M. Dearborn, both of Dover.
GUPTILL, Ebenezer, m. (1) ----, m. (2) May 16, 1769, by Rev. Matthew Merriam, Sarah (Jellison), Came, wid. of Nicholas.
GUPTILL, Nathaniel, b. Jul. 16, 1754, d. Oct. 13, 1841, aged 85, m. (1) Feb. 24, 1779, by Rev. Matthew Merriam, Mary Chadbourne, d. May 1807, aged 44, dau. of Joseph, both of Berwick, Me., m. (2) Sarah ----, d. Oct. 29, 1842, aged 79.
GUPTILL, Moses, d. Jun. 8, 1874, aged 77, m. (1) int. Jul. 10, 1825, m. Jul. 8, 1825, in Lebanon, Me., by Elder Zebedee Delano, Mary or Nancy Chadburn, d. Aug. 6, 1827.
GUPTILL, Moses, m. int. Nov. 9, 1828, in Lebanon, Me., Tamson Hodsdon, of Ossipee.
GUPTILL, Benjamin H., m. int. Jul. 26, 1851, in Lebanon, Me., Lydia A. Pray, of Acton, Me.
GUPTILL, George W., m. (1) (pub. Mar. 1, 1853, in Great Falls), Harriet Wakefield, m. (2) Oct. 21, 1863, in Great Falls, Martha A. Corson, both of Rochester.
GUPTILL, George, of Milton, son of Daniel, d. Jun. 2, 1889, aged 43, m. Mar. 25, 1866, Sarah F. Morgan.
GUPTILL, Alonzo, m. (pub. Dec. 24, 1868, in Great Falls), Olive Ann Lord, both of Berwick, Me.
GUSHEE, Rev. Edward M., of Wallingford, Conn., m. June 8, 1864, in Dover, Lydia H. Low, of Dover, dau. of Dr. Nathaniel.
HACKETT, Allen, d. 1848, m. Feb. 1800, in Gilmanton, Polly Young, d. Jan. 8, 1854, aged 73.
HACKETT, Jeremiah M., b. Sept. 2, 1802, d. Apr. 30, 1878, m. (1) June 1, 1841, by Elder Enoch Place, Mary Ann S. York, dau. of John, m. (2) int. Sept. 27, 1846, in Dover, Mary A. W. Foss.
HACKETT, William R., of Sandwich, m. Aug. 20, 1866, in S. Tamworth, Olive Marston, of Suncook.
HACKETT, John, of Brookfield, aged 27, m. int. Aug. 30, 1870, in Brookfield, Nellie M. Bennett, of Freedom, aged 26.
HADLEY, Albert H., m. Aug. 14, 1869, in Dover, Abbie M. Leighton, both of Dover.
HAINES, Charles F., son of Capt. John, b. Oct. 2, 1821, m. 1851, Mary Elizabeth Chadbourne, of Sanford, Me.

HAINES, Alanson C., of Newmarket, m. Mar. 4, 1868, in Lee, Larah Clivia Hyley, d. Aug. 6, 1885, aged 41.

HALE, Wright, m. Feb. 12, 1804, by Rev. Benjamin Balch, Sally Waldron, both of Barrington.

HALE, James D., m. Dec. 16, 1813, by Rev. Enos George, Mary Leighton, both of Barrington.

HALE, Thomas W., son of William, d. Jan. 26, 1911, aged 85, m. Nov. 29, 1865, by Rev. Francis E. Abbott, Lizzie K. Hayes, both of Barrington.

HALEY, Robert, of Kittery, Me., b. Dec. 22, 1778, d. Feb. 20, 1845, m. Mar. 14, 1802, Nancy Shillaber, of Portsmouth, b. Jul. 25, 1779, d. Jan. 23, 1832.

HALEY, William, of Tuftonboro, son of Robert, b. Sep. 29, 1806, m. Nov. 9, 1834, in Wolfeboro, Mary Ann Hersey, of Wolfeboro.

HALEY, Capt. John B., of Portsmouth, m. Oct. 1, 1846, Mary Riley Varney.

HALEY, Samuel, of Epping, m. Feb. 20, 1856, in Newmarket, Mrs. Mary Ann Chapman, of Newmarket.

HALEY, Benjamin F., of Springfield, Mass., d. Mar. 25, 1911, aged 81, m. Jan. 29, 1863, in Great Falls, Augusta M. Noyes, of Great Falls.

HALEY, William, m. (pub. Sept. 28, 1865, in Ossipee), Mrs. Betsey F. Dore, both of Tuftonboro.

4) HALL, Rev. Avery, son of Theophilus, b. Dec. 2, 1737, d. Aug. 5, 1820, m. (1) Hannah (or Mary) Chesley, d. June 10, 1771, (Tate), dau. of James, m. (2) May 17, 1772, by Rev. James Pike, Abigail Pike, b. Mar. 30, 1740, d. July 22, 1819, dau. of Rev. James.

4) HALL, Joseph, son of Joseph, b. Dec. 11, 1742, d. Dec. 16, 1826, aged 85, m. in 1763, Mary Coe, b. Mar. 25, 1745, d. May 18, 1822, aged 78.

HALL, Elisha, d. July 28, 1829, aged 67, m. Aug. 1786, Lois Tasker, both of Madbury.

HALL, Joseph, of Barrington, b. July 8, 1767, d. Apr. 27, 1844, m. (1) ---- ----, m. (2) Nov. 5, 1795, by Rev. Benjamin Randall, Polly Shannon Randall, of New Durham, b. Feb. 24, 1774, d. Feb. 23, 1845, aged 71, dau. of Rev. Benjamin.

HALL, Daniel, b. July 28, 1769, m. Jan. 19, 1792, by Rev. Benjamin Balch, Mary Cate, b. Oct. 8, 1773, both of Barrington.

HALL, Solomon Jr., m. (1) Oct. 1, 1792, in Barrington, Lydia Scruton, both of Barrington, m. (2) May 2, 1802, in Barrington, Mrs. Charity Johnson, both of Barrington.

HALL, Winthrop, m. June 18, 1794, by Rev. Benjamin Balch, Hannah Hill, both of Barrington.

HALL, Benning, son of William, b. Oct. 18, 1774, m. Aug. 1797, in Portsmouth, Betsey Sherburne.

HALL, Jacob, m. Sept. 29, 1805, by Rev. Benjamin Balch, Betsey Meserve, both of Barrington.

HALL, Israel Jr., b. 1771, d. Dec. 11, 1870, m. (1) May 28, 1807, by Rev. Benjamin Randall, Hannah Saunders, b. 1784, d. July 22, 1825, both of Barrington, m. (2) May 21, 1826, by Elder Enoch Place, Mary Saunders, d. Mar. 30, 1868, aged 76.

HALL, William, son of Daniel, b. Dec. 11, 1792, d. Sep. 30, 1857, m. Aug. 31, 1820, by Elder Enoch Place, Susanna Cate, b. 1804, d, Jun. 13, 1854, aged 50, dau. of Capt. Joseph.

HALL, William, son of Ebenezer, d. Oct. 30, 1868, m. Aug. 31, 1820, by Elder Enoch Place, Susanna Cate, b. 1804, d. June 13, 1854, aged 50, dau. of Capt. Joseph, both of Barrington.

HALL, Thomas B., of Portsmouth, b. Oct. 1, 1794, m. (1) Mar. 11, 1821, Mehitable L. Bennett, of Newmarket, b. Jan. 15, 1802, d. May 8, 1839, m. (2) int. Sep. 19, 1840, in Lee, Hannah K. Adams, of Warren, R. I., m. (3) Aug. 23, 1866, in Lee, Mrs. Mindwell A. York, b. near 1801, both of Lee.

HALL, Daniel Jr., son of Daniel, b. Feb. 27, 1795, d. Apr. 1857, aged 62, m. Jan. 15, 1824, by Elder Enoch Place, Desdamony Watson, both of Barrington.

HALL, Winthrop, d. Apr. 20, 1844, m. (1) ----, d. Nov. 13, 1825, m. (2) Feb. 8, 1827, by Elder Enoch Place, Abigail Stiles, d. Apr. 12, 1827, aged 38, both of Strafford.

HALL, Deac. Joseph, son of Samuel, d. Mar. 20, 1874, aged 71, m. May 31, 1827, by Elder Enoch Place, Betsey Brock, d. May 28, 1849, aged 42, both of Strafford.

HALL, Samuel D., son of Samuel, d. Aug. 26, 1845, aged 48, m. (1) Apr. 9, 1829, by Elder Enoch Place, Mary Ann Sanders, d. 1840, both of Strafford, m. (2) Polly Brock.

HALL, John Jr., m. May 18, 1830, in Barrington, Nancy Willey, both of Barrington.

HALL, Gilman, son of Daniel, b. Feb. 17, 1810, d. Mar. 8, 1870, m. July 1830, Eliza Tuttle, b. May 8, 1803, d. Nov. 9, 1888, dau. of David.

HALL, Moses, of Dover, son of Daniel, b. Jan. 19, 1806, d. Nov. 14, 1843, aged 38, m. July 7, 1831, in Sanbornton, Ann Kelf, of Sanbornton.

HALL, Moses, son of Isaac, b. May 5, 1800, m. (pub. Oct. 30, 1832, in Dover), Henrietta Horn, b. Aug. 10, 1802, d. Jan. 28, 1847, aged 44, both of Dover.

HALL, Alfred, of Barnstead, son of Daniel, b. June 12, 1816, d. Apr. 27, 1878, m. Mar. 17, 1840, by Rev. Silas Green, Mary Ann Otis, of Dover, d. June 9, 1852, aged 37.

HALL, Everett, m. Feb. 27, 1843, by Elder Samuel Sherburne, Mrs. Mary A. Drew, both of Barrington.

HALL, George, of Barnstead, d. Sept. 28, 1881, aged 81, m. May 28, 1843, by Rev. John C. Nutter, Sally Drew, of Alton, b. in 1812, d. June 12, 1890, dau. of Joseph.

HALL, John B., d. Dec. 19, 1881, aged 62, m. May 18, 1850, by Rev. T. Wells, Lydia S. Foss, d. Nov. 3, 1849, aged 23, dau. of Jacob D., both of Barrington.

HALL, Joseph L., b. Aug. 6, 1835, m. Nov. 10, 1859, in Strafford, Ellen E. Tuttle, b. Apr. 10, 1835, d. Sept. 5, 1897, dau. of Jehoah.

HALL, John F., b. May 18, 1838, d. Dec. 28, 1899, m. Apr. 12, 1860, by Rev. John Winkley, Amie E. Scruton, both of Strafford.

HALL, Andrew J., m. Jan. 23, 1862, in Newcastle, Mary A. Yeaton.

HALL, David O., m. Feb. 18, 1862, in Strafford, Sophronia M. Tuttle, both of Strafford.

HALL, Andrew, m. July 9, 1863, in Barrington, Hannah Hall, both of Barrington.

HALL, Stacy W., of Dover, m. Nov. 7, 1864, in Dover, Hattie A. Chadborune, of Boston, Mass.

HALL, J. Milton, of Fall River, Mass., m. May 17, 1865, in Dover, Lizzie M. Chapman, of Dover.

HALL, Nathaniel Jr., son of Nathaniel, m. Nov. 8, 1865, in Durham, Hannah A. Willey, dau. of Jacob, both of Barrington.

HALL, Gilman Jr., m. Jan. 1, 1866, in Barrington, Mary S. Gray.

HALL, Samuel S., of Barrington, m. Mar. 22, 1866, in Barrington, Addie M. Roberts, of Strafford.

HALL, Asa A., of Strafford, m. Dec. 31, 1866, in Dover, Maria A. Stanton, of New Durham.

HALL, Oram R., m. July 11, 1867, in Dover, Livonia S. Fairbanks, both of Dover.

HALL, Benjamin, m. Oct. 2, 1867, in Barrington, Melissa J. Brown, both of Barrington.

HALL, Charles B., m. May 20, 1869, in Dover, Nellie Meader, of Gonic.

HALL, A. B., m. (pub. June 3, 1869, in Rochester), Sarah B. Waldron, both of Rochester.

HAM, Joseph, of Portsmouth, m. Feb. 13, 1777, in Barrington, Margaret Hayes, of Barrington.

HAM, Jonathan, of Barrington, m. Aug. 12, 1777, in Barrington, Esther Garland, of Madbury.

HAM, John, m. Oct. 31, 1777, in Barrington, Lois Foss, both of Barrington.

5) HAM, Eleazer, son of Ephraim, b. 1763, d. Apr. 5, 1836, m. (1) Sept. 14, 1786, by Rev. Joseph Haven, Lucy Jenness, both of Rochester, m. (2) Susan Wiggin, d. Aug. 21, 1822, m. (3) Sept. 3, 1823, by Rev. Thomas C. Upham, Elizabeth Robinson.

HAM, Nathaniel, m. Aug. 4, 1799, by Rev. Benjamin Balch, Jenna Otis, both of Rochester.

HAM, Jonathan, m. July 21, 1803, by Rev. Benjamin Balch, Susanna Pearey, both of Barrington.

HAM, Thomas, m. Nov. 23, 1809, in Barrington, Nancy Ham, both of Barrington.

HAM, George, Jr., of Barrington, son of George, d. May 9, 1878, aged 90, m. Feb. 6, 1812, by Rev. Enos George, Martha Leighton, of Farmington, d. Nov. 1, 1866, aged 79.

HAM, James, of Rochester, son of James, b. 1785, d. Dec. 11, 1874, m. (1) near 1814, Olive Waldron, b. Apr. 4, 1787, dau. of Joseph, m. (2) Mar. 22, 1827, by Elder Enoch Place, Mary Foss, of Barrington, d. Oct. 25, 1864, aged 60.

HAM, Titus, son of Ephraim, b. 1790, d. Jul. 22, 1855, m. May 30, 1816, Nancy Peirce, b. 1789, d. Nov 7, 1842.

HAM, Thomas, of Madbury, son of Samuel, d. Apr. 15, 1871, aged 79, m. Oct. 29, 1818, by Elder Enoch Place, Mary Caverno, of Barrington, d. Apr. 27, 1877, aged 78, dau. of Capt. Jeremiah.

HAM, Daniel Jr., of Barrington, b. Oct. 2, 1805, m. Apr. 23, 1829, by Rev. William Demeritt, Sarah Bickford, of Rochester, b. Mar. 10, 1809.

HAM, Marshall, m. Oct. 16, 1842, in Lebanon, Me., Olive Applebee, both of York, Me.

HAM, Oliver P., m. (pub. Apr. 4, 1843, in Newmarket), Mehitable Smith, b. 1809, dau. of Samuel, both of Durham.

HAM, Clement, b. near 1812, d. Aug. 8, 1864, m. Dec. 28, 1843, by Elder Enoch Place, Margaret Roberts Foss, b. near 1812, d. Nov. 13, 1857, aged 46, both of Barrington.

HAM, Capt. Benjamin, d. May 30, 1899, aged 83, m. Mar. 12, 1846, in Tuftonboro, Sarah D. Hall, d. May 29, 1907, aged 83.
HAM, Hiram, of Wolfeboro, b. 1810, d. 1888, m. July 8, 1863, in Ossipee, Mary D. Nutter, of Wakefield, b. 1823, d. 1888.
HAM, John F., of Durham, m. May 22, 1864, in Newmarket, Mary N. Nealley, of Newmarket.
HAM, Fernald E., of Boston, Mass., m. Oct. 25, 1866, in Portsmouth, Sarah E. Wyatt, dau. of Eben.
HAM, Samuel C., of Barrington, m. June 5, 1867, in N. Berwick, Me., Mattie A. Guy, of Charlestown, Mass.
HAM, Joshua M., of Dover, son of Walter, b. Apr. 1841, d. Nov. 19, 1888, aged 47, m. June 9, 1867, in Dover, Mary A. Wiggin, of Barrington, d. Jan. 17, 1929, aged 80, dau. of George.
HAM, Edward B., of Dover, m. Sept. 1, 1869, in Dover, Aramantha E. Ham, of Rochester.
HAMILTON, Solomon, son of Abial, bpt. Aug. 19, 1733, b. 1733, d. 1794, m. (1) Jan. 27, 1757, by Rev. John Morse, Sarah Keay, dau. of Peter, m. (2) Elizabeth Peirce.
HAMILTON, John, b. May 25, 1745, d. 1790, m. Dec. 5, 1770, by Rev. Matthew Merriam, Mary Weymouth.
HAMILTON, Sgt. Benjamin Jr., b. 1750, m. Mar. 28, 1771, by Rev. Matthew Merriam, Judith Ricker.
HAMILTON, Henry, of Sanford, Me., b. 1748, d. 1819, m. Oct. 5, 1780, by Rev. Matthew Merriam, Eunice Lord, of Berwick, Me., dau. of Jeremiah.
HAMMOND, Alonzo L., m. Jan. 4, 1863, in Center Ossipee, Georgie A. Merrow.
HAMMOND, Squire B., m. Sept. 13, 1867, by Rev. Robert S. Stubbs, Patience T. Hammon, of W. Paris, Me.
HANSCOM, Pelatiah, b. 1750, d. 1799, m. Jan. 12, 1775, in Kittery, Me., Susanna Cole, d. Jan. 9, 1833.
HANSCOM, John, m. Oct. 28, 1790, by Rev. Benjamin Balch, Abigail Arlen, both of Barrington.
HANSCOM, James, son of Isaac, b. Jul. 24, 1785, d. Dec. 7, 1863, m. int. Jul. 12, 1806, in Lebanon, Me., Experience Pray, b. Mar. 4, 1786, d. Feb. 4, 1865, dau. of Joseph.
HANSCOM, John Jr., m. Jan. 29, 1807, in Barrington, Hannah Foss, both of Barrington.
HANSCOM, Isaac, son of Isaac, d. Nov. 22, 1827, aged 39, m. int. Aug. 12, 1809, in Lebanon, Me., Nancy Libby, d. Oct. 18, 1838.

HANSCOM, Fernald, m. int. Apr. 13, 1816, in Lebanon, Me., Dorcas Chadbourne.

HANSCOM, Abraham, son of Isaac, d. Jan. 7, 1885, aged 80, m. (1) May 16, 1824, in Lebanon, Me., Sarah Goodwin, d. Nov. 8, 1865, aged 62, m. (2) Dec. 2, 1866, in Lebanon, Me., Mrs. Nancy (Goodwin) Hersom, d. Apr. 9, 1874, aged 70, dau. of Elisha.

HANSCOM, Levi, d. Apr. 1875, m. Nov. 4, 1824, in Lebanon, Me., Catharine Pray.

HANSCOM, Oliver, d. Dec. 4, 1878, aged 73, m. int. Dec. 24, 1831, in Lebanon, Me., Draxey Ricker, b. Mar. 20, 1804, d. Oct. 28, 1884, dau. of Ezekiel.

HANSCOM, Warren, d. Oct. 19, 1854, m. Oct. 22, 1840, by Rev. Lucian Hayden, Caroline P. Brock, both of Dover.

HANSCOM, James M., son of James, b. Feb. 16, 1819, d. Dec. 3, 1882, m. int. Nov. 10, 1841, in Lebanon, Me., Cynthia L. Gerrish, of Berwick, Me., Jan. 28, 1889.

HANSCOM, William L., m. (1) near 1845, Susan ----, d. Feb. 8, 1863, aged 38, m. (2) Jan. 25, 1864, in S. Berwick, Me., Sarah W. Nason, b. 1832, d. 1884.

HANSCOM, James E., b. 1821, d. July 27, 1865, m. (pub. Oct. 7, 1845, in Dover), Sarah Ann Gray, b. 1825, d. Sept. 27, 1853, aged 55.

HANSCOM, Willis, d. Jan. 29, 1880, m. Jan. 29, 1846, in Lebanon, Me., Laura Jane Earl, d. Jul. 30, 1890.

HANSCOM, James Hurl, son of Pelatiah, b. Mar. 25, 1822, d. Jan. 29, 1890, aged 67, m. May 10, 1846, in Milton, Sarah Jones, d. Sept. 24, 1889, aged 68, dau. of Nathan.

HANSCOM, Aaron H., of N. Berwick, Me., d. May 22, 1881, aged 60, m. int. Dec. 18, 1847, in Lebanon, Me., Susan Woodsom, b. May 14, 1827, dau. of John.

HANSCOM, Reuben, of No. Berwick, Me., m. Mar. 13, 1853, in Lebanon, Me., Permela Lord, d. Mar. 7, 1865, aged 39.

HANSCOM, Alpheus A., m. Oct. 16, 1853, in Lebanon, Me., Clara Libbey.

HANSCOM, Edwin, m. Dec. 1, 1853, in Lebanon, Me., Olive Libbey.

HANSCOM, Bray, of Ossipee, d. Aug. 19, 1892, aged 75, m. Apr. 18, 1855, in Effingham, Olive Titcomb, of Effingham, d. Aug. 27, 1907, aged 74, dau. of John.

HANSCOM, Sylvester O., b. July 26, 1834, d. Jan. 9, 1876, m. Feb. 13, 1858, by Elder Elias Hutchins, Serena A. Follett, b. July 19, 1839, d. Apr. 2, 1900, both of Dover.

HANSCOM, John F., m. July 18, 1862, in Dover, Julia F. Dore, both of S. Berwick, Me.

HANSCOM, Reuben, of Rollinsford, m. May 24, 1866, in Dover, Lizzie M. Earl, of Acton, Me.

HANSCOM, G. H., m. Dec. 5, 1866, in Strafford, Lucy J. Tasker.

HANSCOM, Samuel, m. (pub. Apr. 25, 1867, in Portsmouth), Mrs. Mary C. Hill.

HANSCOM, Isaac, m. Nov. 7, 1867, in Dover, Carrie J. Hayes, both of Lebanon, Me.

HANSCOM, John, of Strafford, m. (pub. Oct. 8, 1868, in Rochester), C. Amanda Nute, of Rochester.

HANSCOM, Charles N., of Dover, m. (pub. May 12, 1870, in Great Falls), Philinda A. Blanchard, of Newmarket.

4) **HANSON**, Timothy, son of Thomas, d. Feb. 24, 1801, aged 93, m. (1) near 1732, Keziah Chesley, dau. of Samuel, m. (2) July 8, 1755, Mary (Tuttle) Twombly, wid. of Daniel, b. Dec. 29, 1728, d. May 17, 1793, dau. of Thomas.

HANSON, Caleb, m. Dec. 25, 1788, Lucy Brown, d. Mar. 15, 1841, aged 79, both of Barrington.

6) HANSON, John, of Rochester, son of Jacob and Abigail, b. Apr. 7, 1777, d. Mar. 12, 1844, m. Oct. 9, 1806, by Rev. Benjamin Randall, Sally Runnels, of New Durham, d. June 4, 1871, aged 88, dau. of Samuel.

6) HANSON, James P., son of John B., b. May 30, 1791, d. Nov. 18, 1868, m. June 13, 1811, by Rev. Joseph Haven, Hannah Place, b. Apr. 15, 1790, d. May 16, 1882, dau. of James.

HANSON, John Place, son of James, d. Dec. 4, 1894, aged 81, m. (1) int. Dec. 17, 1843, in Dover, Julia Banks, b. Aug. 8, 1821, d. Aug. 8, 1844, dau. of Joseph, m. (2) Jan. 10, 1852, by Rev. Thomas J. Greenwood, Caroline Banks, d. May 16, 1909, aged 84, dau. of Joseph.

HANSON, Charles H., aged 27, m. int. Dec. 13, 1858, in Brookfield, Mary C. H. Buzzell, aged 24, both of Brookfield.

HANSON, Elisha A., m. (pub. Jan. 9, 1861, in Ossipee), Elizabeth A. Fall, d. Aug. 2, 1864, aged 22.

HANSON, John C., m. Feb. 5, 1862, in Dover, Elizabeth A. Demeritt, of Madbury.

HANSON, Daniel Jr., m. (pub. June 5, 1862, in Ossipee), Mrs. Sarah Tuttle.

HANSON, Nathaniel E., of Dover, m. Oct. 30, 1862, in Wells, Me., Martha A. Locke, of Wells, Me., dau. of Stacey H.

HANSON, Andrew, of Madbury, m. Nov. 16, 1862, in Strafford, Margaret Caverno, of Strafford.

HANSON, Joshua M., of Rochester, m. May 9, 1864, in Dover, Alma J. Webber, of Somersworth.

HANSON, Luther F., of Somersworth, m. Nov. 12, 1864, in Dover, Martha A. Rogers, of Freeport, Me.

HANSON, Micah, m. Jan. 1, 1865, in Milton, Mrs. Phebe Ann (Huntress) Morse, wid. of Darwin, b. May 2, 1827, d. Dec. 21, 1907.

HANSON, Hiram, m. Nov. 29, 1865, in Great Falls, Mrs. Sarah Melcher.

HANSON, Jonathan A., m. Dec. 10, 1865, in Dover, Leonora A. Deland, d. Nov. 5, 1890, aged 53, dau. of John, both of Dover.

HANSON, William, m. Dec. 10, 1865, in Dover, Christine Daniels, d. Jan. 2, 1887, aged 83, both of Dover.

HANSON, Caleb, m. Jan. 20, 1867, in Barrington, Mrs. Mary Peavey, both of Barrington.

HANSON, R. H., of S. Danvers, Mass., m. June 17, 1867, in Sandwich, Nettie E. Pierce, of Sandwich.

HANSON, Jacob, of Wolfeboro, b. Apr. 5, 1830, d. Aug. 16, 1885, m. (1) (pub. Feb. 3, 1870, in Ossipee), Wilhelmina D. Nutter, of Ossipee, d. Mar. 26, 1879, aged 37, dau. of Samuel, m. (2) Emma F. Brown, b. Aug. 27, 1843, d. Oct. 9, 1898, dau. of James L.

HANSON, James W., of Rochester, m. (pub. May 12, 1870, in E. Rochester), Clara E. Horne, of Farmington.

HANSON, George H., m. Nov. 23, 1870, in Dover, Arabella F. Drew, dau. of Reuben W.

HARDISON, Joseph, m. int. Oct. 6, 1814, in Lebanon, Me., Lucy Libbey.

HARDISON, Freeman, m. Feb. 10, 1863, in Dover, Nancy B. Chaney, both of S. Berwick, Me.

HARFORD, Solomon, m. Sep. 13, 1774, by Rev. Isaac Hasey, Mercy Farnham.

HARFORD, John, m. July 4, 1797, by Rev. Benjamin Balch, Betsey Babb, both of Barrington.

HARGRAVES, William, m. (pub. Apr. 22, 1869, in Rochester), Ann Wright, both of E. Rochester.

HARMON, Nelson S., m. Dec. 21, 1850, in Lebanon, Me., Sarah E. Pray.

HARMON, Charles A., of Great Falls, m. Dec. 25, 1867, in Great Falls, Hannah McKenney, of Biddeford, Me.

HARMON, John E., of Portsmouth, m. (pub. Dec. 24, 1868, in Great Falls), Mary A. Dixon, of Great Falls.

HARMON, William F., m. (pub. Nov. 17, 1870, in Great Falls), Lizzie Bracy.

HARRIMAN, Ambrose, m. int. Feb. 24, 1844, in Lebanon, Me., Eliza J. Wentworth.

HARRIMAN, Darius G., of Farmington, son of David L., d. Jan. 27, 1889, aged 56, m. Nov. 24, 1860, in Farmington, Sarah J. Penney, of New Durham, dau. of Louis.

HARRIMAN, Charles, of Somersworth, m. (pub. Feb. 15, 1866, in Portsmouth), Abbie Linscott, of Berwick, Me.

HARRIMAN, Rev. George G., of Fisherville, m. (pub. Nov. 19, 1868, in Great Falls), Susan I. Fielden, of Great Falls.

HARRIS, Samuel, of Springfield, Mass., m. Feb. 2, 1869, by Rev. J. C. Foster, Mrs. Harriet M. Hutchinson, of Dover.

HARRISON, Joseph, m. Mar. 20, 1868, in Newmarket, Eliza Booth.

HART, John, son of Nathaniel, d. Feb. 9, 1854, aged 68, m. Nov. 17, 1811, in Wakefield, Elizabeth Nutter, of Milton, d. Jun. 19, 1866, aged 80, dau. of Hatevil.

HART, Daniel Q., of Milton, son of Mark A., d. Sep. 29, 1916, aged 79, m. (pub. Dec. 27, 1860, in Great Falls), Ellen V. Ricker, of Farmington, d. May 8, 1904, aged 73, dau. of William.

HART, Almon, of Eaton, d. Jan. 6, 1885, aged 44, m. Jan. 29, 1866, in Lebanon, Me., Rachel Wentworth.

HART, John R., m. (pub. Aug. 6, 1868, in Rochester), Fannie J. Sawtell, both of E. Rochester.

HARTFORD, Solomon, m. Sep. 13, 1774, by Rev. Isaac Hasey, Mercy Farnham.

HARTFORD, Solomon, b. 1800, d. Mar. 20, 1872, m. (pub. Mar. 30, 1830, in Rochester), Ruth Tebbetts, d. Sep. 25, 1914, aged 102, dau. of Ezekiel.

HARTFORD, Benjamin P., m. (1) Nov. 11, 1836, in Conway, Betsey P. Kelley, d. May 13, 1855, m. (2) Sep. 4, 1855, in Lebanon, Me., Hannah S. Brown, both of Wakefield.

HARTFORD, David P., d. 1891, aged 74, m. Jan. 23, 1841, in Lebanon, Me., Mary Thurston, of Rochester.

HARTFORD, Eliakim, d. Jan. 25, 1860, m. Nov. 20, 1853, in Lebanon, Me., Sarah E. Shapleigh, of Rochester.

HARTFORD, James M., m. Jul. 4, 1857, by Rev. John Winkley, Mahalia F. Hayes, d. Dec. 21, 1913, aged 73, dau. of James, both of Strafford.

HARTFORD, Moses B., d. Jun. 19, 1911, aged 72, m. Apr. 1, 1859, in Barrington, Lucy A. Otis, d. Dec. 15, 1911, aged 69, dau. of Job.
HARTFORD, Lyman, of Rochester, m. Feb. 21, 1863, in Dover, Salome J. Whittier, of W. Amesbury, Mass.
HARTFORD, Charles E., m. July 29, 1865, in Dover, Hattie S. Goodwin, dau. of Capt. James, both of Rollinsford.
HARTFORD, Charles T. Jr., son of Charles T., d. Dec. 2, 1900, aged 54, m. Aug. 10, 1866, in Rochester, Hannah E. Jenness.
HARTFORD, John T., son of Solomon, d. Aug. 22, 1905, aged 71, m. June 14, 1868, in Great Falls, Nellie M. Twombly, both of Dover.
HARTFORD, Charles T., m. (pub. Aug. 11, 1870, in Rochester), Lavinia J. Smallcorn.
HARTWILL, Rev. Philander, m. Feb. 22, 1831, in Lebanon, Me., Esther Fernald, both of Sanford, Me.
HARVEY, Charles A., of N. Berwick, Me., m. Nov. 18, 1865, in Dover, Hannah G. Moulton, of Salmon Falls, dau. of James R.
HARWOOD, Peter, m. Jan. 22, 1787, by Rev. Benjamin Balch, Sally Armit, both of Madbury.
HASEY, Rev. isaac, aged 23, m. Aug. 22, 1765, by Rev. Isaac Lyman, of York, Me., Rebecca Owen, aged 31.
HASTY, George B., m. Nov. 28, 1865, in S. Berwick, Me., Sarah J. Brown.
HATCH, Stephen, m. int. Mar. 22, 1818, in Lebanon, Me., Mary Murray.
HATCH, Sylvanus, of Somersworth, m. Oct. 6, 1842, in Lebanon, Me., Mary Jane Gerrish.
HATCH, Enoch F., of Madison, m. Aug. 25, 1857, in Sandwich, Sarah E. Frost, of Tamworth.
HATCH, William H., of Milton, m. June 6, 1864, in Farmington, Mary Briggs, of N. Berwick, Me.
HATCH, George B., d. Dec. 5. 1908, aged 63, m. Feb. 26, 1867, in Wolfeboro, Hattie S. Horne, d. Dec. 6, 1909, aged 59, both of Wolfeboro.
HATCH, George A., m. Apr. 17, 1868, in Dover, Clara A. Roberts, both of Milton.
HAWKINS, William, of Barrington, m. Jan. 20, 1778, in Barrington, Lydia Bickford, of Barnstead.
HAWKINS, Benjamin, d. July 16, 1823, aged 68, m. in 1779, by Rev. William Parsons, Susan Bunker.
HAWKINS, Joseph, of Wakefield, m. July 10, 1796, by Rev. Benjamin Balch, Molly Davis, of Barrington.

HAWKINS, George, m. Nov. 21, 1813, by Rev. Joseph Boody, Esther Cook, both of Barrington.

HAWKINS, Elder Benjamin, d. Dec. 5, 1874, aged 80, m. (1) ---- ----, d. Mar. 29, 1823, aged 30, m. (2) Jan. 8, 1824, by Elder Enoch Place, Sarah Gray, d. June 15, 1885, aged 81, both of Strafford.

HAWKINS, Andrew, son of Benjamin, b. 1804, d. 1859, m. Dec. 22, 1825, by Elder Enoch Place, Mary L. Jenness, both of Barnstead.

HAWKINS, Hosea, b. 1810, d. Oct. 15, 1889, aged 80, m. Sept. 26, 1826, by Elder Enoch Place, Mary Caswell, b. 1806, d. May 21, 1894, both of Strafford.

HAWKS, N. Mortimer, of Lynn, Mass., m. Dec. 2, 1867, in N. Berwick, Me., Mary Buffum, of N. Berwick, Me., dau. of Benajah.

HAYDEN, James H., m. Nov. 12, 1862, in Dover, Matie E. Dockum, both of Newmarket.

HAYES, Hezekiah, m. Dec. 6, 1785, by Rev. Benjamin Balch, Sobriety Cate, both of Barrington.

HAYES, Jonathan, of New Durham, m. July 3, 1794, by Rev. Benjamin Balch, Polly Ham, of Barrington.

HAYES, David, m. Dec. 4, 1794, by Rev. Benjamin Balch, Polly Hayes, both of Barrington.

HAYES, Isaac, m. Feb. 26, 1797, by Rev. Benjamin Balch, Lovey Emerson, both of Barrington.

HAYES, Joseph, of Barrington, m. Oct. 29, 1801, by Rev. Benjamin Balch, Elizabeth Wingate, of Madbury.

HAYES, Daniel, m. Oct. 31, 1805, by Rev. Benjamin Balch, Tamson Montgomery, both of Barrington.

HAYES, Moses Jr., of Rochester, m. Aug. 24, 1813, in Barrington, Betty Hall, of Barrington.

HAYES, Moses, m. June 14, 1816, in Barrington, Hannah Otis, both of Barrington.

HAYES, James W., m. June 9, 1836, in Barrington, Desdamonia Watson, both of Barrington.

HAYES, Samuel, of S. Berwick, Me., m. Mar. 16, 1841, by Elder Samuel Sherburne, Sarah Seavey, of Portsmouth.

HAYES, Ivory, m. May 31, 1846, in Barrington, Mary E. Perkins, both of Barrington.

HAYES, Samuel, of Barrington, m. Oct. 28, 1847, by Rev. Homer Barrows, Caroline Shackford, of Somersworth.

HAYES, Charles H., of Strafford, m. Mar. 9, 1848, by Elder Enoch Place, Sarah Jane Foss, of Rochester, dau. of Benjamin.

HAYES, Alphonzo E., m. Apr. 26, 1866, in New Durham, Sarah E. Willey, both of New Durham.

HAYES, George, m. Apr. 26, 1866, in Rochester, Mrs. Betsey Cross.

HAYES, Levi, m. Dec. 5, 1867, in Farmington, Mary E. Hanson, both of Farmington.

HAYWOOD, William, of E. Rochester, m. Aug. 12, 1865, in Rochester, Abbie M. Chamberlain, of Alton.

HAZELTINE, Charles, of Newburyport, Mass., m. Jul. 4, 1842, Mary Young.

HEARD, Jacob, of Rochester, m. near 1805, in Barrington, Eunice Libbey, of Pittsfield.

HEARD, Enoch P., m. int. Oct. 23, 1810, in Lebanon, Me., Susanna Woodsum.

HEARD, Daniel, m. Nov. 1827, in Lebanon, Me., Eliza Miller, both of Shapleigh, Me.

HEARD (HURD), Ira, son of Jacob, b. June 7, 1798, d. Apr. 9, 1876, m. Oct. 16, 1823, in Berwick, Lorana Allen, b. Mar. 7, 1804, d. June 15, 1888, dau. of Elijah.

HEARD (HURD), Benjamin, m. Nov. 1825, by Elder Roger Copp, Hannah Knox.

HEARD, (HURD), Benjamin C., n. Dec. 14, 1841, in Lebanon, Me. Olive Ann Weymouth, both of No. Berwick, Me.

HEARD (HURD), Willard, of Needham, Mass., m. June 29, 1863, in Rochester, Caroline Young, of Barrington.

HEARD (HURD), Romeyn, m. Dec. 15, 1863, in Wolfeboro, Sarah V. Varney, both of Alton.

HEARD (HURD), Samuel F., <u>of Gonic</u>, m. Jan. 4, 1865, in Dover, Charlotte <u>Bell</u> Drew, <u>of Barrington, b. May 19, 1843, dau. of John T</u>.

HEARD (HURD), Marquis, m. Sept. 1, 1867, in Alton, Lizzie Hanscomb, both of Alton.

HEARD (HURD), Herbert I., of Dover, m. Dec. 13, 1870, in Pittsfield, Mary O. Butters, of Pittsfield.

HEATH, Benjamin, m. Sept. 15, 1786, by Rev. Benjamin Balch, Dolly Willey, both of Barrington.

HEATH, Franklin W., m. (pub. Sept. 13, 1866, in Ossipee), Amanda M. Tasker, dau of Moses S.

HEATH, William A., of New Durham, m. Aug. 30, 1867, in S. Lebanon, Me., Mary C. Dame, of Farmington.

HEDDLE, William, of Laconia, m. 1847, Louisa Hadley.

HEDERWICK, William, m. (pub. Sept. 9, 1869, in Rochester), Eunice H. Horn.

HEMMINGWAY, Phineas W., of Somersworth, m. (pub. July 22, 1869, in Rochester), Anna C. Perkins, of Strafford.

HENDERSON, John S., of Dover, m. Aug. 24, 1863, in Canajoharie, N.Y., Fanny Vanzundt, dau. of Rev. B. Vanzundt.

HENDERSON, Charles W., m. Nov. 7, 1864, in Dover, Martha J. Goodwin, of S. Berwick, Me.

HENSHAW, Josiah A., m. July 6, 1869, in Salmon Falls, Martha M. Putnam, both of Leicester.

HERSEY, William Jr., of Sanbornton, m. Nov. 26, 1807, by Rev. Isaac Smith, Ruth Bean, of Gilmanton, dau. of David.

HERSEY, D. S., of Danvers, Mass., m. (pub. May 30, 1867, in Great Falls), Sarah E. Smith, of Ossipee.

HERSOM, Stephen, m. int. Dec. 1803, in Lebanon, Me., Molly Runnels.

HERSOM, Samuel, m. Aug. 4, 1811, in Lebanon, Me., Betsey Hayes.

HERSOM, Jonathan, m. Jul. 2, 1812, by Rev. Isaac Hasey, Eunice Knox.

HERSOM, Samuel Jr., m. int. Sep. 10, 1814, in Lebanon, Me., Esther Ricker.

HERSOM, Oliver, m. Mar. 27, 1816, by Rev. Paul Jewett, Phebe Ricker.

HERSOM, Mark, m. May 28, 1816, in Lebanon, Me., Sally Hodsdon, both of Berwick, Me.

HERSOM, Ivory, m. int. Jun. 14, 1817, in Lebanon, Me., Polly Dore.

HERSOM, Joel, m. Dec. 3, 1818, in Lebanon, Me., Dorcas Jones.

HERSOM, Isaac, m. Dec. 8, 1818, in Lebanon, Me., Sarah Hersom.

HERSOM, Jacob, m. int. Jul. 31, 1819, in Lebanon, Me., Lucy Butler.

HERSOM, Daniel, m. Mar. 2, 1823, by Elder Zebedee Delano, Olive Goodwin.

HERSOM, James Jr., m. Mar. 7, 1824, in Lebanon, Me., Tammy Blaisdell.

HERSOM, John Jr., m. int. Aug. 21, 1824, in Lebanon, Me., Asenath Shorey, of Shapleigh, Me.

HERSOM, Joseph, m. Mar. 22, 1827, in Lebanon, Me., Betsey Lord.

HERSOM, Samuel 3rd, m. int. Mar. 26, 1828, in Lebanon, Me., Margaret Blaisdell, of Jay, Me.

HERSOM, Naham, m. Feb. 20, 1831, in Lebanon, Me., Betsey Pray, b. May 23, 1803.

HERSOM, David M. m. int. Mar. 13, 1834, in Lebanon, Me., Prudence L. Rollins.

HERSOM, Lucius, m. (1) int. Feb. 28, 1835, in Lebanon, Me., Theodocia Goodwin, m. (2) int. Sep. 10, 1841, in Lebanon, Me., Martha Ann Reynolds, of Acton, Me.

HERSOM, Joseph, m. Mar. 3, 1839, in Lebanon, Me., Nancy Goodwin. [Was this a second marriage?]

HERSOM, Joshua, m. int. Mar. 5, 1839, Sally Gerrish.

HERSOM, Benjamin, m. int. Nov. 24, 1839, in Lebanon, Me., Sarah H. Ricker.

HERSOM, Oliver, m. Apr. 21, 1840, in Lebanon, Me., Mrs. Mary Ricker. [Was this a second marriage?]

HERSOM, Ira, m. Dec. 11, 1842, in Lebanon, Me., Margaret Hersom.

HERSOM, Stephen, m. Dec. 9, 1845, in Lebanon, Me., Priscilla Broughton.

HERSOM, Lyman, m. Jun. 14, 1849, in Lebanon, Me., Martha Jane Smith.

HERSOM, Dr. Naham A., m. (1) Sep. 13, 1852, in Lebanon, Me., Martha Balcom, m. (2) int. Nov. 13, 1865, in Lebanon, Me., Jane S. Lord.

HERSOM, Benjamin, m. Apr. 26, 1855, in Lebanon, Me., Mrs. Lois Clark.

HERSOM, Thomas S., m. 1862, in Lebanon, Me., Torrey Bryant.

HERSOM, Martin V., m. June 1, 1862, in Dover, Ellen M. Williams, both of Waterville, Me.

HERSOM, Jacob (Joel?) G., m. Oct. 24, 1863, in Lebanon, Me., Emily J. Prescott, of Acton, Me.

HERSOM, John S., son of John Jr., aged 30, m. Nov. 19, 1864, in Lebanon, Me., Mrs. Martha A. (Jones) Butler, aged 19, wid. of Francis, b. May 2, 1845, dau. of James.

HERSOM, Stephen M., m. int. Dec. 22, 1864, in Lebanon, Me., Mary M. Prescott, of Acton, Me.

HERSOM, Oliver, of Lebanon, Me., m. Oct. 6, 1867, in Dover, Mrs. Melissa A. Durgin, of Dover.

HERSOM, John, m. Apr. 5, 1869, by Rev. Robert S. Stubbs, Mary Jane Varney, both of Dover.

3) **HICKS**, Joseph, of Madbury, son of Joseph, d. June 20, 1807, aged 62, m. (1) near 1750, Lydia Brewster, of Portsmouth, d. May 15, 1804, m. (2) Deborah Ham, b. 1754, dau. of Joseph.

HICKS, George H., of Alton, m. int. Sep. 1, 1869, in Lebanon, Me., Abby M. Chamberlin.

HIDDEN, George D., of Tamworth, m. Jul. 22, 1836, in Lebanon, Me., Maria Blaisdell.

HIDDEN, Dr. William B., of Concord, m. (pub. Dec. 3, 1863, in Tamworth), Angeline Boyden, of Tamworth.

HIGGINS, James T., of Rochester, m. Oct. 29, 1862, in Dover, Annie Dow, of S. Danvers, Mass.

HIGHT, William, son of Temple, b. Oct. 20, 1773, d. Apr. 18, 1847, m. Jan. 1, 1797, by Rev. Jonathan Tompson, Abigail Goodwin, d. May 27, 1851, aged 74.

HIGLEY, Eben N., of Great Falls, m. (pub. Jan. 21, 1869, in S. Berwick), Hannah B. Morrison, of Parsonsfield, Me.

HILDRETH, William E., m. Oct. 26, 1869, in Dover, Ellen Mack, dau. of John.

5) **HILL**, Andrew, son of Benjamin, b. Apr. 3, 1744, d. Feb. 10, 1826, m. Judith Gerrish, d. July 28, 1837, aged 94.

HILL, Joseph, m. Nov. 10, 1785, by Rev. Benjamin Balch, Elizabeth Peavey, both of Barrington.

HILL, Jeremiah, m. Oct. 3, 1787, by Rev. Isaac Hasey, Abigail Stevens.

HILL, George, of Lee, m. Oct. 4, 1787, by Rev. Benjamin Balch, Molly Stanton, of Barrington.

6) HILL, Deac. William, son of Andrew, b. June 30, 1780, d. Oct. 1870, m. Mary Clark.

HILL, Isaac, of Dover, b. Dec. 25, 1759, d. May 2, 1823, m. Feb. 20, 1791, Julianna Reader, b. Jan. 17, 1773.

HILL, Reuben, of Wakefield, m. Feb. 9, 1795, by Elder John Buzzell, Sarah Whitehouse, of Middleton.

HILL, Daniel, of Barrington, m. Jul. 14, 1796, Esther Caswell, dau. of Timothy.

HILL, David, m. July 8, 1802, in Barrington, Molly Otis, both of Barrington.

HILL, Benjamin, m. Nov. 20, 1806, by Enos George, Polly Ham, both of Barrington.

HILL, John, m. Nov. 8, 1827, by Elder Zebedee Delano, Lydia Butler.

HILL, David Smith, son of Isaac, b. Oct. 5, 1805, m. Jan. 3, 1828, Martha G. E. Thompson, b. Dec. 25, 1808.

HILL, Daniel, of Lebanon, Me., son of Jeremiah, b. Mar. 7, 1798, d. Dec. 13, 1880, aged 83, m. Feb. 8, 1828, Sarah Downs, of Milton, d. Oct. 20, 1861, aged 59, dau. of John.

HILL, Joseph, 4th, of Strafford, d. Apr. 28, 1851, aged 50, m. Jan. 25, 1829, by Elder Enoch Place, Polly Sampson, of Farmington.

HILL, Capt. Andrew, of Strafford, son of Benjamin, d. Apr. 20, 1841, aged 33, m. (pub. Jan. 21, 1834, in Gilmanton), Plooma D. Mudget.

HILL, John B., d. June 23, 1869, aged 44, m. June 3, 1845, by Rev. E. C. Cogswell, Emily M. Dow, both of Northwood.

HILL, Orin T., son of Nicholas D., d. Jan. 18, 1904, aged 78, m. (1) Hannah H. Matthews, d. Mar. 18, 1854, aged 30, dau. of Samuel, of W. Sumner, Me., m. (2) Dec. 2, 1854, in Strafford, Mary E. Foss, b. Nov. 10, 1822, d. Aug. 2, 1896, aged 73, dau. of William, both of Strafford.

HILL, Charles A., m. Sept. 24, 1854, by Elder Enoch Place, Adeline W. Foss, both of Strafford.

HILL, Daniel W., son of Daniel S., b. Mar. 4, 1827, d. Jan. 13, 1903, aged 75, m. Mar. 11, 1855, in Milton, Betty Rankins, b. Sept. 1, 1828, d. Dec. 23, 1902, aged 74, dau. of John.

HILL, Samuel, m. Jan. 21, 1858, in Sandwich, Eliza Mudgett, both of Sandwich.

HILL, Moses D., b. Dec. 17, 1830, d. Apr. 20, 1886, m. (1) Sept. 12, 1858, by Elder Elias Hutchins, Mary E. Mason, b. Mar. 18, 1829, d. Sept. 21, 1857, both of Dover, m. (2) June 14, 1861, by Rev. Arthur Caverno, Irene Joy, b. Mar. 28, 1833, d. Nov. 11, 1872, aged 39, m. (3) Anna J. ----, b. Apr. 19, 1845, d. May 25, 1886.

HILL, Henry, m. Mar. 3, 1859, in Dover, Mary J. (Waldron) Caswell, wid. of Andrew, b. 1808, d. Jul. 1, 1881, dau. of Isaac, both of Madbury.

HILL, Samuel H. Jr., m. (1) June 19, 1859, in Strafford, Lydia C. Parshley, d. Feb. 4, 1860, aged 25, dau. of Ebenezer, both of Strafford, m. (2) Nov. 26, 1862, in Strafford, Mary Ann Swan.

HILL, Robert W., m. (pub. Apr. 10, 1862, in Wakefield), Mary A. Horne, both of Wolfeboro.

HILL, Albert, of Saybrook, Conn., son of Abram, m. June 16, 1864, in Durham, Harriet (Berry) Hall, widow, of Strafford, dau. of Ezra.

HILL, Andrew S., m. Dec. 20, 1864, in Great Falls, Maggie C. Hanson.

HILL, John Tilton, b. Aug. 7, 1839, d. Sept. 11, 1922, m. (1) Mar. 9, 1865, in Dover, Vienna C. Locke, b. 1840, d. 1867, both of Dover, m. (2) Sept. 28, 1868, in Dover, Sarah A. Foss, b. Apr. 9, 1829, d. Jan. 11, 1911.

HILL, Newell, of N. Sandwich, m. Apr. 19, 1865, in Dover, Hannah L. Clough, of Dover.

HILL, David H., of Sandwich, m. June 4, 1865, in S. Parsonsfield, Me., Mary E. Moulton, of S. Parsonsfield, Me., dau. of William E.

HILL, Warren B., m. Aug. 6, 1865, in New Durham, Malvenah L. Emerson, both of Barnstead.

HILL, Joseph W., of Barrington, m. (1) Apr. 3, 1866, by Rev. James Rand, Sarah E. Tibbetts, of Wolfeboro, m. (2) (pub. June 11, 1874, in Rochester), Mrs. Sarah Berry.

HILL, Daniel, m. June 7, 1866, in Great Falls, Abby Downs, both of Milton.

HILL, Joseph C., of Wakefield, m. Apr. 9, 1867, by Rev. James Rand, Addie Morrison, of Lewiston, Me.

HILL, Amos G., of Barnstead, m. June 2, 1867, in Strafford, Hannah J. Avery, of Strafford, d. May 18, 1900, aged 60, dau. of David.

HILL, S. Augustus, of Great Falls, m. Jan. 26, 1868, in Berwick, Me., Sarah E. Smith, of Charlestown, Me.

HILL, Charles W., of Dover, m. Sept. 7, 1868, in Exeter, Alice C. Hardy, of Exeter.

HILL, Charles E., m. Sept. 28, 1868, in Great Falls, Etta I. Carpenter, both of Great Falls.

HILL, John B. m. (pub. Oct. 8, 1868, in Rochester), Emma A. Goodwin, both of Barnstead.

HILL, Robert, m. Mar. 13, 1869, in Rochester, Jennie Howard, both of Barrington.

HILL, Isaiah, of Melrose, Mass., aged 64, m. Aug. 1, 1869, in Brookfield, Mrs. Martha S. Chamberlain, of Brookfield, aged 57.

HILL, Albert F., of Boston, Mass., m. Oct. 15, 1869, in Dover, Nettie S. Day, of Dover.

HILL, Ambrose C., m. Nov. 23, 1870, in Lynn, Mass., Carrie A. Mathes, both of Lynn, Mass.

HILL (HILLS?), Charles, of haverhill, Mass., n. Nov. 24, 1829, in Brookfield, Hannah F. Hanson, of Brookfield.

HILTON, Nathaniel, m.Oct. 5, 1828, in Lebanon, Me., Hannah Wentworth, of Shapleigh, Me.

HILTON, Andrew F., of Acton, Me., m. Feb. 3, 1861, in Lebanon, Me., Emma A. Hersom.

HILTON, Richard, m. Apr. 13, 1864, in Manchester, Mary S. Jones, both of Portsmouth.

HILTON, Charles H., m. Oct. 22, 1864, in Dover, Lucy E. McCann, both of Buxton, Me.

HILTON, Luther, m. May 23, 1866, in Salmon Falls, Patience Green, both of Wells.

HOAG, Nathan F., aged 38, m. July 10, 1864, in Strafford, Mrs. Antoinette L. (Burleigh), aged 31, wid. of Dr. Tristram, d. Apr. 10, 1875, dau. of Thomas.

HOBBS, Jonathan, of Effingham, d. Mar. 2, 1845, aged 75, m. Nov. 5, 1798, in Tamworth, Sarah Sanborn, of N. Hampton, d. Sept. 20, 1861, aged 85.

HOBBS, Isaac, of Effingham, d. July 11, 1853, aged 46, m. (1) Mar. 22, 1829, by Rev. Clark, Susan Roberts, of Ossipee, d. Mar. 25, 1840, aged 32, m. (2) July 28, 1842, by Rev. J. Milton Coburn, Mary Hyde, of Wolfeboro.

HOBBS, John F., m. Mar. 3, 1863, in Great Falls, Melinda Ham, both of Rochester.

HOBBS, Dr. Benjamin, of Wakefield, m. May 24, 1863, in Rochester, Hattie M. Chase, of Rochester.

HOBBS, Wilson C., of Somersworth, m. Feb. 20, 1866, in Rochester, Mary J. Clark, of Berwick, Me.

HOBBS, William, m. (pub. Mar. 10, 1870, in N. Berwick, Me.), Mary Hill.

HODGDON, Amos, son of Jonathan, d. Oct. 17, 1832, aged 72, m. Jan. 1, 1789, by Rev. Joseph Haven, Elizabeth Ham, d. Dec. 17, 1825, both of Rochester.

HODGDON, Thomas, m. Oct. 4, 1796, by Rev. Benjamin Balch, Anna Felker, d. Mar. 13, 1838, aged 66, both of Barrington.

HODGDON, Parker, m. int. Oct. 1799, in Lebanon, Me., Molly Gerrish.

HODGDON, Stephen, m. 1810, by Rev. John Osborne, Sarah Starboard, of Durham, d. Dec. 6, 1878, aged 93, dau. of Lt. John.

HODGDON, Job S., of Dover, m. Feb. 15, 1816, in Barrington, Margaret Smith, of Rochester.

5) HODGDON, William, son of Caleb, b. 1774, d. Jan. 16, 1842, m. Jan. 30, 1817, by Rev. J. W. Clary, Susan Coffin, b. Mar. 26, 1778, d. Mar. 24, 1842, dau. of Eliphalet.

HODGDON, Samuel H., of Strafford, m. (1) Oct. 8, 1818, by Elder Enoch Place, Betsey Tasker, of Barrington, m. (2) Nov. 3, 1819, by Elder Enoch Place, Betsey Daniels, d. Apr. 30, 1828, of Barrington, m. (3) Nov. 27, 1828, by Elder Enoch Place, Rebecca Waterhouse, of Barrington.

HODGDON, Edward, of So. Berwick, Me., m. Jan. 19, 1823, in Lebanon, Me., Sarah Winn, of Dover.

HODGDON, Daniel, m. Dec. 10, 1845, by Elder Samuel Sherburne, Lucy Walker, both of Barrington.

HODGDON, John C., m. int. Aug. 10, 1850, in Lebanon, Me, Malinda Hodgdon.

HODGDON, Oren C., m. int. Sep. 15, 1854, in Lebanon, Me., Mary Dearborn.

HODGDON, Charles H., of Ossipee, m. (pub. Sept. 11, 1862, in Wolfeboro), Helen B. Garland, of Wolfeboro.

HODGDON, Lyman, of Barnstead, m. Apr. 4, 1866, in Dover, Hattie Delaney, of Dover.

HODGDON, Walter S., of Farmington, m. Dec. 25, 1866, in Farmington, Georgianna B. Allen, of Haverhill, Mass.

HODGDON, Westbury G., of Farmington, m. June 15, 1867, in Tuftonboro, Ellen A. Colbath, of Middleton.

HODGDON, John A., of Newington, m. (pub. May 12, 1870, in Great Falls), Mary E. Powers, of Great Falls.

HODSDON, Isaac, m. Jun. 21, 1821, in Lebanon, Me., Mary Knox.

HODSDON, Charles, of Barrington, m. int. Feb. 21, 1830, in Lebanon, Me., Unice L. Knox.

HODSDON, Elisha, m. int. Oct. 21, 1838, in Lebanon, Me., Hannah Hayes, of Strafford.

HODSDON, Edward P., of Ossipee, son of Deac. Joseph, m. (pub. Feb. 13, 1862, in Rochester), Emma B. Demeritt, of Farmington, b. 1840, d. 1932.

HODSDON, George F., m. Jan. 16, 1870, in Milton, Lucinda J. Jones

HODSON, Daniel, of Great Falls, m. (pub. May 5, 1870, in Lebanon, Me.), Phebe Ricker Shapleigh, of Lebanon, Me., b. May 29, 1849, d. Aug. 5, 1893, dau. of Charles.

HOITT, John, m. Apr. 7, 1807, by Rev. Isaac Hasey, Patience Ross, dau. of Hugh.

HOITT, William, b. 1787, d. Jun. 30, 1843, m. int. Nov. 2, 1812, in Lebanon, Me., Hannah Dore, b. 1789, d. Feb. 18, 1865.

HOITT, Gorham, of Lee, d. Sep. 9, 1867, aged 63, m. int. May 5, 1824, in Lee, Abigail P. Locke, of Barrington, d. Apr. 5, 1878, aged 76.

HOITT, Jesse, of Tuftonboro, d. Mar. 20, 1885, aged 92, m. (1) Sally ----, d. Apr. 14, 1828, aged 33, m. (2) Jan. 11, 1829, in Middleton, Salonia Rand, of New Durham, d. June 3, 1884, aged 83.

HOITT, William, m. Dec. 6, 1850, in Lebanon, Me., Martha Ann Hayes, dau. of Elihu.

HOITT, James, of New Bedford, Mass., m. Oct. 8, 1855, in Lebanon, Me., Esther Jane Montgomery, of Dover.

HOITT, Byron D., m. June 29, 1865, in Northwood, Emma H. Fogg, both of Northwood.
HOITT (HOYT), James William, m. (pub. Oct. 22, 1863, in Newington), Zerviah Furber, dau. of Thomas G.
HOITT (HOYT), James W., of Rochester, m. Nov. 7, 1863, in Exeter, Eliza J. Abbott, of N. Andover, Mass.
HOITT (HOYT), Phineas D., of Portsmouth, m. Apr. 11, 1864, in Great Falls, Mrs. A. Whitehouse, of Great Falls.
HOITT (HOYT), Rufus A., of Rochester, m. Feb. 26, 1866, in Rochester, Lucy A. Drew, of Brookfield, d. Mar. 29, 1909, aged 61, dau. of Benjamin.
HOITT (HOYT), Hanson, of Portsmouth, m. (pub. Aug. 30, 1866, in Newington), Mary Frances Downing.
HOITT (HOYT), Samuel W., m. Oct. 6, 1866, in Newington, Almira O. Martin, of Jackson.
HOITT (HOYT), Winthrop, of Portsmouth, m. Nov. 3, 1866, in Newington, Mahala Jones, of Wakefield.
HOLBROOK, Hiram H., m. Nov. 21, 1868, in Great Falls, Clara B. Moody, both of Great Falls.
HOLLIS, Capt. Abijah, of Milton, m. July 9, 1864, in Cambridge, Mass., Harriette Van Mater French, of Exeter, dau. of Henry.
HOLMAN, Joshua R., of Lowell, Mass., m. int. Sep. 28, 1854, in Lebanon, Me., Mary A. Abbott, of Rochester.
HOLMES, Ephraim, m. Jan. 20, 1751, Betty Libbey, of Portsmouth, dau. of Abraham.
HOLMES, Joshua, b. Dec. 3, 1739, m. Dec. 23, 1757, Abigail ----, b. Feb. 4, 1738.
HOLMES, Ephraim, <u>d. June 1, 1837, aged 80</u>, m. Feb. 6, 1783, by Rev. Joseph Haven, Mary Hall, d. July 17, 1857, aged 92, <u>dau. of Elder Joseph</u>, both of Barrington.
HOLMES, Joseph, d. June 16, 1828, aged 69, m. Dec. 10, 1784, by Rev. Benjamin Balch, Content Otis, d. Nov. 30, 1847, aged 84, both of Barrington.
HOLMES, Ephraim, m. Jan. 20, 1785, by Rev. Benjamin Balch, Mary Remick, d. Mar. 27, 1787, aged 21, both of Barrington, m. (2) Sally ----, d. Mar. 20, 1820, aged 61.
HOLMES, John, d. Apr. 13, 1840, aged 76, m. (1) Sept. 30, 1785, by Rev. Benjamin Balch, Mary Cornell, d. Mar. 27, 1787, aged 21, both of Barrington, m. (2) Sally ----, d. Mar. 20, 1820, aged 61, m. (3) Polly ----, d. Apr. 16, 1872, aged 83.

HOLMES, Joshua, of Rochester, m. Dec. 25, 1796, by Rev. Benjamin Balch, Polly Cater, of Barrington.

HOLMES, John, m. Sep. 15, 1803, by Rev. Isaac Hasey, Molly Lord.

HOLMES, Noah, d. Oct. 18, 1821, aged 21, m. Apr. 20, 1820, by Elder Enoch Place, Nancy Babb, both of Barrington.

HOLMES, Capt. John G., b. Nov. 18, 1823, d. Feb. 18, 1894, m. May 15, 1850, by Elder John C. Holmes, Eliza Jane Foss, b. May 11, 1829, d. Oct. 21, 1915, dau. of Eliphalet.

HOLMES, Charles N., m. (pub. June 22, 1865, in Portsmouth), Annie M. Trefethen.

HOLMES, William F., m. Sept. 18, 1865, by Rev. James Rand, Maria S. Daniels, both of Nottingham.

HOLMES, John L., m. Nov. 1, 1866, in Northwood, Louella K. Jenness, both of Nottingham.

HOLMES, Henry H., of Tuftonboro, m. (1) (pub. July 30, 1868, in Wolfeboro), Abbie Augusta Wiggin, of Wolfeboro, d. Mar. 13, 1879, aged 27, m. (2) Sally Welch, d. 1893.

HOLMES, Thomas, of Berwick, Me., m. Aug. 4, 1868, in Rochester, Mrs. Abbie J. Warren, of Somersworth.

HOLMES, Charles W., of Cambridgeport, Mass., m. Sept. 1, 1869, in Dover, Fanny M. Hooper, of Dover.

HOOPER, William, b. Apr. 29, 1719, d. July 26, 1809, m. Oct. 29, 1743, in Berwick, Me., Elizabeth Emery, b. Sept. 24, 1724, d. 1812, dau. of Daniel.

HOOPER, Daniel, son of William, b. 1744, d. Mar. 24, 1820, m. Sept. 24, 1781, Hannah Heard, both of Berwick, Me.

HOOPER, Rev. Noah, son of Rev. William, b. Oct. 9, 1776, d. Aug. 30, 1854, aged 78, m. June 20, 1796, by Rev. William Hooper, Elizabeth Kelley, d. Jan. 18, 1862, aged 87 yrs., 6 mos., both of Madbury.

HOOPER, John, son of Rev. William, b. July 4, 1778, m. Jan. 22, 1799, by Rev. William Hooper, Susanna Meserve, dau. of Col. Ebenezer.

HOOPER, Samuel Lord, of Madbury, son of Rev. William, b. 1785, d. Sept. 19, 1807, m. Mar. 12, 1807, in Berwick, Me., Polly Clark, of Berwick, Me.

HOOPER, John, son of John, d. July 9, 1880, aged 82, m. Jan. 27, 1825, by Rev. J. W. Clary, Caroline Cushing, d. Dec. 28, 1882, aged 76.

HOOPER, Sylvester I., of Berwick, Me., m. Nov. 4, 1868, in Dover, Mrs. Lucy L. Howe, of S. Yarmouth, Mass.

HOPE, Henry, m. Jan. 5, 1870, in Dover, Elzira Stirling, both of Dover.

HORN, John, d. Sept. 11, 1840, aged 80, m. Nov. 15, 1785, by Rev. Jeremiah Shaw, Jane Rust, b. Nov. 19, 1763, d. July 15, 1843, dau. of Col. Henry, both of Wolfeboro.

HORN, Paul, m. July 7, 1788, by Rev. Benjamin Balch, Margaret Horn, both of Dover.

HORN, Richard, m. Jan. 3, 1805, in Lebanon, Me., Sarah Farnham.

HORN, Samuel, of Tuftonboro, d. May 23, 1840, aged 53, m. (1) June 21, 1812, by Rev. Joseph Boodey, Mary B. Palmer, of New Durham, d. Feb. 15, 1826, aged 37, m. (2) Aug. 28, 1826, in Middleton, Hannah Glidden, d. Apr. 15, 1848, aged 52, both of Tuftonboro.

HORN, Andrew, m. int. Feb. 25, 1815, in Lebanon, Me., Dorca Knox.

HORN, Capt. David J., m. int. Jan. 2, 1847, in Lebanon, Me., Abby G. Robinson, of Limington, Me.

HORN, Elijah, m. int. Jun. 6, 1853, in Lebanon, Me., Mary Jane Stackpole.

HORN, Thomas W., m. Jan. 22, 1859, by Rev. William A. Forbes, Mary E. Nowell, of Sanford, Me.

HORN, Andrew P., m. int. Feb. 14, 1862, in Lebanon, Me., Olive A. Hersom.

HORN, Jackson, of Wakefield, m. (pub. Apr. 10, 1862, in Wakefield), Mary M. Quimby, of Newfield, Me.

HORN, Joseph S., m. Aug. 1, 1863, in Great Falls, Eveline A. Caverly, both of Somersworth.

HORN, Nathaniel, son of Nathaniel, d. Feb. 11, 1911, aged 72, m. Oct. 29, 1863, in Dover, Martha Wilson, d. Apr. 5, 1916, aged 87, dau. of David, both of Dover.

HORN, Charles W., of Middleton, m. Aug. 31, 1865, in Alton, Mary F. Allen, of Wakefield.

HORN, Benjamin F., m. Nov. 28, 1866, in Rochester, S. Jennie Meserve.

HORNE, Samuel, of Newburyport, Mass., son of Amos, b. at Isles of Shoals, d. Aug. 3, 1845, aged 70, not of the Dover family, m. Mary Horne, b. May 29, 1786, d. Sept. 2, 1866.

HORNE, Andrew, son of William, b. 1728, d. May 19, 1812, m. near 1752, Elizabeth Willand, b. 1720, d. Feb. 11, 1804, dau. of William.

HORNE, Paul, b. 1747, m. (1) Oct. 27, 1774, by Dr. Belknap, Hannah Smith, d. Dec. 3, 1786, m. (2) Margaret Horne, dau. of Samuel.

HORNE, Ephraim, son of Andrew, b. Jun. 10, 1762, m. Nov. 30, 1786, by Rev. Joseph Haven, Molly Wentworth, both of Somersworth.

HORNE, Ebenezer, of Tuftonboro, m. Sep. 30, 1813, by Rev. Joseph Boodey, Anna Garland, of Middleton, d. Apr. 13, 1864, aged 71.

HORNE, William C., d. Dec. 12, 1845, aged 49, m. May 29, 1817, by Rev. Joseph Boodey, Mercy Tibbetts, d. Nov. 15, 1834, aged 37, both of Farmington.

HORNE, George, of Wakefield, m. int. Jul. 10, 1824, in Lebanon, Me., Pamela Roberts.

HORNE, John, m. Mar. 3, 1825, in Lebanon, Me., Martha Wentworth.

HORNE, Samuel M., b. Sep. 2, 1802, d. Aug. 23, 1876, m. (1) Sep. 1826, Mary Bodge, d. Apr. 13, 1850, aged 46, m. (2) 1853, Miriam Pinkham.

HORNE, Enoch Jr., d. Oct. 21, 1884, aged 75, m. Dec. 27, 1832, by Rev. Joseph Boodey, Louisa Littlefield, d. May 8, 1900, aged 87, dau. of John, d. May 8, 1900, aged 87, both of Farmington.

HORNE, Francis Drew, son of James, b. Sept. 12, 1815, d. Nov. 26, 1865, m. in 1841, Sarah D. Ricker, b. Apr. 21, 1818, d. June 24, 1890, dau. of Elmer.

HORNE, Samuel P., of Rochester, d. Feb. 1, 1904, aged 82, m. (pub. Sep. 13, 1842, in Wolfeboro), Mary Ann Ham, of Farmington, d. Dec. 25, 1891, aged 70, dau. of Moses W.

HORNE, Veranus, son of Wentworth, d. Aug. 1, 1895, aged 67, m. Jun. 3, 1847, by Elder Jacob Bodge, Mary Ann Gilbert, d. Feb. 13, 1908, aged 79.

7) HORNE, James G., son of James H., d. May 18, 1886, aged 61, m. Apr. 30, 1848, by Rev. Nathaniel Barker, Abba Applebee, d. June 8, 1875, aged 47, both of Milton.

HORNE, James F., of Dover, m. Jan. 21, 1864, by Rev. James Rand, Leonora Varney, of Rochester, d. June 15, 1920, aged 76, dau. of George W.

HORNE, Charles Adams, of Dover, m. Mar. 24, 1864, in Dover, Florence Allen, of Rollinsford.

HORNE, Ebenezer, of Moultonboro, m. July 8, 1864, in Farmington, Mrs. Dorothy (Ricker) Horn, of Farmington, wid. of David Y.

HORNE, Horace E., son of Daniel, d. Sep. 1, 1909, aged 65, m. Sept. 3, 1864, in Rochester, Susan C. Kimball, both of Rochester.

HORNE, Benjamin F., m. Dec. 1864, in Lebanon, Me., Mrs. Augusta Morrison, of Great Falls.

HORNE, Albert M., son of Jessie, d. Nov. 25, 1913, aged 76, m. Mar. 1, 1865, Helen S. Horne, both of Rochester, d. Jan. 24, 1901, aged 60, dau. of Gershom.

HORNE, Alonzo P., son of Enoch, b. Nov. 12, 1845, d. Apr. 23, 1905, m. Apr. 1, 1865, in Alton, Sarah Abby Canney, b. Aug. 23, 1847, d. Jul. 10, 1905, dau. of William.

HORNE, Jethro, of Haverhill, Mass., m. (pub. Dec. 14, 1865, in Rochester), Mrs. Janette Durgin, of Madbury.

HORNE, Harlan P., m. Apr. 28, 1866, in Milton, Katie Edgerly, both of Rochester.

HORNE, John C., m. June 13, 1866, in Dover, Sarah E. Tuttle, both of Rochester.

HORNE, Gustavus H., m. Oct. 18, 1866, in Dover, Ellen Hampsen, both of Dover.

HORNE, Henry B., son of Gershom, d. Nov. 8, 1899, aged 55, m. Nov. 4, 1866, in Rochester, Lavina J. Colcord.

HORNE, J. H., of Lebanon, Me., m. Feb. 23, 1869, in Milton, Sarah D. Nute, of Dover.

HORNE, Henry S., son of Henry, d. May 21, 1896, aged 62, m. (pub. Aug. 5, 1869, in Rochester), Rosina J. Cilley, both of Rochester

HORNE, Charles H., of Tiftonboro, m. Oct. 17, 1869, by Rev. David B. Cowell, Mary A. Peirce. [Remarried Oct. 17, 1870.]

HORNE, George A., of Berwick, Me., m. (pub. June 2, 1870, in Rochester), Annie Champion, of Wakefield.

HORNE, Charles A., of Great Falls, m. (pub. July 14, 1870, in Great Falls), Chrissie Varney, of Rochester.

HORNE, Charles H., m. (pub. Oct. 27, 1870, in Milton), Maggie Emerson, both of Rochester.

HORNE, Henry, m. int. Apr. 30, 1872, in Lebanon, Me., Clarinda A. Guptill, of No. Berwick, Me.

HORNER, Daniel W., of Tiftonboro, b. 1829, d. 1899, m. int. Nov. 16, 1858, in Brookfield, Lizzie A. Cotton, of Brookfield, b. 1828, d. 1913.

HORNEY, William H., son of Gilbert, d. Sep. 6, 1920, aged 73, m. (pub. May 19, 1870, in Rochester), Mary A. Colby, both of Rochester.

HORSUM, Stephen, m. int. Dec. 1803, in Lebanon, Me., Molly Runnels.

HORSUM, Jonathan, m. Jul. 2, 1812, by Rev. Isaac Hasey, Eunice Knox.

HORSUM, Samuel Jr., m. int. Sep. 10, 1814, in Lebanon, Me., Esther Ricker.
HORSUM, Oliver, m. Mar. 17, 1816, by Rev. Paul Jewett, Phebe Ricker.
HORSUM, Mark, m. May 28, 1816, in Lebanon, Me., Sally Hodsdon, both of Berwick, Me.
HORSUM, Ivory, m. int. Jun. 14, 1817, in Lebanon, Me., Polly Dore.
HORSUM, Joel, m. Dec. 3, 1818, in Lebanon, Me., Dorcas Jones.
HORSUM, Daniel, m. Mar. 2, 1823, by Elder Zebedee Delano, Olive Goodwin.
HORSUM, Joseph, m. Mar. 22, 1827, in Lebanon, Me., Betsey Lord.
HORSUM, Samuel 3rd, m. int. Mar. 26, 1828, in Lebanon, Me., Margaret Blaisdell.
HORSUM, Oliver, m. int. Apr. 13, 1839, in Lebanon, Me., Mrs. Mary Ricker.
HOUGH, George H. S., of Dover, m. Mar. 10, 1867, in Malden, Mass., Mary A. Sampson, of Malden, Mass.
HOUGHTON, William H., of Boston, Mass., m. Apr. 4, 1867, in Great Falls, Mary E. Ames, of Dover.
HOUSTON, Enoch, of Somersworth, m. Dec. 24, 1846, in Lebanon, Me., Louisa Hinkman Farnham, b. Feb. 22, 1825, dau. of Mathew.
HOVEY, George H., of Charlestown, Mass., m. Nov. 6, 1862, in Dover, Melissa F. Davis, of New Durham.
HOWARD, Samuel, son of Amos, b. 1754, d. May 2, 1824, m. Jan. 15, 1778, by Dr. Belknap, Sarah Hanson, d. 1836, aged 77.
HOWARD, Richard, m. May 27, 1795, in Barrington, Polley Drown, both of Barrington.
HOWARD, Samuel, m. Nov. 26, 1799, in Barrington, Abigail Drown, both of Barrington.
HOWARD, William, b. near 1779, m. Nov. 12, 1812, in Barrington, Polly Hanson, b. near 1782, both of Barrington.
HOWARD, Daniel, m. Dec. 18, 1813, in Barrington, Abigail Young, both of Barrington.
HOWARD, James, b. 1785, d. Sept. 25, 1825, m. near 1814, Susan Otis.
HOWARD, Samuel, m. July 5, 1817, in Barrington, Polly Miles.
HOWARD, Moses, m. Dec. 29, 1818, in Barrington, Charity Pearl, both of Rochester.
HOWARD, James, m. Sept. 19, 1819, in Barrington, Mary Hodgdon, both of Barrington.

HOWARD, Asa, d. May 8, 1840, aged 34, m. int. July 13, 1828, in Dover, Harriet Clark.

HOWARD, George W., son of James, b. 1821, d. Jan. 13, 1895, aged 73, m. Apr. 8, 1845, by Elder, Enoch Place, Sarah Ann Otis, b. 1823, d. 1889, dau. of Joshua, both of Strafford.

HOWARD, Ira T., son of Richard, m. Jan. 17, 1847, in Barrington, Sarah Leathers.

HOWARD, Emery, m. Feb. 6, 1849, in Barrington, Mrs. Elizabeth Ann Leathers, both of Barrington.

HOWARD, Samuel, m. Jan. 1855, Eliza Burrows, d. Sep. 23, 1878, aged 64, dau. of Amos.

HOWARD, Aldo B., m. Mar. 30, 1862, by Rev. John Winkley, Nancy Wallingford, both of Rochester, d. Feb. 27, 1909, aged 65, dau. of Daniel.

HOWARD, Charles, of Rochester, m. July 3, 1866, in Farmington, Ellen Hussey, of Farmington, dau. of Jeremy.

HOWARD, A. J., m. July 31, 1866, in Rochester, E. G. Dadd.

HOWARD, Mathew, m. Sept. 14, 1867, by Rev. Robert S. Stubbs, Lydia A. Nute, both of Dover.

HOWARD, Emery Jr., of Milton, m. Mar. 17, 1869, in Rochester, Emma Kenney, of Dover.

HOWARD, Proctor A., of Rochester, m. Apr. 2, 1870, in Berwick, Me., Sarah A. Peavey, of Dover.

HOWARD, John O., of Rochester, m. Aug. 6, 1870, in Rochester, Bessie M. Horne.

HOWARD, John O., of Rochester, m. (pub. Aug. 18, 1870, in Rochester), Bessie M. Horne, of Lebanon, Me.

HOWE, Thomas, of Barrington, m. Jan. 28, 1788, by Rev. Benjamin Balch, Patience Garland, of Rochester.

HOWE, Samuel, m. Nov. 18, 1790, by Rev. Benjamin Balch, Hannah Clark, both of Barrington.

HOWE, John, m. Oct. 20, 1791, in Barrington, Lydia Swain, both of Barrington.

HOWE, Jonathan, d. Dec. 18, 1866, aged 84, m. Oct. 20, 1805, by Rev. Joseph Haven, Mehitable Twombly, b. Jul. 26, 1782, dau. of Samuel.

HOWE, Thomas, of Rochester, m. (1) Patience ----, d. Nov. 17, 1830, aged 64, m. (2) int. Feb. 19, 1832, in Farmington, Mrs. Betsey (Heard) Nutter, of Farmington, wid. of Lt. James, d. Mar. 29, 1859, aged 91.

HOWE, Thomas, b. Oct. 16, 1787, m. Nov. 24, 1825, in Barrington, Betsey Rowe, b. May 20, 1807, both of Barrington.

HOWE, Daniel, son of Thomas, b. July 20, 1826, m. Nov. 25, 1847, in Barnstead, Sarah Ann Clay, both of Barrington.

HOWE, Samuel, of Dover, son of Thomas, b. Sept. 11, 1828, d. Aug. 7, 1903, aged 74, m. (pub. May 3, 1853, in Rochester), Temperance A. Bickford, of Rochester.

HOWE, Levi F., son of Thomas, b. Sept. 7, 1830, m. Sept. 6, 1857, in Barrington, Mary Ann Arlin, d. Nov. 9, 1864, aged 23.

HOWE, John F., m. Nov. 20, 1868, in Dover, S. Lizzie Hussey, both of Dover.

HOWORTH, John, m. Nov. 4, 1866, in Dover, Mary A. Ashton, both of Dover.

HUBBARD, Joshua R., m. July 15, 1866, in Rochester, Mrs. Sophia Libbey.

HUBBARD, Calvin H., d. Apr. 17, 1924, aged 82, m. (pub. Dec. 16, 1869, in Great Falls), Lizzie A. Farnham.

HUCKINS, Andrew, of Madbury, d. Sept. 14, 1831, aged 63, m. Sept. 1791, Mary Daniels, of Barrington, d. Feb. 1, 1842, aged 70.

HUCKINS, Robert, son of Andrew, d. Nov. 2, 1880, aged 79, m. May 27, 1824, by Elder Enoch Place, Mary Daniels, d. Sept. 14, 1876, aged 72, dau. of Jacob.

HUCKINS, Joseph, d. Feb. 5, 1840, aged 50, m. (1) Hannah Waldron, d. Dec. 15, 1825, aged 33, m. (2) Mar. 18, 1827, by Elder Enoch Place, Sarah Waldron, d. Aug. 9, 1878, aged 78, both of Strafford.

HUCKINS, Israel, m. (1) ---- Waldron, m. (2) Mary Waldron, d. Feb. 2, 1826, aged 23, m. (3) June 4, 1827, by Elder Enoch Place, Susanna M. Boodey, d. Mar. 11, 1855, aged 44, both of Strafford.

HUCKINS, Asa, b. 1808, d. Sept. 29, 1878, aged 70, m. Oct. 1835, by Rev. David Root, Eliza Seavey, b. Dec. 27, 1807, d. Jan. 7, 1894.

HUCKINS, John, b. 1815, d. 1889, m. Nov. 12, 1840, by Elder Enoch Place, Hannah Abbie Hill, b. 1818, d. 1893, dau. of Andrew, both of Strafford.

HUCKINS, Lieut. Andrew, son of John D., d. Oct. 6, 1894, aged 74, m. (pub. Nov. 25, 1845, in Alton), Maria J. Chamberlain, d. Apr. 27, 1893, aged 70, dau. of John.

HUCKINS, Robert, b. July 8, 1821, d. Jan. 2, 1888, m. July 3, 1852, in Dover, Mary Ann Paul, b. Mar. 13, 1828, d. Apr. 16, 1910, both of Rollinsford.

HUCKINS, Jonathan D., of Lee, son of Moses, d. Jan. 23, 1860, aged 54, m. (1) Elinor H. Page, of Rochester, d. Aug. 5, 1842, aged 32,

m. (2) Nancy D. ----, d. Mar. 19, 1853, aged 34, m. (3) (pub. Dec. 13, 1853, in Haverhill, Mass.), Mary A. L. Dame, of Durham.

HUCKINS, R. L., m. Mar. 15, 1863, in Dover, Sarah J. Tucker, of Dover.

HUCKINS, Zachariah B., of Northwood, m. Apr. 30, 1865, in Barrington, Caroline R. Gear, of Barrington.

HUCKINS, George H., of Madbury, son of Robert, d. Sept. 15, 1871, aged 24, m. Dec. 10, 1870, in Dover, Sarah M. Tucker, of Fisherville.

HUFF, Edward R., m. Jan. 4, 1864, in Salmon Falls, Hattie Lee, both of Saco, Me.

HULL, William, son of Richard, m. May 6, 1790, Betsey Knowlton.

HULL, Samuel, of Northwood, son of Richard, d. Jun. 3, 1856, aged 80, m. Jan. 27, 1803, Sally Burnham.

HULL, John B., d. July 31, 1888, aged 68, m. (1) July 3, 1842, by Rev. Eben Francis, Elizabeth R. Wentworth, d. Jan. 6, 1846, aged 28, m. (2) Jan. 11, 1849, by Rev. Thomas J. Greenwood, Sarah Ann Horn, d. Dec. 19, 1874, aged 61, dau. of Samuel.

HULL, Cyrus G., b. Mar. 11, 1820, d. Nov. 7, 1898, m. Aug. 28, 1842, Harriet Willey, b. Dec. 27, 1821, dau. of Mark.

2) **HUNKING**, William, son of John, b. 1667, d. 1723, m. May 12, 1692, by Rev. John Pike, Sarah Partridge, dau. of John.

3) HUNKING, Capt. Mark, son of William, b. May 6, 1700, d. Aug. 6, 1782, m. (1) July 30, 1725, Mary Leavitt, b. July 11, 1699, dau. of John, m. (2) ---- Bradford, of Boston.

HUNKING, Benjamin, m. June 12, 1788, by Rev. Benjamin Balch, Betty Bunker, both of Madbury.

HUNKING, Mark, of Strafford, son of Nathaniel, b. Aug. 25, 1807, d. Jan. 2, 1872, m. 1825, Betsey Downs, b. Jul. 15, 1805, d. Apr. 16, 1859, dau. of John.

HUNT, Henry K., of Wakefield, Mass., m. Nov. 24, 1870, in Union, Mrs. Mary Frances (Canney) Beacham, wid. of George A., b. Sept. 23, 1830, d. 1913, dau. of Moses.

HUNTOON, Daniel R., of Sacramento, Calif., m. Mar. 5, 1867, in Lowell, Mass., Laura E. Wallace, of Dover.

HUNTRESS, Dyer Place, of Strafford, m. (1) ---- ----, m. (2) Sarah Elizabeth Bacon, of Roxbury, Mass., d. Mar. 11, 1853, aged 16, dau. of Marshall.

HUNTRESS, Dr. Joseph, of Tamworth, m. (pub. June 30, 1864, in Tamworth), Mrs. Julia A. Slade, of Charlestown, Mass.

HUSSEY, Benjamin, m. Mar. 7, 1774, by Rev. Isaac Hasey, Sarah Harmon.

HUSSEY, John, b. 1753, d. 1836, m. Feb. 12, 1776, by Rev. Isaac Hasey, Joyce Clark, b. 1755, d. 1831.

HUSSEY, Richard, of Lebanon, Me., b. Feb. 14, 1759, m. near 1783, Betsey Drew, of Madbury, b. Nov. 8, 1761.

HUSSEY, Reuben, m. Jul. 26, 1786, by Rev. Isaac Hasey, Experience Yeaton.

HUSSEY, Daniel, son of Paul, b. 1760, d. 1839, m. Apr. 28, 1788, by Rev. Isaac Hasey, Margaret Garland, b. 1768, d. 1841.

HUSSEY, Zachery, m. Jun. 23, 1788, Rev. Isaac Hasey, Elizabeth ---.

HUSSEY, Deac. Thomas, son of Thomas, b. Sept. 6, 1786, d. June 10, 1878, aged 91, m. Dec. 12, 1814, by Rev. Joseph Haven, Susan Hale, d. Apr. 9, 1887, aged 93, dau. of Thomas W., both of Barrington.

HUSSEY, Ezekiel, of Rochester, d. Apr. 3, 1823, m. Dec. 7, 1815, by Rev. J. W. Clary, Mercy Horne, of Dover, d. June 10, 1860, aged 65.

HUSSEY, Joseph, son of Richard, d. Jan. 11, 1871, aged 82, m. (1) Jan. 19, 1817, Anna Wiggin, d. July 17, 1853, aged 57, m. (2) Susan E. ----, d. Mar. 21, 1886, aged 51.

HUSSEY, Levi, son of Samuel, d. Mar. 13, 1872, aged 75, m. Sarah Edgerly, d. May 19, 1851, aged 54, dau. of Jonathan.

HUSSEY, Reuben, son of Richard, b. June 16, 1792, m. Feb. 8, 1821, by Elder Enoch Place, Alice Perkins, both of Barrington.

HUSSEY, Daniel Jr., son of Silas, d. Jun. 11, 1905, aged 73, m. Apr. 22, 1855, in Rochester, Mary F. Evans, of Rochester, d. Mar. 27, 1912, aged 79, dau. of William.

HUSSEY, Charles P., of Rochester, son of Samuel, d. Jul. 30, 1894, aged 62, m. Nov. 27, 1856, in Dover, Caroline Watson, of Dover, d. Mar. 17, 1915, aged 86, dau. of Winthrop.

HUSSEY, Edward R., son of Joseph, d. Apr. 8, 1900, aged 80, m. Dec. 20, 1857, in Milton, Bathsheba W. Goodwin, d. Nov. 30, 1889, aged 69, dau. of Jeremiah.

HUSSEY, John S., d. May 27, 1907, aged 65, m. (pub. Jan. 3, 1861, in Great Falls), Mary E. Boyle, of Rochester, d. Mar. 27, 1905, aged 61.

HUSSEY, Miles, of Exeter, Me., m. Oct. 5, 1862, in Alton, Lucy Whitehouse, of Alton.

HUSSEY, Charles, m. Apr. 29, 1865, in Dover, Joanna Bodwell, of Great Falls.

HUSSEY, Oliver W., son of Silas, d. Nov. 27, 1919, aged 81, m. Apr. 29, 1865, in Rochester, Melvina M. Varney.

HUSSEY, Samuel L., of Somersworth, m. (pub. Oct. 4, 1866, in Great Falls), Ella F. Curtis, of Bingham, Me.

HUSSEY, Albert F., of Dover, m. Jan. 1, 1868, in Gorham, Me., Carrie B. Fogg, of Gorham, Me.

HUSSEY, Dr. Charles E., of Dover, m. Oct. 13, 1870, in Buxton, Me., Lizzie L. Hutchinson, of Kennebunk, Me., dau. of Mahlon.

HUTCHINS, James, m. Dec. 8, 1785, by Rev. Benjamin Balch, Ruth Davis, both of Madbury.

HUTCHINS, John, of Dover, m. June 28, 1794, by Rev. Benjamin Balch, Keziah Howard, of Barrington.

HUTCHINS, Joseph, m. July 2, 1812, by Rev. Enos George, Hannah Waldron, both of Barrington.

HUTCHINS, Alpheus, of Northumberland, m. int. Sep. 6, 1851, in Lebanon, Me., Olive Corson.

HUTCHINS, Elder Elias, d. Sept. 11, 1859, aged 58, m. Dec. 24, 1846, by Rev. Ransom Dunn, Mrs. Marilla Marks.

HUTCHINS, Martin S., son of Remington, d. Oct. 15, 1918, aged 80, m. Dec. 3, 1864, in Dover, Olive A. Champion, d. Oct. 17, 1909, aged 68, dau. of John N., both of Dover.

HUTCHINS, George W., m. Aug. 27, 1866, by Rev. James Rand, Sarah F. Hill, both of Dover.

HUTCHINS, George S., m. Aug. 8, 1867, by Rev. Alden Sherwin, Mary Jane Smith, both of Kennebunkport, Me.

HYDE, Daniel A., m. Jan. 11, 1847, by Rev. Hezekiah D. Buzzell, Livonia D. Piper, d. Mar. 24, 1854, aged 26, dau. of Thomas, both of Alton.

ILLINGSWORTH, Frederick Augustus, of Waltham, Mass., m. int. Dec. 16, 1862, in Lebanon, Me., Ellen Jane Stevens.

INGRAHAM, Orimel C., of Canada, b. May 18, 1822, d. Oct. 9, 1897, m. Sept. 22, 1845, by Rev. Samuel Sherburne, Mary S. Hanson, of Strafford, d. Nov. 24, 1904, aged 83.

3) **JACKSON**, William Jr., son of William, b. in 1715, deposition, will 1757, proved 1760, m. early as 1741, Abigail Follett, dau. of Ichabod, m. (2) Olive Allen, b. 1715, d. Feb. 1, 1813, aged 88, dau. of Jacob.

4) JACKSON, Ebenezer, son of William, m. Aug. 19, 1773, by Dr. Belknap, Dorothy Leighton, d. Dec. 7, 1841, aged 88, both of Barrington.

JACKSON, Samuel Jr., m. Feb. 13, 1825, in Lebanon, Me., Abigail Nisbett.

JACKSON, Thompson, son of Josiah, b. Oct. 5, 1810, d. Apr. 6, 1871, m. (1) June 3, 1833, Mary Ann Page, m. (2) Aug. 29, 1842, Louisa J. (Chesley) Chesley, b. Aug. 31, 1809, d. Jan. 27, 1889, dau. of Lt. James.

JACKSON, Asa, of Rochester, m. Sep. 20, 1844, in Lebanon, Me., Abra Goodwin.

JACKSON, Jacob A., of New Durham, m. Dec. 30, 1855, in Newmarket, Mary Jane Critchett, of Newmarket.

JACKSON, Samuel A., of Kittery, Me., m. Feb. 7, 1865, in Great Falls, Olive D. Wallingford, of Lebanon, Me.

JACKSON, Moses F., m. Dec. 14, 1867, in Dover, Elizabeth A. Merrow, both of Dover.

JACKSON, J. H., m. (pub. Oct. 22, 1868, in Wolfeboro), Sarah F. Cotton, b. 1852, d. 1892.

JACKSON, George F., m. (pub. Nov. 12, 1868, in Rochester), Lizzie E. Howard, both of Rochester.

JACKSON, Charles H., of Rochester, m. (pub. Nov. 26, 1868, in Strafford), Martha A. Seward, of Strafford.

JACOBS, James C., son of Nicholas, m. Sept. 27, 1853, in Lunenburg, Vt., Mary V. Lamson, both of Dover.

JACOBS, Jeremiah, m. Aug. 27, 1864, in Great Falls, Areline M. Shorey, both of Rochester.

JAMES, Elisha, m. Oct. 12, 1774, by Rev. Isaac Hasey, Mercy Tebbetts.

JAMES, John, son of John, b. Jan. 19, 1752, d. Feb. 6, 1844, m. Mar. 26, 1778, by Rev. Isaac Hasey, Lydia Door.

JAMES, Daniel, m. Nov. 13, 1816, in Lebanon, Me., Dolly Blaisdell.

JAMES, Ebenezer, m. Aug. 10, 1828, in Lebanon, Me., Parmela Hanscom.

JAMES, John, m. int. May 10, 1840, in Lebanon, Me., Maria Prescott, of Acton, Me.

JAMES, Andrew D., of Lee, b. Feb. 12, 1815, d. Jul. 6, 1883, m. int. Feb. 22, 1847, in Lee, Lillis Bunker, of Durham, b. Apr. 6, 1816, d. Apr. 20, 1901, dau. of Samuel.

JAMES, Samuel, m. May 23, 1847, in Lebanon, Me., Caroline Blaisdell.

JAMES, Joseph A., of Lee, son of Thomas, d. Aug. 11, 1880, aged 59, m. Feb. 11, 1850, Mary E. Fernald, d. Aug. 19, 1898, aged 67, of Madbury.

JAMES, John H., m. Feb. 3, 1868, in Dover, Roesa A. Roberts, both of Somersworth.

JASPER, Charles A., of Wadleigh's Falls, Me., son of Rev. O. H., m. Sept. 30, 1866, in Dover, by Rev. O. H. Jasper, Anne Danforth, of Brunswick, Me.

JELLISON, Oliver M. of Portsmouth, m. (pub. May 26, 1870, in Wakefield), Lizzie A. Hutchins, of Wakefield.

JENKINS, Nathan, of New Durham, d. Feb. 15, 1872, aged 78, m. Apr. 3, 1814, by Rev. Joseph Boodey, Rose Horn, of Farmington, d. May 10, 1859, aged 70.

7) JENKINS, Elijah, of New Durham, son of Ebenezer and Hope, b. Mar. 14, 1802, m. (1) May 30, 1827, in Dover, Elizabeth Roberts, b. Apr. 24, 1804, d. Jan. 14, 1831, dau. of Joseph and Anna, of Dover, m. (2) Feb. 3, 1833, Abigail B. Drew, d. Jan. 28, 1860, aged 57, dau. of William.

JENKINS, Melville P., of Allenstown, m. Dec. 25, 1861, by Rev. Alvan Tobey, H. Susan Fernald, of Madbury.

JENKINS, George Henry, of Rollinsford, m. Oct. 11, 1865, in Dover, Melissa E. Thurston, of Dover.

JENKINS, Sgt. John S., of Lee, son of John Jr., b. Jun. 2, 1847, d. Oct. 12, 1926, m. Nov. 18, 1865, in Durham, Maria H. Otis, of Newmarket, b. Nov. 13, 1845, d. Mar. 2, 1912, dau. of Simon.

JENKINS, Charles W., m. July 7, 1866, in Great Falls, Abbie W. Horne, both of Rochester.

JENKINS, George W., of Boston, Mass., m. June 5, 1870, in Dover, Emma A. Lawrence, of Dover, dau. of David.

JENKS, Simeon, of N. Providence, R.I., b. Apr. 4, 1756, m. near 1781, Anne Moriah Nutter, of St. George, Me., b. May 12, 1761, dau. of Jonathan.

JENKS, Simeon, m. Sept. 1, 1793, by Rev. Benjamin Balch, Elizabeth Wells, both of Dover.

JENKS, Charles W., m. Feb. 7, 1867, in Dover, Lydia A. Newell, both of Boston, Mass.

JENKS, Joshua E., of Portland, Me., m. Sept. 15, 1869, in Dover, Nettie C. Perkins, of Brunswick, Me.

JENNESS, Mark, m. Aug. 14, 1777, in Barrington, Betty Ham, of Barrington.

JENNESS, Moses, of Rochester, m. Feb. 6, 1806, by Rev. Benjamin Balch, Mrs. Hannah Berry, of Barrington.

JENNESS, John Jr., of Barrington, d. Mar. 21, 1842, m. May 5, 1808, by Rev. Joseph Haven, Sarah Robinson, of Rochester, d. Aug. 20, 1827, aged 45.

JENNESS, Deac. Solomon, of Rochester, d. July 27, 1869, aged 79, m. (1) Nov. 24, 1811, by Rev. Micajah Otis, Elizabeth Seavey, d. Apr. 30, 1823, aged 30, both of Rochester, m. (2) Jan. 11, 1824, by Rev. William Demeritt, Phebe Taylor, d. Dec. 31, 1831, aged 43, m. (3) March 25, 1832, by Rev. William Demeritt, Elizabeth Allen, d. May 21, 1861, aged 61, m. (4) Lydia L. Conner.

JENNESS, Joseph, m. Nov. 22, 1812, in Barrington, Hannah Watson, both of Rochester.

JENNESS, Samuel D. Jr., d. July 16, 1866, aged 68, m. Aug. 24, 1820, by Elder Enoch Place, Sally Sampson, d. Oct. 30, 1875, aged 79, both of Barrington.

JENNESS, Daniel, d. Oct. 17, 1889, aged 84, m. (1) Feb. 12, 1826, in Wakefield, Olive Moulton, of Wakefield, d. Aug. 9, 1845, aged 41, m. (2) Melinda ----, d. Sept. 14, 1885, aged 67.

JENNESS, Benning Wentworth, b. 1806, d. Nov. 16, 1879, m. Sept. 12, 1826, by Elder Enoch Place, Nancy Walker Shackford, b. 1801, d. May 25, 1868, aged 68, dau. of Samuel, both of Strafford.

JENNESS, Hiram, d. Feb. 1, 1870, aged 56, m. Jul. 28, 1835, in Middlton, Sarah Welch, d. Sep. 17, 1895, aged 81, both of Wakefield.

JENNESS, Seth, m. Nov. 26, 1835, by Elder Enoch Place, Esther Brock, d. Nov. 28, 1847, aged 38, dau. of John, both of Rochester.

JENNESS, William, of Farmington, son of Hiram, b. 1839, d. Jan. 5, 1864, n. Nov. 25, 1858, in Milton, Elizabeth Jenness, of Wakefield, b. 1827, d. Jan. 4, 1861, dau. of Hiram.

JENNESS, Franklin H., of Madbury, m. Jan. 13, 1862, by Rev. James Rand, Elvira B. Quimby, of Dover.

JENNESS, R. V., of Dover, m. July 29, 1863, in Brookfield, Emily C. Smith, of Brookfield.

JENNESS, James F., of Portsmouth, m. Dec. 8, 1864, in Malden, Mass., Hannah Hill, of Dover.

JENNESS, Stephen S., of Rochester, son of John J., d. Jan. 11, 1897, aged 56, m. Jan. 4, 1865, in Rochester, Helen M. Wiggin, of Alton.

JENNESS, Gilman, m. Dec. 6, 1866, in Alton, Sarah Freeman.

JENNESS, John W., of Strafford, m. Mar. 28, 1867, in Barnstead, Lizzie M. Parker, of Barnstead.

JENNESS, Charles B., of Durham, m. Sept. 4, 1867, in Wolfeboro, Addie E. Bickford, of Wolfeboro.

JENNINGS, C. P., of Dover, m. Jan. 4, 1869, by Rev. Robert S. Stubbs, Sarah F. Miles, of Madbury.

JEPSON, Rev. John W., of W. Newfield, Me., m. Feb. 17, 1862, in Dover, m. Jennie Brackett, of Berwick, Me.

JEROLD, Charles E., of Wolfeboro, m. Oct. 10, 1867, in Tuftonboro, Sarah A. Moody, of Ossipee.

JEWELL, Milton, b. July 2, 1808, d. Jan. 4, 1869, m. (pub. Feb. 1, 1831, in Strafford), Nancy Calley, b. May 3, 1808, d. Apr. 7, 1880, aged 71.

JEWELL, Charles M., of Barrington, son of Milton, b. May 30, 1840, d. Feb. 19, 1865, m. Nov. 2, 1862, in Strafford, Maria L. Winkley, of Strafford, b. Feb. 23, 1843, d. May 17, 1882.

JEWELL, Samuel F., of Barrington, m. (pub. Dec. 30, 1869, in Rochester), Wenna F. Gray, of Farmington.

JEWETT, John, son of Jacob, b. May 26, 1771, m. Jan. 27, 1796, Anne Frances Clark, b. Jan. 26, 1772.

JEWETT, Daniel G., of Boston, Mass., b. Dec. 8, 1829, m. int. Nov. 22, 1867, in Lebanon, Me., Eliza A. Gerrish, b. Aug. 22, 1836, d. Mar. 13, 1887, dau. of George.

JEWETT, William G., of Rochester, m. Jan. 18, 1868, by Rev. Robert S. Stubbs, Mary E. Ham, of Barrington.

JEWETT, Charles, of Brooklyn, N.Y., m. July 9, 1868, by Rev. Alden Sherwin, Abbie E. Flagg, of Dover.

JOHNSON, James, m. June 4, 1788, by Rev. Benjamin Balch, Hannah Danielson, both of Barrington.

JOHNSON, Thomas Jr., of Barrington, m. Dec. 30, 1811, by Rev. Micajah Otis, Susannah Gray, of Rochester.

JOHNSON, Andrew, of Fryburg, Me., m. Feb. 25, 1813, by Rev. Micajah Otis, Charity Johnson, of Barrington.

JOHNSON, Samuel, m. Sept. 1, 1813, by Rev. Micajah Otis, Mehitable Johnson, both of Barrington.

JOHNSON, James 3rd, of Strafford, d. Jan. 8, 1891, aged 78, m. Dec. 27, 1832, by Elder Enoch Place, Peggy Tuttle, of Barrington, d. Jan. 1, 1875, aged 62, dau. of John.

JOHNSON, Stephen, son of James, d. Feb. 7, 1864, aged 45, m. Sept. 22, 1839, by Elder Enoch Place, Catherine Johnson, d. Jan., 5, 1893, aged 73, both of Strafford.

JOHNSON, James, m. int. Jan. 1, 1843, in Lebanon, Me., Olive Annis, of Sanford, Me.

JOHNSON, Solomon, son of Leighton, b. Mar. 25, 1828, m. Oct. 14, 1851, in Lebanon, Me., ---- [missing].

JOHNSON, Ezra F., son of Ezra, d. Feb. 14, 1889, aged 56, m. Apr. 11, 1853, in Wolfeboro, Elizabeth W. Sanborn, d. Feb. 21, 1920, aged 83, both of Wolfeboro.

JOHNSON, George W., of Sanford, Me., d. Sept. 25, 1907, aged 77, m. (1) (pub. Aug. 1853, in N. Berwick, Me.), Olive J. Chadborne, b. 1831, d. 1862, dau. of Uriah, m. (2) Apr. 3, 1864, in S. Berwick, Me., Louise M. Ferguson, of Great Falls.

JOHNSON, Joseph L. son of Leighton, b. Jul. 23, 1834, m. Aug. 31, 1856, in Lebanon, Me., ---- [missing].

JOHNSON, Samuel, m. (pub. May 8, 1862, in Wolfeboro), Mrs. Mary Sargent.

JOHNSON, Lorenzo A., m. Oct. 4, 1862, in New Durham, Ellen Perkins, of Alton.

JOHNSON, William F., b. Mar. 15, 1834, d. Nov. 8, 1892, m. int. Feb. 10, 1863, in Lebanon, Me., Ada A. Libbey, of Sanford, Me., b. Apr. 28, 1831, d. Oct. 7, 1870.

JOHNSON, Samuel F., m. Mar. 17, 1864, by Rev. James Rand, Helen A. Hoitt.

JOHNSON, Sgt. James W., of Wolfeboro, m. (pub. Apr. 13, 1865, in Milton), Julia A. Hatch, of Milton, dau. of Elijah.

JOHNSON, Henry, m. Sept. 9, 1865, by Rev. Asa Piper, Melissa M. Cotton, of Gilmanton.

JOHNSON, Augustus, of Barnstead, m. Jan. 1, 1868, in Dover, Abbie Dicey.

JOHNSON, A. W., m. (pub. Apr. 22, 1869, in Farmington, Me.), Mary A. Backus.

JOHNSON, George H., of Charlestown, Mass., m. Jan. 4, 1870, in Gonic, Fannie E. Locke, of Gonic.

JOHNSON, George, m. (pub. Nov. 10, 1870, in Great Falls), Mrs. Deborah Jenness.

JONES, Eliphalet, son of Nathaniel, b. 1752, d. 1820, m. Apr. 20, 1775, by Matthew Merriam, Ruth Roberts, b. May 12, 1758, d. May 12, 1828, aged 70, dau. of Joshua, both of Berwick, Me.

JONES, Jeremiah, m. May 26, 1791, by Rev. Benjamin Balch, Molly Howard, both of Barrington.

JONES, Joseph, d. Dec. 30, 1847, aged 78, m. Apr. 23, 1793, by Rev. Benjamin Balch, Anna Ayers, both of Barrington.

JONES, Capt. Levi, son of Ebenezer, m. (1) Oct. 15, 1801, Elizabeth Plumer, dau. of Joseph, m. (2) Nov. 23, 1831, by Rev. Isaac Willey, Mrs. Sarah (Webster) Wallingford, d. Jan. 12, 1863, aged 69, wid. of Samuel, both of Milton.

JONES, John P., b. May 9, 1772, m. near 1804, Nancy Chesley, b. Aug. 13, 1769, d. Sept. 28, 1848, dau. of Capt. Jonathan.

JONES, Joseph Jr., of Rochester, m. Nov. 15, 1810, by Rev. Micajah Otis, Eliza Brock, of Barrington.

JONES, Edward, m. Nov. 20, 1811, by Rev. Micajah Otis, Martha Maloon, both of New Castle.

JONES, John, m. Nov. 15, 1818, in Barrington, Hannah Hill.

5) JONES, John S., son of William, b. Apr. 8, 1793, d. Sept. 2, 1880, m. Feb. 24, 1819, Abigail Drew, b. 1796, d. Apr. 4, 1886.

JONES, Joseph Jr., d. May 30, 1854, aged 67, m. Oct. 31, 1819, by Elder Enoch Place, Susan Hill, d. May 14, 1854, aged 61, both of Barrington.

JONES, Hiram, d. Oct. 2, 1855, aged 55, m. (1) int. May 12, 1824, in Lebanon, Me., Joanna Stevens, of Shapleigh, Me., d. Sep. 27, 1836, aged 33, m. (2) int. Nov. 7, 1839, in Lebanon, Me., Mary C. Stevens, of Acton, Me., d. Dec. 1, 1882, aged 80.

JONES, Jonathan R., d. Mar. 29, 1866, m. (1) 1825, by Rev. James Weston, Rebecca Knox, d. Nov. 14, 1848, aged 43, m. (2) Oct. 12, 1851, in Lebanon, Me., Mrs. Esther H. Corson, d. Jul. 2, 1883, aged 77.

JONES, Jonathan, m. (1) int. Jun. 26, 1825, in Lebanon, Me., Rebecca Knox, m. (2) Oct. 12, 1851, in Lebanon, Me., Mrs. Esther H. Corson.

JONES, Samuel, m. int. Mar. 27, 1826, in Lebanon, Me., Molly Lord.

JONES, Ephraim S., m. int. Nov. 11, 1826, in Lebanon, Me., Katharine Wentworth.

JONES, Peter (Clark?), d. Oct. 16, 1858, m. Feb. 25, 1827, in Lebanon, Me., Ada Hersom.

JONES, Samuel 3rd, m. int. Nov. 4, 1827, in Lebanon, Me., Louisa Parsons, of Newfield, Me.

JONES, Samuel, m. int. Sep. 5, 1828, in Lebanon, Me., Mrs. Hannah Hooper, of Berwick, Me.

JONES, Dr. Samuel W., son of Samuel Jr., b. Jun. 17, 1808, m. (1) Oct. 26, 1828, Martha Legro, d. Aug. 26, 1835, aged 35, dau. of Moses, m. (2) int. Apr. 27, 1836, in Lebanon, Me., Roxanna Lord.

5) JONES, Ebenezer, son of William, b. June 21, 1802, m. (1) Nov. 26, 1831, Sarah Ann Kennison, m. (2) Apr. 27, 1836, by Elder Enoch Place, Hannah H. Foss, b. June 5, 1811, dau. of Eliphalet, both of Strafford.

JONES, Nathaniel M., d. Jan. 25, 1879, aged 81, m. (pub. June 12, 1832, in Alton), Mary A. Watson, d. July 11, 1882, aged 81.

JONES, Lewis, m. Dec. 9, 1835, by Rev. Nathaniel Berry, Betsey L. Edgerly, b. 1809, d. Feb. 9, 1836, aged 21, dau. of Jeremiah, both of New Durham.

JONES, John, d. Apr. 29, 1884, aged 73, m. int. Dec. 15, 1838, in Lebanon, Me., Rosetta Prescott, of Acton, Me., d. Jan. 1, 1889.

JONES, Ebenezer Jr., m. int. Oct. 1, 1839, in Lebanon, Me., Mrs. Lydia Warren.

JONES, Nathaniel B. of Somersworth, m. int. Nov. 1, 1840, in Lebanon, Me., Vesta H. Tebbets.

JONES, Gershom, b. Jun. 28, 1818, m. (1) int. Jan. 22, 1843, in Lebanon, Me., Nancy J. Hersom, d. Jan. 11, 1845, m. (2) Jul. 5, 1846, in Lebanon, Me., Mary Ricker, d. Aug. 19, 1865, aged 42, m. (3) Dec. 7, 1867, in Lebanon, Mrs., Sarah Butler.

JONES, Joseph B., of Cathage, Me., m. int. Mar. 25, 1843, in Lebanon, Me., Abigail W. Roberts.

JONES, Eli, son of James, b. Jan. 20, 1819, d. Feb. 6, 1863, m. int. Mar. 23, 1844, in Lebanon, Me., Mary Ann Hersom.

JONES, Eben, m. int. Mar. 3, 1849, in Lebanon, Me., Mehitable Jane Ricker.

JONES, Seaver, son of James, b. Sep. 9, 1824, m. Oct. 19, 1849, in Lebanon, Me., Urbana Ricker.

JONES, Ebenezer Jr., m. Dec. 22, 1849, by Elder William H. Littlefield, Permelia J. Fernald.

JONES, James N., b. 1794, d. 1865, m. (1) Mary McDuffee, b. 1796, d. 1848, m. (2) Apr. 7, 1850, by Rev. Nathaniel Berry, Sally Clough, both of Alton.

JONES, William Augustus, son of Joshua, b. Oct. 14, 1828, d. Aug. 8, 1881, aged 52, m. Oct. 11, 1850, in Milton, Emeline C. Ricker.

JONES, John A., m. Nov. 23, 1851, in Lebanon, Me., Ruth F. Hersom, d. Aug. 26, 1853, aged 23.

JONES, Oliver L., son of James, b. Aug. 23, 1828, m. int. Oct. 26, 1854, in Lebanon, Me., Margaret Austin, b. 1831, d. Jan. 17, 1881.

JONES, George W., son of Eliphalet, d. Feb. 20, 1900, aged 66, m. (1) Mar. 16, 1856, in Milton, Lydia Jane Corliss, both of Milton, m. (2) Feb. 29, 1860, in Milton, Charlotte Dixon, of Lebanon, Me., aged 19.

JONES, Joseph M., m. int. Oct. 30, 1856, in Lebanon, Me., Phebe K. Hall, of Yarmouth, Me.

JONES, John S., son of Hiram, b. Aug. 29, 1830, d. Sep. 10, 1886, m. (1) int. Feb. 2, 1858, in Lebanon, Me., Lucretia F. Reynolds, d.

Dec. 12, 1860, m. (2) int. Oct. 24, 1862, in Lebanon, Me., Sarah E. Hayes.

JONES, Thomas, m. int. Sep. 4, 1860, in Lebanon, Me., Lucinda F. Blaisdell.

JONES, John R., m. int. Apr. 20, 1861, in Lebanon, Me., Mary S. Seaward, of Kittery, Me.

JONES, William F., of Durham, m. Jan. 8, 1862, in Sanbornton, Laura Chase, dau. of Thomas.

JONES, Nathaniel D., b. 1839, d. Apr. 2, 1890, m. Dec. 5, 1863, in Lebanon, Me., Mary Olive Hayes, b. 1844.

JONES, John W., of Portland, Me., m. Feb. 7, 1865, in Milton, Addie E. Doldt, dau. of Rev. James.

JONES, George, of Great Falls, m. July 5, 1865, by Rev. James Rand, Louisa A. Richards, of Haverhill, Mass.

JONES, Paul, m. (pub. Apr. 19, 1866, in Portsmouth), Mrs. Nancy Austin.

JONES, Eliphalet, m. June 10, 1866, in Dover, Emma D. Hardison, both of N. Berwick, Me.

JONES, George Albert, of Lebanon, Me., son of James, b. Feb. 26, 1847, m. 1867, in Somersworth, Eunice J. Blaisdell, of Somersworth.

JONES, Augustine, of Boston, Mass., m. Oct. 10, 1867, in Dover, Caroline Alice Place, of Dover, dau. of William.

JONES, J. Henry, m. Nov. 2, 1867, in Saco, Me., H. Jennie Evans, dau. of J. D., both of Rochester.

JONES, Charles A., m. May 26, 1868, by Rev. James Rand, Hannah Jane Otis, both of Dover.

JONES, Daniel B., aged 20, m. Nov. 2, 1868, in Middleton, Emma E. Perkins, b. Aug. 7, 1850, d. Jun. 18, 1907, dau. of Stephen.

JONES, Alfred W., m. (pub. May 12, 1870, in E. Rochester), Ellen S. Kimball, both of Great Falls.

JONES, Dana P., of Lebanon, Me., m. Jun. 21, 1874, in Rochester, Mary F. Dearborn.

JONES, John S. 2nd, m. int. Oct. 11, 1875, in Lebanon, Me., Luella Ricker.

JORDAN, James K., of Denmark, Me., m. int. Oct. 2, 1819, in Lebanon, Me., Nancy Courson.

JORDAN, Charles, d. Jun. 8, 1848, m. Jul. 10, 1828, in Lebanon, Me., Dorcas Stanton.

JORDAN, Frederick B., of Portland, Me., m. Jul. 30, 1856, in Lebanon, Me., Mary M. Clark, of Somersworth.

JORDAN, Ebenezer S., of Wilton, m. int. Oct. 24, 1857, in Lebanon, Me., Clara Stanton.

JORDAN, George I., of Rochester, m. Jan. 26, 1862, in Rochester, Elizabeth Downs, of Milton.

JORDAN, Granville, m. Aug. 1, 1867, in Dover, Sarah E. Emerson, both of Durham.

JOY, Ebenezer, son of Samuel, b. May 30, 1785, d. Aug. 8, 1827, m. Jan. 16, 1815, Nancy Watson, b. 1795, d. Oct. 1, 1827, dau. of Henry.

JOY, Ivory, of York, Me., d. Apr. 24, 1879, aged 84, m. Dec. 16, 1819, in Lebanon, Me., Adah Furbush, d. Feb. 14, 1863, aged 65.

JOY, Samuel, of Durham, b. Apr. 30, 1824, d. 1901, m. Mar. 21, 1857, by Rev. Thomas J. Greenwood, Susan D. Smart, of Newmarket, b. Dec. 31, 1824, d. Aug. 25, 1906.

JOY, Samuel M., of N. Berwick, Me., m. Dec. 24, 1863, in Newcastle, Melinda Yeaton, of Portsmouth.

JOY, Edward, of Portsmouth, m. June 15, 1867, in Portsmouth, Mary E. Bickford, of Rochester.

JOY, Horace A., of N. Berwick, Me., m. Aug. 3, 1867, in S. Berwick, Me., Cynthia A. Hilton, of Salmon Falls.

JOY, Timothy M., of Newmarket, son of Eben, m. Oct. 28, 1867, by Rev. Isaac C. White, Nellie F. Wiggin, of Durham, dau. of Thomas.

JUNKINS, Rufus, of Wakefield, d. Apr. 1854, aged 60, m. (1) Mar. 3, 1822, Sarah Hayes, d. July 12, 1828, aged 25, dau. of James, m. (2) (pub. July 21, 1829, in Milton), Temperance P. Adams, of Milton, d. Mar. 14, 1874, aged 74.

KALLIHER, John, of S. Canton, Mass., m. June 1, 1865, in Dover, Mary E. Gleeson, of Dover.

KEAY, Edmund, b. Oct. 13, 1788, d. Sep. 2, 1841, in Lebanon, Me., Permit Libbey.

KEAY, Otis Jr., m. May 6, 1819, in Lebanon, Me., Dorcas Woodsum.

KEAY, Otis, m. int. Jan. 19, 1829, in Lebanon, Me., Lucy Sawyer, of Wells, Me.

KEAY, Hiram, b. Dec. 17, 1791, m. Jun. 7, 1829, in Lebanon, Me.,Charlotte Libbey, b. Jun. 7, 1805, d. Aug. 30, 1853.

KEAY, David, b. 1807, m. Mar. 14, 1830, in Lebanon, Me., Ruth Jones, b. 1808.

KEAY, Albra, d. Oct. 13, 1870, aged 69, m. (1) int. Dec. 22, 1832, in Lebanon, Me., Phebe Downs, d. Jun. 11, 1840, m. (2) Mar. 23, 1847, in Lebanon, Me., Lydia D. Ross.

KEAY, Nathaniel Washman, son of Hawley A., b. Jun. 18, 1822, m. int. Aug. 3, 1844, in Lebanon, Me., Susan W. Seaver, of China, Me., d. Apr. 30, 1853, aged 40.

KEAY, Everett F., m. Mar. 24, 1866, in Ossipee, Meribah F. Nutter, d. Nov. 20, 1887, aged 45.

KEAY, Gershom J., of Boston, Mass., m. Aug. 19, 1866, in Great Falls, Abbie M. Horne, of Great Falls, dau. of Samuel F.

KEITH, George H., of New York, m. May 7, 1863, in Dover, Lucy A. Wiggin, of Dover.

KELLAM, A. N., of New Haven, Conn., m. July 20, 1864, by Rev. Ezra Haskell, Emma C. Drew, of Dover, dau. of Isaac.

KELLEY, Daniel, m. Nov. 8, 1799, by Rev. Benjamin Balch, Sally Tasker, both of Barrington.

KELLEY, Henry M. m. (pub. Nov. 25, 1858, in Great Falls), Lydia A. Taylor, d. Sep. 10, 1907, aged 68, dau. of Joshua, both of Rochester.

KELLEY, Edward P., of Haverhill, Mass., m. May 12, 1862, in Dover, Lizzie Bateman, of Dover, d. Oct. 6, 1917, aged 70.

KELLEY, George W., son of William, m. Jan. 16, 1867, by Rev. Alvan Tobey, Annie L. Stackpole, dau. of Otis, both of Madbury.

KENDALL, James W., of Boston, Mass., m. (pub. Sept. 27, 1866, in Wolfeboro), Abbie H. Rice.

KENDELL, Stephen, son of Enoch, d. Mar. 21, 1892, aged 85, m. (1) int. Dec. 11, 1836, in Dover, Jane Ann Harlow, m. (2) July 13, 1876, in Madbury, Mary P. (Bunker) Johnson, widow, dau. of Samuel.

2) **KENNARD**, Samuel, son of Michael, d. 1820, aged 88, m. Sept. 29, 1750, in Dover, Elizabeth Allen, dau. of Francis and Mary.

KENNARD, George, aged 60, of Brighton, Me., m. Apr. 22, 1855, in Brookfield, Elizabeth Leavitt, aged 62, of Brookfield.

KENNETT, J. C., of Madison, m. Sept. 25, 1866, in Tamworth, Lizzie Stillings, of Jefferson.

KENNEY, Lafayette D. M., m. (pub. Oct. 21, 1869, in Rochester), Hattie B. Moody, of E. Rochester.

KENNISON, Joseph, m. Oct. 6, 1773, by Rev. Isaac Hasey, Sarah Bean.

KENNISON, John Jr., m. Apr. 1, 1784, by Rev. Isaac Hasey, Betty Fall.

KENNISON, Andrew, of Tuftonboro, d. Oct. 21, 1852, aged 75, m. Mar. 30, 1802, in Wakefield, Sally Roberts, of Ossipee, d. Dec. 4, 1879, aged 98.

KENNISON, Chase, m. Dec. 16, 1810, by Rev. Benjamin Randall, Mrs. Lettice (Bickford) Bodge, wid. of Samuel, both of Middleton.

KENNISON, Solomon, of Brookfield, m. Nov. 26, 1829, in Wakefield, Hannah Colby, of Dover.

KENNISON, Mark, m. May 31, 1846, in Newmarket, Asenath S. Caswell, both of New Market.

KENNISTON, Albert, m. (pub. Sept. 4, 1862, in Ossipee), Eunice Kimball, both of Ossipee.

KENT, Josiah, of Parsonsfield, Me., m. Mar. 9, 1818, in Lebanon, Me., Eunice Dixon.

KENT, John, of Barnstead, d. Sept. 23, 1843, aged 42, m. (pub. Dec. 18, 1827, in Portsmouth), Ruhamah Dearborn, of Portsmouth, dau. of Gen. Asa.

KENT, Jonathan, m. Apr. 2, 1829, Jane Mills, both of Eaton.

KENT, George W., of Boston, Mass., son of William, aged 29, m. Jul. 23, 1866, in Lebanon, Me., Sarah J. Graves, aged 22, dau. of William B.

KENT, James M., of Durham, m. (pub. June 9, 1870, in Rochester), Mary A. Trickey, of Dover.

KEPPEL, John F., of New York City, N.Y., m. Nov. 3, 1868, by Rev. Robert S. Stubbs, Georgia A. Welch, of Dover.

KERSHAW, Edward, m. Mar. 4, 1867, in Salmon Falls, Almira A. Goodwin, both of S. Berwick, Me.

2) **KIELLE**, Ebenezer, b. Mar. 14, 1746, d. Sept. 22, 1820, m. Apr. 26, 1781, Molly Hall, b. Dec. 22, 1755, dau. of Benjamin, d. Jan. 1, 1835, aged 80, both of Barrington.

6) **KIMBALL**, Ephraim, son of Ephraim, b. June 17, 1751, m. Sept. 23, 1773, Hannah Emerson, b. Feb. 13, 1754, d. Sept. 13, 1838, dau. of Solomon.

7) KIMBALL, Solomon, son of Ephraim, of Farmington, b. May 2, 1789, d. Mar. 7, 1832, m. Jan. 10, 1810, by Rev. Micajah Otis, Martha L. Babb, b. Sept. 1783, d. Sept. 19, 1836, dau. of Moses, of Barrington.

KIMBALL, Jesse, of Newfield, Me., m. Dec. 5, 1822, in Lebanon, Me., Betsey Ross.

KIMBALL, Timothy L., m. Mar. 24, 1836, by Rev. James Weston, Betsey H. Lord, dau. of Capt. Benjamin.

KIMBALL, William S., m. Mar. 7, 1855, in Lebanon, Me. Anna L. Palmer, both of Milton.

KIMBALL, Joseph P., d. Sept. 24, 1863, aged 31, m. Aug. 23, 1855, in Alton, Lucy M. Freeman, d. Oct. 30, 1863, aged 29.

KIMBALL, Samuel A., d. Nov. 9, 1860, aged 40, m. (1) int. Apr. 4, 1854, in Lebanon, Me., Adaline Hanscom, both of Milton, m. (2) Mar. 20, 1857, in Milton, Lucy D. Pinkham.

KIMBALL, Col. Samuel S., m. July 8, 1863, in Dover, Emmarilla S. Yeaton, both of Belgrade, Me.

KIMBALL, Parker S., of Providence, R.I., m. Oct. 20, 1863, in New York, Mary Eleanor Hull, of Dover, dau. of John B.

KIMBALL, John D., m. Jan. 14, 1864, by Rev. Arthur Caverno, Adaline Kelley, both of Dover.

KIMBALL, John T., of Dorchester, Mass., m. May 19, 1864, in Rochester, Abra A. Wentworth, of Rochester.

KIMBALL, Benjamin, m. (pub. Apr. 19, 1866, in Wolfeboro), Mary E. Hartshorn.

KIMBALL, George E., b. 1844, d. 1915, m. (pub. Apr. 4, 1867, in Wolfeboro), Nancy J. Chase, of Alton, b. 1844, d. 1937.

KIMBALL, Benjamin, of Bangor, Me., m. Aug. 18, 1867, in Dover, Nellie L. Moulton, of Dover, dau. of Josiah.

KINCAID, David L., of great Falls, m. Nov. 27, 1851, in Lebanon, Me., Susan G. Lord.

KING, Samuel, of Kennebunkport, m. Aug. 25, 1868, by Rev. James Rand, Sarah S. Daney, of Dover.

KING, Thomas J., m. May 28, 1870, in Dover, Jennie A. Getchell, both of Dover.

KING, Benjamin, of Kennebunkport, Me., m. July 12, 1870, in Dover, Abby Pray, of Ossipee.

KINGMAN, John, of Rye, b. Dec. 23, 1747, m. Nov. 18, 1773, in Barrington, Dolley Waterhouse, b. Jan. 17, 1750.

KINGSBURY, James A., of Dover, m. Sept. 2, 1864, in Dover, Georgiana D. Thomas, of Boston, Mass.

KINGSBURY, Byron F., of Boston, Mass., m. Dec. 25, 1867, in Dover, Caroline M. Chick, of Dover.

KINSMAN, Prescott B., of Berwick, Me., m. before Dec. 4, 1868, in Milton, Annette D. Shapleigh.

2) KITTREDGE, Dr. George Washington, d. July 4, 1836, aged 36, m. Nov. 7, 1826, in Portland, Me., Julia Ann Gage, of Portland, Me., d. Jan. 20, 1887, aged 87.

KITTREDGE, John, m. June 30, 1864, in Dover, Harriet H. Peirce, dau. of Andrew.

KNAPP, Isaac B., m. May 30, 1864, in Dover, Angelia P. Speed, both of Rollinsford.

KNAPP, William D., of Somersworth, m. Nov. 29, 1866, in Great Falls, Sarah H. Hussey, of Barrington, d. Jan. 5, 1906, aged 73.

KNIGHT, George, b. 1733, d. 1784, m. near 1760, Susannah Chesley, b. June 28, 1737, d. Apr. 23, 1784, dau. of George.

4) KNIGHT, John, son of George, d. Jan. 30, 1850, aged 89, m. Feb. 16, 1790, Deborah McCutchins, d. Oct. 18, 1829, aged 83.

KNIGHT, Stephen, of Waterboro, Me., m. Mar. 17, 1822, by Elder Zebedee Delano, Mary Pray.

KNIGHT, William, of So. Berwick, Me., m. before Jan. 26, 1841, in Lebanon, Me., Cordelia Cowell, of Sanford, Me.

KNIGHT, Alpha, of Boston, Mass., m. 1843, Elizabeth Wingate Nason, d. Mar. 9, 1846, in Boston.

KNIGHT, James F., of Newmarket, m. Aug. 3, 1862, in Dover, Stalbira A. Nelson, of Eliot, Me.

KNIGHT, Gilman, m. Dec. 11, 1862, in Dover, Mary A. Pinder, both of Salmon Falls.

KNIGHT, Edward W., m. Sept. 15, 1868, in Great Falls, Nettie M. Davis, both of S. Berwick, Me.

KNOWLES, Moses, of Northwood, m. Nov. 26, 1801, by Rev. Benjamin Balch, Polly Caverly, of Barrington.

KNOWLTON, Jonathan, of Northwood, d. July 27, 1853, aged 62, m. (1) Lydia ----, d. Oct. 21, 1838, aged 45, m. (2) July 14, 1839, by Rev. Alpheus D. Smith, Mary Willey, of Dover, d. Sept. 11, 1871, aged 75.

KNOWLTON, Charles T., of Portland, Me., m. May 4, 1869, in Dover, Martha Hodgdon, of Biddeford, Me.

KNOX, Eleazer, m. Mar. 19, 1778, by Rev. Isaac Hasey, Marcy Spencer.

KNOX, David, m. Sep. 6, 1792, by Rev. Isaac Hasey, Molly Hanson.

KNOX, Samuel, m. Nov. 29, 1792, by Rev. Isaac Hasey, Sally Gerrish.

KNOX, John Jr., m. Apr. 16, 1795, by Rev. Isaac Hasey, Sarah Dore.

KNOX, Stephen, m. Nov. 22, 1795, by Rev. Isaac Hasey, Anna Hanson.

KNOX, James, m. Jun. 29, 1800, by Rev. Isaac Hasey, Betsey Lord.

KNOX, Moses Jr., m. Nov. 24, 1803, by Rev. Isaac Hasey, Susannah Perkins.

KNOX, Henry, m. Feb. 4, 1805, by Rev. Isaac Hasey, Rachel Wentworth.

KNOX, Edward, m. Mar. 22, 1810, by Rev. Isaac Hasey, Sally Burrows.

KNOX, Joshua, m. Mar. 10, 1817, by Rev. Paul Jewett, Patience Knox.
KNOX, Benjamin, m. int. Nov. 6, 1819, in Lebanon, Me. Keziah Butler.
KNOX, Benjamin, m. Jun. 30, 1822, in Lebanon, Me., Dorcas Butler.
KNOX, Thomas, m. near 1824, Eleanor Peavey, of Alton.
KNOX, Levi, m. int. Oct. 30, 1825, in Lebanon, Me., Sophia Hodsdon.
KNOX, John Jr., b. 1799, d. 1845, m. 1827, in Lebanon, Me., Elizabeth Jones, b. Jan. 30, 1802, d. 1832, dau. of Thomas.
KNOX, James, m. int. Jul. 23, 1827, in Lebanon, Me., Alice Tuttle.
KNOX, Jesse, of Lebanon, Me., son of John, d. Aug. 29, 1878, aged 76, m. (pub. July 24, 1827, in Milton), Lydia Dore, of Milton, d. Mar. 16, 1860, aged 59.
KNOX, John, m. int. Apr. 8, 1830, in Lebanon, Me., Betsey Lord, of Berwick, Me.
KNOX, Edward, of Somersworth, d. Apr. 16, 1879, aged 67, m. (pub. Mar. 5, 1833, in Lebanon, Me.), Ezobah Roberts, of Lebanon, Me., d. July 28, 1881, aged 76.
KNOX, George J., m. int. Sep. 4, 1842, in Lebanon, Me., Susan G. Farnham.
KNOX, James Jr., m. Jan. 29, 1846, in Lebanon, Me., Betsey Staples, of No. Berwick, Me.
KNOX, Zachariah, d. Aug. 14, 1887, aged 65, m. Jan. 11, 1854, by Rev. Benjamin Webber, Sarah A. Newcomb, d. Nov. 8, 1887.
KNOX, George A., m. Nov. 17, 1864, in Somersworth, Angie I. Canney.
KNOX, Daniel E., m. Jan. 19, 1865, in Rochester, Ellen J. Thompson, both of Berwick, Me.
KNOX, Alonzo, m. Dec. 29, 1866, in Rochester, Avalenia J. Smith, both of Somersworth,.
KNOX, Willard S., m. int. Dec. 9, 1869, in Lebanon, Me., Josephine A. Burrows, d. Jan. 28, 1874, aged 26.
KNOX, Thomas, of Berwick, Me., m. (pub. Nov. 3, 1870, in Great Falls), Jennie Libby, of Great Falls.
LAMB, John W., m. int. Apr. 2, 1860, in Lebanon, Me., Mary Annie Ham, of Rochester.
LAMOS, Nathaniel, d. Jun. 11, 1881, aged 81, m. int. Nov. 8, 1824, in Lee, Rhoda Ricker, d. Sep. 13, 1882, aged 81, both of Lee.
LAMOS, James M., of Somersworth, m. Nov. 13, 1866, in Great Falls, Agnes Hall, of Bucksport, Me.

LAMOS, Horace A., of Great Falls, m. Nov. 24, 1870, by Elmer Hewitt, Jennie Collins, of Boston, Mass.

LANCEY, George, of Dover, m. int. Jun. 16, 1839, in Dover, Sarah G. Knox.

LANCEY, Samuel F., m. Sept. 1, 1845, by Rev. Theodore Wells, Mary K. Hall, both of Barrington.

LANE, Samuel, of Lee, b. Aug. 2, 1801, d. Jul. 30, 1876, m. Elizabeth Hill, b. Dec. 26, 1802, d. May 23, 1888, dau. of William.

LANE, Edward, of Lee, m. Feb. 12, 1801, by Rev. Benjamin Balch, Elizabeth Winkley, of Barrington.

LANE, William, son of John, d. Oct. 29, 1837, aged 38, m. Oct. 28, 1820, by Rev. John Osborne, Charlotte Hill, b. Apr. 1801, d. May 5, 1855, dau. of William.

LANE, Ameries, d. Sep. 21, 1910, aged 77, m. (pub. Apr. 18, 1854, in Middleton), Eliza Ann Furber, d. Jun. 6, 1910, aged 73.

LANE, Edmund, b.1841, m. int. Feb. 14, 1865, in Lee, Hannah M. Jenkins, b. 1840, dau. of John, both of Lee.

LANE, Samuel G., of Concord, m. Nov. 21, 1866, in Center Sandwich, Elvira B. Marston, dau. of Moulton H.

LANE (LAYNE), Edward F., son of Samuel, m. Feb. 20, 1865, in Durham, Melinda H. Jenkins, b. Dec. 27, 1840, d. Jul. 24, 1887, dau. of John, both of Lee.

LANG, Reuben, m. Nov. 15, 1810, in Brookfield, Mary Whitehouse.

LANG, George, d. Sept. 18, 1882, aged 90, m. (1) Susan ----, d. Apr. 17, 1838, aged 45, m. (2) int. Sept. 18, 1841, in Lee, Mrs. Charlotte (Hill) Lane, wid. of William, b. Apr. 1801, d. May 5, 1855, aged 54, dau. of William, both of Lee.

LANG, Henry, son of Lt. Thomas, d. Sep. 18, 1882, aged 90,m. (pub. Jan. 24, 1843, in Brookfield), Caroline A. Drew, both of Brookfield.

LANG, Andrew J., aged 26, m. Oct. 20, 1855, in Brookfield, Mehitable Sanborn, aged 25, both of Brookfield.

LANGLEY, Timothy, m. 1807, by Rev. John Osborne, Ruth Runnels, both of Barrington, d. Apr. 1, 1847, aged 82.

LANGLEY, Warren, d. Apr. 26, 1864, aged 65, m. Nov. 29, 1821, by Rev. William Demeritt, Mary Peirce, d. Feb. 20, 1869, aged 65, dau. of Curtis.

LANGLEY, Amos, of Chichester, m. 1826, in Somersworth, Rebecca Libbey.

LANGLEY, James, b. 1800, d. 1848, m. Jan. 30, 1828, by Rev. Joseph Boodey, Susan Drew, b. Apr. 13, 1792, d. 1866, dau. of John.

LANGLEY, John, son of Obediah, b. Nov. 15, 1812, d. Jan. 15, 1881, aged 69, m. (pub. Nov. 15, 1831, in Durham), Mary Willey, b. May 2, 1808, d. Oct. 10, 1889, dau. of Robert.

LANGLEY, Ephraim, b. 1811, d. 1869, m. Jan. 2, 1834, by Elder Hezekiah D. Buzzell, Sarah B. Roberts, b. 1795, d. 1883, both of Alton.

LANGLEY, Thomas, of Alton, m. (pub. Nov. 19, 1844, in Tuftonboro), Elizabeth M. French, of Tuftonboro, b. Oct. 12, 1825, d. July 19, 1853, aged 27, dau. of Thomas.

LANGLEY, Amos, d. May 20, 1885, aged 58, m. Jun. 14, 1849, in Lebanon, Me., Catherine Brackett, d. Apr. 17, 1857, both of No. Berwick, Me.

LANGLEY, Henry, of Barnstead, m. Feb. 10, 1855, in Newmarket, Mrs. Elizabeth (Drew) Shaw, of Durham.

LANGLEY, Jonathan, of Acton, Me., m. Jul. 10, 1856, in Brookfield, Mrs. Susan E. (Butler) Ricker, wid. of Ebenezer.

LANGLEY, John C., of Madbury, d. Mar. 1857, aged 30, m. Jan. 4, 1857, by Elder Elias Hutchins, Martha A. Hanson, of Lee, b. Apr. 18, 1836, d. Jun. 4, 1920.

LANGLEY, William D., of Durham, m. Aug. 21, 1864, in Barrington, Mary J. Drew, of Barrington, d. Sept. 1864, dau. of Timothy.

LANGLEY, Thomas J., m. July 11, 1867, by Rev. Robert S. Stubbs, Hannah Cook, of Rollinsford.

LANGMAID, Samuel, m. Jan. 22, 1756, Mary Willey, d. Jan. 24, 1831, aged 94, dau. of Samuel.

LANGMAID, Winthrop, d. Oct. 28, 1863, aged 83, m. (1) (pub. May 11, 1805, in Barrington), Frances Kielley, d. Oct. 23, 1847, aged 66, m. (2) Jan. 4, 1855, by Elder Enoch Place, Mrs. Mary Huntress, aged 70, both of Strafford.

LANGMAID, Minot Wesley, son of Jacob, b. Sept. 30, 1811, d. Sept. 19, 1884, aged 73, m. (1) Apr. 15, 1832, by Rev. William Demeritt, Louisa Williams, m. (2) Nov. 1, 1862, in Newmarket, Priscilla Adams Chesley, of Durham, b. June 30, 1837, d. Aug. 12, 1910, dau. of Rev. Alfred.

LANGMAID, Jacob H., son of Minot, d. Apr. 11, 1907, aged 70, m. Feb. 11, 1864, in Dover, Emma F. Davis, b. Mar. 21, 1841, d. Apr. 22, 1879, dau. of David, both of Dover.

LANGMAID, Charles A., son of Minot, m. (1) Oct. 25, 1865, in Dover, Mrs. Lizzie A. Bean, both of Durham, m. (2) Mar. 16, 1876, in Newmarket, S. Josephine Chesley, of Durham, aged 30, dau. of Alfred.

LANGMAID, Alonzo E., son of Samuel, b. Dec. 28, 1841, d. Nov. 11, 1925, m. Jan. 28, 1866, in Lee, Zetta W. Wiggin, dau. of Issacher, b. 1848, d. 1937, both of Lee.

LASKEY, William J., son of Pelatiah, b. May 31, 1825, d. Sept. 1, 1866, m. July 4, 1848, Caroline Goodwin, d. May 21, 1868, aged 40.

LASKEY, Lewis B., son of John, b. Aug. 24, 1846, m. Nov. 19, 1868, in Dover, Lydia Tuttle, both of Dover.

LAWTON, Theodore, of Northbridge, Mass., m. Dec. 25, 1867, in Great Falls, Selena F. Hanners, of Great Falls.

LEACH, Henry, m. Nov. 13, 1837, Naomi E. Whitcher, d. Apr. 21, 1846, dau. of William, both of Epping.

LEACH, William Dudley, m. Jan. 26, 1857, in Sandwich, Sarah Hoyt/Hoitt, b. Dec. 27, 1825, both of Sandwich.

LEACH, George A., of Newmarket, m. Jan. 30, 1869, in Newmarket, Annie M. Chesley, of Barnstead.

LEARNED, A. C., m. (pub. Nov. 12, 1868, in Great Falls), Charlotte Ricker.

LEATHERS, Ebenezer, m. Mar. 26, 1777, in Barrington, Eleanor Moore, both of Barrington.

LEATHERS, Aaron, of Barrington, son of James, b. June 22, 1741, d. 1816, m. Oct. 21, 1779, Molly Murrey, of Northwood, b. Feb. 15, 1757, d. Oct. 8, 1840.

LEATHERS, Benjamin, m. Oct. 8, 1789, by Rev. Benjamin Balon, Sarah Place, both of Lee.

LEATHERS, Thomas, of Barrington, m. July 1, 1795, by Rev. Benjamin Balch, Lydia Sargent, of Northfield.

LEATHERS, Edward, m. Oct. 25, 1798, by Rev. Benjamin Balch, Anna Leathers, both of Barrington.

LEATHERS, Jonathan, m. Mar. 23, 1801, by Rev. Benjamin Balch, Betsey Giles, both of Barrington.

LEATHERS, William, m. Sept. 12, 1802, by Rev. Benjamin Balch, Thankful Arnold, both of Barrington.

LEATHERS, Valintine, m. Sept. 10, 1803, by Rev. Benjamin Balch, Sarah Starbird, both of Barrington.

LEATHERS, Ebenezer Jr., m. May 14, 1804, by Rev. Micajah Otis, Huldah Sawyer, both of Barrington.

LEATHERS, Stephen, m. Sept. 6, 1818, in Barrington, Betsey Hanscom, both of Barrington.

LEATHERS, Daniel, m. May 19, 1830, in Barrington, by Rev. Samuel Sherburne, Estha Capon, both of Barrington.

LEATHERS, Oliver, m. June 19, 1845, by Elder Samuel Sherburne, Sally Tyler, both of Barrington.

LEATHERS, Daniel, m. July 23, 1865, in Nottingham, Mary H. Davis, of Durham.

LEATHERS, Alphonzo D., m. Aug. 16, 1868, in Rochester, Jennie E. Amazeen, both of Farmington.

LEATHERS, Levi, of Nottingham, m. Aug. 3, 1869, in Dover, Emily M. Davis, of Dover.

LEAVITT, Edward, b. 1757, d. July 27, 1831, m. (1) Aug. 27, 1794, in Wolfeboro, Hannah Sias, of Ossipee, m. (2) Jan. 28, 1818, by Rev. Joseph Haven, Abigail Peavey, wid. of Edward, d. Sept. 11, 1858, aged 76, both of Tuftonboro.

LEAVITT, Samuel Quarles, m. (1) in 1806, Lydia Jewell, d. Oct. 13, 1834, m. (2) (pub. Jan. 28, 1840, in Effingham), Elizabeth A. Moore.

LEAVITT, Samuel, d. Jan. 18, 1838, aged 41, m. int. Sept. 1827, in Tuftonboro, Jemima H. Piper, b. Jan. 4, 1803, dau. of John, both of Tuftonboro.

LEAVITT, Capt. Morris W., of Effingham, b. 1815, d. 1862, m. (1) (pub. Apr. 13, 1841, in Parsonsfield, Me.), Martha Knight, b. 1822, d. May 24, 1845, aged 25, m. (2) Catherine ----, b. 1816, d. 1892.

LEAVITT, Levi C., b. Mar. 3, 1817, d. Feb. 4, 1890, m. Feb. 4, 1844, by Rev. J. Milton Coburn, Martha J. Lear, b. July 25, 1819, d. Jan. 15, 1890, both of Effingham.

LEAVITT, James B., son of James, d. Mar. 21, 1865, aged 60, m. (pub. Oct. 21, 1845, of Ossipee), Mary Lamper, dau. of John S., both of Effingham.

LEAVITT, Woodbury L., son of Samuel, d. Oct. 20, 1863, aged 36, m. Mar. 15, 1849, in Boston, Mass., Julia A. Morrill, d. Aug. 24, 1855, aged 25, both of Tuftonboro.

LEAVITT, John A., of Danvers, Mass., b. Apr. 19, 1829, d. Dec. 16, 1911, m. (pub. June 20, 1854, in Effingham), Mary E. Sanders, of Ossipee, b. June 8, 1830, d. Jan. 1, 1915.

LEAVITT, Alphonzo C., m. Feb. 20, 1862, in Effingham, Mary E. Furbush, both of Effingham.

LEAVITT, John H., m. Oct. 11, 1862, in Dover, Paulina A. Cooper, both of Rollinsford.

LEAVITT, Almond, m. Apr. 13, 1867, in Farmington, Nellie Jones.

LEE, Daniel, m. Sept. 1848, by Rev. Theodore Wells, Mehitable Leighton, both of Barrington.

LEE, Frank, of Wakefield, m. (pub. Sept. 3, 1868, in Wakefield), Anna M. Bartlett, of Lee.

LEGG, James A., of Dover, son of Lucian B., d. June 22, 1880, m. (pub. Nov. 17, 1870, in Dexter, Me.), Abiah M. Hill, of Dover, d. Dec. 25, 1925.

LEGRO, John, son of John and Rachel, b. Jan. 29, 1733, d. Aug. 4, 1800, m. near 1755, Sarah Randall, b. Apr. 6, 1736, d. Jan. 8, 1791.

LEGRO, John, b. Jan. 29, 1733, d. Aug. 4, 1800, m. (1) Mar. 22, 1778, by Rev. Isaac Hasey, Patience Blaisdell, m. (2) Feb. 2, 1796, by Rev. Isaac Hasey, Sarah Libbey, b. Mar. 6, 1736.

LEGRO, Moses, d. Mar. 30, 1858, aged 80, m. Nov. 28, 1799, by Rev. Isaac Hasey, Polly Goodwin, d. May 14, 1859, aged 79.

LEGRO, John Jr., of Frankfort, Me., m. Nov. 19, 1808, in Lebanon, Me., Eliza Burrows.

LEGRO, David Jr., son of Thomas, b. Jan. 20, 1791, m. Dec. 3, 1812, in Lebanon, Me., Joanna Hayes.

LEGRO, Daniel, son of Thomas, b. Feb. 7, 1795, d. Sep. 27, 1834, m. (1) Feb. 27, 1817, by Rev. Paul Jewett, Ruth Horne, d. Apr. 1, 1826, m. (2) int. Jul. 9, 1822, in Lebanon, Me., Lydia Plummer, b. Jan. 25, 1795, d. Dec. 19, 1849.

LEGRO, Thomas W. Jr., son of Thomas, b. Jul. 24, 1800, d. Jun. 28, 1854, m. int. Oct. 1, 1822, in Lebanon, Me., Dorcas Goodwin, b. Apr. 28, 1801, d. May 6, 1849.

LEGRO, Ira, son of Daniel, b. Nov. 4, 1819, d. Oct. 2, 1852, m. Oct. 23, 1848, in Lebanon, Me., Ellen Rumney.

LEGRO, David G., son of Thomas Jr., b. Sep. 8, 1833, m. int. Nov. 18, 1856, in Lebanon, Me., Lucinda Furbush.

LEGRO, Ebenezer, son of Thomas Jr., b. Sep. 12, 1840, m. int. Mar. 20, 1863, in Lebanon, Me., Sarah J. Franklin, b. 1843.

LEGRO, J. Irving, m. Oct. 7, 1867, in Rochester, Clara W. Mathes, both of Rochester.

LEGRO, Edger B., m. (pub. July 14, 1870, in Great Falls), Hattie A. Bates.

6) **LEIGHTON**, James, son of James, b. Dec. 31, 1768, d. Jan. 21, 1841, m. Nov. 24, 1790, by Rev. Benjamin Balch, Hannah Buzzell, dau. of Ebenezer, both of Barrington.

LEIGHTON, Andrew, m. June 7, 1792, in Barrington, Margaret Babb, both of Barrington.

LEIGHTON, Robert, m. Nov. 29, 1804, by Rev. Benjamin Balch, Susannah Cater, both of Barrington.

LEIGHTON, John, m. Apr. 13, 1809, by Rev. Micajah Otis, Polly Furber, both of Farmington.

LEIGHTON, William P., of Farmington, m. Jan. 16, 1823, by Elder Enoch Place, Abigail Leighton, of Strafford, d. Mar. 7, 1826, aged 21, dau. of Andrew.

LEIGHTON, Seth S., son of John, d. Feb. 14, 1830, m. in Apr. 1824, in Portsmouth, Martha Ann Mary Winkley, dau. of Francis.

LEIGHTON, Isaac, d. Jan. 22, 1836, aged 33, m. Mar. 29, 1831, by Elder Enoch Place, Maria Cate, dau. of Capt. Joseph, both of Barrington.

LEIGHTON, Francis F., m. int. Jan. 4, 1854, in Lebanon, Me., Elizabeth A. Watson, both of Farmington.

LEIGHTON, Charles H., m. Mar. 10, 1864, in Middleton, Annah E. Whitehouse, both of Middleton.

LEIGHTON, Charles H., m. July 28, 1866, in Farmington, Emma A. Colbath.

LEIGHTON, Samuel R., of Dover, m. Jan. 1, 1867, in Farmington, Ellen L. Colbath, of Farmington.

LEIGHTON, Charles M., m. (pub. Dec. 12, 1867, in Portsmouth), Florence S. Peduzzi.

LEIGHTON, James, m. (pub. Dec. 2, 1869, in Berwick, Me.), Abbie F. Clark, both of Dover.

LEVY, Sampson, m. May 19, 1863, in Dover, Martha C. George, both of Newburyport.

LEWIS, Simon Jr., of Kittery, Me., m. Oct. 15, 1821, in Lebanon, Me., Dorothy Jones.

LEWIS, William B., of Kittery, Me., son of Simon, b. May 19, 1824, m. (1) Apr. 12, 1845, in Lebanon, Me., Paulina Jones, m. (2) Aug. 4, 1853, in Lebanon, Me., Abby Ricker, d. Sep. 23, 1866, aged 66.

LEWIS, Samuel H., m. int. Dec. 15, 1860, in Lebanon, Me., Alice Lord.

LEWIS, Joseph B., m. (pub. July 14, 1870, in Great Falls), Fannie B. Hanson, both of Ossipee.

LIBBEY, Joseph, son of Capt. James, d. Apr. 30, 1827, m. Joanna Hall, (moved to Barrington).

LIBBEY, Jonathan, m. Dec. 27, 1803, by Elder Zebedee Delano, Hannah Knox.

LIBBEY, Daniel (or David?), b. Jan. 18, 1783, m. Dec. 28, 1808, in Lebanon, Me., Anna Smith.

LIBBEY, John Jr., m. int. Jan. 28, 1809, in Lebanon, Me., Nabby Libbey.

LIBBEY, James, m. int. Nov. 5, 1810, in Lebanon, Me., Nabby Goodwin.

LIBBEY, Oliver, m. int. Oct. 29, 1813, in Lebanon, Me., Hannah Delano.

LIBBEY, Nathaniel, m. Nov. 24, 1813, in Lebanon, Me., Tirzah Lord.

LIBBEY, Daniel, d. Aug. 3, 1862, aged 68, m. Mar. 10, 1817, by Rev. Joseph Boodey, Ada Clough, d. Jan. 30, 1882, aged 82, both of Alton.

LIBBEY, Oliver, m. int. Apr. 13, 1817, in Lebanon, Me., Lydia Littlefield

LIBBEY, Asa, of New Durham, son of Benjamin, d. Mar. 6, 1836, aged 44, m. May 18, 1820, by Rev. Joseph Boodey, Nancy Clough, of Alton.

LIBBEY, Oliver, of Eliot, Me., b. Jan. 6, 1799, murdered in the West, 1858, m. Nov. 2, 1823, by Rev. J. W. Clary, Elizabeth Henderson, d. Jun. 5, 1871, aged 70, dau. of Thomas.

LIBBEY, Charles, m. Sep. 4, 1836, by Elder Zebedee Delano, Patience Plumer, both of Sandford, Me.

LIBBEY, Isaac, of Bradford, Mass., m. Mar. 12, 1837, by Elder Zebedee Delano, Mary Worster.

LIBBEY, Robert, m. Apr. 4, 1838, by Elder Zebedee Delano, Hannah Murray.

LIBBEY, John M., son of Daniel, d. Mar. 7, 1889, aged 70, m. (1) Dec. 5, 1839, by Elder William Blaisdell, Polly H. Wiggin, d. Apr. 17, 1854, aged 35, dau. of Josiah, both of Tuftonboro, m. (2) Ann M. ----, d. Mar. 22, 1864, aged 27.

LIBBEY, James, m. near 1840, Mrs. Mehitable (Hanson) Ham, wid. of Capt. Moses, d. Jan. 9, 1852, aged 76, dau. of William.

LIBBEY, Thomas H., m. Apr. 15, 1843, in Lebanon, Me., Miriam Goodwin.

LIBBEY, William K., of Tuftonboro, d. May 14, 1906, aged 83, m. Nov. 14, 1844, by Rev. Joseph Boodey, Betsey N. Colbath, of Farmington, d. Apr. 12, 1890, aged 69.

LIBBEY, Edward P., m. Jan. 23, 1848, by Rev. Noah Hooper, Eliza Hersom.

LIBBEY, Ebenezer, m. Aug. 19, 1850, by Elder William H. Littlefield, Lusetta Fall.

LIBBEY, Ivory Jr., m. Nov. 29, 1852, in Lebanon, Me., Nancy Hanscom.

LIBBEY, Daniel, son of Levi, b. Nov. 18, 1830, d. May 1, 1918, m. Oct. 10, 1857, in Tuftonboro, Ann Elizabeth Canney, b. June 4, 1836, d. June 22, 1921, dau. of Ira.

LIBBEY, Ham, of Wakefield, m. (pub. Dec. 17, 1857, in Ossipee), Mary Ann Fogg, of Ossipee, d. Sept. 8, 1865, aged 57, dau. of Abner.

LIBBEY, Frank, m. int. Oct. 21, 1859, in Lebanon, Me., Irene L. Usher, of Biddeford, Me.

LIBBEY, John, m. int. Sep. 2, 1862, in Lebanon, Me., (married Sep. 11, 1862, in No. Berwick, Me.), Sabina Dillingham, of No. Berwick, Me.

LIBBEY, Elder A. W., pastor of the Advent Christian Church, E. Boston, Mass., m. Feb. 12, 1865, in Biddeford, Me., Julia A. Libbey, of Biddeford, Me.

LIBBEY, Charles W., of Newfield, Me., d. Jan. 14, 1903, aged 61, m. Oct. 13, 1866, in Great Falls, Mary Abbie Nason.

LIBBEY, Marion W., of Berwick, Me., m. (pub. Oct. 13, 1870, in Great Falls), Lizzie J. Hersom, of Great Falls.

LIBBEY, Owen, m. Dec. 21, 1870, in Lebanon, Me., Lucie L. Guptill, of No. Berwick, Me.

LINDSEY, Charles R., of Wells, Me., m. Nov. 5, 1846, in Lebanon, Me., Mary E. Murray.

LINDSEY, W. K., of Rochester, m. Jan. 20, 1865, in Brookfield, Hattie E. Churchill, of Brookfield, dau. of John T.

LINDSEY, George S., of Rochester, m. July 3, 1866, in Farmington, Mary E. Perkins, of Farmington, dau. of Ephraim.

LINSCOTT, Nathaniel, of Sanford, Me., m. Oct. 22, 1866, in Rochester, Ruth A. Wormwood, of N. Berwick, Me.

LINSCOTT, George H., of Rochester, m. Feb. 6, 1869, in Rochester, Mary Abby Howe, of Barrington.

LITCHFIELD, Leonard, m. Aug. 22, 1848, in Lebanon, Me., Betsey Jones.

LITTLE, Edmund Jr., m. Aug. 20, 1789, Judith Bartlett, b. Dec. 3, 1770, dau. of Joseph.

LITTLEFIELD, Henry, m. Apr. 1806, by Rev. Micajah Otis, Deborah Foss, both of Barrington.

LITTLEFIELD, John, m. Mar. 26, 1812, by Rev. Joseph Boodey, Polly Ham.

LITTLEFIELD, Daniel, of Wells, Me., m. Dec. 13, 1821, in Lebanon, Me., Mary Littlefield, of Sanford, Me.

LITTLEFIELD, Samuel, of Sanford, Me., m. May 15, 1825, in Lebanon, Me., Huldy Webber, of Shapleigh, Me.

LITTLEFIELD, Solomon, m. Dec. 27, 1825, in Lebanon, Me., Sally Morrison, both of Sanford, Me.

LITTLEFIELD, John, m. Feb. 19, 1827, by Elder Zebedee Delano, Mercy Barker, both of Sanford.

LITTLEFIELD, John, of Dover, b. 1801, d. 1875, m. in 1828, in Barnstead, Charlotte G. Munsey, of Dover, d. July 20, 1882, aged 74.

LITTLEFIELD, Moses, m. Dec. 22, 1831, in Lebanon, Me., Ruth Littleford, both of Sanford, Me.

LITTLEIFLED, Horace, m. int. Oct. 11, 1832, in Lebanon, Me., Mary E. Chase, of Roxbury, Mass.

LITTLEFIELD, George, m. Apr. 29, 1841, by Elder Jairus E. Strong, Clarissa Libbey.

LITTLEFIELD, Hiram, m. Aug. 31, 1844, by Elder Jairus E. Strong, Louisa Goodwin, both of No. Berwick, Me.

LITTLEFIELD, Joshua F., m. Jul. 6, 1845, by Elder Elias Hutchins, Jennette Q. Miller, d. Jan. 5, 1904, aged 82.

LITTLEFIELD, Horace, b. Apr. 1, 1818, d. Aug. 25, 1898, m. Nov. 12, 1848, in Dover, by Rev. Thomas J. Greenwood, Sarah P. Locke, b. Apr. 16, 1830, d. Feb. 13, 1905, dau. of Elisha.

LITTLEFIELD, James D., of Melrose, Mass., son of Joshua, d. Jan. 20, 1890, aged 55, m. Oct. 20, 1857, by Rev. Benjamin F. Parsons, Rhoda P. Swett, of Dover.

LITTLEFIELD, B. F., of Kittery, Me., m. Feb. 5, 1866, in Great Falls, Ruba R. Weaver, of Weymouth, Nova Scotia.

LITTLEFIELD, William H., of Manchester, m. Jan. 16, 1867, in Dover, Emma T. Hutchinson, of Bangor, Me.

LITTLEFIELD, Alpheus, of Berwick, Me., son of John, b. Feb. 2, 1845, d. Sept. 8, 1930, aged 84, m. Oct. 31, 1868, in Dover, Atsy L. Pierce, of Lebanon, Me., b. Oct. 29, 1840, d. Feb. 4, 1898.

LITTLEFIELD, Cyrus H., m. (pub. Aug. 18, 1870, in Great Falls), Deborah H. Williams, both of Alfred, Me.

LITTLEFIELD, Morris C., of Farmington, m. Aug. 29, 1870, in Dover, Elvira Thurston, of Conway.

LITTLEFIELD, Stephen E., of Dover, m. (pub. Oct. 27, 1870, in Great Falls), Olive A. Edson, of Great Falls.

LIVINGSTON, Josiah E., of Manchester, m. Nov. 13, 1866, in Wolfeboro, Nancy S. Haley, dau. of Abel.

LIVINGSTONE, James, m. (pub. Apr. 26, 1866, in Portsmouth), Mary Thompson.

LOCK, Jethro, m. Feb. 16, 1786, by Rev. Benjamin Balch, Abigail Howard, both of Barrington.

LOCK, John, of Alton, m. Apr. 11, 1799, by Rev. Benjamin Balch, Sarah Stanton, of Barrington.

LOCK, Samuel, of Barrington, m. Jan. 27, 1801, in Barrington, Mrs. Tamsin Hayes, of Farmington. (was this a second marriage?)

LOCK, William, m. Apr. 20, 1802, in Barrington, Mrs. Mary Hayes, both of Barrington. (was this a second marriage?)

LOCK, Isaac, m. Oct. 19, 1812, in Barrington, Betty Patrick, both of Barrington.

LOCK, Jeremy, son of Jeremiah, b. Apr. 9, 1811, d. May 7, 1850, aged 48, m. Feb. 14, 1828, in Dover, Elizabeth Wentworth, d. Aug. 17, 1848, aged 41.

LOCK, Joshua, of New Durham, m. int. Oct. 25, 1829, in Lebanon, Me., Abra W. Furbish.

LOCK, Henry W., son of Elisha, b. Sept. 28, 1828, d. Mar. 19, 1895, m. (1) Elizabeth Whitehouse, b. 1826, d. May 9, 1855, dau. of Nicholas, m. (2) Evengline Hayes, b. 1839, d. Mar. 18, 1919, dau. of Watson.

LOCKE, Jethro, of Rye, m. Hannah Rand, d. Feb. 14, 1831, aged 103.

LOCKE, Samuel, m. Mar. 1, 1792, by Rev. Benjamin Balch, Lucy Cate, both of Barrington.

LOCKE, John, of Barrington, m. Sept 20, 1792, by Rev. Joseph Haven, Abigail Page, of Rochester, d. Apr. 5, 1829, dau. of Daniel.

LOCKE, Elisha, b. Oct. 26, 1780, d. Dec. 15, 1854, aged 74, m. in 1806, by Rev. John Osborne, Sophia Pinkham, of Durham, b. Feb. 20, 1790, d. Feb. 15, 1876, dau. of Thomas.

LOCKE, Benjamin Babb, of Barrington, m. Nov. 23, 1815, by Rev. Joseph Haven, Elizabeth Heard, d. Mar. 25, 1831, aged 40.

LOCKE, Howard, of Somersworth, m. int. May 11, 1833, in Lebanon, Me., Eunice Wentworth.

LOCKE, James E., of Northwood, m. Nov. 8, 1833, in Barrington, by Rev. Samuel H. Merrill, Elizabeth H. Hayes, of Barrington.

LOCKE, Alfred, of Barrington, son of Elisha, b. Dec. 19, 1811, m. Aug. 5, 1834, by Rev. Isaac Willey, Mary Ann Seavey, of Rochester.

LOCKE, Sampson B., son of John, b. June 17, 1811, d. July 31, 1863, m. Dec. 25, 1835, in Barrington, Sarah Canney, b. Feb. 8, 1809, d. Sept. 23, 1879, dau. of Samuel.

LOCKE, Elisha Jr., of Barrington, son of Elisha, b. Nov. 18, 1814, d. Oct. 1886, aged 72, m. Jan. 27, 1841, by Rev. Lucian Hayden, Lavina French, of Dover.

LOCKE, Lyman, son of Elisha, b. Jan. 22, 1821, m. Dec. 25, 1842, by Rev. Samuel Nichols, Susan Cater.

LOCKE, James M., of Barrington, son of Elisha, b. July 1, 1823, m. Jan. 28, 1846, in Wolfeboro, Izetta I. Plummer, of Wolfeboro.

LOCKE, Samuel A., m. Apr. 28, 1850, by Elder Samuel Sherburne, Sophronia Adeline Sherburne. b. May 31, 1832, dau. of Elder Samuel.

LOCKE, Oliver Babb, son of Elisha, b. Feb. 28, 1835, d. Apr. 11, 1911, aged 76, m. Jan. 23, 1858, in Barrington, Martha A. Fernald.

LOCKE, Andrew J., m. Mar. 9, 1859, by Rev. Elias Hutchins, Sarah A. Smith, d. Jun. 3, 1915, aged 78, dau. of John, both of Madbury.

LOCKE, George W., of Buxton, Me., b. Oct. 5, 1843, m. Jan. 15, 1863, in Dover, Mary E. Dorr, of S. Berwick, Me., b. Nov. 17, 1846, d. Jan. 7, 1893.

LOCKE, James H., of Hartford, Conn., m. (pub. Jan. 5, 1865, in Portsmouth), Sarah A. Trefethen, of Kittery, Me.

LOCKE, Edward A., m. Jan. 9, 1867, in Great Falls, Emma A. Daniels.

LOCKE, Ira W., m. May 27, 1869, by Rev. Jesse Meader, Mary A. Babb, both of Barrington.

LOCKE, E. Frank, of Rochester, m. (pub. Sept. 9, 1869, in Great Falls, Julia E. Janvrin, of Great Falls.

LOOMIS, Charles A., of Skowhegan, Me., m. Sept. 24, 1865, in Conway, Maria Osgood, of Conway.

LOONEY, Francis C., b. 1802, d. 1854, m. Feb. 22, 1848, by Rev. E. G. Page, Rhoda A. Leighton, b. 1817, d. 1896, dau. of Thomas.

LORD, Joseph Jr., son of Nicholas, m. Aug. 23, 1773, by Rev. Matthew Merriam, Hannah Kilgore, b. Apr. 14, 1752, d. Mar. 19, 1851, both of Berwick, Me.

LORD, William, of Barnstead, m. Jan. 14, 1777, in Barrington, Hannah Hawkins, of Barrington.

LORD, Richard, son of Joseph, d. Aug. 18, 1833, aged 78, m. Oct. 1, 1787, by Rev. Jonathan Tompson, Mary Gerrish, d. Feb. 22, 1836, aged 75.

LORD, John L., of Ossipee, m. int. Oct. 1828, in Tuftonboro, Henrietta Grant, of Tuftonboro, d. Mar. 22, 1829, aged 23, dau. of John.

LORD, William Allen, of Berwick, Me., b. Mar. 20, 1801, d. July 28, 1879, m. (pub. Feb. 28, 1832, in Milton), Clarissa Lyman, of Milton, b. Oct. 29, 1802, d. Mar. 18, 1892, dau. of Theodore C.

LORD, Francis H., of Ossipee, b. Apr. 6, 1825, d. Sept. 2, 1912, m. (pub. May 21, 1857, in Tamworth), Hannah E. Blaisdell, of Tamworth.

LORD, William H., d. May 14, 1871, aged 37, m. Oct. 24, 1858, in Acton, Me., Susan S. Hart, d. Nov. 17, 1905, aged 78, dau. of John.

LORD, George B., m. July 8, 1862, by Rev. James Rand, Lizzie C. Mott, d. Oct. 17, 1902, aged 61, both of Somersworth..

LORD, William C., m. Nov. 24, 1862, in Great Falls, Eleanor Morrill, both of Lowell, Mass.

LORD, Franklin, of Porter, Me., m. (pub. Dec. 11, 1862, in Brookfield), Eliza Jane Cate, of Brookfield.

LORD, George, of Water Village, m. (pub. Mar. 26, 1863, in Wolfeboro), Mrs. Nancy Wingate, of Wolfeboro.

LORD, Thomas B., m. Sept. 7, 1864, in Effingham, Hattie P. Burbank, both of Effingham.

LORD, Charles E., m. Sept. 28, 1865, in Dover, Mrs. Clara R. Stiles, wid. of William I., both of Dover.

LORD, John A., of Rochester, m. Nov. 11, 1865, in Lebanon, Me., Annie M. Brock, of Lebanon, Me.

LORD, Charles E., of Lebanon, Me., m. Jan. 3, 1866, in Milton, Abbie A. Blanchard, of Chelsea, Mass.

LORD, Horace W., of Rollinsford, m. May 7, 1866, in Salmon Falls, Awilda A. Wentworth, of Barnstead.

LORD, John C., of Lebanon, Me., m. Nov. 28, 1866, in Great Falls, Mary J. Blanchard, of Chelsea, Me.

LORD, George W., of Berwick, Me., m. Dec. 24, 1867, in Great Falls, Eunice E. Hill, of Great Falls.

LORD, William F., of Auburn, Me., m. Apr. 27, 1868, in Dover, Josie P. Daicy, of Lewiston, Me.

LORD, Henry W., of S. Berwick, Me., m. Aug. 24, 1868, in Dover, Arabella M. Clark, of Rochester.

LORD, William E., m. (pub. Nov. 12, 1868, in Salmon Falls), Cornelia J. Alley.

LORD, Horace B., of Berwick, Me., son of Samuel, b. Sept. 8, 1846, d. July 25, 1893, m. Jan. 10, 1869, in Great Falls, Nellie K. Hoitt, of Dover.

LORD, James, of Somersworth, m. (pub. July 29, 1869, in Great Falls), Mary W. Chick, of Parsonsfield, Me.

LORD, Edwin A., m. (pub. Mar. 3, 1870, in Great Falls), Emma Grant.

LORD, John A., m. Apr. 30, 1870, in Dover, Abby F. Baker, d. Sept. 10, 1890, aged 42, dau. of Otis, both of Dover.

LORD, Parker W., of Dover, m. Aug. 6, 1870, in Great Falls, Ada M. Stokes, of Concord.

LORD, Coleman F., of Norway, Me., m. Dec. 26, 1870, in Dover, Elizabeth (Lizzie) A. Furber, of Newmarket.

LORING, Rev. Joseph, m. int. Aug. 12, 1837, in Lebanon, Me., Susan K. Hancock, of Franklin.

LOTHROP, John C., son of Daniel, d. Apr. 28, 1895, aged 66, m. (1) (pub. Feb. 13, 1849, in Rochester), Lydia B. Hanson, d. July 8, 1868, aged 39, m. (2) Jan. 26, 1870, in E. Rochester, Abby J. Mills, both of Great Falls.

LOTHROP, Dr. S. K., m. Nov. 22, 1869, in Boston, Mass., Alice L. Webb.

LOUD, John Henry, m. Oct. 8, 1862, in Wolfeboro, Lizzie A. Cotton.

LOUD, William H., of Portsmouth, m. (pub. July 18, 1867, in Great Falls), Martha W. Fernald.

LOUGEE, Leavitt, of Gilmanton, d. Dec. 20, 1857, aged 56, m. May 11, 1826, by Rev. Joseph Boodey, Mahala Stockbridge, of Alton, d. Apr. 28, 1854, aged 51.

LOUGEE, Franklin W., son of James, m. (pub. Mar. 23, 1847, in Somersworth), Sarah L. Jones.

LOUGEE, Chester N., m. Dec. 22, 1861, by Rev. Alvan Tobey, Ella M. Sall, both of Dover.

LOUGEE, George G., of Exeter, m. (pub. Apr. 12, 1866, in Portsmouth), Josephine Adams, dau. of Joseph B.

LOUGEE, Dr. I. W., of Alton, m. Oct. 25, 1866, in Barnstead, Ellen Wheeler, of Barnstead.

LOUGEE, Barry H. m. Oct. 18, 1867, in Rochester, Mrs. Sarah E. Foss, both of Somersworth.

LOUGEE, John H., d. Jan. 1, 1886, aged 72, m. Jan. 19, 1870, in Berwick, Me., Mrs. Hannah A. Seavey, d. Apr. 9, 1899, aged 60, both of Berwick, Me.

LOUGEE, Amos D., of Great Falls, d. Jun. 17, 1919, aged 82, m. (pub. Sept. 29, 1870, in Ossipee), Nancy E. Hodsdon, of Center Ossipee, d. Dec. 17, 1916, aged 81.

LOVEJOY, Warren F., m. June 30, 1866, in Dover, Mrs. Angeline P. (Gilman) Starbird, of Dover, wid. of James W.

LOVERING, Isaac S., of Freedom, b. 1814, d. 1897, m. (1) Harriet M. Hodsdon, d. Dec. 17, 1859, aged 47, m. (2) (pub. Nov. 22, 1860, in Wolfeboro), Ruth E. Bassett, of Wolfeboro, b. 1820, d. 1898.

LOW, Capt. Nathaniel Jr., m. Sept. 5, 1862, in Dover, Lucy J. Niles, both of Dover.

LOWD, Wentworth Jr., of Acton, Me., m. Jun. 11, 1853, in Lebanon, Me., Abba C. Roberts, of Great Falls.

LOWE, George M., of Wells, Me., m. Oct. 10, 1870, in Dover, Mary D. Gerrish, of Alfred, Me.

LOWELL, Lendal B., of Standish, Me., m. Sept. 8, 1865, in Conway, Abby W. Hunt, of Gorham, Me.

LOWELL, Nathan S., m. Sept. 9, 1865, in Farmington, Melissa J. Richards, both of Biddeford, Me.

LOYNDS, William A., m. Oct. 13, 1870, in Dover, Sophia Drinkwater, both of Dover.

LUCAS, Benjamin, b. 1820, d. 1896, m. Apr. 25, 1840, in Wolfeboro, Polly Willey, b. 1805, d. 1894, both of Wolfeboro.

LUCAS, James, of Durham, m. June 21, 1862, in Dover, Celestia E. Powers, of Rollinsford.

LUCAS, John, of Milton, b. 1824, d. 1873, m. June 11, 1865, by Rev. Asa Piper, Sarah E. Trask, of Brookfield, b. 1836, d. 1920.

LUCAS, Isaac, m. Dec. 21, 1867, in Great Falls, Martha Ann Elliott, of Dover, dau. of Arthur F. R.

LUCAS, George H., of Wolfeboro, m. Jan. 30, 1869, by Rev. Robert S. Stubbs, Zelia Churchill, of Brookfield.

LUKE, Addis E., b. Aug. 27, 1837, d. Nov. 18, 1902, m. Apr. 9, 1859, by Elder Elias Hutchins, Eliza A. Dorr, b. Feb. 9, 1842, d. Mar. 12, 1917, both of Rollinsford.

LYFORD, John, m. Oct. 27, 1825, in Brookfield, Polly Shortridge, both of Brookfield.

LYMAN, Capt. William B., of Milton, son of Theodore C., b. Apr. 23, 1807, d. Nov. 13, 1889, m. Dec. 29, 1833, by Rev. Gibbon Williams, Lydia Jones, of Dover, d. Mar. 1, 1890, aged 76, dau. of John.

LYNDE, Henry, of Melrose, Mass., m. (pub. Oct. 13, 1870, in Great Falls), Sarah A. Hanson, of Great Falls.

MACE, Levi S., m. int. Jun. 17, 1848, in Lebanon, Me., Caroline Ingalls, of Canterbury.

MACE, Charles W., of Rye, m. (pub. July 23, 1868, in Great Falls), Eliza J. Tucker, of Great Falls.

MACY, James E., m. Sep. 8, 1846, Hannah Whidden.

MADDOX, Daniel, m. int. Apr. 23, 1836, in Lebanon, Me., Lucinda Lord.

MADDOX, Daniel, m. Sep. 23, 1838, in Lebanon, Lucy Lord.

MADDOX, Ivory, of Somersworth, m. (pub. Oct. 11, 1866, in Portsmouth), Susan Upham, of Portsmouth.

MADDOX, G. W., of Lawrence, Mass., m. July 24, 1869, in Dover, Lessie D. Smith, of Hudson, Me.

MANN, George W., d. Sept. 24, 1888, aged 86, m. May 23, 1859, in Sandwich, Mary H. Frye, d. May 11, 1897, aged 83, both of Sandwich.

MANSON, James, d. Oct. 6, 1862, aged 52, m. June 4, 1843, by Elder Samuel Sherburne, Zerviah Sherburne, both of Barrington.

MANSON, Dr. Charles A., of Portsmouth, m. Sept. 4, 1865, in Wakefield, Helen Frances Wadleigh, of Wakefield, dau. of Elijah.

MANSON, George W., of Limerick, Me., m. Sep. 26, 1868, in Rochester, Hattie N. Shorey.

MARBLE, George F., m. (pub. Oct. 13, 1870, in Great Falls), Hannah B. Boston, both of Barrington.

MARCH, Joseph Delaney, m. Mar. 9, 1854, Olive Ham, d. Nov. 26, 1857, aged 39, dau. of Joshua.

MARDEN, James Jr., son of James, b. Aug. 17, 1761, d. Mar. 1817, aged 54, m. Oct. 16, 1783, by Rev. Joseph Haven, Frederica Seavey, d. Dec. 1837, aged 72.

MARDEN, Jacob K., m. May 6, 1871, in Dover, Augusta A. Chesley, b. Sep. 1, 1843, d. Oct. 26, 1932, dau. of Samuel.

MARLAND, Noah, m. (pub. June 23, 1870, in E. Rochester), Elizabeth Firth.

MARSH, Thomas H., of Boston, Mass., m. (pub. Sep. 1, 1846, in Brookfield), Melinda Warren, of Brookfield, dau. of Josiah.

MARSTON, John, of Manchester, m. Dec. 13, 1846, by Elder Alexander Tuttle, Sarah Ann McDaniel, of Barrington.

MARSTON, Charles D., of Newmarket, d. Jun. 9, 1868, aged 31, m. Nov. 29, 1855, in Newmarket, Mary Jane Moulton, aged 23, of Nottingham.

MARSTON, John A., aged 35, m. Sept. 20, 1864, in Strafford, Celestia M. Marston, aged 22, both of Sandwich.

MARSTON, James W., d. Oct. 30, 1908, aged 76, m. Mar. 25, 1869, in Great Falls, Mrs. Olive J. Ham, d. Oct. 30, 1919, aged 81, both of Great Falls.

MARTIN, Robert, of Brookfield, m. int. Dec. 25, 1823, in Wolfeboro, m. Jan. 7, 1824, in Brookfield, Julia Ann Huggins, of Wolfeboro.

MARTIN, Nathaniel, of Brighton, Mass., m. int. Oct. 31, 1835, in Lebanon, Me., Lydia Peirce.

MARTIN, William B., of Somersworth, d. May 30, 1908, aged 81, m. Feb. 7, 1848, in Lowell, Mass., Clara M. Wallingford, of Lowell, Mass.

MASON, Capt. Lemuel Bickford, of Barnstead, son of Robert, b. Jan. 14, 1759, d. Mar. 3, 1851, m. (1) Sarah Nutter, d. 1786, m. (2) Nov. 16, 1786, by Rev. Joseph Haven, Molly Chamberlain, of Rochester, d. Feb. 4, 1851, aged 82, dau. of Ephraim.

MASON, Rev. Lemuel, son of Capt. Lemuel Bickford, b. Aug. 24, 1797, d. June 6, 1850, m. Mar. 3, 1818, by Rev. Jeremiah Shaw, Hannah Watson, d. Feb. 21, 1863, dau. of Asa.

MASON, Dr. Ward B., m. Sept. 25, 1831, by Elder Enoch Place, Sarah Ann Montgomery, d. Aug. 25, 1848, aged 36, dau. of Capt. Paul, both of Straford, moved to Pleasant Grove, Ill.

MASON, George E., of Franklin, m. Oct. 23, 1853, in Lebanon, Me., Mary E. Young, of Strafford.

MASON, Albert, of Milton, m. Oct. 31, 1861, in Milton, Mrs. Mary J. Tebbetts, of Tuftonboro.

MASON, Enoch T., of Milton, m. Jan. 29, 1862, in Milton, Sarah E. Quint, of Ossipee.

MASON, David T., aged 45, son of Edward, d. June 4, 1892, m. Oct. 7, 1864, in Sandwich, Mrs. Martha Eaton, aged 36, d. June 7, 1869, both of Sandwich.

MASON, Charles E., aged 19, m. Sept. 11, 1865, in Sandwich, Hester Ann Hoag, aged 25, d. Jan. 5, 1894, aged 62, dau. of James, both of Sandwich.

MASON, Octavius C., aged 34, son of Nathan, m. Oct. 15, 1865, in Sandwich, Martha E. Quimby, aged 32, dau. of Charles.

MASON, Calvin, of Milton, m. Apr. 9, 1867, in Great Falls, Lydia A. Quint, of Ossipee.

8) **MATHES**, Valentine, son of Valentine, b. Mar. 23, 1807, d. Aug. 1, 1883, m. (1) June 30, 1833, Frances Mathes, d. Aug. 5, 1854,

aged 38, dau. of John, m. (2) May 11, 1867, Emeline S. Chesley, dau. of Asa.

MATHES, Elder Sherburne, m. Feb. 15, 1837, in Barrington, Elizabeth Babcock, dau. of Elder William.

MATHES, Samuel H., of Milton, son of William, b. Jan. 27, 1817, d. Feb. 21, 1888, aged 71, m. int. Apr. 30, 1837, in Dover, Marty T. Perkins.

MATHES, Burnham, son of John, b. Aug. 20, 1836, d. Feb. 4, 1895, m. Apr. 26, 1862, in Durham, Elizabeth A. Stevens, both of Durham.

MATHES, George, of Rollinsford, m. Nov. 13, 1862, in Dover, Susan J. Bunker, of Durham.

MATHES, Constantine B., m. Jan. 22, 1865, in Newmarket, Elizabeth Kinston, both of Newmarket.

MATHES, Charles H., of Durham, m. Aug. 20, 1865, in Barrington, Mary E. Chesley, of Barrington.

MATHES, Robert H., of Durham, m. Apr. 28, 1866, by Rev. James Rand, Mary E. Cousens, of Surry, Me.

MATHES, Valentine, of Durham, m. May 11, 1867, in Durham, Emeline S. Chesley, of Barrington.

MATHES, Hamilton Augustus, of Durham, son of John, m. Dec. 5, 1867, by Rev. Alvan Tobey, Belle S. Hoitt, of Lee, dau. of Gorham.

MATHES, Benjamin F., of Dover, m. June 3, 1868, in Newmarket, Josie M. Hodgdon.

MATHES, John H., son of Samuel H., d. Sept. 26, 1912, aged 65, m. May 21, 1870, in Dover, Alice A. Brown, both of Dover.

MATHES, Valentine Jr., of Durham, son of John, aged 24, m. Jan. 18, 1872, by Rev. Alvan Tobey, Nellie M. Pendexter, of Durham, aged 20, dau. of James.

MATHES, Mark H., of Durham, son of Jacob, aged 35, m. Sept. 26, 1875, in Newmarket, Emma F. Clark, of Durham, aged 21, dau. of George Edney.

MATHEWS, Horatio N., of Dover, son of Francis, m. (1) (pub. Apr. 22, 1834, in Berwick, Me.), Eunice G. Butler, of Berwick, Me., d. Dec. 26, 1851, aged 36, dau. of James, m. (2) Jun. 8, 1852, by Elder Elias Hutchins, Lydia Spencer, both of Berwick, Me.

MATHEWS, James Franics, m. Jul. 12, 1857, in Berwick, Me., Annie Day.

MAXWELL, John S., of Dover, m. Oct. 7, 1867, by Rev. James Rand, Hattie S. Wiggin, of Barrington.

MAYALL, Miles, of Somersworth, m. May 30, 1839, by Rev. Joseph Loring, Polly Furbish, both of Somersworth.

MCCANN, David, m. Nov. 17, 1796, in Barrington, Molley Foss, both of Barrington.

MCCANN, William A., of Poland, Me., m. Nov. 5, 1863, in Dover, Hannah S. Tash, of Dover.

MCCRILLIS, John, m. Nov. 25, 1765, by Rev. Isaac Hasey, Mary Garland.

MCCRILLIS, William, m. May 1, 1814, by Rev. Paul Jewett, Jane Furbish.

MCCRILLIS, George, m. int. Nov. 11, 1820, in Lebanon, Me., Joanna Jones.

MCCRILLIS, John Jr., m. Dec. 5, 1822, in Lebanon, Me., Eunice Foss.

MCCRILLIS, John, m. Dec. 4, 1823, in Lebanon, Me., Mary Rankins.

MCCRILLIS, Andrew, son of Henry, b. Mar. 27, 1801, d. June 19, 1872, aged 71, m. Oct. 17, 1824, in Tamworth, Mary C. Webster, d. Jan. 8, 1859, aged 55, both of Sandwich.

MCCRILLIS, Dr. John, of Berwick, Me., son of Henry, b. Dec. 30, 1779, d. Sept. 18, 1854, m. (1) Mar. 15, 1826, in Farmington, Betsey Furber, of Farmington, dau. of Gen Richard, m. (2) ---- ----.

MCCRILLIS, James, m. int. Feb. 13, 1828, in Lebanon, Me., Susan Peirce, of Berwick, Me.

MCCRILLIS, George, m. Aug. 26, 1849, by Rev. David B. Cowell, Julia Goodwin.

MCCRILLIS, John R., b. 1818, m. Dec. 24, 1848, in Strafford, Maria Babb, b. 1823, d. Sept. 10, 1876, dau. of Sampson.

MCCRILLIS, William, son of Neal, b. Apr. 30, 1821, m. Jan. 28, 1851, Mary S. Watson, of Tamworth, b. May 25, 1825.

MCCRILLIS, Lewis, m. Apr. 26, 1851, in Lebanon, Me., Ruth Hoitt.

MCCRILLIS, John G., m. int. Oct. 1, 1853, in Lebanon, Me., Lydia A. Cole, of Newfield, Me.

MCCRILLIS, George, m. int. Feb. 4, 1854, in Lebanon, Me., Eunice Peirce, of Berwick, Me.

MCCRILLIS, David, m. int. Aug. 6, 1855, in Lebanon, Me., Mary Jane Eaton.

MCCRILLIS, Daniel, m. Apr. 25, 1857, in Lebanon, Me., Jane E. Ramsey.

MCCRILLIS, John, of Nottingham, m. May 15, 1862, in Durham, Mary Jane Emerson, of Durham, b. Nov. 10, 1830, dau. of Timothy.

MCCRILLIS, John, m. int. Dec. 28, 1864, in Lebanon, Me., Relief Ann Blaisdell.

MCCRILLIS, Thomas, m. (pub. Jan. 17, 1867, in Great Falls), Mrs. Sarah F. Wiggin, both of E. Rochester.

MCDANIEL, David, m. Feb. 14, 1799, by Rev. Benjamin Balch, Betsey Ham, both of Barrington.

MCDANIEL, True William, d. May 23, 1892, aged 79, m. Jan. 22, 1852, in Dover, Rebecca Daniels, d. May 8, 1895, aged 74, dau. of Isaac, both of Barrington.

MCDANIEL, John, of Barrington, son of Andrew, b. 1829, d. 1883, m. May 9, 1853, in Lee, Hannah Rundlett, of Lee, b. 1833, d. Jan. 13, 1887.

MCDONALD, Rev. R., m. Dec. 26, 1864, in Tamworth, Mrs. Mary Ann Nute, both of Sandwich.

MCDONALD, Albert, m. Aug. 3, 1867, in Great Falls, Carrie L. Peaks, both of Portland, Me.

4) **MCDUFFEE**, John Flagg, son of Jacob, b. 1806, d. Dec. 27, 1888, m. (1) Nov. 21, 1830, by Rev. Isaac Willey, Lucy Flagg, b. 1805, d. 1866, both of Rochester, m. (2) Feb. 13, 1868, Mrs. Martha (Ham) Varney, wid. of Daniel, b. 1824, d. 1891.

MCDUFFEE, Daniel, m. Oct. 20, 1844, in Rochester, Lydia L. York, both of Rochester.

MCDUFFEE, Dana, d. Jan. 25, 1890, aged 61, m. Feb. 4, 1852, Lydia Gilman, b. Mar. 10, 1830, dau. of Moses.

MCDUFFEE, John W., of Lewiston, Me., m. May 28, 1863, in Dover, Matilda J. Hutchinson, of Dover.

MCDUFFEE, Henry H., of Lewiston, Me., m. Nov. 29, 1866, in Wolfeboro, Seddie T. Brackett, dau. of John M.

MCDUFFEE, Daniel H., m. (pub. Oct. 8, 1868, in Rochester), Fannie Foss, of Rochester.

MCDUFFEE, George C., m. June 3, 1869, by Rev. Jesse Meader, Abby E. Parsons, both of Rochester.

MCDUFFEE, George A., m. (pub. June 10, 1869, in Rochester), Emma S. Hoyt, both of Rochester.

MCFARLIN, Jackson, of Howesville, Tenn., m. July 14, 1865, in Lawrence, Mass., Mary A. Hurd, of Freedom.

MCILROY, John, m. June 4, 1863, in Rochester, Mrs. Hannah B. Hanson, both of Rochester.

MCINTIRE, Stephen, d. May 4, 1880, aged 78, m. Nov. 22, 1825, in Wolfeboro, Pamela Welch, d. June 8, 1876, aged 74, both of Wolfeboro.

MCINTIRE, Jason, b. 1818, d. 1876, m. (1) June 25, 1843, by Rev. Joseph Boodey, Ann Thurston, d. Nov. 1849, aged 28, of Alton, m. (2) Oct. 20, 1850, by Elder Josiah Glines, Hannah Garland, both of Alton, d. Jan. 6, 1907, aged 77, dau. of Thomas.

MCINTIRE, William, son of Joseph, d. Apr. 7, 1910, aged 88, m. Aug. 18, 1850, by Rev. Nathaniel Berry, Melissa B. Nute, b. near 1834, d. Oct. 19, 1887, aged 52, both of Alton.

MCINTIRE, Nathaniel, of Aton, m. Apr. 22, 1863, in Rochester, Emma Colbath, of New Durham.

MCINTIRE, Frederic, m. June 24, 1864, in Rochester, Elizabeth A. Nicholson.

MCINTIRE, Samuel C., of Dover, m. Dec. 31, 1865, in Farmington, Isabell A. Sanborn, of Farmington.

MCINTIRE, John A., of S. Berwick, Me., m. Sept. 2, 1868, by Rev. Robert S. Stubbs, Amanda M. Ford, of Dover.

MCINTIRE, James Frank, of Boston, Mass., m. Nov. 24, 1870, in Dover, Phebe P. Libbey, dau. of Rev. Charles O.

MCNEAL, John, of Rochester, m. Nov. 25, 1802, by Rev. Benjamin Balch, Frances Clark, of Barrington.

MCNEAL, William, m. Feb. 3, 1812, by Rev. Joseph Boodey, Nancy Emerson.

MCNEAL, Daniel W., of Barnstead, m. (pub. Jan. 7, 1864, in Wolfeboro), Addy M. Moulton.

MEADER, Lemuel B., b. Apr. 12, 177[9?], d. May 19, 1839, m. May 24, 1798, by Rev. Joseph Haven, Mary Kimball, b. Apr. 17, 1779, d. Jul. 24, 1845, dau. of Ephraim and Hannah.

MEADER, Benjamin, m. Dec. 4, 1808, by Rev. Micajah Otis, Nabby Munsey, both of Barrington.

MEADER, Rev. Jesse, son of Lemuel and Mary, b. Dec. 12, 1802, d. July 11, 1881, m. Oct. 8, 1832, by Elder Enoch Place, Hannah D. York, b. Nov. 2, 1811, d. Feb. 14, 1889, dau. of John, both of Rochester.

MEADER, James J., of Rochester, d. July 3, 1909, aged 69, m. Oct. 14, 1865, in Dover, Anna M. Johnson.

MEADER, Dudley P., of Durham, m. July 11, 1867, in Dover, Julia E. Hill, of Barnstead.

MEADER, Charles H., m. Dec. 24, 1867, in Rochester, Jennie McDuffee.

MEADER, David F., m. Oct. 11, 1868, in Fairhaven, Mass., Mary A. Chandler, both of Dover.

MEADER, Eli, m. (pub. Apr. 22, 1869, in Rochester), Sarah M. Vickery.

MEADER, James D., of Durham, m. Sept. 4, 1869, in Dover, Emma A. Perkins, of Newmarket.

MEARS, Joseph, m. May 1, 1863, in Dover, Sarah J. Warren, both of Dover.

MELLEN, Edwin, m. int. Feb. 20, 1857, in Lebanon, Me., Orrilla R. Manson, of Limerick, Me.

MELLEN, George N., m. Oct. 5, 1861, in Lebanon, Me., Mary Rankin.

MELLEN, Erastus, m. Feb. 23, 1864, in Rochester, Margaret Shorey, of Great Falls.

MELLOWS, Samuel, of New Durham, d. July 25, 1878, aged 82, m. (1) Mar. 26, 1820, by Rev. Joseph Boodey, Patience Leighton, of Alton, d. Nov. 24, 1847, aged 55, m. (2) Nov. 23, 1851, in Alton, Mrs. Elizabeth Sanborn, of Alton.

MELLOWS, Aaron L., m. Jan. 3, 1847, by Rev. Hezekiah D. Buzzell, Lucretia Adams, b. 1828, d. 1850, both of Alton.

MELVIN, George, of Dover, m. Apr. 18, 1870, in Dover, Mary J. French, of Farmington.

MERRILL, Elder Eliphalet, d. Feb. 6, 1853, aged 87, m. Oct. 9, 1794, by Rev. James Miltimore, Miriam Green.

MERRILL, Isaac, of Dover, son of Joseph, b. July 14, 1803, d. Mar. 17, 1885, aged 81, m. in 1829, in S. Berwick, Me., Hannah Jane Lord, b. Feb. 7, 1809, d. July 6, 1892, dau. of Edmond.

MERRILL, William G., of Dover, m. Apr. 21, 1867, in Union, Serepta Edmunds, of Wolfeboro.

MERRILL, T. T., of Farmington, m. Sept. 15, 1867, in Lewiston, Me., Fannie S. White, of Lewiston, Me.

MERRILL, Edward H., of S. Dedham, m. Oct. 31, 1867, in Dover, Jane E. Moore, of Dover.

MERROW, James, m. Oct. 6, 1816, in Lebanon, Me., Lucy Betel, of Alfred, Me.

MERROW, Isaac, m. Jan. 14, 1849, in Lebanon, Me., Mary Wentworth.

4) **MESERVE**, Daniel, son of Daniel, b. Mar. 18, 1734, d. Mar. 25, 1808, aged 74, m. May 5, 1764, Sarah Demeritt, b. Apr. 3, 1736, dau. of Eli.

MESERVE, Joseph, m. Nov. 5, 1789, by Rev. Benjamin Balch, Betty Hayes, both of Barrington.

5) MESERVE, Simon, son of Clement, b. June 14, 1773, m. June 20, 1798, by Rev. Benjamin Balch, Abigail Snell, d. Dec. 1861, both of Barrington.

5) MESERVE, George, son of Clement, b. Oct. 24, 1780, m. Jennie Swain.

5) MESERVE, Andrew, son of Clement, b. Aug. 27, 1786, d. Dec. 6, 1865, m. July 13, 1806, by Benjamin Balch, Patience Hall, b. Nov. 16, 1782, d. Sept. 23, 1872, both of Barrington.

5) MESERVE, Curtis, son of Clement, b. Dec. 22, 1795, m. (1) in 1817, Olive Lunt, m. (2) Lydia Stone.

5) MESERVE, John, son of Clement, b. Mar. 11, 1793, m. (1) in 1831, Eleanor Pennell, m. (2) ---- Huse.

MESERVE, Samuel, d. Mar. 3, 1900, aged 91, m. (1) Abigail ----, d. Nov. 26, 1831, aged 31, m. (2) Dec. 5, 1833, by Rev. Nathaniel Thurston, Mary A. Hanson, b. 1810, d. Nov. 18, 1887, dau. of John, both of Rochester.

MESERVE, Isaac H., b. June 21, 1813, d. Mar. 1, 1875, m. (1) Feb. 18, 1838, by Rev. Samuel Nichols, Martha B. Waterhouse, d. July 25, 1847, aged 34, m. (2) Dec. 26, 1848, in Barrington, Nancy W. Shackford, d. Feb. 5, 1905, aged 94, dau. of Samuel.

MESERVE, John C., d. Nov. 14, 1845, aged 25, m. May 19, 1845, by Elder Aaron Ayer, Susan Ham, d. July 4, 1847, aged 23.

6) MESERVE, Charles R., son of Samuel, b. July 24, 1825, d. Apr. 5, 1898, aged 72, m. (1) Jan. 8, 1846, in Dover, Sophronia R. Tucker, b. June 1, 1826, d. Sept. 18, 1876, aged 50, dau. of Ezra, m. (2) July 4, 1888, by Rev. Ithamar W. Beard, Annie E. Brown, b. Dec. 25, 1864, d. July 20, 1893, dau. of William H., m. (3) Mar. 27, 1845, in Concord, Clara L. Nason.

MESERVE, Isaac H., of Roxbury, Mass., m. Dec. 26, 1848, by Rev. Theodore Wells, Mary W. Shackford, of Barrington.

MESERVE, Winthrop S., of Durham, b. Feb. 9, 1838, d. Feb. 14, 1915, m. Nov. 30, 1861, in Dover, Eliza E. Tuttle, of Dover, b. Oct. 31, 1839, d. July 18, 1871.

MESERVE, Eben, of Dover, m. Sept. 29, 1863, in Boston, Mass., Martha J. Shepard, of Boston, Mass.

MESERVE, George, of Dover, m. July 4, 1864, in Dover, Hannah J. Bickford, of Durham.

MESERVE, Maj. William Neal, of Roxbury, Mass., m. Nov. 30, 1864, in Dover, Abby Augusta Hill, b. Aug. 16, 1842, d. Dec. 21, 1912, of Dover, dau. of Dr. Levi G.

MESERVE, George, of Madbury, m. Sept. 3, 1867, by Rev. Jesse Meader, Emma J. Hiller, of Portland, Me.

MESERVE, Gen. John S., of Salmon Falls, m. Dec. 25, 1867, in S. Berwick, Me., Mary Jane Antwine, of S. Berwick, Me.

MESERVE, George W., of Lee, son of Charles R., m. Nov. 9, 1869, in Durham, Helen M. Stanton, of Strafford, dau. of Ezra.

MESERVE, James, m. (pub. Aug. 4, 1870, in Great Falls), Lizzie Carney, both of Dover.

MEYERS, Rudolph H., of Portland, Me., m. Dec. 14, 1866, in Dover, Hannah Bobbott, of Windham, Me.

MILES, Laban, m. (pub. Jan. 23, 1862, in Concord), Augusta Kimball, both of Dover.

MILES, Reuben M., of Madbury, m. Aug. 10, 1862, by Rev. James Rand, Susan L. Pray, of Dover.

MILES, William H., of Madbury, m. Nov. 28, 1866, in Dover, Hattie C. Kimball, of Durham.

MILES, Charles H., of Great Falls, m. Jan. 16, 1869, in Great Falls, Sarah A. Pierce, of Augusta, Me.

MILLER, Granville Dow, of Dover, m. Jan. 9, 1863, in Portsmouth, Belinda Waterman, of Portland, Me.

MILLER, Benjamin F., of Acton, Me., m. Mar. 12, 1863, Mary Ross, b. Apr. 13, 1834, dau. of James.

MILLER, James A., m. July 4, 1866, by Rev. James Rand, Jane M. Berry, both of New Durham.

MILLER, James, of Rollinsford, d. Jan. 23, 1890, aged 45, m. Aug. 4, 1866, in Dover, Flora E. Ford, of Effingham.

MILLER, Levi, b. Aug. 1, 1836, d. Apr. 21, 1899, m. Dec. 2, 1866, in Strafford, Sarah A. Babb, b. May 5, 1836, d. Jan. 23, 1923.

MILLS, John Jr., m. Apr. 1, 1784, by Rev. Isaac Hasey, Margaret Kennison.

MILLS, James, m. Nov. 25, 1790, by Rev. Isaac Hasey, Rachel Courson.

MILLS, Isaiah, m. Aug. 11, 1810, in Lebanon, Me., Betsey Cottle.

MILLS, Benjamin, m. Oct. 29, 1815, in Lebanon, Me., Sally Guppy, of Rochester.

MILLS, Joseph, m. Jul. 26, 1818, in Lebanon, Me., Polly Jones.

MILLS, John Jr., m. Mar. 12, 1822, in Lebanon, Me., Sophia Hersom.

MILLS, Jeremiah, son of Samuel, b. 1805, d. Sept. 26, 1882, aged 77, m. (1) Betsey ----, d. Jan. 6, 1836, aged 27, m. (2) Nov. 27, 1836, by Elder Enoch Place, Sarah Foss, b. 1812, d. June 11, 1852, both of Strafford.

MILLS, George, of Rochester, m. Apr. 6, 1844, in Lebanon, Me., Sally J. Furbush.

MILLS, Francis H., of Wakefield, son of Elisha, d. May 1, 1873, aged 44, m. Oct. 6, 1853, in Haverhill, Mass., Mary J. Ellis, of Middleton, b. 1833, d. Oct. 22, 1882.

MILLS, William F., m. Nov. 3, 1866, by Rev. James Rand, Mrs. Nancy M. Hawkins, both of Dover.

MILLS, Albert H., m. Apr. 2, 1868, in Great Falls, Martha J. Blaisdell, both of Lebanon, Me.

MITCHELL, Thomas E., b. Jul. 3, 1831, d. Mar. 11, 1905, m. Nov. 19, 1853, by Elder Elias Hutchins, Lydia A. Perkins, b. May 3, 1833, d. Mar. 14, 1907.

MITCHELL, William F., of Campton, aged 24, m. Apr. 25, 1864, in Strafford, Sarah J. Hall, of Sandwich, aged 22.

MONTGOMERY, Jonathan, m. Mar. 13, 1777, in Barrington, Mary Hayes, both of Barrington.

MONTGOMERY, Capt. Paul, of Barrington, d. Apr. 12, 1841, aged 59, m. May 6, 1805, by Rev. William Hooper, Mary Emerson, of Madbury, d. July 7, 1880, aged 94.

MONTGOMERY, Moses, b. 1805, d. 1871, m. (1) Mar. 5, 1829, by Elder Enoch Place, Sarah Ann Peavey, d. Nov. 18, 1843, aged 31, dau. of Hudson, both of Strafford, m. (2) Jan. 7, 1849, in Barnstead, Hannah W. Parshley, of Barnstead, b. 1827.

MONTGOMERY, John Jr., d. May 3, 1846, m. Dec. 30, 1830, by Elder Enoch Place, Eliza W. Otis, b. 1806, d. Jan. 16, 1888, dau. of Joshua, both of Strafford.

MONTGOMERY, Capt. Nathaniel, d. July 19, 1856, aged 50, m. (pub. Feb. 7, 1832, in Strafford, Love Tuttle, b. Mar. 19, 1807, d. May 12, 1875, aged 68, dau. of James, both of Strafford.

MONTGOMERY, Capt. David, m. Sept. 17, 1835, by Rev. John Winkley, Mary Ann Winkley, dau. of Rev. John, both of Strafford.

MONTGOMERY, Jonathan H., b. 1822, d. Apr. 21, 1835, m. Nov. 25, 1850, by Elder Elias Hutchins, Sarah E. Stiles, b. 1827, d. 1910, both of Strafford.

MONTGOMERY, John S., son of Capt. David, m. May 26, 1861, by Elder Enoch Place, Hattie J. Parshley, dau. of Thomas.

MOODY, John Jr., m. (1) Jun. 16, 1818, by Rev. Paul Jewett, Eliza Powers, m. (2) int. Oct. 22, 1826, in Lebanon, Me., Phebe G. Merrill, of Brownfield, Me., m. (3) int. Aug. 28, 1830, in Lebanon, Me., Mary Jane Libbey, of Eliot, Me.

MOODY, Gardner S., m. Jul. 21, 1846, in Lebanon, Me., Lucy Jane Todd.

MOODY, Joseph C., of Ossipee, m. (pub. Aug. 27, 1863, in Meredith), Lizzie J. Kelly.

MOODY, George, of Tamworth, m. May 9, 1865, in Ossipee, Mary A. Hobbs, of Ossipee.

MOODY, William M., of Great Falls, m. (pub. Dec. 24, 1868, in Great Falls), Lizzie A. Huntress, of Tamworth.

MOODY, James F., of Brookfield, son of Jonathan, aged 22, m. Mar. 2, 1869, in Wolfeboro, Hannah H. Canney, aged 17, dau. of Simeon.

MOONEY, Capt. Jeremiah Burnham, son of Lt. Benjamin, b. Apr. 23, 1767, d. Mar. 17, 1807, m. Jan. 12, 1792, Abigail Mathes, b. 1772, d. May 11, 1827, dau. of Valentine.

MOONEY, Jeremiah, son of Lt. Benjamin, d. Sep. 30, 1857, aged 68, m. Nov. 11, 1813, by Rev. Joseph Boodey, Jane Coffin, d. Mar. 31, 1875, aged 87, dau. of Stephen, both of Alton.

MOONEY, Hiram, m. (pub. Dec. 23, 1845, in Farmington), Lucretia B. Tredick, b. July 7, 1822, d. Feb. 26, 1901, aged 78, dau. of William, both of Alton.

MOONEY, Dana J., of Newmarket, m. Dec. 27, 1865, in Alton, Abba Wentworth, of Alton.

MOORE, Peter, m. July 28, 1785, by Rev. Benjamin Balch, Jane Bumford, both of Barrington.

MOORE, John, m. July 4, 1833, in Barrington, Hannah Parshley.

MOORE, John, of Sanford, Me., m. Sep. 12, 1844, by Elder Abram Sanborn, Sabrina Gerrish.

MOORE, Joel T., of Stratham, m. Oct. 8, 1844, by Rev. Joseph Loring, Adeline J. Corson.

MOORE, Joseph, of Ossipee, son of Andrew, m. Feb. 12, 1864, by Rev. Alvan Tobey, Martha E. (Wentworth) Bennett, of S. Berwick, Me., dau. of Moses.

MOORE, Frank B., of Lawrence, Mass., m. Feb. 18, 1864, in Lawrence, Mass., Emma Ricker, of Dover.

MOORE, Delmont, m. Nov. 29, 1864, in Dover, Caroline M. Varney, of N. Berwick, Me.

MOORE, William E., m. June 9, 1867, in Milton, Sarah E. Downs, both of Milton.

MOORE, Calvin D., of Newburyport, Mass., m. (pub. Oct. 3, 1867, in Salisbury, Mass.), Flora A. Hobbs, of Ossipee.

MOORE, Samuel, m. July 4, 1868, in Dover, Hannah L. Smith, both of Biddeford, Me.

MOORE, John B., m. Aug. 27, 1868, by Rev. James Rand, Sarah E. Rose, both of Rochester.

MOORE, Moses H., m. Oct. 3, 1868, by Rev. Robert S. Stubbs, Nancy J. Kendall, both of Dover.

MORGAN, Harris W., b. 1827, d. 1889, m. Apr. 30, 1849, in Wolfeboro, Jane C. Edgerly, b. July 4, 1817, d. 1909, dau. of Daniel, both of Wolfeboro.

MORRILL, Henry T., of Lincoln, Me., m. Oct. 8, 1842, by Rev. Joseph Loring, Hannah Sherman.

MORRILL, David, of Holderness, m. June 2, 1853, by Rev. Levi B. Tasker, in Sandwich, Eliza P. Smith, of Sandwich.

MORRILL, Ephraim L., of N. Berwick, m. (pub. Mar. 31, 1864, in Great Falls), Elizabeth Silloway, of Great Falls.

MORRILL, Alphonso, of Amesbury, Mass., m. June 4, 1864, in Dover, Helen C. Twombly, of Dover.

MORRILL, Winfield S., of Gilford, m. Aug. 5, 1866, in W. Alton, Ruhamah Coleman, of W. Alton.

MORRISON, Nicholas, m. Sep. 26, 1809, by Rev. Isaac Hasey, Nancy Peirce.

MORRISON, Dr. John, of Alton, d. May 17, 1878, aged 87, m. Mar. 11, 1816, by Rev. John Osborne, Mary Randall, of Lee, b. 1794, d. Mar. 10, 1879, aged 85.

MORRISON, Gen. Nehemiah, of Alton, b. Aug. 21, 1794, d. Jan. 31, 1871, aged 77, m. Jan. 2, 1817, by Rev. Joseph Boodey, Polly French, of New Durham, d. Sept. 1, 1866, aged 66.

MORRISON, Jonathan Jr., of Tuftonboro, d. Jan. 21, 1875, aged 81, m. (1) Dec. 18, 1820, in Wolfeboro, Belinda Libbey, of Wolfeboro, d. May 19, 1846, aged 46, dau. of Ichabod, m. (2) June 30, 1847, in Tuftonboro, Mary Gould, d. Apr. 18, 1878, aged 73.

MORRISON, Ebenezer, son of Jonathan, d. June 12, 1847, m. (1) int. Jan. 1828, in Tuftonboro, Nancy Ladd, d. Aug. 12, 1844, aged 45, both of Tuftonboro, m. (2) Drusilla B. ----, d. Apr. 28, 1846, aged 32.

MORRISON, Nathan, d. Nov. 20, 1852, aged 38, m. (1) Apr. 20, 1844, in Wolfeboro, Ann C. Fullerton, d. Aug. 6, 1850, aged 30, both of Wolfeboro, m. (2) Feb. 8, 1851, in Wolfeboro, Alice A. Doe, both of Wolfeboro.

MORRISON, James H., of Boston, Mass., m. Mar. 6, 1845, by Elder Enoch Place, Abigail Stiles, of Strafford, dau. of John.

MORRISON, J. M., aged 51, m. Feb. 19, 1864, in Strafford, Emily McGaffey, aged 38, both of Strafford.
MORSE, Abner, b. 1801, d. 1885, m. (1) Jerusha ----, b. 1802, d. 1833, m. (2) (pub. May 6, 1845, in Gilmanton), Mrs. Abigail (Foss) Dow, wid. of Taylor, b. 1798, d. 1877, both of Gilford.
MORSE, Thomas J., b. June 17, 1824, d. June 24, 1871, m. (1) (pub. Nov. 28, 1848, in Great Falls), Elmira B. Walker, b. June 3, 1831, d. Nov. 3, 1852, m. (2) Mary E. Philbrick, b. Apr. 23, 1829, d. Nov. 22, 1899.
MORSE, Silas Marshall, Jr., son of Silas Marshall, b. Aug. 22, 1826, d. Nov. 21, 1893, m. May 29, 1849, in Effingham, Sabrina A. Hayes, b. 1828, d. 1906.
MORSE, John M., of Somersworth, m. June 1, 1867, in Great Falls, Caroline E. Wood, of Exeter.
MOSES, Phineas, m. May 13, 1811, by Rev. Micajah Otis, Nancy Arlen, both of Barrington.
MOSES, Phineas S., m. (1) int. Oct. 29, 1826, in Dover, Eliza Allen, m. (2) Mar. 26, 1828, in Barrington, Thankful Leathers, both of Barrington.
MOSES, Leonard, m. Aug. 2, 1837, in Barrington, Elizabeth Aren, of Barrington.
MOSES, John H., m. (pub. June 2, 1864, in Portsmouth), Delia II. Wells.
MOULTON, Jacob Jr., d. Dec. 10, 1870, aged 83, m. June 18, 1815, by Rev. Jeremiah Shaw, Eunice Dean, d. Mar. 17, 1875, aged 84.
MOULTON, Jonathan, m. Feb. 15, 1820, by Rev. Jeremiah Shaw, Nancy E. Moulton, b.1799, d. Dec. 8, 1867, aged 68.
MOULTON, Samuel A. M., son of Samuel, b. 1805, m. Feb. 22, 1829, Mary Young, b. 1810, both of Somersworth.
MOULTON, George, m. Dec. 6, 1830, in Lebanon, Me., by Rev. Abner Flanders, Anna Clark, both of Sanford, Me.
MOULTON, Robert, d. Feb. 4, 1848, aged 79, m. (1) Hannah ----, b. 1764, d. Jun. 2, 1831, m. (2) 1833, in Middleton, Mary Burrows, d. Feb. 18, 1848, aged 62, both of Wakefield.
MOULTON, Jonas, b. 1811, d. Mar. 15, 1872, m. (1) Mary W. Burroughs, b. 1814, d. Aug. 21, 1861, m. (2) Feb. 10, 1870, in Union, Elizabeth Mills, both of Wakefield.
MOULTON, Frederic Brown, son of Samuel, b. Oct. 12, 1816, d. Dec. 16, 1857, m. (1) Nov. 6, 1838, Lydia Maria Brown, b. Sept. 15, 1819, d. June 4, 1843, m. (2) Hannah George.

MOULTON, Seth Shackford, son of Capt. Joseph, b. July 3, 1812, m. (1) Oct. 20, 1842, by Rev. Eben Francis, Betsey Smith, dau. of John, m. (2) July 15, 1845, by Rev. William G. Anderson, Caroline Hanson, d. Mar. 16, 1854, aged 40.

MOULTON, Gilman, b. June 27, 1825, d. Oct. 15, 1893, m. July 4, 1849, by Rev. Levi B. Tasker, in Sandwich, Abby T. Quimby, b. July 23, 1829, d. Feb. 9, 1860, dau. of J. Smith Quimby.

MOULTON, Alvah, son of Samuel, b. Mar. 27, 1819, d. Aug. 16, 1904, aged 85, m. Sept. 26, 1855, in Dover, Susan Preston Tapley, b. Apr. 29, 1828, d. Sept. 22, 1913, aged 85, dau. of John, both of Dover.

MOULTON, Benjamin, m. Mar. 2, 1862, in Tamworth, Mrs. Hannah S. Swett.

MOULTON, Gilman, m. (pub. Apr. 24, 1862, in Center Sandwich), Lydia A. Dearborn.

MOULTON, Trueworthy, m. May 11, 1862, in Milton, Isabella Page, both of Wakefield.

MOULTON, Horace S., m. (pub. June 4, 1863, in Moultonboro), Sarah A. Whitten, both of Moultonboro.

MOULTON, Nathaniel W., of Dover, m. July 6, 1863, in Boston, Mass., Linda Whitney, of Augusta, Me.

MOULTON, Josiah S., b. Sept. 24, 1843, d. Jan. 29, 1918, aged 74, m. Feb. 15, 1865, in Dover, Ella Mary Mathes, b. June 29, 1844, d. Mar. 25, 1925.

MOULTON, Erastus, m. July 6, 1867, by Rev. Alden Sherwin, Georgia B. Chick, both of Boston, Mass.

MOULTON, Moses P., m. Feb. 9, 1869, by Rev. Robert S. Stubbs, Susan F. Hanson, both of Dover.

MUNSON, Henry, m. July 3, 1866, in Newburyport, Mass., Mrs. Phebe Maria Austin, of Dover.

MURDOCK, Walter C., of Great Falls, m. (pub. Oct. 21, 1869, in Great Falls), Mary A. Marden, of Salmon Falls.

MURPHY, Hiram G., of Dover, m. May 19, 1866, in Great Falls, Clara A. Hubbard, of Great Falls.

MURRAY, George, m. int. Apr. 9, 1815, in Lebanon, Me., Dorcas Bean.

MURRAY, James, m. int. Jun. 7, 1823, in Lebanon, Me., Mercy Downs.

MURRAY, Ebenezer, of Standish, Me., m. Jun. 20, 1830, by Elder Zebulon Delano, Sarah Stackpole.

MURRAY, Thomas, of Ireland, d. Mar. 15, 1891, aged 68, m. Apr. 6, 1854, in Lebanon, Me., Sarah Ann Earnshaw, d. July 25, 1895, aged 59.

MURRAY, James Jr., m. May 20, 1854, in Lebanon, Me., Almira Peirce.

MURRAY, Lewis, m. Oct. 1, 1850, by Rev. John Hubbard, Arabella (Isabella?) Goodwin.

MURRAY, Capt. Thomas M., m. Dec. 2, 1863, in Portsmouth, Elizabeth Jane Thomas, of Dover.

MURRAY, David, m. Oct. 1, 1867, in Lawrence, Mass., Lizzie W. Watson, both of Newmarket.

MURRAY, Eusaph, m. Oct. 2, 1870, in Dover, Catherine Megan, both of Dover.

NASH, John R., of Somersworth, m. Jul. 26, 1846, in Lebanon, Me., Hannah H. Blaisdell.

2) **NASON**, Benjamin, d. in 1714, m. (1) June 30, 1687, by Rev. John Pike, Martha Canney, b. Feb. 5, 1669, d. before 1708, dau. of Thomas, m. (2) Sarah (Bolles) Chadbourne, wid. of Humphrey, b. Jan. 26, 1657, dau. of Joseph, m. (3) Dec. 28, 1708, by Rev. Nathaniel Rogers, Elizabeth (Martyn) (Kennard) Furber, wid. of Edward Kennard and Lt. William Furber, dau. of Hon. Richard.

NASON, Joseph, d. Jan. 7, 1843, m. June 17, 1807, Mehepsabar Tebbets, b. Mar. 31, 1786, dau of Aaron.

NASON, Peter, m. int. Jan. 2, 1834, in Lebanon, Me., Sarah Goodwin.

NASON, Oliver, m. Apr. 9, 1860, in Lebanon, Me., Mary A. Fall.

NASON, Luther, b. Feb. 13, 1840, d. Jan. 16, 1915, m. (1) Mary E. Butler, m. (2) int. Jun. 27, 1861, in Rollinsford, Emily J. Burke, d. Oct. 1884, aged 41, dau. of James, both of S. Berwick, Me.

NASON, Robert, m. Aug. 18, 1862, in Dover, Ellen E. Oxford, both of S. Berwick, Me.

NASON, Reuben, m. Apr. 23, 1863, in Dover, Vienna M. Davis, both of Dover.

NASON, William, m. Nov. 1, 1863, in Campton, Sarah E. Lake, both of Rollinsford.

NASON, Albion F., m. Oct. 31, 1866, in Dover, Clara L. Whitney, both of Windham, Me.

NEAL, Joshua, b. June 23, 1786, d. Nov. 4, 1840, m. June 17, 1776, Mary Tarleton, d. Dec. 10, 1825, aged 69.

NEAL, John, m. May 11, 1806, by Rev. Micajah Otis, Martha Church, both of Barrington.

NEAL, John, of Tuftonboro, d. Sept. 23, 1855, aged 62, m. Mar. 1, 1819, in Wolfeboro, Abigail Hersey, of Wolfeboro, d. May 9, 1872, aged 82.

NEAL, Oliver, son of Nathaniel, d. Sept. 27, 1850, aged 52, m. int. Apr. 1825, in Tuftonboro, Sally Burbank, d. Oct. 2, 1846, aged 49, both of Tuftonboro.

NEAL, Richard B., b. Mar. 13, 1820, d. Sept. 26, 1890, m. (pub. Apr. 26, 1842, in Tuftonboro), Nancy N. Piper, b. Oct. 22, 1820, d. July 24, 1882.

NEAL, Enoch B., son of Oliver C., d. Oct. 27, 1890, aged 62, m. (1) (pub. May 31, 1855, in Somersworth), Lizzie M. Winchell, d. Oct. 1872, aged 44, m. (2) (pub. Apr. 17, 1874, in Great Falls), Mrs. Nancy J. (Fox) Tibbetts, wid. of Charles D., d. Jun. 22, 1898, aged 64, dau. of Ira.

NEAL, James H., b. Jan. 29, 1835, d. Nov. 12, 1906, m. (pub. Dec. 20, 1860, in Ossipee), Adaliza J. Copp, b. Apr. 4, 1835, d. Nov. 20, 1913, both of Tuftonboro.

NEAL, Jacob S., m. Jan. 7, 1863, in Strafford, Annie M. Clark, both of Barrington.

NEAL, Henry, of S. Newmarket, m. June 1, 1867, in Dover, Ellen Cole, of Dover.

NEAL, George W., of Kittery, Me., m. Aug. 11, 1868, by Rev. George G. Field, Delia A. Henderson, of Dover, d. Sept. 17, 1914, aged 71, dau. of Samuel H.

NEALEY, Benjamin Mason, son of Sgt. Joseph, b. Apr. 4, 1782, d. Oct. 16, 1859, aged 74, m. in 1807, by Rev. John Osborne, Sarah Ford, of Nottingham, b. Oct. 22, 1784, d. Sept. 7, 1849, aged 65, dau. of Capt. Eben.

NEALEY, Sylvester L., of Newmarket, aged 30, b. June 23, 1827, d. Nov. 16, 1862, m. Aug. 20, 1857, by Rev. Alvin Tobey, Sarah A. Hanson, of Madbury, b. Dec. 8, 1835, d. Dec. 24, 1906, aged 71, dau. of Sargent.

NEALLEY, Edward Bowdoin, son of Sgt. Joseph, b. Dec. 28, 1784, d. Jan. 1839, m. Jan. 7, 1809, Sally True, b. Oct. 25, 1789, d. Dec. 28, 1850.

NEALLEY, Benjamin Mason, son of Benjamin, b. Oct. 3, 1811, d. July 29, 1888, m. Aug. 8, 1836, Abby Pray, b. Mar. 1, 1817, d. Jan. 29, 1895, dau. of James.

NEALLEY, Benjamin Frank, son of Benjamin M., b. July 16, 1816, d. 1867, m. Feb. 16, 1840, Susan Emerson Bartlett, of Lee, b. Mar. 24, 1819, d. Mar. 26, 1905, dau. of William.

NEALLEY, Benjamin Frank, son of Benjamin M., b. Oct. 24, 1839, d. Mar. 27, 1911, aged 71, m. Aug. 1, 1866, in Dover, Hattie Ruth Colby, b. May 14, 1846, d. Oct. 12, 1903, dau. of Rev. John, both of Dover.

NELSON, Frank, of Wakefield, m. (pub. May 12, 1870, in Great Falls), Grace M. Tebbets, of Great Falls.

NEWCOMB, James A. G., m. Oct. 14, 1850, in Berwick, Me., Olive G. Manning, both of Berwick, Me.

NEWELL, Burley B., of Wolfeboro, m. Oct. 19, 1865, in Natchez, Miss., Fernandia M. Lachenwitz.

NEWELL, Edwin C., of Brookfield, aged 25, m. int. Dec. 31, 1867, in Brookfield, Elizabeth F. Martin, of Wolfeboro, aged 24.

NEWELL, Edwin C., of Brookfield, m. (pub. June 4, 1868, in Wolfeboro), Elizabeth F. Martin, of Wolfeboro, dau. of Daniel.

NEWELL, Dr. A. C., m. (pub. Jan. 7, 1869, in Gonic), Jennie S. Hayes.

NICHOLS, George Washington, son of george, b. Oct. 16, 1816, d. May 29, 1888, m. May 27, 1838, Lovina Knox, b. May 18, 1811, d. Jul. 16, 1892.

NICHOLS, Rev. Jacob W., d. Nov. 16, 1863, aged 40, m. July 19, 1846, in Ossipee, Nancy King, d. Feb. 27, 1889, aged 70.

NICHOLS, Henry A., of Amherst, Me., m. Nov. 28, 1867, in Nashua, Mary E. Varney, of Boston, dau. of Shubael, late of Dover.

NICKERSON, Robert, of Tamworth, b. Apr. 8, 1818, d. Sept. 25, 1865, m. June 28, 1853, by Rev. Levi B. Tasker, in Sandwich, Mary Ann Quimby, of Sandwich, b. Feb. 21, 1822, d. June 1, 1858, dau. of J. Smith Quimby.

NICKERSON, Joseph R., of Tamworth, Oct. 14, 1862, in Sandwich, Sarah P. Marston, of Sandwich.

NIGHSWANDER, Jacob, of Toronto, Canada, m. Oct. 13, 1869, in Dover, Costilla Lacoste Horton, of Dover, d. June 17, 1911, aged 66, dau. of Charles H.

NILES, William H., of Webster, Me., son of John, m. Apr. 21, 1866, by Rev. William Wilmot, Lydia E. Davis, of Alton, dau. of Andrew.

NISBETT, Charles, m. int. Jan. 30, 1806, in Lebanon, Me., Mercy Austin.

NISBETT, Samuel, m. int. Sep. 20, 1826, in Lebanon, Me., Sophia Brackett, of Shapleigh, Me.

NISBETT, Charles, m. int. Dec. 9, 1827, in Lebanon, Me., Nancy Hodgdon, of Ossipee.

NORRIS, Arthur F. L., of Manchester, m. 1846, Olive Willard Wallace.

NORRIS, Joseph S., m. (pub. Sept. 8, 1870, in Farmington), Isabella M. Ricker, both of Farmington.

NORWOOD, Epraim Francis, of Dover, b. 1830, d. June 10, 1921, m. (1) Abby S. ----, b. 1830, d. 1854, m. (2) (pub. July 16, 1868, in Portsmouth), Anna B. Drake, of Portsmouth, b. 1834, d. 1878, m. (3) Mary Elizabeth ----, b. 1841, d. 1927.

NOWELL, Mark, of N. Berwick, Me., m. Dec. 5, 1867, in Great Falls, Elmira H. Tolman, of Great Falls.

NOWELL, George Dana, of Wolfeboro, son of George H., d. July 6, 1902, aged 61, m. Jan. 16, 1870, in Rochester, Nellie F. Cate, of Brookfield, d. Oct. 16, 1881, aged 36.

NOYES, Dr. William H., of Gloucester, Mass., m. May 14, 1848, by Elder Enoch Place, Sarah M. Parshley, of Strafford, dau. of Ebenezer, moved to Newburyport, Mass.

NOYES, Henry C., m. (pub. May 3, 1853, in Great Falls), Sabra R. Hamilton, d. Aug. 11, 1892, aged 66, dau. of Adrial.

NOYES, Washington, of Hampstead, m. int. Nov. 8, 1864, in Lebanon, Me., Sabrina D. Corson.

NOYES, Charles, of Boston, Mass., m. Dec. 25, 1867, in Dover, Abbie M. Blaisdell, of Dover.

NUTE, John, m. June 11, 1799, by Rev. Benjamin Balch, Susanna Pearl, both of Rochester.

NUTE, Israel, d. Feb. 15, 1836, aged 44, m. Sept. 28, 1817, by Rev. Joseph Haven, Hannah Fish, b. Sept. 3, 1797, dau. of John, both of Milton.

7) NUTE, John C., son of Francis, b. Dec. 14, 1794, d. Apr. 26, 1872, m. (1) Feb. 22, 1818, Sarah Ann Varney, d. Nov. 2, 1856, aged 57, m. (2) Nov. 4, 1858, in Dover, Rhoda, Ann Varney, d. Nov. 28, 1875, aged 73, both of Dover.

NUTE, Sewell, of Barrington, m. (1) Oct. 17, 1825, in Barrington, Lydia Merrill, of Dunbarton, m. (2) Apr. 22, 1838, by Rev. Samuel Nichols, Elizabeth Brown, both of Barrington.

NUTE, Parker, d. Jun. 8, 1812, d. Oct. 30, 1887, m. Apr. 10, 1834, by Rev. Nathaniel Berry, Mariah Horne, b. Oct. 12, 1815, d. Apr. 11, 1877, both of Barrington.

NUTE, Suel, m. Apr. 22, 1838, in Barrington, Elizabeth Brown, both of Barrington.

NUTE, Thomas, son of Meserve, b. Nov. 10, 1817, d. Nov. 9, 1902, m. Sep. 3, 1843, Maria Brock, d. Apr. 12, 1886, aged 69, dau. of Paul.

NUTE, Hopley Y., d. Apr. 4, 1877, aged 53, m. (1) Oct. 7, 1845, by Rev. Seth W. Perkins, Lydia C. Pinder, d. Sept. 28, 1860, aged 43, m. (2) Aug. 20, 1862, in Portsmouth, Mrs. Sarah W. Webster, both of Durham.

NUTE, Stephen, of Wolfeboro, m. (pub. Sept. 25, 1862, in Wolfeboro), Sarah M. Nichols, of Ossipee.

NUTE, Charles A., of Wakefield, m. Sept. 5, 1866, in Ossipee, Almira N. Glidden, of Ossipee.

NUTE, James, m. Sept. 10, 1866, in Dover, Emeline Stillings, both of Bartlett.

NUTE, Daniel A., m. (pub. Nov. 29, 1866, in Wolfeboro), Ellen E. Clark.

NUTE, George A., m. Mar. 8, 1867, in Methuen, Mass., Nellie M. Hall.

NUTE, Charles Henry, of Dover, m. Dec. 8, 1868, in Dover, Sarah Elizabeth Chesley, of Durham, b. Oct. 18, 1910, dau. of Daniel.

NUTE, George A., m. (pub. Jul. 10, 1873, in Dover), Annie L. Parsons, d. Jun. 4, 1898, aged 56, dau. of John, both of Rochester.

NUTTER, Isaac, b. 1793, d. Jan. 13, 1873, m. Lydia Jeffers, b. 1798, d. Nov. 3, 1880.

NUTTER, Jethro, d. Jan. 26, 1854, aged 90, m. (1) Aug. 31, 1774, by Rev. Isaac Hasey, Sarah Downs, m. (2) 1784, Polly Elliott.

NUTTER, John H., of Farmington, m. Dec. 14, 1810, by Rev. Micajah Otis, Hannah Hall, of Barrington.

NUTTER, Samuel, of Rochester, d. Feb. 14, 1865, aged 74, m. Nov. 12, 1815, by Elder Enoch Place, Miriam Clark, of Barrington, d. 1856.

NUTTER, John 4th, d. Mar. 21, 1847, aged 42, m. (pub. Jan. 12, 1830), in Barnstead), Hannah Nutter, d. Mar. 18, 1874, aged 67.

NUTTER, John H., m. Aug. 16, 1866, in Newmarket, Abby R. Leary.

NUTTER, Henry C., m. Jan. 8, 1868, in Farmington, Arabella M. Leighton, both of Farmington.

NUTTER, H. F., m. Aug. 7, 1868, in Rochester, Fannie Hammett, both of Rochester.

NUTTER, Charles E., m. Aug. 9, 1868, in Rochester, Elzina Downs, both of Milton.

NUTTER, Sidney H., m. (pub. July 8, 1869, in Rochester), Arabell Corson, both of Milton.

NUTTER, Charles F., of Saco, Me., m. Dec. 11, 1869, in Dover, Mary E. Owen, of Buxton, Me.

OAKES, Thomas Edmund, of Dover, m. Apr. 26, 1866, in Brookline, N.J., Hester A. Patterson, of Brookline, N.J.

O'NEAL, James, m. before Apr. 17, 1858, in Somersworth, Abby Clark.

ORDWAY, Walter S., of S. Newmarket, m. July 3, 1866, in Dover, Charlotte W. Horne, of Dover.

ORNE, Frederick A., of Middleton, m. (1) Feb. 28, 1859, by Rev. Benjamin F. Parsons, Emma C. Tasker, of Dover, m. (2) Oct. 24, 1863, in Rochester, Jennie E. Springfield.

ORRELL, Charles S., of Lee, m. (pub. Jan. 3, 1867, in Berwick, Me.), Myra B. Hersey, of Milton.

OSBORNE, John Henry, of Rochester, son of Elijah, b. Aug. 13, 1836, d. Mar. 27, 1917, aged 80, m. Jan. 1, 1861, in Rochester, Sarah Jane Hanson, of Barrington, d. Mar. 24, 1914, aged 73, dau. of Jonas.

OSBORNE, George F., of Boston, Mass, m. Dec. 24, 1866, in Boston, Mass., Abbie B. Peirce, of Dover, dau. of J. Kittredge Peirce.

OSBORNE, Daniel G. (or David), of Pittsfield, m. Sept. 20, 1867, by Rev. James Rand, Clara Chase, of Dover.

OSGOOD, Ebenezer, of Milton, m. int. Sep. 15, 1829, in Lebanon, Me., Eleanor Burrows.

OSGOOD, Addison, of Ossipee, aged 26, m. Dec. 11, 1858, in Sandwich, Mary A. Watson, of Moultonboro, aged 24.

OSGOOD, A. J., m. Sept. 14, 1865, in Haverhill, Mass., Lydia E. Wentworth, both of Rochester.

OSGOOD, Napoleon B., m. (pub. Oct. 5, 1865, in Portsmouth), Helen B. Knox, both of Biddeford, Me.

OTIS, Rev. Micajah, son of Joshua, b. May 21, 1747, d. May 20, 1821, m. near 1769, Sarah Foss, d. Jan. 20, 1827.

OTIS, Job, son of Rev. Micajah, b. Aug. 23, 1770, d. Sept. 28, 1854, m. Oct. 12, 1795, Sarah Kimball, b. Feb. 7, 1777, d. Feb. 26, 1853, dau. of Ephraim and Hannah.

OTIS, Lemuel, son of Elijah, d. Dec. 28, 1863, aged 91, m. June 1, 1796, by Rev. Benjamin Balch, Leah Pearl, d. Apr. 2, 1855, aged 91.

OTIS, Joshua, son of Elder Micajah, d. July 18, 1839, aged 66, m. (1) Nov. 26, 1799, by Rev. Micajah Otis, Abigail Young, d. Oct. 11, 1818, aged 36, m. (2) Apr. 23, 1820, by Elder Enoch Place, Abigail Cate, d. June 21, 1857, aged 65, dau. of Eleazer.

OTIS, Simon, of Barrington, son of Micajah, d. Jan. 6, 1871, aged 93, m. (1) Mar. 4, 1803, by Rev. Micajah Otis, Abigail Giles, of Rochester, d. Mar. 13, 1818, aged 34, m. (2) Elizabeth Ring Walker, d. Aug. 4, 1831, aged 41, dau. of William.

OTIS, Jethro, b. Mar. 1, 1781, d. Aug. 13, 1863, m. Mar. 24, 1803, by Rev. Benjamin Balch, Esther Howard, both of Barrington.

OTIS, Micajah Jr., m. Jan. 23, 1806, by Rev. Micajah Otis, Hannah Allard, d. Nov. 10, 1845, aged 74, both of Barrington.

OTIS, Elijah, m. Nov. 21, 1811, by Rev. Micajah Otis, Jane Otis, both of Barrington.

OTIS, Capt. Stephen, son of Micajah, d. Jan. 7, 1834, aged 50, m. near 1812, Joanna ----, d. July 15, 1852, aged 58.

OTIS, Joseph Jr., of Barrington, m. Oct. 23, 1812, in Barrington, Lucy Place, of Rochester.

OTIS, Capt. Joshua, of Rochester, son of Job, d. Aug. 2, 1826, aged 40, m. Nov. 11, 1813, by Elder Enoch Place, Love Elkins, of Farmington.

OTIS, Samuel, b. 1802, d. Sep. 11, 1887, aged 87, m. Feb. 5, 1824, by Elder Enoch Place, Lydia Smith, b. 1803, d. Feb. 29, 1875, aged 75, both of Strafford.

OTIS, Nicholas, m. Nov. 29, 1827, by Elder Enoch Place, Judith Young, d. Jan. 25, 1830, aged 39, both of Strafford.

OTIS, John, of Dover, m. Feb. 10, 1838, in Lebanon, Me., Mrs. Patience (Young) Randall, wid. of Arthur. [Was this a second marriage?]

OTIS, Thomas Jefferson, son of Micajah, b. Dec. 9, 1806, d. Nov. 15, 1892, m. (1) Susan ----, d. Sept. 23, 1843, aged 39, m. (2) in 1846, Elmina P. Canney, b. Sept. 3, 1829, d. Oct. 27, 1908, dau. of Daniel.

OTIS, Walter B. K., of Somersworth, , m. Apr. 3, 1842, by Elder Enoch Place, Sarah P. Rand, of Rochester, d. June 14, 1855, aged 34.

OTIS, Micajah, son of Elijah, d. Dec. 12, 1864, aged 80, m. (1) Hannah Allard, d. Nov. 10, 1845, aged 74, m. (2) Oct. 6, 1846, in Farmington, Mrs. Polly Hall, both of Farmington.

OTIS, Joshua, of Strafford, son of Job, b. 1821, m. May 11, 1848, by Elder Enoch Place, Rebecca Fidelia Ricker, b. 1827, d. Mar. 16, 1879, of Farmington.

OTIS, Joseph G., of Lee, b. 1818, m. May 30, 1856, by Elder Elias Hutchins, Abby D. Stanton, of Strafford, b. 1822, d. Oct. 13, 1858, dau. of Ezra.

OTIS, Jethro, of Strafford, son of L. H. Otis, d. Jan. 31, 1900, aged 60, m. (pub. Jul. 19, 1860, in Rochester), Anna Jordon, of Somersworth.

OTIS, John, m. Aug. 16, 1862, in Rochester, Mrs. Mary Pearl, of Rochester.

OTIS, John H., m. Sept. 8, 1862, in Dover, Lucy A. Cole, of Dover.

OTIS, Hiram D., of Strafford, m. Feb. 25, 1864, in Strafford, Sarah A. Pitman, of Barnstead.

OTIS, William T., m. May 23, 1864, by Rev. James Rand, Clara A. (Cole) Osgood, wid. of John Jr., both of Dover.

OTIS, James T., of Kittery, Me., m. May 23, 1865, in Portland, Me., Addie York, of Biddeford, Me.

OTIS, Ai D., of Farmington, b. 1836, d. 1906, m. Nov. 29, 1866, in New Durham, Harriet Canney, of Barnstead, b. Dec. 29, 1836, d. 1919, dau. of Joseph.

OTIS, John H., m. (pub. Jan. 27, 1870, in Great Falls), Sarah J. Hobbs, both of N. Berwick, Me.

PAGE, Capt. Benjamin, d. Nov. 2, 1838, aged 78, m. Aug. 6, 1767, Keziah Guptill, dau. of Thomas.

PAGE, David Copp, of Rochester, m. Feb. 2, 1804, by Rev. Benjamin Balch, Sarah Ham, of Barrington.

PAGE, Joseph W., of Durham, d. Mar. 9, 1834, aged 43, m. Nov. 30, 1823, by Rev. Federal Burt, Mary Ann Gilman, of Dover, d. May 21, 1882, aged 84.

PAGE, David W., of Rochester, b. 1818, d. Feb. 11, 1878, m. Dec. 7, 1846, by Rev. Robert B. Stacy, Sylvesty Canney, of Farmington, b. Sept. 23, 1824, d. June 17, 1904, dau. of Isaac.

PAGE, Daniel A., of Rochester, m. Feb. 3, 1863, in Dover, Melissa E. Peirce, of Dover.

PAGE, Josiah E., son of Joseph, b. Apr. 30, 1834, d. Feb. 9, 1911, m. July 27, 1864, by Rev. Asa Piper, Hannah E. Marsh, of Wakefield, b. Nov. 14, 1840, d. Feb. 5, 1925, dau. of John.

PAGE, Moses D., m. Nov. 10, 1864, in Dover, Emma L. Vickery, both of Dover.

PAGE, Albert R., of Gilmanton, m. (pub. June 25, 1868, in Farmington), Addie E. Clements, of New Durham.

PAINE, John, of Moultonboro, m. Nov. 8, 1832, in Milton, Mrs. Comfort (Jones) Laskey, of Milton, wid. of Jonathan, d. Dec. 15, 1866, aged 90.

PALMER, Henry A., m. (pub. Sept. 17, 1863, in Portsmouth), Frances L. Goodwin.

PALMER, John R., of Dover, m. Aug. 22, 1867, in Barrington, Nellie A. Gray, of Barrington.

PALMER, Aaron, of Weare, m. Oct. 11, 1867, in Dover, Myra Goodwin, of Suncook.

PALMER, E. Burritt, of Philadelphia, Pa., m. May 29, 1868, in Dover, Abby Y. Cate, of Dover

PALMER, Benjamin W., m. (pub. June 24, 1869, in Great Falls), Charlotte A. Redfield, both of Dover.

PARISH (PARIS), Charles Samuel, of Wolfeboro, b. 1842, d. 1924, m. June 13, 1869, Susan Amanda Cook, of Wakefield, b. 1841, d. 1932.

PARKER, Pierce, of Kittery, Me., m. int. Dec. 2, 1834, in Lebanon, Me., Hannah Lord.

PARKER, Dr. Alvah, of Lebanon, Me., d. Jun. 3, 1851, m. May 8, 1836, Lucinda Jones, b. Nov. 17, 1817, d. Sep. 25, 1900, dau. of Stephen.

PARKER, Dr. John S., m. (1) Oct. 26, 1853, by Rev. Clement Parker, Miriam B. Wood, d. Apr. 17, 1862, aged 27, m. (2) May 17, 1863, by Rev. Clement Parker, Carrie M. Wood.

PARKER, Dr. N.C., m. May 1, 1862, in Farmington, Adelaide H. Cilley, only dau. of Rev. D. P. Cilley.

PARKER, Thomas, of London, Eng., m. (pub. Feb. 23, 1865, in Portsmouth), Annie Wheeler.

PARKER, Charles E., m. June 26, 1865, in Dover, Anna A. Clifford, both of Epping.

PARKER, Riley H., of N. Andover, Mass., son of Nathan, m. Feb. 1, 1866, by Rev. Leonard Withington, in Newburyport, Mass., Julia F. Yeaton, of New Castle, dau. of Edward S.

PARKER, Dr. Henry R., m. (pub. May 31, 1866, in Wolfeboro), Ella M. Thompson, dau. of Moses.

PARKER, Jeremiah L., of Manchester, m. Sept. 29, 1866, in Dover, Mrs. Emily J. Jones, of Great Falls.

PARKER, Charles F., of E. Rochester, m. July 18, 1867, in Farmington, Hattie A. Thurston, of Manchester.

PARKER, Lewis C., of Bartlett, m. Nov. 8, 1867, in Great Falls, Emma Roby, of Dover.

PARKER, Charles L., of Bartlett, m. July 8, 1869, in Dover, Mary E. Roby, of Cambridge, Mass.

PARKER, Enoch, m. (pub. Dec. 8, 1870, in Rochester), Mrs. Sarah E. J. Holman, both of Epping.

3) **PARSHLEY**, George, d. Mar. 28, 1829, aged 78, m. (1) Mar. 5, 1778, in Barrington, Betty Demeritt, both of Barrington, m. (2) Nov. 24, 1814, in Barrington, by Rev. Micajah Otis, Mrs. Meribah Sloper, b. 1784, d. June 19, 1860.
PARSHLEY, Richard, m. Aug. 11, 1782, in Northwood, Anna Sloper, d. Dec. 6, 1836, aged 76.
PARSHLEY, Paul, m. Nov. 1, 1807, by Rev. Micajah Otis, Lydia Caverly, both of Barrington.
PARSHLEY, John, d. Nov. 24, 1856, aged 71, m. Nov. 26, 1811, in Barrington, by Rev. Joseph Boodey, Polly Parshley, d. Dec. 21, 1872, aged 90.
PARSHLEY, Richard Jr., m. Jan. 31, 1814, in Barrington, by Rev. Micajah Otis, Polly Caverly, both of Barrington.
PARSHLEY, Thomas 3rd, b. near 1794, m. Nov. 25, 1824, by Elder Enoch Place, Betsey Foss, b. near 1800, d. Jul. 30, 1870, aged 70, both of Strafford.
PARSHLEY, John W., b. 1809, d. Dec. 25, 1864, m. Mar. 15, 1836, by Elder Enoch Place, Mary A. Foss, b. 1810, both of Strafford.
PARSHLEY, John Gilman, son of John, b. Apr. 11, 1816, d. Oct. 26, 1845, m. Oct. 17, 1840, by Rev. John Parkman, Betsey R. Hayes, d. Feb. 11, 1849, aged 35.
PARSHLEY, John D., m. June 2, 1862, in Strafford, Orissa A. Foss, d. Feb. 18, 1908, aged 66, dau. of Warren.
PARSHLEY, Ebenezer James, of Strafford, son of Ebenezer, d. June 22, 1918, aged 86, m. Nov. 22, 1864, by Rev. James Rand, Mrs. Lizzie (Kimball) Thompkins, of Dover, wid. of Charles A., d. Nov. 22, 1874, aged 37.
PARSHLEY, Sanborn, d. Mar. 1, 1895, aged 63, m. Nov. 16, 1866, by Rev. James Rand, Rufina Smith, d. Jan. 27, 1917, aged 76, both of Strafford.
PARSHLEY, Frank B., of Newmarket, m. Feb. 27, 1869, in Great Falls, Sarah B. Whitehouse, of S. Berwick, Me.
PARSONS, Ebenezer, d. May 26, 1865, aged 92, m. Jan. 18, 1798, Sally Joy, b. Nov. 10, 1771, d. July 7, 1850, dau. of Samuel.
PARSONS, William, of Shapleigh, Me., son of John, d. Apr. 19, 1895, aged 77, m. Jun. 13, 1850, in Lebanon, Me., Elizabeth Merrow, of Somersworth.
PARSONS, Bradley E., of Rochester, son of John, d. Nov. 15, 1918, aged 80, m. Oct. 4, 1857, by Elder Elias Hutchins, Sophia Young, of Madbury.

PARSONS, Everett, son of John, d. May 16, 1900, aged 72, m. (1) July 18, 1858, in Rochester, Susan Hilton, d. May 12, 1864, aged 40, both of Rochester, m. (2) May 20, 1870, in E. Rochester, Lenora Babb, of Manchester, d. Nov. 18, 1897, aged 63, dau. of James.

PARSONS, Ebenezer J., of Durham, m. May 26, 1862, in Durham, Mary J. Tasker, of Strafford.

PARSONS, George W., of Salem, m. Nov. 25, 1863, in Rochester, Louise T. Bickford, of Rochester.

PARSONS, Solomon B. G., m. Apr. 2, 1864, in Dover, Eugenia F. Brown, both of Somersworth.

PATTERSON, George H., m. Feb. 20, 1861, in Dover, Lydia A. Drew, b. Aug. 19, 1841, dau. of John T.

PAUL, Benjamin, son of Moses, b. Sep. 26, 1755, m. Anna Bampton, b. Jul. 27, 1750, dau. of Ambrose.

PAUL, Stephen, b. Nov. 1, 1777, d. Feb. 15, 1862, m. Oct. 2, 1800, by Rev. William Hooper, Temperance Ellison, b. Dec. 23, 1789, d. Nov. 5, 1859, both of Barrington.

PAUL, Ellison, son of Stephen, b. Apr. 15, 1802, d. Nov. 11, 1865, m. July 11, 1830, Clarissa Gleason, b. Apr. 26, 1801, d. Jan. 19, 1879, aged 77.

PAUL, Lorenzo Clay, of St. Peters, Minn., b. July 8, 1837, d. Sept. 14, 1920, m. Oct. 29, 1857, in Newmarket, Mary C. Smith, of Newmarket, b. Apr. 29, 1838, d. Apr. 20, 1912.

PAUL, Henry M., m. (pub. Oct. 2, 1862, in S. Eliot, Me.), Mary E. Tetherly.

PAUL, Henry G., m. (pub. Aug. 25, 1864, in Portsmouth), Augusta H. Witham, both of Kittery, Me.

PAUL, Samuel F., m. (pub. Nov. 17, 1870, in Portsmouth), Lizzie R. Mathews, both of Kittery, Me.

PEAREY, Benjamin F., m. Dec. 9, 1864, in Farmington, Mrs. Mary E. (Legro) Richardson, dau. of Jacob, both of Farmington.

PEARL, John, m. Oct. 12, 1789, by Rev. Benjamin Balch, Abigail Gray, both of Barrington.

PEARL, Isaac, d. May 1, 1826, m. May 15, 1792, by Rev. Joseph Haven, Jane Tucker, b. 1776, d. Jun. 14, 1860, both of Rochester.

PEARL, Thomas, d. May 3, 1850, aged 90, m. Feb. 7, 1793, in Barrington, Betty Stanton, d. Oct. 7, 1852, aged 82, dau. of William, both of Barrington

PEARL, Abraham, m. June 1, 1796, by Rev. Benjamin Balch, Molly Jones, both of Barrington.

PEARL, Nathaniel, m. Nov. 28, 1833, in Barrington, by Rev. Samuel H. Merrill, Mary Hall, b. Jan. 21, 1814, dau. of Daniel, both of Barrington.

PEARL, Peter, m. Aug. 20, 1862, in Farmington, Nancy W. Leighton, both of Farmington.

PEARL, Sgt. Maj. Rufus K., m. Mar. 4, 1865, in Farmington, Lizzie S. Cloutman, dau. of Hersey, both of Farmington.

PEASE, Thomas G., of Strafford, m. Mar. 13, 1867, in Strafford, Sarah A. Wallingford, of Milton, d. Jun. 22, 1893, aged 47, dau. of Daniel.

PEASE, Daniel H., of Strafford, m. Oct. 27, 1867, in Strafford, Carrie A. Pearce, of Little Compton R.I.

PEAVEY, Joseph, of Barrington, d. Mar. 14, 1830, aged 90, m. July 16, 1764, by Rev. Jos. Adams, Arabella Nutter, d. Feb. 1830.

PEAVEY, William Jr., m. Oct. 17, 1788, in Barrington, Sarah Neal, both of Barrington.

PEAVEY, Joseph, of Barrington, m. Dec. 18, 1788, by Rev. Benjamin Balch, Abigail Chesley, of Durham.

PEAVEY, John Jr., son of John, b. 1791, d. Dec. 6, 1864, m. Mar. 11, 1818, by Rev. Joseph Haven, Mary Caverly, b. 1800, d. Feb. 1, 1857, dau. of John, both of Barrington

PEAVEY, Joseph Jr., d. Dec. 21, 1830, aged 33, m. Mar. 15, 1821, by Elder Enoch Place, Hannah Foss, dau. of Timothy, both of Strafford.

PEAVEY, Enoch, m. July 2, 1829, by Rev. Joseph Boodey, Betsey Garland, d. Aug. 27, 1879, aged 83, both of Alton.

PEAVEY, Benjamin F., m. Jan. 9, 1865, in Farmington, Mary E. Richardson, of Farmington.

PEDUZZI, George S., of Portsmouth, m. July 8, 1863, in New Durham, N.J., Mary B. Perry, of New Durham, N.J., dau. of H. F. Perry.

PEEL, Charles F., b. 1845, d. 1939, m. June 1, 1867, by Rev. Alden Sherwin, Emma A. Howard, b. 1849, d. Jan. 19, 1881, both of Dover.

PEIRCE, Benjamin, d. Nov. 29, 1833, aged 72, m. Dec. 27, 1792, by Rev. Jonathan Tompson, Peace Thompson.

PEIRCE, Curtis, of Barrington, son of Israel, d. Oct. 26, 1837, aged 60, m. Jun. 16, 1800, by Rev. William Hooper, Olive Woodhouse, of Madbury, d. Apr. 29, 1844, aged 61.

PEIRCE, Joshua, m. int. Sep. 1801, in Lebanon, Me., Marcy Peirce.

PEIRCE, John Jr., m. Jul. 28, 1805, by Rev. Isaac Hasey, Mehitable Pray.

PEIRCE, Stephen, m. May 10, 1818, in Lebanon, Me., Betsey Yeaton, both of Berwick, Me.

PEIRCE, John Hussey, b. Feb. 11, 1798, d. Aug. 6, 1876, m. Dec. 17, 1820, Abigail Mills, b. Apr. 7, 1801, d. Apr. 18, 1889.

PEIRCE, John, m. (1) Mar. 13, 1822, by Elder Enoch Place, Abigail Foss, d. Jan. 7, 1832, aged 49, of Strafford, m. (2) Dec. 2, 1832, by Elder Enoch Place, Molly Foss, widow, d. Aug. 26, 1839, aged 59, both of Strafford.

PEIRCE, Daniel, m. int. Apr. 8, 1830, in Lebanon, Me., Lydia Peirce.

PEIRCE, Ebenezer Jr., m. int. Jun. 24, 1831, in Lebanon, Me., Emelu Hanson.

PEIRCE, Noah, b. 1802, d. Aug. 12, 1873, m. int. Oct. 19, 1831, in Lebanon, Me., Adah Goodwin, d. Aug. 29, 1877.

PEIRCE, Luke, d. Sep. 18, 1861, m. int. Oct. 12, 1833, in Lebanon, Me., Caroline Libbey, of No. Berwick, Me., b. Nov. 1, 1814.

PEIRCE, Ephraim, of Boston, Mass., d. Jun. 1, 1879, aged 79, m. Jul. 13, 1834, by Rev. Abner Flanders, Sarah Chick.

PEIRCE, Moses, b. 1815, m. (1) Oct. 23, 1836, Hannah Lord, m. (2) int. Mar. 9, 1868, in Brookfield, Mrs. Maria Briggs, of Haverhill, Mass.

PEIRCE, James, d. Aug. 13, 1872, aged 64, m. int. Sept. 2, 1838, in Dover, Naomi Dearborn, d. Mar. 9, 1875, aged 60.

PEIRCE, William H., m. int. Feb. 3, 1839, in Dover, Charlotte Langley, both of Dover.

PEIRCE, Cyrus H., of Concord, d. Aug. 15, 1869, aged 46, m. Dec. 14, 1845, by Rev. Nathaniel Berry, Abigail Berry, of Barnstead, b. 1812, d. 1847, dau. of John.

PEIRCE, Leighton, son of Stephen, b. 1825, m. int. Jun. 17, 1848, in Lebanon, Me., Berlinda Lord, b. 1813, d. Feb. 12, 1874 or 1879.

PEIRCE, Ezekiel R., son of James, b. 1810, m. Jan. 1, 1854, in Lebanon, Me., Olive Johnson, b. 1821.

PEIRCE, Caleb S., m. int. Apr. 19, 1856, in Lebanon, Me., Louisa Horn, of Sanford, Me.

PEIRCE, John C., son of John H., b. Jul. 1, 1839, m. (1) 1858, in Rochester, Mary F. Brackett, of Berwick, Me., b. 1837, d. Nov. 22, 1864, dau. of James, m. (2) Martha E. ----, b. 1834.

PEIRCE, Charles F., b. 1837, m. int. Dec. 27, 1860, in Lebanon, Me., Almira L. Webber, b. Jun. 15, 1842, dau. of Hezekiah.

PEIRCE, William, m. Sep. 17, 1861, in Lebanon, Me., Amanda J. Jenniss.
PEIRCE (PIERCE), Andrew D., of Barrington, b. Oct. 16, 1825, d. Jul. 27, 1870, m. Mar. 5, 1857, in Great Falls, Sarah A. Demeritt, of Madbury, b. Apr. 17, 1832, d. Jan. 21, 1903.
PEIRCE (PIERCE), Ira M., of Barnstead, Vt., m. May 31, 1866, in Dover, Fannie M. Ingraham, of Dover.
PEIRCE (PIERCE), Curtis H., m. Feb. 13, 1867, in S. Berwick, Me., Lottie A. P. Hill, both of Barrington.
PEIRCE (PIERCE), Joseph, of Berwick, Me., m. (pub. Dec. 10, 1868, in Great Falls), Lucy M. Russell, of Wellington, Conn.
PEIRCE (PIERCE), John, of Boston, Mass., m. (pub. June 9, 1870, in Great Falls), Ada E. Ripley, of Paris.
PEIRCE (PIERCE), Charles O., m. (pub. Nov. 10, 1870, in Great Falls), Erva E. Jones.
PELREN, Severe, of Alton, m. Apr. 18, 1866, in New Durham, Alma Knox, of New Durham.
PEMBERTON, C. H., of Somersworth, m. Sept. 17, 1866, in Rochester, Lucy Ellen Lee, of Biddeford, Me.
3) **PENDERGAST**, James, son of Stephen, b. 1784, d. Sept. 7, 1850, m. (1) in 1808, by Rev. John Osborne, Hannah Emerson, of Durham, b. June 25, 1790, d. Aug. 7, 1826, dau. of Capt. Smith, m. (2) Mar. 31, 1830, by Rev. John Osborne, Mary Hill, of Nottingham, b. 1783, d. Mar. 23, 1863, aged 80.
4) **PENDERGAST**, Solomon, son of Edmund, b. Apr. 7, 1808, d. July 9, 1882, m. (1) Apr. 26, 1832, Lydia Wiggin, b. Nov. 6, 1811, d. Aug. 20, 1848, dau. of Capt. William, m. (2) (pub. June 11, 1850, in Newmarket), Judith Matilda Mathes, of Lee.
PENDERGAST, Stephen Jr., m. Apr. 1, 1860, in Strafford, Anna A. Hill, d. Apr. 26, 1930, aged 95, dau. of John, both of Barnstead.
PENDEXTER, Alfred, of Dover, son of Edward, d. Dec. 12, 1850, aged 46, m. (pub. May 29, 1832, in Newington), Phebe Pickering, d. Mar. 20, 1867, aged 61.
PENDEXTER, Edward Jr., of Durham, son of Edward, m. Nov. 12, 1840, in Concord, Martha C. Stickney, of Concord, d. Jan. 10, 1892, aged 73, dau. of Nathan.
PENNEY, Joseph J., of New Durham, d. Nov. 30, 1903, aged 76, m. Jan. 1, 1867, in Middleton, Almira B. Cook, of Middleton, d. Apr. 20, 1894, aged 66, dau. of Isaiah.
PENNEY, John C., m. Jan. 1, 1870, in Union, Arabelle E. Stevens, both of Middleton.

PERKINS, Joseph, d. Feb. 16, 1829, aged 70+, m. Dec. 1779, Anne Canney, d. July 15, 1832, aged 81, dau. of Ichabod, both of Madbury.

PERKINS, John, of Middleton, m. Jan. 28, 1794, in Brookfield, Olive Clark, of Epping.

PERKINS, William, of New Durham, d. Aug. 4, 1858, aged 84, m. (1) near 1795, Rachel Varrell, d. Mar. 28, 1837, aged 63, m. (2) Oct. 10, 1837, Mrs. Deborah (Pendexter) Spinney, d. Oct. 26, 1848, aged 70.

PERKINS, Samuel, m. Dec. 15, 1796, in Barrington, Lydia Babb, both of Barrington.

PERKINS, Alcut, b. Oct. 21, 1791, m. Mar. 25, 1813, in Barrington, Nancy Davis, b. July 9, 1793, both of Barrington.

PERKINS, John, d. Mar. 16, 1864, aged 72, m. Dec. 28, 1818, by Rev. Joseph Boodey, Sally Libbey, b. 1798, d. 1879, dau. of Benjamin, both of Alton.

PERKINS, John, b. 1803, d. 1864, m. Apr. 20, 1823, by Rev. Phinehas Crandal, in Newmarket, Sarah Morrison, b. 1798, d. 1879, both of Dover.

PERKINS, Stephen Jr., son of Stephen, b. 1808, d. 1860, m. (1) (pub. Sep. 13, 1831, in Middleton), Abigail Perkins, d. 1856, m. (2) Feb. 10, 1858, in Middleton, Martha Ann Morgan, b. 1835.

PERKINS, Nathaniel, of Middleton, m. Oct. 6, 1831, by Elder Enoch Place, Harriet Otis, of Strafford, dau. of Job.

PERKINS, Paul Jr., m. Aug. 26, 1832, by Elder Enoch Place, Abigail Otis, dau. of Joshua, both of Strafford.

PERKINS, Darius, m. Feb. 12, 1839, by Elder Enoch Place, Lanora F. Ham, dau. of George, both of Strafford.

PERKINS, William, m. Mar. 3, 1839, in Barrington, by Rev. Samuel Nichols, Abigail Fuller, both of Somersworth.

PERKINS, John B., m. Mar. 28, 1847, by Rev. Theodore Wells, Julia Ann Robinson, both of Barrington.

PERKINS, James S., of Somersworth, d. Oct. 2, 1882, m. Nov. 16, 1848, by Rev. Alpheus D. Smith, Eliza W. Wentworth, of Berwick, Me.

PERKINS, John B., m. Mar. 24, 1850, in Barrington, Betsey Seavey.

PERKINS, Joseph F., aged 27, m. Feb. 11, 1860, in Middleton, Sarah A. Young, aged 22, of Dover.

PERKINS, Warren H., b. 1832, d. 1910, m. May 15, 1861, by Elder Enoch Place, Nancy L. Foss, b. 1841, d. Feb. 27, 1919, dau. of Eliphlet.

PERKINS, James H., of Rochester, m. (pub. Oct. 24, 1861, in Milton), Clarinda Knox, of Lebanon, Me., d. May 23, 1871, aged 28.
PERKINS, Timothy R., of Dover, m. Aug. 26, 1862, in Dover, Mary Ann Covercy, of Boston, Mass.
PERKINS, Peleg D., m. Nov. 30, 1863, in Gilmanton, Sarah E. Dow.
PERKINS, Edward R., of Strafford, d. Nov. 27, 1888, aged 77, m. (1) Sarah M. ----, d. Nov. 13, 1852, aged 50, m. (2) Jul. 9, 1864, by Rev. John Winkley, Lavina Sanders, of Laconia, d. Mar. 7, 1912, aged 76.
PERKINS, Augustus J., m. Nov. 5, 1865, in W. Milton, Anna J. Wallace, both of Middleton.
PERKINS, Samuel, m. Nov. 17, 1865, in Dover, Abby Jane Goodwin, d. May 17, 1910, aged 67, dau. of William.
PERKINS, Michael R., m. June 27, 1866, in Portsmouth, Dorah F. Kingsbury, dau. of Samuel, both of Portsmouth.
PERKINS, Ruel, of Berwick, Me., m. Nov. 30, 1866, in Great Falls, Nancy Bowden, of Bucksport, Me.
PERKINS, James P., of New York City, m. Dec. 20, 1866, by Rev. Francis E. Abbott, Helen F. Everett, of Dover, dau. of Lucius.
PERKINS, William T., m. (pub. Apr. 25, 1867, in Portsmouth) Lizzie H. Berry, both of Great Falls.
PERKINS, Charles, m. May 5, 1869, in Middleton, Emma Chesley.
PERKINS, George A., of Portsmouth, m. May 25, 1869, in Dover, Lizzie A. Rothwell, of Dover.
PERKINS, Winslow T., d. Jan. 15, 1920, aged 83, m. July 14, 1869, in Dover, Carrie S. Durant, b. 1844, d. 1933, both of Dover.
PERKINS, Seth B., of Manchester, m. (pub. Aug. 26, 1869, in Great Falls, Lavina V. Ward, of Great Falls.
PERKINS, Walter T., of Dover, m. May 16, 1870, in Salmon Falls, Abby A. Andrews, of Stowe, Me.
PERKINS, Cyrus B., m. Jan. 17, 1878, in Middleton, Mary A. Kimball.
PETERSON, John A., of Portsmouth, m. Nov. 24, 1864, in Dover, Mary A. Stackpole, of Dover.
PETTENGILL, Hosea A., of Rindge, son of Asa, b. Sept. 16, 1808, d. Apr. 2, 1889, m. Nov. 27, 1851, by Rev. Levi B. Tasker, in Sandwich, Polly M. Skinner, b. Nov. 1, 1818, d. Oct. 20, 1896, dau. of Elijah.
PEVERLY, Charles, m. Nov. 26, 1869, in Rochester, Mrs. Mary S. Varney, both of Middleton.

PHILBRICK, Josiah, d. Sept. 26, 1873, aged 48, m. (1) Apr. 12, 1849, in Newfield, Me., Nancy R. Thompson, d. 1853, both of Effingham, m. (2) Mar. 24, 1856, in Effingham, Elizabeth Ann Kennerson.

PHILBRICK, Ivory E., m. Mar. 5, 1864, in Great Falls, Ellen A. Tuttle, of Dover.

PHILBRICK, Daniel, of Alton, m. July 4, 1867, in Newmarket, E. J. Chase, of Newmarket.

PHILBROOK, John M., d. Aug. 19, 1861, aged 54, m. (pub. Jul. 8, 1828, in Ossipee), Ann Maria Haslett, b. 1810, d. 1898.

PHILLIPS, Albert O., of Alton, m. Oct. 20, 1869, in Dover, Mary S. Frost, of Portland, Me.

PHILPOT, Benjamin, of Somersworth, son of James, b. Apr. 27, 1747, m. Dec. 28, 1775, Olive Roberts.

PICKERING, Levi, d. Oct. 25, 1841, aged 76, m. Nov. 27, 1788, by Rev. Joseph Haven, Abigail Downs, b. 1765, d. Mar. 6, 1837, both of Rochester.

PICKERING, James, of Wakefield, son of Levi, b. 1784, d. Aug. 12, 1877, m. Jan. 13, 1828, in Wakefield, Betsey Henderson, of Rochester, b. 1794, d. Oct. 12, 1872.

PICKERING, John Jr., of Dover, m. int. Dec. 19, 1830, in Dover, m. Jan. 9, 1831, in Barrington, Abigail S. Leathers, of Barrington.

PICKERING, Charles W., of Gilford, m. Apr. 10, 1853, by Rev. Levi B. Tasker, in Sandwich, Mary Eliza Bean, of Sandwich.

PICKERING, John B., of Newington, son of Thomas, aged 46, m. May 28, 1868, by Rev. Alvan Tobey, Sarah Jane Hodgdon, of Barnstead, aged 31, dau. of Charles.

PIDGIN, William C., m. Nov. 4, 1868, by Rev. Robert S. Stubbs, Mrs. Eunice A. Applebee, both of Dover.

PIKE, Daniel, son of Rev. James, b. Dec. 2, 1732, d. May 2, 1806, m. near 1756, Anne Carr, sister of Dr. Moses.

PIKE, Nicholas G., of Somersworth, son of John, b. Oct. 4, 1779, d. Dec. 14, 1810, aged 31, m. Oct. 1, 1809, by Rev. William Hooper, Sarah Hayes, of Dover.

PIKE, Joseph, b. Nov. 22, 1785, m. Nov. 30, 1809, Sarah Gordon, of Newburyport, Mass.

PIKE, Robert, b. 1809, d. 1858, m. Apr. 7, 1844, in Middleton, Betsey Tibbetts, b. 1817, d. 1898, both of Middleton.

PIKE, George C., d. Oct. 18, 1889, m. (1) Dec. 8, 1844, in Middleton, Abigail Hanson, d. Aug. 6, 1851, aged 35, both of Middleton, m.

(2) (pub. Apr. 20, 1852, in Middleton), Maria S. Cook, ?Clark?, d. Nov. 14, 1902, aged 74, dau. of Lewis, of Middleton.

PIKE, Col. John L., d. Oct. 9, 1863, aged 56, of Middleton, m. (1) Cynthia ----, d. May 5, 1848, aged 39, m. (2) Sept. 3, 1848, by Rev. Joseph Boodey, Mrs. Betsey Pinkham, of Milton, d. Dec. 16, 1881, aged 70.

PIKE, James D., of Middleton, d. Nov. 10, 1914, aged 80, son of Jacob J., m. Apr. 1, 1860, in Milton, Susan L. Cloutman, of Middleton.

PIKE, John, m. (pub. Apr. 3, 1862, in Farmington), Mary M. Cloutman, both of Middleton.

PIKE, John, of Ossipee, m. June 11, 1864, in New York, Jane Aikin, of New York.

PIKE, John G., of Salmon Falls, m. July 18, 1867, in Dover, Mrs. Alice W. Horn, of Dover.

PIKE, John G., of Boston, Mass., m. Oct. 24, 1867, in Boston, Martha A. Horne, of Dover, dau. of Oliver S.

PIKE, John K., of Lawrence, Mass., m. (pub. Apr. 7, 1870, in Great Falls), Mrs. Mary Connor Yeaton.

PIKE, George H., of Wakefield, d. Sep. 2, 1901, aged 54, m. Sep. 12, 1872, by Rev. Asa Piper, Lovey Sanborn, of Milton.

PINKHAM, Stephen, d. Feb. 28, 1806, aged 89, m. early as 1741, Mary ----.

PINKHAM, Samuel, son of Samuel, b. Sept. 1, 1768, d. Dec. 4, 1838, m. Nov. 1789, Sally Chesley, of Lee, b. Nov. 20, 1770, d. Feb. 26, 1838.

PINKHAM, Otis, b. Jan. 13, 1765, d. Jan. 5, 1814, m. Hannah Young, d. Mar. 17, 1838, aged 68.

PINKHAM, Daniel, b. 1775, d. 1853, m. (1) May 7, 1796, by Rev. William Hooper, Anne Garland, b. 1764, d. 1828, both of Dover, m. (2) May 18, 1829, by Elder Nathaniel Berry, Mrs. Mary Brackett, b. 1790, d. 1862, both of Alton.

PINKHAM, Augustine U., b.May 25, 1791, m. Nov. 25, 1813, in Lebanon, Me., Mary Hanscom, b. Dec. 12, 1791, d. Nov. 24, 1848, dau. of Isaac.

PINKHAM, Alfred, son of Daniel, b. May 27, 1810, m. (1) in 1831, Harriet Burnham, of Newmarket, d. Jan. 14, 1885, aged 72, m. (2) Oct. 21, 1886, in Durham, Claire A. (Pinkham) Smart, dau. of Daniel.

PINKHAM, Janverin, m. Feb. 16, 1832, in Lebanon, Me., Lucetta Knox.

PINKHAM, John S., of Great Falls, son of Augustine, b. Apr. 1, 1820, m. Mar. 16, 1843, in Lebanon, Me., Lydia A. Haridson, of Lebanon, Me., b.Apr. 24, 1822, d. Mar. 13, 1856, dau.of John.

PINKHAM, W. H. H., m. Nov. 21, 1861, in Farmington, Sarah A. Pinkham, both of Farmington.

PINKHAM, Charles H., m. Apr. 10, 1862, in Dover, Alice J. Foss, both of Dover.

PINKHAM, Levi L., m. Mar. 25, 1865, in Farmington, Augusta R. Cooper, both of Farmington.

PINKHAM, John E., of Dover, m. Nov. 23, 1865, in Farmington, Mrs. Emilee J. Pinkham, of Casco, Me.

PINKHAM, Elder Joseph D., m. Feb. 28, 1867, in Alton, Caroline L. York, of Alton.

PINKHAM, Stephen F., m. Jul 26, 1868, in Middleton, Betsey A. Perkins.

PINKHAM, Cyrus Gates, aged 24, m. Oct. 27, 1868, in Middleton, Lena Labonte, aged 33, of Dover.

PINKHAM, George H., son of Luther H., d. Nov. 12, 1888, aged 46, m. Feb. 6, 1869, by Rev. Robert S. Stubbs, Olive A. Hurd, both of Dover.

PINKHAM, Asa J., m. Jan. 1, 1870, in Dover, Mary A. Brownell, both of Dover.

PINKHAM, William T., m. Sept. 6, 1870, in Dover, Lizzie A. Ricker, both of Dover.

PINKHAM, George E., m. Aug. 1872, in Middleton, Laura Main.

PIPER, Rev. Asa, of Acton, Mass., son of Josiah, b. Mar. 7, 1757, d. May 17, 1835, m. (1) Mary Cutts, of Portsmouth, b. 1766, d. Jan. 4, 1802, dau. of Edward, m. (2) Sarah Little, of Kennebunk, Me., b. 1765, d. Oct. 15, 1827, dau. of Rev. Daniel.

PIPER, Timothy, of Tuftonboro, d. Apr. 27, 1852, aged 78, m. int. Dec. 1799, in Tuftonboro, Hannah Neal, of Wolfeboro, d. Aug. 23, 1865, aged 84.

PIPER, Stephen, d. July 12, 1846, aged 64, m. (1) June 12, 1806, in Wolfeboro, Hannah Whitten, d. Dec. 26, 1833, aged 52, both of Wolfeboro, m. (2) Rhoda ----.

PIPER, Col. David, b. Nov. 19, 1800, d. Sept. 14, 1864, aged 64, m. int. July 1820, in Tuftonboro, Sally Haley, d. Sept. 9, 1870, aged 77, both of Tuftonboro.

PIPER, Samuel, d. Dec. 20, 1884, aged 82, m. 1823, by Rev. Jeremiah Shaw, Eley Haley, d. May 4, 1895, aged 97, both of Tuftonboro.

PIPER, James, d. Dec. 22, 1893, aged 86, m. Oct. 31, 1828, in Wolfeboro, Sally Wiggin, d. June 16, 1898, aged 88, both of Wolfeboro

PIPER, Samuel T., of Tuftonboro, son of Israel, d. Aug. 9, 1874, aged 68, m. Nov. 22, 1837, in Wolfeboro, Eleanor Knox, of Wolfeboro, d. Jan. 31, 1865, aged 47.

PIPER, Elder Thatcher William, son of Samuel, b. May 9, 1824, d. Nov. 21, 1893, m. Nov. 27, 1845, in Tuftonboro, Nancy Mahaley Allen, b. June 2, 1828, d. Aug. 1, 1915.

PIPER, Benjmain Y., son of John, of Lee, m. (1) Hannah Evans, d. Oct. 5, 1856, aged 36, m. (2) Apr. 6, 1858, in Marblehead, Mass., Sarah Bell Evans, of Marblehead, Mass., b. May 9, 1823, d. Jan. 21, 1897.

PIPER, Moses H., of Strafford, m. Apr. 10, 1864, in Strafford, Mary Jane Downing, of Rollinsford.

PIPER, William H., m. May 5, 1866, in Laconia, Anna M. Jackson, both of Laconia.

PITMAN, Joseph, d. Dec. 3, 1800, aged 37, m. Dec. 1788, Molly Bickford, both of Madbury.

PITMAN, Joseph, m. Jan. 24, 1827, in Brookfield, Nancy H. Martin, both of Brookfield.

PITMAN, Alonzo J., of Boston, Mass., m. June 26, 1870, in Dover, Sarah A. Legg, of Dover, dau. of Lucian B.

PLACE, James, b. Feb. 25, 1755, d. Jan. 24, 1837, m. Sept. 26, 1785, by Rev. Joseph Haven, Abigail Hayes, b. Feb. 9, 1761, d. Aug. 2, 1855, dau. of Moses, both of Rochester.

PLACE, Joshua, d. Feb. 1, 1856, aged 75, m. Mar. 13, 1806, by Rev. Benjamin Randall, Sally Willey, b. 1790, d. 1875, both of New Durham.

PLACE, Rev. Enoch, son of James, b. July 13, 1786, d. Mar. 23, 1865, m. Sept. 29, 1808, Sally Demeritt, b. Feb. 26, 1789, d. Jan. 1, 1880, aged 91, dau. of Capt. Daniel.

PLACE, Moses, son of James, d. Apr. 8, 1858, aged 60, m. (pub. Mar. 8, 1826, in Strafford), Patience Drown, d. July 4, 1866, aged 64, both of Rochester.

PLACE, Noah, son of James, b. 1800, d. Oct. 29, 1873, m. Charlotte Ham, of Rochester, b. 1802, d. 1884.

PLACE, H. Joseph, b. 1809, d. 1873, m. (pub. June 11, 1833, in Alton), Lydia Hurd, b. 1813, d. 1878.

PLACE, Demeritt, son of Elder Enoch, m. July 13, 1837, in Barrington, Mary Jane Foss, dau. of William Jr.

PLACE, Capt. William Smith, of Strafford, son of Elder Enoch, m. (pub. Jan. 19, 1841, in Charleston, Me.), Mary Jane Foss, of Charleston, Me., b. Mar. 19, 1818, d. Sept. 13, 1859.

PLACE, John, m. Nov. 27, 1848, by Elder Samuel Sherburne, Emily Powers, both of Barrington.

PLACE, James F., son of James, d. Jan. 1, 1869, aged 39, m. Dec. 16, 1852, in Dover, Hannah E. Tuttle, d. June 23, 1876, aged 40, both of Dover.

PLACE, John Kezer, son of Elder Enoch, m. Nov. 16, 1854, in Strafford, Hannah M. Pearey, of Barrington, d. June 14, 1911, aged 80, dau. of Smith Pearey.

PLACE, David Marks, son of Elder Enoch, of Lowell, Mass., m. June 12, 1859, by Elder Elias Hutchins, Caroline H. Crockett, of Dover, d. May 10, 1885.

PLACE, James A., m. June 2, 1864, in Salmon Falls, Jennie Converse, both of Salmon Falls.

PLACE, James Frank, of Rochester, m. (pub. Sept. 14, 1865, in S. Danvers, Mass.), Sarah H. Potter.

PLACE, Charles A., m. (pub. Apr. 19, 1866, in Wolfeboro), Abby Cate, both of Alton.

PLACE, Ira S., of Farmington, m. May 25, 1867, in New Durham, Melvina A. Gilman, of Strafford.

PLACE, William, m. Apr. 1, 1868, in Middleton, Lydia A Whitchouse.

PLAISTED, Sidney G., of York, Me., m. int. Jan. 25, 1865, in Lebanon, Me., Lydia R. Goodwin.

PLUMER, Ephraim, b. Apr. 30, 1766, d. May 4, 1843, m. Feb. 2, 1791, Nancy McDuffee, b. May 1, 1768, d. Dec. 26, 1851.

PLUMER, Daniel M., son of Ephraim, b. Mar. 10, 1794, d. Aug. 9, 1872, aged 78, m. Nov. 9, 1820, by Rev. Joseph Boodey, Eunice Card, d. Apr. 11, 1870, aged 77, dau. of Thomas, both of Milton.

PLUMER, James, of Gilmanton, m. int. Dec. 22, 1839, in Dover, Nancy Daniels, of Dover.

PLUMER, Walter S., of Dover, m. Dec. 20, 1846, in Dover, Rebecca R. Ross, of Great Falls, d. Jul. 20, 1898, aged 68, dau. of Thomas.

PLUMER, John C., son of Daniel, b. June 17, 1829, d. Sept. 20, 1902, aged 73, m. (1) June 17, 1855, in Milton, Lydia Augusta Durrell, b. Nov. 4, 1823, d. Aug. 22, 1859, aged 35, both of Milton, m. (2) June 15, 1862, in Dover, Amelia C. Witherell, b. May 3, 1831, d. May 16, 1898.

PLUMER, Joseph, of Milton, m. Oct. 1, 1863, in Saxonville, Mass., Hannah D. Clark, of Sanbornton, dau. of John H.

PLUMER, John N., m. June 11, 1864, in Rochester, Mary E. Bracket, both of Rochester.

PLUMER, Joseph E., of Milton, m. Oct. 20, 1869, in Concord, Susan E. Pecker, of Concord.

PLUMMER, Joseph, son of John, b. 1752, d. Apr. 27, 1821, aged 69, m. Nov. 30, 1778, by Rev. Joseph Haven, Hannah Bickford, b. 1754, d. Feb. 1811, dau. of Lemuel.

PLUMMER, Capt. Beard, of Milton, son of John, b. Aug. 12, 1754, d. Oct. 7, 1816, m. Sept. 7, 1780, by Rev. Joseph Haven, Susanna Ham, d. Feb. 20, 1803, aged 41, dau. of Jonathan.

PLUMMER, William, d. Nov. 6, 1901, aged 79, m. (pub. Oct. 17, 1843, in Great Falls), Mary Ann Horn, d. Feb. 20, 1901, aged 78.

PLUMMER, William H., m. Jan. 1, 1866, in Rochester, Abbie L. Lane, both of Farmington.

PLUMMER, Cyrus, m. (pub. Apr. 26, 1866, in Portsmouth), Mary E. Martin.

POOLE, Charles H., of Great Falls, m. June 5, 1870, in Boston, Mass., Susie A. Crosby, of Melrose, Mass.

POORE, Benjamin I., m. (pub. Nov. 12, 1868, in Salmon Falls), Lucy A. Alley.

POPE, Charles O., m. Dec. 31, 1867, in Wells, Me., Nancie W. Locke, of Dover, dau. of Stacy H.

PORTER, Charles, of Danvers, Mass., m. Nov. 27, 1866, in Dover, Sarah E. Applebee, of Dover.

PRATT, Alvan S., m. (pub. May 19, 1870, in Rochester), Mary T. Knight.

PRAY, Thomas, d. Nov. 19, 1814, aged 54, m. Jan. 3, 1784, by Rev. Isaac Hasey, Molly Taylor.

PRAY, John, son of Joshua, b. Sep. 17, 1767, m. Dec. 24, 1787, by Rev. Isaac Hasey, Anna Austin.

PRAY, Chadburn, m. int. Nov. 1803, in Lebanon, Me., Abigail Brackett.

PRAY, Hiram, of Berwick, m. (1) int. Apr. 5, 1809, in Lebanon, Me., Parmela Libbey, m. (2) Dec. 29, 1811, in Lebanon, Me., Polly Libbey, d. Aug. 8, 1819, aged 39.

PRAY, Benjamin, m. int. May 27, 1815, in Lebanon, Me., Anne Hanscom.

PRAY, Stephen Jr., m. int. Sep. 12, 1816, in Lebanon, Me., Nabby Delano.

PRAY, Isaac N., m. Aug. 1, 1819, in Lebanon, Me. Patience Horn.

PRAY, Alexander, of Berwick, Me., m. Dec. 24, 1820, in Lebanon, Me., Sarah Lord.

PRAY, Amos, son of John Jr., b. 1799, d. Jul. 17, 1863, m. Dec. 5, 1824, Judith Hodgdon, dau. of William.

PRAY, Samuel, m. Apr. 14, 1825, in Lebanon, Me., Esther Hersom.

PRAY, Amos, of Shapleight, m. int. Apr. 9, 1826, in Lebanon, Me., Jerusha Knox

PRAY, Benjamin, b. Oct. 7, 1807, d. Jan. 27, 1900, aged 92, m. int. Oct. 12, 1834, in Dover, Dorcas Pray, d. Aug. 12, 1883, aged 76.

PRAY, John, m. Oct. 4, 1838, in Parsonsfield, Me., Patience B. Moulton, of Parsonsfield, Me.

PRAY, William M. of Boston, Mass., m. Jun. 19, 1849, in Lebanon, Me., Elizabeth Marsh, of Sanford, Me.

PRAY, Dr. Thomas J. W., son of Moses and Lydia, b. Sept. 2, 1819, d. Dec. 7, 1888, aged 69 yrs., 3 mos., 7 das., m. (1) Nov. 20, 1850, by Rev. Homer Barrows, Sarah E. Wheeler, d. Apr. 15, 1857, aged 29, dau. of John H., m. (2) June 1, 1870, in Dover, Martha A Mathews.

PRAY, John W., b. Jan. 9, 1826, d. Oct. 15, 1904, m. (pub. Jan. 18, 1855, in Rollinsford), Harriet T. Lang, b. Nov. 28, 1826, d. Dec. 12, 1904, aged 78.

PRAY, Robert, of Acton, Me., m. Jan. 3, 1856, in Somersworth, Sarah F. Hersom.

PRAY, Amos, of Acton, Me., m. Oct. 16, 1858, in Lebanon, Me., Mary Jones.

PRAY, Ivory, d. Mar. 14, 1880, aged 48, m. (pub. Jun. 13, 1861, in Salmon Falls), Elizabeth C. Tucker, b. Feb. 20, 1840, d. Jan. 15, 1904, both of Salmon Falls.

PRAY, Sylvester, of Lebanon, Me., son of Moses, b. Nov. 18, 1836, d. Jun. 29, 1872, m. Aug. 30, 1862, in Dover, Martha S. Twombly, of Newmarket.

PRAY, Amasa, son of Ezra, d. Mar. 7, 1909, aged 70, m. Sept. 13, 1865, in Rochester, Laura A. Trickey.

PRAY, Dr. Thomas J. W., son of Moses, b. Sept. 2, 1819, d. Dec. 7, 1888, aged 69, m. (1) Nov. 20, 1850, by Rev. Homer Barrows, Sarah E. Wheeler, d. Apr. 15, 1857, aged 29, dau. of John H., m. (2) June 1, 1870, in Dover, Martha A. Mathews, b. Apr. 18, 1841, d. Nov. 5, 1900.

PRAY, George H., of Dover, m. Nov. 25, 1870, in Farmington, Vianna Angenette Hilton, of Rollinsford.

PRESCOTT, Woodbury T., d. Mar. 14, 1871, aged 68, m. Dec. 29, 1829, by Rev. Samuel K. Lothrop, Frances E. Banks, d. Mar. 11, 1871, aged 61.
PRESCOTT, Alfred, of Gilmanton, son of Timothy, m. Nov. 13, 1838, Octavia Bean, of Great Falls, dau. of Deac. Joseph.
PRESCOTT, Daniel F., of Acton, Me., m. Nov. 23, 1842, in Lebanon, Me., Mary Cowell.
PRESCOTT, Jonathan, m. Nov. 25, 1847, in Lebanon, Me., Deborah Ann Gile.
PRESCOTT, James, of Madbury, m. May 1848, by Rev. Theodore Weils, m. Jane Hall, of Barrington.
PRESCOTT, Sewell, of Acton, Me., m. Sep. 26, 1849, in Lebanon, Me., Merilla M. Hersom.
PRESCOTT, George B., son of Woodbury, b. Oct. 20, 1833, d. June 22, 1900, m. May 31, 1864, by Rev. Thomas G. Salter, Melvina A. Swain, b. May 28, 1838, d. Oct. 28, 1928, aged 90, dau. of Israel, both of Dover.
PRESCOTT, Benjamin F., d. Sep. 23, 1919, aged 78, m. Oct. 20, 1865, in Dover, Rebecca Foss.
PRESCOTT, John R. S., of Nottingham, m. Jan. 27, 1867, by Rev. James Rand, Phymelia A. Hutchins, of Lebanon, Me.
PRESCOTT, Safford W., of Deerfield, m. Jan. 21, 1869, by Rev. Isaac G. White, Susan Chesley, of Durham.
PRESCOTT, John W., of Brookfield, aged 23, m. Oct. 25, 1870, in Dover, Addie Jewett, of Milton, aged 21.
PRESTON, Charles E., of Dover, m. Sept. 27, 1870, in Dover, Mary E. Daley, of Great Falls.
PRICE, Moses, son of William, bpt. Mar. 26, 1799, m. (pub. Jan. 27, 1829, in Gilmanton), Sarah Page.
PRIEST, Nathan, d. before June 3, 1825, m. Apr. 15, 1813, Jane Vennard, d. 1848.
PRIEST, Peletiah, of Pittsfield, d. June 8, 1860, aged 54, m. Sept. 26, 1833, by Elder Enoch Place, Betsey F. Hill, of Strafford, d. Oct. 18, 1858, aged 49, dau. of William.
PUGSLEY, John, m. Dec. 22, 1866, in Rochester, Sarah M. Varney, d. July 21, 1881, aged 35, both of Lebanon, Me.
PUTNAM, Albert E., m. Dec. 4, 1870, in Farmington, Abbie E. Wingate, both of Farmington.
QUARLES, Col. Samuel D., of Ossipee, son of Col. Samuel, b. Jan. 16, 1833, d. Nov. 22, 1889, m. (pub. Jan. 31, 1887, in Ossipee),

Susan Augusta Brown, of Wolfeboro, b. June 18, 1834, d. Dec. 26, 1891, dau. of Moses P.

QUIMBY, Jacob, son of <u>Benjamin,</u> b. Oct. 16, 1743, m. near 1767, Tamson Wentworth.

QUIMBY, John M., m. int. Jan. 2, 1831, in Dover, <u>m. Mar. 27, 1831, in Barrington,</u> Sarah Meader, <u>both of Dover.</u>

QUIMBY, John M., m. Mar. 27, 1831, by Rev. Samuel Sherburne, Sarah Meader, both of Dover.

QUIMBY, Thomas C., son of Elder Daniel, m. (1) Oct. 5, 1834, Hannah Brackett, m. (2) Feb. 14, 1867, Selina Meigs.

QUIMBY, Daniel W., son of Daniel, b. Aug. 14, 1822, m. Aug. 1845, Laura A. W. Jones, <u>d. Aug. 9, 1912, aged 86,</u> dau. of Stephen.

QUIMBY, Albert W., son of John, aged 30, d. Sept. 8, 1885, m. Feb. 5, 1852, by Rev. Levi B. Tasker, in Sandwich, Sarah A. Hackett, aged 18, d. July 1863, dau. of John.

QUIMBY, Harrison M., son of J. Smith Quimby, aged 26, d. Apr. 10, 1898, m. Sept. 30, 1857, in Sandwich, Betsey W. Severance, aged 23, dau. of J. Smith Severance.

QUIMBY, J. T., of Biddeford, Me., m. (pub. Jan. 8, 1863, in Great Falls), Lucy E. Whitehouse, of Great Falls.

QUINT, James, of Dover, m. July 21, 1867, in Strafford, Lydia S. Drew, of Barrington.

RADFORD, Charles F., of Salem, Mass., m. Nov. 10, 1862, in Dover, Abby C. Aldrich, of Somersworth.

RAITT, John F., of Eliot, Me., m. Nov. 1, 1862, in S. Berwick, Me., Susan A. Lord, of S. Berwick, Me.

RAITT, William F., <u>of Eliot, Me.</u>, m. Nov. 24, 1866, in Dover, Carrie C. Gage, <u>of Dover.</u>

RAND, Samuel, <u>d. Sept. 18, 1841, aged 49,</u> m. Dec. 3, 1812, by Rev. Joseph Haven, Sarah Foss, both of Rochester.

RAND, Jeremiah, of Farmington, m. Sept. 8, 1846, by Rev. Nathaniel Berry, Cynthia D. Tuttle, of New Durham, <u>b. May 20, 1820, d. Jan. 15, 1889.</u>

RAND, Leonard S., m. Nov. 23, 1862, by Rev. James Rand, <u>Mrs.</u> Elizabeth H. Sawyer.

RAND, John E., <u>son of Rev. James</u>, m. Apr. 20, 1865, by Rev. James Rand, Lizzie S. Randall, <u>of Lebanon, Me.</u>

RAND, William E., m. Feb. 28, 1867, in Portsmouth, Emily Bell.

RAND, John C., of Medford, Mass., m. (pub. June 13, 1867, in Great Falls), Kate M. Bates, dau. of Moses.

RAND, William E., m. Feb. 1868, in Gonic, Hannah M. Howard.

RAND, Mark F., m. Nov. 9, 1869, in Dover, <u>Mrs</u>. Laura A. Hurd, <u>both of Dover</u>.

RAND, John H., of Rochester, b. 1853, d. 1894, m. Nov. 25, 1869, in Rochester, Cyrena A. Preston, of Barrington, b. 1854, d. 1921.

2) **RANDALL**, <u>Capt</u>. Nathaniel, son of Richard, d. Mar. 9, 1748/9, aged 54, m. early as 1720, Mary Hodgdon, d. Jan. 3, 1775, aged 76, dau. of Israel.

RANDALL, Rev. Benjamin, son of Capt. Benjamin, b. Feb. 7, 1749, d. Oct. 22, <u>1818</u>, m. Nov. 1, 1771, Joanna Oram, b. Feb. 1748, d. May 12, 1826, dau. of Capt. Robert.

RANDALL, John, d. Apr. 29, 1875, aged 79, m. Nov. 12, 1825, by Rev. John Osborne, Mrs. Hannah <u>(Currier)</u> Giles, both of Lee, <u>wid.</u> of Paul.

RANDALL, Samuel, of Berwick, Me., m. int. Sep. 29, 1838, in Lebanon, Me., Ann Wallingford.

RANDALL, Jeremiah D., b. 1838, m. (1) Nov. 4, 1858, in Dover, Mary E. Merrill, d. Aug. 30, 1860, aged 19, dau. of John, both of Dover, m. (2) int. Apr. 10, 1862, in Lee, Susan F. Bartlett, b. 1833, <u>both of Lee</u>.

RANDALL, George W., m. July 3, 1862, in New Durham, Elizabeth Towle, both of New Durham.

RANDALL, George H., m. Jan. 24, 1863, in Great Falls, Julia A. Burns, both of Great Falls.

RANDALL, John H., of Roxbury, Mass., m. (pub. Feb. 25, 1864, in Wolfeboro), Ora T. Cotton.

RANDALL, Aaron W., of Berwick, Me., <u>son of Samuel, d. Oct. 31, 1896, aged 57</u>, m. June 13, 1864, by Rev. Asa Piper, Emily S. Colomy, of Newfield, Me., <u>d. Sept. 28, 1913, aged 68, dau. of Isaac</u>.

RANDALL, Charles P., m. (pub. Sept. 27, 1866, in Wolfeboro), Ruth E. Pinkham.

RANDALL, Leonard O., m. July 26, 1867, in Great Falls, Carrie Jackson.

RANDALL, John H., m. Apr. 26, 1869, in Dover, Elizabeth F. Card, <u>both of Dover</u>.

RANDALL, James E., m. (pub. June 17, 1869, in Great Falls), Arabelle Chandler, of Great Falls.

RANDALL, Horace, m. (pub. June 16, 1870, in Rochester), Addie M. Durgin, both of Rochester.

RANDALL, Nehemiah, of Dover, m. (pub. Aug. 4, 1870, in Newmarket), Lovina Clay, of Madbury.

RANDALL (RENDALL), William, m. Feb. 19, 1818, in Lebanon, Me., Rebecca Haridson.
RANKIN, John, m. Oct. 1, 1769, by Rev. Isaac Hasey, Peggy Dore.
RANKIN, Jonathan, m. (1) Mar. 12, 1784, by Rev. Isaac Hasey, Molly Champion, m. (2) Jun. 27, 1812, in Berwick, Me., Olive Guptill.
RANKIN, James, m. Mar. 29, 1786, by Rev. Isaac Hasey, Sarah Champion.
RANKIN, Thomas, m. Mar. 24, 1796, by Rev. Isaac Hasey, Joanna Wallingford.
RANKIN, John, of Rochester, m. May 4, 1820, in Lebanon, Me., Lydia Furbush.
RANKIN, Daniel, m. Nov. 29, 1828, in Lebanon, Me., Lydia Blaisdell.
RANKIN, Charles, m. Nov. 24, 1840, in Lebanon, Me., Lucretia Peirce.
RANKIN, Eli C., m. (1) Oct. 19, 1843, in Lebanon, Me., Elizabeth Dixon, m. (2) Apr. 20, 1845, in Lebanon, Me., Abba Jane Carlisle.
RANKIN, Jonathan Jr., m. Dec. 13, 1849, in Lebanon, Me., Maria A. Cowell.
RANKIN, Isaac W., m. Sep. 18, 1850, in Berwick, Me., Frances E. Buzzell.
RANKIN, Daniel Jr., m. Jun. 12, 1851, in Lebanon, Me., Cordelia S. Varney.
RANKIN, Charles D., m. Jul. 13, 1851, in Lebanon, Me., Mary E. Varney.
RANKIN, Jonathan F., m. Feb. 27, 1862, in Lebanon, Me., Mrs. Dorcas Hayes.
RANKIN, Charles O., m. Dec. 4, 1867, in Lebanon, Me., Nancy A. Tobey, of Portsmouth.
RANKIN, James E., m. Dec. 29, 1867, in Lebanon, Me., Eunice V. Stevens.
RANKIN, Louis, m. int. Jun. 20, 1872, in Lebanon, Me., Nellie M. Tebbetts, of Rochester.
READ, John S., m. Oct. 6, 1814, by Rev. Micajah Otis, Mary Allard, both of Farmington.
READ, David, m. Dec. 7, 1867, by Rev. Jesse Meader, Letitia Brooks, of Dover (colored).
REED, Jacob, m. Sep. 22, 1822, in Lebanon, Me., Dolly Frost, both of Sanford, Me.

REED, Hanson O., of Dover, m. Aug. 27, 1867, in Exeter, Helen Morrison, of New Durham.

REED, Augustus H., of Newfield, Me., m. Oct. 21, 1867, in Dover, Hannah E. Moore, of Dover.

REED, James G., of Newburyport, Mass., m. (pub. Nov. 12, 1850, in Strafford), Hannah E. Parshley, of Strafford, dau. of Ebenezer, moved to Newburyport, Mass.

REMICK, Joseph Jr., m. Oct. 18, 1804, by Rev. Isaac Hasey, (pub. Jan. 19, 1805, in Lebanon, Me.), Dolly Burrows, dau. of Joseph.

REMICK, Samuel, of Eliot, Me., d. Sept. 14, 1871, aged 50, m. (pub. Nov. 12, 1847, in Tuftonboro), Susan A. Burleigh, d. May 4, 1904, aged 82.

REMICK, Andrew J., son of Nathaniel, b. Dec. 3, 1835, d. Feb. 22, 1895, m. (pub. Dec. 16, 1858, in Great Falls), Lydia A. Hart, b. June 2, 1826, d. June 17, 1906, both of Milton, dau. of Mark.

REMICK, Colby, of Milton Mills, m. Aug. 24, 1870, in Dover, Isabel Goodwin, of Sanford, Me.

RENSHAW, William H., m. June 23, 1862, in Cambridge, Mass., Ellen F. Garland, both of Dover.

REYNOLDS, Capt. Daniel, son of Col. Daniel, b. Oct. 7, 1771, d. Oct. 25, 1809, aged 39, m. Aug. 6,. 1797, Elizabeth Leighton, b. Apr. 19, 1778, d. Sept. 12, 1851, dau. of James.

REYNOLDS, Samuel, m. int. Mar. 9, 1811, in Lebanon, Me., Hannah Farnham.

REYNOLDS, Ephraim F., m. Mar. 23, 1826, by Elder Enoch Place, Mary P. Locke, b. Apr. 4, 1807, dau. of Elisha, both of Barrington.

REYNOLDS, James A., son of Stephen, d. May 11, 1919, aged 82, m. Mar. 16, 1864, by Rev. James Rand, Miriam S. Hanson, both of Madbury.

RICE, David Hall, of Savannah, Ga., m. Feb. 25, 1868, by Rev. Alden Sherwin, Elizabeth H. Garland, of Dover, dau. of Thomas B.

RICHARDS, Ichabod, m. Oct. 1, 1804, in Brookfield, Anna ----.

RICHARDS, Orin I., b. Nov. 1, 1820, m. Oct. 5, 1847, in Andover, Mass., Eliza Moore.

RICHARDS, Winslow Abraham, son of Rev. Abraham, m. Mar. 10, 1854, by Rev. Abraham, Richards, Eliza Taylor, of Norridgewick, Me., b. Aug. 4, 1831.

RICHARDS, James, m. int. Sep. 1, 1854, in Lebanon, Me., Priscilla R. Cousins, of Lyman, Me.

RICHARDS, Joseph B., m. Apr. 2, 1864, in Farmington, Mary E. Hanson, of Somersworth.

RICHARDS, Gorham D., of Farmington, m. (pub. June 2, 1870, in Barnstead), Mary J. French, of Barnstead.

RICHARDSON, Benjamin, of Gilmanton, m. Nov. 19, 1787, Deborah Edgerly, b. Nov. 7, 1766, d. Aug. 1790, dau. of James.

RICHARDSON, Stephen, m. Aug. 25, 1830, in Barrington, by Rev. Samuel Sherburne, Abigail Hanscom, both of Barrington.

RICHARDSON, John A., of Durham, m. int. Feb. 3, 1835, in Durham, Frances J. (Farrand) Murdock, of Concord, wid. of Rev. Thomas J., d. Mar. 29, 1880, aged 79, dau. of Daniel.

RICHARDSON, Charles H., of Northwood, b. Oct. 5, 1829, d. Apr. 9, 1899, m. Sept. 15, 1853, in Durham, Emeline S. Hanson, of Newmarket, b. July 20, 1832, d. Dec. 3, 1893, dau. of Robert.

RICHARDSON, George W., m. Mar. 26, 1863, in Farmington, Sarah E. Locke, both of Barrington.

RICHARDSON, Stephen, m. Oct. 14, 1864, in Farmington, Melissa Spurling, both of Barrington.

RICHARDSON, George A., m. Jan. 23, 1865, in Dover, Mary J. Rothwell, both of Dover.

RICHARDSON, Charles R., of Farmington, m. Nov. 12, 1865, in Farmington, Charlotte Hayes, of Alton.

RICHARDSON, Stephen H., m. May 26, 1866, in Great Falls, Mary E. Jackman, both of Dover.

RICHARDSON, Lucian, of Moultonboro, m. (pub. Apr. 25, 1867, in Portsmouth), Clara H. Pinder, of Newmarket.

RICHARDSON, Charles, of Alton, m. (pub. Dec. 12, 1867, in Wolfeboro), Eliza Clark, of Wells, Me.

RICHARDSON, Charles T., of Boston, Mass., m. Dec. 25, 1867, in Dover, Charlotte A. Esterbrook, of Dover.

RICHARDSON, Orlando, of Tuftonboro, b. 1843, d. 1912, m. (1) June 24, 1869, in Dover, Abbie L. Trafton, of Dover, b. 1849, d. 1876, m. (2) Ella A. ----, b. 1850, d. 1889.

RICHARDSON, Bradbury, m. (pub. July 21, 1870, in N. Berwick, Me.), Emma L. Buzzell, both of Rochester.

RICHARDSON, George F., of Rochester, m. (pub. Sept. 22, 1870, in Wells, Me.), Mary A. Donnell, of Wells, Me., d. Mar. 23, 1913, aged 77, dau. of Samuel.

RICHMOND, James A., d. May 29, 1879, aged 51, m. (pub. Jun. 25, 1850, in Somersworth), Eunice Earl, d. Oct. 16, 1896, aged 65, dau. of Mark.

RICKER, Ephraim, son of John, b. Jul. 15, 1759, m. Mar. 16, 1780, by Rev. Matthew Merriam, Dolly Nock, both of Berwick, Me.

RICKER, Henry, m. Jan. 1789, by Rev. Isaac Hasey, Betsey McCrillis.
RICKER, Thomas, son of Capt. Ebenezer, b. Jun. 26, 1772, m. Jan. 9, 1797, by Rev. Matthew Merriam, Sally Hodsdon.
RICKER, Samuel, m. int.Oct. 25, 1806, in Lebanon, Me., Phebe Ricker.
RICKER, Reuben, d. Feb. 24, 1843, aged 58, m. Dec. 24, 1807, in Lebanon, Me., Sarah Horn, d. Jan. 18, 1853, aged 71, dau. of Benjamin.
RICKER, Moses Jr., d. Dec. 17, 1873, aged 84, m. int. May 1, 1809, in Lebanon, Me., Kezia Hodgdon, d. Jan. 17, 1862, aged 72.
RICKER, John, m. int. Sep. 16, 1809, in Lebanon, Me., Nancy Glass.
RICKER, Ebenezer Jr., m. int. Feb. 3, 1810, in Lebanon, Me., Suky Stevens.
RICKER, Samuel, m. int. Oct. 12, 1811, in Lebanon, Me., Eunice Jones.
RICKER, Simon, m. int. Sep. 6, 1813, in Lebanon, Me., Polly Goodwin.
RICKER, Jabez, m. int. Jan. 7, 1815, in Lebanon, Me., Alice Pray.
RICKER, Enoch, m. int. Jul. 13, 1816, in Lebanon, Me., Love Lord.
RICKER, Edmund G., m. Sep. 14, 1819, by Rev. Paul Jewett, Sally Horne.
RICKER, James S., of Dover, d. July 18, 1867, aged 70, m. Sept. 1, 1819, Elizabeth C. Whitten, of Wolfeboro, b. Nov. 24, 1796, d. Oct. 10, 1882, dau. of Jesse.
RICKER, Ebenezer Jr., d. May 1, 1859, aged 68, m. int. Apr. 15, 1820, in Lebanon, Me., Naomi Sherman, d. Sep. 7, 1864, aged 65.
RICKER, Ezekiel, m. Nov. 21, 1822, in Lebanon, Me., Mary Shorey.
RICKER, Ebenezer 3rd, d. Dec. 2, 1841, aged 38, m. int. Jul. 23, 1826, in Lebanon, Me., Susan Butler, d. Sep. 12, 1877, aged 91.
RICKER, Tilly H., m. Dec. 21, 1826, in Lebanon, Me., Vesta Hayes, d. Sep. 26, 1889.
RICKER, John L., of Dover, b. 1805, d. Dec. 16, 1896, m. Apr. 3, 1829, by Rev. Joseph Boodey, Pamelia Chamberlin, of Alton, b. 1809, d. 1896.
RICKER, James, m. int. Dec. 5, 1830, in Lebanon, Me., Eunice Goodwin, d. Jan. 21, 1872, aged 73, dau. of Reuben.
RICKER, Ebenezer 4th, m. int. Jan. 23, 1836, in Lebanon, Me., Mercy Ricker, d. Sep. 16, 1880, aged 77.
RICKER, Eli, m. int. Oct. 8, 1837, in Lebanon, Me., Maria Jacobs.

RICKER, Samuel, m. int. Dec. 19, 1837, in Lebanon, Me., Lydia Hersom, d. Oct. 1840.

RICKER, Elza W., of Boston, Mass., m. Nov. 15, 1840, in Lebanon, Me., Nancy Pray, b. Aug. 11, 1818, d. Aug. 24, 1884, dau. of Samuel.

RICKER, Samuel, m. int. Jul. 9, 1843, in Lebanon, Me., Dorcas Leach, of Effingham.

RICKER, John Y., m. Dec. 4, 1846, in Lebanon, Me., Experience Wentworth.

RICKER, Ezekiel, son of William, d. May 28, 1895, aged 72, m. (1) (pub. May 11, 1847, in Effingham), Martha Ann Jones, d. 1869, aged 37, both of Farmington, m. (2) (pub. Oct. 20, 1870, in Rochester), Mrs. Lorinda Cousens, of Rochester.

RICKER, Willis Seaver, d. Mar. 19, 1889, aged 67, m. Jan. 27, 1849, in Lebanon, Me., Sarah Ann Hersom.

RICKER, Charles Coffin, son of Ezekiel, m. Feb. 22, 1850, in Lebanon, Me., Mary E. Ross.

RICKER, Asa H., d. Sep. 19, 1877, aged 50, m. Dec. 19, 1850, in Lebanon, Me., Esther Jane Jones, d. Nov. 1858.

RICKER, Winslow W., d. Jan. 8, 1885, aged 53, m. (1) int. Jan. 4, 1851, in Lebanon, Me., Harriet Hersom, d. Aug. 16, 1862, m. (2) Sep. 6, 1865, by Rev. Asa H. Gould, Mary A. Gowen.

RICKER, Lewis Downs, son of Elijah, b. Aug. 3, 1820, d. Sep. 17, 1884, m. May 23, 1851, in Lebanon, Me., Eliza J. Hartford.

RICKER, Stephen F., son of Aaron, b. Feb. 3, 1824, m. int. Jul. 3, 1855, in Lebanon, Me., Elmira Reading Prescott, d. 1884.

RICKER, Thomas Jr., son of Thomas, b. Aug. 14, 1826, m. int. Feb. 8, 1856, in Lebanon, Me., Elizabeth F. Fernald.

RICKER, Daniel D., m. int. Nov. 2, 1861, in Lebanon, Me., Olive A. Pray, of No. Berwick, Me., d. Aug. 26, 1862, aged 27.

RICKER, Phineas A., m. Dec. 22, 1862, in Great Falls, Lucy M. Smith, both of Great Falls.

RICKER, Martin V., b. Jan. 17, 1839, d. June 8, 1915, m. (pub. Apr. 23, 1863, in Ossipee), Leonora E. Leighton, b. Aug. 28, 1842, d. Feb. 4, 1885.

RICKER, Capt. John S., d. Nov. 4, 1874, aged 33, m. Sept. 5, 1863, in Sandwich, Mary A. Ham, both of Dover.

RICKER, Capt. Ephraim W., m. July 16, 1865, in E. Alton, Clara Hurd, of Alton, dau. of John S.

RICKER, Charles E., son of Timothy, d. Jan. 8, 1916, aged 73, m. Aug. 19, 1865, in Rochester, Abbie Foss.

RICKER, John Q., m. Sept. 5, 1865, in Dover, Laura E. Horne, both of Farmington.
RICKER, Albert M., m. Oct. 9, 1866, in Dover, Julia A. J. Howe, d. Jan. 10, 1909, aged 60, both of Dover.
RICKER, George K., of Dover, m. Nov. 28, 1866, in Dover, Emma P. Newell, of Dover, Mass.
RICKER, Oliver P., m. Dec. 22, 1866, in Dover, Susan A. Corson, both of Dover.
RICKER, Nathaniel J., m. (pub. May 30, 1867, in Great Falls), m. Jennie Byers, both of Rochester.
RICKER, Lafayette, of Rollinsford, m. June 29, 1867, in Great Falls, Nellie J. Hill, of Berwick, Me.
RICKER, Joseph D., of Farmington, m. Sept. 25, 1867, in Rochester, Fanny G. Jewell, of Augusta, Me.
RICKER, John H., m. Oct. 23, 1867, in Great Falls, Charlotte Cockran.
RICKER, Nathaniel M., m. Mar. 11, 1868, in Great Falls, C. Ella Grant.
RICKER, Edward F., m. (pub. Aug. 11, 1870, in Rochester), Bessie Byers.
RICKER, William H., m. (pub. Sept. 1, 1870, in Rochester), Clara F. Jones, both of Farmington.
RICKER, George F., m. (pub. Oct. 27, 1870, in Berwick, Me.), Lizzie A. Downs, both of Berwick, Me.
RIDLEY, Andrew J., m. Dec. 23, 1866, in Great Falls, Lydia J. Pray.
RINES, Henry, son of Henry, b. July 1730, d. Oct. 15, 1815, m. Nov. 26, 1761, Mary Fall, b. Jan. 1733, d. May 17, 1823, dau. of John.
RINES, Samuel, son of Henry, b. 1800, d. 1886, m. Feb. 6, 1824, in Milton, Louisa Miller, b. 1804, d. 1868, dau. of Richard.
RINES, Nathaniel, m. (1) Martha Wiggin, m. (2) Apr. 13, 1828, in Middleton, Nancy Cook, d. Oct. 10, 1855, aged 68, both of Middleton.
RINES, Samuel, of Milton, m. (pub. Oct. 13, 1870, in Rochester), Mrs. Esther Grant, of Rochester.
RING, Anson J., of Hampstead, m. int. Sep. 12, 1859, in Lebanon, Me., Delana D. Corson.
ROA, Jacob C., of No. Andover, Mass., m. Jan. 30, 1862, in Strafford, Martha S. Berry, of Strafford.
ROAK, Cyrus A., of Durham, m. Feb. 16, 1867, in Boston, Mass., Sarah E. Earley, of Epping.

ROBERSON, Francis W., of Boston, Mass., m. Nov. 14, 1870, in Dover, Mrs. Mary M. Nutter, of Cambridgeport, Mass.

ROBBINS, William T., m. Apr. 15, 1865, in Dover, Mrs. Mary J. Daniels, both of Boston, Mass.

ROBERTS, William, b. 1759, d. Jan. 1813, m. (1) Elizabeth Conway, of Rochester, N.Y., m. (2) Lydia Allard, d. 1858.

ROBERTS, Samuel, son of Hatevil, b. Dec. 12, 1686, m. (1) Abigail Perkins, m. (2) Sep. 20, 1716, Sarah Lord, b. Mar. 28, 1696, dau. of Nathan.

ROBERTS, Ebenezer, son of John and Frances, b. Feb. 5, 1721/2, d. 1804, m. early as 1757, Sarah Miller, b. 1731, d. 1799, dau. of Dr. Thomas.

ROBERTS, Aaron, of Somersworth, son of John, m. May 5, 1768, by Dr. Belknap, Mary Hanson, widow, of Dover, b. Jun. 19, 1737.

ROBERTS, John Jr., of Somersworth, son of John, b. 1741, d. 1819, m. Dec. 13, 1768, by Rev. Jacob Foster, Elizabeth Hodgdon, b. 1740, d. 1825.

ROBERTS, Ebenezer, of Somersworth, son of John, m. Mar. 12, 1771, Rachel Philpot, b. Jul. 1, 1755, dau. of John, of Somersworth.

ROBERTS, Ichabod, b. Sep. 17, 1748, son of John, m. Dec. 21, 1772, by Rev. James Pike, Susannah Roberts, dau. of Joseph, of Somersworth.

ROBERTS, Samuel, son of John, d. Apr. 1, 1821, aged 69, m. Mar. 7, 1782, by Rev. Joseph Haven, Lydia Tebbetts, d. Nov. 21, 1820, aged 58, dau. of David.

ROBERTS, Jonathan, m. Jan. 15, 1789, by Rev. Benjamin Balch, Betsey Foss, both of Barrington.

ROBERTS, Silas, son of Aaron, d. Dec. 8, 1851, aged 90, m. July 19, 1789, by Rev. Joseph Haven, Sarah Davis, d. Apr. 10, 1855, aged 86, dau. of Zebulon, both of New Durham.

ROBERTS, Nicholas, m. Sept. 13, 1789, in Barrington, Molly Fernald, both of Barrington.

ROBERTS, Nicholas, m. June 20, 1813, in Barrington, Mary Arlen, both of Barrington.

ROBERTS, Hanson, son of David, b. Jan. 29, 1793, d. Aug. 27, 1870, m. Feb. 5, 1814, by Rev. J. W. Clary, Lydia Henderson, b. Nov. 13, 1794, d. Mar. 24, 1872, dau. of Thomas.

ROBERTS, Capt. Joseph Jr., m. Apr. 15, 1827, by Rev. Joseph Boodey, Priscilla Edgerly, b. 1802, d. June 2, 1840, aged 38, dau. of Josiah, both of Farmington.

ROBERTS, Owen Swain, son of James, b. Apr. 4, 1813, d. 1853, m. (pub. Jan. 23, 1838, in Milton), Harriet L. Foss, b. 1814, d. 1895, dau. of William.

ROBERTS, John, of Dover, b. Feb. 12, 1819, d. Aug. 20, 1891, m. Sept. 29, 1844, in Boston, Mary Jane Banks, of Nottingham, b. Sept. 5, 1818, d. Nov. 27, 1880, aged 62.

ROBERTS, Joshua, of Ossipee, d. June 18, 1876, aged 82, m. (1) Dorothy Hanson, d. May 7, 1854, aged 57, dau. of Daniel, m. (2) Oct. 19, 1854, in Ossipee, Mrs. Hannah S. Abbott, of Rollinsford.

ROBERTS, Thomas H., of Dover, d. June 21, 1900, aged 75, m. May 17, 1855, in Boston, Mass., Anatis A. Whitney, of Boston, Mass., d. Sept. 22, 1887, aged 55.

ROBERTS, John W., of Rochester, m. (1) Jul. 4, 1855, in Lebanon, Me., Abby D. Roberts, of N. Berwick, Me., dau. of William, m. (2) Jun. 14, 1868, in Rochester, Carrie C. Ellis.

ROBERTS, Amos, of Charlestown, Mass., m. (pub. Jan. 29, 1857, in Barrington), Sarah Elizabeth Buzzell, of Barrington, b. Dec. 18, 1838, dau. of Ebenezer.

ROBERTS, Daniel W., d. Jan. 19, 1879, aged 45, m. Apr. 18, 1858, in Dover, Lucy Wentworth, of Milton, d. Feb. 11, 1911, aged 81, dau. of Isaac.

ROBERTS, Moses, of Rollinsford, m. Sept. 8, 1861, in S. Berwick, Me., Lydia M. Hussey, of Somersworth.

ROBERTS, Ira, d. 1875, m. (1) Belinda ----, d. 1860, m. (2) Oct. 26, 1861, in Rochester, Mrs. Caroline L. (Foss) Ricker, wid. of Joshua.

ROBERTS, Joshua, of Ossipee, m. (pub. Mar. 20, 1862, in Ossipee), Mrs. Sally Tripp, of Kennebunk, Me.

ROBERTS, George Thomas, m. May 1, 1862, in S. Berwick, Me., Lydia E. Smith, both of Rollinsford.

ROBERTS, Jeremiah B., m. June 12, 1862, in Durham, Sarah E. Willey, both of Farmington.

ROBERTS, Sewall T., of Alton, m. (pub. July 3, 1862, in Concord), A. E. Beacham, of Wolfeboro.

ROBERTS, James, m. Aug. 17, 1862, in Dover, Mrs. Mary Faye, both of Dover.

ROBERTS, Seth, m. Mar. 30, 1863, in Farmington, Ellen M. Bennett, both of Dover.

ROBERTS, Aaron P., b. July 30, 1864, d. Aug. 24, 1904, m. July 7, 1864, in Boston, Mass., Laura A. Dame, b. Feb. 20, 1846, d. Dec. 2, 1913, both of Ossipee.

ROBERTS, Elijah E., of Rochester, m. June 18, 1865, in Tewsbury, Mass., Martha S. Herrick, of Tewsbury, Mass.

ROBERTS, William Estes, of Dover, m. Dec. 5, 1865, in Dover, Rosetta Marie Chesley, of Durham, b. Dec. 12, 1845, dau. of Daniel.

ROBERTS, Edmond, of Farmington, m. Dec. 6, 1865, in Farmington, Agnes Locke, of New Durham.

ROBERTS, John W., m. July 25, 1866, in Rochester, Martha A. Sherburne.

ROBERTS, Harrison F., m. Aug. 26, 1866, in Farmington, Abbie Horn.

ROBERTS, Henry K, of Rochester, m. Mar. 16, 1867, by Rev. James Rand, Ellen A. Kimball, of Dover.

ROBERTS, Hermon W., m. May 7, 1867, in Great Falls, Emma A. Snow, both of Rochester.

ROBERTS, Lyman, m. Aug. 20, 1867, by Rev. Alden Sherwin, Susan F. Roberts, both of Biddeford, Me.

ROBERTS, John W., of Rochester, m. June 16, 1868, in Rochester, Carrie C. Ellis, of Lebanon, Me.

ROBERTS, Benjamin, of New York City, m. (pub. July 23, 1868, in Great Falls), Addie O. Thompson, of Great Falls.

ROBERTS, James, of Farmington, m. Aug. 25, 1869, in Laconia, Ann M. Thompson, of Gilford.

ROBERTS, William C., of Farmington, m. (pub. May 19, 1870, in Farmington), Annie J. Tucker, of Kennebunkport, Me.

3) **ROBINSON**, Stephen, son of Timothy, b. Feb. 14, 1742, d. Aug. 23, 1820, m. June 19, 1777, in Salem, Mass., Content Alley, b. July 23, 1752, d. Nov. 18, 1818, dau. of Samuel Jr.

ROBINSON, Samuel, m. Dec. 3, 1777, in Barrington, Deliverance Clark, both of Barrington.

ROBINSON, Levi, m. Jan. 16, 1806, by Rev. Joseph Haven, Martha Hanson, d. July 7, 1826, aged 42, both of Rochester.

ROBINSON, Meshach, m. Sept. 3, 1818, by Rev. Micajah Otis, Sarah Whitehouse.

ROBINSON, James, m. May 11, 1830, in Barrington, by Rev. Samuel Sherburne, Betsey Brown, both of Barrington.

ROBINSON, Eli, of Barrington, m. Apr. 30, 1843, by Rev. Samuel Sherburne, Sarah Pearl, of Rochester.

ROBINSON, Noah, m. Oct. 5, 1845, in Brookfield, Judith Cook, both of Brookfield.

ROBINSON, William M., of Charlestown, Mass., m. Nov. 30, 1863, in Boston, Mass., Mary Fanny Canney, of Dover.

ROBINSON, Benjamin F., m. (pub. June 9, 1864, in Portsmouth), Lydia V. Tobey.

ROBINSON, William, of Lawrence, Mass., m. Sept. 15, 1865, in Dover, Mrs. Margaret Gallager, of Dover.

ROBINSON, Addison R., of Tamworth, m. Aug. 15, 1866, in Meredith, Nellie M. Swasey, of Ossipee.

ROBINSON, Charles H., m.Oct. 14, 1866, in Lebanon, Me., Alice J. Shapleigh.

ROBINSON, Edward H., son of William, d. Feb. 17, 1914, aged 76, m. Nov. 24, 1867, in Dover, Emma B. Wallace, d. July 19, 1917, aged 69, dau. of Jasper G., both of Dover.

ROBINSON, George H., m. Oct. 29, 1870, in Dover, Fannie Leighton, both of Dover.

ROGERS, Brackett R., of Parsonsfield, Me., d. Feb. 1877, m. int. Apr. 30, 1858, in Lebanon, Me., Olivia ----.

ROGERS, Tyler, of Sandwich, m. Aug. 24, 1865, by Rev. James Rand, Caroline Felch, of Tamworth,

ROGERS, John, son of Samuel, d. Apr. 21, 1869, aged 28, m. Mar. 31, 1868, in Milton, Olive (Downs) Wentworth, wid. of John C., b. Aug. 20, 1822, d. Apr. 3, 1888, dau. of James.

ROGERS, David, of Acton, Me., m. Aug. 14, 1868, in Rochester, Mrs. Clarecy Hoyt, of Rochester.

ROGERS, Amasa A., of Somersworth, d. Feb. 17, 1902, aged 75, m. Jan. 15, 1870, in Dover, Allie W. Blaisdell, of Dover.

ROLFE, Edward, m. (pub. Aug. 11, 1870, in Great Falls), Mary Jane Hodgdon.

ROLLINS, Capt. Ichabod Jr., son of Ichabod, b. 1746, d. Feb. 18, 1787, m. July 4, 1768, Ruth Philpot, b. Feb. 2, 1747, d. Sept 2, 1801, dau. of Richard.

5) ROLLINS, James, son of Judge Ichabod, d. Dec. 1813, aged 58, m. (1) Aug. 20, 1777, Hannah Carr, b. Dec. 9, 1754, d. July 1789, aged 33, dau. of Dr. Moses, m. (2) near 1800, Lucy Gerrish, d. Oct. 1815, aged 55.

ROLLINS, Ichabod, of Chichester, son of Ichabod, b. Dec. 14, 1772, d. Dec. 26, 1853, m. Aug. 9, 1793, by Rev. Isaac Smith, Sarah Leighton, of New Durham Gore, d. Jan. 16, 1859, aged 87, dau. of Jonathan.

ROLLINS, Elisha, son of John, b. Jan. 29, 1794, d. Dec. 6, 1872, m. Apr. 21, 1814, by Rev. Paul Jewett, Prudence Lord, d. May 8, 1871.

ROLLINS, John Jr., son of John, b. Feb. 28, 1799, d. Jun. 23, 1860, in Kansas, m. May 20, 1824, by Rev. James Weston, Hannah Lord, d. Dec. 14, 1855.

ROLLINS, Augustus, of Somersworth, son of Capt. Hiram, b. 1797, d. Jan. 27, 1870, m. May 29, 1824, by Rev. Thomas C. Upham, Abiah Winkley, d. Feb. 24, 1881, aged 81, dau. of Samuel.

5) ROLLINS, Steven J., son of Ichabod, b. Aug. 10, 1797, d. Nov. 2, 1891, m. (1) Nov. 11, 1824, Abigail Severance, b. Jan. 22, 1804, d. Feb. 15, 1830, m. (2) Oct. 1, 1830, Mehitable Severance, b. July 15, 1810, d. Nov. 2, 1891, both daus. of Jonathan.

6) ROLLINS, John N., son of Jonathan, b. Oct. 28, 1800, d. 1871, m. Dec. 9, 1824, Hannah Wilkinson, b. 1802, d. 1865.

ROLLINS, Ichabod, son of Ichabod, b. Mar. 15, 1801, d. Jan. 14, 1847, m. Jan. 15, 1826, Sarah Walker, b. Jun. 20, 1804, d. Apr. 13, 1866.

ROLLINS, Richard, m. Sep. 9, 1827, in Lebanon, Me., Betsey Hayes.

5) ROLLINS, Jeremiah M., son of Jonathan, b. Oct. 2, 1811, d. Aug. 23, 1886, m. (pub. Feb. 19, 1833, in Alton), Martha Libbey, d. Sept. 23, 1888, dau. of Benjamin.

ROLLINS, Aaron B., of Sandwich, d. Aug. 30, 1835, aged 29, m. Nov. 27, 1834, by Elder Enoch Place, Elizabeth A. Wentworth, of Dover, dau. of David.

ROLLINS, Calvin, of Somersworth, son of Moses, d. Jan. 1, 1887, aged 72, m. Aug. 25, 1844, by Rev. Jacob Stevens, Rebecca Thompson, of Dover, d. Jan. 2, 1888, aged 77, dau. of Daniel.

ROLLINS, Joseph P., m. (pub. Mar. 16, 1847, in Alton), Anna Woodman, b. 1813, d. 1881.

ROLLINS, Edwin J. E., son of Stephen J., b. Jan. 27, 1842, d. Feb. 17, 1879, m. Apr. 17, 1860, Betsey J. Stevens, d. May 15, 1909, aged 66.

ROLLINS, Thomas C., of Brookfield, aged 21, m. int. Dec. 29, 1862, in Brookfield, Anna L. Goodwin, of West Newfield, Me., aged 23.

ROLLINS, George W., son of George F., d. Dec. 13, 1914, aged 69, m. Sept. 9, 1864, in Concord, Mary A. Gray, both of Dover.

ROLLINS, James A., m. Mar. 7, 1866, in Alton, Mrs. Emma F. Clough, d. Feb. 6, 1868, aged 22.

ROLLINS, Warren S., of Lee, m. June 15, 1866, in Nottingham, Mrs. Huldah H. Witham.

ROLLINS, Benjamin F., m. July 21, 1870, in Dover, Rosa Dearborn, both of Dover.

ROOD (ROOT?), Marshall, m. Dec. 11, 1845, by Elder Enoch Place, Mary Foss, dau. of James, both of Portsmouth.

ROSS, Hugh Jr., d. Jan. 21, 1881, aged 89, m. (1) int. Apr. 30, 1814, in Lebanon, Me., Hannah Downs, d. Nov. 12, 1857, aged 70, m. (2) May 6, 1858, Mrs. Hannah Rowell.

ROSS, William L., m. Dec. 31, 1854, in Lebanon, Me., Mary L. Welch, both of Shapleigh, Me.

ROSS, Barton H., of Great Falls, m. Dec. 25, 1866, in Great Falls, Irena E. Williams, of Lewiston, Me.

ROSS, Joseph B., of Shapleigh, Me., m. Apr. 30, 1867, by Rev. Alden Sherwin, Mary E. Johnson, of N. Berwick, Me.

ROSS, William J., son of James M., d. Jan. 1, 1907, aged 73, m. Aug. 20, 1870, in Dover, Linna H. Thurlow, both of Dover.

ROSS, Joseph H., of Beverly, Mass., m. Nov. 24, 1870, in Dover, Mrs. Mary A. Goodale, of Dover, wid. of Abner.

ROTHWELL, Jeremiah, of Dover, son of Richard, d. Feb. 3, 1908, aged 89, m. Sept. 10, 1865, in Portsmouth, Josephine E. Chase, of Portsmouth, d. Dec. 28, 1898, aged 59.

ROWE, James, of Barrington, m. Jan. 22, 1777, in Barrington, Betty Boodey, of Madbury.

ROWE, James, d. Aug. 30, 1851, aged 79, m. Elizabeth Boodey.

ROWE, David T., of Farmington, m. (1) Jul. 11, 1861, by Rev. J. H. Harmon, Araminda D. Gerrish, m. (2) Jul. 4, 1876, by Rev. Charles N. Sinnett, Estella J. Kennedy.

ROWELL, James, m. May 1, 1823, in Lebanon, Me., Lois Varney, both of Brentwood.

RUGG, James A., of Portsmouth, m. Sept. 4, 1865, in Portsmouth, Susan E. Canney, dau. of Benjamin.

RUNDLETT, Asa, m. May 14, 1801, by Rev. Isaac Hasey, Hannah Horn.

RUNDLETT, Josiah, m. int. Oct. 29, 1808, in Lebanon, Me., Betsey Fall.

RUNDLETT, David, of Lee, m. 1817, by Rev. John Osborne, Lydia Hall, of Barrington, b. Aug. 31, 1797, dau. of Daniel.

RUNDLETT, Nathaniel, of Lee, m. (1) Mary ----, d. Aug. 22, 1835, aged 46, m. (2) int. Feb. 17, 1836, Mary G. Simpson, of Nottingham.

RUNDLETT, Samuel, son of Charles, b. Apr. 11, 1814, m. Oct. 23, 1843, Sarah Ann French, b. June 1, 1819, d. June 29, 1884, <u>dau. of William</u>.

RUNDLETT, Charles H., of Durham, m. (pub. Dec. 10, 1850, in Barrington), Lucy L. Reynolds, of Barrington, <u>d. May 4, 1908, aged 78, dau. of Ephraim</u>.

RUNNELS, Winthrop, m. Jan. 4, 1792, by Rev. Benjamin Balch, Hannah Lock, both of Barrington.

RUNNELS, Samuel, m. <u>(2)</u> Nov. 19, 1844, by Rev. Nathaniel Berry, Mrs. Dorcas Ricker, d. June 8, 1847, aged 80, both of New Durham.

RUNNELS, John S., m. Jan. 14, 1865, in New Durham, Elizabeth F. Evans, both of New Durham.

RYAN, James M., b. 1820, d. <u>Dec. 14</u>, 1848, m. Jan. 16, 1848, by Rev. Samuel Kelley, Martha Ann Young, d. Nov.11, 1851, aged 24, both of Dover.

ST. JOHN, Marcus M., of Dover, Kansas, son of Lewis Lathrop and Sarah (Russell) St. John, b. Jan. 8, 1847, d. Feb. 16, 1890, m. May 21, 1870, in Dover, Kansas, Bettie C. Haskell, formerly of Dover, N.H., b. 1834, d. 1915, dau. of Jacob.

SAMPSON, Jonathan, m. Nov. 13, 1817, in Barrington, Abigail Clark, b. 1799, both of Barrington.

SAMPSON, Luther, of Rochester, m. May 9, 1867, in Pembroke, Me., Philandia C. Garnett, of Pembroke, Me.

SANBORN, Oliver W., of Rochester, <u>son of William</u>, d. Apr. 18, 1887, aged 73, m. Betsey ----, b. 1809, d. Jun. 25, 1865.

SANBORN, Jonathan R., m. Aug. 22, 1824, in Lebanon, Me., Mary R. Burrows.

SANBORN, Alonzo F., son of Isaac, b. Feb. 24, 1827, d. July 24, 1885, m. Aug. 31, 1848, in Sandwich, Elvira B. Quimby, b. Jan. 26, 1826, d. June 28, 1870, dau. of J. Smith Quimby, both of Sandwich.

SANBORN, J. B., m. before Dec. 8, 1849, in Boston, Mass., Mary T. T. Fairbanks, of Somerville, Mass.

SANBORN, Lowell, of Gilmanton, aged 30, m. June 27, 1850, by Rev. Levi B. Tasker, in Sandwich, Sarah A. Bean, of Sandwich, aged 21, dau. of Moody.

SANBORN, Dr. Tristram, of Sanbornton, aged 22, d. Dec. 6, 1859, m. (1) Aug. 18, 1850, by Rev. Levi B. Tasker, in Sandwich, Hannah M. Burleigh, of Sandwich, aged 19, d. Feb. 27, 1853, dau.

of Thomas, m. (2) Nov. 14, 1853, Antoinette L. Burleigh, d. Apr. 10, 1875, dau. of Thomas.

SANBORN, Ambrose, of Acton, Me., m. Oct. 18, 1854, by Elder James Rand, Betsey Linscott, of No. Berwick, Me.

SANBORN, Jonathan N., b. 1818, m. Apr. 5, 1855, in Brookfield, Elizabeth A. Buzzell, b. 1833, both of Brookfield.

SANBORN, Joel Sawyer, m. (pub. July 30, 1857, in Great Falls), Mrs. Sarah (Roberts) Low, wid. of Nehemiah P.

SANBORN, Alfred B., of Brookfield, aged 51, m. int. Apr. 19, 1860, in Brookfield, Sarah T. Sanborn, of Newfield, Me.

SANBORN, Abner J., m. June 16, 1861, in Strafford, Ester J. Knowles, of Epson.

SANBORN, Nathan, m. Jan. 1, 1863, in Rochester, Hannah M. Varney, both of Rochester.

SANBORN, John W., d. Oct. 30, 1920, aged 74, m. May 27, 1867, in Wakefield, Ellen E. Felker, both of Rochester.

SANBORN, Isaac E., m. Oct. 23, 1867, in Great Falls, Ellen Linscott, both of Farmington.

SANBORN, William Henry, m. Dec. 24, 1868, in Rochester, Sarah A. Beede, both members of Dover Monthly Meeting.

SANBORN, Martin Luther, of Wakefield, aged 20, m. Mar. 14, 1869, in Ossipee, Nellie C. Blake, of Brookfield, aged 17.

SANBORN, William H., of Milton, m. June 29, 1869, in Portland, Me., Georgie A. Crockett, of Portland, Me.

SANBORN, Newton P., of Effingham, m. (pub. Oct. 21, 1869, in Great Falls), Hattie J. Kimball, of Great Falls.

SANBORN, Hiram W., of Boston, Mass. M. Nov. 27, 1871, in Dover, Hattie A. Yeaton.

SANDERS, Levi, m. Oct. 25, 1792, by Rev. Benjamin Balch, Betsey Cate, both of Barrington.

SANDERS, William F., of Strafford, d. June 29, 1835, m. May 18, 1830, by Elder Enoch Place, Abigail M. Miles, of Barnstead.

SANDERS, William, m. Aug. 4, 1839, by Elder Enoch Place, Mrs. Abigail (Miles) Sanders, d. Oct. 25, 1847, aged 44, wid. of William F.

SANDERS, Gideon D., d. June 11, 1907, aged 88, m. (1) June 6, 1846, Sarah Jane Welch, both of Ossipee, m. (2) Mary J. ----, d. Mar. 20, 1896, aged 73.

SANDERS, Dr. Laban M., m. Aug. 24, 1864, in Barnstead, Sarah Tucker.

SANDERSON, Reuben, of Tamworth, m. Feb. 2, 1786, by Rev. Benjamin Balch, Nancy McDaniels, of Barrington.

SANDERSON, C. S., m. Dec. 24, 1863, in Dover, Frances M. Allen, of Dover, dau. of George W.

SANDERSON, George A., of Dover, m. Apr. 21, 1867, in Haverhill, Mass., Emma Smith.

SARGENT, Edwin, of Amesbury, Mass., m. Sept. 17, 1862, in Farmington, Adeline E. Merrill, of Farmington, dau. of Isaac.

SAVORY, George P., son of Richard, b. June 12, 1801, d. <u>Nov. 26, 1882</u>, m. May 25, 1823, by Rev. William Demeritt, Lydia Ham, b. May 9, 1799, d. Aug. 29, 1879, both of Dover.

SAVORY, Charles F., of Rochester, m. May 2, 1864, in Great Falls, Abbie A. Clement, of Rollinsford.

SAWYER, Daniel, of Eaton, m. Oct. 21, 1804, Bridget Blanchard, of Sandwich.

SAWYER, Bitfield, of Strafford, d. Feb. 24, 1862, aged 68, m. July 29, 1824, <u>in Barrington</u>, Patience Brown, of Barrington.

SAWYER, Rev. Seth, son of Enoch, b. 1806, d. Feb. 4, 1892, m. (1) Jan. 10, 1830, in Alton, Elizabeth Ann Wiggin, d. May 27, 1833, dau of Benjamin, m. (2) Aug. 6, 1835, Sarah Eliza Stevens, d. Nov. 10, 1869, dau. of John, m. (3) Oct. 2, 1870, in Acton, Me., Lucy Jane Tupper, d. July 19, 1880.

SAWYER, Jason G., of Porter, Me., m. int Sep. 23, 1848, in Lebanon, Me., Hannah Brown.

SAWYER, Franklin, of Lee, <u>son of Josiah, d. Apr. 18, 1878, aged 45</u>, m. <u>(1)</u> int. Feb. 8, 1850, in Lee, Lydia A. Perkins, of Greenland, <u>d. Sep. 15, 1861, aged 38, m. (2) Addie ----, d. Nov. 15, 1865, aged 23, m. (3) Feb. 6, 1868, in Lee, Sarah P. Fernald, of Waltham, Mass., b. near 1833</u>.

SAWYER, Alonzo Havington, son of Daniel, b. May 17, 1827, d. Jul. 17, 1885, m. Nov. 7, 1850, Martha J. Shapleigh, <u>b. 1831, b. 1918</u>, dau. of Samuel.

SAWYER, Israel Jr., b. 1816, d. 1895, m. (1) Metilda ----, b. 1814, d. Oct. 1852, of Alton, m. (2) Apr. 29, 1859, in Dover, Mrs. Emily L. Smith, of Dover.

SAWYER, George W., of Porter, Me., m. (pub. May 19, 1864, in Brookfield), Christina C. Cook, of Brookfield.

SCALES, John, of Wolfeboro, son of Samuel, b. Oct. 6, 1835, m. Oct. 22, 1865, in Center Harbor, Ellen A. Tasker, of Strafford, dau. of Deac. Alfred.

SCATES, Rev. John, m. June 30, 1745, in Rochester, by Rev. Amos Main, Abigail Hayes, d. Aug. 18, 1782.
SCATES, Ithiel, of Rochester, son of John, d. 1825, m. Oct. 9, 1793, by Rev. Matthew Merriam, Ruth Clark, of Berwick, Me.
SCATES, Benjamin, of Lebanon, Me., son of John, d. Aug. 9, 1833, aged 83, m. (1) Lydia Jenness, d. May 16, 1802, dau. of John, m. (2) Sept. 11, 1803, by Rev. Asa Piper, Rebecca Ham, dau. of Dobavar, m. (3) Feb. 6, 1814, Abigail Folsom, b. Apr. 13, 1772.
SCATES, Zimri, of Ossipee, son of John, d. May 19, 1886, aged 84, m. Dec. 23, 1830, in Effingham, Susan W. S. Clark, of Effingham, d. Mar. 28, 1859, aged 50, dau. of Dr. David W.
SCATES, Eri N., b. Dec. 21, 1818, d. Jan. 7, 1877, m. int. Feb. 19, 1837, in Dover, Mary N. Smith, b. Oct. 8, 1815, d. Apr. 20, 1853.
SCATES, Alvah, m. Oct. 9, 1867, in Farmington, Mrs. Helen M. Butters, of Haverhill, Mass.
SCRIBNER, Stephen, of Washington, m. Feb. 25, 1783, Abigail Church, of Barrington, dau. of Ebenezer.
4) **SCRUTON**, Benjamin O., son of Jonathan, b. May 29, 1803, d. Oct. 27, 1835, m. (1) Apr. 7, 1825, Charlotte Brock, m. (2) Nov. 10, 1831, Nancy Collins.
SCRUTON, Joseph, d. Jul. 16, 1886, aged 76, m. Apr. 1, 1838, by Rev. John Winkley, Lavina Brock, d. Jan. 15, 1885, aged 72, both of Strafford.
SCRUTON, Clark, of Strafford, aged 24, son of Joseph, d. Dec. 26, 1894, aged 66, m. Jan. 9, 1853, in Strafford, Vianna J. Scruton, of Farmington, d. Jul. 2, 1900, aged 76.
SCRUTON, James M., of Strafford, m. (pub. Jan. 9, 1862, in Barrington), Sarah A. Hall, of Dover.
SCRUTON, G. H., of Strafford, m. June 2, 1863, in Barrington, Fannie Bennett, of Nottingham.
SCRUTON, Stephen B., son of Joseph, d. Oct. 10, 1918, aged 80, m. Nov. 25, 1863, by Rev. James Rand, Martha A. Wallingford, d. Dec. 13, 1907, aged 60, dau. of Job.
SCRUTON, Daniel H., b. 1840, d. 1928, m. Apr. 2, 1868, in Strafford, Vienna E. Brock, b. 1849, d. 1920, both of Strafford.
SCRUTON, Dr. John E., of Farmington, m. Aug. 15, 1870, in Center Lebanon, Me., Laura E. Hersom, d. Mar. 20, 1886, aged 38, dau. of Ira.
SEARS, Amos G., of Dover, m. Jun. 1, 1847, in Rockingham, Susan A. Davis, of Rockingham.

SEAVER, Nathaniel, m. Jun. 21, 1812, by Rev. Isaac Hasey, Dorcas Keay.

SEAVEY, William, b. Aug. 3, 1761, m. May 11, 1780, Molly Foss, b. May 8, 1781.

SEAVEY, Isaac, son of William, b. Dec. 10, 1780, m. Aug. 27, 1801, by Rev. Benjamin Balch, Polly Twombly, both of Barrington.

SEAVEY, John, son of William, b. Oct. 26, 1782, m. May 8, 1806, by Rev. Micajah Otis, Lucy Cate, both of Barrington.

SEAVEY, Samuel, son of William, b. Oct. 15, 1784, m. Oct. 23, 1806, by Rev. Benjamin Balch, Mrs. Abigail Davis, both of Barrington.

SEAVEY, William, son of William, b. Jan. 25, 1790, m. Dec. 24, 1807, by Rev. Micajah Otis, Hannah Cate, both of Barrington.

SEAVEY, Elijah Jr., son of William, b. Mar. 1, 1787, m. Oct. 15, 1812, in Barrington, Sally Parshley, both of Barrington.

SEAVEY, William Jr., m. Dec. 24, 1812, by Rev. Micajah Otis, Mrs. Hannah Foss, both of Barrington.

SEAVEY, Ebenezer, of Rochester, m. Jan. 9, 1814, by Rev. Micajah Otis, Hannah Berry, of Barrington.

SEAVEY, Henry, son of William, b. Aug. 3, 1794, d. Jan. 28, 1877, aged 82, m. in 1822, Rachel Corson, d. Feb. 17, 1857, aged 56.

SEAVEY, Ichabod, son of William, b. Nov. 29, 1796, d. July 29, 1847, aged 50, m. Mar. 4, 1824, by Rev. Thomas C. Upham, Relief Corson, d. Apr. 11, 1881, aged 86.

SEAVEY, John, b. 1805, d. 1892, m. Nov. 15, 1832, by Daniel Boodey, J.P., Mehitable Nason, b. 1810, d. 1900, both of New Durham.

SEAVEY, Ebenezer, of Rochester, d. Nov. 4, 1842, aged 77, m. (1) Hannah ----, d. May 11, 1836, aged 51, m. (2) Aug. 2, 1837, by Elder Enoch Place, Dorothy (----) Seavey, of Farmington, wid. of Samuel, b. 1780, d. Nov. 24, 1859.

SEAVEY, Mark H.W., m. Nov. 26, 1845, by Rev. Theodore Wells, Mary Susan Foss, both of Barrington.

SEAVEY, Daniel A., of Dover, b. May 23, 1829, d. Oct. 15, 1897, m. July 13, 1863, in Rochester, Sarah Varney, of Barrington, b. Jan. 18, 1837, d. Oct. 30, 1918..

SEAVEY, Charles H., m. Aug. 5, 1863, in Dover, Julia A. Seavey, both of Dover.

SEAVEY, S. Augustus, of Somersworth, d. Jul. 10, 1905, aged 67, m. Dec. 7, 1865, in Dover, Annie L. Hussey, of Dover.

SEAVEY, Wilmon A., of Alexandria, m. May 7, 1868, by Rev. Robert S. Stubbs, Jennie Richardson, of Springfield.

SEAVEY, Charles H., of Barrington, m. Jan. 11, 1869, in Rochester, Mrs. Sarah A. Howe, of Rochester.

SECOMB, Edward A., of Brooklyn, N.Y., m. July 27, 1865, in Rochester, Mary C. Turner, of Rochester.

SELLEA, John H., son of Charles H., of Saco, Me., b. 1846, d. Mar. 24, 1916, m. Apr. 8, 1869, in Dover, Annie E. Brown, b. 1845, d. Nov. 21, 1924.

SEVERANCE, Asa, son of Lt. Asa, aged 22, m. Nov. 20, 1850, by Rev. Levi B. Tasker, in Sandwich, Hannah M. Webster, aged 22, both of Sandwich.

SEWELL, Benjamin C., of Spmersworth, m. int. Aug. 10, 1828, in Lebanon, Me., Paulina F. Wentworth.

SHACKFORD, Samuel Burnham, son of Samuel, b. Jan. 1, 1817, d. Jan. 1, 1881, m. (1) Apr. 5, 1837, by Rev. Enoch Place, Martha Susan Hale, d. May 24, 1845, aged 29, dau. of James D., both of Barrington, m. (2) Lydia J. Pendexter.

SHACKFORD, Seth, of Barnstead, m. Apr. 2, 1865, in Farmington, Roxanna Nute, of Farmington.

SHACKFORD, Charles B., of Conway, b. Dec. 28, 1840, d. Jan. 2, 1881, m. Oct. 26, 1869, in Dover, Caroline Cartland, of Lee, b. July 6, 1847, d. Nov. 21, 1897, dau. of Moses A.

SHACKLEY, John, m. Aug. 7, 1865, in Great Falls, Louisa Norwood, dau. of Seth, both of Beverly, Mass.

3) **SHANNON**, Lt. William, of Rochester, son of Capt. Thomas, d. in 1813, aged 34, at Sackett's Harbor, m. Sept. 27, 1801, by Rev. Benjamin Balch, Mary Waldron, of Barrington, dau. of Isaac.

SHAPLEIGH, Samuel, d. Oct. 11, 1848, aged 66, m. (2) Jun. 26, 1816, by Rev. Paul Jewett, Eunice Wentworth, d. Feb. 6, 1843, aged 57.

SHAPLEIGH, James Waldron, of Eliot, Me., m. (1) Mar. 10, 1819, in Lebanon, Me., Hannah Lee Chandler, m. (2) (pub. Mar. 30, 1841, in Somersworth), Betsey Lamber Baker, dau. of Moses.

SHAPLEIGH, Elisha Jr., d. Dec. 8, 1849, aged 46, m. int. Sep. 7, 1828, in Lebanon, Me., Betsey Wentworth, d. Aug. 5, 1886.

SHAPLEIGH, Andrew, of Eliot, Me., m. int. Oct. 10, 1830, in Lebanon, Me., Caroline Rollins, d. Feb. 13, 1880.

SHAPLEIGH, Samuel, m. (3) Oct. 8, 1844, by Rev. Joseph Loring, Phebe Ricker, d. Sep. 5, 1871, aged 77.

SHAPLEIGH, Edwin, son of Richard, d. Sep. 29, 1874, m. int. Nov. 10, 1845, in Lebanon, Me. (married in Somersworth), Abby H. Carpenter, of Somersworth.

SHAPELIGH, Moses W., m. Sep. 14, 1847, by Rev. Edward F. Abbott, Abby Jane Drew, of Milton.

SHAPLEIGH, Samuel Chandler, son of Samuel, d. Mar. 2, 1885, m. Sep. 3, 1856, in Lebanon, Me., Fannie Hammond.

SHAPLEIGH, Elisha Bacon, m. Jun. 5, 1864, in Lebanon, Me., Anna S. Lord.

SHAPLEIGH, Dr. Orrin Q., m. Jan. 5, 1865, in Great Falls, Belle D. Weeks, of Rochester.

SHAPLEIGH, George A., m. Oct. 31, 1865, in Lebanon, Me., Abbie E. Bartlett, of New Portland, Me.

SHAPLEIGH, Nicholas Blaisdell, m. Nov. 23, 1869, in East Boston, Mass., Orianna Maria Prescott, dau. of George Washington Prescott.

SHAPLEIGH, Oliver Waldron, son of Oliver, b. Apr. 11, 1844, d. Jul. 13, 1879, m. Dec. 16, 1869, in Acton, Me., Myra S. Prescott, of Acton, Me.

SHAPLEIGH, Samuel, of Eliot, Me., m. Oct. 29, 1863, in Dover, Susan A. Whitehouse, of Dover.

SHATSWELL, Joseph Augustus, of Salem, m. Nov. 19, 1863, in Boston, Mass., Mary Esther Woodman, of Dover.

SHAW, Lebbeus, m. Nov. 18, 1841, Dorcas Worster, b. Nov. 30, 1818, dau. of Samuel.

SHAW, Jackson, of Freedom, d. Feb. 18, 1907, aged 78, m. (1) June 8, 1861, in Dover, by Rev. D. P. Leavitt, Hannah S. Foss, of Rochester, m. (2) Nov. 2, 1865, in Dover, Lorinia N. Foss, both of Rochester.

SHAW, O.W., m. Jan. 7, 1862, in Great Falls, Sarah J. Rollins, dau. of D. G. Rollins.

SHAW, Gilbert, of Canada, d. May 7, 1902, aged 65, m. Sept. 6, 1863, in Concord, Mary A. Foss, both of Strafford.

SHAW, Andrew J., of Kensington, son of Abraham, m. Feb. 13, 1867, by Rev. Alvan Tobey, Mary E. Giles, of Lee, dau. of Paul.

SHEA, John O., of Great Falls, m. (pub. Sept. 22, 1870, in Great Falls), Frances J. Wentworth, of Saco, Me.

SHEPARD, Jacob, m. June 15, 1800, by Rev. Benjamin Balch, Elizabeth Hill, both of Lee.

SHEPARD, Charles H., of Boston, Mass., m. 1849, in Boston, Mass., M. H. Pray, of Lebanon, Me.

SHEPARD, Jacob, d. Sept. 25, 1887, aged 63, m. (pub. Apr. 3, 1849, in Durham), Hannah Butler, d. Nov. 24, 1904, aged 87.

SHEPARD, Charles H., b. Jan. 31, 1837, d. Aug. 20, 1919, m. Mar. 24, 1861, in Tuftonboro, Carrie F. Bean, b. 1839, d. 1900, dau. of Rev. Silas F.

SHEPARD, Joseph F., of Lake Village, m. Oct. 6, 1869, in Lebanon, Me., Lavinia A. Orrell.

SHERBURNE, Gideon, m. June 12, 1803, by Rev. Benjamin Balch, Betsey Chesley, d. Nov. 21, 1861, aged 80, both of Barrington.

SHERBURNE, Elder Samuel, son of Gideon, b. Oct. 23, 1803, d. Aug. 8, 1861, aged 58, m. July 12, 1831, by Rev. William Demeritt, Elizabeth Swain, b. Oct. 21, 1810, dau. of Deac. Daniel, both of Barrington.

SHERBURNE, Joel F., m. (pub. Jan. 9, 1862, in Barrington), Eliza A. Young, both of Barrington.

SHERBURNE, Alphonzo Lafayette, son of Elder Samuel J., b. Feb. 1, 1840, m. May 7, 1863, in Dover, Hannah O. Batchelder, both of Barrington.

SHERMAN, Martin W., d. Sep. 23, 1878, aged 68, m. int. Jun. 20, 1841, in Lebanon, Me., Olive A. Hersom, d. Sep. 30, 1891, aged 79.

SHERMAN, Thomas Jr., m. May 6, 1855, in Acton, Me., Abby Elizabeth Fox, of Acton, Me., d. Jun. 16, 1877, aged 54, dau. of Jonathan.

SHERMAN, Enoch Piper, m. (1) int. Dec. 11, 1858, in Lebanon, Me., Jane N. Guptill, d. Oct. 1, 1861, aged 29, m. (2) May 16, 1863, in Lebanon, Me., Mary Ricker, b. Apr. 10, 1837, d. Jun. 1, 1889, dau. of Ebenezer.

SHERMAN, Hiram W., of Pawtucket, R. I., m. Nov. 8, 1864, in Rochester, Susan Sanborn, of Rochester.

SHERMAN, Edward B., of Tiverton, R. I., m. Oct. 16, 1868, by Rev. Alden Sherwin, Hannah A. Wallace, of Farmington.

SHOREY, Ichabod, m. int. Jan. 1801, in Lebanon, Me., Polly Hilton.

SHOREY, John, m. int. Aug. 1801, in Lebanon, Me., Sally Wentworth.

SHOREY, Henry L., m. (1) (pub. Mar. 20, 1849, in Great Falls), Margaret A. Decater, m. (2) int. Sept. 29, 1858, in Rollinsford, Ruth M. Goodwin, of Berwick, Me., d. Oct. 9, 1863, aged 25, dau. of Ichabod.

SHOREY, John G., d. 1885, m. Jun. 30, 1857, in Dover, Amanda Austin, both of Somersworth.

SHOREY, Ezra, m. Jan. 1, 1866, in Rochester, Abbie J. Parshley, d. Apr. 29, 1897, aged 50, dau. of John.

SHOREY, Nathaniel L. Jr., of Rochester, son of Nathaniel, d. Sep. 27, 1914, aged 75, m. Feb. 20, 1866, in Great Falls, Mary E. Corson, of Lebanon, Me.

SHOREY, Stephen F., son of Stephen, d. Mar. 12, 1905, aged 67, m. (pub. Dec. 13, 1866, in Portland, Me.), Abby L. Horne, both of Rochester.

SHOREY, John, of S. Berwick, Me., m. Dec. 21, 1867, in N. Berwick, Me., Abby E. Fernald, of N. Berwick, Me.

SHORTRIDGE, John S., of Brookfield, aged 31, m. int. Dec. 27, 1867, in Brookfield, Susan E. Mitchell, of New Durham, aged 19.

SHORTRIDGE, George F., of Brookfield, aged 34, m. int. Feb. 3, 1869, in Brookfield, Carrie M. Mason, of Somersworth, aged 28.

SHUTE, Albert T., b. Sept. 11, 1846, d. Feb. 10, 1896, m. June 4, 1867, by Rev. James Rand, Josephine A. Dame, b. 1854, d. Sept. 25, 1936, both of Dover.

SIAS, Archelaus, m. int. Nov. 12, 1838, in Lebanon, Me., Melissa Hodsdon.

SIMES, William, of Milton, son of Bray W., b. Dec. 22, 1803, d. Dec. 17, 1907, aged 76, m. (1) Jan. 3, 1858, in Wakefield, Sarah E. Churchill, of Brookfield, b. Sept. 7, 1834, d. May 24, 1863, aged 25, dau. of Eben C., m. (2) Feb. 26, 1865, in Dover, Amanda Vickery.

SIMES, John U., son of Bray U., b. June 7, 1836, d. Sept. 28, 1927, m. Oct. 1, 1863, in Dover, Nancy R. Jewett, b. Jan. 31, 1839, d. Apr. 4, 1904, dau. of Asa, both of Milton.

SIMES, Edward S., son of Bray U., b. Sept. 30, 1842, d. Sept. 9, 1927, m. Mar. 29, 1868, Mary E. Lowd, b. Feb. 28, 1845, d. Dec. 25, 1920, dau. of Sylvester.

SIMMONS, William R., m. Dec. 27, 1865, by Rev. James Rand, Martha C. Rust, both of Rochester.

SIMPSON, Capt. Andrew Lapish, son of Andrew, b. Oct. 2, 1800, m. Sep. 23, 1840, Lydia Kelley, b. Jan. 31, 1814, d. May 31, 1895, dau. of Benjamin.

SINCLAIR, Leander D., d. Oct. 28, 1889, aged 83, m. (1) (pub. Mar. 6, 1832, in Ossipee), Olive W. Kimball, d. May 28, 1867, aged 55, m. (2) Sept. 18, 1867, in Great Falls, Mrs. Ada Spencer.

SINCLAIR, Moses, d. May 24, 1904, aged 62, m. Oct. 31, 1864, in Ossipee, Achsa A. Wentworth, d. Mar. 4, 1906, aged 66.

SINCLAIR, Jeremiah, of Ossipee, d. June 10, 1888, aged 54, m. Dec. 22, 1868, in Ossipee, Susie M. Gilman, of Wakefield, d. Nov. 18, 1883, aged 38.

SLEEPER, John V. B., of W. Alton, m. Oct. 26, 1862, in W. Alton, Abbie E. Sanborn, of Gilford.

SLEEPER, George W., of Alton, m. Sept. 26, 1869, in Middleton, Mrs. Lydia J. (Pinkham) Horne, of Farmington, wid. of William B.

SLOPER, Joshua, m. Apr. 13, 1789, by Rev. Benjamin Balch, Sarah Brown, both of Barrington.

SLOPER, John F., m. Mar. 12, 1868, in Strafford, Marilla J. Swain, both of Strafford.

SLYDER, Jacob D., of York, Pa., m. Jan. 14, 1869, in Clayton, Ill., Mary A. Tuttle, of Dover.

SMALL, Edwin E., m. (pub. Sept. 2, 1869, in Rochester), Annie R. Hall.

SMALLCORN, Robert, b. Jul. 14, 1804, m. Oct. 14, 1831, in Lebanon, Me., Eunice Wentworth, b. Dec. 28, 1813, dau. of Jedediah, both of Dover.

SMART, James, illegitimate son of F. Sharp, b. Sept. 12, 1796, d. Sept. 24, 1863, m. Oct. 12, 1818, by Rev. John Osborne, Lois Grover, b. Apr. 27, 1795, d. Oct. 19, 1875, both of New Durham.

SMART, Samuel, of Newmarket, m. (pub. June 21, 1853, in Newmarket), Alice Ann Jones, of Durham, b. Jun. 19, 1820, d. Jul. 9, 1912, dau. of Thomas.

SMART, Amos, of Durham, d. Apr. 6, 1863, aged 26, m. Nov. 28, 1860, by Rev. Alvin Tobey, Harriet E. Gage, of Boston, Mass,

SMART, Samuel G., m. (pub. Apr. 19, 1866, in Portsmouth), Mary W. Garland, of Rye.

SMELLIE, John, m. Apr. 8, 1869, in Dover, Martha Southwick, both of Dover.

SMITH, George J. O., son of John, b. 1808, d. Nov. 14, 1888, m. Abigail A. Downs, b. 1810, d Apr. 14, 1900, dau. of Jonathan.

SMITH, James, of Durham, d. Aug. 15, 1811, aged 50, m. Dec. 5, 1784, by Dr. Belknap, Eleanor Waldron, b. May 28, 1766, d. Dec. 4, 1792, aged 26, dau. of Thomas Westbrooke Waldron.

SMITH, William, of Rye, m. Oct. 19, 1807, by Rev. Micajah Otis, Peggy Felker, of Barrington.

SMITH, Daniel, m. Apr. 2, 1820, by Elder Enoch Place, Sally Tuttle, d. Mar. 28, 1851, aged 49, dau. of Enoch, both of Barrington.

SMITH, Capt. Alfred, m. May 25, 1823, Clarissa Blydenburgh, b. June 16, 1793, d. Mar. 29, 1861, dau. of John.

SMITH, William Blake, b. Apr. 20, 1804, d. Jan. 23, 1867, m. (1) Apr. 10, 1829, Hannah Diman, b. Jan. 19, 1808, d. May 3, 1835, dau. of Capt. Samuel, m. (2) in 1836, Mary A. Hardy, b. July 2, 1814, d. Dec. 17, 1888, aged 73 yrs., 5 mos., 15 das., dau. of Stephen.

SMITH, John S. Jr., of Barrington, b. 1810, d. 1880, m. July 23, 1833, by Elder Enoch Place, Sarah Ann Smith, of Strafford, d. June 25, 1871, aged 64, dau. of Ebenezer.

SMITH, Deac. Ebenezer Jr., of Strafford, son of Ebenezer, d. Jan. 13, 1894, aged 83, m. Apr. 6, 1834, by Elder Enoch Place, Mary Smith, of Barrington, dau. of John, d. Dec. 6, 1887, aged 74.

SMITH, Lewis E., m. (pub. Jul. 27, 1847, in Somersworth), Emeline S. Beal, d. Jan. 19, 1888, aged 61, dau. of Woodman.

SMITH, Jacob B., of Bradford, Mass., b. 1818, d. Dec. 30, 1888, m. May 3, 1849, by Elder Enoch Place, Mary Ann Parshley, of Strafford, dau. of John, b. 1818, d. Oct. 18, 1870.

SMITH, Bartlett, son of John, aged 24, m. Apr. 2, 1850, by Rev. Levi B. Tasker, in Sandwich, Rosannah George, aged 21, dau. of Levi, both of Holderness.

SMITH, John, of Dover, b. 1829, d. Dec. 4, 1898, m. June 3, 1850, by Elder Elias Hutchins, Ruth Ella Seavey, of Alton, b. 1831, d. Mar. 23, 1899.

SMITH, George, m. June 4, 1850, by Rev. Levi B. Tasker, in Sandwich, Hannah M. Frost, dau. of Joseph, both of Sandwich.

SMITH, Joseph Harris, aged 26, born in Meredith, m. (1) June 26, 1850, by Elder Enoch Place, Olive Ann Foss, aged 20, born in Strafford, d. Dec. 25, 1852, aged 22, dau. of Isaac, m. (2) Aug. 2, 1865, in Malden, Mass., Mrs. Harriet S. Wiggin, of Dover.

SMITH, Jacob G., m. (pub. Nov. 9, 1852, in Somersworth), Betsey E. Gerrish, d. Mar. 1, 1866, aged 38.

SMITH, John Q. A., b. Oct. 3, 1825, d. Aug. 12, 1885, m. June 8, 1853, in Dover, Mary Riley, d. Oct. 10, 1863, aged 38, dau. of Capt. John.

SMITH, Stephen, of Nottingham, aged 31, m. Nov. 21, 1855, in Newmarket, Mary A. Burley, of Newmarket, aged 23.

SMITH, Capt. George J. O., b. near 1826, m. Aug. 27, 1856, Connie Waldron Riley, b. near 1834, dau. of Capt. John, both were lost at sea, in 1865, on way to China.

SMITH, Samuel E., d. Feb. 15, 1865, aged 34, m. Nov. 26, 1856, by Rev. Alvin Tobey, Ann Demeritt, d. June 4, 1916, aged 77, both of Durham.

SMITH, Dr. Jeremiah, b. July 14, 1837, m. (1) Oct. 10, 1858, in Dover, Angeline Horn, both of Dover, m. (2) int. Apr. 5, 1865, in Lee, Hannah M. Webster, of Dover, b. Jan. 29, 1835, dau. of Daniel K.

SMITH, Wesley M., of Dover, son of Irving, d. Mar. 27, 1890, aged 52, m. Aug. 10, 1859, in Dover, Olive S. Edwards, of Lyman, Me.

SMITH, Jacob Jewett, of Rowley, Mass., m. Oct. 1859, Harriet Boardman, dau. of Capt. George Young.

SMITH, Noah, m. (pub. Oct. 11, 1860, in Great Falls), Georgiana Prior, d. Jul. 31, 1889, aged 45, dau. of Joseph, both of Great Falls.

SMITH, Andrew P., of Somersworth, m. Jan. 24, 1863, in Great Falls, Fannie F. Bray, of Kittery Point, Me.

SMITH, Wesley G., of Somersworth, m. Feb. 25, 1864, in Dover, Lizzie Y. Carle, of Hollis, Me.

SMITH, Andrew, of Effingham, m. June 16, 1864, in Lawrence, Mass., Laura B. Pilling, of N. Andover, Mass.

SMITH, Charles B., of Strafford, d. Jan. 28, 1868, aged 24, m. Aug. 7, 1864, in Dover, Sarah W. Kimball, of Dover, d. Sept. 30, 1873, aged 27.

SMITH, John Q. A., m. Jan. 3, 1865, by Rev. Ezra Haskell, Lucretia Riley, d. Feb. 20, 1916, aged 86, dau. of Capt. John.

SMITH, James C., of Berwick, Me., m. Jan. 6, 1865, in Berwick, Me., Mrs. Luella Wentworth, of Sanford, Me.

SMITH, Samuel R., of Limerick, Me., son of Samuel B., m. Oct. 9, 1865, in Durham, Carrie E. Doe, of Durham, dau. of Alfred S.

SMITH, Herman J., of Dover, m. Oct. 26, 1865, in Woodstock, Vt., Belle S. Anderson, of Woodstock, Vt., dau. of Dexter.

SMITH, Alvin, of Winthrop, Me., m. Apr. 27, 1867, in Rochester, Vienna Wentworth, of Rochester.

SMITH, Andrew J., m. (pub. June 20, 1867, in Portsmouth), Mrs. Mary L. Whitten, of Rochester.

SMITH, John M., of Kennebunkport, Me., m. Aug. 6, 1867, by Rev. Alden Sherwin, Elvira R. Hanscom, of Lyman, Me.

SMITH, John W., of Dover, son of Henry, d. Jan. 1, 1925, aged 83, m. June 28, 1868, by Rev. Robert S. Stubbs, Sarah J. Embry, of Buxton, Me., d. Sept. 6, 1889, aged 53, dau. of Josiah.

SMITH, Byron W., m. Jan. 2, 1869, by Rev. James Rand, Josephine H. Bennett, both of Northwood.

SMITH, Josiah, m. Apr. 4, 1869, in Rochester, Mrs. Mary (Cowell) Prescott, wid. of Daniel, d. Aug. 24, 1889, aged 65.

SMITH, Charles A., of Milton, m. (pub. May 27, 1869, in Great Falls), Susie S. Stover, of Blue Hill, Me.

SMITH, David F., m. Nov. 25, 1869, in Dover, Nellie F. Chick, of Portland, Me.

SMITH, Robert, of Brookfield, aged 26, m. int. May 1870, in Brookfield, Mrs. Ruhama Geralds, of Brookfield, aged 41.

SMITH, John N., m. (pub. Dec. 22, 1870, in Rochester), Delia McDuffee.

SNELL, Nathaniel, son of John, d. Aug. 16, 1863, aged 62, m. Feb. 6, 1832, by Rev. William Demeritt, Avis Williams, d. Feb. 26, 1862., aged 55.

SNELL, Alfred, m. int. Jun. 19, 1853, in Lee, Emily A. Page, d. Jan. 11, 1915, aged 80, dau. of Daniel, both of Lee.

SNELL, Rev. Nehemiah C., of Lee, son of Paul, d. May 17, 1893, m. Dec. 14, 1858, in Barrington, Mrs. Martha A. (Hanson) Langley, of Madbury, wid. of John C., b. Apr. 18, 1836, d. Jun. 4, 1920.

SNELL, Timothy H., of Dover, m. May 4, 1862, in Center Strafford, Amanda M. Foss, of Barrington.

SNELL, George C., m. May 14, 1868, in Dover, Hannah M. Pierce, both of Dover.

SNOW, John, m. Oct. 1, 1788, in Barrington, Hannah Watson, both of Barrington.

SNOW, Martin, of Farmington, m. (pub. Aug. 18, 1870, in Rochester), Lydia A. Goodwin, of Rochester.

SPAULDING, Alanson, of Manchester, m. July 30, 1866, in Dover, Clara M. Philpot, of Great Falls.

SPEAR, Alphonzo Augustus, of W. Buxton, Me., d. Jan. 29, 1912, aged 69, m. Jan. 13, 1867, in Ossipee, Sarah E. Hodsdon, d. July 18, 1924, aged 80.

SPENCER, Ebenezer, of Nottingham, m. July 14, 1791, in Barrington, Mehitable Buzzell, of Barrington.

SPENCER, Israel, m. July 30, 1792, by Rev. Benjamin Balch, Betsey Sloper, both of Barrington.

SPENCER, John, of Berwick, Me., m. Feb. 2, 1820, by Elder Zebedee Delanop, Abigail Wentworth.

SPENCER, Allen, m. Nov. 22, 1866, in Rochester, Mrs. Elizabeth McQuesten.

SPINNEY, Ephraim, d. June 24, 1807, m. Feb. 11, 1796, by Rev. William Hooper, Deborah Pendexter, d. Oct. 26, 1848, aged 70, both of Durham.

SPINNEY, Elias, of Acton, Me., m. Mar. 12, 1863, in Wakefield, Nancy Pinkham, of Milton, dau. of Charles.
SPINNEY, James T., of Wakefield, m. Nov. 1, 1863, in Wakefield, Mary A. Farnham, of Milton.
SPRAGUE, Levi A. H., of Newfield, Me., m. Aug. 5, 1868, in Effingham, Lydia Treadwell, of Kennebunk, Me.
SPRINGER, George H., m. Mar. 16, 1868, in Dover, Cynthia E. Blanchard, of Yarmouth.
SPRINGFIELD, Charles W., of Rochester, m. Sept. 6, 1863, in Rochester, Mary E. Cate, of Alton, d. Apr. 29, 1921, aged 77, dau. of Eleazer R.
SPURLIN, Hanson, son of Jonathan L., d. Oct. 19, 1883, aged 53, m. (1) Aug. 18, 1852, in Dover, Abby Freeman, both of Dover, m. (2) Mar. 13, 1862, in Dover, Lydia Whitehouse, m. (3) July 29, 1864, in Dover, Mrs. Hannah Yeaton, of Newcastle.
SPURLIN, Charles F., of Pittsfield, son of Thomas Jr., b. Jan. 3, 1843, d. Oct. 19, 1916, m. (1) Dec. m. Dec. 8, 1869, in Dover, Mary E. Tucker, of Dover, b. Feb. 10, 1857, m. (2) Sept. 5, 1870, by Rev. James Thurston, Mary Eliza Cook, b. Feb. 10, 1851, both of Dover.
SPURLING, Robert, of Madbury, m. int. Mar. 13, 1823, in Lebanon, Me., Betsey Lord.
1) SPURLING, Thomas, d. July 6, 1840, aged 86, m. Bridget Bunker, d. Nov. 22, 1831, dau. of James.
SPURLING, George A., b. Nov. 16, 1844, d. Sept. 28, 1931, aged 86, m. Nov. 11, 1866, in Dover, Ellen A. Hall, d. Dec. 2, 1882, aged 34, both of Dover.
4) **STACKPOLE**, Lt. Samuel, son of Joshua, b. Oct. 17, 1740, d. July 23, 1834, m. near 1766, Zervia or Zibiah Watson, d. Oct. 12, 1820, aged 79, dau. of Isaac.
STACKPOLE, Edmund, m. (1) Feb. 19, 1792, by Rev. Isaac Hasey, Lydia Haridson, m. (2) int. Oct. 5, 1805, in Lebanon, Me., Sarah Abbott.
STACKPOLE, William, m. (1) Nov. 19, 1795, by Rev. Isaac Hasey, Sally Haridson, m. (2) int. May 10, 1806, in Lebanon, Me., Sally Gerrish.
STACKPOLE, Otis, son of Joshua, m. early as 1797, Dorcas ----, d. Aug. 29, 1836, aged 78.
STACKPOLE, Joshua, m. Sep. 9, 1798, by Rev. Isaac Hasey, Aphia Keay.

STACKPOLE, Samuel, m. Jul. 2, 1806, by Elder Zebedee Delano, Sally Brock.
STACKPOLE, George, m. Feb. 6, 1823, in Lebanon, Me., Joanna Jones.
STACKPOLE, Edmund, m. Dec. 7, 1823, in Lebanon, Me., Eunice Pray.
STACKPOLE, James, of Dover, m. Mar. 18, 1827, in Lebanon, Me., Dorothy Pray.
STACKPOLE, Isaac, m. int. Aug. 27, 1831, in Lebanon, Me., Syrena Marston, of Parsonsfield, Me.
6) STACKPOLE, Peter Morrill, son of Thomas, b. May 5, 1803, d. Feb. 22, 1881, m. May 22, 1834, Mary D. Canney, b. Nov. 14, 1809, d. May 3, 1915, dau. of John.
STACKPOLE, Edwin L., of Rollinsford, d. Jan. 21, 1883, aged 52, m. (pub. Aug. 6, 1850, in S. Berwick, Me.), Mary Jane Welch, of S. Berwick, Me., b. 1830, d. 1906.
STACKPOLE, Thomas, of Somersworth, son of Moses, b. Jul. 5, 1826, d. Feb. 7, 1890, m. Jan. 1, 1858, by Rev. Arthur Caverno, Mary E. Mudget, of Dover, b. Jul. 9, 1836, d. Feb. 5, 1898, dau. of Isaac.
STACKPOLE, George L., of Tuftonboro, m. Aug. 4, 1866, by Rev. James Rand, Martha A. McDuffee, of Rochester, d. Oct. 27, 1911, aged 65, dau. of Daniel.
STACKPOLE, Albert S., m. Mar. 8, 1867, in Lebanon, Me. Lavinia M. Curry.
STACKPOLE, Charles H., of Dover, m. Mar. 15, 1868, in Dover, Annie M. Carter, of E. Kingston.
STACKPOLE, Simon R., m. Oct. 31, 1869, by Rev. Ezra Haskell, Martha J. Horne, of Kittery, Me.
STACY, Elder Robert B., m. (1) Dec. 9, 1827, by Rev. William Demeritt, Lydia Ann Wiggin, b. Jan. 16, 1811, d. July 3, 1863, dau. of James, m. (2) Oct. 1, 1863, in Newmarket, Mehitable (Smith) Ham, wid. of Oliver P., b. 1809, dau. of Samuel.
STACY, Oliver C., m. Jan. 30, 1866, in Dover, Lydia A. Emery, b. May 7, 1851, d. Aug. 19, 1921, dau. of King, both of Eliot, Me.
STANTON, William, son of William, b. 1768, d. July 28, 1828, aged 60, m. Apr. 9, 1792, by Rev. Benjamin Balch, Margaret Holmes, d. Apr. 6, 1848, aged 79, both of Barrington.
STANTON, James, son of Benjamin, b. Dec. 11, 1790, d. Aug. 28, 1867, m. Jan. 16, 1812, by Rev. Isaac Hasey, Sabra Wentworth, b. Dec. 24, 1792, d. Apr. 6, 1872.

STANTON, Simon, m. Jan. 12, 1814, in Brookfield, by Elder Benjamin Burnham, Sally Martin, both of Brookfield.
STANTON, Ezra, son of John, d. Jan. 30, 1872, aged 79, m. Dec. 1819, by Rev. Micajah Otis, Polly Otis, d. May 26, 1878, aged 76.
STANTON, Brackett, m. Mar. 19, 1851, in Saco, Me., Catharine White.
STANTON, Levi W., of Newburyport, Mass., son of James, aged 29, m. Aug. 17, 1858, in Sandwich, Anna T. Burleigh, of Sandwich, aged 20, dau. of Thomas.
STAPLES, Nathaniel, m. int. Sep. 3, 1814, in Lebanon, Me., Mary Wentworth.
STAPLES, Nicholas W., d. Jan. 12, 1849, m. Nov. 23, 1814, by Rev. Paul Jewett, Olive Ricker, d. Dec. 4, 1871.
STAPLES, Oliver, of Berwick, Me., m. Nov. 1, 1821, in Lebanon, Me., Mary Wentworth.
STAPLES, John P., m. int. Jul. 23, 1843, in Lebanon, Me., Harriet Libbey, of No. Berwick, Me.
STAPLES, John Henry, aged 38, m. Apr. 4, 1850, in Sandwich, Mrs. Mary Ann (Quimby) George, aged 40, wid. of John.
STAPLES, John, m. int. Dec. 19, 1854, in Lebanon, Me. May Roberson, both of Milton.
STAPLES, Christopher C. B., of Effingham, m. June 26, 1864, in Effingham, Julia A. Welch, of Ossipee.
STAPLES, John W., m. June 8, 1867, by Rev. Robert S. Stubbs, <u>Mrs</u>. Nellie M. Hawkins, <u>both of Dover</u>.
STARBIRD, Stephen, d. Dec. 15, 1869, aged 80, m. (1) Jan. 18, 1818, by Rev. Federal Burt, Tamson Nute, m. (2) Caroline (Teague) Davis, wid. of Daniel, <u>b. Mar. 1, 1795, d. Feb. 22, 1882</u>.
STARK, William, m. before Oct. 7, 1848, in Lebanon, Me., Sarah Honesly.
STEARNS, <u>Col</u>. William, m. Dec. 12, 1826, by Rev. R. Porter, in Barrington, Martha Winkley, of Barrington, <u>dau. of John</u>.
STEARNS, Samuel F., of Watertown, Mass., m. June 22, 1867, in Lynn, Mass., Carrie M. Glines, of Dover.
STEEL, James C., m. Apr. 2, 1862, in Dover, <u>Mrs</u>. Sarah A. Spinney, <u>both of Dover</u>.
STEEL, James H., of Ellington, Conn., m. May 24, 1865, in Portsmouth, Sarah B. Kenney, dau. of Capt. Hamti.
STERLING, Capt. Henry H., b. 1849, d. 1917, m. Sept. 18, 1867, in Dover, Mary A. Buzzell, b. 1849, d. Feb. 4, 1926, dau. of Miles R., <u>both of Dover</u>.

STERLING, Walter S., m. Dec. 31, 1868, by Rev. Robert S. Stubbs, Abby Coleman, both of Dover.

STEVENS, Henry, m. Apr. 22, 1778, by Rev. Isaac Hasey, Mary Farnham.

STEVENS, John, b. July 30, 1778, d. 1847, m. 1802, Lydia Horne, b. Nov. 12, 1773, d. 1848.

STEVENS, Benjamin, m. Mar. 16, 1786, in Lebanon, Me., Elly Stanton.

STEVENS, Joseph, m. int. May 6, 1809, in Lebanon, Me., Molly Canney.

STEVENS, Joseph, of Lee, d. before Aug. 30, 1820, m. 1810 by Rev. John Osborne, Catharine T. Gile, of Durham, d. Apr. 6, 1860, aged 68.

STEVENS, Paul, m. Nov. 24, 1814, by Rev. Paul Jewett, Mary Clark.

STEVENS, Henry, of Shapleigh, m. Apr. 18, 1824, in Lebanon, Me., Isabella Chaney, of Sanford, Me.

STEVENS, Ivory, d. May 4, 1878, aged 79, m. Mar. 17, 1825, in Berwick, Me., Dordana Richmond, b. Oct. 14, 1805, d. Feb. 12, 1890.

STEVENS, Emery, of Effingham, b. Nov. 2, 1811, d. Sept. 21, 1880, m. (1) Oct. 15, 1845, by Rev. Moses Dow, Eliza Ann Prescott, b. Aug. 4, 1809, d. Jan. 23, 1846, m. (2) Abigail H. ----, b. Nov. 4, 1806, d. Aug. 27, 1871.

STEVENS, Benjamin, son of John, d. Sep. 12, 1905, aged 82, m. Dec. 9, 1847, by Rev. Alpheus D. Smith, Louisa J. Young, d. Apr. 11, 1897, aged 77, dau. of Paul D.

STEVENS, Parker Jr., m. Sep. 19, 1849, by Elder John Hubbard, Elizabeth Gowell, both of Durham.

STEVENS, Charles P., m. May 4, 1852, by Elder Charles Corson, Sarah Wallingford.

STEVENS, Daniel, b. 1827, d. 1868, m. Nov. 27, 1855, in Sandwich, Mary E. Hoitt, b. 1835, d. 1927, both of Tuftonboro.

STEVENS, Mark, m. Nov. 22, 1856, in Brookfield, Mary M. Trask, both of Brookfield.

STEVENS, Caleb F., m. int. Oct. 27, 1864, in Lebanon, Me., Carrie M. Swett, of Knox, Me.

STEVENS, James D., of Alton, m. Apr. 30, 1865, in Washington, D. C., Caroline F. Brown, of Wolfeboro.

STEVENS, Herbert F., m. Mar. 18, 1868, in Exeter, Nancy H. Adams, both of Wakefield.

STEVENS, Orrin, of Great Falls, m. (pub. July 30, 1868, in Great Falls), Mary E. Marston, of Parsonsfield, Me.
STEVENS, Charles A., <u>of Lawrence, Mass.</u>, <u>aged 22, m. int. Jun. 6, 1868</u>, m. Sept. 14, 1868, by Rev. Robert S. Stubbs, in Brookfield, Laura A. Blake, <u>of Brookfield, aged 20</u>.
STEVENS, Jacob B., of Acton, Me., m. Jun. 4, 1870, by Rev. Ira C. Guptill, Charlotte M. Shapleigh.
STEVENSON, W. S., of Portland, Me., m. (pub. Jan. 13, 1870, in Great Falls), Icilia T. Whitehouse.
STEWARD, Elder James, m. Aug. 26, 1827, by Elder Zebedee Delano, Anna Chadbourne, <u>both of Berwick, Me</u>.
STEWART, Charles M., of Kenduskeag, Me., m. int. Jul. 9, 1869, in Lebanon, Me., Julia A. Hall.
STILES, Samuel <u>Jr</u>., m. Nov. 26, 1778, <u>in Barrington</u>, Anna Foss, <u>d. Dec. 20, 1837, aged 78, both of Barrington</u>.
STILES, Samuel, of Barrington, m. June 6, 1785, by Rev. Benjamin Balch, Hepsibath Twombly, of Madbury.
STILES, William, m. Feb. 21, 1808, in Barrington, Susanna Foss, both of Barrington.
STILES, Lewis, b. 1821, <u>d. 1894</u>, m. Jan. 29, 1845, by Elder Enoch Place, Hannah <u>Susan</u> Sloper, b. 1823, <u>d. Nov. 5, 1903</u>, dau. of <u>John</u>, both of Strafford.
STILES, Moses, of Somersworth, <u>d. Sept. 15, 1907, aged 79</u>, m. (pub. Sept. 15, 1846, in S. Berwick, Me.), Hannah Walker, of S. Berwick, Me., <u>d. July 17, 1909, aged 85</u>.
STILES, William L., Jr., <u>of Watertown, Mass</u>., m. Apr. 27, 1864, in Dover, Mary A. Glines, <u>of Dover</u>.
STILES, John H., m. May 30, 1866, in Strafford, Salinda I. Brown.
STILLINGS, Alfred, m. Oct. 11, 1865, by Rev. James Rand, Leonora L. Hayes, <u>both of Bartlett</u>.
STILLINGS, Albert D., of Ossipee, son of Richard, d. Apr. 7, 1914, aged 81, m. July 28, 1866, in N. Conway, Emma B. Fogg, of Minot, Me.
STILLINGS, James G., of Acton, Me., m. Feb. 23, 1867, in New Durham, Sophronia E. Corson, of New Durham.
STILLINGS, Eli N., m. Mar. 9, 1868, in Great Falls, Mary E. Guptill, both of Berwick, Me.
STILLINGS, Albert F., of Boston, Mass., m. (pub. Apr. 22, 1869, in Boston, Mass.), Electa A. Shapleigh, of Great Falls.
STOCKBRIDGE, John, of Alton, m. Feb. 12, 1803, by Rev. Benjamin Balch, Abigail Gray, of Barrington.

STOCKBRIDGE, Capt. George, d. May 27, 1859, aged 73, m. Mar. 28, 1811, by Rev. Joseph Boodey, Jamima Leighton, d. Aug. 15, 1855, aged 67, both of Alton.

STOCKBRIDGE, Reuben, d. Dec. 27, 1884, aged 80, m. int. Oct. 1826, in Tuftonboro, Hannah Piper, d. June 27, 1888, aged 84, both of Tuftonboro.

STOCKBRIDGE, Abednego, son of John, m. (1) Mar. 11, 1838, by Rev. Israel E. Jones, Maria Clough, d. Apr. 30, 1854, aged 45, both of Alton, m. (2) July 14, 1856, in Barnstead, Mary Thurston, both of Alton.

STONE, Asa F., of Ipswich, Mass., m. Mar. 26, 1865, in Strafford, Mary Ann Foss, of Strafford.

STONE, Edwin A., m. Jan. 22, 1866, by Rev. Francis E. Abbott, Jennie P. Clement, both of Franklin.

STONE, James L., m. (pub. Sept. 9, 1869, in Great Falls), Laura E. Guptill, both of N. Berwick, Me.

STORER, Jedediah, m. Nov. 23, 1828, in Lebanon, Me., Mary Emery, both of Sanford, Me.

STORER, George H., of Wells, Me., m. Aug. 4, 1863, in Rochester, Lavina York, of Dover.

STRATTON, Ephraim M., m. Mar. 11, 1849, by Rev. Theodore Wells, Elizabeth H. Seavey, both of Barrington.

STRAW, Alonzo, of Alton, m. (pub. Feb. 16, 1865, in Alton), Ruth Ellen Varney, of Tuftonboro.

STREETER, Reuben M., of Toledo, Ohio, m. Aug. 24, 1870, in Durham, Lucia M. Olcott, of Boston, Mass.

STUBBS, Rev. Robert S., of Dover, m. May 15, 1867, in Nashua, M. E. Otterson, of Nashua.

2) **SULLIVAN**, Benjamin, b. 1736, d. 1767, m. near 1760, Kesiah Grant, dau. of Charles.

2) SULLIVAN, James, b. Apr. 22, 1744, d. Dec. 10, 1808, m. (1) Feb. 22, 1768, Mehitable Odiorne, of Durham, b. June 26, 1748, d. Jan. 26, 1786, dau. of William, m. (2) Dec. 20, 1786, in Charlestown, Mass., Martha (Langdon) Simpson, d. Aug. 26, 1812, wid. of Thomas.

SWAIN, Daniel, b. Jan. 14, 1766, d. Dec. 20, 1843, m. June 15, 1789, by Rev. Benjamin Balch, Elizabeth Ayers, b. Oct. 20, 1770, d. Nov. 27, 1856, both of Barrington.

SWAIN, Richard, m. May 1, 1804, by Rev. Benjamin Balch, Abigail Bunker, both of Barrington.

SWAIN, Richard, of Barrington, m. Aug. 5, 1804, by Rev. John Osborne, Lydia Daniels, of Madbury, d. Nov. 19, 1828, aged 55.

SWAIN, Richard Jr., m. Mar. 7, 1831, in Barrington, by Rev. Samuel Sherburne, Sally Sherburne, both of Barrington.

SWAIN, Joel, m. Mar. 2, 1840, by Rev. John Winkley, Abigail Daniels, both of Strafford.

SWAIN, Greenleaf H., m. (1) June 18, 1859, in Dover, Marcia O. Brock, both of Barrington, m. (2) Oct. 2, 1867, in Lowell, Mass., Sarah E. P. Bodge, both of Barrington.

SWAIN, Truman C., of Dover, son of Daniel, d. Dec. 10, 1863, aged 22, m. Aug. 23, 1862, in Dover, Lizzie Mitchell, of Lawrence, Mass.

SWAIN, Charles G., of Barrington, m. Mar. 7, 1865, in Strafford, Hester A. Brown, of New Hampton.

SWAN, Edmund M., m. Nov. 23, 1864, in Dover, Susan F. Clark, both of Dover.

SWASEY, George A., of Milton, m. Nov. 24, 1859, in Milton, Lizzie M. Fernald, d. Jan. 27, 1887, aged 47.

SWASEY, John R., of Brentwood, m. Dec. 25, 1863, in Lebanon, Me., Martha J. Fall.

SWEAT, John, son of Josiah, m. Nov. 3, 1811, by Rev. Jeremiah Shaw, Sarah Pierce, both of Turftonboro.

SWEAT, Robert, son of Josiah, b. 1789, d. 1835, m. Dec. 1812, by Rev. Jeremiah Shaw, Polly Wiggin, b. 1792, d. 1865, both of Tuftonboro.

SWEAT, Dr. Moses, of Parsonsfield, Me., m. Mar. 21, 1863, in Ossipee, Mary Abbie Young, of Wakefield.

SWETT, Samuel, of Wolfeboro, d. Aug. 1, 1867, aged 80, m. May 23, 1813, in Wolfeboro, Mehitable Neal, of Tuftonboro, d. Oct. 24, 1870, aged 85.

SWETT, John, son of Samuel, d. Mar. 15, 1886, aged 72, m. (pub. Nov. 12, 1839, in Tuftonboro), Lydia S. McIntire, d. May 7, 1878, aged 63.

SWINERTON, Dr. John L., son of John, b. 1805, d. Nov. 2, 1882, m. Apr. 25, 1832, by Rev. Samuel Nichols, Ann A. Robinson, b. 1803, d. Sep. 13, 1880, both of Wolfeboro.

SWINERTON, Charles, son of Dr. John L., b. 1834, d. 1903, m. Oct. 23, 1864, by Rev. Asa Piper, Abby C. Wentworth, b. 1798, d. 1887.

SYKES, George, m. July 20, 1868, by Rev. Alden Sherwin, Mary E. Flack, both of Dover.

SYMMES, William, son of Timothy, b. June 10, 1820, d. Apr. 12, 1907, m. Feb. 22, 1847, by Rev. Mr. Greely, Nancy G. Hanson, d. Nov. 3, 1901, aged 72, dau. of Robert, both of Somersworth.

SYMMES, Ebenezer H., of Newfield, Me., m. May 31, 1862, in Great Falls, Mrs. Olive A. Brown, d. Sep. 12, 1878, of Great Falls.

TALBOT, Edwin R., of Boston, Mass., m. July 1, 1869, in Dover, Mary A. Wentworth, of Dover.

TANNER, George, m. July 3, 1869, in Dover, Ellen Young, both of Rochester.

TAPLEY, Charles W., of Cape Neddick, Me., m. Jan. 18, 1863, in New Durham, m. Abby Berry, dau. of Rev. N. Berry.

TAPLEY, William R., of Dover, m. Oct. 1, 1863, in Portsmouth, Clara A. Haley, dau. of Capt. J. B. Haley.

TARBOX, Thomas B., of Biddeford, Me., m. (pub. Feb. 17, 1870, in Portsmouth), Emma Hutchins, of Wakefield.

TARLTON, Capt. Herman A., m. Oct. 11, 1866, in Portsmouth, Anna Louise Ham, dau. of Henry.

TARR, John W., m. Dec. 1, 1869, in Dover, Clara J. Peasley, both of Whitefield, Me.

TASH, Deac. John, d. Aug. 3, 1811, aged 71, m. Mary Ham, d. Dec. 3, 1848, aged 98, dau. of James.

TASKER, James, m. Mar. 4, 1786, Charity Church, both of Barrington.

TASKER, Israel, m. Jan. 29, 1798, by Rev. Benjamin Balch, Sally Young, both of Barrington.

5) **TASKER**, Capt. William, son of Samuel, b. Aug. 11, 1781, d. June 14, 1848, m. near 1808, Lydia Batchelder, b. June 20, 1786, d. Feb. 8, 1863.

TASKER, Elisha, m. near 1809, Mary Buzzell, d. Dec. 28, 1844, aged 55, dau. of Levi.

TASKER, Nahum, of Dover, son of Nahum, d. July 12, 1888, aged 81, m. (1) Apr. 1825, in Milton, Mary Wallingford, of Milton, d. Jan. 5, 1868, aged 69, dau. of David, m. (2) Oct. 26, 1879, Mrs. Mary Hanson, aged 48, widow.

TASKER, Rev. Levi Buzzell, son of Elisha, b. Mar. 21, 1814, d. Aug. 29, 1875, m. Aug. 19, 1838, Hannah P. Caswell, dau. of William.

TASKER, Lorenzo, of Northwood, m. July 28, 1845, by Rev. Homer Barrows, Mary L. Allen, of Barrington.

TASKER, Paul Jr., m. (1) Hannah Smith, of Strafford, d. May 18, 1847, aged 41, dau. of Ebenenzer, m. (2) (pub. Jan. 18, 1848, in Northwood), Ruth S. Hanscom, both of Strafford.

TASKER, George W., m. Sep. 20, 1855, in Lebanon, Me., Lydia S. Jones.
TASKER, Nathaniel H., m. (1) (pub. Nov. 15, 1855, in Northwood), Betsey D. Garland, of Strafford, m. (2) Oct. 11, 1865, in Strafford, Mrs. Susan A. Cobb, both of Northwood.
TASKER, Andrew H., of Northwood, m. Oct. 3, 1862, in Durham, Louisa M. Snell, of Lee.
TASKER, John, of Barnstead, m. Nov. 16, 1865, in Strafford, Sarah C. Johnson, of Pittsfield.
TASKER, Hiram H., of Milton, son of Naham, aged 26, m. Oct. 28, 1866, in Lebanon, Me., Jennie M. Wiggin, aged 22, dau. of Tobias.
TASKER, John C., b. 1844, d. Jan. 2, 1919, m. Mar. 26, 1868, by Rev. Robert S. Stubbs, Mary F. Winkley, b. 1840, d. 1881, both of Dover.
TASKER, William H., m. (pub. Nov. 26, 1868, in Strafford), Sarah L. Tuttle, both of Strafford.
TASKER, Charles W., m. Oct. 9, 1869, in Dover, Maria B. Newcomb, d. Jan. 8, 1926, aged 82, both of Dover.
TATE, Palatiah, m. Mar. 15, 1799, by Rev. Isaac Hasey, Anna Hanson, bpt. Jun. 9, 1776, dau. of Daniel.
TATE, Josiah C., b. 1815, d. 1885, m. (pub. Jan. 31, 1837, in Dover), Annar Hull, b. 1813, d. 1878.
TAYLOR, Capt. Daniel, d. Oct. 23, 1821, aged 47, m. Dec. 2, 1802, Hannah Thompson, b. Oct. 26, 1765, dau. of Sgt. John.
TAYLOR, Hiram B., m. Apr. 23, 1863, in Dover, Almira Ham, both of N. Berwick, Me.
TAYLOR, Timothy C., m. Mar. 21, 1866, in Effingham, Hattie B. Brown.
TAYLOR, Truman J., of Woodbury, Vt., b. 1834, d. 1871, m. May 30, 1866, by Rev. James Rand, Caroline E. Wortman, of Dover, b. 1844, d. June 17, 1913, dau. of Capt. Richard.
TAYLOR, Col. J. D., of Cambridge, Ohio, m. Dec. 11, 1866, in Boston, Mass., E. A. Hill, of N. Berwick, Me.
TEBBETS, Ebenezer, son of Moses, b. Mar. 16, 1739, m. Apr. 21, 1757, by Rev. Amos Main, Olive Dore of Lebanon, Me., dau. of Philip.
5) TEBBETS, Elijah Jr., son of Elijah, b. Mar. 18, 1740, d. Jan. 18, 1832, m. (1) Sept. 1, 1761, Lydia Robinson, d. Sept. 1762, dau. of Timothy, m. (2) Sept. 13, 1763, Hannah Furbush.
TEBBETS, Peter, dead 1768, m. early as 1763, Elizabeth (Robinson) (Tebbets) Hussey.

TEBBETS, Reuben, son of Moses, b. Sept. 5, 1743, m. July 23, 1770, Betty Carr, b. Jan. 12, 1750, dau. of Dr. Moses, of Somersworth.

TEBBETS, Aaron, m. (1) Mehepsabah Hussey, m. (2) Jan. 14, 1785, by Rev. Matthew Merriam, Hannah (Smith) Wentworth, wid of Paul.

TEBBETS, Moses, m. Aug. 4, 1785, by Rev. Isaac Hasey, Abigail Knox.

TEBBETS, Joseph, m. Sept. 21, 1786, by Rev. Benjamin Balch, Hannah Roberts, both of Barrington.

TEBBETS, Daniel, son of Aaron, b. June 1768, m. 1795, Hannah Abbott.

TEBBETS, William J., m. Jul. 8, 1795, in Wakefield, Sarah Winkley, of Brookfield, d. Feb. 23, 1855, aged 88, dau. of John.

TEBBETS, Jacob, m. Dec. 29, 1811, in Lebanon, Me., Polly Hersom.

TEBBETS, George, b. Mar. 12, 1795, m. Jul. 1, 1821, in Lebanon, Me., Mary Foss, b. Nov. 15, 1803, d. Apr. 13, 1888, aged 84.

TEBBETS, Robert, of barnstead, m. Jan. 30, 1822, by Rev. Joseph Boodey, Hannah B. Mooney, of Alton, d. Dec. 23, 1834, aged 34, dau. of Maj. Joseph.

TEBBETS, Hiram, d. Mar. 13, 1870, aged 66, m. Aug. 18, 1824, in Lebanon, Me., Aseneth Mills, d. Jun. 9, 1853, aged 46.

TEBBETS, John, of Berwick, m. Mar. 1, 1829, in Lebanon, Me., Dorcas McCrillis.

TEBBETS, Hezekiah, m. May 12, 1831, by Elder Hiram Holmes, Mary Edgerly, b. May 5, 1805, d. June 3, 1877, aged 72, dau. of Daniel, both of Wolfeboro.

TEBBETS, Dudley, m. Nov. 11, 1841, in Berwick, Me., Martha Guptill, d. Oct. 28, 1846.

TEBBETS, Benjamin B., of Wolfeboro, m. Nov. 27, 1841, in Wolfeboro, Frances Jane Dearborn, of Wakefield.

TEBBETS, Orland H., b. Oct. 19, 1823, d. Mar. 22, 1870, m. Nov. 28, 1844, in Lebanon, Me., Lydia Ann Clark, of Rochester, b. Nov. 4, 1823, d. Feb. 10, 1872.

TEBBETS, Eri, son of Edward, b. near 1827, d. May 15, 1885, aged 59, m. (1) Oct. 1, 1848, by Rev. Joseph Boodey, Elvira Colbath, both of Farmington, m. (2) int. Sept. 29, 1859, in New Durham, Eliza B. Pinkham, b. near 1837, of New Durham.

TEBBETS, Elijah, m. int. Jun. 7, 1853, in Lebanon, Me., Susan Chick, b. Nov. 20, 1825, dau. of Simon F.

TEBBETS, Meshach R., m. Sep. 15, 1853, in Lebanon, Me., Rebecca Corson, both of Rochester.

TEBBETS, Stephen, m. Nov. 24, 1853, by Rev. Joseph Loring, Ruth Clark, both of Rochester.

TEBBETS, Isaac, of Lebanon, Me., d. Sep. 16, 1863, aged 31, (Civil War), m. Dec. 21, 1853, by Elder Elias Hutchins, Melissa Chapman, of Somersworth.

TEBBETS, Hiram, m. int. Jan. 30, 1854, in Lebanon, Me., Lydia G. Wentworth, of Great Falls.

TEBBETS, Clark James, of Brookfield, b. Jan. 26, 1829, d. Mar. 11, 1904, m. Oct. 18, 1854, in Rochester, Mary R. Page, of Dover, b. Jan. 3, 1835, d. Nov. 12, 1893.

TEBBETS, James L., of Haverhill, Mass., b. 1831, m. (1) (pub. Dec. 19, 1854, in Haverhill, Mass.), Caroline M. Tebbets, of Farmington, d. Apr. 21, 1863, aged 35, dau. of Charles, m. (2) int. Aug. 12, 1867, in Brookfield, Eliza A. Avery, of Wolfeboro, aged 23.

TEBBETS, William R., m. Jul. 20, 1855, in Lebanon, Me., Sarah A. Varney, both of Milton.

TEBBETS, John W., m. Nov. 11, 1856, in Rollinsford, Clara W. Blaisdell, d. Apr. 22, 1896, aged 60, dau. of Jonathan.

TEBBETS, Andrew J., son of George, b. 1839, d. Dec. 30, 1913, aged 74, m. (pub. Aug. 5, 1858, in Great Falls), Lucinda Knox, d. Feb. 14, 1920, aged 79, dau. of Alfred, both of Berwick, Me.

TEBBETS, James H., of Brookfield, aged 27, m. int. Sep. 7, 1858, in Brookfield, Martha E. Cotton, of Wolfeboro, aged 25.

TEBBETS, Rev. Charles W., d. Jan. 29, 1879, aged 38, m. (pub. Dec. 9, 1858, in Great Falls), Mehitable Webster, d. Oct. 20, 1866, aged 22, both of Berwick, Me.

TEBBETS, Charles G., of Wolfeboro, m. May 28, 1861, in Dover, Nancy J. Fox, of Tuftonboro, d. Jun. 22, 1898, aged 64, dau. of Ira.

TEBBETS, Richard B., m. Dec. 15, 1861, in Barrington, Mrs. Nancy H. Hanson.

TEBBETS, Samuel H., of Rochester, m. Dec. 22, 1861, in S. Berwick, Me., Mary E. Shapleigh, of Dover.

TEBBETS, William, of Berwick, Me., m. Sept. 27, 1862, in Great Falls, Lizzie A. Hodgdon, of S. Berwick, Me.

TEBBETS, Charles E., of Lee, son of Ephraim, m. July 15, 1864, in Durham, Sarah A. Demeritt, of Madbury, dau. of Eben.

TEBBETS, George W. O., m. Nov. 24, 1864, in Dover, m. Abby Cotton, of Wolfeboro.

TEBBETS, Henry H., m. Feb. 12, 1865, in Rochester, Annie A. Clark.

TEBBETS, George S., of Berwick, Me., son of Lewis, d. Jan. 11, 1916, aged 80, m. Feb. 24, 1865, in Dover, Hattie S. Roberts, of Rochestor.

TEBBETS, David T., of Wolfeboro, son of Dr. Thomas J., b. Mar. 23, 1832, d. Aug. 13, 1893, m. July 8, 1865, in Ossipee, Lucinda Idella Nichols, of Ossipee, d. June 1, 1909, aged 67.

TEBBETS, Charles B., of Rochester, m. Aug. 10, 1865, in Boston, Mass., Georgia B. May, of Lynn.

TEBBETS, Ezra K., of Somersworth, m. May 14, 1866, in Great Falls, Lizzie Rothwell, of Lawrence, Mass.

TEBBETS, James H., m. Feb. 1, 1867, in Rochester, Mary E. Wakeham, both of Milton.

TEBBETS, Charles H., m. (pub. July 4, 1867, in Wolfeboro), Mary E. Gilman.

TEBBETS, Isaac H., of Brookfield, son of John K., aged 18, m. int. Oct. 5, 1867, in Lebanon, Me., Dorothy C. Varney, of E. Rochester, aged 21, dau. of Moses.

TEBBETS, George H., m. Dec. 15, 1867, in Dover, Ellen E. Young, dau. of Jonathan.

TEBBETS, George B., m. Apr. 22, 1868, in Dover, Abbie C. Drew, both of Dover.

TEBBETS, Noah, of Rochester, m. (pub. Nov. 4, 1869, in Newton, Mass.), E. Fannie Whipple, of Newton, Mass., dau. of Orrin.

TEBBETS, Hall W., m. May 10, 1870, in Lynn, Mass., Kate P. Hood, dau. of George, both of Lynn, Mass.

TEBBETS, Charles W., m. Jun. 4, 1870, by Rev. Ira C. Guptil, Hannah C. Shapleigh.

TENNANT, Joseph, m. Mar. 25, 1865, in Rochester, Elizabeth Graham.

TENNEY, John Jr., of Rowley, Mass., m. Aug. 9, 1777, in Barrington, Patience Young, of Barrington.

TENNEY, Jonathan, of Newton Center, Mass., m. Sept. 17, 1866, in Great Falls, Ellen J. Legro.

THAYER, Henry B., of Winona, Minn., m. (pub. Apr. 16, 1868, in Sumner, Minn.), Sadie A. P. Fernald, of Boston, Mass., dau. of Dr. Fernald, of Barrington.

THING, H. Y., m. Oct. 10, 1862, in Dover, Abbie Clifford, both of Epping,.

THING, R. W., of Shapleigh, Me., m. (pub. Jan. 8, 1868, in Great Falls), Celia A. Fisk, of Lebanon, Me.

THOMAS, John R., b. Apr. 23, 1834, d. Mar. 20, 1906, m. (pub. Sept. 18, 1862, in Wolfeboro), Hattie S. Holmes, b. Apr. 27, 1845, d. Apr. 15, 1915, both of Tuftonboro.

THOMPSON, Noah, of Rochester, son of Noah T., d. July 9, 1829, aged 56, m. Apr. 29, 1796, by Rev. Benjamin Babb, Polly Clark, of Barrington.

THOMPSON, Samuel, m. May 27, 1798, by Rev. Benjamin Balch, Anna Snell, both of Lee.

THOMPSON, James G., m. Jan. 5, 1804, by Rev. Isaac Hasey, Mary Fall, dau. of Ebenezer.

THOMPSON, Stephen, of Shapleigh, Me., m. Aug. 25, 1816, in Lebanon, Me., Polly Wentworth.

THOMPSON, Noah, of Lee, d. Jan. 30, 1883, aged 87, m. int. Oct. 11, 1822, in Lee, Sukey Kelsey, of Nottingham, d. Apr. 12, 1862, aged 58, dau. of John.

6) THOMPSON, Deac. Benjamin, of Greenland, son of Col. Ebenezer, b. Mar. 31, 1804, d. Apr. 23, 1875, m. Dec. 23, 1833, by Rev. Samuel H. Merrill, Lucinda J. Drew, of Barrington, b. Nov. 29, 1812, d. Feb. 22, 1862, dau. of Jonathan.

THOMPSON, Daniel, m. Feb. 1835, in Lebanon, Me., Hannah Wentworth.

THOMPSON, Hiram, of Tuftonboro, d. May 1, 1879, aged 61, m. (pub. Mar. 22, 1842, in Ossipee), Sabrina Beacham, of Ossipee, d. Aug. 7, 1884, aged 62.

THOMPSON, Washington, of Tuftonboro, b. Nov. 4, 1811, d. Jan. 9, 1892, aged 80, m. (pub. June 6, 1843, in Ossipee), Joanna Beacham, of Ossipee, b. May 1, 1817, d. Sept. 6, 1902, aged 85.

THOMPSON, George W., of S. Berwick, Me., son of Isaac, d. Mar. 28, 1892, aged 53, m. Jul. 21, 1861, in S. Berwick, Me., Susan L. Cooper, of York, Me., d. Oct. 30, 1905, aged 65.

THOMPSON, Charles H., son of John, aged 25, m. July 29, 1861, by Rev. Alvin Tobey, Mrs. Olive (Bean) Twombly, wid. of Samuel T., aged 38, dau. of Jeremiah.

THOMPSON, Samuel D., m. Nov. 28, 1861, in N. Conway, Ellen M. Chase, dau. of Jacob.

THOMPSON, Alonzo, m. Aug. 2, 1863, in Wakefield, Mrs. Elizabeth Abbott, both of Wolfeboro.

THOMPSON, Burnham, of Newmarket, m. Mar. 23, 1864, in Rochester, Nelly F. Hoopen, of Hanson, Me.

THOMPSON, J. W., of Durham, m. June 1, 1864, in Lee, Fannie C. Jenkins, of Lee.

THOMPSON, Sgt. Thatcher M., b. Feb. 18, 1836, d. Apr. 11, 1915, m. Sept. 17, 1864, in Tamworth, Fannie H. Tibbetts, b. Aug. 15, 1847, d. Jan. 5, 1931, both of Ossipee.

THOMPSON, John W. E., of Deerfield, son of Daniel, m. Dec. 14, 1865, in Durham, Susan A. Clough, of Shifton, Canada, dau. of Benjamin.

THOMPSON, Dr. George N., of Boston, Mass., m. Mar. 1, 1866, in Rochester, Lydia Pray, of Rochester.

THOMPSON, Elder William, m. (pub. May 31, 1866, in Wolfeboro), Mrs. Mary Lucas.

THOMPSON, Amos H., m. July 24, 1867, in Great Falls, Orinda H. Hurd.

THOMPSON, Charles, m. Apr. 28, 1868, in Dover, Mary J. Meader, both of Dover.

THOMPSON, Joseph, of Salem, m. Sept. 2, 1868, in Rochester, Augusta M. Welch, of Sanford, Me.

THURSTON, Cyrus, m. Dec. 2, 1866, in Effingham, Mary L. Shackford, both of Eaton.

TILTON, Albert, of Sandwich, son of Ebenezer, b. Sept. 20, 1825, d. May 23, 1895, m. Feb. 4, 1852, by Rev. Levi B. Tasker, in Sandwich, Sarah A. Hoit/Hoitt, of Tuftonboro.

TILTON, Elbridge G., m. (pub. Mar. 18, 1862, in Tamworth), Elizabeth Jackson.

TILTON, James F., m. June 9, 1862, in St. Augustine, Fla., Mary A. Walton, of St. Augustine, Fla.

TILTON, James H., m. Jan. 24, 1867, in Laconia, Eliza B. Lovell, dau. of Warren, both of Laconia.

TITCOMB, John, son of Col. John, b. Aug. 3, 1760, d. Aug. 9, 1816, m. May 2, 1782, by Dr. Belknap, Sarah Ham, b. 1761, d. Apr. 25, 1857, dau. of Capt. Samuel.

TITCOMB, Joshua, of Effingham, d. Sept. 23, 1836, aged 68, m. Sept. 27, 1791, in Wakefield, Margaret Mordough, of Wakefield, d. Nov. 10, 1857, aged 87.

TITCOMB, Oliver, of Acton, Me., m. Feb. 12, 1832, in Lebanon, Me., Hannah Wentworth.

TITCOMB, Joshua T. Jr., of Effingham, d. Apr. 28, 1872, aged 63, m. (1) (pub. Aug. 16, 1836, in Ossipee), Hannah R. Fogg, d. May 21, 1847, aged 35, dau. of Abner, m. (2) Dorothy Cooper, d. July 1899, aged 71.

TITCOMB, Charles W., of Parsonsfield, Me., m. June 14, 1863, in Alton, by Rev. Seth Sawyer, Jennie S. Chamberlain, of New Durham.
TITCOMB, Benjamin, of Acton, Me., m. Jun. 7, 1864, in Lebanon, Me., Hannah A. Fox, d. Feb. 4, 1877, aged 49, dau. of Jonathan.
TITCOMB, Oliver C., d. Jun. 15, 1890, aged 44, of Acton, Me., m. Jun. 13, 1867, in Lebanon, Me., Annah D. Roberts, of Milton.
TITUS, Charles E., of Boston, Mass., m. May 11, 1867, in Durham, Susan A. Mathes, of Dover, dau. of Valentine.
TOBEY, Charles, m. Dec. 8, 1868, by Rev. Robert S. Stubbs, Philomelia Stackpole, both of Dover.
TODD, Samuel Jr., son of Samuel, b. Feb. 3, 1824, m. Jul. 11, 1846, in Lebanon, Me., Mary A. Frost.
TOMKINS, Charles A., m. June 1, 1857, by Rev. Arthur Caverno, Elizabeth M. Kimball, <u>d. Nov. 2, 1874, aged 37</u>, both of Dover.
TORR, Lt. Andrew, b. Aug. 25, 1744, d. Mar. 8, 1817, m. (1) early as 1777, Mary Jones, d. Sep. 10, 1808, aged 56, dau. of Joseph, m. (2) Oct. 22, 1809, by Rev. William Hooper, Deborah (Ham) Hicks, of Madbury, <u>b. 1754</u>, wid. of Joseph.
TORR, George H., m. Nov. 2, 1865, in Andover, Mass., Lucretia W. Richardson.
TOWLE, David, of Chichester, aged 34, m. July 4, 1846, Nancy Kezer, aged 38, dau. of John.
TOWLE, John C., of Center Harbor, m. Sept. 23, 1863, in Sandwich, Laura B. Mudgett, of Holderness.
TOWLE, Capt. G. Frank, m. (pub. Jan. 5, 1865, in Portsmouth), Alexine D. Chase, dau. of Capt. C. H. Chase.
TOWLE, John W., of Dover, m. Apr. 29, 1865, in Center Ossipee, Lizzie M. Goldsmith, of Ossipee.
TOWLE, Jeremiah, of Newington, m. (pub. May 11, 1865, in Portsmouth), Virginia A. Vaughan.
TOWNSEND, Henry H., of Boston, Mass., m. June 7, 1870, in Milton, Agnes J. Brierly, of Milton Mills, dau. of Edward.
TREFETHEN, S. F., m. (pub. June 26, 1862, in Portsmouth), Mary E. Clark, both of Rye.
TREFETHEN, John L., m. Dec. 10, 1864, in Newington, Arieine N. Nutter, both of Newington.
TREFETHEN, John W., son of Capt. Archelaus, b. 1841, d. 1886, <u>of Dover</u>, m. May 8, 1870, in Dover, Francenia Runnels, b. 1852, d. May 15, 1927, dau. of Alvah, <u>of Lee</u>.

TREVETT, Joseph, m. May 8, 1803, by Rev. Benjamin Balch, Elizabeth Noble, both of Barrington.

6) **TRICKEY**, William, son of Deac. William, b. Jan. 8, 1771, d. July 22, 1852, m. (1) Feb. 6, 1793, by Rev. Benjamin Balch, Lois Meader, b. July 7, 1768, d. Aug. 8, 1834, dau. of Lemuel, m. (2) Jan. 12, 1836, Martha Horn, b. 1777, d. Dec. 3, 1862.

TRICKEY, Charles W., of Stoneham, Mass., m. May 22, 1847, by Rev. Theodore Wells, Martha S. Cater, of Barrington.

TRICKEY, Charles Wesley, b. June 3, 1824, d. June 21, 1896, aged 72, m. Oct. 10, 1855, by Elder Elias Hutchins, Ellen Frances Page, both of Dover.

TRICKEY, Maj. William H., b. 1841, d. 1931, m. (pub. Aug. 18, 1864, in Wolfeboro), Celeste Deland, of S. Wolfeboro, b. 1839, d. 1915, dau. of William.

TRICKEY, Charles Henry, son of Charles W., b. July 20, 1848, d. Sept. 9, 1899, m. Dec. 4, 1869, in Dover, Ada J. Bond, both of Dover.

4) **TRIPE**, Thomas, son of Richard, d. Jan. 3, 1831, aged 46, m. near 1815, Mary ----, d. Dec. 28, 1863, aged 72.

TRIPP, William, m. Sept. 16, 1865, by Rev. Francis E. Abbott, Nancy E. Perkins, both of Epping.

TRIPP, George H., m. (pub. July 21, 1870, in Portsmouth), Susie Tucker.

TRUE, Simeon S., d. Mar. 20, 1845, aged 43, m. Oct. 24, 1822, Lucy Sturdivant, b. Aug. 26, 1802, d. Jan. 28, 1886.

TRUE, John S., of Holderness, aged 49, m. Aug. 4, 1850, in Sandwich, Mrs. Lucy (Sturdivant) True, of Centre Harbour, b. Aug. 26, 1802, d. Jan. 28, 1886, wid. of Simeon.

TRUE, John S., aged 49, m. Sep. 1850, Lucy S. (Sturdivant) True, wid. of Simeon S., b. Aug. 26, 1802, d. Jan. 28, 1886.

TRUE, John M., m. (pub. May 12, 1864, in Moultonboro), m. Annie Beede, of Sandwich.

TRUE, Solomon, of Rochester, m. (pub. Nov. 24, 1870, in Rochester), Mary Jane Ogden, of New York City.

TUCK, Frank J., m. Aug. 1, 1864, in Rochester, Abby M. Howe.

TUCKER, Nahum N., b. Jan. 27, 1828, d. Jan. 22, 1890, m. (pub. Aug. 17, 1852, in Ossipee), Sarah Pinder, d. Nov. 1, 1867, aged 34.

TUCKER, John E., m. Apr. 10, 1867, in Great Falls, Ellen M. Remington, both of Berwick, Me.

TUCKER, William H., of Eliot, Me., m. Dec. 5, 1869, in Kennebunk, Me., Augusta Chick, of Berwick, Me.

TURNER, Henry A., of Boston, Mass., m. (pub. Apr. 19, 1866, in Portsmouth), Sarah F. Moulton, dau. of John.

TURNER, George, m. Feb. 8, 1867, in Portsmouth, Mrs. Ann Staples.

TURNER, James W., m. (pub. May 12, 1870, in Portsmouth), Bell Graham.

TUTTLE, Levi, m. Mary Welch, d. Dec. 1818.

TUTTLE, Nathaniel, m. Feb. 16, 1794, by Rev. Isaac Hasey, Alice Hartford.

6) TUTTLE, Elijah, son of Elijah, b. 1774, d. May 24, 1866, m. (1) Apr. 5, 1798, by Rev. Benjamin Balch, Sally Tasker, b. June 16, 1783, d. Feb. 3, 1819, dau. of Samuel, both of Barrington, m. (2) Polly ----, d. Feb. 26, 1841, aged 66.

TUTTLE, James Jr., b. Sept. 15, 1779, m. June 30, 1799, in Barrington, Sarah Clark, b. Oct. 25, 1779, d. Nov. 30, 1842.

TUTTLE, Samuel H., m. Feb. 27, 1812, by Rev. Micajah Otis, Mrs. Judith Johnson, both of Barrington.

TUTTLE, James Jr., d. Dec. 7, 1823, aged 24, m. (Aug. 30, 1821, by Elder Enoch Place, Lavina Tuttle, b. May 26, 1802, d. Jan. 8, 1881, aged 78, dau. of James, both of Strafford.

TUTTLE, William, son of Elijah, b. Apr. 9, 1802, d. Jan. 8, 1859, m. Oct. 3, 1822, by Elder Enoch Place, Mary Starbard, b. 1796 or Nov. 5, 1797, d. Aug. 14, 1858, dau. of Stephen, both of Strafford.

TUTTLE, Job. N., of Providence, R.I., m. June 1, 1823, by Rev. Joseph Haven, Esther C. Blake, of Rochester, d. Feb. 24, 1859, aged 68.

TUTTLE, Daniel, d. Oct. 30, 1869, aged 73, m. Jul. 4, 1825, by Rev. Peter Holt, Judith French, d. Jan. 25, 1879, aged 82.

TUTTLE, Lt. Daniel C., of Strafford, b. 1798, d. June 24, 1864, m. Sept. 27, 1825, by Elder Enoch Place, Sarah Drew, of Barrington, b. in 1800, d. Nov. 28, 1864, dau. of Meshack.

TUTTLE, Rev. Alexander, son of Joseph, b. Jan. 2, 1804, d. July 4, 1863, m. Aug. 18, 1831, by Rev. William Demeritt, Lucinda A. Bennett.

TUTTLE, Col. Enoch Jr., d. Mar. 9, 1844, aged 39, m. May 4, 1833, by Elder John Caverly, Hannah Colley, dau. of Richard, both of Strafford.

TUTTLE, Samuel, of Barrington, m. May 10, 1838, by Rev. Samuel Nichols, Abigail Tebbets, of Dover.

TUTTLE, Asa, d. Oct. 17, 1857, m. Nov. 24, 1842, by Rev. John Winkley, Clarissa Caverly, d. Nov. 15, 1888, aged 70, dau. of Ephraim, both of Strafford.

TUTTLE, Joseph, b. 1826, d. June 3, 1864, aged 36, m. July 13, 1848, by Elder Enoch Place, Mahala Howard, b. Feb. 7, 1825, d. Sept. 10, 1890, dau. of Daniel, both of Wakefield.

TUTTLE, Alonzo, b. Jan. 1, 1833, d. Sep. 2, 1902, m. May 20, 1854, by Elder Samuel Sherburne, Cynthia A. Lang, b. Mar. 28, 1836, d. Jan. 21, 1919, both of Strafford.

TUTTLE, Alonzo F., m. Mar. 31, 1863, in Dover, Fannie L. Tuttle, both of Nottingham.

TUTTLE, Joseph E., m. Dec. 22, 1863, in Dover, Caroline H. Paul, both of Dover.

TUTTLE, Joseph W., of Strafford, m. (pub. May 12, 1864, in Dover), Frances A. Hoitt, both of Dover.

TUTTLE, Hazen M., of Durham, m. Nov. 2, 1864, in Newmarket, Mary A. Stevens.

TUTTLE, H. Freeman, son of Hezekiah, d. Apr. 17, 1882, aged 35, m. Dec. 25, 1865, by Rev. John Winkley, Jennie Caswell, both of Strafford.

TUTTLE, Woodbridge W., of Newmarket, m. Dec. 31, 1865, in Durham, Annie E. Ham, of Durham.

TUTTLE, Hiram O., b. May 29, 1836, d. Mar. 30, 1909, m. Jan. 14, 1866, in Wolfeboro, Julia A. Hayes, b. Sept. 14, 1844, d. Feb. 8, 1917, both of Alton.

TUTTLE, Horace, son of Ami, of Lawrence, Mass., m. Sept. 25, 1866, by Rev. Francis E. Abbott, Anna Kerby, of Dover.

TUTTLE, Joseph W., of Strafford, m. May 18, 1867, by Rev. Jesse Meader, Nellie J. Hodgdon, of Lee.

TUTTLE, Loring O., son of Silas, d. Aug. 26, 1907, aged 59, m. (pub. Apr. 22, 1869, in Strafford), Sarah E. Waldron.

TUTTLE, Henry O., of Nottingham, m. Nov. 18, 1869, in Dover, Nettie G. Cummings, of Dover.

TWOMBLY, James, m. (1) Abigail Gilman, m. (2) Sep. 26, 1833, in Middleton, Eliza Ellis, both of Middleton.

2) TWOMBLY, John, b. in 1659, d. in 1724, m. (1) Apr. 18, 1687, by Rev. John Pike, Mary Canney, b. Jan. 17, 1671, dau. of Thomas, m. (2) Oct. 3, 1692, by Rev. John Pike, Rachel Allen, dau. of Edward.

3) TWOMBLY, Ensign Benjamin, son of John, d. in 1762, m. July 10, 1721, Hannah Evans, of Salisbury, Mass., b. Apr. 5, 1698, dau. of Thomas.

5) TWOMBLY, Ezekiel, son of Daniel, d. May 27, 1837, aged 75, m. Nov. 1782, Abigail Nute, d. Mar. 17, 1849, aged 85, both of Madbury.

5) TWOMBLY, Jotham, son of Ralph, m. in 1786, Lydia Baker.

TWOMBLY, William, of Madbury, m. Nov. 18, 1788, by Rev. Benjamin Balch, Jerusha Runnels, of Barrington.

6) TWOMBLY, Paul, son of James, b. Oct. 3, 1774, m. Feb. 6, 1799, in Northwood, Hannah Hayes, b. July 20, 1774, d. Apr. 30, 1819.

TWOMBLY, Benjamin, of Lancaster, son of Benjamin, d. Apr. 6, 1834, aged 66, m. Feb. 28, 1799, by Rev. Joseph Haven, Judith Twombly, of Rochester, d. June 21, 1851, aged 75.

TWOMBLY, Aaron, b. Apr. 10, 1781, m. Feb. 18, 1802, in Barrington, Sarah ----, b. May 22, 1779.

TWOMBLY, Ezekiel, of Portsmouth, m. (1) May 20, 1810, in Portsmouth, Hannah Redman, of Dover, m. (2) June 3, 1825, in Portsmouth, Mrs. Jane (Vennard) Priest, of New Castle, wid. of Nathan, d. 1848.

6) TWOMBLY, Hurd, of Madbury, son of John, b. Dec. 31, 1789, d. Mar. 1, 1872, m. (1) May 5, 1813, by Rev. Joseph Boodey, Sarah Caverno, of Barrington, b. June 25, 1792, d. Aug. 19, 1827, m. (2) Dec. 9, 1828, by Elder Enoch Place, Mrs. Lavina (Tuttle) Tuttle, wid. of James Jr., b. May 26, 1802, d. Jan. 8, 1881, aged 78, dau. of James.

TWOMBLY, Silas, son of Samuel, b. Dec. 22, 1798, d. July 29, 1865, m. Mar. 28, 1822, by Elder Enoch Place, Sally Caverly, b. Sept. 2, 1794, d. Sept. 1840, aged 48, both of Strafford.

TWOMBLY, Isaac, d. May 13, 1851, aged 43, m. July 3, 1831, by Elder Samuel Sherburne, Lucy Brock, both of Barrington.

TWOMBLY, John Plumer, of Barrington, d. Sept. 1, 1861, aged 47, m. Oct. 1, 1831, by Rev. John Winkley, Lois Clark, of Strafford, d. Feb. 6, 1865, aged 59.

TWOMBLY, Nathaniel, d. Nov. 24, 1839, aged 37, m. Nov. 27, 1831, Elizabeth Seavey, d. Jan. 21, 1843, aged 29, dau. of Elijah.

6) TWOMBLY, Capt. Wingate J., son of Ephraim, b. Oct. 2, 1806, d. Oct. 7, 1890, m. (1) int. Mar. 10, 1833, in Dover, by Rev. William Demeritt, Louisa Curtis, d. Feb. 23, 1836, aged 21, m. (2) in 1839, in Stratham, Sarah Chapman, of Greenland, d. Mar. 5, 1891, aged 70, dau. of Samuel.

TWOMBLY, Samuel T., of Somersworth, m. Nov. 25, 1838, by Rev. Rufus O. Williams, Olive Bean, of Avon, Me., b. 1823, dau. of Jeremiah and Olive.

TWOMBLY, Benjamin, son of Moses, b. Jan. 16, 1807, d. Dec. 2, 1869, m. Dec. 23, 1839, Mary Jane Ayers, b. Mar. 8, 1816, d. Apr. 1, 1888, dau. of Jonathan.

TWOMBLY, Benjamin F., of Barrington, son of Isaac, b. May 11, 1817, m. Jan. 1, 1841, by Rev. John Winkley, Rosamond N. Colby, of Dover.

TWOMBLY, Isaac S., son of Isaac, m. July 4, 1842, by Elder Mayhew Clark, Polly Willey.

TWOMBLY, Nathaniel, 2nd, of Dover, b. 1821, m. May 15, 1845, by Elder Daniel P. Cilley, Sarah W. Evans, of Barrington, b. 1820, dau. of Levi.

TWOMBLY, Isaac S., of Barnstead, son of Isaac, b. Sept. 23, 1821, m. Nov. 23, 1847, by Rev. Enos George, Lovey W. Libbey, of Pittsfield

TWOMBLY, Reuben H., b. 1827, d. Jan. 21, 1893, m. (1) (pub. June 13, 1854, in Boston, Mass.), Susan J. Nute, b. 1833, d. June 19, 1867, aged 34, m. (2) Ann M. Drew, b. 1839, d. Dec. 17, 1916, dau. of Hiram.

TWOMBLY, Ezra H., of Milton, b. 1827, d. Dec. 13, 1883, aged 54, m. Mar. 5, 1855, in Dover, Lucinda K. Hanson, of Dover, b. 1828, d. July 19, 1910, aged 82, dau. of Israel.

7) TWOMBLY, William H., of Dover, son of William, b. Apr. 22, 1831, d. Apr. 10, 1902, aged 70, m. Mar. 12, 1857, by Elder Elias Hutchins, Malvina Nutter, of Madbury, b. June 20, 1839, d. Nov. 3, 1907, aged 68, dau. of Charles H.

TWOMBLY, Henry W., b. 1835, d. June 2, 1904, m. Jan. 17, 1862, in Dover, Ann Janette Libbey, both of Dover, b. 1841, d. Sept. 12, 1930, dau. of Ira.

TWOMBLY, Stephen, m. (pub. Apr. 14, 1864, in Portsmouth), Mrs. Georgiana H. Young.

TWOMBLY, Joseph F., m. Jan. 2, 1865, in Farmington, Eliza Berry, both of New Durham.

TWOMBLY, William Henry Harrison, of Madbury, son of Hurd, b. Oct. 16, 1840, m. June 4, 1865, in Dover, Esther Hall, of Barrington.

TWOMBLY, James L., of Milton, m. Aug. 15, 1865, in Farmington, Lizzie A. Downs, of Farmington, dau. of Otis P.

TWOMBLY, John W., m. (pub. Apr. 26, 1866, in Middleton, Clara A. Place, dau. of Isaiah H.

TWOMBLY, John, m. Oct. 29, 1866, in Dover, Mrs. Melissa J. Burleigh, both of Dover.

TWOMBLY, Henry H., m. Sept. 18, 1867, in Dover, Jennie M. Flanders, both of Dover.
TWOMBLY, John E., of Milton, son of James M., b. Jan. 3, 1836, d. Aug. 24, 1888, m. July 26, 1868, in Great Falls, Annie Lydia Waterhouse, of Dover, b. Jan. 4, 1840, d. July 16, 1910, dau. of Benjamin.
TWOMBLY, Everett F., m. (pub. Nov. 12, 1868, in Rochester), Mary A. Allen, both of Farmington.
TWOMBLY, George H., of Dover, m. Sept. 14, 1869, in Davenport, Ind., Marion Thackrah, of Davenport, Ind., d. Dec. 29, 1869.
TYLER, John, m. June 10, 1849, by Elder Samuel Sherburne, Martha Arlin, both of Barrington.
UNDERWOOD, Jarvis, A., of Fort Edward, N. Y., m. Jun. 14, 1860, in Lebanon, Me., Eunice K. Shapleigh.
UPHAM, Henry B., of Saugus, Mass., m. Sept. 10, 1867, in Dover, Mary H. Clark, of Dover.
VALLEY, Frank, d. Aug. 16, 1888, aged 42, m. Sept. 25, 1869, in Dover, Julia A. Weeks, both of Dover.
VAN TASSELL, J. N., of Terrytown, N.Y., m. Aug. 25, 1867, in Dover, Hannah P. Smith, of Candia.
VARNEY, Andrew, son of Dominicus, b. Aug. 17, 1818, d. Apr. 21, 1900, m. Nancy Watson, d. Mar. 14, 1896, dau. of Winthrop.
VARNEY, Elijah, d. Apr. 14, 1822, m. Nov. 25, 1779, by Dr. Belknap, Sarah Roberts, d. Oct. 31, 1847, aged 88, dau. of Aaron.
VARNEY, Samuel, m. int. 1802, in Lebanon, Me., Nabby Farnham.
VARNEY, Elias, m. Dec. 19, 1805, in Barrington, Hannah Lock, both of Barrington.
6) VARNEY, Capt. Paul, son of Thomas, b. 1798, d. Mar. 11, 1864, aged 66, m. Dec. 25, 1823, by Rev. Joseph Boodey, Polly Chamberlain, b. 1802, d. June 8, 1878, aged 76, dau. of Capt. Jacob, both of Alton.
VARNEY, Elder Moses, m. Dec. 26, 1824, in Lebanon, Me., Betsey Blaisdell, d. Nov. 22, 1844, aged 42.
VARNEY, David, d. Aug. 17, 1872, aged 71, m. in 1826, in Rochester, Lucy Smith, d. May 22, 1881, aged 70.
5) VARNEY, Elias, son of Shubel, d. Oct. 29, 1861, aged 78, m. (1) Hannah H. ----, d. Aug. 8, 1830, aged 41, m. (2) May 1, 1831, by Elder Enoch Place, Mary Foss, d. June 8, 1878, aged 80, dau. of Maj. Samuel, both of Barrington.

VARNEY, Joshua A., son of Thomas, b. Oct. 11, 1803, d. Sep. 19, 1894, m. (pub. Dec. 16, 1834, in Alton), Deborah Varney, b. Nov. 7, 1814.

6) VARNEY, Obed, of Farmington, son of Festus, b. Apr. 20, 1811, d. Mar. 13, 1840, m. May 1837, in Barrington, Sarah W. Locke, of Rochester, b. Mar. 10, 1818, d. Dec. 30, 1844, dau. of Edward.

VARNEY, Isaac, of No. Berwick, Me., m. Nov. 24, 1839, in Lebanon, Me., Sarah B. Cloutman, of Rochester, d. Apr. 17, 1845, aged 52.

VARNEY, Moses E., son of Isaac, b. Nov. 23, 1819, m. Apr. 27, 1844, in Lebanon, Me., Sarah Ann Blaisdell, d. Oct. 5, 1875, aged 55.

VARNEY, John A., m. Feb. 8, 1846, by Rev. Mr. McCollom, Sarah A. Foye, b. Aug. 16, 1827, d. Oct. 29, 1886, aged 56, dau. of Richard, both of Dover.

VARNEY, Alfred N., d. Sep. 13, 1860, aged 38, m. Dec. 30, 1849, by Elder Elias Hutchins, Almira N. Foss, d. Mar. 1, 1903, aged 74.

VARNEY, Elias Jr., son of Elias, d. July 27, 1850, aged 28, m. Nov. 7, 1846, by Rev. Samuel Kelley, Eliza A. Foss, both of Barrington.

VARNEY, Samuel, son of Joseph, d. Mar. 20, 1858, aged 29, m. Sept. 20, 1848, by Elder Elias Hutchins, Sophia Moody, d. Nov. 17, 1849, aged 18.

VARNEY, Jacob, m. int. Oct. 29, 1848, in Dover, Mary Woodes, both of Dover.

VARNEY, Humphrey Jr., d. Nov. 22, 1888, aged 71, m. Nov. 26, 1849, in Lebanon, Me., Phebe J. Gordon, of Somersworth, d. Jun. 30, 1889, aged 62.

VARNEY, David F., b. 1829, d. 1871, m. Apr. 14, 1850, in Lebanon, Me., Sarah A. McCrillis, b. 1832.

VARNEY, Joel, of Milton, m. Dec. 1, 1852, in Lebanon, Me., Mrs. Patience Foss.

VARNEY, asa, of Rochester, m. Oct. 1, 1853, by Rev. Joseph Loring, Sara A. Clough, of Effingham.

VARNEY, Arthur H., m. May 7, 1854, in Lebanon, Me., Nancy J. Tebbets, both of Rochester.

VARNEY, Andrew J., son of Paul, d. July 20, 1906, aged 76, m. (pub. Dec. 18, 1856, in Alton), Loella Woodman, b. 1836, d. 1883.

VARNEY, Freeman, son of Solomon, b. Dec. 6, 1836, d. Feb. 24, 1917, m. Aug. 24, 1859, in Somersworth, Mary Ham Hayes, b. Jun. 7, 1836, d. Mar. 11, 1900.

VARNEY, Charles Ayer, son of John H., b. May 19, 1834, <u>d. June 2, 1893</u>, m. May 18, 1860, by Rev. Benjamin F. Parsons, Sophia J. Nute, <u>b. Apr. 27, 1842, d. July 12, 1927, dau. of John C.</u>, both of Milton.

VARNEY, Daniel, m. Nov. 21, 1861, in Farmington, Sarah J. Peasley, both of Gilmanton.

VARNEY, Jonathan M., of Alton, m. Jan. 1, 1862, in Barnstead, Dora S. Lougee, of Barnstead.

VARNEY, George F., m. Mar. 3, 1863, in Great Falls, Eliza C. Ham, both of Rochester.

VARNEY, Charles W., m. (pub. Mar. 12, 1863, in Exeter), Nellie N. Lane.

VARNEY, Edwin H., m. Mar. 19, <u>1863</u>, in Dover, Rebecca A. Young, <u>both of Dover</u>.

VARNEY, Daniel W., m. (pub. Oct. 6, 1864, in Haverhill, Mass.), Mary A. Horn, both of Rochester.

VARNEY, Andrew 2nd, m. Dec. 18, 1864, in S. Berwick, Me., Mariah H. Leighton, both of Dover.

VARNEY, Thomas G., <u>son of Andrew, d. Dec. 23, 1901, aged 62</u>, m. May 21, 1865, in Dover, Lydia J. Trickey.

VARNEY, Stephen, m. May 27, 1866, in Rochester, Mrs. Rebecca Barnard, of Farmington.

VARNEY, J. S., of Tamworth, m. July 31, 1866, in Rochester, Mrs. Lydia Frances (Cotton) Wakeham, of Milton, wid. of James Henry.

VARNEY, Albert, of Farmington, m. Feb. 8, 1867, in Farmington, Antoinette Crockett, of Alton, dau. of Amos.

VARNEY, Elihu, of Alton, m. May 12, 1867, in New Durham, Ellen E. Roberts, of Farmington.

VARNEY, Benajah P., of Dover, m. Aug. 7, 1867, in Portsmouth, Ann Lizzie Moulton, of Portsmouth, dau. of Daniel.

VARNEY, Nehemiah E., m. Jan. 1, 1868, by Rev. Alden Sherwin, Mrs. Marcia O. Brock, <u>both of Barrington</u>.

VARNEY, George E., of Alton, m. (pub. May 6, 1869, in Wolfeboro), Mary A. Cotton, of Wolfeboro.

VARNEY, George W., of Rochester, m. (pub. July 8, 1869, in Rochester), Sarah J. Scruton, of Farmington.

VARNEY, Robert, m. Feb. 19, 1870, in Dover, Caroline H. Locke, <u>both of Dover</u>.

VARNEY, John F. Jr., of Farmington, m. May 6, 1870, m. (pub. May 12, 1870, in Rochester), Hattie C. Wentworth, of Lebanon, Me.

VARNEY, M. R., m. July 1, 1870, in Berwick, Me., Mrs. E. M. J. Thurston, both of Dover.

VARNEY, Isaac, m. Aug. 11, 1870, in Rochester, Emma J. Mathes, both of Rochester.

VEASEY, Henry W. of Exeter, m. Aug. 14, 1855, in Newmarket, Mary Deborah Doe, of Newmarket.

VESSELL, Thomas O., m. May 17, 1869, in Dover, Mattie Woods, both of Dover.

VICKERY, William H., of Dover, m. (pub. May 14, 1863, in Charlestown, Mass.), Ellen A. Barker, of Charlestown, Mass.

VICKERY, William H., of Rochester, son of John S., d. Mar. 10, 1916, aged 77, m. Mar. 11, 1869, by Rev. Robert S. Stubbs, Fanny Evans, of N. Berwick, Me.

VICKERY, Frank, m. Nov. 2, 1870, in Dover, Augusta Leach, of New York City, dau. of William.

VINCENT, William, m. Jan. 14, 1808, in Barrington, Lucretia Willey, both of Durham.

VINTON, Josiah Otis, of E. Bridgewater, Mass., m. Dec. 10, 1867, in Dover, Mary S. Page, of Dover.

VITTUM, David P. S., of Sandwich, m. (pub. Jan. 18, 1866, in Albany), Susannah Mason, of Albany.

VITTUM, Frank H., of Laconia, m. Mar. 13, 1869, in Center Sandwich, Flora L. Merrill, of Alton.

WADLEIGH, Eben R., m. Dec. 24, 1866, in Great Falls, Eliza A. Willey, both of S. Berwick, Me.

WADLEIGH, N. G., of Dover, m. Sept. 3, 1867, in Portsmouth, Olive J. Warren, of Wells, Me., dau. of James.

WADLEIGH, Erastus, m. Sept. 26, 1867, in Sutton, Olive F. Davis.

WADLEIGH, Curtis E., of Salem, Mass., m. (pub. Nov. 5, 1868, in Wolfeboro), Mrs. Lucy E. Rust, of Wolfeboro.

WADLEIGH, Lt. Com. George H., m. Oct. 12, 1869, in Lexington, Mass., Clara E. Robinson, of San Francisco, Calif.

3) **WALDRON**, Aaron, son of Aaron[2] and Hannah Boodey Waldron, Richard Canney Waldron[1], d. Jan. 26, 1825, aged 45, m. Mary Huckins, d. July 9, 1863, aged 77, dau. of John.

2) WALDRON, Col. Isaac, son of Richard Canney Waldron, b. Mar. 16, 1747, d. May 3, 1841, aged 94, in Barrington, m. Sarah Boodey, b. Mar. 8, 1755, d. Jul. 8, 1799, dau. of Azariah.

WALDRON, Jesse, m. int. Jan. 16, 1817, in Lebanon, Me., Eunice Clark.

WALDRON, Daniel, m. Sept. 22, 1819, by Elder Enoch Place, Eliza K. Woodbury, b. Nov. 4, 1796, d. June 27, 1821, dau. of Dr. Robert, both of Barrington.

WALDRON, Zachariah, son of Richard, d. Oct. 27, 1827, aged 28, m. Dec. 30, 1824, by Elder Enoch Place, Polly Willey, b. 1803, d. 1877, both of Strafford.

WALDRON, Daniel, of York, Me., d. Oct. 7, 1843, aged 45, m. (pub. Oct. 23, 1827, in Portsmouth), Irene Dearborn, of Portsmouth, dau. of Gen. Asa.

WALDRON, Daniel B., m. (pub. May 19, 1835, in Strafford), Druzilla W. Parshley, b. Oct. 21, 1857, aged 47, dau. of John B.

WALDRON, John, m. Mar. 4, 1841, in Barrington, by Rev. Samuel Nichols, Lydia Babb, both of Barrington.

WALDRON, Jonathan C., b. 1817, d. 1898, m. Apr. 2, 1846, by Elder Enoch Place, Emeline S. Parshley, b. 1818, d. Nov. 20, 1881, aged 64, dau. of Ebenezer, both of Strafford.

WALDRON, William Bradley, of Rochester, m. (pub. June 29, 1847, in Lebanon, Me.), Abby Hanson Blaisdell, of Lebanon, Me., dau. of Elder Edward.

WALDRON, William W., b. 1822, d. 1908, m. Aug. 27, 1848, by Elder P. S. Burbank, Mary E. Peavey, b. 1828, d. 1908.

WALDRON, Aaron, son of Richard, m. Feb. 12, 1855, in Strafford, Emily P. Otis, dau. of Samuel, both of Strafford.

WALDRON, John D., of Wakefield, m. (pub. Aug. 13, 1863, in S. Berwick, Me.), Maria E. McDaniel, of S. Berwick, Me.

WALDRON, Wells, of Dover, m. Oct. 8, 1867, in S. Berwick, Me., Annie Linton, of S. Berwick, Me.

WALDRON, Ira, of Dover, b. July 14, 1841, m. Nov. 26, 1868, in Toledo, Ohio, Sophie Freeman, of Toledo, Ohio, dau. of John P.

WALDRON, Dudley B., son of James, d. Jul. 9, 1904, aged 65, m. (pub. Mar. 6, 1874, in Rochester), Celia C. Waldron.

WALKER, Samuel, d. May, 19, 1854, aged 76, m. Mar. 31, 1803, by Rev. Benjamin Randall, Susanna Twombly, b. 1784, d. 1872.

WALKER, Nathan D., son of Dependence, b. Apr. 3, 1804, d. Oct. 9, 1889, m. (1) Nov. 23, 1823, Sophia Dore, of Milton, d. Dec. 7, 1873, aged 69, m. (2) Elizabeth N. (Joy) Miles, d. Aug. 9, 1879, aged 75, wid. of Abraham, dau. of Jacob.

WALKER, Nathan P., son of George, b. Feb. 29, 1804, d. 1893, m. int. Jan. 19, 1834, in Dover, Martha Hicks, d. Dec. 7, 1873, aged 69.

WALKER, Sgt. Henry, m. Aug. 15, 1864, by Rev. James Rand, Annette Gilman, of Madbury.

WALKER, John S., m. (pub. Feb. 23, 1865, in Portsmouth), Emma F. Moulton, both of Newmarket.

WALKER, James, of Fryburg, Me., m. Sept. 20, 1865, in Conway, Marion E. Farrington, of Conway.

WALKER, Lt. Thomas H., m. Aug. 24, 1866, in Newmarket, Mary L. Edgerly, both of Durham.

WALKER, Henry F., of Strafford, m. June 23, 1867, in Strafford, Lydia J. Kimball, of Dover.

WALKER, Benjamin T., of Portland, Me., m. July 18, 1867, in Dover, Fannie C. Smith, of Eastport, Me.

WALKER, Asa, m. (pub. Dec. 26, 1867, in Portsmouth), Ruth L. Brooks, dau. of Joshua.

WALKER, Joseph H., m. Oct. 11, 1868, by Rev. Alden Sherwin, Elizabeth S. Tibbets, d. Dec. 14, 1914, aged 70, both of Dover.

WALLACE, Edwin, son of Rev. Linzey, b. 1823, d. Oct. 29, 1894, aged 71, m. Susan R. Whitehouse, dau. of William.

WALLACE, Nelson J., d. Dec. 14, 1876, aged 46, m. Nov. 13, 1856, in Dover, Frances J. Foster, dau. of Jonathan, both of Dover.

WALLACE, Sylvester B., of Middleton, m. Oct. 2, 1862, in Dover, Maggie I. Hoitt, of Dover.

WALLACE, James S. m. Sept. 3, 1864, in Dover, Esther Tucker, of Rochester.

WALLACE, George F., of Sandwich, m. Nov. 27, 1865, in Dover, Sarah Austin, of Dover.

WALLACE, Alijah B., m. Jul. 4, 1866, in Alton, Mary Elizabeth Canney, b. Mar. 16, 1842, d. Mar. 20, 1910, dau. of William.

WALLACE, Simeon Parker, d. Nov. 30, 1905, aged 74, m. (1) Feb. 2, 1868, in Ossipee, Mrs. Emily (Merrow) Palmer, wid. of Joseph F., m. (2) Josephine L. Hurd, d. Jan. 8, 1914, aged 75.

WALLACE, John, m. Nov. 28, 1869, in Milton, Olive (Downs) (Wentworth) Rogers, wid. of John S., b. Aug. 20, 1822, d. Apr. 3, 1888, dau. of James.

5) **WALLINGFORD**, David, son of Peter, b. 1770, d. 1815, m. Nov. 8, 1789, by Rev. Joseph Haven, Sarah Corson, b. 1772, d. Nov. 22, 1864, both of Rochester.

WALLINGFORD, Aaron, d. Dec. 27, 1858, aged 80, m. int. Oct. 24, 1801, in Lebanon, Me., Betsey Downs.

WALLINGFORD, Levi, m. Nov. 24, 1811, in Lebanon, Me., Lydia Critchet.

WALLINGFORD, Thomas, m. Oct. 22, 1815, in Lebanon, Me., Anne McCrillis.
WALLINGFORD, Amos P., son of Jacob, b. 1794, d. Aug. 21, 1825, m. Feb. 11, 1819, in Lebanon, Me., Rhoda Blaisdell, b. 1800, d. Aug. 9, 1863.
WALLINGFORD, William, m. Feb. 11, 1819, in Lebanon, Me., Joanna Peirce.
WALLINGFORD, Jonathan, m. int. Jul. 1, 1820, in Lebanon, Me., Rachel Knox, of Berwick, Me.
WALLINGFORD, Daniel, m. Jan. 19, 1823, in Lebanon, Me., Lydia Wallingford.
WALLINGFORD, James, d. Apr. 29, 1854, aged 47, m. Jun. 16, 1830, in Lebanon, Mary Estes, of Berwick, Me.
WALLINGFORD, John, m. Jun. 16, 1833, in Lebanon, Me., Susan Wallingford, of Alton.
WALLINGFORD, Stephen, m. int. Nov. 29, 1833, in Lebanon, Me., Mercy Wallingford.
WALLINGFORD, Henry, d. Oct. 2, 1877, aged 60, m. int. Apr. 2, 1838, in Lebanon, Me., Alice Young, d. Mar. 30, 1888, aged 72.
WALLINGFORD, Giles, m. int. Jan. 27, 1849, in Lebanon, Me., Merlindia Wallingford.
WALLINGFORD, Lafayette, m. Feb. 14, 1850, in Lebanon, Me., Sally McCrillis.
WALLINGFORD, Ebenezer, m. int. Dec. 8, 1852, in Lebanon, Me., Charlotte Wallingford.
WALLINGFORD, Capt. John G., m. Oct. 4, 1864, in Dover, Nellie P. Cook, d. May 24, 1911, aged 67, dau. of Jedediah.
WALLINGFORD, Reuben H., m. Nov. 19, 1864, in Berwick, Me., Patience Wallingford, both of Berwick, Me.
WALLINGFORD, Mark F., m. Nov. 10, 1866, in Rochester, Mary A. Worster, of N. Berwick, Me.
WALLINGFORD, Joseph D., of Lebanon, Me., m. Dec. 10, 1866, in Dover, Nellie D. Hutchins, of Dover.
WALLINGFORD, David W., of Milton, m. Feb. 13, 1870, in Barnstead, Mary Jane Tuttle, of Barnstead.
WALLAINGFORD, Joseph L. of Berwick, Me., m. Jun. 15, 1870, in Lebanon, Me., Augusta L. Stevens.
WALLINGFORD, Samuel W., m. (pub. Nov. 24, 1870, in Milton), Mary B. Plumer.
WARBURTON, Edward H., m. Aug. 30, 1868, by Rev. Robert S. Stubbs, Mary E. Shorey, both of Rochester.

WARBURTON, James H., of Rochester, m. (pub. June 23, 1870, in E. Rochester), Clara A. Shorey, of E. Rochester.

WARD, Samuel, m. Jan. 1, 1806, in Barrington, Tamsin Hall, both of Barrington.

WARD, Freeman J., m. June 24, 1869, in Dover, Nettie J. Flagg, both of Dover.

WARREN, Benjamin Jr., son of Benjamin, b. Dec. 9, 1750, m. Nov. 26, 1770, Abigail Philpot.

WARREN, Chadbourne H., son of Chadbourne, d. May 3, 1909, aged 84, m. (1) int. May 15, 1844, in Dover, Clara E. Twombly, b. 1822, d. Aug. 18, 1867, dau. of Isaac, m. (2) Apr. 18, 1868, in Great Falls, Martha Allen, b. 1823, d. Nov. 26, 1919, dau. of Ethan.

WARREN, Frederick A., m. Sept. 16, 1861, in Dover, Lizzie F. Hanscom, both of Dover.

WARREN, Moses F., of Rollinsford, son of Moses, b. Aug. 13, 1838, d. Aug. 7, 1889, m. int. Dec. 4, 1861, in Rollinsford, Mary A. Emery, of Somersworth, b. Feb. 3, 1837, d. Oct. 22, 1913.

WARREN, Edwin, m. Dec. 25, 1861, in Dover, Sarah J. Scully, both of Dover.

WARREN, George W., m. (pub. Dec. 11, 1862, in Wolfeboro), Emeline Kimball.

WARREN, Charles W., m. Jan. 1, 1867, in Great Falls, Mary A. Tuok.

WARREN, Charles W., of Dover, m. July 18, 1868, by Rev. Robert S. Stubbs, Sarah F. Bedell, of S. Berwick, Me.

WARREN, Charles E., of Great Falls, m. Aug. 16, 1868, in Great Falls, Estelle S. Groves, of Bangor, Me.

WARREN, Wilber F., m. Oct. 17, 1868, in Rochester, Sarah H. Byers, both of Rochester.

WATERHOUSE, Timothy, of Barrington, d. Dec. 18, 1834, aged 88, m. Mary Tibbetts, b. 1754, d. Dec. 10, 1799, dau. of Jeremiah.

WATERHOUSE, George, b. Mar. 15, 1746, m. June 20, 1771, in Barrington, Elizabeth ----, b. Mar. 31, 1748.

WATERHOUSE, Benjamin, m. Jan. 20, 1780, in Barrington, Abiah Garland, both of Barrington.

WATERHOUSE, Jeremiah, of Barrington, m. June 5, 1806, by Rev. Benjamin Babb, Susanna Twombly, of Madbury.

WATERHOUSE, Daniel, m. Aug. 10, 1806, by Rev. Benjamin Balch, Mrs. Lydia Brown, both of Barrington.

WATERHOUSE, Jeremiah, son of Jeremiah, d. Nov. 16, 1887, aged 68, m. Sept. 29, 1841, by Rev. Francis V. Pike, Martha A. Winkley, of Barrington, b. Nov. 9, 1819, d. Jan. 18, 1894, aged 74, dau. of William.

WATERHOUSE, Benjamin Augustus, m. Oct. 31, 1842, by Elder Samuel Sherburne, Eliza Leathers, d. Aug. 3, 1884, aged 60, both of Barrington.

WATERHOUSE, Dr. William, m. Feb. 27, 1849, by Rev. Theodore Wells, Martha W. Buzzell, both of Barrington.

WATERHOUSE, John, m. Sept. 9, 1855, by Rev. John Winkley, Betsey Gray, dau. of Ebenezer, both of Rochester.

WATERHOUSE, William E., m. Feb. 1, 1869, in Portsmouth, Elizabeth S. Hale, dau. of William, both of Dover.

WATERS, Aja (?) T., m. Apr. 15, 1824, Mylo Hill, b. Aug. 8, 1807, dau. of Isaac.

WATSON, Jeremiah F., b. Sept. 18, 1800, m. Oct. 2, 1822, in Barrington, Hannah Hall, b. Jan. 28, 1802, dau. of Daniel.

WATSON, William, m. May 11, 1826, in Barrington, Sally Seavey, both of Barrington.

WATSON, Edward F., of Lowell, Mass., m. Mar. 22, 1835, by Rev. Isaac Willey, Meribah Ann Main, of Rochester, dau. of Amos.

WATSON, George Pary, son of Jeremiah F., b. Dec. 23, 1828, m. Apr. 17, 1847, by Rev. Homer Barrows, Mary E. Thompson, both of Dover.

WATSON, Jeremiah W., of Alton, m. Dec. 23, 1858, in Sandwich, Harriet E. Duntley, of Sandwich, dau. of Blaisdell Duntley.

WATSON, Charles Westley, son of Jeremiah, b. Jan. 1, 1832, m. Feb. 14, 1859, by Rev. Benjamin F. Parsons, Mary Oliver, both of Biddeford, Me.

WATSON, Elias M., son of Jeremiah, b. Mar. 27, 1841, m. Jan. 19, 1862, in Rochester, Mary A. Pearl.

WATSON, John, of Exeter, m. July 17, 1865, in Dover, Mrs. Clara A. Carleton, of Durham.

WATSON, Elihu B. Jr., of Gonic, m. Dec. 7, 1865, in Gonic, Emma A. Foss, of Barrington, dau. of Charles A.

WATSON, Issac N., of Dover, m. Feb. 13, 1869, in Lee, Susan J. Thompson, of Lee.

WATSON, John L., m. May 1, 1869, in Great Falls, Mary A. Tebbetts, both of Dover.

WATSON, Chase G., of Marlborough, Mass., m. Nov. 18, 1869, in Durham, Annie M. Griffiths, of Durham, dau. of John B.

WATSON, John M., of Rochester, m. (pub. Apr. 14, 1870, in Rochester), Annie E. Mooney.

WEBB, Samuel, m. (pub. Nov. 24, in Great Falls), Catherine P. Leavitt, both of Lawrence, Mass.

WEBBER, Hezekiah, d. May 27, 1890, aged 94, m. (1) Apr. 19, 1819, in Lebanon, Me., Susanna Hanson, d. May 13, 1834, m. (2) Jul. 22, 1838, in Lebanon, Me., Mrs. Julia Ann (Smith) Goodwin, wid. of Amos, b. Mar. 21, 1810.

WEBBER, John, m. int. Dec. 11, 1827, in Lebanon, Me., Hannah Staples, of Sanford, Me.

WEBBER, Hezekiah Jr., son of Hezekiah, m. int. May 31, 1851, in Lebanon, Me., Laura Jane Goodwin, b. May 18, 1835, d. Sep. 3, 1884, aged 49.

WEBBER, David H., son of Hezekiah, b. Jul. 5, 1822, m. Nov. 22, 1855, by Rev. Elias Chapman, Mary E. Hanson, of Berwick, Me.

WEBBER, John T., m. May 9, 1864, by Rev. James Rand, Julia E. Pierce, both of Dover.

WEBBER, Wesley, m. May 20, 1865, in Rochester, Abbie E. Wentworth, both of Rochester.

WEBBER, Charles H., of Kennebunk, Me., m. Oct. 25, 1867, by Rev. Alden Sherwin, Laura E. Hutchins, of Wells, Me.

WEBBER, Joseph A., of Cape Elizabeth, Me., m. Mar. 21, 1869, in N. Berwick, Me., Jerusha G. Hatch, of N. Berwick, Me.

WEBBER, Freeman H., m. (pub. Oct. 20, 1870, in Great Falls), Mrs. Addie A. Blaisdell.

WEBBER, Amos Henry, m. Nov. 10, 1872, in Somersworth, Ellen Elizabeth Magoon, dau. of Benjamin.

WEBSTER, William Gage, son of Ebenezer, b. Aug. 26, 1803, d. Oct. 4, 1877, m. May 15, 1828, by Rev. Benjamin Hoyt, Hannah Jane Foss, b. Aug. 25, 1804, d. Nov. 23, 1881, aged 77, dau. of George.

WEBSTER, Augustus A., son of Matthias, b. Sep. 9, 1829, d. Jul. 24, 1919, m. Jul. 29, 1850, in Lebanon, Me., Euia A. Shorey, b. May 18, 1832, d. Nov. 4, 1902, dau. of Stephen, both of Rochester.

WEBSTER, George A., of Dover, son of John, d. Mar. 13, 1911, aged 71, m. Feb. 27, 1865, in Dover, Annie E. Young, of Strafford.

WEBSTER, Charles A., b. Aug. 8, 1815, d. Nov. 21, 1887, m. Nov. 7, 1866, in Strafford, Seddie E. Tuttle, of Strafford, b. 1836, d. 1918, dau. of James.

WEDGEWOOD, Rev. Dearborn, son of Jonathan, b. Oct. 29, 1810, d. Oct. 7, 1876, aged 66, m. int. Aug. 29, 1835, in Dover, Ursula P. Dealand, of Brookfield, d. Mar. 29, 1887, aged 72.

WEDGEWOOD, Elbridge G. L., m. Dec. 2, 1866, in Lebanon, Me., Ursula Hartford.

WEEDEN, Capt. Amos, m. Oct. 1, 1863, in Providence, R. I., Sarah E. Whitten, dau. of Moses, both of Dover.

WEEDEN, George, of N. Berwick, Me., m. (pub. Aug. 11, 1870, in Great Falls), Nellie F. Currier, of Strafford.

WEEKS, George B., of Portsmouth, m. Oct. 29, 1864, in Dover, Catherine E. Shields, of Providence, R.I.

WELCH, Stephen, m. Nay 2, 1813, in Lebanon, Me., Nancy Paul, both of Sanford, Me.

WELCH, Ebenezer, m. Nov. 20, 1838, in Barrington, by Rev. Samuel Nichols, Abia G. Waterhouse, both of Barrington.

WELCH, Charles W., of Boston, Mass., m. Feb. 26, 1846, by Rev. Joseph Loring, Malvina B. Fernald.

WELCH, Joseph A., of Wakefield, m. (pub. Apr. 10, 1862, in Wakefield), Roxanna T. Greely, of Cumberland, Me.

WELCH, Joseph M., m. June 2, 1866, in Tuftonboro, Sarah F. Thompson, of Ossipee, b. May 29, 1843, d. Oct. 23, 1918.

WELCH, Samuel F., of Lawrence, Mass., b. Aug. 7, 1835, d. Jun. 21, 1902, m. Oct. 10, 1866, in New Durham, Betsey J. Miles, of Somersworth, b. May 4, 1843, d. mar. 24, 1912, dau. of Jeremiah.

WELCH, Joseph, of Biddeford, Me., m. Oct. 8, 1867, in Salmon Falls, Anna E. Cole, of Saco, Me.

WELCH, John D., of Pittsburg, m. Apr. 2, 1868, in Great Falls, Mary E. Hurd, of Great Falls.

WELD, Dr. Charles, m. int. Jun. 15, 1828, in Lebanon, Me., Theodotia Wentworth.

WELLS, Brenton R., of Chicago, Ill., m. Jan. 10, 1870, in Dover, Abby W. Kittredge, of Dover, dau. of Thomas W.

WENDELL, Oliver C., of Dover, m. July 11, 1870, in Augusta, Me., Sarah Butler, of Augusta, Me.

WENTWORTH, Richard, m. Dec. 20, 1791, by Rev. Samuel Shephard, Deborah Burleigh.

WENTWORTH, John, m. Nov. 28, 1813, by Rev. Joseph Boodey, Betsy Clark.

WENTWORTH, Elder James J., m. July 8, 1832, by Elder Enoch Place, Clarissa Hall, of Strafford, dau. of Israel.

WENTWORTH, Albra, d. Jun. 3, 1875, aged 68, m. (1) Jan. 19, 1829, in Wakefield, Rhoda Cook, of Wakefield, d. Jun. 15, 1845, aged 35, m. (2) Eliza V. ----, d. Jan. 24, 1905, aged 83.

WENTWORTH, Charles K., of Berwick, Me., m. Dec. 31, 1863, in Industry, Me., Ellen M. Plummer, of S. Berwick, Me.

WENTWORTH, James F., of Denmark, Me., m. (pub. Apr. 26, 1866, in Great Falls), Fidelia J. Swinnerton.

WENTWORTH, L. J., of Waterford, Me., m. (pub. July 5, 1866, in Strafford), Sarah E. Caverly, of Strafford.

WESCOTT, Clarendon F., m. (pub. Aug. 11, 1870, in Great Falls), m. Abbie Frost, both of Rochester.

WESLEY, Samuel, m. Aug. 30, 1847, in Lebanon, Me., Joanna McCrillis.

WEST, George W., of Omaha, Neb., m. (pub. Oct. 8, 1868, in Omaha, Neb.), Adelia A. Janvrin, of Great Falls, dau. of Rufus.

3) **WHEELER**, Dr. James Henry, of Dover, son of John B., b. Sept. 17, 1831, d. Jan. 26, 1893, m. Oct. 21, 1862, in New York City, Hannah Draper French, of New York City, b. Apr. 1, 1839, d. Sept. 15, 1910, dau. of Eli.

WHITE, Joseph, m. Jan. 5, 1786, by Rev. Isaac Hasey, Jane Copps, dau. of Deac. Samuel.

WHITE, Lewis, of Canotn, Mass., m. Apr. 12, 1838, in Lebanon, Me., Cynthia Drew.

WHITE, Nathaniel, b. Oct. 1, 1818, d. Jan. 2, 1912, m. (1) (pub. Oct. 11, 1842, in Ossipee), Clarinda Tasker, d. Apr. 4, 1865, aged 42, m. (2) Oct. 14, 1867, in Ossipee, Mrs. Sarah M. Nute, d. Jan. 30, 1891, aged 56, both of Ossipee.

WHITE, John C., of Roxbury, Mass., m. Mar. 15, 1846, by Elder Josiah Wetherbee, Lydia B. Stanton.

WHITE, James Elliott, of Northfield, Mass., son of William, aged 23, d. 1864, m. Sept. 8, 1853, by Rev. Levi B. Tasker, in Sandwich, Sophia Watson, aged 25, dau. of Jedediah, both of Sandwich.

WHITE, Lemuel, of Great Falls, m. Dec. 24, 1863, in Portsmouth), Elizabeth N. Clark.

WHITE, James C., of Somersworth, m. Jan. 8, 1864, in S. Berwick, Me., Mary J. Wentworth, of S. Berwick, Me.

WHITE, David N., b. 1844, d. 1922, m. Apr. 26, 1865, in Ossipee, Eunice A. Nutter, b. 1844, d. 1916.

WHITE, Joseph F., of New Castle, son of Joseph A., m. Jan. 8, 1869, by Rev. Alvan Tobey, Lizzie Ellis, of Portland, Me., dau. of Hiram.

WHITE, George B., of Boston, Mass., m. (pub. Aug. 26, 1869, in Great Falls), Mary Frances Butler, of Berwick, Me.

WHITE (WHYTE), Benjamin F., m. Mar. 30, 1835, in Barrington, Ellen Jane Hall.

WHITEHORN, (?) Ebenezer, m. Aug. 16, 1798, by Rev. Benjamin Balch, Sarah Langmaid, both of Barrington.

WHITEHORN, James Y., m. (pub. May 11, 1865, in Portsmouth), Mary Ann Hoyt, both of Newington.

WHITEHOUSE, James, d. Apr. 7, 1844, aged 75, m. Dec. 19, 1776, by Rev. Isaac Hasey, Mary Dore, d. Mar. 26, 1848, aged 97.

WHITEHOUSE, Robert, m. Jan. 21, 1791, by Rev. Isaac Hasey, Lydia Wallingford.

WHITEHOUSE, Enoch, son of Turner, d. Oct. 1804, m. Nov. 15, 1798, by Rev. Benjamin Balch, Sally Smith, both of Barrington.

WHITEHOUSE, Daniel, son of Joseph, b. in 1781, d. Nov. 8, 1852, m. (1) Mar. 25, 1803, by Rev. Benjamin Balch, Mary Leathers, d. near 1850, both of Dover, m. (2) Sept. 6, 1850, by Elder Enoch Place, Mrs. Delia Corson.

WHITEHOUSE, Thomas, m. Sep. 21, 1815, in Lebanon, Me., Sobriety Hartford.

WHITEHOUSE, Turner, m. Oct. 9, 1823, in Brookfield, Hannah Martin, both of Brookfield.

WHITEHOUSE, Andrew, of Somersworth, m. Jun. 14, 1827, by Elder Zebedee Delano, Mary J. Wise, of Sanford, Me.

WHITEHOUSE, Leonard, m. Nov. 23, 1830, in Barrington, Phebe Hall, both of Barrington.

WHITEHOUSE, John Cotton, d. July 5, 1859, aged 47, m. Feb. 2, 1834, in Middleton, Mary Emeline Kimball, both of Middleton.

WHITEHOUSE, Jacob, d. May 8, 1904, aged 91, m. int. Sep. 4, 1836, in Dover, Lydia A. Horn.

WHITEHOUSE, Leonard, m. Feb. 19, 1850, in Barrington, Martha A. Welch, both of Barrington.

WHITEHOUSE, Edmund H., of Somersworth, d. Oct. 21, 1862, m. (pub. Sept. 10, 1850, in Somersworth), Caroline E. Boyle, of Bucksport, Me., d. Apr. 1851, aged 22.

WHITEHOUSE, George W., m (1) May 22, 1853, in New Durham, Lydia M. Ransom, both of Dover, m. (2) Apr. 10, 1862, by Rev. James Rand, Fannie Carpenter, both of Dover.

WHITEHOUSE, Franklin, of Tuftonboro, d. Feb. 20, 1923, aged 87, m. Dec. 2, 1855, in Wolfeboro, Martha A. Moody.

WHITEHOUSE, John M., m. May 25, 1862, in Dover, Sarah A. Foye, both of Strafford.

WHITEHOUSE, Mark, of Great Falls, m. Oct. 18, 1864, in Great Falls, Alvina Haughton, of Biddeford, Me.

WHITEHOUSE, Charles E., of Dover, m. May 31, 1865, in Portsmouth, Dorcas E. Cole, of Newcastle.

WHITEHOUSE, Charles W., of Tuftonboro, m. Feb. 18, 1866, in Ossipee, Phebe F. Hanson, of Ossipee, b. 1840, d. 1932.

WHITEHOUSE, Jonas W., m. Jul. 16, 1866, in Middleton, Abbie M. Harvey.

WHITEHOUSE, Turner, m. Nov. 18, 1866, in Strafford, Mary Bumford, both of Barrington.

WHITEHOUSE, John M., of Strafford, m. Jan. 31, 1867, in Rochester, Abbie H. Peirce, of New Durham.

WHITEHOUSE, Daniel F., m. May 28, 1868, in Dover, Annie E. Scott, both of Dover.

WHITEHOUSE, Charles, of Kensington, m. Oct. 9, 1869, in Rochester, Mary J. A. Lougee, of Sanbornton.

WHITEHOUSE, Benjamin F., m. Sept. 20, 1870, by Rev. Ezra Haskell, Harriet A. Young, both of Dover.

WHITEHOUSE, Charles E., m. Jun. 10, 1876, in Middleton, Susan J. Amazeen.

WHITLEY, William, m. (pub. July 22, 1869, in Great Falls), Elizabeth Hart, both of Great Falls.

WHITNEY, Leonard S., d. Oct. 6, 1839, m. Jan. 14, 1838, by Rev. Eleazer Smith, Rolina Dolloff.

WHITNEY, Leonard P., m. Feb. 26, 1862, in Dover, Emma A. Griffin, both of Dover.

WHITNEY, Edward H., m. Nov. 29, 1866, by Rev. Ezra Haskell, Jennie H. Hooper, d. Nov. 29, aged 72, dau. of John, both of Dover.

WHITNEY, Charles H., m. May 18, 1867, in Portsmouth, Flora E. Harding, both of Kittery, Me.

WHITTEN, David E., b. May 26, 1839, d. Oct. 28, 1908, m. Oct. 14, 1865, in Ossipee, Nettie A. Tebbetts, b. Sept. 27, 1840, d. Dec. 11, 1875, both of Wolfeboro.

WHITTIER, William, m. Aug. 11, 1810, in Lebanon, Me., Sally Hardison.

WHITTIER, Horace P., m. Nov. 10, 1864, in Dover, Emma D. Freeman, both of Dover.

WHITTIER, Joseph F., m. Apr. 26, 1866, in S. Berwick, Me., Jennie Downs, both of Dover.

WHITTIER, Phineas C., m. Mar. 11, 1869, in Dover, Emma F. Patten, both of Amesbury, Mass.

WIGGIN, Andrew, m. Aug. 19, 1777, by Rev. Isaac Hasey, Mary Whitehouse.

WIGGIN, Chase, son of Mark, b. Jan. 26, 1772, d. May 12, 1835, m. Jul. 10, 1794, Nancy French.

WIGGIN, Richard, d. Jan. 17, 1873, aged 84, m. int Feb. 1813, in Tuftonboro, Eleanor Chamberlain, d. July 24, 1867, aged 75.

WIGGIN, William, d. Feb. 14, 1865, aged 78, m. int. Nov. 1814, in Tuftonboro, Dolly Snell, d. Mar. 29, 1865, aged 74, both of Tuftonboro.

WIGGIN, Mark Jr., son of Mark, b. Oct. 27, 1778, d. Jun. 20, 1848, m. Mar. 30, 1815, in Wakefield, Hannah Poor Hardy, b. Dec. 7, 1793, d. Jun. 23, 1849, dau. of Maj. Dudley.

WIGGIN, David, d. May 5, 1820, aged 39, m. Dec. 5, 1816, by Rev. Isaac Smith, Betsey Pervier, d. May 21, 1850, aged 72.

WIGGIN, Robert, d. Nov. 9, 1886, aged 85, m. (1) Nov. 12, 1822, in Wolfeboro, Polly Maria Craton, d. Apr. 16, 1871, aged 73, both of Wolfeboro, m. (2) Mary E. ----, d. Mar. 4, 1913, aged 69.

WIGGIN, Tobias H., b. May 27, 1804, d. Jul. 30, 1870, m. Mar. 21, 1824, in Lebanon, Me., Judith Peirce, b. May 29, 1804, d. Sep. 16, 1882.

WIGGIN, Capt. George Jerry, of Durham, son of Lt. Davis, b. Oct. 14, 1801, d. 1891, m. (1) Apr. 17, 1827, Abigail Thompson, of Lee, b. Dec. 12, 1800, d. Feb. 2, 1872, dau. of Edmund, m. (2) Feb. 8, 1873, in Durham, Mrs. Alice Ann (Jones) Smart, wid. of Samuel, dau. of Thomas.

WIGGIN, Rev. Daniel A., son of Richard, b. Oct. 13, 1826, d. Mar. 30, 1900, m. (1) (pub. Jan. 26, 1847, in Tuftonboro), Shuah Morrison, b. Aug. 31, 1828, d. Sept. 13, 1857, aged 29, dau. of Ebenezer, m. (2) Feb. 18, 1858, in Wolfeboro, Susan P. Wiggin, b. May 8, 1824, d. Dec. 21, 1887, dau. of Tufton, both of Tuftonboro.

WIGGIN, Joseph W., d. Jan. 3, 1871, aged 49, m. May 20, 1847, by Rev. Homer Barrows, Lavinia A. G. Clark, d. Feb. 22, 1873, aged 49.

WIGGIN, Woodbury, of Barrington, b. Jan. 7, 1823, d. Apr. 1, 1905, m. (1) Martha Ann ----, d. Oct. 18, 1850, aged 24, m. (2) Apr. 27, 1852, in Lebanon, Me., Mrs. Rebecca O. (Barrows) Felker, wid. of Elias R., d. May 14, 1871, aged 49.

WIGGIN, John T., son of Richard, d. Aug. 2, 1870, aged 42, m. (1) (pub. Aug. 30, 1853, in Tuftonboro), Ellen M. Wiggin, dau. of Richard, m. (2) Mehitable E. ----, d. May 18, 1891, aged 64.

WIGGIN, Hiram, m. (pub. Jun. 18, 1857, in Stratham), Ruth Gerrish, of Nottingham, d. Jun. 27, 1901, aged 79.

WIGGIN, Capt. Augustus, of Dover, son of Richard, b. July 21, 1826, d. May 25, 1898, m. (1) Dec. 20, 1857, in Wolfeboro, Martha S. Leavitt, of Tuftonboro, b. Nov. 16, 1833, d. Oct. 21, 1880, aged 46, dau. of Samuel, m. (2) Lizzie E. Cotton, b. Jan. 1, 1836, d. Jan. 17, 1907.

WIGGIN, Charles F., of Ossipee, b. 1829, d. 1906, m. (pub. May 27, 1858, in Wolfeboro), Arvilla M. Beacham, of Wolfeboro, b. 1840, d. 1905.

WIGGIN, Freeman W., son of Tobias H., b. May 13, 1840, m. int. Feb. 20, 1861, in Lebanon, Me., Sarah E. Burleigh, of Union Village.

WIGGIN, Joseph H., m. Feb. 5, 1862, in Dover, Susan A. Rogers, both of Dover.

WIGGIN, Russel B., son of Benjamin, b. Nov. 25, 1836, d. Nov. 14, 1886, m. Mar. 27, 1862, in Dover, Emily J. Paul, b. Apr. 13, 1839, d. Dec. 23, 1890, both of Dover.

WIGGIN, John A., of Epping, m. Nov. 4, 1862, in Lee, Abby S. Hanson, of Lee.

WIGGIN, Benaiah, of Stratham, m. Nov. 23, 1862, in Dover, Mrs. Jennie M. Hall, of Dover.

WIGGIN, George W., m. Mar. 5, 1863, by Rev. John H. Garmon, Rachel A. Knox, of Berwick, Me.

WIGGIN, A. E., of Tamworth, m. (pub. Apr. 16, 1863, in Lawrence, Mass.), Mary F. Drown, of Nottingham.

WIGGIN, James M., of Stratham, m. Apr. 18, 1863, in Dover, Angie A. Osborne, of Dover.

WIGGIN, John, m. Oct. 20, 1863, in Wakefield, Sarah Farnham, of Wakefield.

WIGGIN, Joseph D., of Lee, b. 1841, m. int. Dec. 17, 1863, in Lee, Hannah M. Beardslee, of Salem, b. 1844, d. May 3, 1930, aged 86.

WIGGIN, Charles, of Tuftonboro, m. (pub. Nov. 23, 1865, in Wolfeboro), Jane N. Thompson, of Ossipee.

WIGGIN, John H., b. 1843, d. 1910, m. Dec. 4, 1866, by Rev. James Rand, Sarah E. Tibbetts, b. 1838, d. 1917, both of Portland, Me.

WIGGIN, Lyford M., of Tuftonboro, m. Mar. 2, 1867, in Dover, Hattie E. Rogers, of Rochester.

WIGGIN, Jacob H., of Dover, m. June 23, 1867, in Rochester, Lydia A. Tebbetts, of Barrington.

WIGGIN, A. Dana, m. July 4, 1867, in Newmarket, Annie M. Mathes.

WIGGIN, James S., of Tuftonboro, m. Nov. 18, 1867, in Rochester, Ettia N. Merrill, of Somersworth.

WIGGIN, Joseph M., of Dover, son of Nathaniel, m. Jan. 10, 1868, by Rev. Alvan Tobey, Jennie M. Morrison, of Madbury, dau. of Abraham.

WIGGIN, Charles W., of Boston, Mass., m. Mar. 11, 1868, in Great Falls, Emma E. Randall, of Somersworth.

WIGGIN, Walter, m. Mar. 23, 1868, in Newmarket, Sarah A. England, both of Newmarket.

WIGGIN, Albert H., of Dover, m. Feb. 22, 1869, in Biddeford, Me., Rebecca S. Waterhouse, of Biddeford, Me.

WIGGIN, Daniel C., of Alton, b. 1831, d. Oct. 24, 1898, m. June 3, 1869, in Dover, Abby H. Snell, of Dover, b. 1837, d. Dec. 16, 1919.

WIGGIN, John W., of Dover, m. Sept. 5, 1870, in Sherman, Me., Josephine E. Young, of Sherman, Me.

WILCOX, Carlos, of Fall River, Mass., m. Sept. 22, 1869, in Lawrence, Mass., Abbie A. Parsons, of Lawrence, Mass.

WILDES, Joseph, b. 1795, d. Oct. 6, 1868, of Kennebunk, Me., m. Nov. 5, 1823, by Elder Zebedee Delano, Betsey Goodwin, b. 1797, d. Nov. 14, 1857.

WILDES, Joseph Jr., d. 1856, m. Jun. 5, 1851, by Elder Samuel Goodwin, Judith G. Gerrish.

WILDES, Jacob G., m. int. Aug. 22, 1859, in Lebanon, Me., Abba J. Goodwin, of Newfield, Me.

WILDES, John F., m. int. Dec. 19, 1863, in Lebanon, Me., Sophia J. Young.

WILEY, Charles R., of Roxbury, Mass., m. Nov. 28, 1866, by Rev. James Rand, Mrs. Olivia Worthing, of Chelsea, Mass.

WILKINS, Zadock, of Salem, Mass. M. Nov. 10, 1828, in Lebanon, Me., Sarah Knox.

WILKINSON, Rufus, d. Feb. 5, 1868, aged 68, m. Nov. 1825, by Rev. William Demeritt, Catherine Bunker, d. May 11, 1874, aged 68, dau. of Aaron.

WILKINSON, James, m. Sep. 9, 1832, in Lebanon, Me., Lydia D. Goodwich, both of Berwick, Me.

WILKINSON, Isaiah N., m. Jun. 28, 1855, in Lebanon, Me., Lucy D. Hayes, both of Rochester.

WILKINSON, Albra 2nd, of Effingham, m. July 26, 1863, in Ossipee, Vienner Moulton, of Newfield, Me.

WILKINSON, W. H., of Salmon Falls, m. (pub. Dec. 29, 1870, in Great Falls), Emma A. Haydon, of Wells, Me.

WILLAND, Edward, of Ossipee, m. (pub. Jan. 21, 1834, in Wolfeboro), Diedmaia Brown, of Tuftonboro, d. Dec. 26, 1840, aged 28.

WILLAND, Edward A., of Great Falls, son of Nathaniel H., d. July 8, 1915, aged 69, m. Dec. 25, 1870, in Dover, Calista A. Chesley, of Barrington, d. July 17, 1915, aged 66, dau. of Samuel.

WILLAND, Noah, son of Charles, d. Sep. 24, aged 58, m. (pub. Jun. 11, 1874, in Rochester), Mary A. Wentworth.

6) **WILLEY**, Capt. Mark, son of Robert, b. Apr. 10, 1791, d. Apr. 21, 1878, m. Dorothy Cilley, d. Mar. 11, 1876.

WILLEY, Nathaniel, son of William, b. Aug. 9, 1765, d. Sep. 23, 1860, m. Apr. 20, 1786, Dorothy Quimby, b. 1768, d. 1862.

WILLEY, Isaac, b. 1776, d. Mar. 24, 1838, m. Sept. 11, 1796, by Rev. Benjamin Balch, Hannah Otis, d. Apr. 16, 1838, aged 63, both of Barrington.

WILLEY, Benjamin, m. June 4, 1798, by Rev. Benjamin Balch, Rachel White, both of Barrington.

WILLEY, Samuel, m. Aug. 30, 1798, by Rev. Benjamin Balch, Deborah Willey, both of Barrington.

WILLEY, Ezekiel, m. June 30, 1802, in Barrington, Martha Willey, both of Barrington. (was this a second marriage?)

WILLEY, Thomas, m. May 29, 1806, by Rev. Benjamin Balch, Sally Hall, both of Barrington.

WILLEY, Daniel, of Durham, d. Jan. 8, 1825, aged 31, m. 1817, by Rev. John Osborne, Jane Leathers, of Nottingham.

WILLEY, Phinehas, of Newmarket, d. Feb. 22, 1825, aged 27, m. Mar. 25, 1818, by Rev. John Brodhead, Welthern Sias, b. Jan. 8, 1794, d. May 17, 1830, dau. of Maj. Nathaniel.

WILLEY, Moses, of Northwood, m. July 4, 1822, by Elder Enoch Place, Abigail Caverly, of Strafford, dau. of Charles.

WILLEY, Aaron, m. Jan. 27, 1823, in Barrington, Sukey Mills, both of Barrington.

WILLEY, John Jr., m. Dec. 15, 1823, in Barrington, Nancy Whitehouse, both of Barrington.

WILLEY, Isaac, d. Sept. 9, 1845, aged 50, m. Feb. 15, 1826, by Elder Enoch Place, Sally Peirce, both of Barrington.

WILLEY, Jacob, m. May 4, 1833, by Rev. Samuel Sherburne, Sarah D. Roberts, of Barrington, d. Feb. 10, 1845, aged 38.

7) WILLEY, Henry, son of Mark, b. Dec. 20, 1812, d. Jan. 22, 1892, m. (1) Feb. 26, 1836, Susan F. Runlett, b. Mar. 3, 1816, d. Oct. 30, 1864, m. (2) Jan. 23, 1866, Abby R. Emerson, b. Nov. 17, 1832, d. Jan. 18, 1914, dau. of Jonathan W.

WILLEY, Moses C., son of Moses, d. May 20, 1846, aged 43, m. Oct. 30, 1836, by Rev. Joseph Boodey, Mary Garland, both of Farmington.

WILLEY, Moses Cheney, son of Isaac, d. Apr. 6, 1889, aged 74, m. (1) int. May 13, 1840, in Dover, Sarah D. Watson, d. May 10, 1846, aged 33, m. (2) May 9, 1854, in Strafford, Betsey K. Leighton, d. Oct. 27, 1854, aged 42.

6) WILLEY, Ira, son of Mark, b. Jan. 7, 1819, d. May 6, 1906, m. Oct. 19, 1843, Mary Ann Stevens, b. Apr. 4, 1824, d. Oct. 4, 1881, dau. of Parker.

WILLEY, Jonas M., son of Benjamin, b. Feb. 1833, d. Oct. 19, 1862, m. July 2, 1853, Frances J. Pinkham.

WILLEY, Daniel H., of Albany, d. Feb. 24, 1876, aged 28, m. July 13, 1856, in Sandwich, Susan Atwood, of Sandwich, aged 24.

WILLEY, Col. Eliphalet, of Wakefield, m. May 13, 1862, in Brookfield, Mrs. Abigail Cater, of Wolfeboro.

WILLEY, Edwin, of Kennebunk, Me., m. July 19, 1862, in Great Falls, Clara K. Parsons, of Great Falls.

WILLEY, Nathaniel S., m. Apr. 18, 1863, in Eddyville, Iowa, Elizabeth H. S. Tuttle.

WILLEY, B. Frank, m. June 23, 1863, in Rochester, Anna A. Cater, both of Barrington.

WILLEY, John W., of New Durham, m. July 15, 1865, in New Durham, Mary E. Tufts, of Middleton.

WILLEY, James, m. June 16, 1866, in Dover, Mrs. Elizabeth B. Watson, both of Dover.

WILLEY, Frank J., of Portsmouth, son of Enoch, d. Dec. 19, 1926, aged 82, m. Mar. 1, 1869, by Rev. Robert S. Stubbs, Mary E. Willey, of Barrington.

WILLEY, William H., of Barrington, m. Mar. 9, 1869, in Barrington, Fannie S. Wentworth, of Strafford.

WILLEY, Elijah, m. Sept. 30, 1869, in Dover, Elizabeth E. Ashton, both of Dover.

WILLEY, Albert C., m. (pub. Jan. 27, 1870, in Great Falls), Hattie A. Campbell.
WILLEY, Daniel H. of Albany, aged 28, d. Feb. 24, 1876, m. Jul. 13, 1856, in Sandwich, Susan Atwood, aged 24.
WILLIAMS, Robert, m. Jan. 13, 1777, in Barrington, Sarah Pinkham, both of Barrington.
WILLIAMS, Ivory, m. int. Sep. 15, 1849, in Lebanon, Me., Jean Grant.
WILLIAMS, Horace, m. int. Aug. 21, 1855, in Lebanon, Me., (married in Somersworth), Ann E. Corson.
WILLIAMS, Charles, of Alton, m. Aug. 22, 1865, in Rochester, Mrs. Mary E. (Curtis) Gilbert, of Farmington, wid. of David M.
WILSON, George W., of Newfield, Me., m. Aug. 17, 1834, by Rev. Abner Flanders, Rhoda Chick, b. Jan. 15, 1809, dau. of Aaron.
WILSON, Elias S., of Freeport, Me., m. int. Sep. 10, 1853, in Lebanon, Me., Georgiana A. Poor, of Portland, Me.
WILSON, Moses E., of Beverly, Mass., m. Aug. 14, 1858, in Lebanon, Me., Cary J. Ricker, of Alton.
WINCHELL, Frank H., m. Nov. 2, 1864, in Great Falls, Hattie M. Prescott, both of Acton.
WINGATE, Jonathan, d. Nov. 13, 1850, aged 92, m. Feb. 1782, Sarah Drew, <u>d. Mar. 20, 1821</u>, both of Barrington.
WINGATE, John, of Farmington, m. Nov. 23, 1801, by Rev. Benjamin Balch, Polly Cate, of Barrington.
WINGATE, Jeremiah B., of Alton, <u>d. Nov. 25, 1851, aged 53</u>, m. Sept. 16, 1824, in Middleton, Nancy H. Stevens, of New Durham, <u>d. July 17, 1884, aged 80</u>.
WINGATE, Aaron P., of Rochester, m. May 15, 1856, in Dover, Lizzie E. Goodwin.
WINGATE, Daniel D., of Tuftonboro, <u>son of Jeremiah, d. Sept. 5, 1924, aged 98</u>, m. Oct. 29, 1857, in Newmarket, Mary W. Wood, of Newmarket, <u>b. Apr. 22, 1833, d. Jan. 7, 1900</u>.
WINGATE, John of Strafford, m. Jan. 5, 1865, in Farmington, Nellie E. Wallingford, of Milton, dau. of David.
WINGATE, John J., of Portland, Me., m. Feb. 4, 1868, in Boston, Mass., Anne E. Davis, of Dover.
WINKLEY, Francis, son of Samuel, b. 1689, d. Apr. 23, 1776, m. Mary Emerson, <u>d. Mar. 17, 1745, aged 41</u>, dau. of Rev. John.
WINKLEY, Francis Jr., of Barrington, <u>son of Samuel, b. Mar.28, 1759, d. June 20, 1847</u>, m. Sept. 16, 1781, by Dr. Belknap, Sarah Libbey, d. Apr. 25, 1843, dau. of Benjamin.

WINKLEY, Deac. John, son of John, of Kittery, Me., b. Feb. 20, 1767, d. Jan. 8, 1843, m. (1) Lydia Hight, d. Sept. 3, 1839, aged 61, m. (2) Mary ----, d. Feb. 26, 1854, aged 90.

WINKLEY, William, son of Samuel, b. Aug. 31, 1763, d. July 29, 1845, m. (1) Nov. 20, 1785, by Rev. Benjamin Balch, Martha Clark, d. Oct. 11, 1786, aged 23, both of Barrington, m. (2) Dec. 27, 1787, by Rev. Benjamin Balch, Mary Winkley, b. Feb. 15, 1766, d. Oct. 16, 1835, dau. of Francis.

WINKLEY, Hunkin, son of Francis, b. Oct. 28, 1763, d. Sept. 28, 1842, m. Aug. 25, 1791, by Rev. Benjamin Balch, Tamson Hayes, dau. of Paul, both of Barrington.

WINKLEY, John, son of Samuel, b. Nov. 17, 1766, d. Jan. 8, 1843, m. Nov. 17, 1791, by Rev. Benjamin Balch, Mary Swain, d. Feb. 21, 1854, aged 90, both of Barrington.

WINKLEY, Benjamin, son of Samuel, b. Jan. 3, 1772, d. Sept. 30, 1851, m. Apr. 7, 1795, by Rev. Benjamin Balch, Elizabeth Pitman, both of Barrington.

WINKLEY, Francis, of Barrington, son of Francis, d. Apr. 7, 1855, aged 81, m. (1) Feb. 28, 1798, by Rev. Benjamin Balch, Sara Drew, of Alton, d. Mar. 26, 1846, aged 68, dau. of Capt. John, m. (2) (pub. Feb. 2, 1847, in Madbury), Abigail (Peirce) Church, wid. of Benjamin, d. May 14, 1865, aged 63, dau. of Israel.

WINKLEY, John, son of Francis, b. Oct. 8, 1769, d. Apr. 8, 1859, m. Mar. 19, 1801, by Rev. Benjamin Balch, Ruth Foye, dau. of Stephen, both of Barrington.

WINKLEY, Col. David, d. Dec. 19, 1852, aged 78, m. July 4, 1802, by Rev. Benjamin Balch, Anna Hussey, d. Nov. 7, 1848, aged 64, both of Barrington.

WINKLEY, Daniel, of Orford, son of Deac. John, d. Feb. 4, 1883, aged 90, m. Mar. 20, 1816, by Rev. Micajah Otis, Sarah Otis, of Barrington, d. Mar. 13, 1886, aged 88.

WINKLEY, William, son of William, b. Jan. 23, 1789, d. May 23, 1866, aged 77, m. Nov. 26, 1818, by Rev. J. W. Clary, Sarah Hussey, d. Jan. 10, 1862, aged 67, dau. of Richard, both of Barrington.

WINKLEY, Benjamin Jr., of Dover, son of Benjamin, b. Feb. 1800, m. Nov. 23, 1826, in Newmarket, by Rev. John Brodhead, Eliza C. Hoitt, of Newmarket.

WINKLEY, Capt. Asa, of Barrington, son of John, d. June 27, 1854, aged 53, m. Jan. 29, 1828, by Rev. J. W. Clary, Hannah Wingate, of Madbury, d. Oct. 1, 1841, aged 39, dau. of Jonathan.

WINKLEY, Samuel, son of William, d. Apr. 17, 1863, aged 57, m. (1) Dec. 28, 1828, by Rev. Cephas H. Kent, Nancy Foss, b. May 13, 1808, d. Mar. 20, 1836, both of Barrington, m. (2) Mar. 12, 1839, by Rev. Silas Green, Lydia Foye, d. Oct. 28, 1881, aged 77.

WINKLEY, Jeremiah, of Lowell, Mass., son of John, m. int. Sept. 4, 1831, in Lee, Maria Jane Langley, of Lee.

WINKLEY, George, of Barrington, son of Francis, b. Mar. 16, 1802, m. Feb. 19, 1832, by Rev. Joseph, Boodey, Tamson Stanton, of Strafford.

WINKLEY, John H. Jr., son of John H., d. May 27, 1878, aged 72, m. (1) Mar. 1836, by Rev. David Root, Keziah Y. Brock, d. Feb. 7, 1850, aged 39, m. (2) Susan Brock.

WINKLEY, Paul T., m. May 4, 1836, by Elder Enoch Place, Abigail K. Otis, d. Sept. 2, 1861, aged 78, dau. of Job, both of Strafford.

WINKLEY, Joseph, son of Francis, b. June 1814, d. Oct. 30, 1890, aged 76, m. Apr. 11, 1841, by Rev. Elihu Scott, Mary Cater, b. 1817, d. Aug. 12, 1875, dau. of John, both of Barrington.

WINKLEY, Benjamin, d. Sept. 29, 1851, aged 79, m. Oct. 17, 1841, by Rev. Enos George, Mrs. Betsey (Peavey) Cate, wid. of Daniel, d. Apr. 28, 1863, aged 80, dau. of Joseph.

WINKLEY, Darius, son of Francis, b. June 17, 1807, m. (1) pub. Nov. 16, 1841, in Barrington, Ursula R. Hall, b. Aug. 17, 1811, d. Oct. 6, 1844, aged 33, dau. of Joseph, m. (2) Oct. 20, 1846, by Elder David Garland, Maria G. Daniels, d. Aug. 26, 1847, aged 26, m. (3) Mar. 24, 1850, by Rev. Homer Barrows, Mrs. Sarah Cate, of Dover, b. 1818, d. 1891.

WINKLEY, Charles E., of Newmarket, m. May 30, 1864, in Newmarket, Mary E. Allen, of Wells.

WINKLEY, Dennis, b. Apr. 24, 1828, d. Jul. 24, 1905, m. Nov. 11, 1865, in Dover, Betsey M. Hawkins.

WINKLEY, John Langdon, m. Mar. 15, 1870, in Dover, Ellen T. Young, of Barrington, dau. of William H.

WINKLEY, John F., of Dover, son of Joseph, d. Oct. 30, 1908, aged 62, m. July 9, 1870, in Dover, Lucinda Ladd, of Saco, Me.

WINN, Jotham, d. Apr. 14, 1866, aged 70, m. Oct. 28, 1821, in Lebanon, Me., Mary Wentworth, d. Nov. 11, 1869, aged 67.

WINN, Josiah, m. int. Oct. 3, 1830, in Lebanon, Me., Sarah Lord.

WINN, Ebenezer, m. May 30, 1839, by Rev. Joseph Loring, Sally J. Hayes.

WINN, Caleb Wentworth, b. Apr. 12, 1835, m. Sep. 14, 1861, in Lebanon, Me., Sarah Wentworth.

WISE, Daniel, of Sanford, Me., m. int. Sep. 19, 1812, in Lebanon, Me., Ann Jones, b. Jul. 17, 1788, dau. of Samuel.

WISWALL, Henry T., of Washington, D.C., m. (pub. Feb. 20, 1868, in Milford), Mrs. Elizabeth (Ayer) Clapp, of Milford, dau. of Rev. O. Ayer.

WITHAM, Josiah, m. int. May 27, 1809, in Lebanon, Me., Dorcas Hersom.

WITHAM, Ira L., son of Obadiah, m. (pub. Nov. 27, 1838, in Milton Mills), Climera P. Witham.

WITHAM, George F., of Somersworth, m. Feb. 16, 1865, in Great Falls, Emily J. Jones, of Lebanon, Me.

WITHAM, Jerome B., m. July 24, 1866, in New Durham, Flora A. Tebbetts, both of New Durham.

WITHERAL, James, son of Thomas, b. Nov. 24, 1755, m. Apr. 17, 1781, by Rev. Isaac Hasey, Matha Gerrish, b. Sep. 9, 1760, dau. of William.

WITHERAL, Thomas, son of Thomas, m. Mar. 21, 1786, by Rev. Isaac Hasey, Elizabeth Knox.

WOOD, John, m. Sep. 17, 1772, in Lebanon, Me., Mary Emerson.

WOOD, Daniel, b. Feb. 5, 1767, d. Jul. 19, 1846, m. Mar. 15, 1795, in Lebanon, Me., Miriam Bodwell, d. May 16, 1848, aged 70.

WOOD, John B., son of Daniel, b. Feb. 8, 1802, d. Aug. 15, 1870, m. int. May 27, 1827, in Lebanon, Me., Arabella S. Goodwin, of Kennebunkport, Me.

WOOD, Temple, of Shapleigh, Me., m. int. Oct. 25, 1829, Charlotte Maria Wood.

WOOD, Daniel Jr., son of Daniel, b. Jun. 30, 1807, d. Jul. 30, 1884, m. Apr. 18, 1830, by Elder Zebedee Delano, Mary Pray.

WOOD, George W., m. Mar. 30, 1864, in Farmington, Lucy J. Jones, both of Farmington.

WOOD, Hiram H., m. June 19, 1864, in Barringotn, Lydia S. Ham, of Dover.

WOOD, Charles J., of Dover, m. Jan. 15, 1867, in Tuftonboro, Sarah E. Piper, of Tuftonboro.

WOOD, Charles G., of Wakefield, m. (pub. Jan. 13, 1870, in Rochester), Sarah F. Horne, of Farmington.

WOOD, William W., of Boston, Mass., m. (pub. Sept. 1, 1870, in Great Falls), Ettie Noyes, of Great Falls.

WOODBURY, Dr. Robert, son of Capt. Elisha, b. Aug. 16, 1767, d. June 15, 1856, m. (1) Aug. 30, 1789, by Rev. Benjamin Balch, Abiah Kingman, d. Nov. 26, 1821, aged 59, dau. of William, both of Barrington, m. (2) in 1825, Content (Sawyer) Neal, of Dover, wid. of James, b. 1774, d. Feb. 13, 1833, dau. of Jacob, m. (3) Mary Ingersol, d. Aug. 29, 1859, aged 87.

WOODES, Charles, m. Nov. 25, 1830, in Barrington, by Rev. Samuel Sherburne, Patience Foye, both of Barrington.

WOODES, John H. C., son of Samuel, d. Mar. 20, 1909, aged 66, m. May 19, 1866, by Rev. James Rand, Jennie N. Decatur, d. Aug. 11, 1916, aged 74, dau. of William, both of Dover.

WOODHOUSE, Nathaniel W., m. Apr. 19, 1868, by Rev. Robert S. Stubbs, Luella D. Clark, of New Durham.

WOODMAN, John, m. Dec. 6, 1787, in Barrington, Sarah Foye, both of Barrington.

WOODMAN, Timothy, m. Mar. 26, 1828, in Barrington, Charity Berry, d. June 30, 1841, aged 43, both of Barrington.

WOODMAN, William, d. Apr. 28, 1880, aged 60, m. int. Aug. 28, 1842, in Lee, Abigail Buzzell, d. Feb. 24, 1897, aged 76.

WOODMAN, Seth W., m. Jan. 16, 1843, by Rev. Samuel Sherburne, Louisa M. Gear, both of Barrington.

WOODMAN, Charles F., of Durham, son of Nathan, b. July 10, 1827, d. Mar. 6, 1861, m. Jan. 1, 1850, in Concord, Sarah A. Perkins, of Pittsfield, b. Oct. 27, 1833, d. Mar. 21, 1894.

WOODMAN, Charles W., of Dover, m. June 26, 1866, in Roxbury, Mass., Frances J. Soren, of Roxbury, Mass., dau. of John J.

WOODSUM, John, b. Nov. 12, 1791, m. Nov. 13, 1820, by Elder Zebedee Delano, Betsey Brock.

WOODSUM, J. Hamilton, m. Jan. 26, 1860, in Lebanon, Me., Dora E. Rowell, both of Roxbury, Mass.

WORCESTER, Mark P., of Rochester, m. May 5, 1866, in Great Falls, Flora A. Clough, of Barnstead.

WORCESTER, Ichabod, of Great Falls, m. (pub. July 30, 1868, in Great Falls), Lydia Laird, of Berwick, Me.

WORMWOOD, James, of N. Berwick, Me., m. Oct. 27, 1866, in Rochester, Julia A. Linscott, of Rochester.

WORSTER, William, son of Moses, m. Feb. 12, 1712/13, by Rev. Nathaniel Rogers, Mary Stevenson.

WORSTER, John, son of Thomas, bpt. Nov. 2, 1718, m. Jul. 15, 1731, Lydia Remick, bpt. Aug. 28, 1820, dau. of Joshua.

WORSTER, William, son of Simeon, b. Jan. 28, 1754, d. Aug. 7, 1842, m. (1) Jul. 15, 1789, Susannah Dixon, b. Jan. 23, 1770, d. Apr. 26, 1802, m. (2) Eleanor Hurd, b. Jun. 1752, d. Dec. 1, 1852.

WORSTER, Exekiel, son of George, m. Jul. 3, 1797, by Rev. Jacob Foster, Anne Pray, of Lebanon.

WORSTER, Moses Remick, son of John, m. Sep. 4, 1799, by Rev. Isaac Hasey, Lydia Hodgdon.

WORSTER, Samuel, son of Samuel, b. July 28, 1780, d. Sept. 20, 1805, m. Oct. 14, 1802, by Rev. Joseph Hilliard, Patty Brown, d. May 28, 1803, aged 20, adopted dau. of Samuel Colley.

WORSTER, John, m. May 3, 1803, by Rev. Isaac Hasey, Dolly Dore.

WORSTER, John Jr., m. Sep. 15, 1803, by Rev. Isaac Hasey, Eunice Tebbets.

WORSTER, Samuel, of Sanford, Me., son of William, b. Nov. 24, 1791, m. Oct. 12, 1817, in Lebanon, Me., Susannah Fernald, b. Sep. 10, 1795.

WORSTER, Ichabod, m. int. Dec. 5, 1818, in Lebanon, Me., Judith Goodwin.

WORSTER, Thomas, son of Ezekiel, b. Apr. 23, 1798, d. Apr. 23, 1841, m. Oct. 1, 1820, in Lebanon, Me., Ruth Dixon, d. Jul. 27, 1884, aged 82.

WORSTER, Ebenezer, son of Alexander, b. Oct. 15, 1797, d. Feb. 9, 1870, m. Aug. 1821, in Lebanon, Me., Rachel Stackpole.

WORSTER, Isaac, of Milton, son of Isaac, b. Aug. 8, 1801, m. Jan. 11, 1827, by Rev. Joseph Hilliard, Julia Hilliard, of Berwick, Me.

WORSTER, Mark, son of Mark, m. (pub. Dec. 11, 1827, in Somersworth), Rachel Dunnell, both of Somersworth.

WORSTER, James, of Berwick, Me., son of Isaac, b. Jan. 8, 1804, m. int. Feb. 10, 1828, in Lebanon, Me., Sarah Fernald, b. May 21, 1803.

WORSTER, Oliver, of Berwick, Me., son of Mark, b. June 7, 1799, d. Jan. 15, 1864, m. (pub. Aug. 12, 1828, in Eliot, Me.), Abigail Lord, b. Mar. 1, 1803, d. Dec. 13, 1899.

WORSTER, Adoniram N., m. Mar. 10, 1834, by Rev. Daniel Reynolds, Lucy Downs.

WORSTER, George, son of Alexander, b. Nov. 12, 1810, m. int. Feb. 8, 1836, in Lebanon, Me., Louisa Hanscom, d. Oct. 25, 1876, aged 67.

WORSTER, Mark, son of Mark, b. Jan. 10, 1817, d. Jan. 4, 1904, m. int. Dec. 2, 1838, Elizabeth Wentworth.

WORSTER, Lemuel, son of Alexander, b. Sep. 22, 1803, m. Aug. 1, 1841, in Lebanon, Me., Margaret Pray.

WORSTER, Fernald H., of Sanford, Me., son of Samuel, b. Nov. 30, 1818, m. int. Oct. 7, 1843, in Lebanon, Me., Angelina P. Smith.

WORSTER, Jethro H., son of John, b. Jul. 4, 1824, m. Aug. 7, 1845, Elizabeth B. Johnson, of Amesbury, Mass., b. Dec. 9, 1822.

WORSTER, Ebenezer, of Somersworth, son of John, b. Nov. 15, 1822, d. Mar. 15, 1910, m. (pub. Oct. 1, 1850, in Somesworth), Mary Ann Keay, of Berwick, Me., b. June 21, 1827, d. Dec. 22, 1895.

WORSTER, William, m. May 7, 1854, in Lebanon, Me., Betsey H. Chaney, d. 1881, both of Sanford, Me.

WORSTER, George, son of Oliver, b. Dec. 14, 1830, m. May 28, 1854, Augusta P. Hayes.

WORSTER, Alexander, m. Sep. 30, 1854, in Portsmouth, Eunice Amy Goodwin.

WORSTER, Eben, m. int. Apr. 25, 1857, in So. Berwick, Me., Nancy Carroll, of Sanford.

WORSTER, Isaac Hanscom, of Lebanon, Me., son of George, b. May 22, 1842, d. Feb. 23, 1890, m. June 20, 1867, in Great Falls or Somersworth, Lizzie H. Francis, of Great Falls.

WYMAN, George K., m. Dec. 20, 1855, in Newmarket, Julia A. Getchell, both of Newmarket.

WYATT, Ira, of Wenham, Mass., d. Feb. 10, 1889, aged 81, m. Aug. 16, 1838, by Elder Enoch Place, Louisa Ann Wingate, of Farmington, d. May 3, 1892, aged 75, dau. of Stephen.

WYATT, Lyman, m. Jan. 17, 1865, in Farmington, Mary H. Garland.

WYMAN, George K., m. Dec. 20, 1855, in Newmarket, Julia A. Getchell, both of Newmarket.

YEATON, Richard, son of Richard, b. Apr. 6, 1768, m. Nov. 29, 1792, by Rev. Matthew Merriam, Molly Guptill, dau. of William

YEATON, John, m. Mar. 21, 1811, in Barrington, Lydia Danielson, both of Barrington.

YEATON, Charles, of Lebanon, Me., m. Jun. 18, 1846, by Rev. Linzey Wallis, Sally Fernald, of Somersworth.

YEATON, Richard A., of New Castle, son of Benjamin, d. Dec. 24, 1925, aged 90, m. (pub. May 10, 1860, in Rochester), Melissa J. Wigglesworth, of Farmington.

YEATON, Sylvester, m. July 5, 1863, in Newcastle, Lucena A. Yeaton, of Moultonboro.

YEATON, Thomas B., m. Feb. 7, 1866, in Dover, Lorinda N. Hall, both of Dover.

YEATON, Richard B., of Farmington, m. Nov. 14, 1868, in Farmington, Elma E. Norris, of Alton.

YEATON, Charles T. m. (pub. Nov. 10, 1870, in Great Falls), Sarah A. Holt, both of Rochester.

YORK, John, of Middleton, d. 1837, m. near 1769, Eleanor Durgin, b. Jan. 13, 1748, d. Oct. 20, 1836, dau. of Jonathan.

YORK, George, m. Jan. 25, 1794, in Brookfield, Margaret Guppy, both of Middleton.

YORK, John, son of Eliphalet, d. Jun. 26, 1851, aged 68, m. (1) May 7, 1803, by Rev. John Osborne, Rebecca Durgin, of Lee, b. Sep. 22, 1791, d. Jan. 11, 1856, aged 71, dau. of Josiah, m. (2) Deborah Durgin.

YORK, Enoch, son of John, d. 1867, m. Nov. 17, 1808, by Rev. Joseph Haven, Sarah Hayes, d. 1868, both of Middleton.

YORK, Simeon D., d. Apr. 7, 1927, aged 85, m. (1) Nov. 28, 1866, in Dover, Mary E. Keith, b. Feb. 26, 1847, d. Dec. 10, 1885, both of Dover, m. (2) Aug. 7, 1894, in Dover, Josephine McGroty.

YOUNG, William, m. June 5, 1791, in Barrington, Charity Howe, both of Barrington.

YOUNG, Eleazer, son of Peter, b. Nov. 8, 1780, d. Oct. 13, 1844, m. (1) Sept. 20, 1801, by Rev. Benjamin Balch, Alice Kingman, d. in 1833, both of Barrington, m. (2) int. May 7, 1837, in Dover, Deborah (Ham) Tebbets, wid. of John, dau. of Samuel.

YOUNG, Benjamin, m. Feb. 2, 1812, by Rev. Micajah Otis, Abra Montgomery, both of Barrington.

YOUNG, Reuben H., m. Aug. 31, 1813, by Rev. Joseph Boodey, Hannah Simpson.

YOUNG, Jonathan Franklin Jr., b. July 19, 1799, d. Oct. 22, 1850, aged 55, m. Aug. 27, 1818, by Elder Enoch Place, Hannah Hall, b. Apr. 13, 1800, d. Oct. 1, 1847, aged 47, both of Barrington.

YOUNG, Eleazer, of Madbury, d. Mar. 11, 1868, aged 82, m. Nov. 13, 1823, by Rev. William Demeritt, Kezia Rowe, of Dover, d. Mar. 31, 1865, aged 67, dau. of John.

YOUNG, Jonathan Jr., m. Dec. 18, 1834, by Elder Enoch Place, Sally Sanders, dau. of Levi, both of Strafford.

YOUNG, Eleazer, of Barrington, m. int. May 7, 1837, in Dover, Mrs. Deborah Tebbetts, of Dover.

YOUNG, Jeremiah L., d. Oct. 4, 1876, aged 59, m. Oct. 16, 1837, in Wolfeboro, Mary A. Jackson, d. Jan. 28, 1894, aged 81, both of Wolfeboro.

YOUNG, Joseph, of Durham, d. Apr. 1, 1864, aged 54, m. (pub. Dec. 20, 1842, in Newmarket), Martha D. Bassett.

YOUNG, Furber, m. Sep. 25, 1845, in Lebanon, Rhoda E. Goodell, both of Farmington.

YOUNG, Isaac, son of Isaac, d. Aug. 13, 1861, aged 76, m. Sept. 27, 1848, by Elder Samuel Sherburne, Mrs. Caroline Neal, both of Barrington.

YOUNG, William H., m. (1) Sarah ----, d. Mar. 22, 1848, aged 34, m. (2) Jan. 24, 1849, in Barrington, Sophia Locke Hall, d. Oct. 21, 1898, aged 70, dau. of Jacob, both of Barrington.

YOUNG, Edwin A., m. Mar. 22, 1862, in Durham, Lizzie I. Drew, both of Durham.

YOUNG, John R., m. July 13, 1862, in Madbury, Abby M. Clay, both of Madbury.

YOUNG, Moses F., m. Oct. 4, 1862, in Dover, Anna L. Varney, both of Dover.

YOUNG, Ezra D., m. Nov. 25, 1863, in Dover, Hattie M. Rogers, both of Dover.

YOUNG, James M., of Rochester, m. May 21, 1864, in Farmington, Mary S. Jones, of Middleton.

YOUNG, Albert, son of Daniel, m. June 12, 1864, in Durham, Mary A. Gleason, dau. of John, both of Durham.

YOUNG, Joseph, m. July 19, 1865, in Dover, Lizzie E. Spurlin, both of Dover.

YOUNG, John S., of Kittery, Me., son of Thomas C., m. Dec. 7, 1865, by Rev. Alvan Tobey, Mary Ann Thompson, of Boston, Mass., dau. of Alfred.

YOUNG, Elijah R., of Ossipee, m. Mar. 10, 1867, in E. Alton, Ann F. Brackett, of Wolfeboro.

YOUNG, Augustine, of Haverhill, Mass., m. Aug. 11, 1868, in Dover, Mary E. Locke, of Dover, dau. of Elisha.

YOUNG, John F., of Strafford, m. Apr. 15, 1869, in S. Berwick, Me., Mrs. Elizabeth H. Perkins, of S. Berwick, Me.

YOUNG, George F., m. May 28, 1869, in Middleton, Caroline H. Perkins.

YOUNG, George F., of Farmington, m. (pub. June 17, 1869, in Farmington), Sarah E. Ellis, of Alton.

YOUNG, J. Frank, of Barrington, son of Jonathan, aged 39, m. Jan. 19, 1871, in Durham, W. Frances (Hoitt) Bean, of Lee, widow, aged 31, dau. of Alfred.

ERRATA

CHAMBERLAIN, Amos, of Lebanon, Me., son of Capt. William, b. Aug. 26, 1764, d. Nov. 4, 1809, m. Jan. 1, 1788, by Rev. Isaac Smith, Sally Rogers, of New Durham Gore.

CHICK, Aaron, b. Jun. 25, 1767, d. Mar. 16, 1851, m. (1) Susan ----, b. Apr. 29, 1771, d. Dec. 28, 1797, m. (2) Dec. 5, 1804, in Lebanon, Me., Nabby Libbey, d. Mar. 29, 1817, aged 42.

CLARK, James, b. Jun. 17, 1775, m. Jul. 3, 1800, by Rev. Isaac Hasey, Lydia Brock, b. Sep. 14, 1780.

CLARK, Rufus, son of James, b. Mar. 3, 1808, m. int. Nov. 10, 1833, in Lebanon, Me., Hannah Chick, b. Dec. 23, 1811, dau. of Aaron.

DOWNING, John B., b. 1811, d. Dec. 1 or Dec. 14, 1871, aged 61, m. (1) Jun. 27, 1847, by Rev. Mathes, Sarah Burnham, m. (2) (pub. Apr. 29, 1869, in Farmington), Mrs. Betsey B. (Lord) Legro, wid. of Benjamin F., d. Mar. 19, 1872, aged 52, both of Farmington.

DOWNS, William King, of Berwick, Me., d. Jan. 11, 1891, aged 67, m. 1842, Isette Tibbetts, dau. of Daniel.

FALL, Ivory Jr., son of Ivory, b. Aug. 16, 1820, m. (pub. Oct. 13, 1845, in Lebanon, Me.), Abby Fernald, b. Mar. 6, 1819, d. Nov. 24, 1894, dau. of James.

FOLSOM, David J., of Rochester, d. Aug. 4, 1882, m. (pub. Aug. 12, 1869, in Rochester). Mary E. Chamberlain, of Lebanon, Me.

FOSS, Chadbourne, d. Dec. 1844, m. Dec. 23, 1824, in Lebanon, Me., Patience Varney.

FOYE, William G., of Berwick, Me., d. Jan. 5, 1883, aged 55, m. Nov. 13, 1852, by Elder Enoch Place, Nancy H. Hill, of Somersworth, d. Jan. 5, 1854, aged 30, dau. of Deac. William.

GRANT, Daniel Jr., son of Capt. Daniel, b. Aug. 22, 1806, d. Nov. 11, 1889, m. Dec. 31, 1827, in Lebanon, Me., Susan Foss.

GRANT, Dependence, son of Capt. Daniel, b. Oct. 10, 1814, d. Nov. 12, 1863, m. Nov. 13, 1844, Mercy Hartford, b. May 29, 1819, dau. of William.

GUPTILL, Moses, d. Jun. 8, 1874, aged 77, m. (1) int. Jul. 10, 1825, in Lebanon, Me., Nancy Chadburn, d. Aug. 6, 1827, aged 25, m. (2) int. Nov. 9, 1828, in Lebanon, Me., Tamson Hodsdon, of Ossipee, d. May 2, 1867, aged 64.

JONES, Peter, son of Moses, b. Jun. 1, 1800, d. Oct. 16, 1858, m. Feb. 25, 1827, in Lebanon, Me., Ada Hersom.

KNOX, Benjamin, d. Mar. 10, 1826, aged 31, m. (1) int. Nov. 6, 1819, in Lebanon, Me., Keziah Butler, d. Jun. 21, 1820, aged 26, m. (2) Jun. 30, 1822, in Lebanon, Me., Dorcas Butler.
KNOX, James, m. int. Jul. 23, 1827, in Lebanon, Me., Alice Tuttle, d. Oct. 1, 1860.
KNOX, David, m. Apr. 1, 1813, Priscilla Cowell, d. Nov. 1861.
KNOX, George J., b. Feb. 14, 1798, d. Jan. 12, 1869, m. (1) int. Sept. 4, 1842, in Lebanon, Me., Susan G. Farnham, d. Feb. 21, 1852, aged 35, m. (2) Sarah J. ----, d. Mar. 8, 1858, aged 41.

INDEX
To Brides' Names

----, Abby S 181 Abigail 14 32 80 125 171 Abigail H 232 Abra W 76 Addie 218 Alice 36 Ann E 76 Ann M 156 Anna 205 Anna J 121 Belinda 60 211 Betsey 172 216 Caroline 6 Catherine 153 Clarissa 57 Cynthia 195 Dorcas 229 Drusilla B 175 Eliza 58 Eliza V 260 Elizabeth 17 26 29 134 256 Elizabeth W 68 Ella A 206 Emeline 65 Emma C 7 Hannah 15 57 176 Hannah H 103 249 Jane 14 Jerusha 176 Joanna 184 Judith 80 Keziah 97 Lizzie 78 Lois 15 Lydia 148 Martha A 190 Martha Ann 263 Mary 27 195 215 244 269 Mary E 263 Mary Elizabeth 181 Mary F 88 Mary J 217 Mehitable 23 Mehitable E 264 Melinda 138 Metilda 218 Nabby 14 Nancy D 133 Nancy N 96 Olivia 213 Patience 131 Polly 125 245 Rhoda 196 Rose L 41 Sally 65 124-125 Sally S 66 Sarah 57 97 105 247 276 Sarah Ann 32 Sarah H 30 Sarah J 278 Sarah M 51 193 Susan 27 111 150 184 277 Susan E 134 Tamson 14

ABBOTT, Anna 96 Eliza J 125 Elizabeth 241 Hannah 238 Hannah S 211 Julia A 30 Maria E 95 Mary A 125 Mary Ann 11 Saddie A 44 Sarah 229 Tamson 23

ACKERMANN, Karen 13

ADAMS, Elizabeth 27 Hannah K 107 Josephine 162 Lucretia 170 Lydia 11 Mary J 53 Nancy H 232 Onissa E 63 Rosamond P 21 Sally 35 Sarah F 69 Susan 21 Temperance P 144

AIKIN, Jane 195

ALDRICH, Abby C 202

ALLARD, Charity 102 Hannah 184 Lydia 210 Mary 204 Sally 2 Sarah F 100

ALLEN, Abigail 3 Apphia 4 Catherine 4 Dorcas 3 Elizabeth 80 138 145 Florence 128 Frances M 218 Georgianna B 124 Keziah G 4 Lorana 117 Louisa L 5 Lucinda 4 Lydia 31 Martha 256 Mary A 249 Mary E 270 Mary F 127 Mary L 236 Nancy Mahaley 197 Olive 135 Rachel 246

ALLEY, Content 212 Cornelia J 161 Lucy A 199

ALVORD, Della P 89

AMAZEEN, Jennie E 153 Susan J 262

AMBROSE, Hannah 45

AMES, Mary E 130

ANDERSON, Belle S 227 Martha 21

ANDREWS, Abby A 193 Lucy 99 Roxanna 69

ANNIS, Olive 139

ANTWINE, Mary Jane 172

APPLEBEE, Abba 128 Eunice A 194 Olive 109

APPLEE, Sarah E 199

AREN, Elizabeth 176

ARLEN, Abigail 110 Joanna 23 Mary 210 Nancy 176

ARLIN, Martha 249 Mary Ann 132 Nancy 22

ARLING, Adeline D P 30

ARMIT, Sally 115

ARNOLD, Thankful 152

ASHTON, Elizabeth E 267 Mary A 132

ATKINSON, Carrie M 26

ATWOOD, Susan 267-268

AUSTIN, Amanda 223 Anna 199 Catharine 76 Dorcas A 65 Elizabeth 91 Lydia 89 Margaret 142 Mercy 180 Nancy 143 Phebe Maria 177 Sarah 254

AVERY, Eliza A 239 Hannah J 122 Ruth H 43-44

AYER, Betsey 94 Elizabeth 271

AYERS, Abbie K 24 Anna 140 Elizabeth 234 Mary Jane 248

AYERS (continued)
  Olive 30 Phebe 46 55 Sarah S 67
  Susan L 67
BABB, Abigail 34 Alice 81 Ann 34
  Betsey 81 113 Charlotte 8 Dolley
  82 Elizabeth L 90 Lenora 188
  Lydia 92 192 253 Margaret 81 155
  Maria 167 Martha L 146 Mary 25
  Mary A 160 Meribah 81 Miriam 34
  Nancy 126 Sarah A 172 Sarah J 90
BABCOCK, Elizabeth 166
BACKUS, Mary A 140
BACON, Sarah Elizabeth 133
BAILEY, Sarah G 30
BAKER, Abby F 162 Betsey Lamber
  221 Elizabeth M 62 Lydia 247
BALCH, Dolla K 36 Polly 92
BALCOM, Martha 119
BALISDELL, Eliza E 19
BAMPTON, Anna 188
BANFIELD, Joanna 37
BANKS, Caroline 112 Julia 112 Julia
  M 87 Lizzie 13 Mary Jane 211
BARBER, Julia 67
BARKER, Ellen A 252 Mercy 158
BARNARD, Rebecca 251
BARNES, Ann 1 Mary Elizabeth 79
BARROWS, Rebecca O 77 263
BARTLETT, Abbie E 222 Anna M
  154 Esther 92 Judith 157 Susan
  Emerson 179 Susan F 203
BARTON, Luella 99
BASSETT, Martha D 275 Ruth E 163
BATCHELDER, Hannah O 223 Lydia
  236 Mehitable A 48 Sarah 88
BATEMAN, Lizzie 145
BATES, Hattie A 154 Kate M 202
BATSON, Sarah L 47
BEACHAM, A E 211 Arvilla M 264
  Joanna 241 Mary Frances 133
  Sabrina 241
BEACHER, Fanny W 9
BEADSLEE, Hannah M 264
BEAL, Emeline S 226
BEAN, Carrie F 223 Dorcas 177
  Elizabeth 17 Hannah A 41 Lizzie A
  152 Mary 17 65 Mary Eliza 194
  Octavia 201 Olive 241 247 Ruth
  118 Sarah 145 Sarah A 216 W
  Frances 276

BEANE, Abby W 64
BEARSE, Mary O 59
BEDELL, Sarah F 256
BEEDE, Annie 244 Sarah A 217
BELL, Emily 202 Julia E 19
BENNETT, Ellen M 211 Fannie 219
  Josephine H 227 Lucinda A 245
  Lydia 92 Martha E 174 Mehitable
  L 107 Nellie M 105 Rhoda E 25
BERREY, Flora J 87
BERRY, Abby 16 236 Abigail 190
  Betsey F 84 Carrie 38 Charity 272
  Eleanor 42 Eliza 14 248 Elizabeth
  10 Fanny B 103 Hannah 137 220
  Harriet 121 Hattie S 77 Jane M 172
  Lizzie H 193 Lydia 8 Marcy 81
  Martha S 209 Mary 56 Mary F 69
  Melissa Ann 23 Olive 25 Rachel 61
  Sarah 46 85 122 Vienna S 86 Viola
  87
BETEL, Lucy 170
BICKFORD, Addie E 138 Esther F 50
  Eveline 80 Georgia A 25 Hannah
  199 Hannah J 171 Hannah W 72
  Jane R 49 Lettice 146 Louise T 188
  Lydia 115 Mary E 9 25 144 Molly
  197 Olive 72 Priscilla 50 Sarah 109
  Temperance A 132
BILLINGS, Clara A 26
BLAISDELL, Abba E 55 Abbie M 181
  Abby Hanson 253 Abigail 97
  Addie A 258 Allie W 213 Betsey
  249 Caroline 136 Clara W 239
  Dolly 136 Ella J 104 Esther Ann
  101 Eunice J 143 Hannah 90 94
  Hannah E 161 Hannah H 178
  Lorania 28 Lucinda F 143 Lydia
  204 Margaret 118 130 Maria 120
  Martha J 173 Nabby 51 Patience
  154 Rebecca 64 Relief Ann 168
  Rhoda 255 Rhoda B 29 Ruth 97
  Sarah Ann 250 Tammy 118
BLAKE, Abigail 81 Elizabeth 50
  Esther C 245 Laura A 233 Nellie C
  217
BLANCHARD, Abbie A 161 Bridget
  218 Cynthia E 229 Mary J 161
  Philinda A 112
BLAZO, Jane 79
BLODGETT, Isabel 75

BLYDENBURGH, Clarissa 225
BOARDMAN, Harriet 227
BOBBOTT, Hannah 172
BODGE, Lettice 146 Mary 128 Sarah E P 235
BODWELL, Joanna 134 Miriam 271
BOLLES, Sarah 178
BOND, Ada J 244
BOODEY, Ariana E 85 Asenath Abigail 36 Betty 215 Elizabeth 215 Joanna 32 Sarah 252 Susanna M 132
BOOKER, Nellie 99
BOOTH, Eliza 114 Elizabeth 93
BOSTON, Fanny D 86 Hannah B 164
BOSWELL, Sarah J 85
BOWDEN, Nancy 193
BOYDEN, Angeline 120
BOYLE, Caroline E 261 Mary E 134
BRACKET, Mary E 199
BRACKETT, Abigail 199 Ann F 276 Betsey 54 Catherine 151 Clara E 70 Hannah 202 Hannah B 25 Jennie 139 Lois 43 Mary 96 195 Mary F 190 Phebe 69 Seddie T 168 Sophia 180
BRACY, Lizzie 114
BRADBURY, Mary S 2
BRADEEN, Sarah F 68
BRADFORD, 133
BRAGDON, Electra J 99
BRANKS, Frances E 201
BRASSBRIDGE, Hannah 22
BRAWN, Alice N 55
BRAY, Fannie F 227
BREWSTER, Abby A 73 Abigail 54 Eliza 16 Lydia 119 Mary 37 Mary Jane 4 Peggy 36 Susan C 4
BRIERLY, Agnes J 243
BRIGGS, Maria 190 Mary 115
BRIMMER, Mary E 98
BROCK, Annie M 161 Betsey 107 272 Caroline P 111 Charlotte 219 Eliza 141 Esther 138 Hannah 14 Keziah Y 270 Lavina 219 Lucy 247 Lydia 277 Marcia O 235 251 Maria 182 Mary 83 Polly 107 Rosina 93 Sally 230 Susan 270 Vienna E 219

BROOKS, Ellen G 28 Letitia 204 Lucretia W 87 Nellie 44 Ruth L 254
BROUGHTON, Priscilla 119
BROWN, Abigail 102 Alice A 166 Anna 35 Annie E 171 221 Betsey 212 Caroline F 232 Diedmaia 266 Elizabeth 181 Emma F 113 Esther F 75 Eugenia F 188 Fannie 38 Hannah 218 Hannah S 114 Hattie B 237 Hester A 56 235 Lois 96 Lovey 14 Lucy 112 Lydia 256 Lydia Ann 79 Lydia Maria 176 Mary Ann 24 Mary E 5 Mary L 24 Melissa J 108 Olive A 16 236 Olivea 31 Patience 218 Patty 273 Salinda I 233 Sarah 23 225 Sarah J 24 115 Susan 44 Susan Augusta 202 Susan P 2
BROWNELL, Mary A 196
BRYANT, Isabella 24 Polly 82 Torrey 119
BUCK, Louisa 39
BUFFUM, Lydia 3 Mary 116
BUMFORD, Jane 174 Mary 262
BUNKER, Abigail 234 Betty 133 Bridget 229 Catherine 265 Deborah 61 Hannah 15 Lillis 136 Mary M 73 Mary P 145 Susan 35 115 Susan J 166
BURBANK, Hattie P 161 Mary Jane 12 Sally 179
BURKE, Betsey J 51 Ellen 99 Emily J 178 Hannah J 51
BURLEIGH, Anna T 231 Antoinette L 123 217 Deborah 259 Hannah M 216 Louise 69 Melissa J 248 Sarah E 264 Susan A 205
BURLEY, Elizabeth G 51 Mary A 226 Mary S 37
BURNHAM, Betsey 60 Harriet 195 Sally 133 Sarah 277
BURNS, Julia A 203
BURROUGHS, Mary W 176
BURROWS, Abigail 104 Dolly 205 Eleanor 183 Eliza 131 154 Elizabeth J 89 Josephine A 149 Mary 176 Mary R 216 Sally 148

BUTLER, Clara 62 Dorcas 149 278
   Eunice G 166 Hannah 223 Keziah
   149 278 Lucy 118 Lydia 65 120
   Martha A 119 Mary E 99 178 Mary
   Frances 261 Ruth 47 Sarah 9 142
   259 Susan 207 Susan E 151
BUTTERS, Helen M 219 Mary O 117
BUZZELL, Abigail 272 Anna 30
   Bridget 73 Caroline A 56 Celissa
   17 Elizabeth A 217 Emma L 206
   Eunice 28 Frances E 204 Hannah
   154 Isett 29 Louise 28 Margery 28
   Martha W 257 Mary 60 236 Mary
   A 231 Mary C H 112 Mehitable
   228 Sarah Elizabeth 68 211
BYERS, Bessie 209 Jennie 209 Sarah
   H 256
CALDWELL, Hannah 10 29
CALL, Eva 44
CALLEY, Nancy 139
CAME, Sarah 105
CAMPBELL, Fanny 94 Hattie A 268
CANNEY, Abigail 68 Angie I 149
   Ann Elizabeth 157 Anne 192
   Augusta M 67 Betsey 55 82
   Deborah M 40 Elizabeth B 45
   Elmina P 184 Hannah H 174
   Harriet 185 Lydia 57 Martha 178
   Mary 246 Mary A 27 Mary D 230
   Mary Elizabeth 254 Mary Fanny
   213 Mary Frances 11 133 Molly
   232 Olive Ann 86 Rebecca 17 Ruth
   H 7 43-44 Sarah 160 Sarah Abby
   129 Susan E 215 Susannah 42
   Sylvesty 185
CAPON, Estha 153
CARD, Abbie L 69 Elizabeth F 203
   Eunice 198 Sarah J 28
CARER, Annie M 230
CARLE, Lizzie Y 227
CARLETON, Clara A 257
CARLEY, Martha J 23 Mary E 45
CARLISLE, Abba Jane 204
CARNEY, Lizzie 172
CARPENTER, Abby H 222 Addie E 7
   Etta I 122
CARR, Anne 194 Betty 238 Clara W
   35 Hannah 213
CARROLL, Ellen M 99 Nancy 274
CARTER, Eliza J 20

CARTLAND, Caroline 221
CASEY, Elizabeth 2
CASWELL, Asenath S 146 Edna E 23
   Esther 120 Hannah P 236 Jennie
   246 Mary 116 Mary J 121
CATE, Abby 198 Abby Y 186 Abigail
   32 183 Betsey 33 217 270 Eliza
   Jane 161 Elizabeth 87 Hannah 14
   220 Louisa A 90 Lucy 159 220
   Lydia 8 65 Mahalah 58 Maria 155
   Mary 106 Mary Ann 27 Mary E
   229 Nellie F 181 Phebe Jane 6
   Polly 268 Sarah 270 Sobriety 116
   Susan G 103 Susanna 107
CATER, Abigail 267 Abigail F 8 Anna
   A 39 267 Ellen M 62 Martha 8
   Martha S 244 Mary 270 Molly 23
   Nancy 56 Polly 6 126 Susan 160
   Susannah 155
CAVERLY, Abigail 266 Betsey 42 56
   Clarissa 245 Eliza Ann 70 Eliza
   Jane 66 Elizabeth A 58 Elizabeth D
   85 Eveline A 127 Florence E 13
   Hannah 57 Lydia 187 Mary 189
   Mary S 35 Polly 148 187 Sally 247
   Sarah E 260 Sarah H 78
CAVERNO, 109 Margaret 113 Sarah
   29 247 Sarah E 32
CHADBORNE, Olive J 140
CHADBORUNE, Hattie A 108
CHADBOURNE, Anna 233 Dorcas
   111 Mary 105 Mary Elizabeth 105
   Sarah 178
CHADBURN, Mary 105 Nancy 105
   277
CHAMBERALIN, Jennie S 243 Molly
   165 Polly 249
CHAMBERLAIN, Abbie M 117 Abby
   D 67 Almira 59 Almira Boody 70
   Annie 50 Eleanor 263 Elizabeth
   Jane 53 Maria J 132 Martha S 122
   Mary A 40 Mary E 277
CHAMBERLIN, Abby M 119 Pamelia
   207
CHAMPION, Annie 129 Molly 204
   Olive A 135 Sarah 204
CHANDLER, Arabelle 203 Hannah
   Lee 221 Mary A 169
CHANEY, Betsey H 274 Isabella 232
   Nancy B 113

CHAPIN, Emma Frances 31
CHAPMAN, Laura C 89 Lizzie M 108
    Lucy A 100 Mary Ann 106 Melissa
    239 Sarah 247
CHASE, A Amanda 52 Abbie A 104
    Abigail 38 Alexine D 243 Anna 70
    Annie L 89 Clara 183 E J 194 Ellen
    M 241 Emily A 62 Hattie M 123
    Josephine E 215 Laura 143 Louisa
    H 102 Lucinda 90 Mary A 78 Mary
    C 104 Mary E 158 Nancy J 147
    Phebe 91 Ruth E 101
CHESLEY, Abigail 189 Annie M 152
    Augusta A 164 Betsey 223 Calista
    A 266 Emeline S 166 Emma 193
    Frances J 93 Hannah 63 106
    Keziah 112 Louisa J 136 Martha 57
    Mary 106 Mary E 166 Nancy 141
    Nancy B 16 Olive M 16 Polly 102
    Priscilla Adams 151 Rosetta Marie
    212 S Josephine 152 Sally 195
    Sarah Elizabeth 182 Susan 201
    Susannah 148
CHESWELL, Charlotte 56 Emily B 1
CHICH, Augusta 244
CHICK, Annie E 11 Caroline M 147
    Emma F 76 Georgia B 177 Hannah
    42 277 Lydia A 76 Mary W 162
    Nellie F 228 Rhoda 268 Sarah 190
    Susan 238
CHRISTIE, Lizzie Wheeler 26 Sarah J
    79
CHURCH, Abigail 219 269 Charity
    236 Hannah 8 Martha 178 Mercy
    77 Nancy 30
CHURCHILL, Hattie E 157 Hattie S
    46 Mary Jane 47 Sarah E 224 Zelia
    163
CILLEY, Adelaide H 186 Dorothy 266
    Rosina J 129
CLAPP, Elizabeth 271
CLARK, Abbie F 155 Abby 183
    Abigail 8 216 Amanda J 41 Anna
    176 Anne Frances 139 Annie A
    239 Annie M 179 Arabella M 161
    Betsy 259 Catherine H 100
    Charlotte 29 Deliverance 212 Eliza
    206 Eliza J 56 Elizabeth N 260
    Ellen E 182 Emma F 166 Eunice
    252 Frances 169 Frances A 41

CLARK (continued)
    Hannah 131 Hannah D 199 Harriet
    131 Jennie L 95 Jennie M 91 Joyce
    134 Katharine 78 Katherine M 98
    Lavinia A G 263 Lois 119 247
    Luella D 272 Lydia 53 Maria S 195
    Martha 269 Mary 65 120 232 Mary
    Ann 81 84 Mary E 76 243 Mary H
    249 Mary J 123 Mary M 143
    Mercy 53 Miriam 182 Nancy L 45
    Olive 192 Phebe J 2 Polly 126 241
    Rebecca 53 Ruth 219 239 Sally 102
    Sarah 3 17 245 Sarah W 43 Susan
    F 235 Susan W S 219
CLARY, Lydia Ann 238
CLAY, Abby M 276 Eliza L 103
    Hannah 96 Lovina 203 Sarah 17
    Sarah Ann 132
CLEAVES, Carrie Nancy 46
CLEMENT, Jennie P 234
CLEMENTS, Abbie A 218 Addie E
    185 Betsey Ann 45 Martha A 49
CLIFFORD, Abbie 240 Anna A 186
CLOUGH, Ada 156 Amanda 75 Emma
    F 214 Flora A 272 Hannah L 121
    Jennie A 60 Maria 234 Nancy 156
    Phebe R 47 Sally 142 Sara A 250
    Susan A 77 242
CLOUTMAN, Lizzie S 189 Mary M
    195 Sarah B 250 Susan L 195
COBB, Ellen D 20 Susan A 237
COCHRAN, Jennie 11
COCKRAN, Charlotte 209
COE, Mary 106
COFFIN, Betsey 76 Christina B 53
    Jane 174 Lydia 31 Polly 55 Susan
    123
COLBATH, Belinda E 41 Betsey N
    156 Ellen A 124 Ellen L 155 Elvira
    238 Emma 169 Emma A 155
    Hannah 33
COLBY, Hannah 146 Hattie Ruth 180
    Mary G 33 Mary A 129 Rosamond
    N 248 Sarah 52
COLCORD, Lavina J 129 Rebecca B
    51
COLE, Anna E 259 Clara A 185
    Dorcas E 262 Ellen 179 Judith 4
    Lucy A 185 Lydia A 167 Susanna
    110

COLEMAN, Abby 232 Eliza 48 Ruhamah 175
COLLEY, Hannah 245
COLLINS, Jennie 150 Nancy 219 Sarah T 12
COLOMEY, P Abbie 50
COLOMY, Emily S 203 Patience 59
CONNACHER, Hannah 99
CONNER, Amanda J 48 Lydia L 138
CONVERSE, Elizabeth S 49 Jennie 198
CONWAY, Elizabeth 210
COOK, Almira B 191 Anna V 5 Christina C 218 Elizabeth 103 Esther 116 Hannah 151 Judith 212 Maria S 195 Mary A 43 Mary Eliza 229 Nancy 209 Nellie P 255 Rhoda 260 Susan 13 Susan Amanda 186
COOPER, Augusta R 196 Dorothy 242 Esther A 98 Mary E 20 Paulina A 153 Sarah Smith 37 Susan L 241
COPP, Adaliza J 179 Clara E 12 Sarah M 30
COPPS, Jane 260
CORLIS, Julia A 63
CORLISS, Lydia Jane 142
CORNELL, Abigail 15 Mary 125
CORSON, Abigail 92 Adeline J 174 Ann E 268 Arabell 182 Comfort 53 Delana D 209 Delia 261 Ellen J 39 Esther H 141 Evelyn R 73 Martha A 105 Mary Ann 103 Mary E 224 Mary L 58 Olive 135 Polly 82 Rachel 220 Rebecca 238 Relief 220 Sabrina D 181 Sarah 254 Sophronia E 233 Susan A 209 Susanna 48
COTTLE, Betsey 172
COTTON, Abby 239 Betsey A 33 Lizzie A 129 162 Lizzie E 264 Lydia Frances 251 Martha E 239 Mary A 251 Melissa M 140 Ora T 203 Sarah F 136 Sarah Jane 92
COURSON, Nancy 143 Rachel 172
COUSENS, Lorinda 208 Mary E 166
COUSINS, Priscilla R 205
COVERCY, Mary Ann 193
COWELL, Cordelia 148 Maria 60 Maria A 204 Mary 201 227 Priscilla 278

CRATON, Polly Maria 263
CRITCHERSON, Hannah M 72
CRITCHET, Lydia 254 Mary Jane 35
CRITCHETT, Mary Jane 136
CROCKETT, Antoinette 251 Caroline H 198 Georgie A 217
CROSBY, Susie A 199
CROSS, Betsey 117 Martha 68
CUMMING, Eliza Ann 52
CUMMINGS, Nettie G 246
CUMMINS, Julia H 52
CURRIER, Hannah 203 Hannah H 46 Nellie F 259
CURRY, Lavinia M 230
CURTIS, Ella F 135 Louisa 247 Mary E 268 Sophia B 102
CUSHING, Caroline 126 Eliza 18 Louisa W 10
CUSHMAN, Lizzie J 1
CUTTS, Mary 196
DADD, E G 131
DAICY, Josie P 161
DALEY, Mary E 201
DAME, Betsey 53 Eleanor R 104 Elizabeth A 71 Jane 10 Josephine A 224 Laura A 211 Martha 2 Mary A L 133 Mary C 117 Mehitable 71 Olive W 12 Sophia H 18
DANEY, Sarah S 147
DANFORTH, Anne 137 Mary 15
DANIELS, Abigail 235 Betsey 123 Christine 113 Emma A 160 Lydia 82 235 Maria G 270 Maria S 126 Mary 132 Mary J 210 Mehitable 57 Molly 81 Nancy 198 Rebecca 168 Sarah 41
DANIELSON, Hannah 139 Lydia 274 Molly 34
DAVID, Sally 27
DAVIS, Abbie L 54 Abigail 54 220 Anne E 268 Belle 99 Betsey 12 Betsey N 12 Caroline 231 Clara A 18 Clara M 68 Emily M 153 Emma 48 Emma F 151 Emma J 74 Hannah J 103 Judith A 18 Lizzie P 60 Lydia E 180 Maria A H 50 Marianna 46 Martha 58 Mary 37 Mary Ann 69 Mary H 153 Melissa F 130 Miriam 31 Molly 115 Nancy 192 Nettie M 148 Olive F 252

DAVIS (continued)
  Olive Frost 103 Orissa J 26 Pamelia
  Ann 98 Polly 46 Ruth 27 135 Sarah
  210 Sarah E 54 Sarah J 57 Susan A
  219 Susannah 32 Vienna M 178
DAVISON, Anna 65
DAY, Annie 166 Nettie S 122 Sabrina
  S 38
DEABORN, Lucy 92 Naomi 190
DEALAND, Ursula P 259
DEAN, Eunice 176
DEARBORN, Abra 79 Annie M 105
  Dolly 91 Ellen S 18 Hannah Jane
  49 Irene 253 Lydia A 177 Mary
  124 Mary F 143 Rosa 215 Rowena
  76 Ruhamah 146
DECATER, Margaret A 223 Martha
  27
DECATUR, Jennie N 272
DEERING, Mary 60
DELAND, Celeste 244 Leonora A 113
  Mary J 71
DELANEY, Hattie 124
DELANO, Adelaide A 19 Hannah 156
  Nabby 199 Ruth 42
DEMERITT, Ann 60 226 Annie 78
  Betsey 61 Betty 187 Elizabeth 22
  Elizabeth A 112 Emma B 124
  Frances L 2 Hannah Y 61 Isabella
  F 90 Mary 6 Mehitable 39 Mercy E
  87 Polly 23 39 Sally 197 Sarah 170
  Sarah A 73 191 239
DENNETT, Elizabeth 3 Laura 73
  Mary Jane 2
DEXTER, Eliza A 1
DICEY, Abbie 140
DILL, Lucretia W 87
DILLINGHAM, Sabina 157
DIMAN, Hannah 226
DIXON, Charlotte 142 Elizabeth 204
  Eunice 146 Mary A 114 Ruth 273
  Sally 74 Susannah 272
DOCKHAM, Lucy A 61 Sarah 58
DOCKUM, Matie E 116
DOE, Alice A 175 Carrie E 227 Lydia
  P 60 Mary Deborah 252 Nancy N
  38 Susie A 56
DOLBY, Vienna E 73
DOLDT, Addie E 143
DOLLIVER, Georgia A 44

DOLLOFF, Rolina 262
DONNELL, Mary A 206
DOOR, Lydia 136
DORE, Abby A 71 Betsey F 106 Dolly
  273 Emeline 87 Hannah 124 Julia F
  112 Lydia 149 Mary 261 Olive 237
  Peggy 204 Polly 118 130 Ruth A
  13 Sarah 148 Sarah Jane 23 Sophia
  253
DORMAN, Carrie A 62
DORR, Eliza A 163 Mary E 160
DOW, Abigail 176 Ann 73 Annie 120
  Emily M 121 Livona 95 Sarah E
  193
DOWNING, Anna M 43 Mary A 18
  Mary E 31 Mary Frances 125 Mary
  Jane 197 Patience 49
DOWNS, Abbie F 102 Abby 122
  Abigail 194 Abigail A 225 Adah 42
  Betsey 133 254 Elizabeth 144
  Elzina 182 Eunice 63 Hannah 215
  Hannah P 43 Jennie 263 Lizzie A
  209 248 Lucy 273 Lydia A 72
  Mary 82 Mercy 177 Olive 213 254
  Phebe 144 Sarah 120 182 Sarah E
  174 Sophia 101
DRAKE, Anna B 181 Emma S 59
  Huldah Jane 41
DREW, Abbie C 240 Abby J 32 Abby
  Jane 222 Abigail 92 141 Abigail B
  137 Ann M 248 Anna Hurd 66
  Arabella F 113 Betsey 134
  Caroline A 150 Charlotte Bell 117
  Cynthia 260 Elizabeth 151
  Elizabeth W 104 Emma C 145
  Hannah 98 Isabel B 95 Isabella 24
  Jane 80 Laura E 50 Lizzie I 276
  Lois 81 Lucinda J 241 Lucy A 125
  Lydia 57 Lydia A 188 Lydia S 202
  Mary A 108 Mary Ellen 87 Mary J
  151 Molly 81 Nancy 78 Olive 20
  Polly 78 Sally 88 108 Sara 269
  Sarah 91 245 268 Susan 151 Susan
  K 21
DRINKWATER, Sophia 163
DROWN, Abigail 130 Mary F 264
  Patience 197 Polley 130
DUGRIN, Lucretia 2
DUNKINS, Anna 2
DUNNEL, Hannah 47

DUNNELL, Rachel 273
DUNTLEY, Harriet E 257 Lorana 52
DURANT, Carrie S 193
DURGIN, Addie M 203 Deborah 275 Eleanor 275 Fannie D 16 Hannah A 62 Janette 129 Lizzie A 64 Margery 49 Mary J 16 Melissa A 119 Phoebe 35 Rebecca 275 Sophronia D 71
DURRELL, Lydia Augusta 198 Susan A 62
DUTCH, Charlotte 91
DYER, Emeline 66
EARL, Eunice 206 Laura Jane 111 Lizzie M 112
EARLEY, Sarah E 209
EARNSHAW, Sarah Ann 178
EASTMAN, Mary 65
EATON, Martha 165 Mary Jane 167
EDGERLY, Ann Augusta 40 Betsey L 142 C Augusta 50 Deborah 206 Jane C 175 Jennie M 95 Katie 129 Mary 238 Mary L 254 Priscilla 210 Sarah 134
EDMUNDS, Serepta 170
EDSON, Olive A 158
EDWARDS, Olive S 227
ELA, Sarah Ann C 15
ELKINS, Love 184 Ruth 12
ELLIOT, Betsey 13
ELLIOTT, Martha Ann 163 Polly 182
ELLIS, Carrie C 211-212 Eliza 246 Lizzie 260 Mary J 173 Rosannah 63 Sarah E 276 Thankful 3
ELLISON, Temperance 188
EMBRY, Sarah J 227
EMERSON, Abby R 267 Abigail 27 Annie E 30 Esther 72 Hannah 146 191 Lovey 116 Maggie 129 Malvenah L 122 Mary 268 271 Mary Jane 167 Nancy 169 Sarah E 144
EMERY, Almira 47 Elizabeth 126 Lydia A 230 Mary 234 Mary A 256 Mary D 12 Mary J 96
EMRSON, Mary 173
ENGLAND, Sarah A 265
ESTERBROOK, Charlotte A 206
ESTES, Joanna 69 Mary 255 Mary E 19

ETHRIDGE, Lydia A 52
EVANS, Betsey Jane 6 Charity 67 Elizabeth 61 Elizabeth F 216 Fanny 252 H Jennie 143 Hannah 13 60 246 Lydia 32 Mary F 134 Sally 32 Sarah Bell 197 Sarah W 248 Susan M 23
EVERETT, Helen F 193
FAIRBANKS, Livonia S 108 Mary T T 216
FALL, Abigail 14 Abra W 76 Betsey 215 Betty 145 Elizabeth A 112 Harriet W 74 Lusetta 156 Martha J 235 Mary 209 241 Mary A 178 Sarah F 99 Susan E 74
FARNHAM, Alice 28 Dorothy 93 Hannah 205 Lizzie A 132 Louisa Hinkman 130 Mary 232 Mary A 229 Melvina 75 Mercy 113-114 Nabby 249 Polly 68 Sarah 127 264 Susan G 149 278
FARRAND, Frances J 206
FARRINGTON, Marion E 254
FAYE, Mary 211
FELCH, Caroline 213
FELKER, Abbie 16 Anna 8 123 Ellen E 217 Hannah 8 Joanna 14 Peggy 225 Rebecca O 263 Sarah 20
FERGUSON, Abigail 74 Louise M 140 Miriam 93
FERNALD, Abby 76 277 Abby E 224 Ann Maria 29 Elizabeth F 208 Esther 115 Josie M 30 Lizzie M 235 Louisa N 91 Malvina B 259 Martha A 160 Martha W 162 Mary 97 Mary E 136 Mary J 71 Molly 210 Permelia J 142 Sadie A P 240 Sally 274 Sarah 273 Sarah E 36 Sarah P 218 Susan 137 Susannah 273
FIELDEN, Susan I 114
FIRTH, Elizabeth 164
FISH, Hannah 181
FISHER, Caroline A 35
FISK, Celia A 240
FLACK, Mary E 235
FLAGG, Abbie E 139 Lucy 168 Nettie J 256

FLANDERS, Adaline L 95 Isabel A 67 Jennie M 249 Lucy Ann 95 Mary Anna 87 Miriam 28 Polly 29
FLOOD, Eliza 63
FOGG, Carrie B 135 Emma A 7 Emma B 233 Emma H 125 Hannah R 242 Mary Ann 157 Susannah 40
FOLLETT, Abigail 135 Serena A 111
FOLSOM, Abigail 219 Mary Eliza 1
FOOTE, Martha A 72
FOOTMAN, Catherine 68
FORD, Amanda M 169 Flora E 172 Sarah 179
FORST, Abbie 260 Mary A 243
FOSS, Abbie 208 Abigail 63 81 83 176 190 Adelaide 86 Adeline W 121 Alice J 196 Almira N 250 Amanda M 228 Anna 233 Betsey 14 47 187 210 Caroline E 46 Deborah 157 Deborah H 103 Dorothy 82 Eliza A 250 Eliza Ann 86 Eliza Jane 126 Emily A 27 Emma A 257 Eunice 167 Fannie 168 Fanny 46 Flavilla Ann 55 Frances M 16 Hannah 84 86 110 189 220 Hannah H 141 Hannah Jane 258 Hannah S 222 Harriet L 211 Hattie A 95 Jane 15 Judith 13 Lois 109 Lorinia N 222 Lovina 75 Lydia 102 Lydia Ann 96 Lydia D 84 Lydia S 108 Margaret Roberts 109 Maria 84 Martha Ann 46 Martha J 85 Mary 109 215 238 249 Mary A 83 187 222 Mary A W 105 Mary Ann 234 Mary E 59 67 91 121 Mary Jane 86 197-198 Mary Susan 220 Molley 167 Molly 190 220 Nabby 57 Nancy 270 Nancy L 192 Olive Ann 226 Olive H 36 Orissa A 187 Patience 250 Priscilla M 85 Rebecca 201 Sally 82 Sarah 83 172 183 202 Sarah A 121 Sarah E 8 10 162 Sarah Jane 116 Sarah M 46 Susan 101 277 Susanna 233 Tamson 102
FOSTER, Frances J 254 Louisa E 26
FOWLER, Betty 14
FOX, Abby Elizabeth 223 Hannah A 243 Nancy J 179 239

FOYE, Hannah 27 Lydia 270 Olly 72 Patience 272 Ruth 269 Sarah 272 Sarah A 250 262
FRANCIS, Lizzie H 274
FRANKLIN, Sarah J 154
FREEMAN, Abby 229 Emma D 262 Lavina 25 Lucinda B 56 Lucinda T 101 Lucy M 146 Mary C 2 Sarah 138 Sophie 253
FREESE, Margaret 14
FRENCH, Elizabeth M 151 Hannah Draper 260 Harriette Van Mater 125 Jane C 64 Judith 245 Lavina 160 Lizzie J 89 Mary 91 Mary J 20 170 206 Nancy 35 263 Polly 175 Sarah Ann 216
FROST, Carrie A 88 Dolly 204 Hannah M 226 Love 100 Lucy 100 Mary S 194 Sarah E 115
FRYE, Mary H 164
FULLER, Abigail 192
FULLERTON, Ann C 175
FURBER, Betsey 167 Eliza Ann 150 Elizabeth 178 Elizabeth A 162 Elizabeth Downing 39 Hannah 7 Lizzie A 162 Mary 70-71 Mary M 10 Melissa Jane 10 Nellie A 99 Polly 155 Rosa J 28 Sally 21 Zerviah 125
FURBISH, Abra W 159 Catherine 2 Elizabeth Thompson 93 Jane 89 167 Lydia 3 Polly 167 Sabra 90
FURBUSH, Adah 144 Ann 90 Betsey 91 Hannah 237 Lucinda 154 Lydia 204 Mary E 153 Sally J 173
FUSBISH, Sarah Ann 4
GAGE, Carrie C 202 Elizabeth 38 Harriet E 225 Julia Ann 147 Lydia 55
GALE, Martha A 95 Mary S 94
GALLAGER, Margaret 213
GARLAND, Abiah 256 Abigail H 38 Anna 128 Anne 195 Betsey 189 Betsey D 237 Elizabeth H 205 Ellen F 205 Esther 109 Hannah 20 169 Helen B 124 Lydia 21 Margaret 134 Mary 32 167 267 Mary H 274 Mary W 225 Patience 131 Rebecca 63 Susan B 33

GARNETT, Philandia C 216
GEAR, Caroline R 133 Louisa M 272
  Mary Ann 19 Rebecca 19
GEORGE, Belinder A 26 Hannah 176
  Judith B 77 Martha C 155 Mary
  Ann 231 Rosannah 226
GERALDS, Ruhama 228
GERRISH, Anabel 16 Araminda D
  215 Betsey E 226 Catherine 17
  Catherine T 89 Cynthia L 111 Eliza
  A 139 Elizabeth 93 Judith 17 120
  Judith G 265 Lucy 213 Mary 160
  Mary D 163 Mary Jane 115 Matha
  271 Molly 123 Polly 76 Ruth 264
  Sabrina 174 Sally 119 148 229
GETCHELL, Jennie A 147 Julia A 274
GILBERT, Mary Ann 128 Mary E 268
GILE, Catharine T 232 Catherine T 12
  Deborah Ann 201
GILES, Abigail 184 Betsey 152
  Deborah 32 Hannah 203 Mary E
  222
GILMAN, Angeline P 163 Annette
  254 Dolly 95 Elizabeth 44
  Elizabeth T 95 Emily A 33 Emma
  48 Hannah 3 Lavinia 52 Lydia 168
  Mary Ann 185 Mary E 12 240
  Mary P 22 Melvina A 198 Molly
  67 Rachel 11 Sally 46 Sarah H 95
  Susie M 225
GILMORE, Mary S 90
GLASS, Nancy 207
GLEASON, Clarissa 188 Mary A 276
GLEESON, Mary E 144
GLIDDEN, Almira N 182 Drusilla 56
  Elma P 99 Hannah 127 Mary A 56
  Melissa Jane 98
GLINES, Carrie M 231 Mary A 233
  Mary Jane 1
GLOVER, Abigail 44 Mary A 44
  Sarah F 53
GOLDSMITH, Lavinia 96 Lizzie M
  243
GOODALE, Hattie M 75 Mary A 215
GOODALL, Almira N 85 Mary H 34
GOODELL, Rhoda E 276
GOODWICH, Lydia D 265
GOODWIN, Abba J 265 Abby Jane
  193 Abigail 120 Abigail A 60 Abra
  136 Adah 190 Almira A 146

GOODWIN (continued)
  Anna L 214 Arabella 178 Arabella
  S 271 Bathsheba W 134 Betsey 92
  265 Betsey H 40 Caroline 152
  Dorcas 98 154 Elizabeth 94
  Elizabeth L 98 Emma A 122
  Eunice 207 Eunice Amy 274
  Eunice T 43 Frances L 185 Hannah
  98 Harriet 69 Hattie S 115 Isabel
  205 Isabella 178 Judith 273 Julia
  167 Julia Ann 258 Laura Jane 258
  Leah Helen 62 Lizzie 49 Lizzie E
  268 Louisa 158 Lydia 49 Lydia A
  228 Lydia R 198 Martha J 118
  Mary E 12 69 88 Miriam 156
  Molly 5 Myra 186 Nabby 156
  Nancy 111 119 Olive 118 130
  Olive M 56 Paulina 45 Polly 154
  207 Ruth M 223 Sarah 111 178
  Sarah Jane 97 Sophia 93 Susie 62
  Theodocia 119 Vanna 79
GORDON, Phebe J 250 Sarah 194
GOULD, Julia A 87 Mary 175
GOWELL, Betsey 98 Elizabeth 232
  Sally 98
GOWEN, Helen E 99 Mary A 208
GRAHAM, Bell 245 Elizabeth 240
GRANT, C Ella 209 Emily O 73
  Emma 162 Esther 89 209 Henrietta
  161 Jean 268 Kesiah 234 Mercy 94
  Sarah E 26
GRANVILLE, Eliza J 28
GRAVES, Sarah J 146
GRAY, Abigail 188 233 Betsey 257
  Carrie S 68 Genny 42 Hannah H 88
  Huldah F 68 Jennie 12 Livonia 86
  Mary A 214 Mary S 108 Nellie A
  186 Patience 6 Polly 102-103 Sarah
  116 Sarah Ann 111 Sarah E D 68
  Sarah F 103 Susannah 139 Wenna
  F 139
GREELY, Roxanna T 259
GREEN, Miriam 170 Patience 122
GREENE, Harriet 62
GRIFFIN, Emma A 262 Pamelia B 6
GRIFFITHS, Annie M 257
GROVER, Ellen M 10 Lois 225 Mary
  33 Sarah E 104
GROVES, Estelle S 256
GUPPEY, Emily 47

GUPPY, Betsey 37 Margaret 275 Sally 172
GUPTILL, Agnes 63 Clarinda A 129 Jane N 223 Keziah 185 Laura E 234 Lucie L 157 Martha 238 Mary E 233 Molly 274 Olive 204 Sylvina 65
GUY, Mattie A 110
HACKETT, Sarah A 202
HADLEY, Louisa 117
HAINES, Abbie 20 Calista 31 Phebe 33 Sarah J 86
HAL, Olive 164
HALE, Elizabeth S 257 Martha Susan 221 Susan 134
HALEY, Clara A 236 Eley 196 Nancy S 159 Sally 196
HALL, Abigail 57 Agnes 149 Amanda F 98 Ann 83 Annie R 225 Betty 116 Clarissa 259 Ellen A 229 Ellen Jane 261 Esther 44 248 Georgie A 22 Hannah 94 108 182 257 275 Harriet 121 Jane 201 Jennie M 264 Joanna 155 Julia A 233 Kezia 61 Lizzie M 86 Lois 66 Lorinda N 274 Lydia 215 Mary 125 189 Mary K 150 Matilda 66 Molly 146 Nellie M 182 Patience 171 Phebe 261 Phebe K 142 Polly 184 Sally 266 Sarah 14 42 Sarah A 219 Sarah D 110 Sarah J 173 Sophia Locke 276 Susan P 19 Tamsin 256 Ursula R 270
HAM, Almira 237 Anna Louise 236 Annie E 246 Aramantha E 110 Betsey 168 Betty 137 Caroline 31 Charlotte 197 Deborah 119 243 275 Eliza C 251 Elizabeth 91 123 Hannah 92 Lanora F 192 Lydia 8 218 Lydia A 67 Lydia S 271 Margaret 82 Martha 168 Mary 236 Mary A 208 Mary Ann 128 Mary Annie 149 Mary E 139 Mary Harriet 72 Mehitable 156 230 Melinda 123 Nancy 109 Olive 60 Olive J 165 Phebe Leighton 21 Polly 92 116 120 157 Rebecca 219 Sarah 3 185 242 Susan 18 171 Susanna 199 Wealthy C B 20

HAMILTON, Hannah 31 Jane G 67 Lydia S 17 Sabra R 181
HAMMETT, Fannie 182 Lizzie P 9
HAMMON, Patience T 110
HAMMOND, Fannie 222 Olive W 43
HAMPSEN, Ellen 129
HANCOCK, Susan K 162
HANKS, Bell 20
HANNERS, Selena F 152
HANSCOM, Abigail 206 Adaline 147 Anne 199 Betsey 153 Catharine 100 Elvira R 227 Julia 101 Julian Ann 97 Lizzie F 256 Louisa 273 Mary 195 Nabby 100 Nancy 157 Parmela 136 Peggy 45 Ruth S 236
HANSCOMB, Lizzie 117 Sally 31 Thesta D 7
HANSON, Abby S 264 Abigail 41 194 Anna 148 237 Anne 31 Caroline 177 Dorothy 211 Ellen A 71 Emeline E 206 Emelu 190 Esther 101 Fannie B 155 Hannah 35 Hannah B 168 Hannah F 122 Ida S 36 Judith 42 Lauretta M 88 Lizzie J 10 Lucinda K 248 Lucy 86 Lydia B 162 Maggie C 121 Martha 212 Martha A 151 228 Mary 210 236 Mary A 171 Mary E 117 205 258 Mary J C 56 Mary S 135 Mehitable 156 Miriam S 205 Molly 148 Nancy G 236 Nancy H 239 Orissa O 20 Patience 41 Phebe F 262 Polly 130 Sarah 23 30 130 Sarah A 45 164 179 Sarah Jane 183 Susan F 177 Susanna 258 Syrene 46
HARDING, Flora E 262
HARDISON, Emma D 143 Sally 262
HARDY, Alice C 122 Hannah Poor 263 Mary A 226
HARIDSON, Lydia 229 Lydia A 196 Rebecca 204
HARLOW, Jane Ann 145
HARMON, Sarah 134
HARRIMAN, Orrville E 72
HART, Elizabeth 262 Lydia A 205 Susan S 161
HARTFIELD, Ellen F 74
HARTFORD, Alice 245 Alice M 40 Eliza J 208 Jane 72 Louisa F 104

HARTFORD (continued)
   Mary F 9 Melissa A 16 Mercy 277
   Sobriety 261 Ursula 259
HARTSHORN, Caroline C 2 Mary E
   147
HARVEY, Abbie M 262 Melissa 89
HASEY, Hannah Owen 2
HASKELL, Bettie C 216
HASLETT, Ann Maria 194
HATCH, Albertine 13 Amanda 103
   Dorothy 4 Emily A 21 Hannah 67
   Jerusha G 258 Julia A 103 140
   Louisa 4 Mary J 5 Susan 25
HAUGHTON, Alvina 262
HAWKINS, Betsey 25 Betsey M 270
   Hannah 160 Nancy M 173 Nellie
   M 231 Rebecca 82
HAYDON, Emma A 266
HAYES, 73 Abigail 197 219 Ari Pearl
   59 Asenath 55 Augusta P 274
   Betsey 6 118 214 Betsey R 187
   Betty 170 Carrie J 112 Charlotte
   206 Dorcas 204 Eliza J 70
   Elizabeth 81 Elizabeth H 66 159
   Elizabeth Lucy 34 Elizabeth R 88
   Evengline 159 Freelove J 22
   Hannah 45 51 124 247 Hattie E 22
   Jennie S 180 Joanna 154 Julia A
   246 Leonora L 233 Lizzie K 106
   Lizzie P 58 Lovie D 44 Lucy D 266
   Lydia 21 Mahalia F 114 Margaret
   109 Martha 84 Martha Ann 124
   Mary 15 159 173 Mary Ham 250
   Mary J 55 Mary Olive 143
   Mehitable 54 Meribah 103 Phebe H
   18 Polly 15 116 Rachel 15 Rebecca
   75 Sabrina A 176 Sally J 270 Sarah
   144 194 275 Sarah C 15 Sarah E
   143 Susannah 81 Tamsin 159
   Tamson 269 Vesta 207
HAYFORD, Delia E 64
HEARD, Betsey 131 Elizabeth 159
   Hannah 3 126
HEATH, Betsey S 38
HENDERSON, Amanda 21 Betsey
   194 Delia A 179 Elizabeth 156
   Louise 18 Lydia 210 Nancy 54
HERRICK, Martha S 212
HERSEY, Abigail 179 Emily M 98
   Mary Ann 106 Myra B 183 Nancy
   M 71
HERSOM, Abigail 55 Ada 141 277
   Dorcas 271 Eliza 156 Elizabeth M
   94 Emma A 122 Esther 200 Harriet
   208 Laura E 219 Lizzie J 157
   Lydia 208 Margaret 119 Mary Ann
   142 Merilla M 201 Nancy 111
   Nancy J 142 Olive A 127 223 Polly
   238 Ruth F 142 Sarah 118 Sarah
   Ann 208 Sarah F 200 Sophia 172
HICKS, Deborah 243 Martha 253
HIGHT, Lydia 269
HILL, Abby Augusta 171 Abiah M
   154 Anna A 191 Augusta 30
   Betsey 25 Betsey F 201 Caroline 5
   Charlotte 150 Clara A 88 Darinda
   A 9 E A 237 Elizabeth 150 222
   Emily A 13 Eunice E 161 Hannah
   82 107 138 141 Hannah Abbie 132
   Hannah H 36 Jane 82 Judith G 63
   Julia E 169 Lois 3 Lottie A P 191
   Mary 123 191 Mary C 112 Mary E
   85 Mary Ellen 44 Mary Jane 74
   Mylo 257 Nancy H 277 Nellie J
   209 Sarah 42 Sarah F 135 Susan
   141
HILLER, Emma J 172
HILLIARD, Julia 273
HILTON, Cynthia A 144 Polly 223
   Sarah 94 Susan 188 Vianna
   Angenette 200
HOAG, Ann 165 Mariah J 89
HOAR, Susanna 102
HOBBS, Abbie 72 Flora A 174 Mary
   A 174 Phebe H 94 Sarah J 185
HODGDON, Annie P 93 Clarissa Jane
   78 Deborah 102 Elizabeth 53 210
   Esther 7 Joanna 65 Josie M 166
   Judith 200 Kezia 207 Lizzie A 239
   Lydia 273 Malinda 124 Martha 96
   148 Mary 7 130 203 Mary Jane 213
   Nancy 180 Nellie J 246 Sarah C 18
   Sarah Jane 194 Tamson 102
HODGKINS, Henrietta 47

HODGON, Sally 94
HODSDON, Harriet M 163 Melissa 224 Nancy E 163 Sally 83 118 130 207 Sarah E 228 Sophia 149 Tamson 105 277
HOIT, Sarah A 242
HOITT, Belle S 166 Eliza C 269 Frances A 246 Georgianna O 37 Helen A 140 Lydia 104 Maggie I 254 Mary Ann 5 Mary E 232 Nellie K 162 Olive 16 Ruth 167 Sarah 6 152 Sarah A 242 Sarah Jane 66 W Frances 276
HOLBROOK, Hattie H T 72
HOLEMAN, Mercy R 100
HOLLAND, Alice 82
HOLMAN, Sarah E J 186
HOLMES, Betsey 34 Elizabeth 65 Hattie S 241 Margaret 230 Mary 40 Mary A 13 Nellie 38 Polly 34 Sally L 7 Sarah A 16 Susan 77 Susanna 33
HOLT, Annie E 69 Sarah A 275
HONESLY, Sarah 231
HONNERS, Margaret 43
HOOD, Kate P 240
HOOPEN, Nelly F 241
HOOPER, Fanny M 126 Hannah 141 Jennie H 262 Sally 39
HOPE, Susan A 68
HORN, Abbie 212 Alice W 195 Angeline 227 Dorothy 128 Eunice H 118 Hannah 215 Henrietta 108 Jennie E 18 Josephine A 37 Louisa 190 Lydia A 261 Margaret 127 Martha 244 Mary A 251 Mary Ann 199 Patience 82 200 Peazy 97 Rose 137 Sarah 84 207 Sarah A 64 Sarah Ann 133 Sarah L 52 Vianna F 16
HORNE, Abbie M 145 Abbie W 137 Abby 52 Abby L 224 Anna 80 Attie A 65 Bessie M 131 Betsey Adams 37 Betty 42 Camela Abby 48 Charlotte W 183 Clara E 113 Dorcas D 76 Dorcas Downs 76 Emma C 99 Fanny H 88 Hattie S 115 Helen S 129 Laura E 209 Lizzie W 40 Louisa S 49 Lucy 103 Lydia 232 Lydia J 225 Margaret 127 Maria M 10 Mariah 181

HORNE (continued) Martha A 195 Martha J 230 Mary 127 Mary A 121 Mercy 134 Nancy 37 Ruth 154 Sally 207 Sarah F 271 Sarah R 65
HORTON, Costilla Lacoste 180
HOWARD, Abigail 159 Betsey 57 Deborah 92 Emma A 189 Esther 184 Hannah M 202 Jane 23 Jennie 122 Keziah 135 Lizzie E 136 Mahala 246 Molly 140
HOWE, Abby M 244 Charity 275 Julia A J 209 Lucy L 126 Mary 68 Mary Abby 157 Sarah A 221
HOYT, Clarecy 213 Ellen F 43 Emma S 168 Martha Adeline 52 Mary Ann 261 Sarah 152
HUBBARD, Clara A 177 Harriet A 77 Margaret T 43
HUCKINS, Mary 8 252 Olive J 104 Sally 58
HUGGINS, Julia Ann 165
HULL, Annar 237 Love 39 Mary Eleanor 147 Sarah 10
HUNT, Abby W 163 Elizabeth 81 Rhoda 94 Sarah E 71
HUNTRESS, Lizzie A 174 Mary 151 Phebe Ann 113
HURD, Betsey 74 Clara 208 Cyclene 3 Eleanor 272 Eliza 15 Emma J 16 Josephine L 254 Laura A 203 Lydia 197 Mary A 168 Mary E 259 Olive A 196 Orinda H 242 Sarah 102
HUSE, 171
HUSSEY, Adelaid 9 Anna 269 Annie L 220 Eliza 38 Elizabeth 91 237 Elizabeth Jane 53 Ellen 131 Emily C 80 Lizzie H 24 Lydia M 211 Martha F 47 S Lizzie 132 Sarah 269 Sarah H 148
HUTCHINS, Emma 236 Laura E 258 Lizzie A 137 Nellie D 255 Phymelia A 201
HUTCHINSON, Emma T 158 Harriet M 114 Lizzie 7 Lizzie L 135 Matilda J 168
HYDE, Asenath 55 Mary 123
HYLEY, Larah Clivia 106
INGALLS, Caroline 164

INGERSOL, Mary 272
INGRAHAM, Fannie M 191
JACKMAN, Mary E 206
JACKSON, Anna M 197 Carrie 203 Elizabeth 242 Hannah 94 Mary 17 36 Mary A 275 Viola U 79
JACOBS, Maria 207 Nancy E 60
JANVRIN, Adelia A 260 Julia E 160
JEFFERS, Lydia 182
JELLISON, Sarah 105
JENKINS, Catherine 33 Elizabeth 3 Fannie C 241 Hannah M 150 Harriet A 88 Keziah 37 Mary E 29 Melinda H 150 Phebe 4 Sarah F 74 Sophia B 102
JENNESS, Abigail 92 Belinda 14-15 Betsey 48 Deborah 140 Elizabeth 138 Hannah E 115 Josephine S 94 Louella K 126 Lucy 109 Lydia 219 Mary A 24 Mary B 40 Mary L 116 Patience 17 Sarah 17 Sarah J 30 Serena A 86
JENNISS, Amanda J 191
JEWELL, Fanny G 209 Lydia 153
JEWETT, Addie 201 Nancy R 224
JOHNSON, Anna M 169 Betsey 78 Catherine 139 Charity 106 139 Elizabeth B 274 Elvira A 59 Esther 14 Hannah 34 Irene 55 Judith 245 Mary 51 Mary E 215 Mary P 145 Mehitable 139 Nabby 82 Olive 190 Sarah 15 Sarah C 237 Sophronia 10
JOICE, Mary L 67
JONES, Abby M 11 Abigail 57 Adah 38 42 Alice Ann 225 263 Ann 271 Betsey 1 157 Clara F 209 Comfort 185 Dorcas 118 130 Dorothy 155 Elizabeth 64 149 Ella Adelia 79 Emily J 186 Erva E 191 Esther Jane 208 Eunice 101 207 Joanna 167 230 Laura A W 202 Leah 66 Lucinda 186 Lucinda J 124 Lucy J 271 Lydia 98 163 Lydia S 237 Mahala 125 Martha A 119 Martha Ann 208 Mary 2 200 243 Mary S 122 276 Meily J 271 Molly 188 Nellie 154 Paulina 155 Polly 102 172 Relief 97 Ruth 144 Sarah 111 Sarah C 94 Sarah L 162 Sophia 90 Susannah 88

JORDAN, Dorcas 19
JORDON, Ann 185
JOY, Elizabeth N 253 Fanny A 62 Irene 121 Sally 187 Susanna 63
JUDKINS, Mary L 19
KEATING, Joanna 72
KEAY, Aphia 229 Dorcas 220 Mary Ann 274 Sarah 110
KEITH, Mary E 275
KELF, Ann 107
KELLEY, Adaline 147 Betsey P 114 Caroline E 59 Elizabeth 126 Eunice 46 Fannie E 22 Lydia 224 Mary Jane 71
KELLY, Lizzie J 174
KELSEY, Sukey 241
KENDALL, Nancy J 175
KENNARD, Elizabeth 178 Ellen N 69
KENNEDY, Estella J 215
KENNERSON, Elizabeth Ann 194
KENNEY, Emma 131 Sarah B 231
KENNISON, Margaret 172 Sarah Ann 141
KENNISTON, Jennie C 90
KERBY, Anna 246
KEZER, Nancy 243
KIDDER, Margaret A 48
KIELLEY, Frances 151
KILGORE, Amy 38 Hannah 160 Martha 53
KIMBALL, Augusta 172 Eliza 14 Elizabeth M 243 Ellen A 212 Ellen S 143 Emeline 256 Eunice 146 Hannah S 28 Hattie C 172 Hattie J 217 Lizzie 187 Lydia J 254 Mahala 58 Martha C 75 Mary 169 Mary A 193 Mary Emeline 261 Olive W 224 Sarah 183 Sarah W 227 Susan C 128 Tryphina 52
KING, Nancy 180
KINGMAN, Abiah 271 Alice 275 Elizabeth 9 Phebe H 24 Polly 81
KINGSBURY, Dorah F 193
KINNISON, Anna 11
KINSTON, Elizabeth 166
KITTREDGE, Abby W 259
KNIGHT, Martha 153 Mary T 199
KNIGHTS, Mary A 96
KNOWLES, Ester J 217
KNOWLTON, Betsey 133

KNOX, Abigail 238 Alma 191
Clarinda 193 Dorca 127 Eleanor
197 Elizabeth 271 Eunice 118 129
Hannah 117 155 Helen B 183
Jerusha 200 Lovina 180 Lucetta
195 Lucinda 239 Mary 124 Molly
93 Patience 149 Rachel 255 Rachel
A 264 Rebecca 141 Sarah 265
Sarah G 150 Unice L 124
LABONTE, Lena 196
LACHENWITZ, Fernandia M 180
LADD, Lucinda 270 Nancy 175
LAIRD, Lydia 272
LAKE, Sarah E 178
LAMPER, Mary 153
LAMSON, Mary V 136
LANE, Abbie L 199 Charlotte 150
Electa A 73 Eliza A 1 Hannah J 33
Jenny 21 Nellie N 251
LANG, Cynthia A 246 Harriet T 200
LANGDON, Martha 234
LANGLEY, Charlotte 190 Ellen M 6
Maria Jane 270 Martha A 228 Sally
30 Sarah 73
LANGMAID, Sarah 261
LANGTON, Theodotia 101
LASKEY, Comfort 185 Love 10
LAWRENCE, Emma A 137
LEACH, Augusta 252 Dorcas 208
LEAR, Martha J 153
LEARY, Abby R 182
LEATHERS, Abigail 61 Abigail S 194
Anna 152 Eliza 257 Elizabeth Ann
131 Hannah 31 Jane 266 Mary 261
Mehitable 17 Rebecca 77 Sarah 49
57 131 Thankful 176
LEAVITT, Augusta H 79 Catherine P
258 Elizabeth 145 J Abbie 63
Martha S 264 Mary 133 Mary A 64
Mary E 27 Mary J 80
LEE, Hattie 133 Lucy Ellen 191
LEEMAN, Emma 21
LEGG, Sarah A 197
LEGRO, Betsey B 64 277 Ellen J 240
Eunice 63 Laura A 11 Lydia C 63
Martha 141 Mary E 188
LEIGHTON, Abbie M 105 Abigail
102 155 Arabella M 182 Augusta 6
Betsey K 267 Dorothy 135
Elizabeth 205 Fannie 213

LEIGHTON (continued)
Hannah E 29 Jamima 234 Leonora
E 208 Lucinda 8 Lydia 23 Mariah
H 251 Martha 109 Mary 34 106
Mary E 34 Mehitable 154 Nancy
83 Nancy J 95 Nancy W 189 Olive
J 93 Patience 170 Patience M 43
Rhoda A 160 Sarah 83 213 Sarah C
5 Sarah Jane 84
LEONARD, Marcia A 67
LEWIS, Amelia A 1
LIBBEY, Abigail 40 100 Ada A 140
Ann Janette 248 Belinda 175 Betty
125 Caroline 190 Charlotte 144
Clara 111 Clarissa 158 Eunice 117
Fanny C 104 Hannah 70 Harriet
231 Harriet C 91 Julia A 157
Lovey W 248 Lucy 113 Martha
214 Mary Ann 22 Mary Jane 173
Nabby 156 277 Nancy N 69 Olive
57 111 Parmela 199 Permit 144
Phebe P 169 Polly 50 199 Rebecca
150 Sabina 62 Sally 192 Sarah 154
268 Sophia 132 Theodoisa 55
LIBBY, Ella G 20 Jennie 149 Mary
Elizabeth 2 Nancy 110
LINSCOTT, Abbie 114 Betsey 217
Ellen 217 Julia A 272 Martha A 76
Rebecca 104
LINTON, Annie 253
LITTLE, Sarah 196
LITTLEFIELD, Lizzie 49 Louisa 128
Lydia 156 Mary 158
LITTLEFORD, Ruth 158
LOCK, Hannah 216 249 Margaret Ann
26 Maribah 7 Mary F E 44
LOCKE, Abigail P 124 Agnes 212
Caroline H 251 Carrie J 90 Dorothy
S 49 Elizabeth 53 Emily 87 Fannie
E 140 Martha A 112 Mary E 276
Mary P 205 Nancie W 199 Sarah A
86 Sarah E 206 Sarah P 158 Sarah
W 250 Vienna C 121
LORD, Abigail 273 Alice 155 Anna 75
97 Anna S 222 Berlinda 190 Betsey
89 118 130 148-149 229 Betsey B
64 277 Betsey H 146 Cynthia 71
Deborah 49 Elizabeth 41 Emily J
103 Eunice 110 Georgie A 22
Hannah 186 214 Hannah Jane 170

LORD (continued)
   Jane S 119 Joan 41 Love 207
   Lucinda 164 Lucy 164 Mary 58
   Molly 96 126 141 Olive Ann 105
   Perlina 23 Permela 111 Polly 97
   Prudence 214 Roxanna 141 Sarah
   79 200 210 270 Sophia 94 Susan A
   202 Susan G 147 Susie A 76 Tirzah
   156
LOUGEE, Dora S 251 Mary J A 262
   Olive M 55 Sarah M 72
LOVELL, Eliza B 242
LOVERING, Anna M 56
LOW, Lydia H 105 Sarah 217
LOWD, Mary E 224
LUCAS, Hannah 75 Mary 242
LUNT, Mary 12 Olive 171
LYMAN, Clarissa 161
MACE, Mary Jane 86
MACK, Elizabeth C 60 Ellen 120
MADDOX, Sarah Elizabeth 63
MAGOON, Ellen Elizabeth 258 Emma E 95
MAHONEY, Margaret 44
MAIN, Laura 196 Meribah Ann 257
MALOON, Martha 141
MANAHAN, Eliza E 5
MANDAVILLE, Isabella 31
MANNING, Olive G 180
MANSON, Louisa A 32 Orrilla R 170
MARDEN, Abigail 81 Martha A 95
   Mary A 177 Nancy 30 Rachel 19
   Susan 39 Susanna 17
MARKS, Marilla 135
MARSH, Elizabeth 200 Hannah E 185
MARSHALL, Meribah 32
MARSTON, Celestia M 165 Elvira B
   150 Lucy A 24 Mary E 233 Olive
   105 Sarah P 180 Syrena 230
MARTIN, Almira O 125 Bedelia 28
   Elizabeth F 180 Emma M 19
   Hannah 261 Mary E 199 Nancy H
   197 Sally 231
MARTYN, Elizabeth 178
MASON, Carrie M 224 Mary 8 Mary
   E 121 Nancy C 78 Susannah 252
MATHES, Abigail 174 Annie M 265
   Annie R 26 Carrie A 122 Clara W
   154 Ella Mary 177 Emma J 252
   Frances 165 Judith Matilda 191

MATHES (continued)
   Sarah F W 31 Sarah Ida B 54 Susan
   A 243
MATHEWS, Lizzie R 188 Martha A 200
MATTHEWS, Cath 68 Hannah H 121
MAXWELL, Martha L 62
MAY, Georgia B 240
MAYHEW, Mydia 20
MCCANN, Lucy E 122
MCCOY, Lois 73
MCCRILLIS, Anne 255 Betsey 207
   Dorcas 238 Jane 90 Joanna 260
   Mary 19 Mary Ann 5 Sally 255
   Sarah A 250
MCCUTCHINS, Deborah 148
MCDANIEL, Irena 104 Maria E 253
   Sarah Ann 164
MCDANIELS, Nancy 218
MCDUFFEE, Annie M 24 Delia 228
   Ellen L 7 Jennie 169 Martha A 230
   Mary 142 Nancy 198
MCGAFFEY, Emily 176
MCGAFFY, Peggy 77
MCGROTY, Josephine 275
MCILROY, Lizzie S 20
MCINTIRE, Lydia S 235
MCKENNEY, Hannah 113
MCNEAL, Elizabeth 42
MCQUESTEN, Elizabeth 228
MEADER, Almira O 34 Jane 52 Lois
   244 Mary 21 72 Mary E 10 Mary J
   242 Nellie 108 Sarah 202 Sarah A
   9
MEARS, Amelia J 1
MEGAN, Catherine 178
MEIGS, Selina 202
MELCHER, Sarah 113
MERRILL, Adeline E 218 Ettia N 265
   Flora L 252 Frances Marion 85
   Lizzie S 77 Lydia 55 181 Mary A
   101 Mary E 203 Phebe G 173
   Sarah C 101
MERROW, Clara A 5 Elizabeth 187
   Elizabeth A 136 Emily 254
   Georgie A 110
MESERVE, Betsey 107 Lucy A 31
   Mary Ann 78 Mary G 48 Placentia
   C 19 S Jennie 127 Susan 18
   Susanna 126

MILES, Abigail 217 Abigail M 217
  Betsey J 259 Elizabeth N 253
  Lydia B 33 M Augusta 68 Polly
  130 Sarah F 139
MILLER, Eliza 117 Jennette Q 158
  Louisa 209 Rosetta B 45 Sarah 210
MILLET, Fanny 93
MILLS, Abby J 162 Abigail 190
  Aseneth 238 Elizabeth 176 Jane
  146 Lydia 63 Polly 12 Sophia 19
  Sukey 266
MITCHELL, Lizzie 235 Susan E 224
MONTGOMERY, Abra 275 Esther
  Jane 124 Mary E 85 Sarah Ann 165
  Tamson 116
MOODY, Clara B 125 Hattie B 145
  Lucy 76 Martha A 261 Mary A 47
  Olive 97 Sarah A 139 Sarah H 1
  Sophia 250
MOONEY, Annie E 258 Clara 95
  Hannah B 238 Mary F 47 Mary
  Jane 68
MOORE, Abbie J 59 Eleanor 152
  Eliza 205 Eliz A 153 Hannah E 205
  Jane E 170 Mary H 40 Nettie 77
MORDOUGH, Margaret 242
MORGAN, Martha Ann 192 Sarah F
  105
MORRILL, Annie S 49 Eleanor 161
  Hannah W 51 Harriet E 55 Julia A
  153 Mary 83 Sally 83 Sarah Jane
  27
MORRISON, Addie 122 Augusta 128
  Elizabeth 99 Hannah B 120 Helen
  205 Jennie M 265 Mary 42 Mary E
  64 Sally 158 Sarah 192 Shuah 263
MORSE, Caroline L 65 Phebe Ann
  113 Sarah 10 Sarah Ann 21
MORTON, Maria A 20
MOSES, Annie M 52
MOTT, Lizzie C 161
MOULOTN, Mary Jane 164
MOULTON, Abby J 28 Addy M 169
  Alta Augusta 92 Ann Lizzie 251
  Elvira B 9 Emma F 254 Hannah G
  115 Lydia 22 Margaret 14 Mary E
  122 Nancy C 21 Nancy E 176
  Nellie L 147 Olive 138 Patience B
  200 Sally Miller 72 Sarah F 245
  Susan 27 Vienner 266

MUDGET, Mary E 230 Plooma D 121
MUDGETT, Abbie M 2 Eliza 121
  Laura B 243 Lucinda B 98
MULLEN, Elizabeth 101
MUNSEY, Charlotte G 158 Nabby 169
MURDOCK, Frances J 206
MURRAY, Hannah 156 Lorana 2
  Mary 115 Mary E 157
MURREY, Molly 152
NALTY, Agnes A 100
NASON, Clara L 171 Elizabeth
  Wingate 148 Mary Abbie 157
  Matilda 74 Mehitable 220 Phebe 88
  Sarah W 111 Viola 13
NAY, Lydia 46 Sarah 51
NEAL, Anna Maria 50 Caroline 276
  Catharine 3 Content 272 Eliza 48
  Hannah 196 M A 30 Mehitable 235
  Nancy B 54 Sarah 189 Susan T 60
NEALLEY, Mary N 110
NEEDHAM, Mary 2
NELSON, Annie A 88 Julia 64
  Stalbira A 148
NEWCOMB, Maria B 237 Sarah A
  149
NEWELL, Emma P 209 Lydia A 137
NEWTON, Patience 28
NICHOLS, Betsey 93 Emma 60
  Lucinda Idella 240 Polly 91 Sarah
  M 182
NICHOLSON, Elizabeth A 169
NILES, Lucy J 163
NISBETT, Abigail 136 Charlotte 97
NOBLE, Elizabeth 56 244 Sally 57
NOCK, Dolly 206 Sarah 74
NORRIS, Ann E 73 Elma E 274
NORTON, Florence Louisa 94 Frances
  A 62 Hannah 93
NORWOOD, Louisa 221
NOWELL, Mary E 127 Susan J 98
NOYES, Augusta M 106 Ettie 271
  Judith 46
NUTE, Abigail 247 Annie P 56 C
  Amanda 112 Elizabeth 42 Helen A
  71 Isadore 92 Julia A 45 Lydia A
  131 Mary A 14 Mary Ann 168
  Melissa B 169 Roxanna 221 Sarah
  D 129 Sarah F 28 Sarah M 260
  Sophia J 251 Susan H 44 Susan J
  248 Tamson 231 Ursula 40

NUTTER, Anne Moriah 137 Arabella
189 Arieine N 243 Betsey 131
Betsey N 79 Deborah 30 Elizabeth
114 Eunice A 260 Hannah 182
Lucinda 104 Malvina 248 Mary D
110 Mary E 48 Mary M 210
Meribah F 145 Rosemon 73 Sarah
17 165 Sarah A 8 Sarah L 45
Wilhelmina 113
O'BRIAN, Bridget 54
O'CONNER, Lydia E 9
ODEL, Mary 11
ODIORNE, Mehitable 234 Nancy 89
OGDEN, Mary Jane 244
OLCOTT, Lucia M 234
OLIVER, Mary 257
ORAM, Joanna 203
ORRELL, Lavinia A 223
OSBORNE, Angie A 264 Caroline C
69 Leah M 86
OSGOOD, Clara A 185 Frances R 62
Henrietta 37 Maria 160
OTIS, Abigail 192 Abigail K 270
Charlotte 34 Content 125 Dorothy
102-103 Eliza W 173 Emily P 253
Genna 34 Hannah 103 116 266
Hannah Jane 143 Harriet 192 Jane
184 Jenna 109 Joanna 82 Lucy A
115 Maria H 137 Mary Ann 108
Mary Jane 85 Molly 120 Nellie E
80 Polly 231 Rhoda 24 Sarah 269
Sarah Ann 131 Susan 130
OTTERSON, M E 234
OWEN, Mary E 183 Rebecca 115
OXFORD, Ellen E 178
PAGE, Abigail 159 Elinor H 132 Ellen
Frances 244 Emily A 228 Isabella
177 Mary Ann 136 Mary R 239
Mary S 252 Rebecca 58 Sarah 201
Sarah Jane 5
PALMER, Anna L 146 Deborah 29
Emily 254 Hannah E 78 Laura 64
Martha M 64 Mary B 127 Sarah
Fannie 40
PARCHER, Annie M 31 Lizzie L 6
PARKER, Georgia 19 Julia F 39
Lizzie H 75 Lizzie M 138
PARSHLEY, Abbie J 224 Druzilla W
253 Elizabeth 32 Elizabeth R 88
Emeline S 253 Hannah 174

PARSHLEY (continued)
Hannah E 205 Hannah W 173
Hattie J 173 Lydia C 121 Mary
Ann 226 Mary M 19 Polly 187
Sally 220 Sarah M 181
PARSONS, Abbie A 265 Abby E 168
Annie L 182 Clara K 267 Hannah 4
Louisa 141
PARTRIDGE, Sarah 133
PATCH, Meribah 32
PATRICK, Betty 159
PATTEN, Emma F 263
PATTERSON, Hester A 183
PAUL, Emeline 74 Emily 51 Emily J
264 Mary Ann 132 Nancy 259
Sarah Ann 78
PAULCAROLINE, H 246
PEAKS, Carrie L 168
PEARCE, Carrie A 189
PEAREY, Hannah M 198 Susanna 109
PEARL, Ann E 21 Ann Maria 86
Caroline W 46 Charity 130
Elizabeth 14 Hannah 39 Leah 183
Mary 14 185 Mary A 257 Sarah 84
212 Susanna 181
PEASE, Annette J 47 Augusta E 68
PEASLEE, Emily A 91
PEASLEY, Clara J 236 Sarah 3 Sarah
J 251
PEAVEY, Abigail 153 Betsey 33 270
Eleanor 149 Elizabeth 120 Hannah
84 Hannah Rogers 47 Mary 9 113
Mary E 253 Nancy 64 Sarah A 131
Sarah Ann 173 Temperence 23
PECK, Nellie M 80
PECKER, Susan E 199
PEDUZZI, Florence S 155
PEIRCE, Abbie 183 Abbie H 262
Abigail 269 Almira 178 Elizabeth
110 Emily A 62 Eunice 167 Harriet
H 147 Joanna 255 Judith 263
Lucretia 204 Lydia 165 190 Marcy
189 Mary 150 Mary A 129 Melissa
E 185 Nancy 109 175 Sally 267
Susan 167
PENDERGAST, Catherine A 78
Emeline 104
PENDEXTER, Deborah 192 228
Lydia J 221 Nellie M 166
PENNELL, Eleanor 171

PENNEY, Sarah J 114
PEPPERELL, Mary 89
PERCY, Nellie G 100
PERKINS, Abbie 80 Abigail 192 210 Alice 134 Alice G 19 Angelina 51 Anna 7 Anna C 118 Betsey 84 Betsey A 196 Caroline H 276 Elizabeth H 276 Ellen 140 Emma A 170 Emma E 143 Fannie M C 78 Frances P 6 Jennie A 100 Lanora F 31 Lucretia 52 Lydia 103 Lydia A 173 218 Martha A 91 Marty T 166 Mary 58 Mary E 1 116 157 Matilda 6 Miriam F 62 Nancy 39 Nancy E 244 Nancy S 39 Nettie C 137 Sarah A 18 272 Susannah 148
PERRY, Lydia 78 Mary B 189 Myra 85
PERVIER, Betsey 263
PETTINGILL, Abbie H 40
PHILBRICK, Deborah 46 Mary E 176
PHILPOT, Abigail 256 Clara M 228 Rachel 210 Ruth 213
PICKERING, Phebe 191
PIERCE, Atsy L 158 Draxcy A 52 Hannah M 228 Julia E 258 Nettie E 113 Sarah 235 Sarah A 73 172
PIKE, Abigail 106 Eliz B 36 Eugene F 98 Mary A 95 Susanna 100
PILLING, Laura B 227
PINDER, Clara H 206 Lydia C 182 Mary A 148 Sarah 244
PINKHAM, Ann 44 Betsey 195 Carrie M 48 Claire A 195 Eliza B 238 Ellen A 63 Ellen H 27 Emeline 104 Emilee J 196 Evelyn F 74 Frances J 267 Lucretia 28 Lucy D 147 Lydia J 225 Mary D 45 Miriam 128 Nancy 229 Pamelia Ann 98 Ruth E 203 Sally 65 Sarah 268 Sarah A 196 Sophia 159
PIPER, Emily 4 Hannah 234 Jemima H 153 L Augusta 43 Livonia D 135 Lois M 71 Mary 66 Nancy N 179 Patience C 4 Sarah E 271 Susan W 7
PITMAN, Elizabeth 269 Sarah A 185 Vienna 16
PLACE, Abigail 54 85 Caroline Alice 143 Clara A 248 Elmira M 54

PLACE (continued) Emily Y 85 Hannah 112 Lucy 184 Mary Elizabeth 9 Olive W 70 Sarah 152 Sarah E 79 Susan Demeritt 35
PLUMER, Elizabeth 140 Emily 79 Mary B 255 Patience 156
PLUMMER, Almira 86 Ellen M 260 Izetta I 160 Lydia 154 Sarah C 2
POOR, Georgiana A 268
POTTER, Olive M 55 Sarah H 198
POWERS, Celestia E 163 Eliza 173 Emily 198 Mary E 124 Polly 90
PRAY, Abby 147 179 Alice 207 Ann B 41 Anne 273 Betsey 118 Catharine 111 Dorcas 200 Dorothy 230 Eunice 230 Experience 110 Lydia 242 Lydia A 105 Lydia J 209 M H 222 Margaret 273 Martha 75 Mary 148 271 Mary Jane 41 Mehitable 190 Nancy 208 Olive A 208 Sarah E 113 Susan L 172
PRESCOTT, Anna L 60 Eliza Ann 232 Elmira Reading 208 Emily J 119 Emma O 59 Hattie M 268 Maria 136 Mary 227 Mary M 119 Myra S 222 Orianna Maria 222 Rosetta 142 Ruth R 12
PRESTON, Cyrena A 203 Louisa A 105 Sophronia 73
PRIEST, Jane 247
PRIOR, Georgiana 227
PUTNAM, Martha J 118
QUIMBY, Abby T 177 Dorothy 266 Ellen A 105 Elvira B 138 216 Martha E 165 Mary Ann 180 231 Mary M 127 Sarah 92 Sarah C 5 Statira A 101
QUINT, Lydia A 165 Sarah E 165
RAINS, Ellen C 6
RAITT, Miriam 93
RAMSBOTTOM, Emma F 80 Nancy C 50
RAMSEY, Jane E 167
RAND, Clara L 65 Cynthia D 86 Eliza A 18 Hannah 159 Mary 32 Salonia 124 Sarah P 184
RANDALL, Abigail 72 Emma E 265 Lizzie S 202 Mary 175 Mary E 79 Patience 184 Polly Shannon 106 Sarah 154 Sophronia A 85

RANDEL, Sally 33
RANDLETT, Mary A 73
RANKIN, Mary 170
RANKINS, Betty 121 Mary 167
RANSOM, Lydia M 261 Mary A 46
RAYMOND, Betsey 8
RAYNES, Mary Jane 66
READER, Julianna 120
REDFIELD, Charlotte A 186
REDMAN, Hannah 247
REED, Abigail 82 Elizabeth 3 Ellen A 33
REMICK, Alice M 48 Lillie G 20 Lydia 272 Mary 125
REMINGTON, Ellen M 244
RENOLDS, Eliza A 59
REYNOLDS, Eunice 64 Josephine M 16 Lucretia F 142 Lucy L 216 Martha Ann 119
RICE, Abbie H 145
RICHARDS, Emily 80 Louisa A 143 Melissa J 163 Pruddence 29
RICHARDSON, Amanda F 58 Jennie 221 Lucretia W 243 Lydia 50 Mary E 188-189 Nancy L 13
RICHMOND, Dordana 232
RICKER, Abby 155 Augusta Jane 37 Carrie C 33 Cary J 268 Charlotte 152 Deborah 45 Dorcas 216 Dorothy 128 Draxey 111 Elizabeth 75 Ellen V 114 Emeline C 142 Emma 174 Esther 118 130 Hannah 36 Isabella M 181 Judith 110 Lizzie A 196 Lizzie B 10 Lucy 58 Luella 143 Luella J 44 Lydia 51 Mary 119 130 142 223 Mary A 53 Mary C 77 Mehitable Jane 142 Mercy 207 Nancy Jane 35 Olive 100 231 Phebe 118 130 207 221 Rebecca 88 Rebecca Fidelia 184 Rhoda 149 Ruth 98 Sally 74 Sarah 101 119 Sarah D 128 Sarah E 25 Susan E 151 Urbana 142
RIDDY, Eliza 100
RILEY, Connie Waldron 226 Lucretia 227 Mary 226
RINES, Hannah Wiggin 49 Judith 5
RIPLEY, Ada E 191
RITHWELL, Lizzie A 193

ROBERSON, Mariah L 39 May 231
ROBERTS, Abba C 163 Abbie D 86 Abby D 211 Abigail W 142 Addie A 56 Addie M 108 Annah D 243 Clara A 115 Eliza A 9 Elizabeth 137 Ella G 104 Ellen E 251 Ellen F 11 Ezobah 149 Hannah 238 Hattie S 240 Keziah 102 Laura A 59 Martha J 54 Martha T 54 Olive 194 Pamela 128 Roesa A 137 Ruth 140 Sally 145 Sarah 70 217 249 Sarah B 151 Sarah D 267 Sarah F 100 Susan 123 Susan F 212 Susannah 210
ROBINSON, Abby G 127 Ann A 235 Asenath 79 Clara E 252 Elizabeth 109 237 Grace B 20 Julia Ann 192 Lydia 237 M M 19 Polly 42 Sarah 138
ROBY, Emma 186 Mary E 186
ROGERS, Elizabeth J 11 Hannah H 51 Hattie E 264 Hattie M 276 Lydia S 39 Martha A 113 Olive 254 Sally 277 Sarah 27 Susan A 264 Susannah 12
ROLES, Lydia F 89
ROLLINS, Caroline 221 Emily Ann 73 Patience 59 Prudence L 119 Sarah A 80 Sarah J 222
ROSE, Sarah E 175
ROSS, Betsey 146 Lydia D 144 Mary 172 Mary E 208 Patience 124 Rebecca R 198 Sarah H 16
ROTHWELL, Lizzie 240 Mary J 206
ROWE, Betsey 132 Kezia 275 Matilda 61 Sarah 82
ROWELL, Dora E 272 Hannah 215
RUMNEY, Ellen 154
RUNDLETT, Hannah 168
RUNLETT, Susan F 267
RUNNALS, Almena A 7
RUNNELS, Francenia 243 Jerusha 247 Molly 118 129 Ruth 150 Sally 112
RUSSELL, Lucy M 191 Mary F 26 Olive 27 Sarah 216
RUST, Hannah J 26 Jane 127 Lucy E 252 Martha C 224 Susannah 38
SAINTJOHN, Sarah 216
SALL, Ella M 162

SALMON, Emma T 91
SAMPSON, Abigail 8 Mary A 130
    Polly 120 Sally 138 Susanna 83
SANBORN, Abbie E 225 Elizabeth
    170 Elizabeth W 140 Ella H 12
    Isabell A 169 Lovey 195 Mary Ann
    78 Mary E 97 Mehitable 150 Sarah
    123 Sarah T 217 Susan 223
SANDERS, Abigail 217 Betsey Y 36
    Jane H 15 Lavina 193 Mahala 49
    Mary Ann 107 Mary E 153 Sally
    275
SARGENT, Julia 101 Lydia 152 Mary
    140
SAUNDERS, Hannah 23 107 Mary
    107
SAVAGE, Mary S 55
SAWTELL, Fannaie J 114
SAWYER, Adaline L 95 Content 272
    Eleanor 70 Elizabeth H 202 Emma
    R 7 Huldah 152 Julia A 20 Lucy
    144 Mary P 68 Sarah Ann 83
    Sophia 33
SAYWARD, Margaret Ann 84
SCEGGEL, Lydia 51
SCOTT, Annie E 262
SCRUTON, Amie E 108 Lavina H 18
    Louisa A 87 Lydia 106 Patience 84
    Polly 22 Sarah J 251 Vianna J 219
SCULLY, Sarah J 256
SEAVER, Susan W 145
SEAVEY, Betsey 192 Dorothy 220
    Eliza 132 Elizabeth 138 247
    Elizabeth H 234 Frederica 164
    Hannah A 162 Julia A 220 Mary
    Ann 159 Olly 13 Ruth Ella 226
    Sally 257 Sarah 116 Ursula A 11
SEAWARD, Mary S 143
SEIDERS, Mattie E 24
SEVERANCE, Abigail 214 Betsey W
    202 Mehitable 214
SEWARD, Lizzie A 36 Martha A 136
    Nancy M 41 Rhoda 61
SEWARDS, Patty 79
SHACKFORD, Caroline 116 Mary L
    242 Mary W 171 Nancy W 171
    Nancy Walker 138
SHACKLEVE, Abigail 74
SHAPLEIGH, Alice J 213 Amy 97
    Annette D 147 Charlotte M 233

SHAPLEIGH (continued)
    Electa A 233 Eunice K 249 Hannah
    C 240 Martha J 218 Mary E 239
    Nellie F 89 Phebe Ricker 124 Sarah
    E 114
SHAW, Elizabeth 151 Letitia J 12 M
    Abby 67
SHEARDEN, Mary 77
SHEPARD, Martha J 171 Sarah 94
SHEPPARD, Judith A 81
SHERBOURN, Abigail 93
SHERBURNE, Annie 78 Betsey 107
    Martha A 212 Sally 235 Sophronia
    Adeline 160 Zerviah 164
SHERMAN, Hannah 175 Naomi 207
SHIELDS, Catherine E 259
SHILLABER, Nancy 106
SHOREY, Areline M 136 Asenath 118
    Clara A 256 Euia A 258 Hattie N
    164 Margaret 170 Mary 72 207
    Mary E 255
SHORTRIDGE, Polly 163
SIAS, Hannah 153 Mary E 74
    Welthern 266
SILLOWAY, Elizabeth 175
SIMPSON, Elizabeth A 86 Hannah
    275 Martha 234 Mary G 215 Sarah
    A 10
SINCLAIR, Betty 11
SKINNER, Polly M 193
SLADE, Julia A 133
SLOPER, Alice 101 Anna 187 Betsey
    228 Deborah Jane 84 Hannah
    Susan 233 Margaret 85 Meribah
    187 Sally 37
SMALL, Angela A 59 Julia A 28
SMALLCORN, Lavinia J 115
SMART, Alice Ann 263 Claire A 195
    Elizabeth 80 Susan D 144 Vina 87
SMITH, Abigail 78 Amy 97 Angelina
    P 273 Anna 156 Avalenia J 149
    Betsey 177 Ceceline G 24 Eliza P
    175 Elizabeth 72 Elizabeth G 1
    Emily C 138 Emily L 218 Emma
    218 Fannie C 254 Flora M 102
    Hannah 127 236 238 Hannah L 175
    Hannah P 38 249 Hattie R 9 Julia
    Ann 258 Julian 97 Lessie D 164
    Lizzie M 99 Lucy 249 Lucy M 208
    Lydia 184 Lydia E 211 M A 99

SMITH (continued)
   Margaret 123 Martha Jane 119
   Mary 90 226 Mary C 188 Mary E
   94 Mary J 17 Mary Jane 135 Mary
   N 219 Mehitable 109 230 Patience
   49 Rufina 187 Ruth R 12 Sally 42
   261 Sarah 94 Sarah A 160 Sarah
   Ann 226 Sarah B 59 Sarah E 118
   122 Sarah L 87 Wealthy A C 18
SNELL, Abby H 265 Abigail 171
   Anna 241 Deliverance 29 Dolly
   263 Harriet E 101 Louisa M 237
   Mary Ann 101
SNOW, Emma A 212 Julia A 69
SOMERBY, Maria 38
SOREN, Frances J 272
SOULE, Isabel J 36
SOUTHWICK, Martha 225
SPEAD, Susan E 37
SPEED, Angelia P 147
SPENCER, Ada 224 Lydia 166 Marcy
   148 Mary 2
SPINNEY, Deborah 192 Sarah A 231
   Temperance 21
SPRAGUE, Deborah W 103
SPRINGFIELD, Jennie E 183
SPURLIN, Lizzie E 276
SPURLING, Amanda S 67 Melissa
   206
SREVENS, Mary C 141
STACEY, Fanny 76
STACKPOLE, Ada F 62 Annie L 145
   Mary A 193 Mary Jane 127
   Philomelia 243 Rachel 273 Sarah
   177 Sarah A 41
STACY, Mehitable 74
STANLEY, Ella N 11
STANTON, Abby D 184 Betty 188
   Clara 144 Dorcas 143 Elly 232
   Helen M 172 Lydia B 260 Maria A
   108 Mary H 89 Molly 120 Nellie E
   43 Sarah 159 Tamsin 13 Tamson
   270
STANWOOD, Rachel 70
STAPLES, Ann 245 Betsey 149
   Hannah 258 Susie M 43
STARBARD, Mary 245
STARBIRD, Angeline P 163 Sarah
   152
STARBOARD, Sarah 123

STERLING, Eliza Maria 9
STERRITT, Fannie A 102
STEVENS, Abigail 120 Arabelle E
   191 Augusta L 255 Betsey 38
   Betsey J 214 Catherine T 12
   Elizabeth A 166 Ellen Jane 135
   Frances 63 Joanna 141 Mary A 246
   Mary Ann 267 Nancy H 268 Ruth
   B 94 Sarah Eliza 218 Sarah J 57
   Suky 207 Susan 96
STEVENSON, Eliza B 6 Mary 272
STICKNEY, Martha C 191
STILES, Abigail 107 175 Clara R 161
   Sarah E 173
STILLINGS, Emeline 182 Jane C 54
   Lizzie 145 Mary G 33 Sally 70
STILSON, Carrie G 89
STIRLING, Elzira 127
STOCKBRIDGE, Mahala 162 Sally 15
STOKES, Ada M 162 Sally 61
STONE, Lydia 171
STOVER, Susie S 228
STRAW, Abigail P 13 Lucy 2
STUBBS, Robert S 146
STURDIVANT, Lucy 244 Lucy S 244
STYLES, Clara 27
SWAIN, Annie E 60 Elizabeth 223
   Elizabeth Ann 75 Jennie 171 Judith
   9 Lydia 131 Margaret A 39 Marilla
   J 225 Mary 269 Mary E 40 Mary
   Jane 39 Melvina A 201 Sarah 45
SWAN, Mary Ann 121
SWASEY, Eunice C 25 Nellie M 213
SWEANOR, Eliza J 24
SWEAT, Mary 31 Mary A 43
SWEETSER, Martha A 10
SWETT, Carrie M 232 Hannah S 177
   Jessie M S 59 Rhoda P 158
SWINNERTON, Fidelia J 260
TANNER, Mary G 32
TAPLEY, Susan Preston 177
TAPPAN, Adah B 64 Eliza A 89
TARLETON, Mary 178
TASH, Hannah S 167
TASKER, Amanda M 117 Betsey 123
   Clarinda 260 Eliza 35 Ellen A 218
   Emma C 183 Lois 106 Lucy J 112
   Mary D 22 Mary E 87 Mary J 188
   Sally 145 245
TATE, Harriet 1

TAYLOR, Eliza 205 Lydia A 145
   Mary J 24 Molly 199 Phebe 138
TEAGUE, Caroline 58 231
TEBBETS, Abigail 30 245 Caroline 26
   Carolline M 239 Deborah 275
   Elizabeth 237 Eunice 273 Grace M
   180 Lucy Ann 64 Mary 98 Mary B
   8 Mehepsabar 178 Nancy J 250
   Olive E 44 Patty 25 Rebecca 99
   Vesta H 142
TEBBETTS, Cyntihia 87 Deborah 275
   Ella 31 Flora A 271 Lydia 210
   Lydia A 265 Mary A 257 Mary
   Ann 84 Mary J 165 Mercy 136
   Nellie M 204 Nettie A 262 Ruth
   114
TENNYS, Molly 34
TETHERLY, Mary E 188
TEWKSBURY, E 53
THACKRAH, Marion 249
THOMAS, Elizabeth Jane 178
   Georgiana D 147 Paulina 1
THOMPKINS, Lizzie 187
THOMPSON, Abigail 263 Addie O
   212 Amerette F 96 Ann M 212
   Dora J 27 Elizabeth 96 Ella M 186
   Ellen J 149 Hannah 83 237 Huldah
   E 101 Jane N 264 Lavina 75
   Martha G E 120 Mary 159 Mary
   Ann 276 Mary E 257 Mary I 86
   Nancy R 194 Nancy S 26 Peace
   189 Rebecca 214 Sarah 18 Sarah A
   71 Sarah F 259 Sophia E 11 Susan
   29 Susan J 257 Temperance 17
THURLOW, Linna H 215
THURSTON, Ann 169 E M J 252
   Elvira 158 Hattie A 186 Martha E
   61 Mary 114 234 Melissa E 137
TIBBETS, Elizabeth S 254 Mary B 8
TIBBETTS, Abbie M 99 Betsey 194
   Charlotte 29 Fannie H 242 Isette
   277 Jennie L 77 Mary 256 Mercy
   128 Minerva A 54 Nancy J 179
   Sarah E 122 264
TILTON, Isabel A 58
TITCOMB, Olive 111
TOBEY, Eunice V 204 Lydia V 213
TOBIE, Ruth W 5
TODD, Lucy Jane 174
TOLMAN, Elmira H 181

TORR, Mary E 61
TOWLE, Elizabeth 203 Marintha A 65
TRAFTON, Abbie L 206
TRASK, Mary M 232 Sarah E 163
TREADWELL, Lydia 229
TREDICK, Lucretia B 174
TREFETHEN, Alice A C 69 Annie M
   126 Sarah A 160
TRICKEY, Adeline 4 Eliza G 7 Laura
   A 200 Lydia J 251 Martha A 17
   Mary A 146
TRIPP, Laura J 5 Mercy 4 Sally 211
TRUE, Elizabeth H 30 Lucy 244 Lucy
   S 244 Mary B 51 Sally 179
TUCK, Mary A 256
TUCKER, Annie J 212 Eliza J 164
   Elizabeth C 200 Esther 254 Jane
   188 Mary E 229 Mary N 92 Sarah
   217 Sarah J 133 Sarah M 133
   Sophronia R 171 Susie 244
TUFTS, Lydia 102 Mary E 267
TUPPER, Lucy Jane 218
TURAS, Bettey 82
TURNER, Annie M 47 Mary C 221
TUTTLE, Alice 149 278 Almira E 43
   Cynthia S 202 Delia A 103 Eliza
   107 Eliza A 18 Eliza E 171
   Elizabeth 57 Elizabeth H S 267
   Ellen A 194 Ellen E 108 Esther G
   57 Fannie L 246 Frances 59
   Hannah 68 Hannah E 198 Jennie L
   43 Lavina 245 247 Love 173 Lydia
   22 152 Mary 112 Mary A 225
   Mary Jane 255 Pateince 49 Peggy
   139 Sally 225 Sarah 66 112 Sarah
   E 129 Sarah L 237 Seddie E 258
   Sophronia M 108 Susan M 22 89
   Sylvira L 41
TWILIGHT, Helen D 25 Mary P 26
TWOMBLY, Clara E 256 Deborah 61
   75 Emma F 18 Hannah S 28 Helen
   C 175 Hepsibath 233 Judith 247
   Lavinia H 66 Louisa 79 Martha S
   200 Mary 112 Mary E 24
   Mehitable 131 Nancy 23 40 Nellie
   M 115 Olive 23 241 Polly 220
   Sarah 82 96 Susanna 253 256
TYLER, Sally 153
UPHAM, Susan 164
USHER, Irene L 157

VANDUZZA, Hannah 35
VANZUNDT, Fanny 118
VARNEY, Ann 181 Anna L 276
  Annie 1 Caroline A 48 Caroline M
  174 Chrissie 129 Cordelia S 204
  Deborah 250 Dorothy C 240
  Electra Jane 47 Eliza Ann 86 Ellen
  234 Hannah H 77 Hannah M 68
  217 Leonora 128 Lois 215 Maria
  62 Martha 3 168 Mary A 88 Mary
  E 180 204 Mary Jane 119 Mary
  Riley 106 Mary S 193 Melvina M
  135 Pamelia 101 Patience 277
  Polly 42 Sarah 34 220 Sarah A 239
  Sarah Ann 181 Sarah M 201 Sarah
  V 117
VARRELL, Rachel 192
VAUGHAN, Virginia A 243
VENNARD, Jane 201 247
VENNER, Mary A 88
VICKERY, Abby E 38 Amanda 224
  Emma L 185 Mary A 75 Sarah M
  170
VIRGIN, Lucy E 67
WADE, Mary E 27
WADLEIGH, Helen Frances 164 Mary
  M 75
WAKEFIELD, Harriet 105
WAKEHAM, Lydia Frances 251 Mary
  E 240
WALALINGFORD, Lydia 261
WALDRON, Albertina 53 Celia C 253
  Cordelia 70 Eleanor 225 Hannah
  132 135 Lovey 57 Mary 132 221
  Mary J 121 Mary Jane 32 Olive
  109 Sally 106 Sarah 132 Sarah Ann
  58 Sarah B 109 Sarah E 246
WALKER, Calantha D 11 Deborah 90
  Elizabeth Ring 184 Elmira B 176
  Hannah 233 Hannah O 59 Lucy
  123 Sarah 214 Sarah Ella 96
WALLACE, Anna J 193 Catherine H
  100 Emma B 213 Hannah A 223
  Laura E 133 Octavie 59 Olive
  Willard 181
WALLINGFORD, Ann 203 Betsey 96
  Charlotte 255 Clara M 165 Joanna
  204 Judith 15 Lydia 255 Martha A
  219 Mary 236 Mercy 255
  Merlindia 255 Nancy 131

WALLINGFORD (continued)
  Nellie E 268 Olive D 136 Patience
  255 Sarah 140 232 Sarah A 189
  Susan 255
WALTON, Mary A 242
WANTWORTH, Olive 213
WARD, Eliza J 18 Lavina V 193
  Martha C 62
WARE, Abigail E 42
WARREN, Abbie J 126 Eliza 48
  Elizabeth 93 Lydia 142 Martha A
  104 Melinda 164 Olive J 252 Sarah
  J 170
WATERHOUSE, Abia G 259 Alice 66
  Annie Lydia 249 Dolley 147
  Martha B 171 Rebecca 123
  Rebecca S 265
WATERMAN, Belinda 172
WATSON, Abigail 93 Anna 70
  Caroline 134 Desdamonia 116
  Desdamony 107 Elizabeth A 155
  Elizabeth B 267 Hannah 138 165
  228 Lizzie W 178 Mary A 141 183
  Mary S 167 Nancy 144 249 Sarah
  D 267 Sophia 260 Zervia 229
  Zibiah 229
WATT, Helen L 99
WEAVER, Ruba R 158
WEBB, Alice L 162
WEBBER, Alma J 113 Almena 5
  Almira L 190 Huldy 158
WEBSTER, Hannah M 221 227 Mary
  C 167 Mehitable 239 Sarah 140
  Sarah W 182
WEDGEWOOD, 70
WEED, Abby C 5 Marietta 77 Mary B
  6
WEEKS, Belle D 222 Fannie E 37
  Julia A 249 Martha 52
WELCH, Augusta M 242 Dorcas 54
  Hannah 13 Julia A 231 Martha A
  261 Martha C 76 Mary 245 Mary
  Jane 230 Mary L 215 Pamela 168
  Salley 7 Sally 126 Sarah 138 Sarah
  Jane 217
WELLS, Delia H 176 Elizabeth 137
WELSH, Cornelia R 40
WENDELL, Sarah Ann 29
WENTWORTH, Abba 174 Abbie E
  258 Abby C 235 Abigail 228

WENTWORTH (continued)
Abra A 147 Achsa A 224 Almira A 67 Almira P 69 Awilda A 161 Betsey 25 98 221 Charlotte 97 Clara L 73 Eliza J 114 Eliza W 192 Elizabeth 55 159 273 Elizabeth A 214 Elizabeth R 133 Emma A 99 Eunice 221 225 Experience 208 Fannie S 267 Frances D 63 Frances J 222 Hannah 122 238 241-242 Hattie C 251 Joanna 33 Judith 64 Katharine 141 Lucy 211 Luella 227 Lydia 97 Lydia E 183 Lydia G 239 Martha 128 Martha E 174 Mary 53 100 170 231 270 Mary A 59 236 266 Mary E 52 Mary F 40 Mary J 260 Molly 128 Olive 254 Paulina F 221 Polly 241 Rachel 55 114 148 Rebecca 64 Rosetta 1 Sabra 230 Sabrina 45 Sally 223 Sally B 90 Sarah 270 Sarah E 25 Tamson 202 Theodatia 259 Vienna 227

WEST, Frances K 48 Lizzie J 74

WEYMOUTH, Mary 110 Olive Ann 117

WHEELER, Annie 186 Ellen 162 Sarah C 99 Sarah E 200

WHIDDEN, Hannah 164

WHIPPLE, E Fannie 240

WHITCHER, Naomi E 152

WHITE, Betsey 55 Catharine 231 Fannie S 170 Margaret 62 Rachel 266

WHITEHOUSE, A 125 Annah E 155 Elizabeth 159 Emily R 50 Icilia T 233 Lucy 134 Lucy E 202 Lydia 229 Lydia A 198 Mahala 69 Mary 150 263 Nancy 266 Sarah 72 120 212 Sarah B 187 Sarah E 71 Susan A 222 Susan R 254 Tamson 66

WHITNEY, Anatis A 211 Clara L 178 Linda 177

WHITTEN, Elizabeth C 207 Hannah 196 Helen M 60 Louisa 76 Mary L 227 Sarah A 71 177 Sarah E 259

WHITTIER, Salome J 115

WIBIRD, Sarah 28

WIGGIN, Abbie Augusta 126 Anna 134 Betsey 51 Eliza A 52 Elizabeth Ann 218 Ellen A 11 Ellen M 264

WIGGIN (continued)
Harriet S 226 Hattie S 166 Helen M 138 Jennie M 237 Love 42 Lucy A 145 Lydia 191 Lydia Ann 230 Mabelle F 96 Martha 209 Mary 100 Mary A 110 Mary S 70 Nellie F 144 Polly 235 Polly H 156 Rachel 42 Rosannah 60 Sally 197 Sarah F 168 Sophronia 38 Susan 109 Susan P 263 Susannah C 21 Zetta W 152

WIGGLESWORTH, Melissa J 274

WILES, Judith 17

WILKINSON, Hannah 214 Mary E 20 Sarah 50

WILLAND, Elizabeth 127 Ella M 44 Lydia A 100

WILLEY, Abigail M 28 Betsey 10 Deborah 266 Dolly 117 Eliza 6 Eliza A 252 Elizabeth 26 Esther 26 Frances E 27 Hannah A 108 Harriet 133 Julia M 9 Lucinda 88 Lucretia 252 Martha 266 Mary 88 148 151 Mary E 267 Nancy 107 Patty 23 Polly 163 248 253 Sally 197 Sarah E 117 211 Tammy 25

WILLIAMS, Avis 228 Carrie 52 Deborah H 158 Ellen M 119 Irena E 215 Louisa 151 Sarah 19

WILSON, Marion 58 Martha 127 Mary H E 36

WINCHELL, Lizzie M 179

WINGATE, Abbie E 201 Elizabeth 116 Hannah 94 269 Louisa Ann 274 Lydia 83 Nancy 161

WINKLEY, Abiah 214 Ann 29 Elizabeth 65-66 150 Maria L 139 Martha 65-66 231 Martha A 257 Martha Ann Mary 155 Mary 90 269 Mary Ann 173 Mary F 237 Mehitable 77 90 Mercy 80 Molly 70 Sarah 238

WINN, Dorcas A 87 Sarah 123

WINSLOW, Attilo Jane 70

WISE, Mary J 261

WITHAM, Augusta H 188 Climera P 271 Dorcas 74 Dorothy L 80 Emeline S 101 Huldah H 214 Lucy 32 Mary C 6 Nancy E 56 Sarah E 96

WITHERELL, Amelia C 198 Eunice 47 Hannah 92
WOOD, Annie A 71 Caroline E 176 Carrie M 186 Charlotte Maria 271 Mary P 80 Mary S 49 Mary W 268 Miriam B 97 186 Sarah J 85
WOODBURY, Eliza K 253
WOODES, Mary 250
WOODHOUSE, Emeline 104 Olive 189 Olive W 34
WOODMAN, Anna 214 Ellen A 30 Hannah 24 Loella 250 Maria F 41 Mary Esther 222 Rachel A 48
WOODS, Mattie 252
WOODSOM, Betsey 74 Susan 111
WOODSUM, Dorcas 144 Susanna 117
WOODUS, Abby H 34
WORMWOOD, Ruth A 157
WORSTER, Dorcas 222 Julia Ann 98 Louise S 39 Mary 156 Mary A 102 255 Sally 76 97
WORTHING, Olivia 265
WORTMAN, Caroline E 237
WRIGHT, Ann 113
WYATT, Sarah E 110

YEATON, Alice H 55 Betsey 93 190 Emmarilla S 147 Experience 134 Hannah 229 Hattie A 217 Julia F 186 Lucena A 274 Mary A 108 Mary Connor 195 Melinda 144 Molly 97 Sarah F 41
YORK, 234 Abigail F 104 Addie 185 Caroline L 196 Comfort 17 Hannah D 169 Lydia L 168 Mary Ann S 105 Mindwell A 107
YOUNG, Abigail 35-36 95 130 183 Alice 255 Anna 49 Annie E 258 Caroline 117 Clara A 75 Coridle 13 Dorothy 22 Eliza A 223 Elizabeth 60 Ellen 236 Ellen E 240 Ellen T 270 Georgiana H 248 Hannah 195 Harriet A 262 Jane 1 Janette 68 Josephine E 265 Judith 184 Louisa J 232 Lucy Maria 54 Martha 50 Martha Ann 216 Mary 26 45 117 176 Mary Abbie 235 Mary C 15 Mary E 165 Mary Susan 33 Patience 184 240 Polly 22 105 Rebecca A 251 Ruth 32 Sally 236 Sarah A 192 Sarah C 67 Sarah H 50 Sophia 61 187 Sophia J 265 Susan C 80

www.ingramcontent.com/pod-product-compliance
Lightning Source LLC
Chambersburg PA
CBHW052054230426
43671CB00011B/1897